CW01371616

Alanbrooke
The Reluctant Warrior

Julian Horrocks

Copyright © 2023 Julian Horrocks

The moral right of the author has been asserted.

Apart from any fair dealing for the purposes of research or private study, or criticism or review, as permitted under the Copyright, Designs and Patents Act 1988, this publication may only be reproduced, stored or transmitted, in any form or by any means, with the prior permission in writing of the publishers, or in the case of reprographic reproduction in accordance with the terms of licences issued by the Copyright Licensing Agency. Enquiries concerning reproduction outside those terms should be sent to the publishers.

Matador
Unit E2 Airfield Business Park,
Harrison Road, Market Harborough,
Leicestershire. LE16 7UL
Tel: 0116 2792299
Email: books@troubador.co.uk
Web: www.troubador.co.uk/matador
Twitter: @matadorbooks

ISBN 978 1803135 847

British Library Cataloguing in Publication Data.
A catalogue record for this book is available from the British Library.

Printed and bound in the UK by TJ Books Limited, Padstow, Cornwall
Typeset in 12pt Adobe Jenson Pro by Troubador Publishing Ltd, Leicester, UK

Matador is an imprint of Troubador Publishing Ltd

MIX
Paper from responsible sources
FSC® C013056

CONTENTS

Introduction		v
PART ONE		**1**
1	Childhood with the Perfect Mother	3
2	1900–1939	16
PART TWO		**35**
	Author's Note	37
3	France: September 1939–May 1940	39
4	France: May–June 1940	65
5	C-in-C Home Forces: June 1940– November 1941	90
6	CIGS: December 1941–February 1942	127
7	CIGS: March–May 1942	157
8	CIGS: June–July 1942	180
9	CIGS: August–September 1942	203
10	CIGS: October–December 1942	231
11	CIGS: January–April 1943	250
12	CIGS: May–August 1943	270
13	CIGS: September–December 1943	304
14	CIGS: January–May 1944	334
15	CIGS: June–September 1944	366
16	CIGS: October–December 1944	400
17	CIGS: January–April 1945	423
18	CIGS: May 1945–June 1946	447
PART THREE		**473**
19	Alanbrooke	475
20	Strategy	509

| 21 | 1945–1963 | 526 |
| 22 | The Reluctant Warrior | 559 |

Appendix	581
Bibliography	595
Notes	599
Acknowledgements	607

INTRODUCTION

Born in 1883, Alan Francis Brooke served in the British Army between 1902 and 1946. He fought on the Western Front for most of the First World War and by November 1918 had been promoted to lieutenant colonel, awarded the Distinguished Service Order twice and mentioned in despatches six times. In 1927, Brooke gave serious consideration to leaving the army and emigrating to New Zealand; in the event, he did neither. The 1930s saw him appointed to a wide variety of senior commands which led to further promotion. He was a lieutenant general when the Second World War started in 1939; by 1945, he was a field marshal. After the War, he was elevated to the peerage, taking the title of 1st Viscount Alanbrooke of Brookeborough. Brooke died in 1963.

On Thursday, 28 September 1939, twenty-five days after Britain declared war on Germany, Brooke bid farewell to his wife, Benita, and their two young children, Kathleen aged eight and Victor aged six; he was then fifty-six years old and Benita, his second wife, was nine years his junior. The reason for the farewell was that he had been designated to command II Corps which was part of the British Expeditionary Force [BEF] being sent to France. During his journey to Southampton docks, Brooke stopped in Salisbury and bought some small pocketbooks. Later that day, he started what was, in effect, a diary although he clearly did not view it as such. He began with a dedication,

Dedicated to Benita Blanche Brooke

Begun 28 September 1939

This book is not intended to be a diary of events, although it may contain references to my daily life. It is intended to be a record of my thoughts and impressions such as I would have discussed them with you had we been together.

After living the last ten years with you and never being parted for more than a few weeks at a time, I should feel quite lost without an occasional opportunity of a talk with you although such a talk must necessarily be confined to writing: I therefore procured this book in Salisbury on purpose for such conversations with you. It was originally part of Smith's stock of books on the Queen Mary but having failed to sell was reduced from 60/– to 15/–!

The thoughts I express may contradict themselves as I wish to give full scope to free expression and do not care if I am forced to change my mind by events.

ON NO ACCOUNT MUST THE CONTENTS OF THIS BOOK BE PUBLISHED.

Brooke continued to hold his written 'talks' with Benita on a daily basis until 1946, usually writing them late at night. As a result, he created a contemporaneous record of the entire Second World War, as witnessed by him. The significance of his record lies in the fact that Brooke held very senior commands during the War. Initially a corps commander in the BEF in France in 1939-40, he commanded the second BEF in France in June 1940. One month later, he was appointed Commander-in-Chief, Home Forces. This was followed by his appointment as Chief of the Imperial General Staff [CIGS] in December 1941, by virtue of which he became the professional head of the British Army and a member of the Chiefs of Staff Committee; in March 1942, he was appointed chairman of this committee. As CIGS and committee chairman, Brooke became the principal military adviser to the British prime minister and the cabinet.

Brooke's plea to Benita that his 'talks' must not be published may well be explained by wartime regulations which prohibited him from keeping a diary. It may equally be explained by the fact he was a private man who shunned publicity. When, in 1951, the Royal Regiment of Artillery commissioned the historian, Arthur Bryant, to write his biography, Brooke agreed on condition that it was only written and published after his death.

Brooke was, however, to change his mind regarding publication of his 'talks'. In 1954, he agreed to Bryant's suggestion that they be used as the foundation for a book which told the story of the War between Dunkirk and El Alamein and that, once written, this book should be published immediately. In the event, Bryant used the 'talks' to write the story of the entire War, which was published in two volumes, *The Turn of the Tide* [1957] and *Triumph in the West* [1959]: as an aside, he never did write the commissioned biography of Brooke. Bryant's titles generated considerable controversy for two reasons. First, they sought to highlight the significant role played by Brooke and the British chiefs of staff in the War and, second, they questioned Churchill's management of the British war effort and his approach to strategy. The nature of this controversy was accurately captured by Lord Moran, Churchill's personal doctor, in his memoirs; he titled his chapter dealing with the controversy, "Defacing the Legend"[1] – the legend being, of course, Churchill.

Following Brooke's death, his papers were deposited with the Liddell Hart Centre for Military Archives at King's College London in 1971. Many years later, Alex Danchev and Daniel Todman unearthed his 'talks' and published them in their full, unedited form in 2001. Their publication, *War Diaries 1939–1945, Field Marshal Lord Alanbrooke*, attracted this review, "The unexpurgated Alanbrooke diaries have been trailed as the last unfinished business of the Second World War. They are said to be indiscreet, malicious and true, debunking Churchill, Eisenhower, Mountbatten, Marshall and De Gaulle. They are and they do."[2] This was a fair and accurate review, save in one respect. Brooke was not motivated by malice when writing his 'talks': as he stated in his opening dedication to Benita, they were merely "intended to be a record of my thoughts and impressions such as I would have discussed them with you had we been together" and there is no evidence which suggests this motive ever changed. Admittedly, it is possible that Brooke's collaboration with Bryant in the publication of *The Turn of the Tide* and *Triumph in the West* was motivated by an element of malice. This issue is addressed in Part Three.

Taken at face value, Alan Francis Brooke cuts a daunting and formidable figure. Three descriptions provide a flavour of the man, the first of which appeared in an article in *The Economist* magazine in 1957, "In his demanding and abrupt efficiency, he knew when to scold, when to encourage, when to protect. Men admired, feared and liked him: in that order, perhaps."[3] The second, provided by his chauffeur, was in similar vein although it did provide an additional insight into Brooke, "I've never known a greater gentleman… it was obvious the great majority of people were frightened of him." The third, offered by a senior officer in the British Army, revealed how Brooke was viewed by his military colleagues, "We regarded him as a highly efficient military machine."[4] Alan Francis Brooke would appear to be one of those figures who commanded admiration and respect, rather than warmth and affection.

Historians have largely been positive in their treatment of Brooke. Indeed, one eminent military historian, writing in the 1990s, expressed the opinion that he was not only "one of the architects of Allied victory" but also "one of the outstanding soldiers of this century".[5] Yet, many of them appear half-hearted, almost grudging, in their acknowledgement of the role which he played in the War: one is left with the impression that they do so through gritted teeth. There are, I suspect, two reasons for this. First, they disapprove of Brooke's collaboration with Bryant in the publication of *The Turn of the Tide* and *Triumph in the West*, viewing it as an exercise in self-aggrandisement on his part. Second, they do not like Brooke. The barrage of negative adjectives that has rained down on him over the decades tends to support this conclusion – stern, forbidding, aloof, impatient, opinionated, self-assured, blunt, forthright, sharp-tongued, brusque, abrupt, rude, short-tempered, flinty, restless, highly strung, intense, intolerant, pig-headed, stubborn and obstinate. It is, by any standards, an impressive list! In fairness, this sentiment is understandable. Brooke was forthright and abrupt in speech and manner and he could occasionally be abrasive: after the War, he recalled a conversation which he had with his opposite number in the United States

INTRODUCTION

Army, General George Marshall, in May 1943, "As I was walking with Marshall and Dill to one of our meetings, Marshall said to me, 'I find it very hard even now not to look on your North African strategy with a jaundiced eye!!' I replied, 'What strategy would you have preferred?' To which he answered, 'Cross channel operations for the liberation of France and advance on Germany, we should finish the war quicker.' I remember replying, 'Yes, probably, but not the way we hope to finish it!'"

I have written this book for two reasons. First, historians have focused on Brooke the soldier and strategist and chosen – perhaps deliberately and perhaps wisely – not to examine the man behind the soldier. Bryant's titles offered a narrative history of the War as seen though Brooke's eyes but offered little by way of detailed insight into his character. Likewise, the 2001 publication of Brooke's diary offered little editorial comment on the character of the diary's author. There are just two other titles in which he features prominently. The only biography of Brooke that has been published was written by the late General Sir David Fraser who was a professional soldier and military historian. Not unreasonably, Fraser dwelt more on the military aspects of Brooke's life and career rather than his character and whilst it is illuminating in several respects, it left me only slightly the wiser in understanding the man behind the soldier. Andrew Roberts' *Masters and Commanders* was constructed around Roosevelt, Churchill, Marshall and Brooke but since the focus of this title was on the formulation of Anglo-American strategy, he was not studied in any depth. To this day, Brooke the man remains largely unexplored territory.

My interest in Brooke was sparked after I read the 2001 publication of his diary. He appeared – at least to me – to be a complex and rather contradictory character and the more I researched him, the more intrigued I became. Here was a man who had spent his entire adult life in military service, yet he held a deep-rooted and intense dislike of war. Here was a man who devoted all his energies to winning the War, yet he clearly believed that war was utterly futile. Here was an "alert, seemingly iron, man without a nerve in his body"[6], yet he "broke down and wept"[7] in the Dunkirk sand hills. Here was a man who freely admitted he would have sprayed poison gas on German troops landing on British beaches, yet he could be entranced by watching "young water hens being instructed by their mother as to how a bath should be taken. She gave a demonstration first and then those tiny mites followed suit and copied her, a wonderful sight." Here was a man who made scathing judgments of his colleagues – one was "a repulsive creature" – yet he could write to Benita in these terms,

> *Such a treat this evening receiving your parcel and in it the frame with my beloved Pooks and Ti [the nicknames of their two children]! I just loved getting it, though it gave me a most desperate longing to have them here just for one large hug. I have installed them on the small table beside my bed alongside of your photograph. But just at the present moment we are having a little family gathering as I have put both your photograph and that of the Pooks and Ti on the table I am writing at, so that we are all together while I have a talk with you.*[8]

Here was a man who projected "demanding and abrupt efficiency"[9] to the outside world, yet he privately admitted in a letter written to Benita in 1942,

> *As usual, my darling, you are being my mainstay and anchor in life. Without you I should be able to do nothing. Your example and life is the most wonderful inspiration to me and my whole life just hinges around you.*[10]

There were also inconsistencies in his diary. Some entries were at odds with others. Some entries appeared completely out of character for this daunting and formidable figure. Furthermore, there were entries in which he expressed regret or appeared to apologise for what he had said or done. Perhaps it was a mistake to take Alan Francis Brooke at face value? Perhaps there was a depth and complexity to his character hitherto unfathomed? One contemporary's description of him as "a most impenetrable man" suggested there may be. The prospect of exploring the unchartered waters of Alan Francis Brooke's character was appealing.

INTRODUCTION

The second reason is that Brooke is a very good example of the 'unsung hero'. He played a pivotal role in the War yet, with the exception of historians and aficionados of the War, few people have heard of him: the name Montgomery draws recognition but the name Brooke or Alanbrooke tends to draw a blank, even though he was Montgomery's immediate superior throughout the War. One explanation is that in wartime the limelight tends to fall on generals who command in the field, especially the successful ones. Another is the common perception that it was Churchill who won the War. Yet another is that whilst Brooke appears in a great many titles written about the War, references to him tend to be brief and sporadic. As a result, there is a lack of public awareness of the part he played in the Allied victory.

This book is not a biography. Its principal purpose is to offer a detailed character portrait of Brooke which presents him in a markedly different, and more sympathetic, light to the way he has been portrayed to date. He was, according to a contemporary, "a consummate actor"[11]: the aim of this book is to unmask him.

I have constructed the book around his diary for three reasons. First, the character portrait that is offered is largely based on my detailed analysis of his entries; in common with most diaries, they reveal a great deal about their author. Second, in edited form, it not only narrates a fascinating and highly readable story but also contains his shrewd judgments of figures such as Churchill, Stalin, Eisenhower, de Gaulle, Smuts, Eden, Marshall, Mountbatten, Montgomery, Alexander and, to a lesser extent, Attlee, MacArthur and Patton. Third, the value of his diary as an historical record has not, in my view, been fully appreciated. It does far more than raise doubts over Churchill's management of the British war effort and his approach to strategy since it opens a window on issues such as the strained relationship that exists between military and political leaders, the weaknesses of politicians, the interplay between prime minister and cabinet and how military leaders should handle their political masters. His diary also has an educational value because there were a great many lessons to be learnt from Brooke's experiences in the War and the failure to learn, or apply, those lessons led to some of the mistakes being made in the recent wars in Iraq and Afghanistan. All these issues are examined in Chapter 21.

Part One covers the period from 1883 up to the outbreak of the War in September 1939 and comprises a fast gallop through Brooke's childhood, his experiences in the First World War and his rise through the army in the interwar years. It highlights some of Brooke's more obvious character traits such as his high level of energy and drive – he "thought fast, talked fast and moved fast."[12]

Part Two, which forms the backbone of the book, covers the six years of the War and ends with Brooke's retirement in 1946. It comprises edited extracts from his diary and his autobiographical Notes: these Notes elaborated on his diary entries and were written by Brooke in the 1950s to help Bryant write the commissioned biography after his death. I should emphasise that Part Two is an account of Brooke's personal experiences between 1939 and 1946 rather than a narrative history of the War.

Part Three comprises four chapters. The first contains the detailed character portrait of Brooke. The second opens with an analysis of Brooke's first year as CIGS and then examines five aspects of Anglo-American strategy. The third covers Brooke's post-War life, his collaboration with Bryant in the publication of *The Turn of the Tide* and *Triumph in the West* and concludes by listing his achievements in the War: this chapter includes an assessment of Churchill and also identifies the lessons to be learnt from Brooke's experiences in the War. The final chapter explains why I came to sympathise with Brooke and why he was a reluctant warrior.

Five points deserve mention. First, the authenticity of Brooke's diary as an historical document is well-nigh unimpeachable since they were truly contemporaneous notes written daily by a man who was, according to two of his close colleagues, "straight, absolutely honest"[13] and "bone honest". Moreover, their authenticity has never been questioned. On the contrary, they have been, and continue to be, freely quoted in books and television programmes without qualification as to their provenance.

Distinction needs to be drawn between the authenticity of his diary and the opinions Brooke expressed in his entries. It has been argued that since his diary was written late at night when Brooke was exhausted and frustrated, he was just letting off steam and, consequently, little importance should be attached to his criticisms: General Ismay was a notable proponent of this claim, as will shortly become apparent. Whilst plausible, this was almost certainly a disingenuous attempt to belittle Brooke's criticisms and sweep them under the carpet. Far more convincing is the argument that whilst his diary was undoubtedly written when he was exhausted and frustrated, that was exactly what made his opinions so compelling and revealing – Brooke wrote when his guard was down.

Second, Brooke was a conventionally minded man, yet he elected to breach wartime regulations and, moreover, create a very real security risk by maintaining his diary throughout the War: he acknowledged this risk in his 30 July 1942 entry, on the eve of his flight to Cairo, "Shall start new book tomorrow as I dare not risk being caught with this should we be caught or crash." The reason why he did so lies in his opening dedication to Benita, "I should feel quite lost without an occasional opportunity of a talk with you", and also in a letter he wrote to Benita in early 1940,

> *Our evening talks as you say take a long time to travel across from one chair to another, but for all that they are something quite sacred to me, the one moment when we seem to draw very close together, when I can make you say things to me and almost imagine you then saying them, and then answer back on paper.*[14]

His 'talks' with Benita were clearly of huge importance to Brooke and the fact they were "quite sacred" to him suggests he viewed them as his lifeline to Benita.

Third, I offer the reader one notable health warning. Since Brooke was one of the principal architects of Anglo-American strategy in the War, it is well-nigh impossible to write a book about him without addressing the subject of military strategy. Unfortunately, my knowledge of this subject is, at best, limited. Consequently, on matters of strategy, the reader is in the hands of a rank amateur.

Fourth, there is an archive interview of Brooke at http://www.bbc.co.uk/archive/the-alanbrooke-diaries/zf2f2sg which is well worth watching. In the opening shot of Brooke, he appears uncomfortable which is probably explained by his dislike of publicity. His demeanour is notable, in particular his eyes; he seems to glare rather than gaze at people and he conveys an air of impatience, almost irritation. When Brooke was a young man, one of his contemporaries referred to his "restless energy". This was still apparent decades later in this interview.

Fifth, Brooke acquired three nicknames during his life. The first was the 'Barrage King' in the First World War. The second, and the one most frequently used, was 'Brookie'. The third, and by far the most entertaining since it captured his forthright, abrupt manner, was 'Colonel Shrapnel'. I did wonder if he was 'Brookie' to those who admired and liked him and 'Colonel Shrapnel' to those who feared him. In Parts One and Two, I refer to him as Brookie and in Part Three as Alanbrooke.

Brooke's contemporaries have provided interesting – in some cases revealing – insights into his character. The following individuals are British unless stated otherwise and many of their quotes reappear in Part Three.

Field Marshal Harold Alexander.
> "I served under him as a commander in the field most of the war and I could not have had a wiser, firmer or more understanding military chief to guide and look after our interests. Brookie, as we always call him, was the outstanding and obvious man for the job; a fine soldier in every sense and trusted and admired by the whole Army."[15]

Major General R H Allen.
> "Though I know that on occasion he can get a bit cross as I have heard a classic case when at a conference at the War Office he told a prominent Treasury official that he was a 'cheeseparing little pipsqueak'... He was always phenomenally quick and endowed with a great sense of humour which made his repartees devastating but never ill natured... one of the most lovable men I have ever met... I rank Brookie with Archie Wavell as those for whom I have the greatest admiration."

Joan Bright Astley, War Office.

> "I experienced the wrath of two members of the Chiefs of Staff Committee when we detrained that morning. First, a furious Sir Alan Brooke who told me with sharp clarity never again to allocate him a sleeping compartment right above the grinding train wheels… Minutes later, the Chief of the Air Staff was saying something angrily to me… the effects of this attack did not last so long as those produced by General Sir Alan Brooke."[16]

> "Sir Alan Brooke was enjoying himself… The day started when we all sat together in the breakfast-room. As he ate toast with caviar and drank Russian tea laced with vodka, he teased and talked and laughed. After a morning or two of silent surprise we realised that, instead of a formidable and distant figure, we had with us a delightful, amusing and easy companion who treated us with equal and courteous attention, from the brigadiers down to me and the other girls. He was a handsome man, strongly built, with broad slightly bowed shoulders, black eyes and hair, not very tall. He thought and spoke with lightning speed, reaching conclusions which darted into words and caught the listener unprepared. The mental agility revealed his French upbringing and education, and the rapid speech his perfect command of the French language. An abrupt manner and ready impatience misled people who did not know him well; if they had, they would have appreciated that both characteristics belonged to a quick and concentrated thinker; if they had, they would have known that he was kindly to subordinates. Most contradictory of all to these characteristics was his love of bird-watching and fishing – two recreations demanding the greatest patience."[17]

General Sir Cecil Blacker.

> "He was one of those whose brief presence was sufficient to make one perfectly sure that all would come right in the end."[18]

Lieutenant General Sir Frederick Browning.

> "I've [just] had the biggest dressing down of my life – but my God he's a great man."[19]

Richard Casey, Australian statesman.

> "Alan Brooke is a man of unusual quality and intensity. I know of no Service Leader who contributed more to the winning of the Second World War than he did, by his military capacity, by his judgement and by his complete honesty of thought and expression."[20]

Admiral Andrew Cunningham, First Sea Lord and member of the Chiefs of Staff Committee.

> "Straight, absolutely honest and outspoken, he was outstandingly able in his difficult and most responsible position. Though impulsive at times, he always spoke out fearlessly and fluently against what he knew to be wrong. Generous almost to a fault, Alan Brooke was always actuated by the highest motives, and was a very charming companion. Jealousy in any shape or form did not enter into his composition. I am no judge of his capability as a fighting soldier; but feel that had it come his way in the later stages of the war he would have been one of our most brilliant commanders in the field. His long services to the country during war as Chief of the Imperial General Staff and on the Chiefs of Staff Committee were immeasurable."[21]

Anthony Eden, Foreign Secretary.

> "Brookie was the greatest of the Allied military leaders... never [left] the Prime Minister and President in any doubt as to what militarily he and the Chiefs of Staff considered right... and would never be bullied into compromise."

General Dwight Eisenhower (American).

> "Impulsive by nature, as became his Irish ancestry, [Brooke] was highly intelligent and earnestly devoted to the single purpose of winning the War. When I first met him in November 1941, he seemed to me adroit rather than deep, and shrewd rather than wise. But gradually I came to realize that his mannerisms, which seemed strange to me, were merely accidental, that he was sincere and, though he lacked that ability so characteristic of General Marshall to weigh calmly the conflicting factors

INTRODUCTION

in a problem and so reach a rock-like decision, I soon found it easy to work with him. He did not hesitate to differ sharply and vehemently, but he did so forthrightly and honestly, and heated official discussion never affected the friendliness of his personal contacts or the unqualified character of his support. He must be classed as a brilliant soldier."[22]

General Sir Harold Franklyn, commander 5th Division, part of the BEF in France in 1940.

"When Brooke visited me at 10am that morning [27 May 1940], he studied the situation in silence – it was very bad – and then all he said was 'What are you going to do about it?' I replied, 'I'm not worried about my left, but I am uneasy about the 143rd Brigade on my right – they have given and are being pushed back.' Without a word, Brooke left. He apparently went straight to HQ 1st Division... ordered Alexander to send three battalions at once to support 5th Division and sent them to support 143rd Brigade at Comines... Brooke's action in ordering up these reinforcements from I Corps on his own responsibility saved the situation."[23]

"He gave his orders clearly and decisively and one was left in no doubt as to his intentions... Brooke showed his great tactical ability under the most difficult circumstances and later proved himself to be the best strategist among the allies. He would have made a great Commander-in-Chief in the field."[24]

General Sir George Giffard.

"At the end of the war in Europe, the Commanders of the Allied Forces are being properly and warmly congratulated upon their splendid successes, but I have not seen anywhere an adequate tribute to you whom I regard as the architect and builder of our victory over Germany."

Sir James Grigg, Secretary of State for War.

"By almost universal testimony it was due largely to his skill and resolution that not only his own Corps but the whole... BEF escaped

destruction in the retreat to Dunkirk."[25]

"It is no small thing, and it is certainly unusual, that the professional head of the Army should be a man who is admitted, nay proclaimed, by every other soldier of magnitude, to be beyond doubt the most accomplished soldier in the Army."[26]

General Sir Leslie Hollis, Senior Military Assistant Secretary to the War Cabinet.

"Resolute, volatile, vibrant, versatile and sharp-tempered… but he was still a very good war-time CIGS. He was an equally good General in the field."[27]

Lieutenant General Sir Brian Horrocks.

"The more I have studied [the 1940 campaign in France which ended in the evacuation from Dunkirk], the clearer it becomes that the man who really saved the BEF was our own corps commander, Lieutenant-General A F Brooke. I felt vaguely at the time that this alert, seemingly iron, man without a nerve in his body… who gave out his orders in short, clipped sentences, was a great soldier, but it is only now that I realise fully just how great he was. We regarded him as a highly efficient military machine. It is only since I have read his diaries that I appreciate what a consummate actor he must have been. Behind the confident mask was the sensitive nature of a man who hated war, the family man-cum-birdwatcher in fact."[28]

General Hastings 'Pug' Ismay, Military Secretary to the War Cabinet and Churchill's chief staff officer.

"Brooke was by general consent the best all-rounder in his Service [Army]. He had been an unqualified success in all the Staff appointments which he had held in peace and war and had made a great reputation as a fighting commander in the retreat to Dunkirk. In council he was so quick in the uptake that he was sometimes impatient with those who were slower witted; and his habit of expressing his opinions in *positive terms led those who did not know him well to regard him as unnecessarily abrupt... It is a thousand pities that copious extracts from his private diaries have been published verbatim. They were intended for the eyes of his wife alone; many of the entries were made when he was exhausted, irritated or despondent... In these circumstances, the dogmatic, sometimes wounding, and often unjustifiable comments which he makes from time to time on his war comrades, cannot be regarded as considered judgments. There is, however, a danger that posterity, not knowing the circumstances, will take the assertions and criticisms in the diaries at face value, and will get the idea that Brooke was self-satisfied, self pitying, ungenerous and disloyal. He was none of these things. On the contrary, his selflessness, integrity and mastery of his profession earned him the complete confidence, not only of his political chiefs and his colleagues in Whitehall, but also of all our commanders in the field. On that count alone, he was worth his weight in gold. In the course of my eighteen years' service in Whitehall, I saw the work of eight different Chiefs of the Imperial General Staff at close quarters, and I would unhesitatingly say that Brooke was the best of them all."*[29]

Major General Sir John Kennedy, Director of Military Operations, War Office.

"Brooke arrived [as Chief of the Imperial General Staff] on 1st December 1941. It was a delight to work with him. He was quick and decided; his freshness made a new impact; he infected the War Office and the Chiefs of Staff with his own vitality; the change of tempo was immediate and immense."[30]

Marian Long, Arthur Bryant's researcher.

"'Brookie' is not an easy personality to capture and put on paper. There are so many different facets to him, and sometimes when interviewing people, I wonder if they are talking of the same man."

General Sir Charles Loyd.

"Few people will ever realize what you have achieved in this war and how much [your peerage] is deserved."

Field Marshal Bernard Montgomery.

"He arrived at my headquarters [near Dunkirk] to say goodbye and I saw at once that he was struggling to hold himself in check... then he broke down and wept – not because of the situation of the BEF, which indeed was enough to make anybody burst into tears, but because he had to leave us all to a fate which looked pretty bad. He, a soldier, had been ordered to abandon his men at a critical moment – that is what disturbed him... That scene in the sand-dunes on the Belgian coast is one which will remain with me all my life. I was allowed to see the real Brookie."[31]

"One of Alanbrooke's great qualities is sympathy... Another outstanding quality in his make-up is sincerity and loyalty; he is selfless, utterly sincere and entirely loyal... We in the Army knew that we could trust him absolutely."[32]

Letter from Montgomery to Brooke, February 1946.

"My dear Brookie,

Now that it has been announced that I am to succeed you, I must write and tell you how I feel about things.

During the late war you have given me many tasks to carry out; each one has been more difficult than the last, and each one has somehow been brought to a successful conclusion. But there have been moments when I have gone 'off the rails': due to impetuosity, irritation, or some such reason. You always pulled me back on to the rails, and I started off down the course again. I know very well that when I used to go 'off the rails', it increased your own work and anxieties 100 per cent. But you never complained. In the goodness of your heart you lent me a helping hand and asked nothing in return: not that I could have done anything for you. I want to say two things:

First – I am terribly grateful for all you have done for me.

Second – I could never have achieved anything if you had not been there to help me; it has been your wise guidance, and your firm handling of a very difficult subordinate, that really did the business. I could have done nothing alone.

Thank you so very much, Brookie. You have been a true friend at all times.

Your very devoted admirer,
Monty"

Lord Moran, Churchill's personal doctor.

"[Churchill] had said with a sly smile that if the Chiefs of Staff had not agreed with him he might have had to get rid of them. At once I taxed him with a direct question: 'Did you ever think of getting rid of Alanbrooke?' He became serious. 'Never.' There was a long pause. 'Never,' he repeated with complete conviction."[33]

"If Winston did not like a man he would certainly not admire him. I asked him once: 'Don't you think that Brooke is pretty good at his job?' There was rather a long pause. 'He has a flair for the business,' he grunted. That was all he would concede. Soldiers in this country, at any rate, will feel that this is an understatement of the fact. They would readily agree that Brooke was not a Marlborough or even a Wellington; the only claim they make for him is that in the Army he is recognized as the best soldier we could produce in two wars."[34]

"Alanbrooke told me that before he took up soldiering he wanted to be a surgeon. A craftsman by instinct, he knew exactly what could be done with the resources at his command and he had the craftsman's respect for method."[35]

"He recoiled from the idea of gaining ascendancy over men to get his own way. The truth was that the competitive instinct had been left out of his make-up. The brutality of war horrified him, and apart from a natural yearning to practise his profession in the exacting conditions of command in the field, he was without ambition."[36]

"A simple, gentle, selfless soul – a warning to us all not to give up hope about mankind."[37]

Lieutenant General Sir Archibald Nye, Vice Chief of the Imperial General Staff.

"Only a handful of people begin to realize all you did... you are more responsible for the winning of the war on the Allied side than any other individual with the sole exception of Winston himself."

"I was in a better position than anyone else to know all you had to cope with; and could therefore know better than others not only your great gifts but your singleness of purpose, your incorruptibility and your absolute integrity – and a combination of these qualities has made you a gigantic figure which no one could fail to admire."

General Sir Bernard Paget.

"He would have won the war in Europe a year earlier. He would have been decisive and have closely directed the campaign."

Sir Charles Portal, Chief of the Air Staff and member of the Chiefs of Staff Committee.

"I can honestly say that I have an unbounded admiration for the way you handled our [chiefs of staff] affairs and for the forcefulness and complete sincerity and the clearsightedness and soundness with which you always dealt with Ministers on our behalf – no one could ever hold a candle to your record in that respect and it was about the biggest factor in getting results."

Admiral Sir Bertram Ramsay.

"No one will ever know what the country owes to Brooke. His worth is quite uncalculable."

Field Marshal Jan Smuts, South African prime minister, as reported by Sir John Kennedy.

"I have the greatest respect for him. I believe him to be a really great man."[38]

INTRODUCTION

Marshal Joseph Stalin (Russian).
> *"A very clever military leader."*[39]

Colonel Rony Stanyforth, Brooke's military assistant in May 1940.
> *"AB is a most impenetrable man and rarely, if ever, shows what he is feeling."*

Part One

ONE

Childhood with the Perfect Mother

Brookie came from good military stock: his family were known as 'the fighting Brookes'. This strong military tradition can be traced back to Sir Basil Brooke, a captain in the English Army who was based in Ireland in the seventeenth century. Five generations later, Henry Brooke was created 1st Baronet Brooke, of Colebrooke, County Fermanagh, Ireland in 1822. By 1854, the baronetcy had passed to Victor Brooke who clearly had an active and robust approach to life: he was a gifted sportsman, enjoyed big game hunting, travelled extensively and, significantly, was a keen naturalist.

In July 1864, Victor married Alice Sophia Bellingham. He was then twenty-one years old but there is some uncertainty about Alice's age since her date of birth is recorded as circa 1844, possibly February 1845; in his biography of Brookie, David Fraser claimed that Alice was "appreciably younger" than Victor. Interestingly, the Brooke and the Bellingham families had a great deal in common. Both were steeped in military tradition, both had lived in Ireland since the seventeenth century and Alice's father, Sir Alan Bellingham, was also a baronet.

Victor's active and robust approach appears to have extended to every activity in life since between 1865 and 1879 Alice gave birth to eight children. By 1883, she was pregnant yet again and on 23 July of that year Alan Francis Brooke was born – in south-west France. Brookie explained his birthplace in his autobiographical Notes, "owing to my mother's health, my parents had been forced in 1868 to start wintering in the South of France." In the years following 1868, Victor and Alice spent increasing amounts of time in south-west France and by 1879 they had bought the Villa Jouvence in Pau, a fashionable resort town and a popular destination for the British. Fraser hinted that one reason for their relocation to France was that Alice regarded the climate and society in Pau as far more agreeable to that on offer in Ireland.

From the outset, there was an unusually strong bond between Alice and Brookie. She appears to have adored him and he, a delicate child prone to poor health, returned that adoration. Brookie's description of Alice in his Notes strongly suggests she was the central and dominant person in his childhood, "She had the faculty, so rare amongst humans, to be able to enter entirely into all one's activities, aspirations, disappointments, successes and failures and to throw herself wholeheartedly into one's life. She was consequently not only the most perfect mother but one of the very best of companions… I place her on a plane above all other members of my family." This strong bond between Brookie and his "perfect mother" continued unabated until her death in 1920.

Whilst little can be learnt about Brookie's childhood and upbringing from his Notes since he covered this subject in twenty short paragraphs, first-hand evidence is available elsewhere. In 1943, Benita asked Brookie's sister, Hylda Wrench, for information about her husband's childhood. Whilst it is unclear what prompted Benita to make this request, Hylda, who was the eighth of the nine children, duly obliged. Her account is revealing:

Alan was born on July 23 1883 at Bagnères-de-Bigorre. My Mother was 38 at the time and he was her ninth child. Douglas [the eldest of Victor and Alice's children] was 18 when he was born. I remember Mother saying how dismayed she was when she knew he was coming. I, who was the youngest, was four years old, and still called 'Baby' and she had confidently hoped there would be no more. He weighed 11 pounds, and she was very ill indeed. Kathleen and I were taken in to see her for a moment the following morning and she looked so white and shattered that I still remember.

CHILDHOOD WITH THE PERFECT MOTHER

Father had somehow never taken any interest in us as babies but Alan somehow won his heart straightaway. Mother spent most of her time in bed the following year as she could not pick up and I remember so well being in her room often when Father came in and Alan was sitting on her bed, and how he would at once stretch out his arms and was not satisfied till Father took him up. They were always great friends and Father used to call him his 'little Tommy'.

In spite of his record weight at birth, he was a very delicate baby... He had a Nourrice [baby-minder] and when she left was taken charge of by Madame Ernest, a nursery governess who was with him till he was five years old and to whom he was very much attached. Though I was so small myself at the time, I can still see him with his enormous eyes and the little fragile white face; there was something most appealing about him. The great difficulty always was to get him to take his food, right through his babyhood he absolutely refused anything solid and would shake his head with determination if he was coaxed to take even so little as a tiny morsel of bread in his milk or soup; these he called 'petit poissons' when he was able to speak and he would have none of them. The only thing, besides milk, he would submit to was tapioca soup and the only way to get him to take his full cup was by tempting him by pretending each mouthful was for somebody he cared for: 'Cette cuillère pour maman, celle-ci pour Papa'.

Even as a small child he was very dreamy and elusive, his eyes had a far-away heavenly look which very much impressed our German Governess, Frieda; I remember on one occasion her saying she was sure he was thinking of other-worldy things, but when we enquired all that was occupying him was whether a little bump on his knee would be blue the next day! When he was under five we went to Colebrooke [the family home in Ireland] for the summer, and Basil [son of Douglas, the eldest of the nine children] was born. Alan did not take much interest at the time but he evidently fully realised his important relationship to Basil a few years later when he was 8 for he insisted on being called 'Uncle Alan'!

It was the following summer... that Mother hardened her heart and had his hair cut; he wore it in long golden curls which rather suited his romantic little pale, serious face, though I never can imagine how Father submitted to it or to the little Lord Fauntleroy suits with lace collars. I was rather sad at the loss of his curls, I remember, and I kept one which I still have and which I shall look out to give you when we return.

The next summer, when he had his eighth birthday, we went to Colebrooke again, the last time before Father died… We children did not of course realise that he was so ill or indeed that he was ill at all, he lived exactly the same life as usual and refused to adopt any invalid ways… The actual day on which he died, Alan and I were playing in the garden… and all the afternoon we saw carriages driving up to enquire how he was; for the first time it dawned upon us that perhaps he was very ill and we turned and looked at each other in a frightened way. It was that evening, the 23rd, at 7 o'clock, that our governess came into the schoolroom crying and told us that he was dead.

Alan was very young for such an experience and within a year he twice again came face to face with death. That spring, the poor little hunchback son of our coachman died and our governess took us to the house to take flowers I think. We were shown into his room and I feel sure it must have made a deep impression upon Alan, even if he did not realise it, seeing the poor little pathetic creature lying there in his best Sunday clothes with tall lit candlesticks round his bed – a little boy like himself. And then at the end of the summer, Mother's favourite brother came out to Bagnères-de-Bigorre to comfort her and died within three weeks of arriving.

It was a sad summer as Mother was very ill and in bed the whole time, but we children managed to make ourselves happy in spite of it all, as children do. I can still see Alan in the little white sailor suits he wore, shorts of course, on his bicycle.

We did not go back to the Villa Jouvence that winter as Mother felt she could not face it… [Alan] had got stronger by now but every spring he used to have long attacks of slow fever which worried Mother very much and kept him in bed for weeks.

But to go back for a bit to those happy years at the Jouvence. He must, I think, have been a very good little boy for I cannot remember any outbursts of temper or naughtiness, which is far from being the case where the rest of us were concerned. I think one reason for this was that he lived in a world of his own and outward happenings did not affect him much, so that he submitted to existing rules without minding. His education was a slow business, he had his lessons from a very nice Mademoiselle Camilou who came in every day… The worst trouble he ever got into was at his lessons for it was most difficult to get him to give his attention; he sat there dreamily playing with his eyelashes, a far-away look in his big eyes and Mademoiselle C never knew how far he was attending. It seemed impossible to teach him to read, he was always making mistakes in his letters and this of course did mean many reproaches and scoldings. It was only when he was seven and still could not read that he was taken [to] an occulist and the cause of his extraordinary backwardness was discovered – namely that his eyes were not in focus and that he needed spectacles temporarily. He was always good at sums. I need not tell you that he had trouble with his spelling!

It does not seem to me on looking back that he had any little boy friends those early years, I mean not of his own age. Our last two winters at the Jouvence, Jack Browne, who went to Herr Querndt's school, came to us for his half holidays on Saturdays, but he was a year older than me. The last winter Victor Yeats Brown also was at the school and came with Jack, he was only 2½ years older than Alan but he was not at all Alan's sort.

One of the outstanding things in Alan's life was his devotion to Victor [Brookie's brother] who was ten years older than him. Our last winter at the Jouvence, Victor, who was 18, lived in the little Castle Jumbo at the other end of the garden. He was working at shorthand and in my free hours I used to dictate to him; to both Alan and I, the hours we spent there were the happiest hours in our day. Mother was so ill that winter that she was practically always in bed, and for many weeks after Father's death Victor slept in her room so as to be at hand should she have one of her faint turns … The pride of Alan's heart was being Victor's 'valet' as he called him; what his duties exactly consisted of I cannot remember, but I think chiefly in helping him to look after his various collections of birds, stuffed birds, eggs, etc., and running messages. Victor always added a romantic quality to life with his enthusiasms, the discipline he exercised over himself, the difficult things he was always aiming at, both physically and mentally. I remember that that last winter walking on his hands was one of his new accomplishments and he used to come into the dining room walking on them, much to the agitation of Frieda… He was also always doing ambitious and surprising things on his bicycle and was altogether the chief source of colour in our lives.

One never quite knew what was going on in Alan's little mind, one of the tantalising things about him was his un-get-at-able quality. But evidently the sad things that happened in his life so young did leave a very deep mark for I still can hear the urgent pleading sound in his voice when he said his evening prayers to Mother and the sense he gave of trying to ward off further impending calamities: 'Fais que Maman ne meurt pas, et fais que la maison ne brûle pas, et fais que je ne me noie pas' [that Mother does not die and that the house does not burn and that I do not drown]. At the time, as children we were amused but looking back one realises what that prayer revealed of the inner workings of a little heart shaken by the experiences it had lived through – though in no other way did he ever give a hint of such a thing.

At this time, he intended to become a sailor and he enjoyed wearing his sailor suits, but whether the drowning possibilities affected him or whether it was admiration for dear old Doctor Bagnell, I don't know, but he surprised us one day by announcing he was going to be a Doctor and this idea he stuck to for some years.

We were all very keen about daring experiments on our swing and seesaw but he did not take any part in them, in fact at this time he certainly showed no indication of the very masculine being he was going to become – not that he was in any way girlish, far too reserved and unemotional for anything of that kind.

On looking back it seems to me that one of his most outstanding qualities was his capacity for keeping himself occupied, he possessed this quality to a unique extent. I have often thought of it for I have never come across a child like him in this respect. One never had 'to play with him', he was quite independent of anything of the kind, indeed he did not even wish it, he was far too busy with his own avocations and leading his own private life. I do not even remember his sharing much in the games we played but he could sit for hours watching with absorbed interest Victor stuffing a bird or cleaning his rifle.

Till Father died, we went to Colebrooke for the summer when Mother was well enough, but this was not often the case, and we then went to Biarritz or to Normandy, but after Father's death all our summers were spent at Bagnères... Here he again had an experience which must have left a deep impression. Next to the [villa], there was a timber yard to which was attached a carpentering shop and here Alan spent most of his time watching, fascinated, whether the work in the timber yard or the carpentering shop; anything of that kind always absorbed him. The son of the owner was a young man with whom he made friends and with whom he spent many happy hours while he was at work. One morning when I was in the garden, Alan came rushing up to me with a white face and horror in his eyes. He told me that the young man, who was consumptive, though of course we children did not realise this, had had a fit of violent coughing which had brought on a terrible haemorrhage and he had died there and then in the yard choked by it.

As if this were not enough, that afternoon Alan and I were standing at the foot of the garden which looked out on the high road [and] a runaway dogcart came down the road and the woman in it was flung out over a stone wall into a small enclosure, and lay there badly injured... I remember going to bed feeling shattered – but what must his feelings have been.

The following summer we went to the little house at Bagnères, Maison Barutel... One incident stands out that summer; there had been a lot of rabies about owing to the fact that it was a very hot summer and we children were cautioned not to have anything to do with strange dogs. One afternoon we had been for a picnic with the de Bouvouloirs, a large party, quite a procession of carriages. As we were coming back that evening and going through a small village, we noticed a Pyrenean dog who did not look at all right. Alan, who was bicycling, was beside the carriage and we saw the dog go up to the bicycle and brush up against it but did not realise that anything had happened till a few minutes later one of us noticed a large red stain slowly spreading on the little white shorts of his sailor suit. We stopped at once of course and one or two of the married women took him into a cottage and investigated. They were horrified to find a large bite. That evening Kathleen and I took him round to Bag's house next door, and he cauterised the wound; we were not present but he said that Alan was very brave. The point of the story is that Alan never said anything on the subject and we did not think that he realised that there was any cause for anxiety, so I was very much taken aback when, three weeks later, he one day said to me: 'Now there is no longer any danger is there of my going mad?' It just showed what he had been going through inside without ever saying a word.

Mother never had any anxieties or trouble about Alan during his schooling years, the only thing that used to trouble her was that he did not seem to have any ambition or sufficient 'go' to satisfy her. I have sometimes thought that seeing Victor doing everything so brilliantly, he did not feel he could compete and was quite happy just to admire him. But Mother wondered whether he would have been different had Father lived and blamed herself for having failed in some way to stir up his ambitions for his own future. He had by now decided to become a soldier but he took it all very calmly so that one had no idea of the possibilities lying under that quiet exterior.

I did not see him again till the winter of 1902 as I went out to South Africa for 18 months at the time of the Boer War. He was then at Woolwich [Royal Military Academy] and came up to London on Sundays; he used to walk all the way from Waterloo Station to the Zoo and spend the morning there, coming to North Audley Street for lunch. I so wanted to ask him for the weekends but there was no spare room... I so minded his only having just the day. He had developed *very much and we had some real talks and I was struck at the way in which he thought things out for himself and did not take them for granted, but he was more reserved than ever and very much of a personality. He had quite outgrown his delicacy and, of all Mother's nine children, he was the only one who never caused her any anxiety about his health after his early childhood.*

Seven points in Hylda's account are worth highlighting. First, the young Brookie displayed little sign of the daunting and formidable personality which was to emerge in later years. The impression created by Hylda is that of a quiet, reserved, well-behaved, obedient and compliant child who was content to fall into line with what was required of him, "He must, I think, have been a very good little boy for I cannot remember any outbursts of temper or naughtiness... I think one reason for this was that he lived in a world of his own and outward happenings did not affect him much, so that he submitted to existing rules without minding."

Second, Hylda recalled "the great difficulty... to get him to take his food, right through his babyhood he absolutely refused anything solid, and would shake his head with determination if he was coaxed to take even so little as a tiny morsel of bread in his milk or soup". One possible explanation is childish stubbornness but, as will become apparent, there was a streak of steely determination in Brookie: in his Notes, "[My mother] had the great quality of making us work to the fullest of our ability and of instilling us with a determination to succeed in life". This determination hinted at the presence of a strong will.

Third, Hylda also created the impression that the perfect mother was a domineering woman who exercised a controlling hold over the young Brookie. There was something rather ominous about this section, "Mother hardened her heart and had his hair cut; he wore it in long golden curls which rather suited his romantic little pale, serious face, though I never can imagine how Father submitted to it, or to the little Lord Fauntleroy suits with lace collars."

In truth, the perfect mother was far from universally admired. Maude Butler, Brookie's cousin, was forthright when she recalled an incident involving one of Brookie's sisters, Kathleen. Whilst her language and grammar are poor, the gist is crystal clear:

> [Kathleen] broke down nursing in War 1 [First World War] and developed TB and it was then they sent for me to go to [the perfect mother]. When Kathleen was dying and had to leave hospital, dear friends at Cambo-les-bains took her in – Aunt Alice [the perfect mother] would not have her for fear of infection! – to me quite incredible, but to [the family] perfectly natural, 'little mother', as they called her, must run no risks.
>
> I'm sure she didn't mean to be selfish but it had become an unbreakable cult. I only went to see Kathleen once at Cambo and she was amazed that [the perfect mother] could be left for a whole day and not have her usual reading aloud. Kathleen kept saying 'but how did you do it?' I simply said [to the perfect mother] 'I'm going' and thought she'd be pleased but she was only surprised I should think of leaving her.
>
> I hope you won't think hardly of what I have said about Alan's mother, everybody adored her, she'd a wonderful natural charm and beauty and I can only think was worshipped into being self-centred. It was extraordinary how she was able to enter into the boys' lives of sport and soldiering, they loved telling her everything. She was always game and 'in it' from shooting tigers to tanks. Just lying in her enormous bed – she slept one side of it and spent the day in the other and used to talk of 'moving across' as if it were a long journey! But she was terrified of thunderstorms and no matter what hour of the night they came, you had to fly to her.

This portrait of the perfect mother is consistent with the recollection of an Englishwoman who lived in Pau and knew the Brooke family: she recalled "a lovely old lady with white hair lying in bed or on a 'chaise longue' and that visiting children rarely saw her but were constantly told not to make too much noise in the house so as not to disturb Lady Brooke."

The whiff of hypochondria that emanates from Maude Butler's story was evident in Hylda's recollections, "Mother spent most of her time in bed the following year as she could not pick up". It was also evident in Brookie's Notes since he recorded that she was bedridden for the "last 15 to 20 years of her life". If Maude Butler's description of the perfect mother as "selfish" and "self-centred" is accurate, which seems likely since hypochondria is a symptom of self-centredness, then this would explain Brookie's education by private governesses followed by attendance at the local school in Pau, St George's: in his Notes, "I had remained at Pau without going to a public school owing to the fact that as a small boy I had been very delicate and that it had been considered better for my health to remain at Pau". Perhaps, but equally convincing is the explanation that the perfect mother was a selfish, controlling parent who kept him in Pau because she wanted to keep her youngest son close to her side. There is a letter in Brookie's papers dated August 1914 which is consistent with this explanation since it refers to "the beautiful thoughts" which the perfect mother had "for her little ones and how she must have watched over and guarded her 'treasures.'"

Hylda's remark, "It does not seem to me on looking back that he had any little boyfriends those early years", shows Brookie had limited contact and interaction with other children. In his Notes, he stated, "owing to the small number of boys [at St George's School], games suffered" and then added "the fact that I had not been to a public school left a serious gap in my early life." In a later section of his Notes when describing his entry into the Royal Military Academy at Woolwich, he made a revealing observation, "I felt that I was not quite one of the herd, I had missed something that they had all had." That "something" was probably exposure to, and experience of, the outside world because the evidence strongly suggests Brookie had a sheltered and protected childhood, despite the number of deaths which he witnessed.

Fourth, there was an element of aimlessness in the young Brookie. Hylda recorded that he was "dreamy and elusive… One never quite knew what was going on in Alan's little mind, one of the tantalising things about him was his un-get-at-able quality… The worst trouble he ever got into was at his lessons for it was most difficult to get him to give his attention, he sat there dreamily playing with his eyelashes, a far-away look in his big eyes". Towards the end of her account, Hylda stated, "the only thing that used to trouble [Mother] was that he did not seem to have any ambition or sufficient 'go' to satisfy her." According to Brookie's Notes, the perfect mother clearly attempted to instil some ambition into her aimless son, "When about 8 years old, I was out driving with my mother at Bagnères-de-Bigorre in her carriage and pair. We passed a house with a tablet on it. I asked my mother what the meaning was of this tablet… shortly afterwards, on the same drive, we passed the house that I was born in and my mother turned to me saying, 'I want to see a similar tablet on this house stating that you were born here'… she used to express her doubts as to whether this tablet would ever be established unless I showed more zeal about my holiday tasks". However, she appears to have failed since decades later Lord Moran would observe of Brookie, "The truth was that the competitive instinct had been left out of his make-up… he was without ambition."[1]

The fifth point worth highlighting was Brookie's devotion to his brother, Victor: he took "pride" in being Victor's "valet". In his Notes, Brookie wrote that he "became my hero… I could not have had a more perfect type of man to emulate". Victor, who was ten years older than Brookie and appears to have excelled at everything he did, was, perhaps, the archetypal Brooke. Hero worship is a common enough characteristic in a young boy yet, interestingly, Brookie was still signing off his letters to Victor with "Your old valet" or "With worlds of love from your old valet" when he was twenty-seven years old. This long-standing admiration of his older brother hinted at the existence of an impressionable streak in Brookie which, as will become apparent, never completely disappeared.

Sixth, Hylda noted that "one of his most outstanding qualities was his capacity for keeping himself occupied, he possessed this quality to a unique extent, I have often thought of it for I have never come across a child like him in this respect. One never had 'to play with him', he was quite independent of anything of the kind". Clearly, the young Brookie was perfectly content with his own company. This "independent" spirit was also evident in one of Hylda's later remarks: when she met him after he had entered the Academy at Woolwich, "I was struck at the way in which he thought things out for himself and did not take them for granted". Her observations suggested he was self-reliant and self-assured.

Finally, Hylda stated that "he surprised us one day by announcing he was going to be a Doctor" and then added, "this idea he stuck to for some years." Towards the end of her account, she used strange language when explaining Brookie's 'decision' to enter the army, "He had by now decided to become a soldier but he took it all very calmly so that one had no idea of the possibilities lying under that quiet exterior." The clear inference was that entering the army may not have been Brookie's own choice of career. In his biography of Brookie, Fraser hinted at the same conclusion, observing that "by the age of sixteen it had been decided that he should seek entry to the Army"[2]: his use of "it" is telling. If someone did exert pressure on Brookie to enter the army, or made the decision for him, then the most likely culprits are either the perfect mother or his eldest brother, Douglas, who Brookie described in his Notes as "my second father" or his older "hero" brother, Victor. Perhaps the importance of upholding the military traditions of the Brooke and Bellingham families was impressed upon him – and the obedient and compliant Brookie, who "submitted to existing rules without minding", acquiesced. Regardless, his destiny had been settled. After a sheltered and protected childhood, Brookie was embarking on a career in the army.

TWO

1900–1939

"At the age of 16 in the spring of 1900, I left St George's School [in Pau] and went to a 'crammer' at Roehampton [in England]", Brookie recalled in his Notes. After attending this intensive six-month preparatory course, he sat and passed the entrance examination into the Royal Military Academy at Woolwich, coming seventh from last in the list of new intakes. The two-year course at the academy, which he entered in December 1900, led to a commission in either the Royal Artillery or the Royal Engineers. With little experience of the outside world, it would have been a demanding challenge for Brookie, as he acknowledged in his Notes, "Whilst at the crammers and at the Royal Military Academy I felt that I was not quite one of the herd, I had missed something that they had all had. As a result, I was inclined to suffer from an inferiority complex which I found very hard to battle against and which stuck to me through my early life. This failing was accentuated by being intensely shy and terrified of doing the wrong thing." One of his contemporaries observed, "At Woolwich it was evident that Brooke was highly strung; he lived on his nerves and found it difficult to relax, finding an outlet for his restless energy in riding, shooting and other activities."

Despite their physical separation, the bond between Brookie and the perfect mother remained as strong as ever, well illustrated by the regular flow of letters which he sent her. In one letter dated 1 July 1902,

My dear little pet,
I shall keep a kind of a diary here for you in my letters but on days

in which there is nothing of interest I shall not write down, I shall send you the letter every Sunday.

Ever your loving little son,
Alan

His unusual greeting of "My dear little pet" was often used, sometimes varied to "My own precious little pet". Likewise, he regularly signed off his letters with "Ever your loving little son" or phrases such as "I must stop now with oceans of love to you and all", "with the very hugest of huge hugs for your own precious wee self" or "with worlds of love and longing to come out". Occasionally, he added "Your Benjamin": when used in this manner, Benjamin means the youngest, and possibly the most beloved, son of a large family.

Throughout his life, Brookie enjoyed drawing and sketching and his letters to the perfect mother often included a sketch. Some of his drawings around the turn of the century – a fox riding on a bloodhound, an animal about to eat a human being and a toad dressed up as an equerry – corroborated Hylda's observation that he "did not take [things] for granted" and hinted at the presence of an open and questioning mind. It was probably around this time that Brookie developed his talent for mimicry: he was, according to Major General Allen, "endowed with a great sense of humour which made his repartees devastating but never ill natured."

Despite living "on his nerves" at Woolwich, Brookie rose to meet the challenge of the two-year course and after passing out in seventeenth place, he was commissioned to join the Royal Regiment of Artillery on 24 December 1902. By this time, according to Hylda, "he had developed very much… he was more reserved than ever, and very much of a personality. He had quite outgrown his delicacy". In his Notes, "I look back on my 2 years at the shop [Woolwich] as a happy but strenuous time during which I learned much… especially in the most important of all accomplishments in life, that of sizing up the relative values of one's fellow men." This final remark is worth highlighting since, as will become apparent, Brookie would prove to be a formidably good judge of his "fellow men": he read people extremely well.

His first posting, which lasted for three years, was to an artillery battery based in Ireland. During this period, he designed a timed percussion fuse and submitted it together with detailed drawings to the War Office for consideration. Even though his submission was rejected, Brookie was displaying resourcefulness and a conscientious attitude.

In 1906, he volunteered for service in India, probably because he was keen to travel and visit foreign countries. He clearly enjoyed the eight years which he spent in what was then the jewel of the British Empire and it was during this period that his love of nature developed, an interest which he may well have inherited, perhaps copied, from his father. In his Notes, "Most of my days shooting consisted in an early rise before dawn, a walk in the dark to some point of vantage on a hill top where we sat waiting for the sun to rise. As the light came the valley was filled with mist which resembled a slightly rippled sea with surrounding hill tops emerging like islands through this sea of mist. Sunrise under those wild surroundings was something never to be forgotten. Personally, I have always felt that when placed in such completely unspoilt beauty of nature, it is easier to realise the greatness of our Maker than in any man-made cathedral. The whole atmosphere is one that is conducive to the deepest thoughts on life, religion and human endeavour. I have certainly obtained more religious and spiritual help throughout my life by close contacts with nature and all its beauties and wonderful conceptions than through books or my contacts with churches and clergy."

Hunting and shooting trips were a common activity for members of the British Army stationed in India. In his Notes, "I derived the most intense thrill from the pursuit of wild game, and the pitting of my own intelligence against that of wild animals on their own ground. And yet from the very start, I had experienced pangs of regret and repentance when a hunt was brought to a successful end by the destruction of some wild creature that I had been the cause of. Strange feeling of deep dissatisfaction with oneself at the very moment of elation at having accomplished the task one had set one's heart on… I had been finding recently that by replacing the rifle more and more by the camera, I still obtained all the thrills of the chase without any of the personal reproaches at its outcome… The feelings that I was experiencing are, I think, exemplified by one of my letters,

> [I] crept up to about 40 yards from [the buffalo] and examined him carefully. All my better feelings were for leaving him but a desperate struggle was going on inside me… I decided to shoot him, got ready and had the rifle on him ready to shoot when he turned a little more broadside on. But he turned the other way and started grazing towards me, he looked absolutely glorious and somehow I could not bring myself to shoot him when in the back of my mind I felt I did not really want him. So I changed my mind and decided to let him off and to take a photograph instead. With the rifle at full cock I crept up to within 30 yards of him and, holding the rifle between my knees in case he should turn nasty, I took 3 snapshots of him.

I have lost most of my shooting trophies and do not miss them much, but I still have those 3 snapshots and they always stir up the happiest memories when I look at them."

One of his many letters to the perfect mother, written in February 1907 when he was twenty-three years old, suggests that Brookie had not by this stage developed much interest in the opposite sex, "Both Norton and I long to be off in the jungle somewhere crawling about for buck or something instead of messing about handing cakes at tea to a lot of ugly and very uninteresting women who all imagine themselves to be goddesses of creation."

Officers serving in India were allowed periods of six months' leave. In 1908, Brookie took his first leave, returned home and promptly became engaged to Jane Richardson who was then twenty-seven years old. The Richardsons, who were neighbours of the Brookes in County Fermanagh, Ireland, were another family steeped in military tradition: in his Notes, "we had known each other for many years." This engagement appears slightly odd. First, Brookie and Janey, as she was called, were markedly different personalities, a fact noted by Fraser in his biography of Brookie. Second, he had been stationed in India since late 1906 and, consequently, there had been no opportunity for this relationship to develop in the intervening period. Third, the engagement then lasted six years. The fact he was stationed overseas is an obvious explanation for this lengthy betrothal. Another, and the one proffered by Fraser, was Brookie's lack of financial means.

Two further sections in his Notes relating to his time in India deserve mention. The first, dated 1908, hinted again at the existence of an impressionable streak in Brookie, "I also disliked parting with Wardrop [his battery commander] who had become an idol to me [and] Main, to whom I was devoted." The second was dated 1911, "About this period, Carlisle and I had been reading articles in the 'Field' on catapults… on railway journeys I used to amuse myself shooting up natives on the backside as they stooped over." Interestingly, Brookie was twenty-seven or twenty-eight years old when he was playing with catapults.

In 1914, Brookie was granted four months' leave to return home and marry Janey. On the day of their wedding, 28 July 1914, Austria-Hungary invaded Serbia which triggered the start of the First World War. Eight days later, his honeymoon was interrupted by a telegram ordering his recall. By early November 1914, Brookie was in command of a troop on the Western Front in France: his troop's quartermaster described him as a "Commanding Officer to whom one could take all problems and be sure of support and solution."[1] Subject to periods of leave and time spent in reserve, Brookie spent the entire war on the Western Front and was present at many of its famous battles such as Neuve Chapelle, Somme, Vimy Ridge and Passchendaele.

In January 1915, he was promoted to staff captain and assumed the role of adjutant to the commander of the 2nd Cavalry Division. Brookie's description of his new commander was a good example of his ability to read people well, "charming… but certainly not one of the world's workers. He had looked upon his profession as a means of providing him with an easy-going life connected with horses, hunting and good friends: his dislike of work was so deeply ingrained that… I very soon found that if things were to run smoothly, I should have to do most of his work for him as well as my own."

In letters written to the perfect mother, Brookie described his experiences in the battle of Neuve Chapelle in 1915. On 11 March, "Messages come in saying some of our shells are dropping among our own infantry, one dashes to the telephone to pass it on to the batteries concerned – knowing every second means mens' lives". Five days later, "the Colonel forwarded my name amongst those for 'mentioning in despatches... whose ability and energy I cannot speak too highly of'. But please do not mention it to anybody yet as of course it is only his report... However, it is at any rate very satisfactory to feel that he appreciated the work". On 21 March, "[The observation post] was a specially good place for looking down on to the lines of trenches and a lovely spring afternoon with lovely warm sun, the birds beginning to sing and everything could be almost felt to be growing". Six days later, "Yesterday I had crawled out to a hay stack to see if it would be suitable to observe from and was coming back when I was spotted by a sniper who made me hurry back faster than I liked, but he did not do any very good shooting".

In another letter to the perfect mother, he described the battle at Festubert in May 1915,

It was a very gruesome sight. But the heartbreaking part of it was to see the poor wounded fellows between the two rows of trenches who could not be fetched back under cover. During the night, they succeeded in getting a lot of them back but they must have had a ghastly day of it lying in the sun.

Brookie elaborated in his Notes, "We supported a series of abortive attacks which seldom penetrated the enemy front line and resulted in one of the worst shambles in no-man's land that I have ever seen. I shall never forget the ghastly sights from the Artillery Observation Posts in the roofs of houses only a couple of hundred yards from the front line. The space intervening between the trenches was covered with dead and dying. The wounded lay in a scorching May sun throughout the day without water and writhing in agony from their wounds."

In November 1915, following his promotion to brigade major, Brookie was assigned to the 18th Infantry Division, commanded by Major General Maxse. An intimidating man with a fierce manner, Maxse was held in high regard. He was a passionate believer in training and a skilled tactician who was open to new ideas, quick to spot their salient points and willing to adopt them. Brookie described him as a "great character", and it is likely that Maxse had a considerable influence on the newly appointed brigade major. At their first meeting, Maxse told Brookie "I don't like your hat" which drew the following reply, "Neither do I and if you give me a week's leave, I shall go home and buy a new one": in his Notes, "I did not get my week's leave but was not attacked again for a bit." During his time with the 18th Infantry Division, one of Brookie's superior officers remarked, "Brooke is magnificent, he does everything but I do wish he'd sometimes tell me what he's doing for I am the CRA [Commander, Royal Artillery]." Another superior officer said of him, "He is a marvel and the best we have got."

Brookie's growing reputation was, in part, due to his refinement and development of the 'creeping barrage'. Traditionally, artillery barrages preceded infantry attacks for time periods ranging from hours to days and were then halted when the infantry attack began. The theory behind the 'creeping barrage' was that artillery fire should continue after the start of an infantry attack, targeted at the area in front of the advancing infantry: consequently, as the infantry moved forward, the artillery barrage would continue moving – or creeping – forward ahead of them. Brookie has on occasions been credited with devising the concept of the 'creeping barrage' but, in truth, it was devised by the French, a fact which he freely acknowledged in his Notes. However, he certainly adapted and improvised the concept to good effect, notably in his sector in the battle of the Somme.

Shortly after the start of the battle of the Somme in July 1916, Brookie was writing in these terms, "A modern battlefield is just about as gruesome a sight as one could ever see. Absolute chaos everywhere… and the most ghastly sights of mutilated and distorted corpses." Two months later, "The ground up near the front line is like nothing on earth! Along the Pozières Ridge the surface of the ground is just like the pictures of the moon, all the craters of the shells touching each other".

In February 1917, he was transferred to the Canadian Corps and appointed chief of staff to the commander of the Corps artillery: it was here that he acquired the nickname, 'the Barrage King'. In his Notes, Brookie assessed his new commander in typically forthright style, "full of bravery and instilled the finest of fighting spirit in the whole of the artillery under his command but as regards the tactical handling of artillery he knew practically nothing."

His description of the battle of Passchendaele suggests that by 1917 he had become hardened to the horrors and brutality of war, "The sights up there are beyond all description; it is a blessing to a certain extent that one becomes callous to it all and that one's mind is not able to take it all in." However, some of his letters to the perfect mother clearly show he was "able to take it all in" and, moreover, did "take it all in". In one letter, written in 1918,

> *Yesterday we attacked Cambrai… I followed into the town at 10am… the scene was beyond description. The contrast between war and peace was the thing that struck me most, one dilapidated house with its end blown off and the inside wrecked but sitting on the mantelpiece of one of the rooms, as if no war was on, a stuffed jay with its head on one side.*
>
> *One trip up to Lens where I wandered among the ruins… such ruin and desolation. I climbed onto a heap of stones which represents the place where the Church once stood and I looked down on the wreckage. One could spend days there just looking down picturing to oneself the tragedies that have occurred in every corner of this place. If the stones could talk and repeat what they have witnessed, and the thoughts they had read on dying men's faces, I wonder if there would ever be any wars.*

In another letter, written a few days before the armistice on 11 November 1918,

Today I had a long walk round Douai cemetery, looking at all the graves, French, English, Russian, Italian and German all equally well cared for… in the middle of the cemetery the Germans had put up a big stone monument like this [he drew a sketch of it in his letter]. On the three corner stones are three medallions with the French, English and German crests, each face turned towards the respective country. On each frontal face at the top is written Pro Patria and at the bottom on each side:

A La Memoire Des Braves Camerades
Den Gefallnen Kameraden Zur Ehre
In Memory of Brave Comrades

One of those brave comrades was Brookie's "hero" brother, Victor, who was killed in action in 1914.

Brookie was in London when the armistice was announced. In his Notes, "I watched London go mad on Armistice night. That wild evening jarred on my feelings. I felt untold relief at the end being there at last but was swamped with floods of memories of those years of struggle. I was filled with gloom that evening and retired to sleep early." If there had been an element of innocence in Brookie at the outbreak of war in 1914, which is a very real possibility, then it had been eradicated by November 1918. There was, however, cause for celebration since he had just become a father, Janey having given birth to their first child, Rosemary, on 25 October 1918.

The hallmarks of Brookie's wartime service between 1914 and 1918 appear to have been diligence, dedication, reliability and, as the war progressed, expertise: he was a conscientious soldier who believed it was his duty to perform to the best of his ability and he applied himself to every task assigned to him. By the end of the War, he had been promoted to lieutenant colonel, awarded the Distinguished Service Order twice and mentioned six times in despatches. More importantly, he had acquired four years' experience of fighting the German Army which, as will become apparent, left him impressed by their fighting abilities and qualities. His respect for Germany's armed forces would shape his thinking in the Second World War.

In 1919, Brookie was selected to attend the Staff College Course at Camberley as a student. It was here that he met and developed his friendship with John Dill, who was an instructor at the college. In his Notes, "I know no other soldier in the whole of my career who inspired me with greater respect and admiration. An exceptionally clear and well-balanced brain, an infinite capacity for work, unbounded charm of personality but, above all, an unflinchable straightness of character". Brookie would succeed Dill as Chief of the Imperial General Staff [CIGS] in 1941 and, thereafter, the two men would work closely together until Dill's death in late 1944.

At the end of the course, Brookie was posted to Newcastle as a member of the general staff of the 50th Northumbrian Division. Two events occurred during his time in Newcastle, namely Brookie and Janey's second child, Tom, was born on 9 January 1920 and the perfect mother died on 27 July 1920.

In January 1923, he returned to the Staff College at Camberley, this time as an instructor. In 1925, halfway through his four years at Camberley, disaster struck when Brookie and Janey were involved in a serious car accident: the man who "thought fast, talked fast and moved fast"[2] also drove fast. The accident was caused by a cyclist pulling out in front of Brookie's car and in taking evasive action he lost control of his vehicle which overturned, leaving Janey paralysed from broken vertebrae. Following an operation, she contracted pneumonia and died a few days later. Brookie, who suffered a broken leg and five broken ribs, blamed himself for the accident. In his Notes, "It took me many months to recover from the shock of this tragedy... It was thanks to Basil [Brookie's nephew] and his wife that I recovered the desire to live and renewal of interest in life... [I chose] to immerse myself as soon as possible in work and to let absorption in my profession smother pangs of memory". The "pangs of memory" were probably pangs of guilt since Brookie was profoundly affected by this tragedy and he withdrew into himself. In his biography of Brookie, Fraser claimed that he became a distant, uncommunicative and strict father to his two children, Rosemary and Tom, who were then six and five years old. If

Fraser is to be believed, and it is reasonable to do so since his claim was based on "personal communications to the author"[3], this was clearly not Brookie's finest hour. The obvious conclusion was that without a wife and partner he did not function well and as a sole parent he floundered badly.

It was not long after Janey's death that Brookie contemplated leaving the army and emigrating to New Zealand. In his Notes, "I had… reached a restless stage in my career… promotion was slowing up… I could see no great prospects of making much of my military career. I seriously contemplated migrating to New Zealand and began to collect all the information I could about the country." At this point in the story, it is necessary to move forward in time. After Brookie's death in 1963, Benita wrote to one of his former colleagues, Captain Short. In his reply, Short referred to two letters which Brookie had written to him decades earlier, "these letters show a little of Lord Alanbrooke's work and views between the wars but the interesting one shows how the course of history might easily have been changed as in 1927 he had serious thoughts of coming to New Zealand as army prospects in those days were rather dim". The "interesting one", written by Brookie on 30 April 1927, revealed the extent to which he was affected by Janey's death,

> *I had serious thoughts myself of coming out to New Zealand as prospects in the Army are not very bright these days and promotion very slow… I had a great misfortune 2 years ago and lost my wife in a motor accident. I had also 5 ribs and my leg broken and very much wish that I could have been finished off at the same time.*

Brookie's choice of New Zealand can be second-guessed. To this lover of nature, New Zealand would have appeared a beautiful, undeveloped country offering a natural wilderness and, perhaps, an escape from unhappy memories. However, as a sole parent of two young children, emigration to the other side of the world was almost certainly an unrealistic option so he remained in the army in England, lonely and withdrawn.

In 1927, he attended the newly created Imperial Defence College as a student. This college had been created on the recommendation of a cabinet committee chaired by Winston Churchill, then Secretary of State for the Colonies. Its principal purposes were the defence of the British Empire and the development of greater understanding between military and civilian leaders on defence, security and strategic issues. This training required Brookie to adopt a more global perspective when considering the higher direction and management of war and is likely to have proved valuable after he became CIGS in 1941.

In 1929, he was promoted to brigadier and appointed commandant of the School of Artillery at Larkhill, a post he held until 1932. The state of the Larkhill camp in 1929 appalled Brookie who, with his customary energy and drive, set about improving the living conditions which earned him widespread respect. One description of him at the time was, "He was not a mixer nor was he a martinet [a stickler for rules]. A pure and simple soldier… as regimental as a button-stick."[4] Another, provided by a fellow officer, was, "He was a thinking soldier, he was head and shoulders above the ordinary officer of his rank at that time. We all thought he should be higher. You felt his presence. He filled a room."[5]

One notable feature of Brookie's time at Larkhill was the importance he attached to training, especially the training of officers: as will become apparent, he regarded leadership as crucially important. Brookie introduced training courses for junior officers which emphasised the importance of collaboration between the different services of the armed forces and, to this end, he invited members of other services to give lectures. He also introduced training courses for commanders of artillery divisions, many of whom were senior in age to Brookie. In his Notes, "I don't think many of them had given much thought to tactics or their development; they certainly had few ideas on the subject. As a result, I had little difficulty in getting them to accept mine."

By now, Brookie was recovering from the aftermath of Janey's death. The explanation for this recovery was almost certainly his developing relationship with Benita Blanche Lees. Benita, the eldest daughter of Sir Thomas Pelly, was a widow, her first husband having been killed in the First World War. She was an intelligent, capable woman but, more importantly, she possessed the quality of calmness which would have appealed to the energetic and restless Brookie. They first met in 1928 and by September 1929 they were engaged. Brookie was now a changed man, well illustrated by two letters he wrote to her in October 1929. In the first,

> *I am continually marvelling at my completely transformed outlook on life generally due to your existence, the increased interest in everything and the complete joie de vivre which I had entirely lost… That perfectly ghastly feeling of being absolutely alone in life… you have absolutely dispelled.*[6]

and in the second,

> *I can't ever explain what balm and comfort you bring… but I do know that a greyness has been there over everything all these years and that though it's been painted over by interests and various activities you are taking it away and each time with you brings a fresh glimpse and feeling of heavenly light and glow of new life and joy.*[7]

They originally planned to marry in the spring of 1930 but brought the wedding forward to December 1929. He was then forty-six years old and Benita was thirty-seven. Childless from her first marriage, it is probably a safe guess that Benita was keen to have children and, given her age, this may explain why the wedding date was brought forward: if this was Benita's wish, Brookie appears to have been only too happy to oblige. Fourteen months after their wedding, Kathleen was born in January 1931, closely followed by the birth of Victor in November 1932. In his late forties, Brookie was starting a new family and more significantly, now had the support of a wife and partner. In his Notes, "It would be quite impossible for me to find words that would do justice to the immeasurable part she has played in shaping my life ever since the day we were married… She has stood as a rock inspiring me with strength and resolution and quite especially as a lighthouse always burning brightly to guide me through life towards those things that really matter and count during our stay on this earth."

Meanwhile, Brookie's professional reputation continued to grow. His 1930 Army Report read, "Great ability, devotion to duty and charm of manner. He is an outstanding officer and highly educated professional soldier far above the average of his rank." In 1932, he returned to the Imperial Defence College, this time as an instructor. After two years at the college, Brookie then took command of the 8th Infantry Brigade in 1934. Yet again, he placed emphasis on training, especially the training of junior infantry officers. In his Notes, "[Junior officers] were sent to their battalions from Sandhurst quite unfit to command a platoon and, as far as I could see, the most usual method to teach them was to put them direct into a platoon to learn for themselves under the very doubtful tutelage of a platoon sergeant." Since he believed that the handling of troops was a skill which needed to be taught, he set up a school for young officers within his brigade. He clearly held strong views on this issue since he later pressed for a specialist school to be set up for all junior infantry officers, not just those in his brigade: in this, he was unsuccessful.

After eighteen months in command of the 8th Infantry Brigade, he was appointed Inspector of Artillery in 1935 and then Director of Military Training in 1936. The following year saw the creation of a new Mobile Division within the British Army and Brookie, now a major general, was appointed its first commander. The British had invented the tank during the First World War as a means of breaking the deadlock of trench warfare but had then failed to develop and exploit its potential in the post-war years. In the 1920s, the more radical British exponents of tanks and armoured forces had projected a visionary role for their use and deployment in future wars, arguing that their rapid mobility offered the benefits of surprise and penetration: the German panzer commander, General Guderian, was of the same opinion. However, their views were not shared by the more traditional and conservative elements of the British military. Brookie's appointment as commander of this new Mobile Division raised the eyebrows of some of these radical British exponents, one of them describing him as "essentially deliberate in his methods as a tactician"[8].

His spell in command of the Mobile Division was short which appears odd. It can be explained, however, by the decision to create a new Anti-Aircraft Corps in 1938 and place Brookie, now a lieutenant general, in command of it. In his Notes, "a new and complicated Corps to raise and an expansion of over 100 per cent in one year. My brain was getting used to mental gymnastics, first, artillery techniques at the Artillery School, then higher direction of war at the IDC, followed by a change to Infantry work with the 8th Infantry Brigade, leading to a return to Artillery Training and organization as Inspector of Artillery, general training matters as DMT, Armoured Forces as Commander of the 1st Mobile Division, and now Anti-Aircraft work at a time when the air threat to this country was becoming daily more menacing." The reason behind Brookie's appointment to these wide-ranging senior commands was almost certainly his efficiency, thoroughness and reliability: General 'Pug' Ismay's observation is worth recalling, "Brooke was by general consent the best all-rounder in his Service [the army]. He had been an unqualified success in all the Staff appointments which he had held in peace and war."[9].

Three aspects of Brookie's character were illustrated during his time in command of the Anti-Aircraft Corps. The first was his sense of fairness. The corps was created to increase Britain's defensive capabilities and since his principal responsibility was to expand its size from two to five divisions, Brookie became heavily reliant on Territorial Army volunteers. In his letter to the Director General of the Territorial Army, he complained that the TA volunteers were being unfairly treated since recent government legislation meant they were "being required to honour a liability for which they did not contract" and that many of them were "hit both financially and in their domestic arrangements".

The second was his ability to analyse problems clearly and logically and then quickly identify the key issue in that problem: in this, Brookie was notably quicker than most of his peers. He had a dissective mind which might explain his skill in mathematics as a child. In his Notes, he recalled a meeting which he attended in 1939 at which he was told that Hitler "might suddenly launch a 'mad-dog attack' on London; on the other hand, as the President of the French Republic was with us [he was visiting London], the Government was anxious to impress him with our strength against aerial attack. He then asked me what I could do as Commander of the AA defence to meet these requirements. I informed him that he had stated two requests which could not be met by the same action. If he wished to defend London, we must deploy guns for this purpose, but in that case the President would see nothing unless he toured the whole of London to visit these guns. On the other hand, if he wished to impress the President, it would be possible to deploy searchlights throughout London and to carry out some illuminating practices, but in this case the security of London would not be provided for. Which did he want?"

The third was his talent for man management. During this period, a situation arose in which an officer, senior in rank to him, found himself under Brookie's command. When this officer retired, Brookie wrote a letter to him which elicited the following reply, "I have never received such a nice letter as yours or one by which I set such store. I always knew it would be easy to work under you and it was for that reason and knowing your ability that I never from the word 'go' felt badly over your going over my head." Brookie set high standards for himself and expected his peers and senior officers to do likewise: he was, however, more tolerant of lower ranking officers. One junior officer under his command in 1939 later wrote to him, "More than anything, I remember your unfailing courtesy and pleasantness to junior officers and your regardless courage in fighting, when necessary, the powers that be."

In May 1939, Brookie was appointed Colonel Commandant, Royal Artillery. This was quickly followed by his appointment as Commander-in-Chief, Southern Command, in August 1939. The latter appointment was significant because in the event of war breaking out, Southern Command had been earmarked to dispatch a corps to France as part of a British Expeditionary Force. In his Notes, Brookie recalled the moment when he learnt of Germany's invasion of Poland on 1 September 1939, "Ronald Adam was tearing down one of the passages [in the War Office] with a worried expression and stopped for one moment to say, 'It has started, the Nazis have advanced into Poland.' I was overwhelmed by a flood of memories of the last war and stood in the passage motionless and aghast at the thought that it was all to be started again."

At this point, four background issues deserve mention. In 1919, the British Government introduced the Ten-Year Rule which required the armed forces to plan on the assumption that Britain and its empire would not be involved in any significant war for the next ten years. This not only led to drastic reductions in defence spending but also created a climate of inertia and helplessness within the armed forces which resulted in the stagnation of their development. Interestingly, the Rule was made self-perpetuating in 1928 at the instigation of Winston Churchill, then Chancellor of the Exchequer, which had the effect of annually resetting the ten-year clock to year one. This Rule was eventually lifted in 1932.

The second concerns the Royal Air Force. The RAF had been founded in 1918 following the merger of the Royal Flying Corps and the Royal Naval Air Service which were the air arms of, respectively, the British Army and Royal Navy. It was the first air force to gain independence from army and navy control and its administration was handled by a separate Air Ministry. Between 1938 and 1940, aircraft production was concentrated on fighters. From 1940 onwards, aircraft production was concentrated on bombers in the belief held by some within the RAF that strategic bombing of Germany would by itself win the War. However, these bombers were largely ill-suited to providing effective air support for land and sea operations. The RAF's capability – and willingness – to support the army and navy during the War was to become a highly contentious issue.

Third, Britain was, first and foremost, a naval power whose principal interest lay in retaining command of the seas to protect itself from invasion and secure its trade routes and communications with its overseas empire and dominions. A key sea route for Britain was the Mediterranean since the Suez Canal provided vital means of access to India, Burma, Malaya, Singapore, Hong Kong, Australia and New Zealand.

Fourth, historically, British policy towards Europe had been to maintain a balance of power between European countries, the aim being to ensure that no single country dominated the continent. In line with this policy, Britain had agreed with France prior to September 1939 that it would send a British Expeditionary Force [BEF] to the continent in the event of hostilities with Germany and to the BEF being placed under the command of a continental ally. Following its declaration of war on Germany, Britain began despatching forces to France. Initially, the BEF comprised two corps. I Corps, which was reasonably well trained and equipped, was commanded by John Dill, Brookie's friend. II Corps, which was poorly trained and equipped, was commanded by Brookie.

Part Two

AUTHOR'S NOTE

Part Two comprises edited extracts from Brookie's diary and autobiographical Notes. The diary entries are dated and, with a few exceptions, indented on the page. Since his diary was voluminous, and many of his entries were lengthy, the editing is extensive. Some extracts may appear to be complete entries when, in fact, they are not.

His autobiographical Notes, which were written in the 1950s, are neither dated nor indented. The possibility that he had an eye on posterity when writing them, or that some sections were coloured by hindsight, cannot be completely discounted.

The diary entries and Notes are, in the main, easy to read and understand since Brookie was succinct in his use of language: he had the ability to express himself clearly using a minimum number of words. He was, however, less proficient with his punctuation, grammar and spelling. Consequently, this has been tidied up for the reader's benefit, without altering the content or tone of his entries.

Brief explanatory notes have, occasionally, been inserted into the text of his diary entries and Notes for the purpose of identifying individuals, explaining code names of operations or whenever an explanation was deemed helpful. These explanatory notes appear in square brackets. In contrast, any text in round brackets was written by Brookie.

He frequently used exclamation and question marks in his diary entries to emphasise a point. One mark denotes mild emphasis and three marks denote maximum emphasis.

Any reference to "you" is a reference to Benita. He referred to his children by their nicknames, Kathleen is "Pooks" and Victor is "Mr Ti".

Part Two also includes extracts from papers, diaries and books written by third parties. These have been inserted to elaborate on, or provide background to, issues mentioned by Brookie in his diary.

The seven years covered by his diary can be broken down into three periods:

September 1939–June 1940: corps commander and then Commander-in-Chief, BEF, France
July 1940–November 1941: Commander-in-Chief, Home Forces
December 1941–June 1946: Chief of the Imperial General Staff.

THREE

France: September 1939–May 1940

Brookie was in a despondent mood as he set off for war. In his first entry on 28 September:

"After seeing you off, Michael and I left for Southampton. I found it quite impossible on that lovely morning as we drove along to realize that I was starting off for the war and that we should not be meeting for some time. Even now surrounded by troops, on the Heysham-Belfast boat disguised under black paint, I find it impossible to realize. It is all too ghastly even to be a nightmare. The awful futility of it all, as proved by the last war! I am glad to say that it does not undermine my belief in an almighty and far-seeing God, working towards one set purpose for the destiny of the human race. I suppose that conflicts between Right and Wrong are still necessary and that we have still got to be taught more fully the futility of war. Eventually we must come to ways of settling our difficulties without war. Evidently, we are not yet sufficiently developed in the process of evolution for such methods. We are now about due to sail down the Solent.

Later: we have now moved out and are anchored close to those forts we watched the Schneider Trophy competitors fly around. It brought me back very vividly to that day we spent together, our dinner at the County Hotel which kept coming back to my mind again and again during the last few days without my daring to refer to it lest I might break down, and finally to our drive back to Thorngrove. The beginning of ten years of happiness such as I should never have thought would be possible on this earth. I cannot tell you what your example has been to me during those 10 years."

By the end of September, Germany had overrun Poland. In October, the German high command set a provisional date of 12 November for the invasion of western Europe. On 29 September, Brookie was still unhappy:

"Both [BEF] Corps to be put into defensive line on Belgium frontier forthwith, this is exactly what I have been trying to guard against in the case of II Corps, the Corps is at present unfit for war and requires at least one to one and a half months' training. I told both Adam [Deputy CIGS] and [illegible] that this was the case and was assured by both of them that the early move of the Corps was a political gesture for the French and that I should be given time to finish training the Corps out here. So much for political promises!! I mentioned to Adam that in war the unexpected often happens. I was assured by him that it was quite impossible for the Germans to attack through Belgium before the winter sets in. I wonder if he is right??"

Brookie judged people according to their efficiency and ability, rather than their nationality. On 30 September:

"French slovenliness, dirtyness and inefficiency are I think worse than ever; but no one could be kinder than they are... We seem to have collected a vast herd at GHQ [British General Headquarters], I wonder if they will all pull their weight??"

1 October saw his first reference to Benita:

"Still no letters today and I am longing to hear from you, it is a horrid feeling to suddenly find yourself cut clean off from those you love and all that means everything to you in the world."

Three days later, he was with his friend and fellow corps commander, John Dill:

"Found him still very depressed about the general state of unpreparedness for war. We condoled with each other on the lack of equipment and shortage of training... I feel desperately sorry for him as he is in the depths of gloom."

He perked up on the following day:

"I received two letters from you today, the first two, they transformed the whole day and seemed to make the sun shine brighter."

On 6 October:

"In the evening, the owner of this chateau [in which he was billeted] came to dine with us in her own dining room! She is rather pathetic, her husband has abandoned her and her only boy who is hidden from the world in the chateau is wanting."

On 9 October, note his respect for Germany's armed forces:

"I am not happy about our general attitude, we are facing this war in a half-hearted way... I feel that the Germans would have been tackling the situation very differently."

On 11 October:

"Gort [Commander-in-Chief, BEF]... gave us details as to present rate of production of various weapons and dates by which we might expect them. The prospects are not cheerful, but the most depressing part of the business is the apparent failure on the part of GHQ to realize how serious these difficulties are. Both the War Office and GHQ appear to be thinking in terms of the war in six months' time. Our immediate danger in the event of an attack does not appear to be fully realized. Let us hope that he does not attack this year and gives us some time to complete our anti-tank and anti-air armament."

Brookie often made dry, occasionally amusing, remarks in his entries. 15 October was a:

"Sunday – and the whole country dressed in their Sunday best, apparently oblivious that they may be sitting on a volcano!"

On 16 October:

> "Lunched with Gort... to meet Gamelin [Commander-in-Chief, French Army]. Billotte [French general] commanding our group of armies was also at lunch, I liked the look of him. Gamelin struck me as looking old and rather tired."

On 19 October, Brookie addressed the issue of whether, in the event of a German invasion of Belgium, British and French forces should advance from their defensive positions on the Franco-Belgian border into Belgium to confront the German forces. This issue clearly concerned him since he returned to it in subsequent entries. Note, again, his respect for Germany's armed forces:

> "Before the conference, Dill and I got hold of Gort and tried to make him realize the serious aspect of the contemplated move. The danger of leaving our present prepared position for one totally unprepared... [Gort] will assume a very light-hearted aspect of the situation and is too inclined to under-estimate the strength and efficiency of the Germans. I sincerely hope that we shall not be forced to advance by a violation of Belgium."

On 20 October:

> "Defences are taking definite shape. Position would be strong except for desperate shortage of men in the long fronts held. With such a frontage, serious resistance becomes impossible. There is no depth to the defence."

On 21 October:

> "Adam [Deputy CIGS] has come out from WO [War Office] for a couple of days. According to him, the Germans will not attack and are themselves starting masses of their rumours about impending attacks, they will instead start another peace offensive with the hope that boredom with the present conditions of war will induce us to make peace. Personally, I feel that if internal conditions become critical the Germans will be forced to start some form of offensive."

On the following day:

> "*Still very short of sandbags, when one remembers the lavish use made of sandbags at home in localities that will never see a bomb, it makes one's blood boil to be so short of them out here.*"

On 23 October:

> "*Fagalde commanding 16th French Corps on my left came to lunch… He is a pleasant ruffian and an amusing companion but does not inspire one with unbounded confidence as far as his efficiency is concerned!*"

Earlier, 6 October, Brookie had criticised the owner of the chateau in which he was billeted. On 24 October:

> "*She is inclined to be pretty sour at times! I don't blame her with strange officers dumped down in her house.*"

On 27 October, note his fear that political considerations might dictate military strategy:

> "*Dill and I asked Gort and Pownall to come to I Corps HQ for a conference to clear up matters as regards dispositions in the event of a move forward to avert a German violation of Belgium or Holland. It is hard to get Gort to realize the seriousness of the situation… He refuses to really face the difficulties we may be up against and makes light of them all. Dill and I feel that the situation is not half as rosy as he tries to make out.*
>
> *Here we are behind the Belgian frontier devoting all our efforts to creating a strong defensive line. And yet should the Germans invade Belgium, in all probability the Belgian army will defend its country. This is however uncertain, the King and his four principal advisors are known to have pro-German tendencies. Meanwhile, we prepare for the possibility of moving forward into Belgium as soon as the Germans begin to invade that country. Our plans however only take us as far as the Scheldt River with delaying actions in advance. For political reasons, this is desirable so as [to] free the industrial centre of Lille-*

Tourcoing-Roubaix from the threat of bombardment. But, and this is the great 'but', shall we even be allowed, again for political reasons, to sit on the Scheldt while the Belgians fight single-handed in the east of their country? This seems highly improbable. Therefore, for political reasons, we may well be forced to abandon what strategy dictates and thus court disaster. Gamelin at all costs wishes to avoid an encounter battle in Belgium and wishes to meet the Germans in well-prepared positions. Will political considerations allow him to follow this wise course? I doubt it??"

On the following day, Brookie was unimpressed:

"Was not at all pleased with the hospital established for Corps troops in a gloomy shed and have ordered it to be moved. I wish my chief doctor had more energy and that old Dawes [brigadier] was a bit younger (by the same token, he is almost 6 months younger than I am but I always feel that he is old enough to be my father!)"

4 November saw another dry comment:

"Eighteen of us got into pillbox, closed down all openings and then fired an anti-tank gun and a Bren gun through the apertures for five minutes to make certain that the fumes and gases from the firing would not be such as to affect the garrison of the pillbox. None of us felt any the worse but it would have assisted promotion considerably if it had been otherwise as there were 1 Lt Gen, 1 Maj Gen, 2 Brigadiers, 1 Colonel and 3 Lt Colonels amongst those in the pillbox! Expensive 'white mice' for such a trial!"

On 5 November:

"Instructed by Gort to attend Armistice Service with Commander of 9th French Army at the spot where Germans came out with a white flag in 1918... The ceremony had been a simple one, lacking finish in every respect, almost comic at times in its lack of thoroughness, and yet there was something in it that gripped one mainly I think the past against the present. I could not help wondering whether the French *are still a firm enough nation to again take their part in seeing this war through."*

Brookie elaborated in his Notes, "On 5 November I had an experience which began to crystallize out the worst fears I had been gradually forming as regards the inefficiency of the French Army... I had been requested by Gort to represent him at a ceremony to be given by General Corap... this was the Corap who became famous in 1940 for crumbling under the first blows of the German advance... I can still see those [French] troops now. Seldom have I seen anything more slovenly and badly turned out. Men unshaven, horses ungroomed, clothes and saddlery that did not fit, vehicles dirty and complete lack of pride in themselves or their units. What shook me most, however, was the look on the men's faces, disgruntled and insubordinate looks, and although ordered to give 'eyes left' hardly a man bothered to do so.

After the ceremony was over, Corap invited me to visit some of his defences... we found a half-constructed and very poor anti-tank ditch with no defences to cover it. By way of conversation, I said that I supposed he would cover the ditch with the fire from anti-tank pillboxes. This question received the reply '*Ah bah! On va les faire plus tard – allons on va déjeuner!*' ['We'll deal with that later – let's go and have some lunch'] and away we went to *déjeuner* which was evidently intended to be the most important operation of the day. I drove home in the depth of gloom".

6 November saw Brookie reminiscing about the First World War:

"In the morning, went to Vimy Ridge Memorial to arrange details of the Armistice ceremony next Saturday... Then went on to Coumbain l'Abbé to see our old Canadian Corps HQ occupied during Battle of Vimy. I saw my old office, the window I used to look out of to see HQ staff playing baseball... and my bedroom hut. It brought back floods of memories and made me feel that the war had never stopped. It had only been interrupted by a happy dream of 20 years. And yet when I came away and thought of the last 10 years of paradise, I felt that the last war and this war were only very trivial matters in my life

as compared with the heavenly happiness which God had granted me by allowing me to share the last ten years with you."

On 7 November, Germany postponed its planned invasion of western Europe on 12 November. Two days later:

"The clouds are gathering fast on the horizon and an invasion of Holland, and possibly also Belgium, seems imminent. I do not relish the role of the 2nd Corps if we move into Belgium. We shall be forced to form 'front to a flank', thus throwing up my left flank in an exposed manner."

On 11 November, Armistice Day:

"The suspense continues, more threats to Belgium and Holland but no further moves on the part of the Germans. This morning, I took part in an Armistice ceremony at the Canadian Memorial at Vimy Ridge. We had two guards of honour, a French one formed by the 51st Division and a British one from the Black Watch. General Pagezy came from Lille for the ceremony. He and I laid wreaths of poppies on the Memorial, the French guard then presented arms whilst their bugles sounded a 'Sonnerie', this was followed by the Black Watch guard presenting arms whilst their pipers played the 'Flowers of the Forest'. The ceremony ended with inspection of each other's guards and by a march past of the guards.

I felt throughout the ceremony as if I were in a dream. The white tall pillars of the monument standing out against the ashy grey sky seemed entirely detached from this earth, whilst the two red wreaths of poppies looked like two small drops of blood on that vast monument. They served as a vivid reminder of the floods of blood that had already been spilt on the very ground we were standing, and of the futility of again causing such bloodshed. I suppose that it is through such punishments that we shall eventually learn to 'love our neighbours as ourselves.'"

Two days later, he returned to the subject of the proposed advance to the River Scheldt:

"*Dill came... to tell me results of his talk with Gort which he asked for to draw attention to our weakness on the proposed line. I gather that he failed to make Gort realize the risks he was taking with the BEF. I am afraid Dill feels the situation clearly, his astute military knowledge makes him see clearly that with such strung out forces, even behind a river, serious resistance is impossible. He feels it his duty to inform Gort who has not quite the same breadth of vision and Dill feels that Gort has the impression that he [Dill] suffers from 'cold feet' and is an alarmist. It is a very sad situation; he is torn between loyalty to his Commander and loyalty to his Corps.*"

On 16 November, he visited various units under his command:

"*In every case interviewed all the officers and had a few words with them. While talking to them, I always have the terrible feeling that I may at one time or another be instrumental towards the issue of orders that may mean death to them. It is I think one of the most trying sides of commanding in war, the haunting thought that you may at any time be forced to issue orders that mean probable death to your friends.*"

Earlier, 28 October, he had referred to 'old Dawes'. On 18 November:

"*Dawes came to see me because he had received a letter from [Military Secretary] appointing him Base Commandant Marseilles. We had a painful interview as he is very upset about it and feels he has been a failure. I had to comfort him — tell him that he had been far from a failure but that his age was too old to be able to do the job should we start active operations [Dawes was six months younger than Brookie].*"

Sundays were significant for Brookie because it was the one day in the week which he would ordinarily spend with Benita. Sunday, 19 November, was significant for another reason: the plan to advance into Belgium up to the River Scheldt had changed. Under the new plan, British forces were to advance to a line on the River Dyle. Brookie had been sceptical about the original plan but now he appeared to change his mind:

> "Sunday again, the one day that is hardest of all to bear being separated from you on! Received new orders from GHQ for yet another scheme of advance into Belgium in the event of violation… This time we plan to go forward to the line Louvain-Wavre with the French on our right and the Belgians on our left. If we can get there in time to organize ourselves properly to meet the German onrush, it is without doubt the right strategy. It is the shortest line possible through Belgium, saves half that country, should give time for coordinated action between the three countries provided the Belgian advance guards on the Albert Canal, at Liège and in the Ardennes can hold out sufficiently long. We must however resolutely resist being drawn in to try and save all Belgium by defending the line of the Albert Canal and Liège. By trying to save the whole of Belgium instead of half, not only would we lose the whole of Belgium but probably the war as well."

Two days later, he met up with Dill to discuss the new GHQ order:

> "As usual… his advice worth its weight in gold. I do wish he was C-in-C instead of Gort, he has twice the vision and ten times the ability. Gort's brain has lately been compared to that of a glorified boy scout! Perhaps unkind, but there is a great deal of truth in it."

On 22 November:

> "GHQ Conference… to discuss order for advance into Belgium… Dill and I having had previous conference yesterday had already settled what we wanted and we got it. Gort is queer mixture, perfectly charming, very definite personality, full of vitality, energy and joie de vivre and gifted without powers of leadership. But he just fails to see the big picture and is continually returning to those trivial details which counted a lot when commanding a battalion but which should not be the main concern of a Commander-in-Chief. Poor old Dill finds it very hard to work under him but is the very soul of loyalty and never

shows anything on the surface... He has risen higher than ever in my estimation since we have been out here."

The duties of a corps commander were varied: 23 November saw Brookie dealing with the subject of venereal disease. His II Corps comprised the 3rd Division, commanded by Bernard Montgomery, and the 4th Division. Montgomery was in trouble because he had issued the following circular to his divisional troops, "I am not happy about the situation regarding venereal disease in the Division. Since the 18th October, the number of cases admitted to field ambulances in the Divisional area totals 44... My view is that if a man wants to have a woman, let him do so by all means: but he must use common sense and take the necessary precautions against infection – otherwise he becomes a casualty by his own neglect, and this is helping the enemy." He then added "The man who has a woman in a beetroot field near his [company] billet will not walk a mile to the Battalion E.T. room... There are in Lille a number of brothels, which are properly inspected and where the risk of infection is practically nil. These are known to the military police and any soldier who is in need of horizontal recreation would be well advised to ask a policeman for a suitable address."[1] Brookie was unimpressed. However, note his protection of Montgomery and his man-management skills – the 'high and low opinions' – when dealing with this difficult subordinate:

"Started the day by having to 'tell off' Monty for having issued a circular to his troops on the prevention of venereal disease worded in such obscene language that both the C.of E. and R.C. senior chaplains had complained to the Adjutant General!... I had already seen the circular and told Monty what I thought of it, namely that [by] the issue of such a document he had inevitably undermined the respect and esteem of the division for him and thus seriously affected his position as commander. The AG originally suggested that Monty should be made to withdraw the document he had issued. I was dead against such a procedure... to make him withdraw it now would be a clear indication of superior authority disapproval which would remove any vestige of respect [the soldiers in Montgomery's division] might have

for him. I told AG that instead I would have him up… and impress on him again the magnitude of his blunder. I therefore pointed out to Monty that his position as a commander of a division had been seriously affected by this blunder and could certainly not withstand any further errors of this kind. I also informed him that I had a very high opinion of his military capabilities and an equally low one of his literary ones. He took it wonderfully well and I think it ought to have done him good. It is a great pity that he spoils his very high military ability by a mad desire to talk or write nonsense."

This was the first of many tickings off to be handed out by Brookie to Montgomery during the War. On 24 November,

"Went down to Raudicourt Chateau, the old 1st Army HQ. The last time I had been there was when we moved out in 1918 to begin the final advance of the war! I felt a desperate longing to have reached the same stage of this war!"

Two days later, he visited a battalion which had just joined his corps in France:

"It is totally unfit for war in every respect and will take at least 2 months to render it fit. It would be sheer massacre to commit it to action in its present state, in addition to endangering the lives of others. I therefore consider that it is a very grave fault by those concerned in sending it out to this country in such a state. Hore-Belisha [Secretary of State for War], when he was out here, asked me whether it would not be advisable to push units and formations out here to complete their training (mainly with the object of impressing people with the numbers he was despatching). I told him that I considered such a procedure was neither fair to the units, the BEF or our allies the French."

His 28 November entry was in similar vein:

"French defences are to all intents and purposes non-existent on this front [Brookie's 4th Division had just taken over the front from the French 51st Division]! When I see this state of affairs and think what might have happened if the Germans had attacked before the winter it makes me shudder!"

On 30 November, he met Gort and Ironside, the CIGS:

"[Ironside] informed me that when Hore-Belisha returned from his trip [to France] he informed both the Cabinet and the Privy Council that the BEF was doing no work and had left their front unprotected. That we were the laughing stock of the French on either flank and a few similar remarks! The true case is that the French have been doing practically nothing on our flanks and that this was the reason why I asked Gort to relieve the 51st Div (French) by my 4th Div on my left flank so that I might prepare defences on this bit of the front and thus secure my flank."

Six days later, Brookie and his II Corps were visited by King George VI:

"The whole show was a first-class turnout and all arrangements ran without a hitch. I felt very proud of the 2nd Corps."

His 9 December entry is unlikely to have impressed Benita:

"Received your letter this evening reminding me that the 7th was the anniversary of our wedding. I had forgotten the actual date but knew that it was about this time in December. It is as well that 10 years ago we did not know that we should be at war again now, it would inevitably have cast a cloud over that sunlit plain of happiness which we have journeyed through together… I never realized that such happiness could exist on this earth… I thank God from the bottom of my heart for having brought us together."

14 December saw him reminiscing again:

"[Drove] through La Bassée and up to main road to Neuve Chapelle with all its memories of fighting in 1915. I also went past the first billet I ever occupied near the front in 1914… I saw the old ditch into which the trench ambulance had fallen on that first night… It was just a mass of memories which were given a bitter twinge through the fact that I was back again starting again what I thought at the time I was finishing for good and all. It gives me a lonely feeling also going back over these old grounds, so many of them that were with me then and are now gone, and so many that are with me now were not born then!"

On 15 December:

"Just finished reading Bouvines: Victoire Créatrice by Antoine Hadingue. It is a very interesting account of the battle fought in 1214... just to the left of my Corps front and I had stood... on the very spot where 100,000 men engaged in deadly combat in 1214!!... it is possible to carry oneself back some 720 years... and follow the whole combat right to the end of the dreadful carnage that resulted from it."

Two days later:

"A very sad tragedy occurred at my Junior Leaders Corps School. An engineer officer was demonstrating the use of the anti-tank mine when one blew up. It killed three officers outright, one more died shortly afterwards, three are very dangerously wounded and two badly wounded. It is very shattering that our anti-tank mines should be as unsafe to handle as that!"

20 December saw an example of his good judgment:

"Left Metz at 7.45am and went to call on the Div Commander of the [French] 42nd Div. Was very much impressed by him, a fine type of officer. From there motored to Kemplich where I met Johnson and Barker and we went round one of the Maginot forts at Welshtenberg [the Maginot Line was a series of supposedly impregnable defensive fortifications built at huge cost by France]. The fort reminded me of a battleship built on land, a masterpiece in its way and there is no doubt that the whole conception of the Maginot Line is a stroke of genius. And yet! It gave me little feeling of security, and I consider that the French would have done better to invest the money in the shape of mobile defences such as more and better aircraft and more heavy armoured divisions than to sink all this money into the ground."

Brookie was due some leave over Christmas. On 21 December:

"Now I am about to pack up in anticipation of starting off on my journey home tomorrow! I cannot get to believe that it can be true and feel rather as if I was moving about in a dream, afraid that any sudden movement might bring the dream to an end."

On 2 January, he returned to France. As will become apparent, new years and anniversaries prompted Brookie to reflect on the past, muse about the future and occasionally philosophise:

"A New Year beginning and pray God that it may bring us Peace. After leaving you this morning, I got into my carriage and tried to reassure myself that the bottom had not dropped out of the world. I comforted myself with the thought of all the memories I am carrying away with me of those 10 heavenly days spent with you and those beloved small persons. Memories that I can call on during the next few months, like turning the leaves of a book".

On 6 January:

"One cheerful bit of news this morning – Hore-Belisha has resigned and we have at last got a new [Secretary of State for War]."

On 10 January 1940 a German pilot, Major Hoenmanns, flew from Munster to Cologne accompanied by Major Reinberger who, unbeknown to Hoenmanns, was carrying detailed plans for the imminent German invasion of Holland and Belgium. Due to a combination of bad weather and pilot error, Hoenmanns became lost and was forced to make an emergency landing in Belgium whereupon both men were arrested. Reinberger attempted to burn his papers but was only partially successful and the remnants fell into Belgian hands. This became known as the Mechelen incident.

On the following day:

"Had to break the news to [Franklyn] that his [5th] division would be leaving the II Corps. I am sorry he is going and should very

much like to have retained the 5th Division. Franklyn is certainly a more attractive type of individual than Montgomery, but I felt that 3rd and 4th Divisions had formed part of II Corps from the start and should go on doing so as long as possible."

On 12 January:

"The war of nerves starts again. A warning from GHQ that Belgium expects to be attacked during the next few days, attack to extend through Holland and Luxembourg… Finally, [I was] able to get back to the one moment of the day that I live for namely when I find your darling letter and later have my evening talk with you on paper."

The next day provided further proof of the wide-ranging duties of a corps commander:

"Then went on to see the Prefet of Lille to express my deep regrets for the murder of a French woman by a man of the 4th Division. He was very nice about it".

14 January saw the British reaction to the Mechelen incident:

"The war of nerves continues. At 3.30am I was woken by Ritchie stating that an early invasion of Belgium was expected… At breakfast time I received orders to attend a conference of the C-in-C… it turned out to be an interesting one. We were told that a German plane had made a false landing in Belgium containing 2 German officers and some plans which they tried to destroy by fire. They were stopped [from] doing so and the plans turned out to be a complete scheme for the invasion of Belgium and Holland by Germany to be carried out shortly. We discussed the whole evidence and came to the conclusion that the whole affair looked like a 'plant' on the part of Germany. It was not likely that officers would fly over Belgium with a plan of this kind in their possession. It seems probable that the whole affair was staged with the object of trying to induce Belgium to call on France and England for military support in the face of such a threat and thus to provide Germany with an excuse for violating the frontier of Belgium *and Holland. We may or may not have been right and so as to leave nothing to chance, we are now at 4 hours' notice to move."*

On 15 January, Brookie was assessing the pros and cons of an advance into Belgium. This issue clearly appealed to his dissective, analytical mind:

"This morning a liaison officer came to inform me that a German invasion of Belgium no longer seemed imminent and that yesterday's scare was as we had thought a plant on the part of Germany… apparently the King of the Belgians has now asked the British and French Governments whether we should be prepared to come to his assistance to meet the possible German threat.

The situation is an intensely interesting one – are we doing just what the Germans have been trying to make us do with the crashed aeroplane 'plant'? Is it to their advantage that we should enter Belgium at the request of the Belgian Government? They would then be given an excuse for violating Belgium and Holland by stating that the attitude of these countries was no longer strictly neutral. They would also be provided with better opportunities for taking advantage of the considerable numerical superiority of forces which they enjoy at present by having a wide front of contact with greater facilities for circulation of forces. Finally, an engagement between our forces in the middle of Belgium would be of the open warfare nature which would suit German forces. On the other hand, we should shorten our front by at least 100 kilometres, allowing us to pull some more divisions into reserve. We should also benefit from the addition of some 18 Belgian divisions to our forces, and finally we should be able to put all the work we are doing now into the defences which we are really likely to require. Since an invasion of Belgium by Germany will always necessitate our moving in. On the whole, I think we should score by going in if invited to do so."

Following the Mechelen incident, Hitler postponed the German invasion which was due to be launched on 17 January. It had been planned on the basis that the main thrust of the attack would be in the north, through Holland and Belgium, with a secondary attack in the south, from the

Ardennes. Subsequently, Germany adopted a new invasion plan in the belief that the original plan was too obvious and unlikely to produce a decisive and successful outcome. Under the new plan, the main thrust of the German attack was switched to the south, through the Ardennes, the intention being to cross the River Meuse and then drive west to the French coast, thereby trapping the British and French forces in the north-east and cutting them off from the rest of France. This new plan anticipated – correctly – that British and French forces would advance into Belgium.

On 16 January:

"Inspected the Indian Mule Company to find they were badly housed, huts unfinished, no glass in windows, stove pipes missing and no palliasses to sleep on. Administered a few 'bites' [reprimands] and hope situation will improve shortly."

On the following day:

"Roger Evans… was most depressing about the progress made about the [1st] Armoured Division [this division was still in Britain, awaiting delivery of its equipment]… it looked to me as if Roger was not 'cutting much ice' and no one was listening to him."

25 January saw an example of Brookie's 'abrupt efficiency'. He had just inspected a battalion, recently arrived in France, commanded by:

"Shaw Stewart who struck me as being no use at all. A good unit being spoilt by a bad C.O. Shall arrange to have him changed."

On 28 January, the War Office's aim of winning the War '3 years from now' illustrated Britain's lack of preparedness for war. Note the lack of coordination in the war policy being devised in London:

"Dewing [Director of Military Operations and Intelligence] at WO [War Office] came out today for a tour of the front… I had an opportunity of pumping him as regards the WO view of the prosecution of the war. The feeling they give me is that whilst concentrating on ensuring that they are going to win the war in 3

years from now, they neglect to realize the danger of losing it this year! Unless we get the Air Ministry and the War Office to realize that they are fighting the same war and that their combined effort is required at the same spot, the same time and with the same object, we are courting disaster against an enemy who adheres to the doctrine of concentration of effort at the vital point at the right time. [For Britain] to contemplate bombing the Ruhr at a time when the Germans are using their combined army and air force effort in one mighty uniform attempt to crush the French and British forces to clear their way into France is, in my mind, sheer folly. Two 'wrongs' will not make a 'right' in this case, and a misuse of our air force will not induce the Germans into a misuse of their own air force by diverting them from their proper task to that of bombing England. When the combined task of the German land and air forces is completed and northern France cleared of the Allies, then and only then will the Germans turn their air might onto England."

On the next day, he watched a French army film which was:

"Mainly intended as propaganda but left one with a feeling of depression as to the lack of real finish in the French army. A very amateur appearance which compares unfavourably with the utter efficiency of the Germans... I only hope [the French] still possess the same fighting qualities which they showed in the last war."

30 January saw an accurate prediction:

"Martel [commander, 50th Division]... was wondering why we were not more concerned with preparing offensive measures to attack the Siegfried Line [Germany's western defence fortifications]; and seemed quite oblivious of the fact that instead of attacking this spring, we are far more likely to be hanging on by our eyelids in trying to check German attacks!"

On the following day:

"The first month of 1940 finished and I wish it was the last one

of the year!... Visited 1/7 Middlesex MG Bn this morning and decided that their commanding officer must go. It is sad the number of territorial commanding officers who are proving quite unsuitable to command a unit out here."

On 1 February:

"No mail this evening and consequently no letter from you and, as a result, a colourless day! The receipt of your letter is the hub round which the day revolves. Without its hub the day turns with an aimless wobble!"

2 February saw Brookie in despair:

"[Gort] wanted to tell us the results of his meetings whilst home on leave. They were not reassuring! Apparently, various expeditions to other theatres of war [Scandinavia] are being considered by the highest [British Government], most of which would it strikes me lead to a dispersal of effort and provide better chances than ever for our losing the war. History is repeating itself in an astonishing way. The same string-pulling as in the last war, the same differences between statesmen and soldiers, the same faults as regards changing key posts at the opening of hostilities and now the same tendency to start subsidiary theatres of war and to contemplate wild projects!! We shall apparently never apply the lessons of one war to the next."

On 3 February:

"The first feelings of spring. A lovely mild day which makes it harder than ever to realize that humanity can be so mad as to be at war again. I went for a walk in the woods and wished that I could wake up out of this nightmare of war and find myself at your side again with the world at peace!"

6 February saw further examples of Brookie's good judgment:

"Up at 6.30am and off at 7.45 first of all to see General Freydenberg [French general] who commands Colonial Corps on this front. A nice, friendly old gentleman who gave me a feeling of quiet efficiency. Then

a visit to the Div Commander of the 22nd Div. A fire eater with curled up moustaches constantly acting and I should think unreliable and useless! Then up to Barnett Hickling commanding 15th [Infantry Brigade] and a tour with him round front-line posts which are as bad and inefficient as they were last December.

I was due at 2.30pm to inspect Fort Hackenburg, one of the big Maginot forts… Most interesting, garrison of over 1000 men, over 7 kilometres of passages, 4 vast great diesel engines… all round an astonishing engineering feat. But I am not convinced that it is a marvellous military accomplishment. Millions of money stuck in the ground for a purely static defence… Their most dangerous aspect is the psychological one, a sense of false security is engendered, a feeling of sitting behind an impregnable iron fence; and should the fence perchance be broken, then French fighting spirit be brought… crumbling down with it!"

Two days later, he attended a conference at British GHQ:

"*The plans, which Gort had told us about after returning from leave [see 2 February], are taking shape! The 42nd and 44th Divisions are being held at home… We may also be called upon to send the 5th Division home. The proposed plans fill me with gloom. They are based on the assumption that the Germans will not attack on this front during the spring. Personally, I hold diametrically opposed views. Any forward move of the Germans on this front must necessarily bring operations in subsidiary theatres to a standstill but unfortunately by then we shall have seriously reduced our strength on this front and will be less well able to meet any attack. We seem to be falling into all the errors that we committed in the last war by starting subsidiary theatres and frittering away our strength.*"

11 February was a Sunday:

"*Sunday again, our day when we should be together… Life without your comradeship is just one long blank. The situation in the Corps is getting more and more confused. Just as we were in the process of giving birth to the new III Corps, the recent proposed diversions to* other theatres have put everything into a state of suspense… It is these uncertainties and counter-orders which are so killing and exhausting for the staffs, forcing them to prepare a multitude of alternative plans".

16 February saw a visit from the new Secretary of State for War, Oliver Stanley, and a former CIGS, Field Marshal Lord Milne. Note Milne's view of the proposed advance into Belgium:

"I… explained to [Stanley] how dangerous I thought any idea of reducing the strength of the BEF at the moment for any ventures in other theatres. He seemed inclined to agree. I told him that I considered this was the only front on which the war could be lost in 1940 if we were not careful and might possibly win if we were fortunate. He expressed the view that he thought it very doubtful whether the Germans would attack on the Western Front this year. I told him I had no doubt about this matter whatsoever and looked upon it as a certainty. I then had a talk with Lord Milne, whose mind is as clear as ever, he was very much of the same opinion as I was. He also expressed the view that, from a military point of view, he considered we were wrong to advance into Belgium."

On 19 February:

"Had to reprimand [illegible] for contravening censorship in a letter home."

Four days later:

"Venning [War Office] came out for a tour. He is another example of those who consider that a state of stalemate prevails on this front and that no active operations are likely to take place. I did my best to convince him that the reverse was the case!"

3 March saw Brookie delivering a speech in French at a memorial ceremony in Lens:

"As we stood there in the main square, I could not help looking back 20 years ago when I was busy writing orders to concentrate the maximum number of guns I could raise to shell this self-same square!… At dinner this evening, I had the fun of hearing my own voice on the wireless on the evening news delivering a bit of my French speech and I wondered whether you were also listening, and hoped you were."

On 6 March, he was at the site of a First World War battle:

"Visited Douaumont Fort at Verdun on the way back. Most impressive sight and one that brings back home to one better than anything I have yet seen what the last war meant as regards devastation and destruction."

On 13 March:

"This morning we heard of the Russo-Finnish peace, I had been expecting it and from the start I had laid 9 to 1 against any [British] expedition ever setting out for Sweden. In my own view, it is a godsend that it should have fallen through. By getting ourselves implicated in the North [Scandinavia] we should have been in grave danger of being defeated in the West through shortage of troops. I wonder what wild scheme may be given birth next!"

On 17 March:

"Orders have now been received for the III Corps to return to this country and take over the same front it should have taken over before we started contemplating wild ventures in Finland. The result is that we have lost a good six weeks in the preparations which we should be making for the defence of this country."

On 22 March:

"Up at 5.30am to see the end of the 4th Div exercise… Rubbed in several of Johnson's mistakes into him and found that he was realizing them himself at last. Weather getting more springlike, daffodils coming up and bushes sprouting which makes war even more objectionable."

2 April saw Brookie preparing to return home for a spell of leave:

"I still don't dare let myself be carried away in a wild flood of joy at the thought of being on my way home… It is the ghastly fear that something might yet crop up at the eleventh hour to stop me… I would feel as if the bottom of the world had dropped out if I was now stopped from coming back to you.

It is now more than 6 months since I started these notes for you and, looking back, I feel that these pages have been filled with quite different accounts from what I had expected to have to enter. It is a very strange war but I sometimes wonder whether if it lasts much longer in its present state we may not on both sides realize that there are better ways of settling our differences than by resorting to war. But this will require a change of mentality and outlook on both sides which are so very far from being reached at the present. However, I am a firm believer that we can ultimately cease from war on this earth, but I am still doubtful whether we have yet reached this high standard of evolution in Europe."

During his leave, Germany invaded Denmark and Norway just as British forces were about to land at various locations in north-west Norway. The subsequent British campaign in Norway was a disastrous failure which led to Neville Chamberlain's resignation as prime minister and the appointment of Winston Churchill as his successor on 10 May 1940.

On 12 April, Brookie returned to France:

"The end of a week in the most perfect heaven with you came to an end this morning at 9.45am just outside Waterloo platform as I drove away… I felt a great tidal wave surging up in my throat which I had to gulp down hard and a desperate flat feeling as if the bottom of the world had dropped out. After the last 6 months of it, I know so well what it means being away from you, the awful longings to be back with you and the incompleteness of everything in life when you are not there to share it with me. The thought of having to face it again is shattering… But when the parting does come, it just comes with a crash. If it was not for your wonderful courage and wonderful calm way of facing trials and difficulties, I do not know what I should do. You are just a tower of strength to me.

So far there are only rumours of impending attacks through Belgium and Holland. Personally, I feel that this is an unlikely eventuality as the Germans have their hands full with Norway for the present, where they require the bulk of their air force."

14 April was a:

"Sunday, and such a different Sunday from the last one spent with you... I slipped off for a short walk through the woods [and] took you with me in spirit".

On 16 April:

"In the afternoon, I went for a walk in the woods nearby and imagined you were at my side. We discussed the lovely carpet of anemones and all the nice green young shoots. In the garden, M. Rosette has found a blackbird's nest that I am watching. I wish I could take photographs of it."

On 17 April:

"[The War Office] consider that the Germans had intended to invade Holland shortly after Norway but his failure in the latter expedition has upset his programme. They still expect him to walk into Holland shortly."

On the following day:

"Today the BEF sustained the most serious loss that it has had since the beginning of the war. Dill was ordered home to take up the appointment of [Deputy CIGS]. I only hope that this may be a preliminary step to his replacing Tiny [Ironside] as CIGS... I felt very sad at seeing him go, he is quite one of the finest men I have ever known."

On 24 April, note his accurate prediction that the British campaign in Norway would end in failure:

> "[Liaison officer] gave us the most recent accounts of the Norwegian campaign. I don't much like our prospects there and feel that matters are so very confused that we shall end by being pushed back into the sea with heavy losses."

On 29 April, he attended a GHQ conference:

> "We spent a bare ½ hour discussing the important plans for an advance into Belgium and their proposed changes, and followed it up with 2 hours of complete details on training matters of minor importance. It is quite maddening not to be able to deal properly with the higher direction of this war without being drawn into minor details."

2 May saw Brookie employing his analytical powers to good effect:

> "Have just been listening to Chamberlain's statement as regards our withdrawal from the south of Trondheim [Norway]. It is a sad blow and one which will, I think, have repercussions in the Mediterranean as it is the first real conclusive proof we have had of the undermining of sea power by air power. However, in the withdrawal and in the strategic logic of such action, I already see evidence of Dill's hand on the tiller and thank God for it."

On 9 May:

> "This evening German planes came over about 10pm. Our new searchlight layout opened up on them and AA engaged them, but I think without result."

FOUR

France: May–June 1940

10 May was the day of the German invasion:

"The German planes returned early this morning between 3 and 4am… A little later Ritchie came to tell me that GHQ had rung up to place us at 6 hours' notice. Shortly afterward he returned and said that the Germans had invaded Belgium and Holland at 3am and that we were at last to put into effect our famous 'D' plan. This entails a rapid move forward to the River Dyle east of Brussels. The II Corps goes onto a one divisional front with the 3rd Div forward and the 4th and 50th Divs back. It was hard to believe on a most glorious spring day with all nature looking quite at its best, that we were taking the first step towards what must become one of the greatest battles of history."

On the following day, Brookie was confronted with a major problem:

"Then crossed frontier into the 'promised land'… went on to 3rd Div HQ in front of Brussels and found out from Monty that the 10th Belgian Div was already holding the front allotted to him [at Louvain]. His men had been fired at by the Belgians, mistaking them for German parachutists, and one man of the Middlesex had been seriously wounded!

Came back… to find order from GHQ to take up front between Belgian [division] and I Corps. Quite impossible! With great difficulty, got through to GHQ and told by Pownall to double-bank [3rd

Division] with the Belgian Div. Not a satisfactory solution. Belgians should be made to sidestep to their left."

On 12 May:

"Rang up Needham at Belgian GQG [GHQ] to try and solve the problem of 3rd Div".

In his Notes, "I soon gathered from [Needham] that he had done nothing and was not likely to do anything! He kept on telling me how upset the whole of the Staff were at the news from the front [German forces had broken through the Belgian line at Maastricht]… under these circumstances he did not think that he could approach them concerning the 10 Belgian Division… I told him that we certainly had not got enough divisions to be able to afford double-banking them on the front."

His 12 May entry continued:

"I then went to see 3rd Div and… explained situation to [Montgomery]."

In his Notes, "[Monty] said that he had settled the matter himself! I expressed surprise and asked him how… He then told me 'Well, I went to the Belgian Divisional Commander and said to him: Mon General, I place myself and my division unreservedly under your orders and I propose to reinforce your front.' He said that the Belgian Commander was delighted with this relationship. I then asked Monty what he proposed to do if the Germans started attacking. He replied 'Oh! I then place the [Belgian] Divisional Commander under arrest and I take command.'"

On 13 May:

"Ritchie came early to tell me that GHQ had wired to say it was now fixed up for 3rd Div to relieve 10th Belgian Div! So all my work of yesterday did bear fruit!… [Then] I found that a whole Belgian Corps, the 1st Corps, was re-forming after being broken up in [the] front, right in the area that the 4th Div was moving into and where *my Corps HQ was to move to... I do not think much of the Belgian Army and am very nervous as to my left flank."*

On 14 May:

"I found as I expected that Gort was not really in the picture as to the troubles and difficulties which I have been having with the Belgians. Nor did he realize their very poor fighting quality... News of the French at Dinant and at Sedan [towns in the Ardennes region to the south] was not good as Germans had broken through at both these points... The [British] Ambassador came in while we were conferring to ask whether he should leave Brussels as he had been informed that the Belgian [Government] was leaving. I advised him to stop and told him that the fact of his leaving could only create a bad and depressing impression."

On 15 May, a mere six days after the start of the German invasion, Brookie scented a looming disaster:

"A day filled with depressing news as to the fate which is befalling the French in the south! I began by being told that the Germans had got into Louvain on the 3rd Div front. This turned out to be false! And really consisted of a party of Belgians, 10 of whom were shot by the Grenadiers!!... Gort gave us bad news that the French 9th Army and Corap (the General I went to for the Armistice ceremony on the 5th November) had broken on the front south of Dinant, also that the Germans had penetrated at Sedan and Mézières... British 1 Corps expecting to be attacked.

On my left the Belgians are in a very shaky and jumpy condition and I would not trust them a yard. The conquest of Holland being completed [by Germany] frees additional forces for the attack on Antwerp. The BEF is therefore likely to have both flanks turned and will have a very unpleasant time in extricating itself out of its current position... I have been busy drawing up plans for our withdrawal to the Charleroi Canal and from there to the Dendre if necessary.

This is enough to make one feel gloomy. But I must say that I still have a firm conviction that Right must conquer over Wrong. Your letters which arrived this evening have been a great inspiration to me, and at present I feel prepared to face the next few days whatever may be in store. Whatever happens, they can never take away from me our years of paradise."

On 16 May, Brookie was ordered to retire from the Louvain front. Two days later:

"I was too tired to write last night and now can barely remember what happened yesterday. The hours are so crowded and follow so fast on each other that life becomes a blur and fails to cut a groove on one's memory. The 3rd Div withdrew successfully out of Louvain… and motored back to the Dendre.

Michael Barker [commander, I Corps] in a very difficult state to deal with, he is so overwrought with work and the present situation that he sees dangers where they don't exist and cannot make up his mind on any points. He is quite impossible to cooperate with. He has been worse than ever today and whenever anything is fixed he changes his mind shortly afterwards [Barker suffered a nervous breakdown].

I finally held a conference of divisional commanders and settled details of my withdrawal in the early hours of tomorrow from the Dendre to the Scheldt. I have taken over 1st and 50th Div and handed over 4th Div to III Corps for the present. The Germans unfortunately got into the 15/19 Regt today and I am afraid did in the HQ and at least 1 squadron."

By 19 May, British GHQ was already considering evacuation from Dunkirk:

"Got up at 5am after a short night and after examining reports started off to examine the new line of defence on the Scheldt. Found travelling difficult owing to masses of refugees but succeeded in covering the whole length of the line… I was called to GHQ for a Corps Commanders conference. It was a momentous one. The news of the French front was worse than ever, they were attempting one *full counter-attack to try and restore the situation. Should this fail, it looked as if the Allied forces would be cut in the centre! The BEF communications to the sea would be completely exposed and so would our right flank. GHQ had a scheme for a move in such an eventuality towards Dunkirk, establishing a defended area around this place and embarking all we could of the personnel of the BEF, abandoning stores and equipment. I preferred pivoting on our left flank which is secure and in contact with the Belgians. To swing our right back onto the River Lys, up the new empty canal to Ypres and thence by Ypres Canal to the sea. By this means, I feel that at any rate we can keep the BEF as a unity and not have it destroyed by bits. If we let go our hold of the Belgians now, I feel certain they will stop fighting and both our flanks will be exposed, in which case there would be little hope.*

I have spent most of the afternoon in considerable anxiety trying to obtain information from 3rd and 1st Div as to whether they are back safe… it was not till after dinner that I got final confirmation of both being on their fronts… The II Corps has now covered a good 150 miles in 9 days and in the process occupied four successive defensive positions. It has entailed excessively hard work on the part of all ranks and has been exceptionally efficiently carried out."

His 20 May entry illustrated the difficulties of conducting an orderly withdrawal:

"I then visited 1st Div and saw Alexander [commander, 1st Division: Alexander features prominently later in his diary] and discussed his withdrawal, he apparently was subjected to flanking pressure owing to I Corps withdrawing too early. His 3rd Brigade, I discovered later, have lost a great deal of material and the rear party finally had to abandon their vehicles and swim the canal owing to bridges being blown. In the afternoon, Gregson-Ellis came to give me the latest news from GHQ, which included German pressure on Arras!! Every possible measure is being taken to try and stop the advance of the [German] tanks and armoured cars in the gap they have made but the situation still remains very serious. CIGS has flown out from London

to discuss future measures. Weygand appointed supreme commander [in place of Gamelin who had been dismissed]. Pagezy has left Lille. The refugees are a desperate encumbrance on all roads."

In his Notes, Brookie provided a flavour of the confusion and panic caused by the lightning speed of the German panzer advance. His dry comment about the Mayor of Roubaix and his scathing opinion of Pagezy, French commander for the Lille region, are worth highlighting, "I had a telephone call from Pagezy asking me where my Corps was. I told him where it was, whereupon he informed me that this was all wrong and that the Germans were in Roubaix. I told him that this was not the case, and that there were no Germans anywhere near Roubaix. He then said that he had been informed by the Mayor, that he knew where they were, and implied that I did not know what the situation was on my front! He was in a very worked-up state and excitable condition, and evidently losing control of his nerves. I told him fairly bluntly that I did not have to go to the Mayor of Roubaix to find out where the Germans were! Within the next 12 hours Pagezy was gone, and I have never seen him to this day. Nor do I wish to see him! He had been full of talk when the danger was non-existent but now, at the moment when his services were most required, he disappeared".

On the following day:

"Got up early to go round front and see divisions… found 3rd Div well established but very thin on the ground… only 1 [battalion] in reserve on whole Div front! Then went forward to look at front… dropped in to HQ 1st Coldstreams… as they had a bad time at Louvain, losing 5 officers and 160 men… very heavy bombardment was going on just south on 1st Div front near Peck Bridge. I therefore went on to 1st Div to find out what was happening. I found out that Germans were across the river… I told Alexander that they must be pushed back.

GHQ conference at 4.45pm. [Gort] gave us an account of the situation which was very gloomy! Germans reported near Boulogne…

Decided that we should have to come back to the line of the frontier defences tomorrow evening. Namely to occupy the defences we spent the winter preparing. Unfortunately, we are too thin on the ground and forced to hold too wide a front."

On 22 May:

"The refugee problem is very bad. The population of Lille, Roubaix, and Tourcoing having left these places and found they could get no food outside are now beginning to crowd back in again... They are the most pathetic sight, with lame women suffering from sore feet, small children worn out with travelling but hugging their dolls and all the old and maimed struggling along. This evening we moved to Armentières in anticipation of the withdrawal of the front. The trouble is that our rear is now also threatened by German tanks."

On 23 May, note Brookie's admiration of the German Army:

"Nothing but a miracle can save the BEF now and the end cannot be very far off! Where the danger lies is in our right rear; the German armoured divisions have penetrated to the coast, Abbeville, Boulogne and Calais have been rendered useless. We are therefore cut off from our sea communications, beginning to be short of ammunition, supplies still all right for 3 days but after that scanty. This evening the Germans are reported to be pushing onto Bethune and on from St Omer namely right in our rear. If only we now had the armoured division, and at least two of them, to clear our rear [the 1st Armoured Division, which had spent the 1939–40 winter in England awaiting delivery of its long overdue equipment, started arriving in France on 20 May: however, most of it was disembarked at Cherbourg and therefore cut off from the BEF by the corridor created by the German advance across north-east France]!

I went to a conference at GHQ. There I discovered that I was... to take over 4th Div again... I went to see 4th Div... and found that the 11th [Infantry Brigade] had lost fairly heavily yesterday, the Northamptons losing 250 men and 2 of the COs being killed. It is a fortnight since the German advance started and the success they have achieved is nothing short of phenomenal. There is no doubt that they are most wonderful soldiers."

On 24 May:

"I attended a conference at GHQ where we discussed the proposed plans for an attack southwards, to join up with one to be carried out by the French from the south [this attack was intended to break through the corridor created by the German advance]. I then waited to discuss plans with Pownall and Adam when General Blanchard came in who commands the French 1st Army. Billotte [French general] had died from the motor accident so that there is no-one up here at present to coordinate the actions of Belgians, British and French 1st Army. This is urgently required if we are to get out of our present position. Received a report this evening that the Germans had penetrated the Belgian front between Menin and Courtrai; I hope this is not correct but feel very nervous about this flank as I have no reserves to hand, should my flank be exposed."

In his Notes, "Was [Billotte's] mantle now to fall on Blanchard? It seemed likely that it would and I therefore took great interest in looking at Blanchard to see what he was like and what confidence he would inspire. He was standing studying the map as I looked at him carefully and I soon gathered the impression that he might as well have been staring at a blank wall for all the benefit he got out of it. He gave me the impression of a man whose brain had ceased to function, he was merely existing and hardly aware of what was going on around him. The blows that had fallen on us in quick succession had left him 'punch drunk' and unable to register events."

On 25 May, note Brookie's anticipation of a German offensive on II Corps' left flank:

"I received information at 2am that German penetration through the Belgian front was growing rapidly and that the Belgians were not *offering much resistance. I came to the conclusion that this was the beginning of a German offensive intended to push right through to our left rear and to join up with the [German] armoured divisions [to the west of Dunkirk] which must have just about shot their bolt. Went to see GHQ to obtain reinforcement of a brigade to hold the Ypres-Comines Canal. I had already sent our MG [battalion] from 3rd Div there. With great difficulty I finally extracted this Brigade. I was informed that the 'Rush for the Sea' plan was abandoned. Thank God for it, I have always hated this plan. The new plan is to try to break through to join the French forces south of the German penetration [this was the 'attack southwards' referred to in his 24 May entry]. It might be possible, but I should doubt it.*

Liaison Officer from 1st Belgian Div came in with very gloomy account of the fighting put up by the Belgians. Personally, I am convinced that the Belgian Army is closing down and will have stopped fighting by this time tomorrow! This of course entirely exposes our left flank [the King of Belgium decided to sue for an armistice on 26 May, requested one on 27 May and when this was turned down, ordered unconditional surrender on 28 May]."

Later that day, Brookie became even more concerned about his left flank. When visiting 3rd Division HQ, he discovered that a British patrol had captured some German staff papers and when these were translated by British GHQ, they revealed that German forces to the east of the retreating BEF were planning a full-scale attack on the Ypres-Comines front, to the left of the line defended by his II Corps. In the final part of his 25 May entry:

"*GHQ had another conference this evening at 7pm. Found the atmosphere entirely changed and was at once presented with 5 Div to hold Ypres-Comines Canal. They have now realized the danger I warned them about this morning. The penetration scheme [the 'attack southwards', see 24 May] is temporarily abandoned [it was abandoned because the 5th Division had been designated to spearhead this attack].*"

On the following day:

> "Went early to see 5th Div… found that they had been getting into position on Ypres-Comines Canal during the night. Motored on to Ypres to find out whether Belgians were defending this place. Found nothing on our left except the Postal Service of the 1st French Motorized Div!! Then examined canal and railway to see what defences were like. Only just escaped being locked out by the blowing of the bridge owing to the arrival of the Germans. Went back to GHQ to try and raise further troops for the defence of Ypres and secured one brigade of 50th Div. Then attended GHQ conference where we were informed of instructions received from home for evacuation of the BEF… It is going to be a very hazardous enterprise and we shall be lucky if we save 25% of the BEF! We are bound to suffer heavily from bombing. I have already been put in the ditch 3 times today to avoid bombing attacks."

27 May saw Brookie attempting to raise additional forces to shore up his defences on the extended II Corps front. His comment about British GHQ in the final paragraph illustrated the chaos and confusion that prevailed:

> "Held conference of Div Commanders of 3rd and 4th Divs at Bondues at 8am to settle details of withdrawal. Called in on 1st Div to ensure that they stop sending traffic on 3rd Div road, which is required to move 3rd Div through back of 5th Div to extend defences northwards from Ypres for flank defence. Then proceeded to Plugstreet to see 5th Div commander [Franklyn] and find out details of his front which was being shelled.
>
> Motored back to GHQ south of Armentières to find that Germans had penetrated 5th Div front. Back to Lomme to my rear HQ to arrange for withdrawal of one brigade of 4th Div to go to assistance of 5th Div. Then proceeded to I Corps to secure assistance of 1st Div and secured 3 [battalions] which had already been withdrawn to rear of Plugstreet. On to GHQ where I secured 7 infantry tanks to be sent at once to help 5th Div.

Returned to Lomme HQ and from there to [British] GHQ to find they had left without saying where they were going. At 8pm closed Lomme HQ and came to L'Allouette Command Post. From there proceeded to 5th Div to discuss results of day's fighting and plans for next day to ensure that road for retirement is kept open. It has been an anxious day. Bad congestion on roads due to French forces spreading over onto roads reserved for us. Belgians have practically given up fighting so that security of eastern flank of retirement rests with II Corps."

He elaborated in his Notes, "I returned to my HQ at Lomme to collect a few papers, leaving Ronnie Stanyforth with the car at the gate of the house serving as our HQ. As I came back to the car, he pointed to a dead body lying in the gutter on the opposite side of the road and said, 'They have just shot that chap!' When I said, 'Who shot him?', he replied 'Oh! Some of these retiring French soldiers, they said he was a spy but I think the real reason was that he refused to give them cognac.' This gives some idea of the lack of discipline in the French retirement which at times looked more like a rout. This lack of discipline and demoralization was by no means universal, and some of the formations were living up to the very highest traditions of the French Army.

The combined effect of [the rapidly deteriorating morale of the French forces and the demoralised refugees] might well have played havoc with the morale of the men of the BEF had it not been for that indescribable quality of detachment and staunchness of the British soldier. He can sympathize with misery, he can rub shoulders with demoralized allies and suffer on their account; he can be subjected to untold fatigues and hardships in the face of disaster. And yet none of these factors affects his balance. To my mind, it is this factor more than any other that has saved us from many disasters and has contributed most to the successes of the British Army. Never have I had greater admiration, respect and affection for the British soldiers than during those anxious days of our retirement from Louvain to Dunkirk."

Brookie also elaborated in his Notes on the movement of Montgomery's 3rd Division to the north, the purpose being to extend his defensive line towards the coast to stop the German forces in the east from cutting off the BEF's access to Dunkirk, "[Montgomery] had to evacuate his present position and lead his division under cover of darkness across the Lys just east of Armentières… and up by second-class roads northward within 4000 yards of the fluctuating front of the 5th Division to north of Ypres. It was a task that might well have shaken the stoutest of hearts, but for Monty it might just have been a glorious picnic.

There was little possibility of sleep that night… and I repeatedly went out to see how they were progressing. They were travelling, as we had so frequently practised for our night moves, with lights out and each driver watching the rear of the vehicle in front of him… lit up by a tail-lamp under the vehicle… However, with the congestion on the roads, road blocks outside villages, and many other blocks caused by refugees and their carts, the division was frequently brought to a standstill. The whole movement seemed unbearably slow… should daylight arrive with the road crammed with vehicles, the casualties from bombing might well have been disastrous. Our own guns were firing… whilst German artillery was answering back and the division was literally trundling slowly along in the darkness down a pergola of artillery fire and within some 4000 yards of a battle-front."

On 28 May:

> "Visited 5th Div to find out situation which is not satisfactory at junction with 50th Div. Germans still pressing on. Gave verbal instructions for further withdrawal… Proceeded north to see Martel who was covering Ypres and to find out what touch he had on his right south of Ypres with 5th Div. Saw Haydon commanding 150th [Brigade] who said he had no contact on his right and that he had thrown back his right flank. Told Martel to send 4th NF to clear up this situation. Then proceeded further north to see whether Monty had reached his front along canal north of Ypres. Found he had as usual accomplished almost the impossible and had marched from Roubaix to north of Ypres, a flank march past front of attack, and was firmly established in the line.

Down again to 5th Div HQ to find situation of day's hard fighting. Division had held on by its eyelids. 17th and 13th [Brigades] greatly reduced by casualties... Line had held, thank God, otherwise 5th and 4th Divisions were lost and II Corps would have been rolled up!"

In his Notes, "It was with a feeling of intense relief that I found Monty in position. It meant that the first, and the most difficult, stage of the move of the II Corps had been accomplished. The 5th Division, plus all the reinforcements that I had given it, had held during the dangerous period of the withdrawal of the 3rd and 4th Divisions from their advance positions. I now had a continuous defensive flank with 5th Division on right, 50th Division in centre and 3rd Division on left stretching from Comines to well north of Ypres and the French Division Lourde Motorisée extending further north"

29 May saw Brookie questioning an order from his commander-in-chief:

"*Received orders from Gort that I was to proceed home and hand over Corps so as to be available for task of reforming new armies. Went to see Gort to find out whether this was an order as I wanted to remain with Corps. Told it was an order which I must obey. Got him to agree that I could stop on until I had finished retiring Corps into perimeter defence covering embarkation... Went back to La Panne [evacuation beach outside Dunkirk] to see how evacuation was proceeding and found arrangements quite inadequate and of a most Heath Robinson nature.*

Then troubles started. 2nd DLM [French Division Lourdes Motorisée] received orders from Blanchard to retire at once to La Panne to embark! I informed his Liaison Officer that if he did so he would uncover my left and cause hopeless road jam. Told Liaison Officer that if General [commanding 2nd DLM] disobeyed my order and I caught him I should have him shot! Then windy officer from 3rd Div came in to say that Germans had got in behind 5th Div on Yser! To complete troubles, the 32nd French Division cut in across from the west right across the lines of retreat of 50th, 5th and 3rd Divs. Utter confusion on roads and complete jam. However matters finally sorted themselves out... The retirement from the Dyle east of Brussels to the perimeter round La Panne was completed!!"

In his Notes, "The order [to return home], I believe, came from the War Office... I felt like a deserter not remaining with [II Corps] till the last. [The 2nd DLM general] did disobey this order but took good care that I did not catch him so that I did not have the satisfaction of shooting him.

On returning to my chateau... I was met by Ciriez our French Liaison Officer: he was in an infuriated condition and livid with rage. He informed me that a squadron of French cavalry had entered the chateau grounds, had commenced to shoot their horses and to throw their arms into the moat of the chateau. He had dashed out to ask them why they were doing this and they informed him that the Germans were on the outskirts of the village and they did not wish to be captured with their arms! He informed them that there were no Germans within 20 miles, that they were a disgrace to the French army".

On 30 May:

"Went round all 4 Divs to ensure that defence of sectors was completed and to find what strength of Corps remained... There is no doubt that the 5th Div in its fight on the Ypres-Comines Canal saved the II Corps and the BEF. I can hardly believe that I have succeeded in pulling the 4 divisions out of the mess we were in, with allies giving way on all flanks... Arranged for Monty to take over Corps. Visited all Div Commanders to say goodbye... Went down to beach at 7.15pm... and with Ronnie Stanyforth and Barney Charlesworth, we paddled out to the destroyer and got aboard.

Finally arrived Dover at 7.15am. Wonderful feeling of peace after the last 3 weeks!"

On the following day, Brookie and General Adam, III Corps commander, drove to London to report to the War Office: Adam later described Brookie's handling of II Corps throughout the German offensive as "perfect".[1] In his Notes, "That drive has always remained so deeply engraved in my memory… It was a most lovely English spring morning, with all the country looking as it only can in spring. Everywhere around us were those spring sights and smells of nature awaking after her winter slumbers. The contrast of this lovely sunlit country and its perfect peacefulness when compared with those Belgian roads crammed with distressed and demoralized humanity, horizons shrouded in smoke-clouds from burning villages, continuous rumbling of guns, bombs and aircraft, smashed houses, dead cattle, broken trees and all those war scars that distort the face of nature. To have moved straight from that inferno into such a paradise… made the contrast all the more wonderful. That drive will always remain one of my most cherished memories".

After a "long sleep of well over thirty-six hours" at home, Brookie returned to the War Office on 2 June for a meeting with John Dill, who had been appointed CIGS a few days earlier. In his Notes: "I was still overcome by the wonderful transformation from war to peace. The awful load of responsibility had been laid aside… life had suddenly assumed a wonderfully rosy outlook and I walked into Dill's room with a light heart… and asked him what he now wished me to do. His reply was: 'Return to France to form a new BEF.' As I look back at the war, this was certainly one of my blackest moments." When interviewed by Anthony Eden, Secretary of State for War, about his new assignment, Brookie was characteristically forthright. In his Notes, "[I informed Eden] that the mission I was being sent on from a military point of view had no value and no possibility of accomplishing anything. Furthermore, that we had only just escaped a major disaster at Dunkirk and were now risking a second such disaster! I continued by stating that possibly this move had some political value and that was not for me to judge, but that I wanted him to be quite clear that the expedition I was starting on promised no chances of military success and every probability of disaster… I was informed that on arrival in France I should take command of all British forces in France, and that I should come under the orders of General Weygand [Commander-in-Chief, French Army]. My role was to support the French".

On 5 June, German forces launched a new offensive against France and by 7 June had broken through the French defensive line. On 12 June, Brookie returned to France, infuriated:

"It took us some time to find the 'Duty Boat' [in Southampton]… it turned out to be a dirty little Dutch steamer with 100 Frenchmen on board and only capable of 12 knots. We sailed at 2pm, no arrangements for food on board and I was very grateful for your excellent sandwiches. At 9.30pm we arrived at Cherbourg to be told that we should have to anchor out in the stream and could not land till 6am tomorrow!! And these are the arrangements the [War Office] has made after pushing me for the last week to get over as quickly as possible!! It's an absolute disgrace and I propose to let them know in no measured terms."

Two points deserve mention. First, Brookie had already decided that little could be achieved from this mission other than to save the British forces in France by repatriating them: in the event, his decision proved to be correct since he was to return to England within six days. In his Notes, "To my consternation, I found that there were still some 100,000 men from the BEF – L of C [lines of communication] troops! In addition, masses of dumps of clothes, equipment, vehicles, stores, petrol, etc. I [issued instructions] to keep on evacuating home as many of these unarmed personnel as [possible], only retaining personnel essential for the maintenance of the four [British] Divisions [still in France]." Second, whereas in May he had been a corps commander, now he was commander-in-chief, responsible only to Weygand, Dill and the British Government. Over the next six days, Brookie was to display quick and incisive leadership.

13 June saw a dry comment and an accurate prediction:

"Left [Cherbourg] at 8am for Le Mans which we did not reach until 2pm but was glad to arrive alive in spite of dangerous driver. Refugees again swarming everywhere and heartbreaking to find oneself back amongst them. Then started off with Swayne to see Weygand.

Another long drive of 170 miles, making some 340 miles in all for the day... am to see Weygand tomorrow. From all I can gather, I can see no hope of the French holding out longer than the next three days."

On 14 June:

"*Went to see Weygand at 8.30am. Found him looking very wizened and tired-looking with a stiff neck from a car smash on previous evening. He said he would speak frankly. That the French army had ceased to be able to offer organised resistance and was disintegrating into disconnected groups. That Paris had been given up and that he had no reserves whatever left. He then stated that at the Inter Allied Council it had been decided to hold a position covering Brittany in front of Rennes [the Brittany Scheme]... He then suggested that I should go with him to Georges' HQ [French general] to draw up an agreement for this manoeuvre."*

In his Notes, "As we were trundling along, [Weygand] turned to me and said: 'This is a terrible predicament that I am in.' I was just preparing to answer that I could well understand how heavy the responsibility must be to be entrusted with the task of saving France in her distress. To my astonishment he continued with: 'Yes, I had finished my military career which had been a most successful one.' I remained dumb and unable to make any adequate remark, it seemed impossible that the man destined to minister to France in her death agonies should be thinking of his military career."

His 14 June entry continued:

"*We then went to see Georges and finally drew up a statement confirming the above plan. But both Weygand and Georges were in agreement with me that the Brittany Defence Scheme was quite impossible owing to lack of troops. I then sent a wire to [War Office] and instructed Howard-Vyse to fly home to explain situation to Dill.*"

Brookie elaborated in his Notes, "[Georges] took me to a large wall-map with a line running across France, showing latest fighting reports. On this line was drawn in red chalk several sausage-shaped indentations along the line. I... was informed by him that they were the penetrations by German armoured forces. I looked at the scale and saw that they were [deep] penetrations of some fifty to a hundred kilometres on a frontage of twenty to thirty. I asked him what reserves he had and, holding his hands up in a gesture of desperation, he replied: 'Absolutely none, not a man, vehicle or gun left!'

We then turned to the question of the defence of Brittany, and Weygand explained that a line was to be held stretching through Rennes with its flanks resting on the sea. While he was talking, I had pulled out my pocket-dividers and, setting them to 50 kilometres, I measured this line and made it out to be 150 kilometres. I drew Weygand's attention to this and he said that it could not be as much. I therefore measured the distance again under his eyes and said that to defend a front of 150 kilometres we should require at least fifteen divisions. Where were these to come from?

I pointed out that the plan as far as I could see had no hope of success. Weygand agreed that the idea was 'fantastic' and Georges, I think, qualified it as 'romantic'. I therefore said that if we, as military men, considered this scheme as doomed to failure with the resources available, it was up to us to represent this fact clearly to the Inter Allied Council. Whereupon he gave me to understand that this had already been done; that it was now considered to be an order".

His 14 June entry continued:

"Arrived back [at Le Mans] at 4pm and called up Dill to explain situation and request that flow of troops out to this country should be stopped at once [Britain was proposing to send more troops to France]. He informed me that he had already done so. I then told him I considered the Brittany Scheme a wild project which was quite impossible and that there was only one course open to us namely to re-embark the BEF as quickly as possible. He said he would see the PM as he had not heard of Brittany Scheme and would call up later

[Dill's ignorance suggests a serious breakdown in communications or a misunderstanding between Britain and France]. Later he informed me that Brittany Scheme was off and that I should proceed with embarkation of troops not under order[s] of French X Army".

Brookie immediately began to issue orders directing units to retire to ports for embarkation back to England. That evening, he was phoned again by Dill. In his Notes, his remark about Churchill's powers of persuasion is worth highlighting, "[Dill] asked me what I was doing about the 52nd Division and I gave him an account of the dispositions... He replied: 'The Prime Minister does not want you to do that.' And I think I replied, 'What the hell does he want?' At any rate Dill's next reply was: 'He wants to speak to you'. To my surprise, I found myself talking to Churchill... He asked me what I was doing with the 52nd Division and after I had informed him, he told me that that was not what he wanted. I had been sent to France to make the French feel that we were supporting them. I replied that it was impossible to make a corpse feel and that the French Army was, to all intents and purposes, dead... He then asked me whether I had not got a gap in front of me. When I replied that this was correct, he asked whether the division could not be put into the gap. I told him that as the gap was some thirty to forty miles broad at that time and would probably be some forty to sixty miles tomorrow, the remainder of the 52nd Division would be of little avail in trying to block this widening chasm. I said that it would again inevitably result in the throwing away of good troops with no hope of achieving any results.

Our talk lasted for close on half an hour and on many occasions his arguments were so formed as to give me the impression that he considered that I was suffering from 'cold feet' because I did not wish to comply with his wishes. This was so infuriating that I was repeatedly on the verge of losing my temper... At last, when I was in an exhausted condition, he said: 'All right, I agree with you.' The strength of his power of persuasion had to be experienced to realize the strength that was required to counter it."

Brookie was now confronted with three problems. First, he needed to detach himself from Weygand's command to secure freedom of decision and action for himself. He secured this on 14 June, according to the final section of his entry:

> "After dinner had another talk with Dill… was informed by him that order had been sent by him placing me on my own and no longer under Weygand."

The second was that London might issue instructions which hampered his repatriation plans. This problem materialised on 15 June:

> "Woken at 3am by arrival of Jimmy Cornwall. Told him that I wanted him to take command of the [British] forces under French X Army as soon as they could be detached… and to then retire on Cherbourg. Gave him a written order to the effect that he was to take command of these troops and whilst rendering all possible assistance to French X Army, to direct his axis of retirement on Cherbourg.
>
> [Dill] called up… to say that the 2 Brigades [of 52nd Division] at Cherbourg were not to be embarked without orders from the UK. This can achieve nothing but lead to chaos… After lunch I had another talk with Dill and was again told that for political reasons it is desirable that the two Brigades… should not be re-embarked for the present. In the evening I was told that shipping was available at Cherbourg to remove [the two] brigades but that owing to WO instruction it could not be made use of! We are wasting shipping and valuable hours; at present bombing is not serious, at any moment it may become so. After dinner had another talk with Dill and Eden and pointed out to them that from a military point of view we were committing a grave error… Subsequently was again called up by Dill and informed that I could embark some of the gunners of the 52 Div and RE at Cherbourg provided I retained the infantry of the two [brigades]."

The third was that the withdrawal of British units had to be implemented without disclosing his intentions to his French ally. In the final section of his 15 June entry:

> "Received Liaison Officer from Jimmy Cornwall with his situation

and statement that [Cornwall] had not yet informed Altmayer [commander, French X Army] of decision to re-embark BEF. Sent him reply not to disclose this fact for the present... Later Guy Rack commanding L of C troops at Rennes called up and said that 2 French generals were enquiring what all this movement towards the ports was implying!! I have replied that we are thinning out Base and L of C organization of BEF... I hope this answer will satisfy them."

16 June was a busy day:

"Got to bed shortly after midnight and had good sleep till 6am when I was called up by CIGS... Told [me] to prepare to carry on embarking 2 brigades of 52nd Div at Cherbourg... At 8.45 had second message by telephone from Dill telling me to fire ahead with 52nd Div but to wait a little longer as regards Cornwall's force.

11.15am. Interview with General Vouez who wanted... to ensure that no misunderstanding existed between me and Weygand. He informed me as to situation on X Army front which is much as I thought but he was inclined to take an over-rosy view of the situation and has now gone back to General Weygand to explain what the situation is as regards the BEF.

1.30pm. Call from Dill... not prepared yet to confirm withdrawal of Jimmy [Cornwall] from X Army. As I had just received message from the latter that X Army were still working on the Brittany Scheme and expecting British cooperation, I told Dill and asked him to ensure that the French Government knows.

6.25pm: I called up again and got Dill who informed me that the decision was that troops with X Army should remain there and continue fighting with the X Army as long as it remained intact. Should X Army begin to disintegrate, they may retire on Cherbourg. This is an unsatisfactory arrangement but possibly inevitable.

Dill in his last call said that Weygand was not satisfied that I should have departed from our signed agreement. But I reminded Dill that I had told [Weygand] that this agreement was based [on] the supposition that the Allied governments had agreed on the Brittany

Scheme. Dill had referred this matter to Winston Churchill who said that there was no such agreement between the governments. I had then specially asked Dill to let Weygand know as I was under an obligation of the document I had signed. I understood that this had been done and that the order taking me from Weygand's orders included such information. However, I do not mind what accusations may be made against me. If I were faced with the same situation again, I should act exactly in the same way and am convinced that any other course of action could only result in throwing good money after bad.

Midnight reports of embarkation are good. Some 45,000 have been embarked in last 24 hours, 12,000 previous 24 hours, giving total of just under 60,000 in 48 hours. Transportation hopeful of making 60,000 figure in next 24 hours which should complete evacuation."

His 17 June entry captured the tension and danger of the rapidly deteriorating situation:

"Received report in early morning that X French Army was in full retreat and that Jimmy Cornwall was retiring British forces under his command on Cherbourg. Informed Naval Commodore and De Fonblanque of necessity to push on with all speed loadings today as this will probably be the last 24 hours clear for all ports. At 10am put call through to Dill to tell him of situation on X Army front and of Jimmy Cornwall's move on Cherbourg. First reaction of Dill was that Jimmy should have remained with X French Army. However, as this army is in full retreat and… Jimmy said that any pressure from Germans would result in disintegration of the X French Army, I cannot see that any other course was open to him.

1.15pm. Call from Dill saying that wireless reports [the] French have stopped fighting. Agreed that we should now concentrate on personnel and that I could start with my HQ this evening. Agreed that I should call up once more if possible but if unable to call up should start off… Made further enquiries about the destroyer to pick us up at St Nazaire tonight.

2.30pm. Have just seen Meric [French liaison officer] who told me he heard the French broadcast by Pétain telling French armies to cease hostilities [Pétain had requested an armistice on 16 June].

3.30pm. Called up [London] again and was told that line to England had been cut and no longer possible to get through. Decided to leave for St Nazaire at 4pm.

4.30pm. We left Redon and motored to the vicinity of St Nazaire. There we parked in a lane hidden from aeroplanes and waited for the destroyer to arrive. We sent Allen the Naval officer on ahead to find out when the destroyer would arrive. He came back about an hour later saying that the Lancastria [British liner] had been bombed with 6000 on board as she was sailing out and sunk. The destroyer detailed for us had to be used to save the survivors and was no longer available!"

Eventually, Brookie and his party found an armoured trawler, the *Cambridgeshire*, to take them back to England:

"When we arrived on board, we found that she had just been saving 900 survivors from the Lancastria. She was in an indescribable mess, soaked in fuel oil and sea water... We are going to have a rough trip from most points of view. But I hope that we may look sufficiently small and insignificant as not to be worth bombing!"

On 18 June, the *Cambridgeshire* left St Nazaire at 4am:

"This morning one of the crew went more or less mad and had to be held down on the deck."

In his Notes: "We spent the whole of this day on the trawler, mostly lying on the deck in the sunshine and thanking God that we were safely out of France for the second time... Suddenly, in the middle of this peaceful scene, we were disturbed by piercing yells emanating from the lower parts of the trawler. The screams drew nearer and finally the individual responsible for them emerged on the deck. It was one of the stokers, a young boy who had been so seriously affected by the men of the *Lancastria* drowning in fuel oil that he had become temporarily unhinged. He started tearing round the deck shouting, 'Can't you see they are all drowning? Why are you not doing anything? Oh God, we must do something for them.' We caught him and held him down, and then hunted for some bromide to give him but there was none. We therefore got several aspirins and ground them down in some milk and poured it down his throat. He gradually quietened down and slept for a couple of hours when the whole procedure had to be repeated.

I gathered from the Captain that he had done excellent work on the previous day and had saved a lot of men himself personally... He must have been of a highly-strung disposition and the sight must have been too much for him and temporarily unhinged him."

His 18 June entry continued:

"The last week has been a very trying one and I hope never to be entrusted with a similar task again! To try and relate political considerations, with which you are not fully informed, with military necessities, which stare one in the face, is a very difficult matter when these two considerations pull in diametrically opposed directions. Politically, it may have been desirable to support our allies to the very last moment even to the extent of being involved in the final catastrophe and annihilation. Militarily, it was self-evident from the start that the very small forces at our disposal could do nothing towards restoring the military situation which would have required at least 2 complete armies to exercise any influence... The difficulty has been to extract the existing forces without giving the impression that we were abandoning our ally in its hour of need. Pétain's order to cease hostilities gave the ultimate necessary relief to this situation but unless this situation had been anticipated in our preparations, I doubt whether we should have saved much."

On 19 June, Brookie was still aboard the *Cambridgeshire*:

"We are in a bad way if we should strike a mine, bomb or torpedo as the whole of the salvage gear is gone in the rescue of survivors of the Lancastria! We have no small boats, rafts, life belts, life buoys...

The crew are a very good lot, very cheerful and have been very good in making us as comfortable as is possible... The one that went queer yesterday is still in a bad way and suffering from a complete nervous breakdown continually shouting about saving people.

At last we set foot on British soil [in Plymouth] and thanked God for again allowing us to come home. I also thanked God that the expedition which I had hated from the start was over... I called up Dill and told him I was home and fixed up to see him at 9am next day... Finally, we caught the midnight train for London."

FIVE

C-in-C Home Forces: June 1940–November 1941

20 June saw Brookie reporting back to Dill. Gratitude was in short supply:

"I saw Dill and told him that if I had to start the whole trip again I should do exactly the same things again. Apparently, the fact that we did not get off more stores from Brest is now looming far larger than the fact that if I had followed out the [Government's] wishes at the start they would have lost both the Canadian and 52nd Divisions besides all stores and L and C personnel!"

Six days later, he was placed in charge of Southern Command:

"The main impression I had was that the Command had a long way to be put on a war footing and that a peace atmosphere was still prevailing."

On 29 June:

"Attended a conference on the [Local Defence Volunteers, later called the Home Guard]… Why do we in this country turn to all the old men when we require a new volunteer force? Old men spell delay and chaos! I wonder whether I have reached the age to stand clear and let younger men replace me!"

Following the fall of France, the German high command concluded that no invasion of Britain should be launched unless and until the

German air force, the Luftwaffe, had gained control of the skies, hence the significance of the Battle of Britain in the summer of 1940. In truth, the window of opportunity for an invasion in 1940 was small because any amphibious assault across the English Channel after September was rendered extremely hazardous, if not impossible, by the deterioration in the weather.

During July, Brookie inspected the state of the defences under his command. He was unimpressed:

"The more I see of conditions at home the more bewildered I am as to what has been going on in this country since the war started! It is now 10 months and yet the shortage of trained men and of equipment is appalling!! At present I fail to see how we can make this country safe from attack."

"Met Green at Crownhill, discussed defence of Plymouth which seems very sketchy. Prior, as Plymouth sub-area commander, does not seem what is wanted and his plans of defence are very sketchy. Green must I am afraid go. He has not got the required qualities... he is too old and lacking in drive."

However, there were exceptions:

"Visited Oxford to see my South Midland Area commanded by McMullen. A good show but not enough troops."

On 17 July, Churchill visited units under Brookie's command. One reason for his visit was that Anthony Eden, Secretary of State for War, had recommended that Brookie be appointed Commander-in-Chief, Home Forces. Two days later:

"I went in to see [Eden] and was told that he wanted me to succeed Tiny Ironside as C-in-C Home Forces... I find it hard to realize fully the responsibility that I am assuming. I only pray to God that I may be capable of carrying out the job. The idea of failure at this stage of the war is too ghastly to contemplate. I know that you will be with me in praying to God that he may give me the necessary strength and guidance."

On the next day, he visited Home Forces' HQ:

"*I was not impressed by the HQ! They are dirty and not very well equipped.*"

In his Notes, "When I arrived there, Ironside had already gone. There was a note from him stating that he had arranged with the owner of the Rolls Royce that he had been using for me to take it over and the best of wishes. That was all! Not a word concerning the defences or his policy of defence, absolutely nothing!"

On 21 July, his first day as C-in-C Home Forces, he attracted the attention of the press:

"*Had to suffer photographer and cine man during the morning.*"

Brookie immediately began a nationwide inspection of the country's defences with his usual energy and drive. In his Notes, he explained his strategy to counter a German invasion, "I... discovered that much work and energy was being expended on an extensive system of rear defence comprising an anti-tank ditch and pillboxes, running roughly parallel to the coast and situated well inland. This static rear line did not fall in with my conception of the defence of the country... we had not got sufficient forces to man this line, even if we had wanted to do so. To my mind, our defence should be of a far more mobile and offensive nature. I visualized a light line of defence along the beaches to hamper and delay landings to the maximum and, in rear, highly mobile forces trained to immediate aggressive action intended to concentrate and attack any landings before they had time to become too well established. I was also relying on heavy air attacks on the points of landing and had every intention of using sprayed mustard gas on the beaches... Another form of defence which I found throughout the country, and with which I was in total disagreement, consisted of massive concrete roadblocks at the entry and exit of most towns and of many villages. I had suffered too much from these blocks in France not to realize their crippling effect on mobility.

There was, however, one point above all others that constituted a grave danger to the defensive organization... There was no form of Combined Command over the three Services... There were far too many commanders... There was no coordinating head to this mass of commanders beyond the Chiefs of Staff Committee and the Admiralty, Air Ministry and War Office... It was a highly dangerous organization. Had an invasion developed, I fear that Churchill would have attempted as Defence Minister to coordinate the actions of these various commands. This would have been wrong and highly perilous with his impulsive nature and tendency to arrive at decisions through a process of intuition".

On 22 July, he dined with Churchill:

"*He is most interesting to listen to and full of the most marvellous courage, considering the burden he is bearing. He is full of offensive thoughts for the future, but I think he realizes the difficulties he is up against! He said he wondered if England had ever been in such straits since the Armada days. He refers to Hitler always as 'that man'!*"

Four days later, he attended a chiefs of staff meeting:

"*Main subject of discussion was the priority of use of fighters in the event of invasion. I came away feeling less confident as to our powers of meeting an invasion. The attitude of representatives of the Naval Command brought [out] very clearly the fact that the navy now realizes fully that its position has been seriously undermined by the advent of aircraft. Sea supremacy is no longer what it was and in the face of strong bomber forces, can no longer ensure the safety of this island against invasion. This throws a much heavier task on the army.*"

On 27 July, Brookie visited:

"*46th Div commanded by Anderson. Found it in a lamentably backward state of training, barely fit to do platoon training... 9th Div is in much the same state as 46th.*"

In June, Italy had declared war on France and Britain, a few days before

France's collapse. Italy's entry into the War imperilled Britain's use of the Mediterranean as a sea route with the result that British shipping was having to use the circuitous, time-consuming route of sailing around Africa via the Atlantic and Indian Oceans to supply its forces in north and east Africa and maintain communications with India, the Far East, Australia and New Zealand. Furthermore, concern was growing in Britain over Egypt because Italy had started building up its military strength in neighbouring Cyrenaica [eastern Libya] and the British forces in the region led by General Wavell, Commander-in-Chief Middle East, were modest.

On 10 August, he attended a meeting with Eden and Wavell:
"The [meeting]… concerned regiments of tanks to be given to [Wavell] at once… I had at this critical time to agree to part with 1 Cruiser Regt, 1 [Light] Tank Regt and 1 Army Tank Regt!"

In his Notes, "This does not seem much… but in the early days even this small contribution constituted a large proportion of the total of my armoured forces."

The desperate shortage of armour in Home Forces brought Brookie into conflict with someone who he came to dislike intensely – Lord Beaverbrook, minister of aircraft production. In his Notes, "[He] began to form an army of his own to protect aircraft factories in the event of invasion. He acquired large proportions of armour plating for the production of small, armoured cars called 'Beaverettes' with which he equipped Home Guard personnel of factories for their protection. This was at a time when I was shouting for every armoured vehicle I could lay my hands on with which to equip regular troops. The whole conception was fantastic. How could individual factories have held out… once the main battle for this country was lost… The more I saw of him throughout the war, the more I disliked and mistrusted him. An evil genius who exercised the very worst of influence on Winston."

On 19 August, he met someone else who he also came to dislike intensely:

"Lunched with Anthony Eden to meet de Gaulle. Was not much impressed by him. In the afternoon, Roger Evans came to see me to ask why he had been removed from the Armoured Division. This resulted in an unpleasant interview."

In his Notes, he offered this damning description of de Gaulle, "Whatever good qualities he may have had were marred by his overbearing manner, his 'megalomania' and his lack of cooperative spirit… In all discussions he assumed that the problem of liberation of France was mine whilst he was concentrating on how he would govern it, as its Dictator, as soon as it was liberated! Added to these disadvantages, his Headquarters were so completely lacking all sense of security that it became quite impossible to discuss any future plans with him."

23 August saw Brookie addressing the subject of British armoured forces. As will become apparent, he invested considerable time on this issue:

"Willoughby Norrie came at 10am and I told him what I wanted done as regards handling of [1st] Armoured Division he takes over [from Evans]… Then to see Cave as regards production of 1st line vehicles and armoured forces… 6pm: Pope [Director of Armoured Fighting Vehicles] to discuss organization of armoured forces and to plan for the winter."

On 31 August:

"Proceeded to Aldershot to inspect the New Zealand Division and was very much impressed with the units I saw. They will be a great loss to Home Forces when they go and a great gain to the Middle East."

3 September was the first anniversary of the start of the War. This prompted Brookie to reflect:

"Looking back, it has been a year of heartbreaking partings from you which stand out for me above all else, a year of unending work and very heavy trials. I am quite convinced that if it had not been for the influence you have had in my life in confirming my belief in an

Almighty and far-seeing God that I should have found it hard to come through such trials… But it is quite impossible to live with you without seeing God's divine heaven radiating from you at all times. I do thank Him for having allowed me to meet you and through you to be able to get so much closer to Him."

The first half of September saw fears of a German invasion intensifying. On 4 September:

"Indications of impending attack before Sept 15th are accumulating."

Three days later:

"All reports look like invasion getting nearer."

8 September was a Sunday, the one day in the week which he usually spent at home:

"Went to the office in the morning where I found further indications of impending invasion. Everything pointing to Kent and E. Anglia as the two main threatened points.

Spent the afternoon and evening in complete paradise with you and those two beloved small persons. It is so wonderful being able to get into such surroundings for a bit and to forget the war and all its horrors. Motored back at 8.30 with air raid on. Searchlights working in all directions and a glowing red sky over London. It seemed so strange leaving you and all the wonderful peace and happiness connected with our combined lives to return here for what may well be the most eventful weeks in the history of the British Empire! I called in at [Home Forces' HQ] on the way back and found that all reports still point to the probability of an invasion starting between the 8th and 10th of this month. The responsibility of feeling what any mistakes or misappreciations may mean in the future of these Isles and of the Empire is a colossal one! And one which rather staggers me at times."

In his Notes, "I do not think I can remember any time in the whole of my career when my responsibilities weighed heavier on me than they did during those days of the impending invasion."

By 14 September, the Italian forces in eastern Libya had begun a tentative advance into Egypt:

"Ominous quiet!! German shipping reserves greatly reduced and air action too. Have the Germans completed their preparations for invasion? Are they giving their air force a last brush and wash-up? Will he start tomorrow or is it all a bluff to pin troops down in this country while he prepares to help Italy to invade Egypt??"

15 September saw some interesting observations:

"Still no move on the part of the Germans... The suspense of waiting is very trying especially when one is familiar with the weakness of our defence! Our exposed coastline is just twice the length of the front the French were holding in France with about 80 divisions and a Maginot Line! Here we have 22 divisions of which only about ½ can be looked upon as in any way fit for any form of mobile operation! Thank God the spirit is now good and the defeatist opinions expressed after Dunkirk are now no longer prevalent. But I wish I could have 6 months now to finish equipping and training the force under my command. A responsibility such as that of the defence of this country under the existing conditions is one that weighs on one like a ton of bricks and it is hard at times to retain the hopeful, confident exterior which is so essential to retain the confidence of those under one and to guard against their having any doubts as regards final success."

On 17 September, Hitler decided against launching an invasion of Britain in 1940. However, German bombing of British cities continued. On 22 September:

"Then went home, where I found you all singing hymns in the drawing room. It was a wet day, but it might have been brilliant sunshine for the joy of being back with you. In the evening, gave Philip a lift back. The approach to London looked like approaching Dante's

Inferno, continuous flashes of guns and sparks of bursting shells in the sky with haloes of searchlights."

27 September was another anniversary:

"*Today is anniversary of my departure for France from Salisbury and our parting outside the County Hotel. I can see your car driving off now when I shut my eyes and can again feel that ghastly desolation that froze into my heart at our having to part.*"

Sunday, 29 September was "*a lovely, peaceful and heavenly day*" spent at home "*sawing wood and just basking in the sunshine of happiness spread by the presence of you and the wee ones. These Sunday afternoons with you are the most wonderful tonic after a hard week's work. When with you, I am able to forget everything connected with the war and its worries and come back refreshed for another week of this burden.*" On 30 September:

"*Attended Chiefs of Staff Committee meeting at 10.15. This organization works surprisingly slowly considering there is a war on! We seem to meander along and there is no snap about it. I only wish that Dill was Chairman.*

[Met] Pope with whom I discussed organization of armoured force, things have been progressing satisfactorily and the organization I wanted has been adopted. We can now forge ahead."

Earlier, 10 August, Brookie had agreed under pressure to some of his armoured regiments being despatched to Egypt. On 2 October, he lost out again to the demands emanating from Cairo:

"*I am to lose the whole of the 1st Armoured Division by 1st November! Worst part of the bargain is that all the cruiser tanks must be pulled back at once for overhaul. I shall therefore be short of 100 Cruisers from now onwards!*"

3 October saw:

"*An interview with Finch [British major general] who proved himself to be an even more poisonous specimen than I thought he* was... Returned to the office to be attacked by Secretary of Jockey Club who wished to carry on with Newmarket race meetings as if no war existed."

On 11 October, Brookie was invited to Chequers. Note his admiration for Churchill:

"Sat up till 2am. PM in great form. Discussing probable course of war, likelihood of German move in Mediterranean... He has a wonderful vitality and bears his heavy burden remarkably well. It would be impossible to find a man to fill his place at present."

On 19 October, he was in a weary and philosophical mood:

"Another day gone and thank God for it! Every day that passes must at least be one day less of this war. But there are times when the madness and folly of war choke one! Why human beings must behave like children at this stage of the evolution of the human race is hard to understand. At any rate, it proves that we have still got to go a long way on the road that leads to perfect human beings. And yet through all its destruction, uselessness and havoc, I can see some progress. Progress that could never be achieved without the upheaval of war. Long-standing institutions and social distinctions are shattered by war and make room for more modern methods of life. Those that would never release what they hold in peace are forced to do so in war, to the benefit of the multitude. Ultimately, I suppose that human beings from much suffering will become wiser and will appreciate that greater happiness can be found in this world by preferring their neighbours to themselves!

Meanwhile, for all my philosophy I am very tired of this war and long for peace. A peace that will allow us to spend the remaining years of our life quietly together in a small cottage with a garden to work in, some trees to look after and perhaps a stream close by where I can watch the fish even if I don't catch them! And above all, somewhere where I can bask in the sublime happiness of the sunshine of your company! But even if I can't be with you at present, I still thank God for having allowed me to know you and for all the wonderful happiness *of seeing you once a week. I am now counting the hours till tomorrow when I hope to start for my Sunday with you."*

On 20 October:

"Sunday is gone and, as usual, has flown like a dream of perfect happiness. You cannot realize what it means after a week of worries, responsibilities, doubts as to whether I am doing all I can, nights of bombing, and the continual desperate longing to be with you, to be able to step out of all that turmoil and at your side find perfect peace and happiness. To be able to mix with the interests of those two beloved wee souls and to enter their world where war does not exist but a thousand simple and healthy interests. To see them developing and to watch bits of your perfect self reflected in them, I cannot tell you, darling, what it all means to me, it is just heaven on earth. I do thank God and you for such a perfect blessing."

On 31 October, he attended a commander-in-chiefs conference held by Churchill:

"We sat from 11am to 1.15 and again from 3pm to 5.15 but, as far as I could see, achieved little! The main subject of discussion was desirability of freeing more destroyers to hunt submarines in the Western Approaches. The Navy for the present seem to have the conviction that they are far better qualified to handle the Army than we are! Personally, I wish they would concentrate their efforts on controlling the naval forces!"

In late October 1940, Italy invaded Greece. By 11 November, Brookie was concerned that Britain might become embroiled in the Greek theatre:

"In evening went to dine with Dill. Anthony Eden was there also but had to go off early as PM was having Chiefs of Staffs meeting to discuss Greek situation. Are we again going to have 'Salonika Supporters' like the last war? Why will politicians never learn the simple principle of concentration of force at the vital point and the avoidance of dispersal of effort?"

On the following day:

"*I attended a skeleton exercise of the 15th Division. A very useful exercise judging by the number of mistakes I saw!*"

On 26 November:

"*Lord Trenchard came to lunch and to discuss with me steps he was taking to rehabilitate the army in the eyes of the country. He is quite right: it has become far too much a habit to run down generals and the army in the press*".

9 December saw the contentious issue of RAF cooperation with the army being addressed:

"*Conference by Anthony Eden on the new Army Cooperation Command of the Air Force... Deplorable situation as regards any cooperation generally. No machines and not likely to materialise for some time. Proposals for training Bomber Command Squadrons also quite inadequate.*"

On Christmas Eve, Brookie spent "*a lovely evening preparing stockings for children.*" Three days later, he was preparing for a training course due to start in early January:

"*Spent most of the day going over my Army Commanders' Course on Armoured Formations. I think it promises fairly well and with luck ought to be of good value.*"

On New Year's Eve, he was in a reflective mood:

"*There are now only 45 minutes left to complete the year 1940! One of the years which will be handed down through history as the year Germany overran Europe... Dunkirk will take its place amongst the many examples of disasters due to political misappreciations of the requirements of war. It should also rank as one of the finest recoveries from disaster. I feel, however, that the air battle for England and the German defeat in its attempt at invasion will probably loom as one of the greatest successes of British arms.*

Personally, I feel that it is the year of my life in which I have had to shoulder the heaviest burdens and face the greatest responsibilities. Looking back at the year in retrospect one fact looms large above all others, namely your influence on my life... If I have succeeded in shouldering my burdens so far, 90% of the credit is due to you and what you mean for me. I thank God for one thing above all others in life and that is for having allowed me to meet you and thus realize what perfection could be realized on this earth."

In his Notes, "1941 began with the fears of invasion abated. The winter was now setting in and any form of seaborne attack was highly unlikely until the spring or early summer... My task as Commander-in-Chief of Home Forces was quite clear. The Home Army must be welded into an effective force capable either to repel any invasion that might be launched against these islands during the year or to form part of Expeditionary Forces in whatever theatre it might be decided to launch offensive operations.

This breathing space, with no immediate fear of invasion, was indeed a welcome one. There was an infinite amount of work required to fit our army for its future role. Units were only partly trained, equipment was still very short especially in armoured forces, formations required a great deal of running in, army-air cooperation was practically non-existent and, most important of all, higher commanders required a great deal of training and weeding out before real efficiency could be achieved."

5 January saw the start of Brookie's training course [see 27 December 1940]:

"Gave opening address after dinner. Very large gathering: all 5 Army Commanders, 6 Corps Commanders and all Armoured [Division and Brigade] Commanders. After opening address, we had a lecture by [Military Intelligence, War Office] on German Armoured Divisions."

On 8 January, note his desire for 'more offensive spirit':

"Finished up final situations of armoured exercise and then had

my final remarks. The latter gave me an opportunity of instilling a little more offensive spirit into the Army and also of expressing my views as regards the present stagnation of training."

On 10 January, he was in a combative mood:
"PM held one of his quarterly conferences of Cs-in-C of the three Services. Attended by the 3 Secretaries of State… [and] the Chiefs of Staff and Pug Ismay. Only 3 points put up for discussion, two of which were mine so I had a busy time. My points were connected with the increased danger of invasion owing to Axis' reverses in the Mediterranean and danger of withdrawal of too many forces from this country. I then had heated argument with Tovey [Commander-in-Chief, Home Fleet] as regards employment of Home Fleet in event of invasion."

In his Notes, "During the discussion I raised the lamentable lack of arms that still prevailed after 1½ years of war… This did not please Winston at all and after the meeting he complained to Dill that he considered it most ungrateful of me to complain of lack of equipment… Considering the period we had been at war, I consider that I had every right, and indeed it was my duty, to draw attention to the shortages that prevailed."

16 January saw the start of a three-day training exercise. On 17 January:
"The exercise is proving very good value and should do a great deal to help to bring on the Armoured Corps."

On 29 January, Brookie implemented some changes in his Home Forces command:
"Conference at the War Office at 4.15pm to settle details concerning split in Eastern Command and organization of my 7 new County Divisions… Paget is shortly to leave us and Budget Loyd take over from him… Paget goes off to organize the new South-Eastern Command. He will be a great loss… Budget might however do very well, I am sure."

In his Notes, there was more than a hint of self-assurance in his remarks about Budget Loyd, "Eastern Command, which covered the main danger area, was far too large to be controlled efficiently by one Commander. It covered the whole of East Anglia from the Wash to the Thames and the South Coast from the Thames to short of Portsmouth. The Thames and London itself split this area in two and made intercommunication difficult and the lateral movement of reserves slow. Guy Williams had been commanding this large front since the beginning, but I was not entirely happy about his methods. Being an engineer, his mind naturally turned to the construction of defensive lines… I decided, therefore, to split Eastern Command in two on the line of the Thames, to retain Williams in command of the Northern Sector for the present and to place Paget, my Chief of Staff, in command of the southern part. I selected Budget Loyd to succeed Paget. I was criticized by many for this decision owing to the fact that Budget had had a nervous breakdown during our retreat to Dunkirk. However, I knew all the circumstances of this breakdown and felt sure that Budget would not break down with me and that he would fill the job admirably."

On 4 February:
"Remained with [Dill] till 8pm discussing proposed cuts in Army Cooperation squadrons of RAF. I am not satisfied that the Air Ministry are transacting this business in an above board method… finally talked over the desirability of making the PM realize more clearly the impending threat of invasion. Apparently both Dill and Pound told him they considered invasion more than probable, but he preferred to believe Portal who considered it improbable [Dill, Dudley Pound, the First Sea Lord, and Charles Portal, Chief of the Air Staff, were the principal members of the Chiefs of Staff Committee]."

13 February illustrated Brookie's dislike of inefficiency:
"After lunch had to attend meeting of Secretary of State's to disentangle hopeless mess [War Office] had made of my proposal to raise County Divisions for defence of beaches. Things looked bad for a

bit as S of S had not got clear picture and had been influenced against scheme by Permanent Under Secretary owing to bad handling of case by Adjutant-General and Quartermaster-General and, especially, by Bob Haining who is quite useless as Vice Chief of [Imperial General] Staff. He understands nothing about military matters and messes everything up. However, I have now got the matter passed by S of S and all is well, except the time unnecessarily wasted. The plan was originally submitted to the WO on Dec 15 and it is now Feb 13 and not yet through."

On 18 February, he demonstrated his commitment and drive:

"A hard day. Started a conference of Commanders-in-Chief at 10am and did not finish till 4.30pm. Secretary of State came to lunch with us… then attended lecture from 5pm till 6.30pm followed by day's work till 7.45. After dinner did 2 hours on our next exercise for Corps Commanders."

By mid-February 1941, Italy had suffered two setbacks. First, its invasion of Greece in late October 1940 had stalled. Second, its half-hearted invasion of Egypt had induced Wavell, Commander-in-Chief Middle East, to launch a counter-attack in December 1940 which resulted in some 100,000 Italians being taken prisoner and large numbers of Italian guns and tanks falling into British hands. Within a few weeks, British forces had occupied the whole of eastern Libya, capturing the ports of Tobruk and Benghazi, and reached El Agheila on the border with Tripolitania [western Libya].

In January 1941, Churchill had proposed to the Greek Government that a British force be sent to their country, the rationale being to assist Greece in the event it was attacked by Germany and, in addition, create a Balkan front in south-east Europe. The Greek Government declined his proposal, fearing that it might provoke Germany into invading their country, and suggested that Britain concentrate its forces in driving the Italians out of north Africa. However, following a change of prime minister in Greece, and further pressing by Churchill, the Greek Government looked upon his proposal more favourably. Consequently, on 12 February, Wavell was ordered to halt his advance in the north African desert and start preparations for the despatch of some of his troops and equipment to Greece. Later that month, Eden and Dill visited Athens and after reporting they were in favour of despatching a force to Greece, Churchill's proposal was approved by the British cabinet. Earlier, 11 November 1940, Brookie had wailed at the prospect of British forces being diverted to Greece: in his Notes, "This is one of the very few occasions on which I doubted Dill's advice and judgment… I have… always considered from the very start that our participation in the operations in Greece was a definite strategic blunder. Our hands were more than full at that time in the Middle East and Greece could only result in the most dangerous dispersal of force."

Britain's intervention in Greece proved disastrous. On 6 April, German forces invaded Greece and by the end of April they had overrun the country resulting in another 'Dunkirk' evacuation by British and Commonwealth troops and the loss of large amounts of equipment and stores. Furthermore, the diversion of forces to Greece meant the opportunity of capturing Tripoli and clearing north Africa of enemy forces in early 1941 was lost. Whilst the prospect of achieving this was, admittedly, slim, hindsight shows this opportunity should have been seized since north Africa was to remain an active battleground until May 1943.

In February 1941, General Rommel was appointed to take command of a German armoured force comprising two small divisions which were hurriedly being sent to north Africa to support the Italian forces. Rommel's arrival in Tripoli on 12 February was closely followed by the arrival of two German battalions and, a few weeks later, a German tank regiment. Rommel had been ordered not to take any offensive action until the remainder of the two divisions arrived in May. Ignoring those orders, Rommel launched a modest attack on the British line at El Agheila in eastern Libya at the end of March. The diversion of forces to Greece had left the British forward positions at El Agheila thinly defended, in some cases by troops who were inexperienced or lacked equipment. When this attack proved successful, Rommel pressed his advantage and by mid-April his forces had retaken Benghazi and the British had retreated to the Libyan-Egyptian frontier, leaving Tobruk under siege.

3 March saw another example of Brookie's dislike of inefficiency:
"*Chief of Staff's meeting in the morning. Dudley Pound is quite the slowest and most useless chairman one can imagine. How the PM abides him, I can't imagine.*"

On 9 March, he attended one of Churchill's house parties at Chequers:
"*Luckily PM decided to go to bed early and by midnight I was comfortably tucked away in an Elizabethan four-poster bed dated 1550! I could not help wondering, as I went to sleep, what wonderful stories the bed could tell of its various occupants during the last 400 years!*"

On 13 March, his forecast regarding Russia would prove accurate:
"*I had to pose for a series of photographs for the National Portrait Gallery and for the Illustrated.*

Where are the Germans going to push next? I would not be surprised to see a thrust into Russia. In many ways this is far the most promising line of action. However, wherever the next thrust may be on the continent, it is certain that the process of attempted strangulation [of Britain] will continue... And if these attempts are sufficiently successful, eventually invasion will be attempted. Meanwhile the preparation of our forces makes good progress."

On 19 March, Brookie inspected the 9th Armoured Division:
"*It is making great strides and should make a grand division eventually. Found from Budget [Loyd] that Bob Haining is messing up matters worse than ever at the War Office [see 13 February].*"

On 21 March, he attended a meeting to discuss a paper prepared by the War Office:

"The whole paper was hopelessly adrift and based on quite a wrong conception of the problems of defence of this country. If only Dill had been here, he would have discussed it with me in its initial stages and the whole matter would have been simple. As it was, I had to crash the whole paper and got S of S to agree that the whole thing required redrafting."

On 1 April:

"Visited units in Portsmouth. Was very much impressed by the results of bombing on Portsmouth, the place has been badly smashed up."

Three days later, Rommel was making his presence felt in north Africa:

"Heard on midnight news that we had lost Benghazi! Not at all a healthy sign and it looks as if we have reinforced Greece at the expense of Tripoli front to a dangerous degree."

On 10 April, Brookie was:

"Rather depressed at the standard of efficiency of Canadian Divisional and Brigade Commanders. A great pity to see such excellent material as the Canadians being controlled by such indifferent commanders."

On 15 April:

"I had a painful interview with Guy Williams [see 29 January Notes] who wanted to refuse the offer to proceed to New Zealand to look after the defences of that country."

On 21 April, he attended a meeting of government ministers. Brookie was to develop a low opinion of politicians:

"Not a very impressive gathering either to look at or to listen to! We were discussing desirability of allowing holidaymakers to visit East Coast. From some of the arguments put forward, one might have imagined that no war was on!

Visit from... Martel to discuss impending withdrawal of some

60 Cruiser tanks from this country for the Middle East [Wavell was now under pressure from Churchill to launch a new offensive against Rommel's forces and secure a decisive victory in north Africa]! It is an appalling blow as far as the defence of this country is concerned."

27 April saw Brookie at Chequers again for another of Churchill's house parties. Amongst the guests was John Kennedy, Director of Military Operations at the War Office:

"[Churchill] was in great form... and kept us up till 3.30am!! Kennedy tried to give PM a rather pompous discourse on strategy in which he contemplated a fairly free evacuation of Egypt! This infuriated the PM and we had some trouble calming him down!"

In his Notes, "The Kennedy incident was a very typical one, poor old John had only intended to express that there might be worse things to lose than Egypt. It was, however, at once taken up by Winston as being a defeatist attitude and Kennedy was relegated amongst those 'many generals who are only too ready to surrender and who should be made examples of like Admiral Byng' [eighteenth-century British admiral sentenced to death for gross dereliction of duty]."

On 5 May, Brookie was at:

"10 Downing Street for what the PM had called a 'Tank Parliament'... On the whole, meeting was I think good value".

In his Notes, "It was a useful meeting, as it brought those responsible for the production of tanks in close contact with those responsible for commanding them in action. I was able to stress the importance of spare parts for tanks and spare tanks, but Winston always disliked the idea of the provision of spares... This failure to provide adequate spare parts for tanks accounted for many of our failures and early difficulties in armoured fighting in North Africa."

11 May was a Sunday, *"A lovely, peaceful day with you. Spent afternoon*

photographing blackbird with cine." Brookie's diary contains many references to his hobbies of bird-watching and bird photography: in his Notes, "These occasional spells of bird-watching did marvels as a means of 'recreation'. I was able for a short spell to forget the war [and] all the nightmare of responsibility."

The next day saw the issue of RAF cooperation with the army being discussed again:

"Next item was air cooperation and assembly was enlarged for this consisting of PM… Portal [Chief of Air Staff] and his awful satellite, Goddard [RAF]. Before we had finished, I became a bit heated and attacked the Air Ministry strongly as regards recent attitude towards Army Cooperation. PM backed me strongly and meeting was a great success!"

On 15 May, he was in Scotland, meeting up with Neil Ritchie who had been a member of his II Corps staff in France:

"A real joy seeing him again… spent rest of afternoon visiting units of the 51st Division… I found considerable improvement since my last visit and Neil Ritchie making a first-class show of the Division."

Another wartime diary keeper was Churchill's private secretary, Jock Colville. When his diaries were published, Colville offered this description of Brookie – "at once spellbound and exasperated by Churchill".[1] There had been hints that Brookie was 'spellbound' in his 22 July 1940, 11 October 1940 and 9 March 1941 entries. 27 May proved the accuracy of Colville's description:

"PM in great form… It is surprising how he maintains a light-hearted exterior in spite of the vast burden he is bearing. He is quite the most wonderful man I have ever met and is a source of never-ending interest studying and getting to realize that occasionally such human beings make their appearance on this earth. Human beings who stand out head and shoulders above all others."

Later diary entries also proved the accuracy of Colville's description since whenever Brookie criticised Churchill, he nearly always matched his criticism with a compliment: seemingly, the impressionable streak which he displayed as a child had not completely disappeared.

On 8 June, a combination of British, Australian, Indian and Free French forces entered Syria and Lebanon, the objective being to remove the Vichy French authorities. This was yet another operation that Wavell was required to undertake, just two months after the Greek debacle and a mere seven days before his new offensive against Rommel in north Africa was due to start. Brookie was appalled. On 17 June, note the 'moth-eaten old admirals':

> "At 12 noon one of the PM's meetings of his C-in-Cs, which in the long run turn out to be mainly a meeting of moth-eaten old admirals! The PM began with a survey of the world situation which was interesting. To my horror, he informed us that the present Libyan operations [Wavell's new offensive] are intended to be a large-scale operation! How can we undertake offensive operations on two fronts in the Middle East when we have not got sufficient for one? From the moment we decided to go into Syria we should have to put all our strength on that front to complete the operation with the least possible delay. If the operation is not pressed through quickly, it may well lead to further complications."

19 June saw another Tank Parliament [see 5 May Notes]:

> "I pressed for better spare parts organization and for the necessity of maintaining some 20% spare [armoured fighting vehicles] per formation. This was not appreciated by the PM who likes to put the whole of his goods in the front window."

On Sunday 22 June, Germany invaded Russia:

> "Had another go at the sparrowhawk. Germany started march into Russia! And with it a new phase of war opens up."

In his Notes, "It certainly was a new phase of the war from my point of view. As long as the Germans were engaged in the invasion of Russia, there was no possibility of an invasion of these islands. It would now depend on how long Russia could last and what resistance she would be able to put up. My own opinion at the time, and an opinion shared by most people, was that Russia would not last long, possibly 3 or 4 months, possibly slightly longer. Putting it at 4 months, and as we were then in June, it certainly looked as if Germany would be unable to launch an invasion of England until October and by then the weather and winter would be against any such enterprise. It therefore looked as if we should now be safe from invasion during 1941. This would put me in the position of devoting the whole of my energies towards converting the defence forces of this island into a thoroughly efficient army capable of undertaking overseas operations, if and when such operations became possible. We were now able to begin to think more offensively".

Meanwhile, in north Africa, Wavell's latest offensive had failed. As a result, Churchill dismissed Wavell and appointed General Auchinleck in his place.

On 30 June:

"[Met] Dill and Portal at 9.45pm to discuss organization of air force to work with army. Did not get home till midnight. It is an uphill battle to try and get an adequate allotment of air force for the army!"

On 9 July, note his disdain for politicians:

"[I attended] meeting of the War Cabinet. The subject to be discussed was my proposed London exercise to deal with a parachute attack. I had to make a statement as to the reason why I considered it advisable to hold the exercise and why we could not hold it as a theoretical exercise. All went well till Beaverbrook started pouring vitriol on the idea. Purely owing to the fact that he has recently taken over the Ministry of Supply and cannot contemplate having his preliminary efforts interfered with! Attlee backed him owing to his fears of the effects of such an exercise on the public. The more I see of politicians the less I think of them! They are seldom influenced directly *by the true aspects of a problem and are usually guided by some ulterior political reason! They are always terrified of public opinion as long as the enemy is sufficiently far but, when closely threatened by the enemy, inclined to lose their heads and then blame all their previous errors on the heads of the military whose advice they have failed to follow. The more I see of democracy, the more I doubt our wisdom of attaching such importance to it! I cannot see how our present system of democracy can produce real qualified leaders of a nation."*

In his Notes, "Our present system of democracy certainly did throw up one of the most wonderful national leaders of our history, Winston Churchill. One of his first acts, however, was virtually to convert the democracy into a dictatorship [following his appointment as prime minister on 10 May 1940, Churchill immediately appointed himself minister of defence: by virtue of holding these two offices, Churchill gained control over the management and direction of the British war effort]! Granted that he still was responsible to a Parliament and granted that he still formed part of a Cabinet; yet his personality was such, and the power he acquired adequate, to place him in a position where both Parliament and the Cabinet were only minor inconveniences which had to be humoured occasionally, but which he held in the palm of his hand, able to swing both of them at his pleasure."

His 10 July entry was in similar vein to the previous day's entry:

"I had to attend another Defence Committee meeting of the Cabinet. The subject for discussion was that of the defence of the aerodromes. There is to be a secret debate in the House [of Commons], and members of the Cabinet are expecting to be cross-examined on our dispositions. Hence considerable quibbling and attempts at defining the indefinable. Attlee made me nearly lose my temper, Margesson [Secretary of State for War since December 1940] confused the issue in imagining he was clearing up matters. After 30 minutes of cross questioning and heating of the air, in the end I succeeded in pacifying them. But they did not rise in my estimation. I remember always

considering that Sir Henry Wilson's description of what he called the 'Frocks' [politicians] must be exaggerated. Now I am surprised how true to life his descriptions are! It is impossible for soldiers and politicians ever to work satisfactorily together – they are, and always will be, poles apart. After the aerodrome defence, we discussed assistance to Russia. Here Anthony Eden surprised me. As a late S of S for War, he must know well what the army's situation is and yet the proposals and suggestions he put forward might have been based on gross ignorance of the weakness of our defence of this country. If this is the best democracy can do, it is high time we moved forward to some other form of government!"

On 17 July:

"Spent the morning watching a bomber squadron carrying out an exercise in close cooperation with the army… Good progress had been made but I was more convinced than ever that we cannot ever expect real close cooperation from bomber squadrons suddenly swinging from an independent role to that of close cooperation with the army".

19 July saw Brookie at Chequers again:

"The First Sea Lord [Dudley Pound] was also there, but not much more awake than usual."

One feature of Brookie's diary is that he assiduously recorded the mileages which he travelled – he appeared to take pride in these. On 22 July, he departed on one week's leave:

"Have now been C-in-C Home Forces for 1 year and 2 days. Have flown just under 14,000 miles during that period and motored some 35,000 miles in my own car. As I have certainly done at least as much in other people's cars when touring round, my total road mileage must be somewhere near 70,000 miles in the year."

On 29 July, he returned to work:

"Motored back to London with a distinct 'going back to school' *feeling. Rather a sinking at heart at the thought of shouldering again the burden of responsibility and all the worries and doubts which endeavour to swamp one's mind and are not always easy to keep down. Those horrible question marks which seem to be everywhere at times! Have I really taken the proper dispositions for the defence of this country? Am I sufficiently insured in the South East? Can I reinforce this corner without taking undue risks in the North? Am I under-appreciating the air threat? Ought I to further denude the beaches to cover the aerodromes? If I do, am I opening the door to sea invasion? Will the air support be as efficient as the Air Ministry would like us to believe? How long will the Navy take to concentrate its forces in home waters? Shall we be able to hold the thrust of Armoured Divisions in Kent during this period? These are all questions where a wrong answer may mean the end of life as we have known it in this country and the end of the British Empire! During the last two years I have frequently felt that my mind was unable to fully realize the volume and magnitude of events I was living through. It is a wonderful provision of nature, otherwise I do not know how one could shoulder heavy responsibility without cracking [before] long."*

On 20 August, he watched:

"*Polish forces carrying out attack with their new tanks. I thought they were very good and promise well for the future.*"

On 28 August, Brookie's language was poor, but the gist was clear:

"*Interview with Walter Elliot, the Director of Public Relations at the WO, whose work is useless. As the only suggestion was that he should remove himself, it was hard to put this to him!*"

8 September saw another dry comment:

"*Arrived in the office after studying briefs for COS [chiefs of staff] meeting in the car to find that another important item had been added. This concerned a mad scheme put up by Joint Planning Committee for a feint attack on Cherbourg Salient [northern France] to relieve* pressure on the Russians. COS meeting lasted from 10.30 to 12.30. It reminds me of the tea party in Alice in Wonderland, with Dill as Alice, Portal as the Hatter and Dudley Pound as the Dormouse. I feel inclined to shout 'put the dormouse in the teapot' to wake him up."

Two days later, Brookie watched another army exercise. This appears to have been so poor, he was moved to take immediate action:

"Spent day with Anderson going round seeing troops. Quite one of the worst divisional advances that I have seen in the last year! Settled on the spot with Anderson that Peters, the Div Commander, must be removed."

On 16 September:

"My visit to Chequers of last Friday is bearing fruit. I had rubbed in the fact that the new 'manpower ceiling' which [Churchill] had imposed was resulting in a reduction of 77 of my infantry battalions, namely a reduction of a ¼ of the infantry force of this country and that the personnel thus provided were to be used for [air defence, coastal defence, ordnance]. He has now taken this matter up with the object of preventing the reduction of these battalions. Nothing but good can come of this, we must stop putting such large proportion of our manpower into purely passive static organization. And again the 'tails' of our formations [those performing administrative and support roles behind front line troops] are far too large. Left 8.30am for the far side of Newmarket to watch exercise by 6th Armoured Div. Most refreshing to see the progress they have made and the state of efficiency that has been reached."

On 19 September, he visited Czech troops based in Britain:

"Found them a most efficient though somewhat dirty force. I am certain that they would give a very good account of themselves if required [two weeks earlier, he described 70 Welsh Young Soldiers Battalion as "dirty, but not a bad lot of boys": for 'dirty', perhaps read violent thugs]."

Later that month, Brookie spent three days at the Combined Operations Training Centre in Scotland:

"Impression that training is far too stereotyped to fit in with varying conditions of possible operations."

"Distinct progress but much more work required. Still thinking much too small in all our plans... went out to watch commandos approach beach in open boats under cover of dark. Much too noisy and voices easily heard."

"I took off at 2.30pm for London. Arrived at 5pm. Went to office where I found Dill wanted to see me at 6.30pm and Margesson at 7pm... Just got back and have been sitting up till close to 1am dealing with last few days' correspondence. Am feeling very weary and sleepy!"

In his Notes, "The whole of my visit to Roger Keyes [Director, Combined Operations] was on his part to try and convince me that our commando policy was right. He failed... and I remained convinced till the end of the war that the commandos should never have been divorced from the army in the way they were. Each division should have been responsible for maintaining a divisional battle patrol capable of any commando work".

Late September saw the start of Operation Bumper, a large, five-day, anti-invasion training exercise organised by Brookie which was designed to test British armoured and mobile units. On 1 October:

"Sad mishandling of armoured forces by Higher Commanders."

And on the following day:

"Another day of manoeuvres... They have been a great success. I am delighted with the way armoured divisions have come on but disappointed at the way Higher Commanders are handling them. They have all got a great deal to learn and the sooner they learn the better."

On 3 October:

"At midnight received special messenger from the War Office with orders to carry out examination for attack on Trondheim [Norway]

and preparation of plan of attack. The whole to be in by next Friday! Also, that I was to dine tonight at Chequers and spend night there to discuss plans.

At 6pm picked up Dill and drove down to Chequers... Dudley Pound, Portal and Attlee formed the party. We sat up till 2.15am discussing the [attack] and I did my best to put the PM off attempting the plan. Air support cannot be adequately supplied and we shall fall into the same pitfall as we did before [the disastrous Norwegian campaign in 1940]."

The Trondheim operation was Churchill's idea: it was prompted by his wish to relieve pressure on Russia which had suffered a series of major defeats since the German invasion in June. In his Notes, "Why [Churchill] wanted to go back [to Norway] and what he was going to do there, even if he did succeed in capturing Trondheim, we never found out... the plan for the capture of Norway had already been examined by the Chiefs of Staff Committee and had been turned down as impracticable owing to insufficient air support for the operation... I felt convinced that I should arrive at similar conclusions."

Five days later:

"Conference with Monty on last week's exercise [Bumper]. It is lamentable how poor we are as regards Army and Corps Commanders. We ought to remove several, but heaven knows where we shall find anything very much better."

In his Notes, "This shortage of real leaders was a constant source of anxiety to me during the war. I came to the conclusion that it was due to the cream of the manhood having been lost in the First World War. It was the real leaders in the shape of platoon, company and battalion commanders who were killed off. These were the men we were short of now. I found this shortage of leaders of quality applied to all three fighting services and, later, I was to observe that this same failing prevailed amongst politicians and diplomats."

On 9 October:

"You and Mr Ti came up to lunch today and turned what might have been a dull, dead day into a red letter day! Our final survey of the [Trondheim] operation convinced us more than ever of its impracticability. I have now been warned to attend Chequers next Sunday again! at 6pm. I have to start for Newcastle the same night."

On 10 October, Brookie held a conference to summarise the lessons learnt from Bumper:

"There were some 270 officers attending it. I began by turning to Monty to act as historian and then I followed on with criticisms. A great relief to have it over. The last fortnight has been a hard one with the large exercise and the PM's task on top of it to examine the Trondheim operation."

On 11 October:

"Had a troublesome morning going through the final appreciation of Trondheim for the PM. I don't like its final shape and would have liked to recast the whole thing. But my conclusion would still remain the same – that the operation is impracticable."

His premonition about its 'final shape' was to prove accurate. On 12 October:

"After having made all arrangements to go to Chequers and for special train to collect me at Wendover station at 1.45am, I suddenly received message during afternoon that PM wanted us at 10 Downing St. instead! Went there at 6.30pm... PM very dissatisfied with our appreciation... [and tried] to make out that I had unnecessarily increased the difficulties! However, I was quite satisfied that there was only one conclusion to arrive at."

Brookie elaborated in his Notes. His reference to Churchill's 'colleagues' is worth highlighting since he would later describe them as "Yes men", "I saw at once from [Churchill's] face that we were in for the hell of a storm! He had with him what he used to classify as some of his 'colleagues', usually Anthony Eden, Attlee, Leathers on this occasion, and possibly a few others. On my side of the table I had the various Naval and Air C-in-Cs who had collaborated with me [and] Paget who was nominated as commander of this expedition. When we were all assembled, he shoved his chin out in his aggressive way and staring hard at me, said: 'I had instructed you to prepare a detailed plan for the capture of Trondheim, with a commander appointed and ready in every detail. What have you done? You have instead submitted a masterly treatise on all the difficulties and on all the reasons why this operation should not be carried out.' He then proceeded to cross-question me for nearly two hours on most of the minor points of the appreciation. I repeatedly tried to bring him back to the main reason – the lack of air support. He avoided this issue and selected arguments such as… 'You state that it will take you some 24 hours to cover the ground between A and B. How can you account for so long being taken, explain to me exactly how every one of those 24 hours will be occupied'!… This led to a series of more questions, interspersed with sarcasm and criticism. A very unpleasant grilling to stand up to in a full room".

Churchill eventually backed down but only after Dudley Pound, the First Sea Lord, refused to send the Home Fleet into Trondheim Fiord, a step deemed necessary to compensate for the lack of air cover. Churchill is reported to have remarked in this meeting, "I sometimes think some of my generals don't want to fight the Germans."[2] John Kennedy, the Director of Military Operations in the War Office, recalled Churchill subsequently instructing the chiefs of staff to "study how the difficulties raised by Brooke could be overcome" and telling Dill that "Brooke should not again be admitted to our counsels."[3]

Dill's relationship with Churchill had been strained since his appointment as CIGS in late May 1940: Churchill referred to him as 'Dilly-dally'. According to John Kennedy, a furious Dill returned from one late-night meeting with Churchill and told him, "What he said about the Army tonight I can never forgive. He complained he could get nothing done by the Army. Then he said he wished he had Papagos [Commander-in-Chief, Greek Army] to run it".[4] By autumn 1941, Churchill was clearly looking to replace Dill and he may have been testing Brookie as a possible successor when he instructed him to examine the Trondheim operation.

By 20 October, the rumour mill was in full flow:
> "Pownall asked to see me and informed me that Beaverbrook was scheming for Tim Pile to be next CIGS after Dill!! There is no knowing what schemes are going on behind our backs!"

In his Notes, "I also began to hear rumours that Beaverbrook was undermining Dill's position with Churchill. It did not take a great deal to do this, as Winston had never been fond of Dill… It would have been impossible for [Churchill and Dill] to hit it off together. They were poles apart in all their outlooks on life… Dill was the essence of straightforwardness, blessed with the highest of principles and an unassailable integrity of character. I do not believe that any of these characteristics appealed to Winston, on the contrary I think he disliked them as they accentuated his own shortcomings in this respect… I know for certain that [Dill] could not abide the easy code of morals of some politicians and Winston's methods were frequently repulsive to him… Beaverbrook filled [Dill] with horror and he found it hard to hide these feelings."

On 21 October, Brookie watched:
> "A demonstration of fighter attacks on lorries, infantry and guns. Most impressive! There is no doubt that the single-seater fighter is destined to play a serious part in ground attacks. Left to their own devices, they could destroy long columns even spaced out at 150 yards between vehicles. I must take steps to provide for their protection in future. The cannon aircraft may later on when equipped with a heavier gun become a formidable weapon against tanks."

On 23 October:
> "Most of the morning was spent sorting out and adjusting senior officers to cover the various changes we must make. There are at least

3 Corps Commanders that must be changed, and possibly 4!... The dearth of suitable higher commanders is lamentable."

On 5 November:

"PM in good form but refusing to realize that there are different types of tanks or, rather, that tactics call for certain types for distinct jobs. Beaverbrook attended meeting and was all smiles, after having written most abusive memo in reply to [Dill's] memorandum. Wonderful bit of acting between Beaverbrook and his production representative by which they ran up the output of tanks for next 3 months from 2,400 to 3,000!!"

On 6 November:

"We have got Copper out of Western Command and Osborne, Massy and Pakenham-Walsh from their Corps [see 23 October]. This is a pretty drastic clearing which ought to make place for the younger material."

On 13 November:

"Anderson and Irwin to interview before they took over their new Corps... spent 1½ hours with Dill discussing various points such as the new quota of aeroplanes which the Air Ministry is now offering us in reply to our claims. It is better but still falls far short. Also discussed with him the various rumours as to successor for him."

In his Notes, "Dill made it clear to me that as far as he was concerned, if he had to go, the one person he wanted to hand over to was me."

On 16 November, Brookie was invited to Chequers. Note his 'greatest respect' and 'real affection' for Churchill, despite their recent clash over Trondheim:

"PM took me off to his study and told me that as Dill had had a very hard time and was a tired man he wanted to relieve him... He then went on to say that he wanted me to take over from Dill and asked me whether I was prepared to do so. It took me some time to reply as I was torn by many feelings. I hated the thought of old Dill going and our very close association coming to an end. I hated the thought of what this would mean for him. The thought of the magnitude of the job and the work entailed took the wind out of my sails. The fact that the extra work and ties would necessarily mean seeing far less of you tore at my heart strings. And, finally, a feeling of sadness at having to give up Home Forces after having worked them up to their present pitch.

The PM misunderstood my silence and said 'Do you not think you will be able to work with me? We have so far got on well together.' I had to assure him that those were not my thoughts, though I am well aware that my path will not be strewn with rose petals! But I have the greatest respect for him and real affection for him, so that I hope I may be able to stand the storms of abuse which I may well have to bear frequently. He then went on to explain the importance he attached to the appointment and the fact that the Chiefs of Staff Committee must be the body to direct military events over the whole world. He also stated that his relations with me must for now approximate [to] those of a Prime Minister to one of his ministers. Nothing could have been kinder than he was and finally when we went to bed at 2am he came with me to my bedroom to get away from the others, took my hand and looking into my eyes with an exceptionally kind look said 'I wish you the very best of luck'.

I got into my bed with my brain in a whirl trying to fathom the magnitude of the task I am about to take on. I have no false conception as to the magnitude of the task and of the doubts whether I shall be able to compete with it. If it was in peace time I should love to try it, but in war the responsibility is almost overwhelming. The consequences of failures or mistakes are a nightmare to think about. I pray God from the very bottom of my heart that He may give me guidance and be at my side in the times I may have to go through. And then I have you, oh my darling, as my lighthouse in all stormy seas. Bless you for the help which you are to me."

Brookie elaborated in his Notes: "[There] was the certain trial of working hand in hand with Winston in handling the direction of the war. I had seen enough of him to realize his impetuous nature, his gambler's spirit and his determination to follow his own selected path at all costs, to realize fully what I was faced with. I can remember clearly that after he had taken me away to his study and had offered me this appointment, he left me alone temporarily to rejoin the others. I am not an exceptionally religious person, but I am not ashamed to confess that as soon as he was out of the room my first impulse was to kneel down and pray".

Churchill's statement that their relations approximated to those of a prime minister and a minister carried the clear message that Churchill could sack Brookie at any time in the same way he could sack a minister. This suggests Churchill had reservations about appointing Brookie and there is evidence that he was not Churchill's first choice to succeed Dill. John Kennedy reported Dill as saying that Churchill almost appointed Archibald Nye [Director of Staff Duties at the War Office]. In his biography of Brookie, Fraser claimed that Nye was Churchill's first choice: however, according to Fraser, when Churchill spoke to Nye on the subject, the latter stated that Brookie was the "only one conceivable choice" which elicited this reply from Churchill, "When I thump the table and push my face towards him what does he do? Thumps the table harder and glares back at me. I know these Brookes – stiff-necked Ulstermen and there's no one worse to deal with than that."[5] The fact that Churchill promoted Nye to Vice Chief of the Imperial General Staff, a move clearly designed to enable Nye to succeed Brookie if he failed or was removed, tends to confirm Fraser's claim.

There is also evidence that Brookie was not universally regarded as Dill's obvious successor. According to Kennedy, "Both Paget and Nye were strongly backed for the job. Much as I admired and liked them both, I was thankful that Brooke had been chosen. One Minister who had been closely involved in the discussions told me… that they felt they 'had to appoint Brooke but very much to their regret and it was hoped it would only be for a year at the outside'. Margesson [Secretary of State for War], no doubt influenced by Dill, had backed Brooke strongly": Kennedy then added that Dill "was glad" that Brookie had been appointed, "I said I was glad too but that I thought the politicians did not, perhaps, realize what they had taken on for Brooke was tough and impatient".[6] Interestingly, Dill appears to have changed his mind since Kennedy reported him saying three months earlier that he regarded Brookie as "too narrow"[7] for the position of CIGS.

Following Brookie's acceptance of his offer, Churchill wrote a letter to him,

My dear Brooke,

Thank you for your letter. I did not expect that you would be grateful or overjoyed at the hard, anxious task to which I summoned you. But I feel that my old friendship for Ronnie and Victor [two of Brookie's elder brothers], the companions of gay subaltern days and early wars, is a personal bond between us to which will soon be added the comradeship of action in fateful events.[8]

On 17 November:

"Had to go to War Office to see Margesson. He was very nice, full of congratulations and full of help. We had long discussion as to how to smooth over the blow for Macready [Assistant CIGS], who is to be passed over by Archie Nye, the latter having been shot up to VCIGS by the PM over Macready's head. This will make matters more difficult."

18 November provided more evidence that Nye was Churchill's first choice:

"Saw Dill this morning who was quite wonderful and is taking the blow just as one would expect. It is a frightful tragedy. He tells me the other two members of the Chiefs of Staff Committee [Pound and Portal] went to see Winston about it to try and get him to reverse his decision. He also told me that the PM first of all wanted to put Archie Nye in to relieve Dill!! Dill had a job to rid him off this idea."

This entry suggests Pound and Portal may also have had reservations about Brookie's appointment: in his biography of Brookie, Fraser claimed that Portal believed he might be "too abrupt."[9]

On 19 November:
> "Today the papers published Dill's departure and my appointment as CIGS... I suppose I ought to be very grateful and happy at reaching the top of the ladder. I can't say that I do. I feel a heavy depression at Dill going after the close contacts I have had with him ever since the war started. I had never hoped or aspired at reaching these dizzy heights and now that I am stepping up onto the plateau land of my military career the landscape looks cold, black and lonely with a ghastly responsibility hanging as a black thunder cloud over me. Perhaps I am feeling liverish for want of exercise today!"

On the next day:
> "Archie Nye came to see me to explain to me that he had not been pulling any strings to obtain the post of VCIGS – I believe he is entirely honest."

Brookie's new appointment meant relinquishing his command of Home Forces. When he said farewell to his colleague General Paget at Home Forces HQ, Brookie is reported to have had "tears in his eyes" and "rushed from the room unable to finish his farewell". As for Dill, he is reported to have said, "I want you to understand that never under any circumstances will I serve under that man Churchill again."[10]

SIX

CIGS: December 1941–February 1942

Officially, Brookie's tenure as CIGS commenced on 25 December 1941. In fact, it started on 1 December 1941. According to John Kennedy, Director of Military Operations at the War Office, "It was a delight to work with him. He was quick and decided; his freshness made a new impact; he infected the War Office and the Chiefs of Staff with his own vitality; the change of tempo was immediate and immense."[1]

As CIGS, Brookie became a member of the Chiefs of Staff Committee. This committee had been formed after the First World War, its role being to advise the prime minister, the cabinet and the minister of defence on all military and strategic matters: to this end, its members attended cabinet and defence committee meetings. In addition, the committee coordinated all the plans and operations of the three armed services. Brookie later described its functions in these terms, "The whole world has now become one large theatre of war, and the Chiefs of Staff represent the Supreme Commanders, running the war in all its many theatres, regulating the allocation of forces, shipping, munitions, relating plans to resources available, approving or rejecting plans, issuing directives to the various theatres. And, most difficult of all, handling the political aspect of this military action and coordinating with our American allies." In effect, the committee was the body through which the British Government conducted the War. It was supported by a Vice Chiefs of Staff Committee and, additionally, a Joint Planning Staff and a Joint Intelligence Staff, members of which were drawn from across all three services.

In December 1941, the members of this committee were Dudley Pound, First Sea Lord, Charles Portal, Chief of the Air Staff, and Brookie, with Pound acting as chairman: they were the professional heads of, respectively, the navy, air force and army. There was a fourth non-voting member, General Hastings 'Pug' Ismay, who was Military Secretary to the War Cabinet and chief staff officer to Churchill in his capacity of minister of defence. In practice, Ismay acted as a bridge between Churchill and the chiefs of staff, his role being that of a conciliator who lubricated their difficult, often grating, relationship. With just four members, the committee was streamlined, effective and, in the main, efficient: it bears close similarity to the small boards of directors that can be found in some large companies in the twenty-first century. It met every day, sometimes more than once.

In early 1939, British and French military staffs had agreed that in the event of war with Germany a defensive strategy of containment would initially be pursued. This strategy reflected their lack of preparedness for war and was designed to give both countries time to mobilise and build up their armed forces: John Kennedy made the point that it takes about three years to build up, train and equip effective armed forces. The lack of preparedness for war explains why Brookie was concerned on 28 January 1940 about 'the danger of losing [the War] this year!' After the fall of France, Britain had pursued a strategy of blockade, bombing of Germany and the encouragement of subversive activities on the continent, the objective being to weaken Germany to the extent that it might be possible to invade the continent – Fortress Europe, as it was called – by 1942. This modest strategy reflected Britain's isolated and relatively weak position.

Britain had, therefore, started the War on the back foot and following its reverses in Norway, France, Greece and the Middle East, it was still on the back foot by the end of 1941. When describing events in mid-1941, Kennedy stated, "At this time, criticism of Churchill was bitter and general... The gist of the criticisms was that we were living from hand to mouth on a diet of improvisation and opportunism; that no clear-cut military appreciations were being laid before the War Cabinet for their discussion and approval or rejection; that from their very inception, military opinions were being distorted and coloured by the formidable advocacy of the Prime Minister, in fact that he was not only advocate but witness, prosecutor and judge. He was also criticized for sending personal directives to the Commanders-in-Chief without professional advice, and for exhausting the Chiefs of Staff to the point of danger"[2]: in a diplomatic tour de force, Kennedy then added "we sometimes longed for a leader with more balance and less brilliance."[3]

Brookie was clearly of the same view. In his Notes, "I remember well being appalled in those early days of my time as CIGS to find the lack of a definite policy for the prosecution of the war. We worked from day to day, a hand to mouth existence with a policy based on opportunism. Every wind that blew swung us like a weathercock. As I was to find out, planned strategy was not Winston's strong card. He preferred to work by intuition and impulse."

In December 1941, British and Commonwealth forces were actively engaged in north and east Africa, the Mediterranean, the Middle East, the Atlantic fighting German U-boats and in bombing Germany. In addition, Britain had to commit and maintain forces in the Far East against the threat posed by Japan whilst also retaining forces in Britain to defend itself from invasion, in the event of Russia's collapse. There was a widely held view that Russia's ability to resist the German invasion would last little more than four to six months, a view clearly held by Brookie according to his Notes, 22 June. Despite the assistance given to Russia in the form of large amounts of equipment supplied via the Arctic convoys, the German Army had reached the outskirts of Moscow by early December 1941. However, the combination of severe wintry conditions and strong resistance from fresh Russian forces brought in to defend Moscow resulted in the exhausted German forces being checked and then subjected to a series of counter-attacks.

Seven days after Brookie's appointment, Japan attacked the American fleet at Pearl Harbor and then invaded Hong Kong, Malaya and the Philippines: as a result, the War became a global conflict. In his Notes, "Dark clouds had been gathering fast and everything pointed towards an early entry of Japan into the war. On the other hand, it was essential that we should take no step that might precipitate hostile actions with Japan without the entry of the USA into the war... [Dill] had told me frankly that he had done practically nothing to meet this threat. He said that we were already so weak on all fronts that it was impossible to denude them any further to meet a possible threat. I think he was quite right... It was undoubtedly correct not to create general weakness on all fronts in an attempt to meet all possible threats, but it left us in a lamentably dangerous position on the entry of Japan into the war."

1 December 1941 was a good example of the new CIGS's working day:

"Arrived [War Office] at 9.15, read telegrams and was briefed by DMO [Director of Military Operations] and DMI [Director of Military Intelligence] for Chiefs of Staff meeting. 10.30 Chiefs of Staff [COS] meeting till 12.15 when we were sent for by PM to 10 Downing Street. There, we discussed advisability of moving into Thailand Peninsular prior to any move by Japan. Decision being to wait until we are certain that USA comes in... Finished meeting 1.30pm. Afternoon prepared my briefs for 6pm Cabinet meeting when I had to give résumé of the week's fighting in Libya, Abyssinia and Russia. Meeting lasted till 7.30pm. At 9.30pm another COS meeting to complete what we had not done this morning. This lasted till 12.30am. Dudley Pound the slowest chairman I have ever seen."

On 2 December:

"Chiefs of Staff meeting from 10.30 to 1.30 at which we discussed possibility of raid on Italian coast. Gave up project owing to threatening situation in Far East. At 5pm another COS meeting which was attended by Anthony Eden [Foreign Secretary] to discuss... offers he could make to Stalin as regards troops for Southern Russia. Owing to Libyan offensive having gone as badly as it has, there will not be much available for Russia [Auchinleck launched a major offensive in mid-November which resulted in the loss of large numbers of British tanks: his offensive did, however, lead to the relief of Tobruk which had been under siege since April]. We then examined latest telegram *from... Halifax [British ambassador to the USA] of conversations with Roosevelt [American president]. It was the most encouraging one received yet as to cooperation of USA with us in the event of war with Japan. Situation in the Far East looking far worse, submarines reported moving south from Saigon this evening."*

Brookie's 3 December entry is significant since it addressed future military strategy. Japan and America had not yet entered the War by 3 December so his strategic eye was therefore focused on Europe, Russia, the Atlantic, the Mediterranean and the Middle East:

"COS [chiefs of staff] meeting at 10.30 where Pug Ismay produced memo from PM to the effect that 18th and 50th Divs were to be offered to the Russians for their Southern front! Eden to make this offer to Stalin during his impending visit to Moscow! This would probably mean having to close down the Libyan offensive whereas I am positive that our policy for the conduct of the war should be to direct both our military and political efforts towards the early conquest of North Africa. From there we shall be able to reopen the Mediterranean and to stage offensive operations against Italy.

Back to [War Office] to prepare brief for Cabinet Defence Committee at 5.30. Here we discussed means of ensuring that the USA comes into Far East war in event of Japanese aggression. Also question of whether Eden was to offer 50th and 18th Divs to Stalin. Luckily, we succeeded in riding PM off such a suggestion but only at expense of some 500 tanks to be sent to Russia, this according to Beaverbrook's suggestion... Tried to begin to make them realize that we must have one definite policy for the conduct of the war. I must get the PM to see the advantages of a real North African offensive policy."

For Brookie, the key issue was lack of shipping. In his Notes, "It is interesting to note that already on December 3rd, my third day as CIGS, I had a clear-cut idea as to what our policy should be. America was not even in the war at that time and it was not possible to foresee our combined landings in Algeria and Morocco. Nevertheless, it was already clear to me that we must clear North Africa to open the Mediterranean [as a sea route] and until we had done that we should never have enough shipping to stage major operations. It is some gratification to look back now knowing that this policy was carried out but only after many struggles and much opposition from many quarters.

[The proposal to send 50th and 18th Divisions to Russia] was a wild one as... there were no troops that could be spared... [and] their employment on that front would have entailed countless administrative problems which had not even been looked into."

4 December saw a good example of the 'spellbound and exasperated' Brookie matching his criticism of Churchill with a compliment:

"I attended War Cabinet at which Anthony Eden's visit to Moscow was again discussed. I had to state results of my investigation as to whether any tanks could be spared for Eden to offer to Stalin. I said best we could do was 300 Churchill tanks by 30th June and that although this offer might be acceptable to Russia, I did not recommend such a gift as we should be seriously denuding this country and prematurely disclosing a new pattern of tank. Painted a picture of possible tank battles in this country such as were taking place in Libya. These gave Kingsley Wood [Chancellor of the Exchequer] the shivers and he appealed to PM not to contemplate denuding this country. Debate became interminable. Anthony Eden like a peevish child grumbling because he was being sent off to see Uncle Stalin without suitable gifts, while Granny Churchill was comforting him and explaining to him all the pretty speeches he might make instead. Finally, Eden succeeded in swinging Churchill round to a gift of some 300 tanks and 300 aircraft. During most of the debate the conduct of the war seemed to have been pushed into the background, self interests seemed to predominate.

COS met at 10pm with the Prime Minister presiding and Attlee and Eden present. During the dinner interval the PM had swung right round again, tanks and aircraft had been put aside, the gift was now to consist of 10 squadrons of aircraft to be made available immediately after the Libyan offensive was finished. Portal agreed, but said offer was too definite. This produced the most awful outburst of temper, we were told that we did nothing but obstruct his intentions, we had no ideas of our own and whenever he produced ideas we produced nothing but objections, etc! Attlee pacified him once, but he broke out again, then Anthony Eden soothed him temporarily but to no avail. Finally, he looked at his papers for some 5 minutes, then slammed them together, closed the meeting and walked out of the room. It was pathetic and entirely unnecessary. We were only trying to save him from making definite promises which he might find hard to keep later on. It is all the result of overworking himself and keeping too late hours. Such a pity. God knows where we would be without him, but God knows where we shall go with him!"

Churchill's style of leadership was confrontational in that he challenged the advice and recommendations of his advisers by robust questioning and cross examination but if he then concluded that their views were sound, he adopted them. Consequently, he often advocated or agreed to a proposal which, initially, he appeared to have opposed. Brookie experienced this on 5 December. Note his perceptive reading of the Japanese:

"*COS meeting at 10.30am where we were greeted by a memorandum from the PM couched practically in identical terms with those we had asked him to accept last night! Also 'Anklet' alterations [commando raid in Norway] which last night raised so much ire were now accepted... After lunch had to see all the military attachés. The Japanese seemed gloomy and I wonder whether we should have them with us much longer!*"

On 7 December, Japanese forces attacked the American base at Pearl Harbor:

"*[We discussed] all the various alternatives that might lead to war [with Japan] and trying to ensure that in every case the USA would not be left out... Then ½ hour with [Secretary of State for War] to put him into the picture and discuss with him advisability of letting Cunningham down as easily as possible on his return from the Middle*

East [General Alan Cunningham had been relieved of command of the British Eighth Army in Egypt], PM being inclined to hold up his dismissal as an example. After dinner listened to wireless to find that Japan has attacked America!! All our work of the last 48 hours wasted! The Japs themselves have now ensured that the USA are in the war."

On the following day:

"[Churchill] also put before the Cabinet his plan to start this week for America to see Roosevelt to ensure that American help to this country does not dry up… he has decided to take Dill which I am delighted at, as it will please Dill I am certain".

Earlier, 2 May and 26 July 1940, Brookie had referred to the vulnerability of sea power to air power. Confirmation of this came on 10 December when he learnt of the sinking of the *Prince of Wales* and *Repulse* by the Japanese in the Far East:

"This on top of the tragedy of [Pearl Harbor] puts us in a very serious position for the prosecution of the war. It means that for Africa eastwards to America through the Indian Ocean and the Pacific, we have lost command of the sea. This affects reinforcements to Middle East, India, Burma, Far East, Australia and New Zealand!"

Throughout his time as CIGS, Brookie was at Churchill's beck and call, hence his frequent use of phrases such as 'sent for' when he was summonsed. 11 December was one of the few instances during the War when Brookie requested a meeting with Churchill, on this occasion to persuade him to appoint Dill as the permanent head of the British Military Mission based in Washington. Since close cooperation between British and American military chiefs was now essential, Brookie clearly felt that Dill, someone he admired, respected and trusted, was the best man to implant into Washington. In the event, this proved to be an astute move:

"In afternoon went to 10 Downing Street to see PM about sending Dill to USA as our representative there – that is to say for him to go with PM and then remain there. PM agreed."

In his Notes, "This agreement was not arrived at without a good deal of discussion. Winston's dislike for Dill was nearly upsetting my plan... I had to press for this appointment and point out to him that with Dill's intimate knowledge of the working of the Chief of Staff Committee and of our strategy, there could be no better man to serve our purposes in Washington at the head of our Mission. Thank heaven I succeeded in convincing Winston, as few men did more in furthering our cause to final victory than Dill. From the very start he built up a deep friendship with Marshall [chief of staff, United States Army] and proved to be an invaluable link between the British and American Chiefs of Staff... I look upon that half hour's discussion with Winston... as one of my most important accomplishments during the War or at any rate amongst those that bore most fruit."

His 11 December entry continued:
"I had to go to COS meeting under PM at 10pm. Meeting began badly and Portal nearly started another brainstorm on the subject of denuding Middle East for the Far East. With some difficulty, we calmed him down and finally I got him to agree [that]... 18th Div to go to Bombay as reinforcement for India and Archie Wavell [now Commander-in-Chief, India] to decide how best to reinforce Burma and how to operate offensively against Jap [lines of communication] through Kra Isthmus. This still leaves possibility of diverting 18th Div up Persian Gulf to Iraq for defence of oil [Iraq was a vital source of oil for Britain] should Germans look like attacking through Turkey. Finished meeting at 12.30am."

On the following day:
"Alan Cunningham, just back from Libya [see 7 December], came to see me, very depressed and hard to comfort."

On 13 December:
"PM and party left last night [for Washington]... At 10.30 started my first Chiefs of Staff meeting as Chairman. Finished at

12 noon instead of 1.30 as we should have done with old Dudley Pound!"

On 14 December, John Kennedy wrote a paper setting out the likely repercussions of Japan's entry into the War. He forecast the fall of Hong Kong within a few weeks and the "strong possibility"[4] of Singapore also falling quite quickly due to deficiencies in its defences. He then highlighted the importance of Rangoon in Burma since this offered the only supply route into China, which was already at war with Japan, and suggested that Rangoon might be more important than Singapore. Brookie's reply was characteristically forthright, "I agree with your paper in so far as it goes. But it does not solve the main problem: (a) Must we skimp the Middle East to save the Far East or (b) Skimp the Far East to ensure success in the Middle East?"[5]

15 December saw some accurate predictions:
"*Far East situation far from rosy! I doubt whether Hong Kong will hold out a fortnight and Malaya a month!*"

On the following day:
"*Far East news no better. Lunched with de Gaulle, a most unattractive specimen. We made a horrid mistake when we decided to make use of him*".

On 17 December:
"*Long COS meeting to discuss reinforcements to Burma and Malaya. A very difficult problem trying to patch holes out there without interfering with Middle East offensive [Auchinleck's offensive was still in progress]. Personally, I do not feel that there is much hope of saving Singapore but feel that we ought to try and make certain of Burma.*"

The next day produced another dry comment:
"*Long COS meeting this morning to consider the desirability of*

seizing North Madagascar to stop Japs getting it. Full of complications... due to de Gaulle wishing to cooperate with the Madagascar operations. His support is more likely to be an encumbrance".

On 19 December, note his disparaging remark:

"A long COS meeting in the morning where we prepared a memorandum on our policy for the Far East. Not an easy document... At 9.30pm Defence Committee meeting with Attlee in the chair to discuss the paper we had prepared this morning. Attlee ran the meeting very well which was not easy as Sir Earle Page, the Australian representative, with the mentality of a greengrocer, wasted a lot of our time. In the end our paper was accepted."

On 20 December:

"Reports came in that Hong Kong Island was half occupied by the Japs but still holding on. Sent wire to the GOC [General Officer Commanding] with congratulations on their defence. The more I look at the situation at present the more I dislike it! My hopes of carrying on with the conquest and reclamation of North Africa are beginning to look more and more impossible every day. From now on the Far East will make ever increasing inroads into our resources. The loss of the American battleships [at Pearl Harbor] and the Prince of Wales and Repulse will take a long time to recover and, meanwhile, we shall suffer many more losses in the Far East."

Christmas Eve was:

"Another hard day. COS meeting in the morning. The situation beginning to become difficult. Winston has arrived in Washington, far from the war, and is pushing for operations by USA and ourselves against North Africa [Churchill was advocating operations in the French territories of Algeria and Morocco, codenamed Gymnast] and banking on further success of Middle East offensive towards Tripoli. On the other side, Duff Cooper in Singapore [British cabinet minister, resident in Singapore] by his demands is inspiring the Australians to *ask for more and more for the Far East. In the middle, Auchinleck struggling along with the forces at his disposal and sending optimistic personal and private messages to the PM, little knowing that his activities must shortly be curtailed owing to transfer of air and sea reinforcements from the Middle East to the Far East. At 3pm Defence Committee meeting to settle… 'scorched earth' policy in Malay peninsular. Had hoped to get home for Xmas but impossible now owing to urgent necessity for COS meeting tomorrow morning."*

At the Washington conference in December 1941, Britain and America agreed that the defeat of Germany should take priority to the defeat of Japan, the rationale being that Germany was the more powerful of the two and that once Germany had been defeated, it was only a matter of time before Japan's defeat would follow: this was called the 'Germany First' policy.

Christmas Day was:

"*My first official day as CIGS!… COS meeting to discuss [Joint Planning Committee's paper on relative importance of the new Far East commitments to the Middle East] and to prepare wire to PM with reference to his desire to carry out 'Gymnast' operation (i.e. reinforcements to French North Africa in event of being called in). Problem complicated by the fact that it does not look as if we are likely to be called in [by the French authorities] and, secondly, that PM is now toying with the idea of carrying out such a plan against resistance [i.e. resisted by French forces] and, finally, owing to the fact that shipping available does not admit of both occupying North Africa at request of French and reinforcing Far East sufficiently to secure Singapore, Burma, and Indian Ocean communications. We have laid down that first of all in importance come security of this country and its communications and after that Singapore and communications through Indian Ocean. This is correct as if the latter go, the Middle East or possibly India may follow… News received this evening that Hong Kong had fallen on Xmas Eve.*"

On 27 December:

> *"A long and wearying COS meeting with a series of difficult problems, mainly connected with the PM and his Chiefs of Staff committee in USA brewing up a series of discrepancies with what we are preparing here... I then escaped home in the hope of being allowed to spend a quiet Sunday and recuperate from the effort of the last 3 weeks!"*

28 December was *"a lovely, peaceful day with you [at home] which was wonderfully restful and fitted me up to stand another week of this strain!"*

The Washington conference also saw agreement on the creation of two new joint command structures. The first, ABDA, was based in South East Asia and was created to counter the Japanese advances in this theatre. The second was the Combined Chiefs of Staff [CCS]: this was, in effect, an amalgamation of the British and American chiefs of staff and its role was to organise, coordinate, direct and manage what was now a global war. Brookie was unimpressed. On 29 December:

> *"I found new wires had been received from the PM at 5am suggesting that [ABDA] should be formed in the Far East under Wavell! with USA deputy C-in-C and American naval forces under Wavell. Special body in Washington to control operations under PM and USA President [CCS]. The whole scheme wild and half-baked and only catering for one area of action, namely Western Pacific, one enemy Japan and no central control... Cabinet was forced to accept PM's new scheme owing to the fact that it was almost a fait accompli!"*

In his Notes, "The two points that worried me about this telegram were that in the first place we were setting up [ABDA] to deal with one specific theatre and one enemy, whilst what was really required was a global organization providing for central control for all fronts and both enemies. Secondly, I could see no reason why at this stage, with American forces totally unprepared to play a major part, we should agree to a central control in Washington... I still feel that in those early months the Combined Chiefs of Staff organisation should have been centred in

London… This would have given us a quicker and more efficient higher control at this period."

On 31 December, in Washington, Britain and America agreed the principles of their military strategy for 1942. Given the circumstances, they were understandably modest: one was "the continuous development of offensive action against Germany" to which was added "It does not seem likely that in 1942 any large-scale land offensive against Germany except on the Russian front will be possible."[6]

The start of a new year prompted Brookie to contemplate the future:

> "Started new year wondering what it may have in store for us. One thing I fully realize is that it has got about as much work in store for me as I can possibly cope with. I pray God that He may give me sufficient strength to devote the energy and drive that it will require. Difficult times with the PM I see clearly ahead of me and there again I pray God to help me by giving me guidance as to how to handle the difficult situations which are certain to confront me.
>
> Cabinet meeting… the time was mainly taken by Anthony Eden describing his recent visit to Moscow. His impressions of Stalin were very interesting and his accounts of the banquets most amusing. The dinner started at 10pm and lasted till 5am! Timoshenko arrived drunk and by continuous drinking, restored himself to sobriety by 5am. On the other hand, Voroshilov, after at least arriving sober, had to be carried out before the evening was through!"

2 January illustrated his energy and drive:

> "COS meeting – as usual I succeeded in finishing it by 12 noon and am beginning to get things moving! Wonder what I shall do when Dudley Pound gets back from the USA and takes the chair again? It will be awful putting up with the delays, I shall have to devise some way of overcoming them."

Four days later:

> "COS as usual which included a long interview with Tennant,

who was captain of the Repulse, sunk off Singapore with the Prince of Wales. He was most interesting in the whole of his account of the action, which apparently lasted under 1½ hours! Spotted at 6am by reconnaissance plane, first attack shortly after 11am and sunk before 1pm!"

On 8 January:
"Long talk with Nye on the organization of the Airborne Division and instructed it to be pushed to the utmost and given preferential treatment."

On the following day:
"COS meeting this morning where we had representatives from the Middle East to discuss with them the possibility of carrying out 'Acrobat' [an attack on Tripoli] in spite of delays that had occurred in capture of [eastern Libya] and new situation in Far East. In view of the fact that operation cannot be carried out for 6 weeks and that during this period reinforcements may well flow [to Rommel] from Italy, I am beginning to wonder whether the operation is on. At any rate I feel that it ought, if possible, to be connected with the operation for occupying [north-west] Africa [Gymnast, see 25 December 1941] on the invitation of the French. But, first secure your invitation!"

On 14 January:
"Heard from America that enterprise called 'Gymnast', to occupy [north-west] Africa, had been put off [the Americans had considerable reservations about Gymnast]."

By 20 January, Churchill and the British delegation had returned to London:
"The COS meetings are very trying again with old Dudley Pound in the chair. He is deadly slow and inefficient!... News from the Far East is bad and I am beginning to be very doubtful whether Singapore will hold out much longer."

In mid-January, Japanese forces invaded Burma. On 21 January:

"COS meeting till 1pm mainly taken up with discussing relative dangers of Singapore and Rangoon and arguing best destiny for further reinforcements."

21 January saw the start of an unexpected counter-offensive by Rommel in eastern Libya which resulted in British and Commonwealth forces being driven back towards the Egyptian border. On the same day, a clearly concerned Brookie wrote a letter to Auchinleck, "I am worried… that you have not got a first-class Armoured Force officer on your staff… There is a colossal amount of work for him in the re-equipping and reforming of your armoured divisions and army tank brigades and in the provision of general advice on armoured matters".

On 23 January:

"COS meeting in morning, mainly concerned with situation in Burma and Singapore. We have now got all the reinforcements on the move and the difficulty now rests in deciding whether these reinforcements should go to Singapore or Burma. Both are in a very dangerous position and each affects the other."

In his Notes, Brookie made a frank admission, "The problem was a difficult one, the retention of Singapore was certainly the most important for the future prosecution of the war and for the protection of our communications through the Indian Ocean. On the other hand, reinforcements for Singapore might well be too late, as turned out to be the case with the 18th Division, whilst reinforcements to Burma might still save the situation there and secure eastern approaches to India. Looking back on our decision to send 18th Division to Singapore, in the light of after events, I think we were wrong to send it to Singapore and that it would have served a more useful purpose had it been sent to Rangoon." One factor which influenced this decision was the pressure being exerted by the Australian Government: on 23 January, the Australian prime minister informed Churchill that an evacuation of Singapore would be viewed as an "inexcusable betrayal".[7]

On 27 January:

"*I was sent for on my way over to COS to see PM. Found him in bed with the red and golden dragon dressing gown on and a large cigar in his mouth*"

The 'spellbound' Brookie expanded in his Notes, "The scene in his bedroom was always the same and I only wish some artist could have committed it to canvas. The red and gold dressing gown in itself was worth going miles to see and only Winston could have thought of wearing it! He looked rather like some Chinese Mandarin! The few hairs were usually ruffled on his bald head. A large cigar stuck sideways out of his face. The bed was littered with papers and despatches."

On 28 January:

"*Dined with Lord Milne [former CIGS, see 16 February 1940] who was kindness itself. Full of advice, let me into many sidelights of political life… informed me as to desire of House to get Margesson [Secretary of State for War] out. Wonderful what a clear and active mind old Milne has maintained in his old age.*"

On the following day:

"*Have just finished dinner and been reading Auchinleck's long letters on his proposed system of reorganization. Some of the ideas are good but others I am not in agreement with.*"

On 30 January:

"*News bad on all sides. Benghazi has been lost again and Singapore is in a bad way. The defence is retiring onto the island tonight. I doubt whether the island holds out very long. The Benghazi business is bad and nothing less than bad generalship on the part of Auchinleck. He has been overconfident and has believed everything his over-optimistic Shearer has told him. As a result, he was not in a position to meet a counter blow. This morning Defence Committee on provision of tanks for Far East. Although it is quite evident that we are incurring grave danger by going on supplying tanks to Russia, it is Beaverbrook's firm intention that we should go on doing so and he controls PM on such matters. At this morning's meeting PM did not attend but left Attlee to take the chair, having decided beforehand that he would not stop sending tanks to Russia!!"*

In his Notes, "I had been questioning [Auchinleck] for some time as regards his intelligence reports which made out Rommel's strength as considerably lower than War Office estimates. I finally discovered that Shearer had been basing his estimate of the enemy strength on far too heavy German and Italian casualties… a considerably heavier proportion than those we had suffered. As we had been attacking the whole time and the enemy had been on the defensive, it was unlikely that their casualties were even as heavy as ours. The results of these underestimates lulled Auchinleck into a sense of false security… Auchinleck, to my mind, had most of the qualifications to make him one of the finest of commanders but, unfortunately, he lacked the one most important of all – the ability to select the men to serve him. The selection of Corbett as his Chief of Staff, Dorman-Smith as his chief advisor and Shearer as head of his intelligence service contributed most of all to his downfall."

Following the fall of Benghazi, Brookie wrote another letter to Auchinleck: he had a talent for managing and guiding his commanders in a direct yet supportive way, "First and foremost, I should like to offer my deep sympathy at the setback that your forces have suffered. I can so well imagine what a deep disappointment this must be to you. Looking at Rommel's counter-stroke from the detached point of view, I cannot help feeling that… over-optimistic intelligence played a large part in accounting for your troubles… It is not my own impression, but one that I have gathered from all quarters."

On 31 January:

"I have now finished two months' work as CIGS and it feels as if it had been ten years!!"

By 2 February, pressure was mounting on the professional head of the British Army:

> "5pm Cabinet meeting. As usual most unpleasant remarks by various ministers in connection with defeats of our forces! As we had retired into Singapore Island… besides being pushed back in Libya, I had a good deal to account for! and found it hard to keep my temper with some of the criticisms that were raised".

In his Notes, "These were very difficult times for me in the Cabinet and Winston was the worst offender. He came out continually with remarks such as: 'Have you not got a single general in that army who can win battles, have none of them any ideas, must we continually lose battles in this way?' Such remarks lowered the confidence of other ministers in the efficiency of the army and could be nothing but detrimental in the present crisis. He could have said anything he liked to me in private, but not in front of the whole cabinet. This… led to other ministers also making offensive remarks at the expense of the army. On one such occasion… I was being bombarded with unpleasant remarks when [Ernest] Bevin asked some question. I thought at the time that the remark was meant offensively and my blood was up. I therefore turned on him and gave him a short and somewhat rude reply. He said nothing more at the time but came up to me as we were going out and in a most charming manner explained that he had not been trying to get at me but was genuinely asking for information. A typical action on his part and nothing could have been nicer. I apologized for the rudeness of my reply".

Yet another wartime diary keeper was Sir Alexander Cadogan, the Permanent Under-Secretary at the Foreign Office. In late January 1942, he described the British Army as "no good" and "very incapable".[8] Cadogan's record of this cabinet meeting on 2 February was revealing, "After last week's debate [the growing disquiet over the Government's handling of the War had prompted Churchill to hold a confidence debate in the House of Commons which he won easily], PM hectors more brutally a more subservient Cabinet. He flew at Amery [Secretary of State for India and Burma]. Latter said, 'Is that the view of the Cabinet?' PM said 'Yes'. No one else said anything."[9]

On 3 February:

"COS meeting mainly concerned with shortage of shipping, and attended by Mountbatten [head of Combined Operations]. During most of the discussion the First Sea Lord [Dudley Pound] went sound to sleep and looked like an old parrot asleep on his perch. Lunch at Claridges… Sikorski [Commander-in-Chief, Polish Armed Forces in the West and prime minister of the Polish Government in exile] sat on my right and was in great form. The more I see him, the more I like him."

In his Notes, "From the very start I was very taken by Sikorski and our acquaintance developed into a real friendship… I had the greatest admiration for his ability."

On 4 February, the key issue of lack of shipping was being addressed:

"Long talk with Bob Haining on situation in the Middle East. The more I find out from various quarters, the more disturbed I am at the situation out there. I do not like the combination of Shearer and the Auk. It is not a good combination!

Then long talk on shipping with Archie Nye, DMO… The situation as regards shipping is most disturbing and one that the PM will not face, and yet it is the one situation which will affect our whole strategy during the coming year."

In the event, Allied shipping losses were to increase alarmingly in the first half of 1942. In his Notes, "Until we could open up the Mediterranean, we should remain one million tons short of shipping and shipping must exercise a stranglehold on all our strategy. Yet for the present, with the entry of Japan into the war and reverses in North Africa, the basic strategy at which I was aiming of clearing North Africa, opening Mediterranean, and threatening Southern Europe had shrunk into the background."

5 February saw another:

> "*Long letter to Auchinleck on the reorganization which he proposes to carry out and on the very indifferent handling of his armoured forces.*"

9 February provided an example of Brookie's good judgment. He was adept at reading situations and detecting ulterior motives:

> "*A long Chiefs of Staff meeting mainly concerned with the Directive for the [new] 'Combined Chiefs of Staff' [organisation]. Ever since Portal and Pound came back from the USA, I have told them that they 'sold the birthright for a plate of porridge' while in Washington. They have, up to now, denied it flatly. However, this morning they were at last beginning to realize that the Americans are rapidly snatching more and more power with the ultimate intention of running the war in Washington! However, I now have them on my side.*
>
> *An unpleasant Cabinet meeting. The news had just arrived that the Japs had got onto Singapore Island. As a result, nothing but abuse for the army. The Auk's retreat in [eastern Libya] is also making matters more sour!*"

Sir Alexander Cadogan was also present at this cabinet meeting. There was a streak of the armchair general in Cadogan, "Very gloomy. Japs have penetrated 5 miles into Singapore island. Our generals are no use, and do our men fight?... As PM says, what will happen if Germans get a footing [in Britain]? I tremble to think. Our army is the mockery of the world. Then about 130,000 tons of shipping sunk in a week! Poor Winston v[ery] desperate."[10]

Brookie's 9 February entry continued:

> "*Finally, this evening, at 10.45, I was sent for by PM to assist him in drafting a telegram to Wavell about the defence of Singapore and the need for Staffs and Commanders to perish at their post.*"

'Perish at their post' was an accurate description. Note Churchill's masterful use of language in the final sentence of his telegram to Wavell, "I think you ought to realise the way we view the situation in Singapore. It was reported to the Cabinet by the CIGS that Percival [British commanding officer in Singapore] has over 100,000 men, of whom 33,000 are British and 17,000 Australian. It is doubtful whether the Japanese have as many in the whole Malay peninsular... In these circumstances the defenders must greatly outnumber Japanese forces who have crossed the straits, and in a well-contested battle, they should destroy them. There must at this stage be no thought of saving the troops or sparing the population. The battle must be fought to the bitter end at all costs. The 18th Division has a chance to make its name in history. Commanders and senior officers should die with their troops. The honour of the British Empire and of the British Army is at stake. I rely on you to show no mercy to weakness in any form. With the Russians fighting as they are and the Americans so stubborn at Luzon [Philippines], the whole reputation of our country and our race is involved. It is expected that every unit will be brought into close contact with the enemy and fight it out. I feel sure these words express your own feeling, and only send them to you in order to share your burdens."[11]

On 10 February:

"I am getting more and more worried about the shipping situation and its effect on our strategy during the coming year. It may well be our undoing!!"

On the following day:

"The news of Singapore goes from bad to worse... PM sent for me this evening to discuss with him last wire from Wavell about Singapore from where he had just returned. It was a very gloomy wire and a depressing wire as regards the fighting efficiency of the troops on Singapore Island. It is hard to see why a better defence is not being put up but I presume there must be some good reason. I can't see the place holding out more than a day or so now. The losses on the island will be vast, not only in men but in material.

I have during the last 10 years had an unpleasant feeling that the British Empire was decaying and that we were on a slippery decline!! I wonder if I was right? I certainly never expected that we should fall to pieces as fast as we are and to see Hong Kong and Singapore go in less than 3 months plus failure in the Western Desert is far from reassuring! We have had a wonderful power of recuperation in the past. I wonder whether we shall again bring off a comeback?"

12 February saw an interesting observation:

"*We are bound to lose [Singapore] before long and I am getting very nervous about [Burma]! We are paying very heavily now for failing to face the insurance premiums essential for security of an Empire! This has usually been the main cause for the loss of Empires in the past."*

On 13 February:

"*News of Singapore getting worse and that of Burma beginning to deteriorate! Added to that the Gneisenau, Scharnhorst and Prinz Eugen [German warships] succeeded in running the gauntlet of the Channel yesterday without being destroyed, whilst we lost some 40 aircraft to the 20 enemy planes brought down! These are black days! Even Russia is no longer doing as well as it was."*

For Sir Alexander Cadogan, 12 February was the "blackest day yet of the war. Singapore evidently only a drawn-out agony. Burma threatened... *Scharnhorst, Gneisenau* and *Prinz Eugen* cockily steamed out of Brest this morning and up the Channel in broad daylight... We are nothing but failure and inefficiency everywhere and the Japs are murdering our men and raping our women in Hong Kong... I am running out of whisky and can get no more drink of any kind. But if things go on as they're going, that won't matter."[12]

By 14 February, Churchill had relented from his earlier 'perish at your post' diktat:

"PM called me up from Chequers to prepare a wire for Wavell stating that 'he alone could judge when further resistance would be useless'".

On 15 February, Singapore surrendered. On the next day:
"Busy afternoon studying repercussions of fall of Singapore on flow of reinforcements. 5pm Cabinet meeting from which I escaped at 7pm. Considering that we have lost Singapore, endangered Rangoon, allowed Gneisenau and Scharnhorst to sail up the Channel and lost 3 transports trying to reinforce Malta I was expecting that the Services would meet with some sarcastic remarks! However, we got off far lighter than I expected. 10pm... Defence Committee under PM... PM on the whole in a very good mood."

In his Notes, "This was typical of Winston, in a real crisis he was always at his best and stood all the heavy shocks without flinching."

The surrender of Singapore resulted in more criticism being levelled at Churchill, on this occasion that he exercised too much power in holding the offices of both prime minister and minister of defence. On 17 February, Brookie addressed this subject:
"½ hour with [Secretary of State for War] mainly to discuss political situation and demand for a Defence Minister separate from the PM. An absolute impossibility with a personality such as his... Am getting more and more worried by old Dudley Pound as First Sea Lord, with an old dodderer like him it is quite impossible for the COS to perform the function it should in the biggest Imperial war we are ever likely to be engaged in! He is asleep during 75% of the time he should be working."

In his Notes, "Frequently when the situation was bad there were suggestions that a separate Chairman for the COS should be found, or a deputy Defence Minister interposed between the PM and the COS. None of these alternatives was either possible or necessary. To my mind, the PM in war must always deal directly with the COS and the members of the COS must defend their actions personally in the Cabinet, using their Chairman as spokesman. The introduction of an outside Chairman will never smooth over differences between members of the COS, if these exist. Should there be such differences there is only one course, to change some or all of the members of the COS. It is essential that these three men should work together as a perfect trinity."

On 18 February:

"Burma news now bad. Cannot work out why troops are not fighting better. If the army cannot fight better than it is doing at present, we shall deserve to lose our Empire!"

On the following day, he returned to the same subject:

"Received reply back from Wavell saying that he was prepared to accept Alexander [General Harold Alexander] to replace Hutton as C-in-C Burma, the latter having proved unsatisfactory as a commander. After lunch, was sent for by PM who said he agreed to Alexander being sent out... Shall try leaving Hutton as CGS [chief of general staff], if this does not work shall have to carry out a change. Only hope Alexander arrives in time as situation in Burma is becoming very critical. Troops don't seem to be fighting well there either which is most depressing.

PM showed me his new Cabinet that he had reconstituted. A smaller one and much more efficient. Beaverbrook is out of it!! That is the greatest Godsend... With a small War Cabinet like that we ought to be able to get on much faster."

The fighting qualities of British troops was a subject which drew some interesting observations from John Kennedy, Director of Military Operations in the War Office, "We had cause on many previous occasions to be uneasy about the fighting qualities of our men. They had not fought as toughly as the Germans or the Russians and now they were being outclassed by the Japanese. There were two reasons for this. The first was that we had only begun to form our army in earnest after the war had broken out and it may be accepted that it takes about three years to organize and train troops and to produce modern equipment for them. The second reason was that we were undoubtedly softer as a nation than any of our enemies except the Italians. This may be accounted for by the fact that modern civilization on the democratic model does not produce a hardy race and our civilization in Great Britain was a little further removed from the stage of barbarity than were the civilizations of Germany, Russia and Japan."[13]

During this period, Kennedy drafted a letter for Brookie to send to all commanders-in-chief. This letter was never sent, presumably through fear a copy may find its way to the press, so its contents were communicated verbally. The following extracts clearly show that the key issues for Brookie were leadership and training:

> *In the German and Japanese armies, we have antagonists who have been trained in the hard school of war itself. The bulk of our army is still untried. The tempo of warfare has so increased that we can no longer season our troops by degrees on the field of battle. If they do not stand up to the first onset of the enemy, they will seldom be given a second chance. Therefore, special measures are needed in preparation for battle.*
>
> *First, there is the question of leadership – the most important of all. I wish all Commanders-in-Chief to devote particular attention to the selection of Commanders. Too many officers have been, and are being, promoted even to high command because they are proficient in staff work, because they are good trainers, because they have agreeable personalities or because they are clever talkers. I do not underrate the difficulties of selecting the best leaders without the test of active service. Mistakes are bound to be made. But let us make as few mistakes as possible. We must be more ruthless in the elimination of those who seem unlikely to prove themselves determined and inspiring leaders in the field. It is essential to select the best men to fill their places. You can rely on my full support.*

Secondly, the morale and the discipline of the Army must be vastly improved. There are strong hopes that the Government will now put a stop to the pernicious criticism of the Forces and the higher command which characterizes certain sections of our Press.

But there is much that we can do ourselves to raise morale and tighten discipline. It is, I fear, true to say that our troops have not always in this war fought as well as they could and should. The reason, in my opinion, has been directly due to a low standard of leadership and true fighting morale. I might define this kind of morale as well-founded pride in fighting efficiency... They must possess a high sense of duty, of comradeship and of discipline; and they must be taught to love the spice of danger and to know its various aspects.[14]

21 February was:

"*A bad day! COS meeting from 10.30am to 1.30pm, and again from 4pm to 7pm... all to do the work which could be done by one man in 1 hour!! And what's worse, when finished the work was not worth the paper it was written on! All connected with the use of Dutch shipping in Java... I know well from personal experience that whatever we may say, the man on the spot is in the end the only one who can judge.*"

His 22 February entry was in similar vein:

"*The night continued to be as damnable as the day! Barely was I asleep when the First Sea Lord called me up at 1.45 about the destiny of convoy with 7th Australian [Division] aboard. It is at present between Colombo [Sri Lanka] and Rangoon marking time pending approval from Australians to use it in Burma. An approval which we are unlikely to obtain in spite of appeals from PM and President of the USA – as a result we shall probably lose Burma!*"

In his Notes, "This division was on its way back from Middle East to Australia when the Burma situation deteriorated rapidly. We had therefore applied to Australian Government for authority to employ this division in Burma as it was the nearest reinforcement available. Meanwhile, in order to save time, we had diverted this convoy from Ceylon towards Rangoon. The Australians were obdurate and insisted on the early return of the division. It must be remembered that this was the first time that Australia had been threatened and allowance must be made for the degree of nervousness created by this threat. Looking back on the event, I still feel that the arrival of this division in Rangoon at that time might well have restored the situation and saved Burma. On the other hand, it was certainly never required for safety of Australia. The outlook prevailing in Australia at that time was definitely parochial and centred solely on its own direct personal security."

His 22 February entry continued:

"Barely was I asleep when the telephone rang again at 3.30am to tell me car was coming down with message from Wavell… Finally, as I was trying to take maybe ¼ hour in bed on Sunday morning, third telephone call to inform me that we were to have a COS meeting at 10.30 to consider Wavell's telegram. It is now quite clear that we can at last dissolve the ABDA organization and run the war on a rational basis! So far there is very little that was settled at Washington [conference in December 1941] which is surviving the test of time… [including] the Combined Chiefs of Staffs – and thank God for it!! We shall now run the war with two main spheres of interest: the Americans running the Pacific up to Asia, including Australia and New Zealand, and a British one running the opposite way round the globe, including Middle East, India, Burma and Indian Ocean."

This entry illustrated Brookie's initial dislike of the Combined Chiefs of Staff organisation He would, however, change his mind, as he admitted in his Notes, "I had little faith in this organization at the time, I think mainly due to the fact that it had been set up in Washington with the USA as the predominant partner whilst they had… not much knowledge in the running of a war and certainly little experience. My views altered completely as time went on and I grew to have the greatest faith in the

Combined Chiefs of Staff organization as the most efficient that had ever been evolved for coordinating and correlating the war strategy and effort of two allies."

23 February saw the appointment of a new Secretary of State for War:
"Then went to say goodbye to Margesson who has been replaced by James Grigg. A good change which will make for efficiency, but I was sorry to see Margesson go as he seemed so very upset and took it so well."

On the next day:
"COS as usual mainly concerned with the future safety of Malta. The serious situation that we are in is not yet fully realized! Unless we advance again in [eastern Libya], I do not think that Malta will be able to hold out as it will no longer be possible to run convoys in from the East or West. The former due to increased air threat and the latter due to deficiency of naval forces."

On 25 February:
"Cabinet meeting… to discuss possibility of diverting temporarily 72 Hurricanes to Russia. As usual, [I] failed to have any deduction made and [was] informed that political aspect of keeping our promise to Russia overtook all strategical considerations! Personally, I consider it absolute madness. We have never even asked Russia to inform us of the real degree of urgency of these reinforcements."

In his Notes, "We had been put on the wrong foot from the very start by Beaverbrook in his mission to Moscow as regards the supply of equipment to Russia. His policy was to pour everything into their lap without even asking whether it was needed and without ever asking anything in return. As a result, we kept on supplying tanks and aeroplanes that could ill be spared and in doing so suffered the heaviest of losses in shipping conveying this equipment to Arctic Russia. We received nothing in return except abuse for handling the convoys inefficiently! We had absolutely no information as to what the Russian situation was as regards equipment. Russia even refused to keep us informed as to the distribution of her forces and the only way in which I knew Russian dispositions was through German messages which we intercepted. I do not pretend for one moment that Russia was not playing a vital role in the war and bearing the maximum brunt of the land warfare. I fully agree that it was essential to retain Russia in the war and to assist her to do so, but this would in no way [have] precluded getting fuller value for what we were doing."

On 27 February:

"Situation in Burma is a little better but appears to be lull before the storm! I cannot see how we are to go on holding Rangoon much longer."

In early March, British forces evacuated Rangoon and began withdrawing to the north and west of Burma.

SEVEN

CIGS: March–May 1942

John Kennedy recorded that by early March, "Brooke seemed to be wilting a little although, as Margesson remarked, he had the great gift of... shaking himself like a dog coming out of the water after awkward interviews with Churchill. But he was showing signs of wear and tear; he was inclined to be irritable; he did not laugh so much as he had during his first weeks in office. It did, in fact, take him some months to adjust himself and establish a satisfactory relationship with the Prime Minister."[1]

2 March was:

> "Another bad Monday... PM had drafted a bad wire for Auchinleck in which he poured abuse on him for not attacking sooner and for sending us an appreciation in which he did not propose to attack till June [Churchill's draft wire included "armies were not intended to stand about doing nothing... soldiers were meant to fight"[2]]!! Long COS till 1.30 mainly deciding form of message from COS to go instead of PM's wire... Defence Committee at 10pm... Much time wasted in hot air but [Churchill] finally accepted wire we had drafted to replace his".

In his Notes, "Here we have another example of Winston's interference with a commander in the field... he [was] trying to force him to attack at an earlier date than [was] thought advisable and, what is more, [tried] to obtain his ends by an offensive wire. Thank heaven we were able to stop the wire and re-word it."

On 3 March:
> "Long interview with McCreery priming him up for his new appointment with Auchinleck."

In his Notes, "I had been worried for some time by Auchinleck's handling of armoured formations… I had therefore informed him that I was sending him out one of our best armoured divisional commanders to act as his advisor at headquarters on the use of armoured forces. I knew that Dick McCreery might have a difficult time with the Auk and I warned him frankly that he might have a difficult furrow to plough. I must say that I had not expected that he would be practically ignored and never referred to by the Auk".

4 March saw another example of Brookie's dislike of inefficiency and delay. On this occasion, he was advocating a change to the command structure, namely replace the usual committee of local army, navy and air commanders with a single supreme commander:
> "A long and protracted COS taken up mainly with a heated argument as regards relative advantages between a single commander (or generalissimo), as opposed to the usual trinity of the three services. I was supporting the former and was being strongly opposed by [Pound and Portal]! The case in point being Ceylon… The argument itself and impossibility of arriving at any agreement convinced me more than anything else that I was right!"

He eventually won this debate but only after Churchill intervened and supported him. Brookie described the role of the supreme commander as follows, "The committee system is not conducive to firm, decisive and quick action which is essential to success in war. When a commander has to modify his decisions to meet the views of colleagues with an equal right to give decisions, he is in effect merely a member of a Council of War, the evils of which have been proved in history. Resulting action is both weakened and slowed up. In an active theatre, a commander must possess an overriding and coordinating authority. For this reason, I consider that there should always be a Supreme Commander in a theatre where active operations are in progress... He should seldom, if ever, exercise direct command of his own Service."[3]

On 7 March, he was presented with a further opportunity to improve efficiency:

"Arrived at COS to find letter from PM saying that I was to be chairman of the COS in future! Also that Mountbatten was to become a member of COS as Chief of Combined Operations!... It will be rather awkward having to take the chair with old Dudley Pound still there, and with Portal whose turn it should have been next! But I do hope that I shall be able to speed up the business. It is quite hopelessly slow at present!"

On Sunday 8 March, Brookie spent a *"lovely, peaceful quiet day at home, forgetting there is any war"*. On the following day:

"First COS in which I took the chair went off all right and both Pound and Portal played up very well."

In his Notes, "Dudley Pound usually was late for our COS meetings and I rather dreaded taking his place in his absence but, to my surprise, dear old Dudley on this morning made a point of arriving before the appointed time and I found him already seated in my chair with his chairman's seat empty. This was typical of the man, I feel certain that this gesture on his part was done on purpose to make matters easier for me".

There is some evidence, albeit circumstantial, which suggests Brookie may have schemed to secure this chairmanship. On 2 January 1942, "Wonder what I shall do when Dudley Pound... takes the chair again? It will be awful putting up with the delays. I shall have to devise some way of overcoming them." When he was commander-in-chief of the second BEF in France in June 1940, the surreptitious way in which he directed the withdrawal of the BEF to Cherbourg indicated a willingness to scheme. Furthermore, as will be seen later, he freely admitted to scheming against the Americans in January 1943.

Whilst no definite conclusion can be drawn one way or the other, two things are, however, clear. First, the crux of Brookie's criticisms was that the Chiefs of Staff Committee was slow and inefficient under Pound's chairmanship. Second, he was motivated by a wish to inject more efficiency, pace and purpose into the committee, rather than personal ambition or self advancement: as Lord Moran observed of him, "he recoiled from the idea of gaining ascendancy over men to get his own way. The truth was that the competitive instinct had been left out of his makeup... he was without ambition."[4]

Dudley Pound was, in fact, seriously ill. He suffered from a highly malignant brain tumour and other health problems which deprived him of sleep, hence his drowsiness and frequent lapses of concentration. Yet, he continued to sit on this committee until September 1943 when illness finally forced him to stand aside: he died a few weeks later. It could be argued that Pound should be admired for continuing to serve as First Sea Lord despite his ill health. However, more convincing is the argument that he should have been forced to step down much earlier since, as Brookie remarked in typically forthright style on 17 February 1942, "with an old dodderer like him, it is quite impossible for the COS to perform the function it should in the biggest Imperial war we are ever likely to be engaged in!"

On 10 March:

"Long COS with Mountbatten attending for the first time. We discussed the problem of assistance to Russia by operations in France with large raid or lodgement... Then painful interview with Alan Cunningham [see 7 December 1941].

At 6pm PM read out new proposals by [Roosevelt] for subdivision of areas of responsibility... Good in places but calculated to drive Australia, NZ and Canada into USA arms and help to bust up Empire!"

11 March saw further discussion of the contentious issue of RAF cooperation with the army:

"Long COS meeting at which we discussed the naval and army calls on the air force. It resulted in rather a heated debate which did not lead us on to much! I expect some pretty stormy passages within the next few weeks."

In his Notes, "Ultimate success lay in the very closest cooperation between all three Services, and not in the individual and un-coordinated effort of one Service. The Air Force was at this time engaged in an all-out air offensive on Germany... many of them held the opinion that given sufficient heavy bombers, Germany could be brought to her knees by air action alone. In these circumstances, it is not surprising that the Air Ministry was anxious to develop its strength in those types of aircraft that were best suited for the attack on Germany. As a result the army was being starved of any types suitable for the direct support of land forces... Everything seemed to be devoted to the production of four-engine bombers which were unsuited for close cooperation with the army. Many doubted that land forces would ever be again employed in large land operations on the Continent – why therefore provide for a contingency that would probably never arise... The Navy were also fighting for greater air support in the anti-submarine war which they were engaged in and on which our very existence depended."

On 13 March, note Auchinleck's suggestion that Brookie and Portal fly out to Cairo:

"Considered Auchinleck's refusal to come home at this morning's COS [Churchill had requested him to return to London "for consultation"]. Drafted letter to PM about it, however he called up from Chequers and I had to tell him about it. He was infuriated and at once again suggested relieving him of his command! Would not agree to Auchinleck's suggestion that I should go out with CAS. In afternoon another telephone call from Chequers, PM saying that he would now send telegram to Auchinleck! I shudder at what he may put in it and we shall have to vet it tomorrow morning!"

On the following day:

"Called up at lunch by PM and told that he wanted [Archie Nye] to go to Middle East to meet Stafford Cripps there and discuss with the Auk prospects of his offensive [Nye was duly despatched to Cairo to assess the situation with Cripps: their report backed Auchinleck]."

On 19 March:

"I had a talk with Pug [Ismay] as to best method of tackling the air problem. With PM in his present mood, and with his desire to maintain air bombardment of Germany, it will not be possible to get adequate support for either the Army or the Navy. This evening, dined with Lord Milne [former CIGS, see 28 January] and had long talk with him, he was as usual most interesting and in great form. His advice on all matters is most valuable. He thinks Winston is drawing near unto his end and that he won't last much longer as PM."

On 23 March:

"A short COS at which Dudley Pound acted as a continual drag and delayed action… A dull day on the whole, with spring sun shining which made the war all the more unpleasant."

On 24 March:

"Called by PM before COS. Found him in bed with the dragon dressing gown on. Evidently still unhappy about delays in Auchinleck's attack. Even suggesting replacing Auchinleck with Archie Nye! I have already ridden him off trying to replace him by Gort! It is very exhausting, this continual protecting of Auchinleck especially as I have not got the highest opinion of him!"

In his Notes: "These impulsive ideas to change Auchinleck were typical of Winston… Archie Nye, although brilliant in most ways, had not yet been tried out as a commander in the field in any capacity."

On 25 March:

> "*COS meeting under PM at which I argued strongly against sending aircraft to Russia from Middle East. [Portal] had been suggesting sending 6 fighter squadrons just at the time when we are at our wits' end as to how to build up an adequate air force for the Middle and Far East. PM finally agreed to postponement of offensive in Cyrenaica till mid-May.*"

On the same day, in a Parliamentary debate on the loss of Singapore, Lord Hankey criticised Churchill for assuming too much power to himself [see 9 July 1941 Notes] and keeping his staffs working until the early hours of the morning.

On 26 March, note the final sentence:

> "*Defence Committee at 10pm. Discussed… postponement of date of offensive in Libya to May 15th. This entailed certain unpleasant remarks [by Churchill] concerning Auchinleck and desire to relieve him. Finished meeting at 11.30pm, which was mainly due to Lord Hankey having asked questions about late sittings!*"

On 27 March:

> "*Decided to go round to 10 Downing Street to attend meeting. Glad I did as I was able to influence withdrawal of aircraft from Middle East to India which PM was intending to carry out. As he had decided on Libyan offensive in May, it was madness to withdraw fighters from Middle East for India now in spite of all risks Calcutta might run.*"

On 28 March:

> "*A difficult COS… We were discussing ways and means of establishing new Western Front [in Europe – see 10 March]. I had propounded theory that a Western Front to be of use must force withdrawal of [German] forces from Russia, that it was impossible with the land forces at our disposal to force the Germans to withdraw land forces from Russia; but that we might induce them to withdraw air forces.*

But to do this, a landing must take place within our air umbrella namely in vicinity of Calais or Boulogne. Mountbatten was still hankering after a landing near Cherbourg where proper air support is not possible."

By 30 March, Churchill had forgotten, more likely brushed aside, Hankey's criticisms:

"Lunched with Margesson who was now feeling happier, having been made a peer.

After dinner had to go round to see PM at 10.30pm. Later: was kept up till 1am discussing possibilities of some kind of offensive in Northern France to assist Russia in the event of German attack being successful, as it probably will be [i.e. the renewal of the German offensive in Russia in 1942 after the winter pause]. A difficult problem – this universal cry to start a western front is going to be hard to compete with and yet what can we do with some 10 divisions against the German masses? Unfortunately, the country fails to realize the situation we are in."

Brookie elaborated on 'this universal cry' in his Notes. His dry comment about Russia is worth highlighting, "This situation grew more and more difficult: the Beaverbrook press influencing public outlook in the direction of a western front, Albert Hall meetings, Trafalgar Square meetings, vast crowds shouting for immediate help for the Russians. Many seemed to imagine that Russia had only come into the war for our benefit! Certainly, very few of them realized that a premature Western Front could only result in the most appalling shambles which must inevitably reduce the chances of ultimate victory to a minimum."

On 31 March, he was in a despondent mood. However, note the resolute tone of the second sentence:

"The last day of the first quarter of 1942, fateful year in which we have already lost a large proportion of the British Empire and are on the high road to lose a great deal more of it! During the last fortnight, I have had for the first time since the war started a growing conviction

that we are going to lose this war unless we control it very differently and fight it with more determination. But to begin with, a democracy is at a great disadvantage against a dictatorship when it comes to war. Secondly, a government with only one big man in it [Churchill], and that one man a grave danger in many respects, is in a powerless way. Party politics, party interests still override larger war issues. Petty jealousies colour discussions and influence destinies. Politicians still suffer from that little knowledge of military matters which gives them unwarranted confidence that they are born strategists! As a result, they confuse issues, affect decisions and convert simple problems and plans into confused tangles and hopeless muddles.

It is all desperately depressing. Furthermore, it is made worse by the lack of good military commanders. Half our Corps and Divisional Commanders are totally unfit for their appointments and yet if I were to sack them, I could find no better. They lack character, imagination, drive and power of leadership. The reason for this state of affairs is to be found in the losses we sustained in the last war of all our best officers, who should now be our senior commanders. I wonder if we shall muddle through this time as we have done in the past? There are times when I wish to God I had not been placed at the helm of a ship that seems to be heading inevitably for the rocks. It is a great honour to find oneself entrusted with such a task, and the hope of saving the ship a most inspiring thought and one that does override all others. But may God help me in my task."

By the following day, despondency had turned to steely determination and resolve:

"Looking back at what I wrote last night, I wonder whether I was liverish! Life looks yellow at times but as long as one can prevent one's thoughts and actions being tinged with yellow all is well! We have got to choose between pulling through and sinking and it does not take long to make that choice! So why look at the black side of life more than is necessary to avoid falling into any unnecessary pitfalls.

A useful COS at which we examined the dangers to which India is exposed and prepared to relate these to those of the Middle East so as to be guided as to the best use of our resources... After lunch had to tell Laurence Carr that he must give up Eastern Command, unpleasant interview but on the whole he took it well."

On 2 April:

"A short COS but somewhat heated one at which I went near to losing my temper with old Dudley Pound. I find it almost impossible to stir him up into action, he is always lagging about 5 laps behind even when he is not sound asleep... I could not get him to realize how essential it is for us to have a concerted plan with the Americans as regards the action of our Naval forces [see next entry]. Without such a plan, we run grave risk of being defeated in detail."

On 5 April, Japanese forces attacked Ceylon [Sri Lanka]. On 6 April:

"I discovered that most of the Japanese fleet appeared to be in the Indian Ocean and our Eastern Fleet retiring westwards. Up to present, no signs of transport. I don't like the situation much as we are very weak in the Indian Ocean, I have been trying to get First Sea Lord to fix up with the Americans some counter move towards Japan to cover this very predicament that we are in but he has failed to do so up to present. At any rate, the air action over Ceylon was successful yesterday and we downed 27 Japs!"

The presence of a powerful Japanese fleet in the Indian Ocean threatened Ceylon, India and the British supply route to the Middle East around Africa. Worse still was the threat that the advancing Japanese forces could link up with the German Army in the Middle East if Rommel overran Egypt or the German forces in southern Russia advanced through the Caucasus into Persia. In his Notes, "We were fighting for our lives to stop gaps. Cairo was none too safe, Persia was threatened with its precious oil by German advance in South Russia, India's eastern flank was threatened, vital communications through Indian Ocean might be cut at any moment and Australia and New Zealand even open to attack."

On 7 April:

> "COS at which we looked into the unpleasant situation created by entrance of Japanese fleet into Indian Ocean. Just what I had been afraid of... frantic calls for air support from Wavell [Commander-in-Chief, India] which, according to Portal, there is little chance of meeting. I suppose this Empire has never been in such a precarious position throughout its history! I do not like the look of things. And yet a miracle saved us at Dunkirk and we may pull through this time. But I wish I could see more daylight as to how we are to keep going through 1942. A very gloomy Cabinet meeting!"

In early 1942, American military planners notably Brigadier General Eisenhower, head of the United States Army's War Plans Division, concluded that the three most important strategic priorities in the War were, first, secure Britain and the Atlantic, second, hold the Middle East and India to avoid any link up between German and Japanese forces and, third, support Russia since it was engaging the bulk of the German forces. The Americans were straightforward and purposeful in their approach to military planning in that they identified the key theatre in any war and then tailored their arms production and training to allow for a decisive engagement with the enemy in that theatre: American planners had previously concluded that north-west Europe was the decisive theatre in a war against Germany.

By March 1942, the Americans were examining the prospect of opening a second front in north-west Europe, the rationale being that this was the most effective way of providing support to Russia: they were also keen to avoid their forces becoming dispersed across various theatres. On 25 March, Eisenhower sent a memorandum to General George Marshall, United States Army chief of staff, recommending that American resources be concentrated on launching cross-Channel operations from Britain. His memorandum was approved by Marshall and President Roosevelt on the same day and Eisenhower was instructed to prepare a plan for those operations. Within two days, an outline plan, later described as "a very simple sketch of the operations"[5], had been produced. On 1 April, this outline plan was presented to Marshall and Roosevelt who, again, immediately approved it. Roosevelt then despatched Marshall and Harry Hopkins, Roosevelt's confidante, advisor and emissary, to London to advocate these operations to the British. Two points are worth noting. First, no detailed planning had been undertaken and, second, the Americans chose to submit their proposals direct to the British Government rather than the Combined Chiefs of Staff. On 8 April, Marshall and Hopkins arrived in London, armed with the American plan.

Their proposals, contained in a document that became known as the Marshall Memorandum, comprised three separate but inter-related operations. The first, Bolero, involved the build up of American forces in Britain in advance of launching cross-Channel operations: Brookie agreed with Bolero since their presence in Britain not only helped secure its defence against invasion but also facilitated the despatch of British troops overseas. The second, Round-up, was the full-scale invasion of north-west Europe scheduled for the spring or summer of 1943: Brookie agreed with the principle but was sceptical about the date. The third, Sledgehammer, was a limited emergency attack on north-west Europe in 1942 if either Russia's defeat appeared imminent or there was a severe deterioration in Germany's situation: Brookie disliked Sledgehammer with a passion.

On 8 April:

> *"Very difficult COS attended by Paget, Sholto Douglas [RAF] and Mountbatten. Subject – attempt to assist Russia through action in France. Plan they had put up was a thoroughly bad one. Then went to Hendon to meet Marshall and Harry Hopkins who had just flown from America."*

By the end of Marshall and Hopkins' nine-day visit, the British had agreed to the proposals in the Marshall Memorandum, the key decision being taken by the defence committee on 14 April. Their agreement was driven by two factors, namely a desire to accommodate the Americans whose support and vast resources were essential to Britain's survival and, second, the fear that rejection of their proposals might prompt America to depart from the agreed Germany First policy and concentrate its military resources in the Pacific. This was a legitimate fear since American domestic opinion was strongly in favour of retaliation against Japan, following the attack on Pearl Harbor.

Much has been written about the British approval of the Marshall Memorandum in April 1942. It has been argued that, at best, the British were somewhat disingenuous and, at worst, they deliberately misled the Americans. The evidence tends to support the latter and, ironically, much of it is provided by the British themselves. Churchill opened the 14 April defence committee meeting by saying "he had no hesitation in cordially accepting the plan".[6] However, he made clear in his subsequent memoirs that at the time he had considerable reservations about the 1942 Sledgehammer operation and that he preferred Operations Gymnast [north-west Africa] and Jupiter [north Norway] over Sledgehammer: Churchill then added, intriguingly, "But I had to work by influence and diplomacy in order to secure agreed and harmonious action with our cherished Ally, without whose aid nothing but ruin faced the world. I did not therefore open any of these alternatives at our meeting on the 14th."[7] General 'Pug' Ismay, Military Secretary to the War Cabinet, also made clear in his memoirs that the British had considerable reservations about the American proposals and then acknowledged, in almost hand-wringing terms, that their failure to articulate these was probably a mistake. Ian Jacob, Military Assistant Secretary to the War Cabinet, was more forthright, admitting that the British thought Sledgehammer was an impossibility but chose not to say so through fear the Americans would transfer their resources to the Pacific.

Brookie's entries over the next few days not only reveal his reservations but also show his attention was focused as much on events in the Indian Ocean, where the British needed immediate assistance, as it was on the American proposals. On 9 April, Marshall, who was Brookie's counterpart in the United States Army, made his pitch to the British chiefs of staff:

"Started COS at 9am as Marshall was due at 10.30. He remained with us till 12.30pm and gave us a long talk on his views concerning

the desirability of starting western front next September [1942] and that the USA forces would take part. However, the total force which they could transport by then only consisted of 2½ divisions!! No very great contribution. Furthermore, they had not begun to realize what all the implications of their proposed plan were! Finally, another COS meeting… examining relative importance of Middle East and Indian theatres and assessing best employment of very limited forces. Large Japanese Naval forces are in the Indian Ocean operating with carriers and have [sunk] two cruisers and one aircraft carrier in the last two days.

I liked what I saw of Marshall, a pleasant and easy man to get on with, rather over-filled with his own importance. But I should not put him down as a great man."

In his Notes, "These first impressions of mine about Marshall… were based on the day's discussions which had made it quite clear that Marshall had up to date only touched the fringe of all the implications of a re-entry into France. In the light of the existing situation, his plans for September of 1942 were just fantastic!… There was a great charm and dignity about Marshall which could not fail to appeal to one. A big man and a very great gentleman who inspired trust but did not impress me by the ability of his brain."

10 April was:

"A very busy day which started with usual COS meeting mainly concerned in trying to save India from the Japs. A gloomy prospect with loss of command of sea and air… in evening had another COS meeting to discuss Joint Planning Staff report on Marshall's scheme for invasion of Europe."

That night, at Chequers, Marshall, Hopkins and the British chiefs of staff were kept up until 2am by Churchill. In his Notes, "I remember being amused at Marshall's reactions to Winston's late hours, he was evidently not used to being kept out of his bed till the small hours of the morning and not enjoying it much! He certainly had a much easier time of it working with Roosevelt, he informed me that he frequently did not see him for a month or six weeks. I was fortunate if I did not see Winston for 6 hours."

On 13 April:

"A bad COS with much loss of time and interruptions trying to frame a reply for Marshall. Then lunch with Portal and Freeman [RAF] to settle 'off the record' the difference between Army and Air Force. Evidently little hope of arriving at any sort of settlement... had Marshall to dine with me. The more I see of him the more I like him."

On 14 April:

"Defence Committee attended by Hopkins and Marshall. A momentous meeting at which we accepted their proposals for offensive action in Europe in 1942 perhaps and in 1943 for certain [the written record of this meeting in Churchill's memoirs shows that Marshall was aware the British chiefs of staff had reservations over Sledgehammer]. They have not begun to realize all the implications of this plan and all the difficulties that lie ahead of us! The fear I have is that they should concentrate on this offensive at the expense of all else! We have therefore been pressing on them the importance of providing American assistance in the Indian Ocean and Middle East."

15 April saw an example of Brookie's good judgment. His assessment of Marshall was impeccable:

"I had Marshall for nearly 2 hours in my office explaining to him our dispositions. He is, I should think, a good general at raising armies and providing the necessary links between the military and political worlds. But his strategical ability does not impress me at all!! In fact, in many respects he is a very dangerous man whilst being a very charming one!... Marshall has started the European offensive plan and is going 100% all out on it! It is a clever move which fits in *well with present political opinion and the desire to help Russia. It is also popular with all military men who are fretting for an offensive policy. But, and this is a very large 'but', his plan does not go beyond just landing on the far coast [of northern France]!! Whether we are to play baccarat or chemin de fer at Le Touquet, or possibly bathe at Paris Plage, is not stipulated! I asked him this afternoon – do we go east, south or west after landing? He had not begun to think of it!!"*

In his Notes, "My conversation with Marshall that afternoon was an eye-opener! I discovered that he had not studied any of the strategic implications of a cross-Channel operation. He argued that the main difficulty would be to achieve a landing. I granted that this would certainly present great difficulties but that our real troubles would start after the landing. We should be operating with forces initially weaker than the enemy and in addition his rate of reinforcement would be at least twice as fast as ours. In addition, [German] formations were fully trained and inured to war whilst ours were raw and inexperienced. I asked him to imagine that his landing had been safely carried out and asked him what his plans would then be… he had not begun to consider any form of plan of action and had not even begun to visualize the problems that would face an army after landing. I saw a great deal of him throughout the rest of the war and the more I saw of him, the more clearly I appreciated that his strategic ability was of the poorest. A great man, a great gentleman and great organizer but definitely not a strategist."

On 16 April:

"Important COS meeting at which we discussed plans for this year's invasion of the continent in collaboration with the Americans, and also plans for 1943. The plans are fraught with the gravest dangers. Public opinion is shouting for the formation of a new western front to assist the Russians. But they have no conception of the difficulties and dangers entailed! The prospects of success are small and dependent on a mass of unknowns, whilst the chances of disaster are great and dependent on a mass of well-established military facts.

> *Took lunch in car and went to see the organization for breaking down ciphers [Bletchley Park] – a wonderful set of professors and genii! I marvel at the work they succeed in doing."*

On 17 April:
> *"A long visit from Casey [Australian statesman and newly appointed minister, resident in the Middle East]. I was very much impressed by him and by his grasp of things – he should be excellent in the ME."*

On 23 April, note Brookie's scepticism regarding the Madagascar attack:
> *"A very difficult COS connected with the proposed operation against Madagascar. The Admiralty who were the original supporters of the necessity for such an attack are now adopting a different attitude and doubting the necessity. I cannot see that the desirability of carrying out the operation (if it ever existed!) has in any way altered, but the change of government in France and the arrival of Laval puts a new complexion on the enterprise [Pierre Laval, who had just been made head of the French Vichy Government, was viewed as a collaborator and supporter of Germany]."*

On 24 April, the chiefs of staff met Churchill and Eden to discuss the Madagascar operation:
> *"The main difficulty was to estimate what effect the operation might have on the new Laval Government and consequently what the repercussions were likely to be. Personally, I feel we have little to gain from carrying out the operation. The main object is to deny the use of Diego Suarez [port in Madagascar] to the Japs, and I don't feel that they are likely to go there! The risks are Laval giving Germans a free run of Dakar or Bizerta or bombing Gibraltar or handing over [French] fleet. Personally, I do not feel operation is worth it. However, Winston decided for it at the present. After lunch another interview with poor Alan Cunningham [see 7 December 1941] who wishes his case judged definitely one way or another."*

Sir Alexander Cadogan, the armchair general in the Foreign Office, also attended this 24 April meeting, "As usual, [Chiefs of Staff] get cold feet when an operation is ready. This time they plead that Laval's accession to power has changed situation. I told [Eden] it had not… and the meeting decided not to interfere with the operation… it is silly planning these things and then calling them off. Let's risk something."[8]

On 29 April:

"At 6.15 I went to the Cabinet meeting, where we were intended to discuss the future operations on the Continent. But instead we got involved in a heavy discussion on army support from the air. I became involved in heated discussion with [Sinclair, Secretary of State for Air], I should have liked to have told him even more plainly that he was deliberately speaking untruths! However, PM backed me up and rubbed into Sinclair the necessity for devoting more love and affection to those air forces destined for army requirements."

Two days later:

"Sent for by PM in the evening to discuss Wavell's latest wire. He is protesting strongly at the fact that land, sea and air forces for defence of India are not being built up quicker. This is partly due to the Madagascar operation. Personally, I wish we were not carrying it out."

On 4 May:

"PM then invited all the Chiefs of Staff to lunch… He was in good form and said he felt elated. I think probably mainly with excitement at thought of attack on Madagascar [due to start the next day]! War Cabinet at 5.30pm… Evatt, the new Australian representative, was there. Not very attractive at first sight!"

On 6 May:

"Arrived just in time to go to COS meeting to turn down proposed attack on Alderney Island [Channel Islands]… After meeting, invited by the PM to sit in garden with him to discuss the Madagascar operation, which has been rather sticky during the last 24 hours!"

On 7 May:

"I was sent for on way to COS meeting to see PM in bed about wire which had come in from Auchinleck about the date of his attack which he is again putting [back] to July or August. PM as usual very upset about the whole business, wishing to bring Alexander back to take over half of Middle East! Luckily, news from Madagascar was better again and this took the edge off the trouble!"

On 8 May, note the conclusion reached regarding the 1942 Sledgehammer operation:

"An unpleasant day! Difficult COS meeting, first of all considering Auchinleck's wire in which he proposes to put off his attack from May 15 to June 15. I do not like his message – it is a bad one based purely on number of tanks and not on the strategical situation. He never takes into account danger Malta is exposed to through his proposed delays. Next, we had to examine the Sledgehammer operation namely proposals for establishing a bridgehead across the Channel. After an examination, Home Forces and Chief of Combined Operations [Mountbatten] had come to the conclusion that the landing craft were insufficient for the operation.

Then Cabinet meeting at 3pm to examine Auchinleck's wire. I had to open the ball and stated that I did not consider that we could order the Auk to attack about May 15 against his advice. That we should give him till June 15 and tell him to coordinate his attack with running of convoy to Malta, whilst being prepared to take advantage of any limited attack enemy might make as expected towards end of May".

Two days later, Brookie was addressing the same subject:

"Called up after breakfast by DMO to be told I was wanted for

Cabinet meeting at 6pm... to discuss latest wire from Auchinleck. He had again stuck his toes in and was refusing to attack till a late date and had sent in a very bad telegram in which he entirely failed to realize the importance of Malta and overestimated the danger to Egypt in the event of his being defeated."

On 11 May:

"Grigg [Secretary of State for War] and I tackled PM again about Cunningham [see 7 December 1941] and Godwin-Austen but without any luck [Churchill held a grudge against General Godwin-Austen who had resigned after one of his orders was countermanded]! I cannot make out his attitude about it – the moment their names are mentioned, one might imagine they were criminals of the worst order."

12 May illustrated Brookie's ability to read people well:

"A difficult COS this morning with a visit from Evatt [Australian politician, see 4 May]... He produced 3 strong blackmail cards and then asked for greater allocation of aircraft from America to Australia. In fact, if we did not ensure that MacArthur's requests were met [Douglas MacArthur, American general based in Australia], we should probably be forced to part with the 9th Aust Div from Middle East, or the Australian Squadron from England, or the diversion of 2nd Inf Div and 8th Armoured Div to Australia! He is a thoroughly unpleasant type of individual with no outlook beyond the shores of Australia."

In his Notes, compare the breadth of Brookie's strategic analysis with Evatt's insularity, "I did my level best to make him listen to a short statement of the global situation and where the main dangers existed. He refused to listen and gave me the impression that, as far as he was concerned, he did not mind what happened to anybody else as long as Australian shores could be made safe. It was quite impossible to make him realize that the security of Australia did not rest in Australia. He failed to see that defeat in the Middle East, India and Indian Ocean must inevitably lead to the invasion of Australia, no matter what reinforcements were sent them now."

On the following day:

"Lunched with Sinclair, Grigg and Portal to discuss army air requirements [see 29 April]. We made no headway at all... Cabinet at 5.30pm where PM decided to send [Arctic] convoy to Russia against advice of Cabinet. He also refused to reconsider employment of either Cunningham or Godwin-Austen."

19 May saw another example of Brookie's good judgment, on this occasion Neil Ritchie. He was very fond of Ritchie but that did not influence his judgment whatsoever. His reservations were to prove well-founded:

"Difficult COS meeting at which we discussed Army and Navy air requirements. It led in the first place to heated arguments between me and Portal and subsequently between Pound and Portal!... It is a depressing situation and the Air Ministry outlook is now so divorced from the requirements of the army that I see no solution except an Army Air Arm.

During afternoon, had interview with Scobie who is back from the Middle East. I am not happy at all from all that I hear of the situation at Middle East Headquarters. Auchinleck's Chief of Staff [Corbett] is nothing like good enough for the job and yet [Auchinleck] insisted on selecting him. On the other hand, I do not feel that Neil Ritchie is a big enough man to command the 8th Army [Ritchie had replaced Cunningham as 8th Army commander – see 7 December 1941] and I fear that the Auk is also losing confidence in him! It is all very depressing with an offensive impending."

On 23 May:

"Went round to 10 Downing Street at 12.30 after COS where Mountbatten and I had long interview with PM discussing invasion possibilities. He was carried away with optimism at times and *establishing lodgements all round the coast from Calais to Bordeaux with little regard to strengths and landing facilities."*

In late May, Russia's Minister of Foreign Affairs, Molotov, visited Britain to sign a new Anglo-Soviet Treaty and took the opportunity to press for the opening of a second front in Europe in 1942 to relieve the pressure on Russian forces.

On 26 May:

"Then went out to lunch at Russian Embassy to meet Molotov again. A memorable lunch party held prior to signing new Anglo-Russian Treaty… Many toasts and many speeches. Somehow the whole affair gave me the creeps and made me feel that humanity has still many centuries to live through before universal peace can be found."

In his Notes, "I was filled with interest to meet Molotov… Not very impressive to look at and with slight impediment in his speech yet gave one a feeling of distinct ability and shrewdness."

Earlier, 8 May, Brookie had noted the shortage of landing craft for the 1942 Sledgehammer operation. 27 May saw further discussion of Sledgehammer:

"At 5.30 went to Downing Street to discuss establishing of Western Front. PM in very good form and quite ready to appreciate that it is impossible to establish a front with landing craft only capable of lifting 4,000 men [in] first flight. He was very amenable to reason but inclined to transfer the scene of action to Northen Norway! Which we are now to examine."

On 28 May, note Brookie's optimism regarding Rommel's new offensive:
"A pretty full COS… we had Dr Evatt again for ¾ hour pleading that Australia should be crammed full of forces at the expense of all other fronts. However, he left with no more than he had come! Rommel

has now started his expected attack and a large-scale battle is raging in the Middle East. A great deal depends on it. The Auk ought to be able to get the better of it and has great chances in pushing a counter stroke home."

On 29 May:

"COS at which we again discussed Madagascar. Again Foreign Office with their mad desire to back de Gaulle are putting us into a position where we shall ultimately be forced to use more force to finally secure our position on the island… Came back [to War Office] to find new telegram from Middle East had arrived which required calling up the PM to give him the latest situation. Found that he is at Chequers looking at a film and not likely to be out till 1am!! I am therefore waiting for him to call up before going to bed!"

On the same day, Molotov, who had travelled on to Washington, met Roosevelt and again pressed for a second front to be opened in Europe in 1942. In reply, Roosevelt "authorized Mr Molotov to inform Mr Stalin that we expect the formation of a Second Front this year."[9]

Two days later, Sir Alexander Cadogan in the Foreign Office was confiding to his diary, "Heard on wireless about our 1,000-plane raid on Germany. Grand! Can't make out what's happening in Libya battle, but nothing seems to have gone irretrievably wrong yet."[10]

EIGHT

CIGS: June–July 1942

By late May, British military planners had concluded that the 1942 Sledgehammer operation offered little prospect of success, the principal reasons being shortage of landing craft, strong German defences in the Pas de Calais area and inadequate air cover for a landing in the Cherbourg peninsular: most telling of all, the invading Allied forces would be vastly outnumbered by the twenty-five German divisions that were believed to be in France. In early June, Mountbatten was despatched to Washington to inform Roosevelt of this conclusion.

On 5 June:

"At this morning's COS we discussed again the various possibilities of helping Russia by proceeding to France, either as a lodgement [Sledgehammer] or as a raid. Prospects not hopeful. We then turned to examine the PM's pet attack on Northern Norway which appears even more impossible".

8 June saw a:

"Long COS meeting with PM... at which we discussed operations on Continent this year, recapture of Burma, Madagascar, alternative of reinforcing India or Middle East i.e. whether 8th Armoured Div and 44th Div were to go to ME or India; the operation for capturing North Norway and finally the sending of a force to Spitzbergen to deny it to the Germans."

On the same day, Churchill wrote a paper for the chiefs of staff in which he argued that, first, no landing in continental Europe should be made in 1942 unless the intention was to stay there, which was a circuitous way of arguing against a raid, and, second, that no attempt should be made to land and stay there in 1942 [i.e. Sledgehammer] unless Germany was demoralised to an extent which justified the risks involved: in the absence of massive German defeats in Russia, this was unlikely.

On 11 June, Churchill effectively killed off Sledgehammer:
"*COS meeting at 10am followed by Cabinet meeting… PM in good form and carried Cabinet with him in his proposed policy that we do not land in France in strength except to stop there, and we do not go there unless German morale is deteriorating.*"

On 13 June:
"*PM… told me he was thinking of starting for Washington on Thursday next and would like me to come with him. He considered Roosevelt was getting a bit off the rails and some good talks as regards western front were required. Escaped home about 4.45pm.*"

On 14 June:
"*A Sunday disturbed by many calls from the PM who was much disturbed at bad turn taken by operations in the Middle East. Rommel certainly seems to be getting the better of Ritchie and to be out-generalling him.*"

On the same day, Sir Alexander Cadogan gave vent to his feelings, "We seem to be being completely worsted and outwitted, as usual, by Rommel. I suppose he's a very good general, but I am quite convinced that our own (including the CIGS) are blockheads who cannot learn anything."[1]

On 15 June:
"*Cabinet meeting and very gloomy owing to bad news from Libya and from Malta convoys. After dinner, 1 hour's hard work before*

10.30 meeting with PM at 10 Downing St. Just back at 1.20am!! And we did nothing except meander round from Burma to France and back. Also discussed upcoming meeting [in] Washington".

A notable feature of Churchill's leadership style was that he kept his advisors and colleagues under constant pressure by bombarding them with papers and notes: in fairness, as a wartime prime minister he was entitled, and indeed probably right, to do so. On 15 June, he wrote a paper for the chiefs of staff on the 1943 cross-Channel invasion, Operation Round-up, in which he envisaged six disembarkations together with six feints at various points between Denmark and Bordeaux whilst, at the same time, his pet Norwegian operation, Jupiter, was also being carried out. This paper is worth reproducing since it not only captured Churchill's passion, enthusiasm and imagination but also illustrated his lack of realism and tendency to be 'carried away with optimism' [23 May].

1. For such an operation, the qualities of magnitude, simultaneity and violence are required. The enemy cannot be ready everywhere. At least six heavy disembarkations must be attempted in the first wave. The enemy should be further mystified by at least half-a-dozen feints, which, if luck favours them, may be exploited. The limited and numerically inferior Air Force of the enemy will thus be dispersed or fully occupied. While intense fighting is in progress at one or two points, a virtual walk-over may be obtained at others.
2. The second wave nourishes the landings effected, and presses where the going is good. The fluidity of attack from the sea enables wide options to be exercised in the second wave.
3. It is hoped that 'Jupiter' will be already in progress. Landings or feints should be planned in Denmark, in Holland, in Belgium, at the Pas de Calais, where the major Air battle will be fought, on the Cotentin Peninsula, at Brest, at St Nazaire, at the mouth of the Gironde.
4. The first objective is to get ashore in large numbers. At least ten Armoured Brigades should go in the first wave. These Brigades must

accept very high risks in their task of pressing on deeply inland, rousing the populations, deranging the enemy's communications, and spreading the fighting over the widest possible areas.

5. *Behind the confusion and disorder which these incursions will create, the second wave will be launched. This should aim at making definite concentrations of armour and motorized troops at strategic points carefully selected. If four or five of these desirable points have been chosen beforehand, concentrations at perhaps three of them might be achieved, relations between them established, and the plan of battle could then take shape.*

6. *If forces are used on the above scale, the enemy should be so disturbed as to require at least a week to organize other than local counter-strokes. During that week a superior fighter Air force must be installed upon captured airfields, and the command of the Air, hitherto fought for over the Pas de Calais, must become general.*

7. *While these operations are taking place in the interior of the country assaulted, the seizure of at least four important ports must be accomplished. For this purpose, at least ten Brigades of infantry, partly pedal-cyclists, but all specially trained in house-to-house fighting, must be used. Here again the cost in men and material must be rated very high.*

8. *To ensure success, the whole of the above operations, simultaneous or successive, should be accomplished within a week of Zero, by which time not less than 400,000 men should be ashore and busy.*

9. *The moment any port is gained and open, the third wave of attack should start. This will be carried from our Western ports in large ships. It should comprise not less than 300,000 infantry with their own artillery plus part of that belonging to the earlier-landed formations. The first and second waves are essentially assaulting forces, and it is not till the third wave that the formations should be handled in terms of Divisions and Corps. If by Zero 14, 700,000 men are ashore, if Air supremacy has been gained, if the enemy is in considerable confusion, and if we hold at least four workable ports, we shall have got our claws well into the job.*[2]

On 17 June, Churchill and Brookie started their journey to Washington:

> *"Travelled up to Stranraer in PM's special train – very comfortable. Had meals alone… with [Churchill] and thus able to settle many points in anticipation of talk with Roosevelt."*

Both men enjoyed overseas trips. For the mercurial, combative and self-confident Churchill, face to face meetings provided the opportunity to exert his will and win debates by the sheer force of his personality. For Brookie, they offered the thrill of flying and an opportunity to visit foreign countries. In his Notes, he provided an insight into Churchill's personality, "We were walking down the quay to embark in the motorboat to take us to the Clipper [flying boat]. He was dressed in his zip-suit and zip-shoes, with a black Homburg hat on the side of his head and his small gold-topped malacca cane in his hand. Suddenly, almost like Pooh-Bear, he started humming, "We are here because we're here – we're here because we're here!" This little song could not have been more appropriate. It was at a time when the Atlantic had not been so frequently flown, we were both somewhat doubtful why we were going, whether we should get there, what we should achieve while we were there, and whether we should ever get back. The next incident was on our arrival in the flying boat. He sent for the steward and said to him: 'The clock is going to do some funny things while we are in the air; it is either going to go backwards or forwards, but that is of little consequence, my stomach is my clock and I eat every four hours!'"

Awaiting Churchill and Brookie in Washington were Roosevelt, Harry Hopkins, Marshall, Henry Stimson, Secretary of War, and Admiral King, Commander-in-Chief, US Fleet. Marshall was still strongly advocating the cross-Channel operations which had been agreed in London in April and, in this, he was firmly supported by Stimson. King's primary interest was in fighting Japan in the Pacific and, as will become clear, this remained his primary interest throughout the War.

If things were difficult in London in June 1942, they were not a whole lot better in Washington – and the architect of the American difficulties was Roosevelt. By June, he had come to the view that

American troops must engage German forces in 1942, probably because mid-term elections were due to be held in November and he needed to justify the Germany First policy to his domestic electorate. This may explain his, arguably rash, assurance to Molotov in late May 'that we expect the formation of a Second Front this year'.[3]

Henry Stimson was also a diary keeper and his entry for 17 June explained the reason for the American difficulties. Roosevelt – memorably described by Stimson as "foxy"[4] – convened a meeting on 17 June at which he instructed his military advisors to re-examine Operation Gymnast, the invasion of north-west Africa: in the meeting, both Stimson and Marshall voiced their opposition to Gymnast but to no avail. Next day, a clearly concerned Stimson sent a firm yet respectful letter to his president in which he argued that Roosevelt should adhere to the plan to launch cross-Channel operations and that it would be a mistake to launch expeditions elsewhere. He also made clear his belief that opening a second front in north-west Europe was the quickest and best way of defeating Germany.

On 19 June, Brookie attended his first Combined Chiefs of Staff [CCS] meeting:

"I gave statement of reasons for our visit which were connected with some of the doubts expressed by President to Mountbatten [during his recent visit to Washington].

After lunch had another [informal] interview with Marshall and his staff at which we made further progress towards defining our policy for 1942 and 1943. Found that we were pretty well of the same accord as to our outlook... On the whole made fine progress today but am a little doubtful as to what PM and President may be brewing up together."

Brigadier Dykes, a member of the British Mission in Washington, also attended this CCS meeting. He was yet another diary keeper and according to his 19 June entry, "The CIGS explained that they had come over largely owing to the President's conversation with Mountbatten when [Roosevelt] had said he was worried because US troops would not be engaged with the enemy on any scale this year. He feared a Continental operation next spring would be too late and was turning toward North-West Africa as a possible let-out this year."[5]

On 20 June:

> "Stinking hot day!! Went up to the office in morning where I looked through the minutes of yesterday's meetings. Then attended another Chiefs of Staff meeting at 11am. Here I met Admiral King for the first time. Meeting was I think a success, at least as a military man he was in agreement as to policy we should adopt. But we fully appreciated that we might be up against many difficulties when confronted with the plans that the PM and the President had been brewing up together at 'Hyde Park' [Roosevelt's residence]. We fear the worst and are certain that North Africa or North Norway plans for 1942 will loom large in their proposals, whilst we are convinced that they are not possible!"

Brookie's statement, 'we are convinced that [north Africa or north Norway] are not possible', is worth highlighting since it is at variance with the minutes of these 19 and 20 June meetings. Both sets of minutes record Brookie suggesting to the Americans that some form of Gymnast operation in 1942 should be considered: they also show that on each occasion his suggestion hit a wall of resistance from the Americans. Following these meetings, the final report of the CCS, dated 21 June, recommended that "Gymnast should not be undertaken under the existing situation."[6] So, why did Brookie suggest staging some form of Gymnast operation in 1942 when he thought it was 'not possible'?

One explanation is that he did believe Gymnast was possible but was persuaded by the force of the American arguments against the operation. However, this is scarcely credible since, as will become clear, it was completely out of character for him to back down in the face of opposition: he always argued tenaciously in favour of the course of action which he believed was right. Far more credible is the explanation that

Brookie tabled Gymnast because Churchill had instructed him to do so – he was doing his political master's bidding.

There are three pieces of evidence which support this conclusion. First, Churchill was also advocating Gymnast. In a paper which he wrote and handed to Roosevelt on 20 June, Churchill stated bluntly that the British believed a cross-Channel operation in 1942 was doomed to failure and then, after highlighting the need to launch an operation in 1942, tabled Gymnast as a possibility. Second, since Brookie knew the CCS rejection of Gymnast would meet with Churchill's disapproval, it was important that the minutes showed he had tabled Gymnast in accordance with his political master's wishes: this explains why on 20 June he 'went up to the office in the morning where I looked through the minutes of yesterday's meetings.' Third, in his 21 June entry which appears shortly, Brookie recorded Churchill as being 'very upset at the decisions we had come to with the Combined Chiefs of Staff'. Churchill's reaction to the CCS decision was confirmed by Brigadier Dykes' diary, "Pug [Ismay] anticipates a major explosion from the PM when he is confronted by this [CCS] document."[7]

In his biography of Brookie, Fraser interpreted Brookie's apparent backing down in the face of American resistance to Gymnast as the only instance when he wavered in his advocacy of a Mediterranean strategy. In truth, he was not wavering – he was just going through the motions of complying with Churchill's instructions.

Earlier, 14 June, Brookie had noted that Rommel was 'out-generalling' Neil Ritchie. On 21 June, Rommel's forces captured Tobruk:

"Pug Ismay called up to say that PM wanted to see me and that he was very upset at the decisions we had come to with the Combined Chiefs of Staff meetings. Found [Churchill] a bit peevish, but not too bad and after an hour's talk had him quiet again. Then went with [Churchill] to see President. I was much impressed by him – a most attractive personality. Harry Hopkins and Marshall also turned up and we had a general discussion of all the possible offensives in France, Africa and the Middle East. After lunch, we had another long

conference lasting till 4.30pm. In the middle, the tragic news of the loss of Tobruk came in!

[Further] meeting with President, PM, Dill, Marshall, King, Harry Hopkins, Little, Ismay and self. Discussed… Middle East position, and accepted offer of American Armoured Div for [Middle East]. This may lead to a USA front in ME at expense of the European front."

On 22 June, Roosevelt and Churchill met again, with Stimson in attendance. Stimson's diary shows that Roosevelt was determined to carry out an operation rather than wait until 1943 when the cross-Channel invasion, Round-up, was due to be launched – the president's "mind was evidently tenaciously fixed to some kind of a diversion from [Round-up]"[8]. This prompted Stimson to express the fear in the meeting that if another operation was carried out, then this might result in Round-up not being launched in 1943: his fear would prove well-founded.

On the same day, 22 June:

"Winston made me drive back with him to the White House in the President's car to discuss necessity to relieve Neil Ritchie. I felt this was bound to come and was prepared for it. I am devoted to Neil and hate to think of the disappointment this will mean to him."

Meanwhile, in London, the loss of Tobruk drew this reaction from the armchair general, Sir Alexander Cadogan, "It held out for 8 months last time and for about as many hours this. I wonder what is most wrong with our army. Without any knowledge, I should say the generals. Most depressing."[9]

Two days later, Churchill and Brookie inspected American troops on exercises:

"Fine hard-looking men… The American system of individual and elementary training seems excellent, but I am not so certain that their higher training is good enough or that they have yet realized the standard of training required."

Brookie elaborated in his Notes, "They certainly had not – and had a lot to learn!... [They] seemed to prefer to learn in the hard school of war itself. As a result, they learned a great deal more in North Africa! But... when they once got down to it, they were determined to make a success of it.

There was a fleet of cars to take us round for the day and as there was a vacant seat in one of the rear cars, Marshall very kindly suggested that Sawyers [Churchill's butler] should accompany us. From then onwards Sawyers became one of the party both as regards watching the displays and as regards absorbing refreshments. The latter he did fairly efficiently and for the rest of the day was distinctly affected by what he had consumed. When we regained the train later on, he was asked by an official if the luggage in front of him belonged to the PM to which, in a thick voice, he replied: 'How the hell should I know!'"

25 June saw another CCS meeting:

"We examined the various alternatives [to] providing an American Armoured Div for Middle East [see 21 June]. A project both PM and President were very keen on. Marshall put forward a new proposal to provide 300 Sherman tanks and 100 self-propelled guns... after examining his proposal, I was all for accepting it but that I might have great difficulty to get the PM to accept it as he would wish to conform to President's desire to produce fighting troops instead of equipment.

Went round to White House to put proposal before PM... Things went better than I expected and I was able to convince PM that military aspect of this problem and its advantages outweighed the political considerations."

Given the contrasting views of the principal participants at the Washington conference, it was perhaps inevitable that the agreement reached at its conclusion amounted to a fudge.

1. Plans and preparations for the Bolero [Round-up] operation in

1943 on as large a scale as possible are to be pushed forward with all speed and energy. It is, however, essential that the United States and Great Britain should be prepared to act offensively in 1942.
2. *Operations in France or the Low Countries in 1942 would, if successful, yield greater political and strategic gains than operations in any other theatre. Plans and preparations for the operations in this theatre are to be pressed forward with all possible speed, energy, and ingenuity. The most resolute efforts must be made to overcome the obvious dangers and difficulties of the enterprise. If a sound and sensible plan can be contrived, we should not hesitate to give effect to it. If on the other hand detailed examination shows that despite all efforts, success is improbable, we must be ready with an alternative.*
3. *The possibilities of operation Gymnast will be explored carefully and conscientiously, and plans will be completed in all details as soon as possible. Forces to be employed in Gymnast would in the main be found from Bolero units which had not yet left the United States. The possibility of operations in Norway and the Iberian Peninsula in the autumn and winter of 1942 will also be carefully considered by the Combined Chiefs of Staff.*
4. *Planning of Bolero [Round-up] will continue to be centred in London. Planning for Gymnast will be centred in Washington.*[10]

It was also somewhat contradictory. Priority was to be given to 'the Bolero [Round-up] operation in 1943' yet it was 'essential... to act offensively in 1942'. Moreover, the fact that 'Forces to be employed in Gymnast would in the main be found from Bolero units which had not yet left the United States' suggested that Gymnast might be given priority over Round-up.

On 26 June, Churchill and Brookie flew back to Britain:
"*I feel now in much closer touch with Marshall and his staff and know what he is working for and what his difficulties are... meeting the President was a matter of the greatest interest, a wonderful charm about him. But I do not think that his military sense is on a par with*

his political sense. As a result, he favours plans which are not possible owing to their administrative aspects."

In his Notes, "The President had no military knowledge and was aware of this fact and consequently relied heavily on Marshall and listened to Marshall's advice. Marshall never seemed to have any difficulty in countering any wildish plans which the President might put forward. My position was very different. Winston never had the slightest doubt that he had inherited all the military genius from his great ancestor Marlborough! His military plans and ideas varied from the most brilliant conceptions at one end to the wildest and most dangerous ideas at the other. To wean him away from these wilder plans required superhuman efforts and was never entirely successful in so far as he tended to return to these ideas again and again. I am convinced that on many occasions Marshall imagined that I was in agreement with some of Winston's wilder ideas; it was not easy for me to explain how matters stood without disloyalty to Winston. On several occasions, I believe that Marshall thought that I was double crossing him. It was in this respect, amongst others, that Dill was such an invaluable help."

On 27 June, it was *"such a joy to be back with you."* On 28 June:
"The next week will be a difficult one, picking up threads and… dealing with the Middle East situation which is about as unhealthy as it can be. And I do not very well see how it will end. As far as I can judge from here, the trouble is due to our tanks being under armed as compared to the Germans. We have been too slow in getting the 6 pdr [pounder] and the 3" AA guns into tanks that are fit to be used out of this country."

Meanwhile, in north Africa, the British were in full retreat. By the end of June, Rommel's forces had advanced into Egypt and were closing in on the British defence line at El Alamein, less than 200 miles from Cairo.

On 30 June:
"[Churchill] informed me that he proposed starting for Cairo by

air on Sunday and that he wanted me to come with him! I told him that it would not be fair on Auk to descend on him unless situation had stabilized a little. I cannot imagine anything more trying than Winston descending on one in the middle of a serious battle!! However, I think he is prepared to accept the fact that the situation must have settled a little before he goes out. Personally, I am longing to go but not in company of PM at the present juncture with the fate of the Delta and Cairo in the balance."

In his Notes, "It is strange that I did not write more about my probable visit [to Egypt]. I had at that time reached the stage where I could no longer handle the situation in Cairo without going out to see for myself. This impending visit was so constantly in my thoughts that I may not ever have thought it necessary to refer to it in my diary."

On 1 July:
"At COS we had a difficult time concerned with possibility of establishing a western front. Russia, USA and the Press all clamouring for a 'Western Front' without thinking what it means or what its implications are!… Nobody stops to think what you can possibly do with some 6 divisions against a possible 20 to 30! PM is well aware of all the implications. And yet for all that we are likely to be forced to undergo all the handicaps of taking up the necessary shipping and sacrificing the required training in order to prepare for an operation which we are convinced is impracticable."

On the following day:
"Dined [at the] Dorchester to meet Eisenhower, the new American general who has come to replace Chaney [commander, European Theatre of Operations, United States Army]."

In his Notes, "[Eisenhower] certainly made no great impression on me… and if I had been told then of the future that lay in front of him, I should have refused to believe it."

On 3 July, Brookie was infuriated:

> "Brendan Bracken caught me and asked me to influence PM not to go to [Middle East] for the present and told me [Leo] Amery's son was coming over to try and induce him to go. I then went in and shortly afterwards a most objectionable young pup turned up who was Amery's son [23-year-old Julian Amery], just back from Cairo. He calmly said that he had landed this morning, that two things were necessary to secure the Middle East, first more equipment and secondly better morale... He considered therefore that the necessity for raising morale was paramount and that this could only be done by the PM flying out to Egypt!! The cheek of the young brute was almost more than I could bear. I cross questioned him as to what he based his deductions on and gathered that it was based on conversations with a few officers in the bar of Shepheard's Hotel, Cairo!"

In his Notes, he recanted a little, "I feel I was somewhat unkind about young Amery when I wrote my diary that evening! But I had been sorely tried by him that day with his attempts to get Winston to go out to the Middle East just when we were trying to stop him from going. In addition, his bumptious manner had annoyed me, sitting there and lecturing Winston and me on the morale of the Middle East force when all he had to base his deductions on were conversations in Shepheard's Hotel in Cairo".

On 6 July, Brookie flew to Northern Ireland to inspect American troops:

> "Went... to see Hartle, the USA general commanding the Southern Force. He was disappointing and had no grip whatever of the situation."

On 7 July, he watched an exercise:

> "It is evident that the USA troops have excellent material but that they require a great deal more training. Good fly back to [London]. Cabinet meeting at 5.30pm. A dreadful exhibition of amateur strategy by Cabinet ministers! Bevin quite at his worst and posing as an authority!

Eden and Cripps offering criticism as if they were leading authorities on strategy! PM unfortunately not in his usual form and unable to keep them in order. A most depressing and lamentable meeting."

On the same day, Sir Alexander Cadogan was noting, "Warned [Eden] of PM's idea of stopping preparations for 2 Front and telling Russians frankly. We can't do this. It will have bad effect. Besides we must be prepared in case there is a break, when we should want to slip on to the Continent without delay."[11] The armchair general's casual remark, 'slip on to the Continent', illustrated Brookie's point that everyone was 'clamouring for a Western Front without thinking what it means or what its implications are!' [1 July]. Cadogan did not attend the 'depressing and lamentable' 7 July cabinet meeting, but he referred to it in his 8 July entry: note the caustic one-liner from Churchill, "'Second Front' in Europe this year definitely off. President wants to do 'Gymnast'. I think that simply a dispersal of effort but if it will keep Russians going, may be worthwhile… Cabinet yesterday seems to have been very depressing. Chiefs of Staff have no ideas and oppose everything. PM said 'We'd better put an advertisement in the papers, asking for ideas'!"[12]

8 July saw the pressure on Brookie mounting:

"Another difficult COS discussing results of yesterday's Cabinet meeting and trying to tidy up this year's policy concerning possible offensives. Also heated debate between [Pound and Portal] on air support. At 12.30pm Cabinet meeting… at which PM ran down [Middle East] army in shocking way and criticized Auchinleck for not showing a more offensive spirit. I had an uphill task defending him and pointing out the difficulties of his present position. Also the fact that any rash move on his part at present would very quickly lose us Egypt. After being thoroughly unpleasant during the Cabinet meeting, with that astounding charm of his he came up to me afterwards and said to me 'I am sorry, Brookie, if I had to be unpleasant about Auchinleck and the Middle East!'… Then you came to lunch, and I forgot about all my worries."

On 9 July, the situation was descending into farce:

"At this morning's COS we had invited Andy McNaughton [commander, First Canadian Army, based in Britain] so as to give him the task of examining the possibility of capturing North Norway with the Canadian Corps! This was according to the PM's orders, it having been suggested by Attlee that with his more flexible and fertile brain he would find a way out where the Chiefs of Staff had failed! After lunch, I sent for [McNaughton]... and informed him privately how matters stood as I did not want him afterwards to imagine that we were suggesting that the Canadians should undertake an operation which we considered impracticable. Alexander turned up in the afternoon having landed home after his trip to Burma and the hard fighting he had there. He looks as if he requires some leave."

On the following day:

"5pm meeting with PM which lasted till 7.30pm. He was in a bad mood and meeting was not pleasant as we were discussing one of his pet schemes namely how it is that Middle East has 750,000 men on its ration strength and only produces 100,000 to fight Rommel!! Dill suffered from this in the past and he will never be convinced by the arguments!"

In his Notes, "In the middle of a Cabinet meeting, [Churchill] would turn to me and say: 'Pray explain, CIGS, how it is that in the ME 750,000 men always turn up for their pay and rations, but when it comes to fighting only 100,000 turn up!! Explain to us now exactly how the remaining 650,000 are occupied!' Not an easy answer to give in the middle of a Cabinet meeting."

11 July saw Churchill causing yet more problems:

"After lunch had difficulties with an unpleasant wire which the PM was insisting on sending to Auchinleck and which would have done no good. Pug Ismay had spent morning trying to stop him sending it without success!"

On 13 July, compare Eden's guile with Brookie's integrity:

"Cabinet meeting at 5.30pm at which PM abused [War Office] owing to the fact that Middle East reported proportion of Valentines [British tank] arrived in bad state. Finally, Defence Committee meeting at 10pm to arrive at final decision about Russia Convoy [Arctic convoy PQ17 was at the time suffering very heavy losses en route to Russia]… finally the meeting became unanimous, the PM gave the verdict against further continuance of convoys for the present. He then discussed alternative methods of helping Stalin and again returned to his attack on Norway. Pointing out how easy such an attack would be! Looked like working up to a storm at one time!!

Just as I was going, was called back owing to wire just received from Smuts [Jan Smuts, South African prime minister and field marshal], very disturbed about Court of Enquiry on surrender of Tobruk [the Tobruk garrison commander was a South African], as rumours had been spread that SA Commander of troops was a fifth columnist!! Eden then suggested that I should wire to Wilson that he should cook his Court of Enquiry to ensure this SA commander should be exonerated! I suggested that Court of Enquiry must report true verdict, this could be kept secret and dealt with by Government as they thought best. This was agreed to."

On 14 July:

"Another difficult COS with First Sea Lord asleep most of the time! In afternoon Selection Board at which Tim Pile [British general] attended. As he gets older, his face discloses more and more to the world his crookedness! He is a repulsive creature!"

On 15 July, he met Neil Ritchie, recently sacked as commander of the British Eighth Army:

"It was a sad meeting as I knew well how much he felt being pushed out of the 8th Army. However, after a bit of a talk he warmed up and was most interesting about his experiences.

At 7pm had to go round to 10 Downing Street… I told

[Churchill] that if he found that he could not go to the Middle East I ought to go out on my own to visit Gibraltar, Malta and Middle East. He agreed. We received news today that Marshall, King and Harry Hopkins are on their way to discuss future operations. It will be a queer party as Harry Hopkins is for operating in Africa, Marshall wants to operate in Europe and King is determined to strike in the Pacific!"

In his Notes, Brookie provided another example of his man-management skills, "Neil Ritchie had done me so wonderfully well in France during the fighting leading to Dunkirk, and I had grown so fond of him that I hated seeing him subjected to this serious reverse. I told him that I considered that he had been pushed on much too fast by Auchinleck, to be put in command of 8th Army in the field when he had never even commanded a division in action. I told him he must regain confidence in himself. To do this, he must go back to what he had done so efficiently before namely the command of a division at home. I told him that when he had regained confidence in himself, I would give him a corps. This is just what happened.

I had by then learned that if you wanted to get Winston's agreement to something, you might have to wait several days for a propitious moment. To ask at the wrong moment was to court disaster… I had been waiting for days, very precious days, to ask him to go to the ME on my own. I knew that the odds would be heavily against getting his sanction… Meanwhile, the situation in the ME was not improving, the Auk was suggesting giving the 8th Army to Corbett. It was essential that I should go out to see for myself what was really wrong."

Meanwhile, in Washington, opinion was growing that the British were resiling from their agreement to launch cross-Channel operations. Sensing the British were more interested in operating in the Mediterranean, the Americans were understandably concerned at the prospect of large numbers of their troops being transferred to Britain under the Bolero plan, only then to become unemployed and inactive. In early July, Marshall recommended to Roosevelt that in the absence of unqualified British commitment to cross-Channel operations, America should withdraw their agreement to the Germany First principle and concentrate its resources in the war against Japan. After overruling him, Roosevelt sent Hopkins, Marshall and King to London, armed with a presidential directive that if they could not persuade the British to agree to launch a cross-Channel operation before the end of the year, then they must find somewhere else for American troops to engage German forces in 1942.

On 17 July, note Brookie's view of the cross-Channel operations:
"Hopkins, Marshall and King… have come over as they are not satisfied that we are adhering sufficiently definitely to the plans for invading France in 1943, and if possible 1942. In my mind 1942 is dead off and without the slightest hope. 1943 must depend on what happens to Russia [by mid-July, the renewed German offensive in Russia was achieving considerable success]. If she breaks and is overrun there can be no invasion and we should then be prepared to go into North Africa instead. But Marshall seems to want some rigid form of plan that we are bound to adhere to in any case!"

In his Notes, "It was evident that if Russia cracked up the Germans could concentrate the bulk of their forces in France and make an invasion quite impossible. Under those circumstances our only hope would be to operate in Africa. But in any case from the moment I took over the job of CIGS I was convinced that the sequence of events should be: (a) liberate North Africa, (b) open up Mediterranean and score a million tons of shipping, (c) threaten Southern Europe by eliminating Italy, (d) then, and only then, if Russia is still holding, liberate France and invade Germany."

On 20 July:
"Troublesome COS with Mountbatten again assuming wild powers unto himself!
At 3pm we met Marshall and King and had long argument with them. Found both of them still hankering after an attack across Channel

this year to take pressure off Russia. They failed to realize that such an action could only lead to the loss of some 6 divisions without achieving any results! Next argument was that we should take advantage of German preoccupation with Russia to establish bridgehead for 1943 operation [i.e. establish a bridgehead in continental Europe in 1942 which could then be developed in 1943]. Had to convince them that there was no hope of such a bridgehead surviving the winter. Next discussed alternative operations in North Africa which they are not much in favour of, preferring the Pacific."

On 21 July, the chiefs of staff met Marshall and King again. Note the final paragraph which suggests Hopkins, who was in favour of 'operating in Africa' [15 July], was Roosevelt's mouthpiece on this trip and may have been undermining Marshall and King:

"Disappointing start! Found ourselves much where we had started yesterday... Except that Marshall admitted that he saw no opportunity of staging an offensive in Europe to aid Russians by September. He missed the point that by September the Russians might be past requiring assistance and that the weather at any rate at that season was such as to make cross-Channel operations practically impossible. We went on arguing for 2 hours, during which time King remained with a face like a Sphinx, and only one idea, i.e. to transfer operations to the Pacific.

At 11pm I had to go back to 10 Downing Street. Both Eden and Hopkins there, I was not allowed to join them for fear that Marshall and King should hear of it and feel that I had been briefed by Hopkins against them according to President's wishes!!"

22 July saw a further meeting with the Americans:

"They handed in written memorandum adhering to an attack on Cherbourg salient as the preliminary move for an attack in 1943. The memorandum drew attention to all the advantages but failed to recognize the main disadvantage that there was no hope of our still being in Cherbourg by next spring! I put all the disadvantages to them.

They did not return to the attack but stated that they would now have to put the matter up to the President and wished to see the PM first. I therefore fixed up for 3pm meeting with PM... You then came to lunch and it was such a joy and rest from my labours having a couple of hours with you. At 3pm... PM informed American chiefs that he was in agreement with opinion of his Chiefs of Staff and would put whole matter before War Cabinet at 5.30pm... I had no trouble convincing Cabinet who were unanimously against it. American Chiefs are therefore wiring to America and we are waiting for the next phase of our meeting."

Roosevelt's reply was immediate and amounted to a fait accompli for Marshall. On 23 July:

"My Birthday! 59! I don't feel like it!... PM wanted Chiefs of Staff to meet him at 3pm. Arrived there to be told... Roosevelt had wired back accepting fact that western front in 1942 was off. Also that he was in favour of attack in North Africa and was influencing his Chiefs in that direction.

Auchinleck started new attack day before yesterday and not very happy with progress he is making."

At the next meeting on 24 July:

"[The Americans] produced a paper containing almost everything we had asked them to agree to at the start... They all agreed to giving up immediate attack on Continent, to prepare plans for attack on North Africa to be carried out if re-entry into Europe was impossible next year [i.e. if the situation on the Russian front by September rendered a cross-Channel invasion in 1943 impracticable, then northwest Africa should be invaded as early as possible in 1942].

At 4.30pm we met PM and I put memorandum to him, he was delighted with it and passed it at once. At 5pm, Cabinet meeting first of all to discuss Stalin's reply to [our] stopping [Arctic] Convoy and [our] intimation that western front was not possible. It was an unpleasant reply! Then PM got me to put up our memorandum to the

Cabinet. From the start things went wrong! Anthony Eden and Cripps thought they saw a flaw in it, they began to argue about things they did not understand, others joined in and very soon we had one of those situations I have now seen frequently in the Cabinet where the real issue is completely lost in arguing out some detail which is misquoted and distorted in the discussion. I perspired heavily in my attempts to pull things straight and was engaged in heated arguments with Eden and Cripps with most of Cabinet taking sides. Bevin, John Anderson, Bruce and PM with me, Attlee, Oliver Lyttelton, Alexander against. In the end, I triumphed and had the memorandum passed without a word being altered. Any changes would have been fatal, the Americans have gone a long way to meet us... A very trying week, but it is satisfactory to think that we have got just what we wanted out of the USA Chiefs."

Earlier, 9 July, the Canadian commander, General McNaughton, had been instructed to examine Churchill's pet Norway operation. On 25 July:

"Saw Andy McNaughton... Found out that he was asking for 5 divisions, 20 squadrons and a large fleet! Was then sent for by PM who wanted to hear results of our morning meeting with Marshall and King. I told him that we had fixed up question of North Africa. USA to find Supreme Commander with British deputy. Under him two Task Force Commanders, one USA for Casablanca front, and one British for Oran front. I wanted Alexander for Task Force Commander. He wanted him to do both Deputy Supreme Commander and Task Force Commander! Had an hour's argument with him".

On 26 July, Brookie *"spent a lovely, peaceful Sunday only marred by one thought, namely that we were not to meet for 3 or 4 weeks owing to your journey to Cornwall and mine to Egypt".* It would have been marred even more if he knew what Sir Alexander Cadogan was recording that same day, *"In Egypt the Auk, after his good old 1916 battle of artillery barrage and infantry attack (!), seems to have been brought to a standstill! I wish de Gaulle were CIGS."*[13]

On 28 July:

> "PM in very depressed mood as result of Auk's second attack being repulsed. Pouring out questions as to why Auk could not have done this or that and never giving him the least credit for doing the right thing. He is quite heart-breaking to work for. It is very trying having to fight battles to defend the Auk when I am myself doubtful at times why on earth he does not act differently."

30 July illustrated the security risks of keeping a wartime diary:

> "Portal broke the news that Winston had decided to follow me at once to the Middle East! I was sent for by [Churchill]… and told that after I left him yesterday, he decided at dinner that he would fly out on Friday! Since then… wire from Ambassador in Moscow had been received suggesting visit from Winston to Stalin was advisable! He was therefore contemplating going on to Russia and wanted me to go with him!! All my plans upset.
>
> Call from PM to go to 10 Downing Street at 11.30. Kept there till 1am discussing details of his journey. He now starts on Saturday and arrives [Gibraltar] after me, disguised in a grey beard! He then flies direct to Cairo so that we arrive there same day. Proposal now is for us to meet Stalin at Astrakhan. Shall start new book tomorrow as I dare not risk being caught with this should we be caught or crash."

With Churchill and Brookie about to descend on them, British commanders in Cairo had good reason to be apprehensive.

Brookie as a toddler. He was "very dreamy and elusive, his eyes had a far-away heavenly look" according to his sister and as a young boy "he certainly showed no indication of the very masculine being he was going to become"

Taken c.1910. Brookie did not enjoy being photographed since he was a private man who was uncomfortable with publicity. On 21 July 1940, his first day as Commander-in-Chief of Home Forces, he recorded in his diary, "Had to suffer photographer and cine man during the morning"

Brookie, centre, aboard the Cambridgeshire in June 1940 after escaping from France for the second time in three weeks. "It is hard at times to retain the hopeful, confident exterior which is so essential to retain the confidence of those under one and to guard against their having any doubts as regards final success." 15 September 1940

Brookie looking immaculate during his Bumper training exercise in September/October 1941. To his right is Barney Charlesworth, Brookie's aide-de-camp, friend and flatmate. Charlesworth's death in February 1945 had a profound effect on him

Churchill and his principal ministers, late 1941. Back row (l to r), Sir Archibald Sinclair, A V Alexander, Lord Cranborne, Herbert Morrison, Lord Moyne, David Margesson, Brendan Bracken. Front row (l to r), Ernest Bevin, Lord Beaverbrook, Anthony Eden, Clement Attlee, Churchill, Sir John Anderson, Arthur Greenwood, Sir Kingsley Wood. Brookie was to develop a low opinion of politicians. Eden and Attlee were dismissed as Churchill's "Yes men" and "the more I see of Herbert Morrison, the more I despise him! If England is to be ruled by that type of man, then we are sunk for a certainty!" 31 July 1944

Brookie in the War Office in December 1941, shortly after taking up the position of Chief of the Imperial General Staff. "Today the papers published… my appointment as CIGS… now that I am stepping up onto the plateau land of my military career, the landscape looks cold, black and lonely with a ghastly responsibility hanging as a black thunder cloud over me." 19 November 1941

Charles de Gaulle, leader of the Free French Forces and head of the French Committee of National Liberation. Churchill produced one of his classic one-liners when he remarked of de Gaulle, "What can you do with a man who looks like a female llama surprised when bathing"

The calm and capable Benita, Brookie's second wife

(l to r), Brookie, Dudley Pound and Charles Portal. They were the professional heads of, respectively, the British Army, Royal Navy and Royal Air Force and the principal members of the British Chiefs of Staff Committee from December 1941. Pound was succeeded by Andrew Cunningham in October 1943

General George Marshall, United States Army chief of staff. "He is, I should think, a good general at raising armies and providing the necessary links between the military and political worlds. But his strategical ability does not impress me at all!!" 15 April 1942

Churchill and Brookie at Fort Jackson in America following the June 1942 Washington conference. To Brookie's right (in foreground) is Henry Stimson, American Secretary of War, looking distinctly colonial in appearance and George Marshall

The "foxy" president. Franklin D. Roosevelt

Cairo, August 1942. Back row (l to r), Arthur Tedder, Brookie, Vice-Admiral Harwood, Richard Casey. Front row (l to r), Jan Smuts, Churchill, Claude Auchinleck, Archie Wavell. Brookie saw his role as that of military chaperone to Churchill and he often positioned himself standing behind his political master when photographs were taken

(l to r) Harold Alexander and Bernard Montgomery. They were respectively appointed Commander-in-Chief, Middle East, and commander, British Eighth Army, during Brookie's visit to Egypt in August 1942.

Joseph Stalin. "A crafty, brilliant, realistic mind, devoid of any sense of human pity or kindness. Gives one almost an uncanny feeling to be in his presence. But undoubtedly a big and shrewd brain with clear cut views as to what he wants and expects to get." 23 August 1942

Brookie, P J Grigg, Secretary of State for War, and General Paget in the War Office

NINE

CIGS: August–September 1942

On 1 August, Brookie departed for Cairo:
"*After a doubtful 2 hours' sleep, called and given breakfast at 1.30am!! We then embarked and by 2am were off into the darkness. I did not sleep over well because plane was very noisy.*"

After a short stop in Gibraltar, Brookie flew on to Malta the same day. In his Notes, "For the next hop it was essential to reach Malta before dawn, otherwise there were chances of being shot down by Italian fighters. Dill and Eden on their way to Greece [in 1941] had missed the island, overshot it and had to turn back to find it only reaching it just in time."

On 2 August:
"*I slept on and off and was snoozing properly when I woke to find the plane bumping badly and thought something had gone wrong till I realized that we were landing in Malta in the dark! It was just before dawn… The destruction is inconceivable and reminds one of Ypres, Arras, Lens at their worst during last war.*"

After another overnight flight, Brookie reached Cairo in the early morning of 3 August:
"*Went over to GHQ after breakfast and had long talk with Corbett [Auchinleck's chief of staff]. The more I saw of him the less I thought of him – he is a very small man. At 5.30pm [Auchinleck]*

came over to Embassy and we had long interview with PM, after which [Churchill] called me in for further talks. He is fretting at the thought that there is to be no offensive till Sept 15th. I see already troublesome times ahead.

After dinner when I was dropping with sleepiness, PM again called me in and kept me up till 1.30am. Back to the same arguments that [Auchinleck] must come back to the command of the ME and leave 8th Army [Auchinleck had assumed direct command of 8th Army following Ritchie's removal]. Exactly what I have always told him from the start! Then argued strongly for Gott to take over whilst I know that Gott is very tired. Finally suggested that I should take over!!"

In his Notes, "One interview with [Corbett] was enough to size him up. He was... unfit for his job of [chief of staff] and totally unsuited for command of the 8th Army, an appointment which the Auk had suggested. Consequently, Corbett's selection reflected very unfavourably on the Auk's ability to select men.

Winston was already selecting Gott without having seen him personally. I knew Gott very well indeed and had the highest opinion of him... He was a brilliant commander, but he had been in the desert since before the beginning of the war and was beginning to feel the effects of it... I happened to know of a letter he had written to his wife in which he expressed feelings that pointed to the fact that he was tired. I did not feel therefore that Gott in his present state was the man to instil a new spirit of self-confidence in the 8th Army. It would require someone like Montgomery... At any rate, I wanted to see Gott for myself to find out how tired he was before putting him down definitely as unfit for the 8th Army.

Winston's suggestion that I should take over the 8th Army personally gave rise to the most desperate longings in my heart! I had tasted the thrill of commanding a formation in war whilst commanding 11 Corps in France. For sheer thrill and excitement, it stood in a category by itself and not to be compared to a staff appointment."

4 August began with a joint commanders-in-chief conference:

"We discussed the relative importance of Egypt as opposed to Abadan [the source of British oil supplies in Persia] and all agreed that the latter's importance was paramount. Then returned to Embassy... to have an hour with Smuts [South African prime minister]... He has a good opinion of the Auk but considers that he selects his subordinates badly and that several changes are desirable. Most of the changes he suggested coincided with my own views. He is the most delightful old man with a wonderfully clear brain.

Returned to GHQ for long discussion with the Auk. A most useful one. I fortunately found that he was in agreement as to the necessary changes, i.e.

(a) new commander for 8th Army, Montgomery
(b) new CGS to be selected vice Corbett
(c) Jumbo Wilson [commander, Ninth Army in Syria and Palestine] too old and to be replaced by Gott
(d) Quinan unsuitable for 10th Army, to be replaced by Anderson.

These changes should lead to improvements, but I must still pass them through the PM and there will be the difficulty. Came back to Embassy for large conference under PM... [who] cross questioned Auchinleck as to the probable date of his offensive. I could see that he did not approve of his replies!

After dinner, I was dragged off into the garden by PM to report results of my day's work. As I expected, my work was not approved of! Montgomery could not possibly arrive in time to hurry on the date of the attack! I told him no one else could. He then pressed for Gott, I told him I had discussed him with Auchinleck who did not consider him up to it and also that he was too tired. I then told him about the project to move Wilson as too old. He then said that I was failing to make use of the two best men: Gott and Wilson... he kept me arguing till 1am!! And we have got to get up at 4.45am tomorrow!!!"

In his Notes, Brookie acknowledged his misjudgment of Wilson, "The relative importance of Egypt as opposed to Abadan was a subject to which I had given a great deal of thought. All the motive power at sea, on land and in the air throughout the ME, Indian Ocean and India was entirely dependent on the oil from Abadan. If we lost this supply, it could not be made good from American resources owing to shortage of tankers and continuous losses of these ships through submarine action. If we lost the Persian oil, we inevitably lost Egypt, command of the Indian Ocean and endangered the whole India-Burma situation.

I felt some very serious doubts as to whether an Auk-Monty combination would work. I felt that the Auk would interfere too much with Monty, would ride him on too tight a rein and would consequently be liable to put him out of his stride. As I was very anxious to put Monty in command of the 8th Army, I felt this might necessitate moving the Auk to some other command.

I was well aware of [Jumbo Wilson's] exceptional ability but had heard… he was showing signs of ageing and had lost his drive. It is interesting to notice how I misjudged at that time the effect that age had had on him. He had become very large and fat and I thought that age was telling fast on him, slowing him up and reducing his value as a commander. I had been misinformed and should not have attached so much importance to rumours. I was totally wrong as I soon discovered and he was still capable of giving the most valuable service. Luckily, I discovered my mistake in time and made full use of him during the rest of the war. An exceptionally clear brain, a strong personality and an imperturbable character."

On the following day:

"I motored south to Gott's HQ and had a useful talk with him. There is no doubt that a rest home would do him a lot of good and I do not feel that he would yet be ready to take over the 8th Army. He requires more experience. It is a strange life that this army leads in the desert, but the men look fit and hard. I was much impressed by the beauty of the turquoise blue of the Mediterranean along the coast. This colour is caused by specially white sand along the coastline."

In his Notes, "[Gott] said, 'I think what is required out here is some new blood. I have tried most of my ideas on the Boche. We want someone with new ideas and plenty of confidence in them.' I knew Gott well enough to know that he would never talk about having 'tried most of his ideas' unless he was tired and had temporarily lost some of his drive. This confirmed my opinion that he was probably not the man to lead the 8th Army."

6 August was:

"One of the most difficult days of my life with momentous decisions to take as far as my own future and that of the war is concerned. Whilst I was dressing and practically naked, the PM suddenly burst into my room... and informed me that his thoughts were taking shape and that he would soon commit himself to paper!

When I went round... [Churchill] said he had decided to split the ME command in two. A Near East taking up to the [Suez] canal and a Middle East taking Syria, Palestine, Persia and Iraq. I argued with him that the Canal was an impossible boundary as both Palestine and Syria are based administratively on Egypt. He... then went on to say that he intended to remove the Auk to the Persia-Iraq Command as he had lost confidence in him. And he wanted me to take over the Near East Command with Montgomery as my 8th Army Commander! This made my heart race very fast!! He said he did not require an answer at once and that I could think it over if I wanted. However, I told him without waiting that I was quite certain that it would be a wrong move. I knew nothing about desert warfare and could never have time to grip hold of the show to my satisfaction before the necessity to attack became imperative.

Another point which I did not mention was that after working with the PM for close on 9 months, I do feel at last that I can exercise a limited amount of control on some of his activities and that at last he is beginning to take my advice. I feel therefore that, tempting as the offer is, by accepting it I should definitely be taking a course which would on the whole help the war the least. Finally, I could not bear the thought that Auchinleck might think that I had come out here on purpose to work myself into his shoes! PM was not pleased with this reply but accepted it well."

Churchill was, however, a man accustomed to getting his own way. Initially rebuffed, he tried again through a different medium. Brookie's 6 August entry continued:

"After lunch, Smuts asked if he could see me for a bit and we retired to a quiet room. He then started on the same story as the PM in the morning. Telling me what importance he attached to my taking it and what a wonderful future it would have for me if I succeeded in defeating Rommel. I repeated exactly what I had said to the PM. Thanked him for his kindness and told him that he did not really know me well enough to be so assured I should make a success of it. However, he replied that he knew I had taken a leading part in saving the BEF in France. At last I got him to agree that Alexander was a better selection than me. I have been giving it a great deal of thought all day and am quite convinced that my decision was a right one and that I can do more by remaining as CIGS.

Sent for by the PM to meet him and Smuts and read their final decision. The telegram was to the War Cabinet recommending a splitting of the Middle East into Near East and Middle East. Auk to vacate the former and take over the latter. Alexander to take over Near East, Gott to take over the 8th Army. Ramsden to leave, Quinan to leave, Corbett and Dorman-Smith also to go. Considering everything, this is perhaps the best solution. I accepted it."

Brookie elaborated in his Notes: "I had been offered the finest Command I could ever hope for and I had turned it down… I could not put the real reasons to Winston which were connected with the fact that, rightly or wrongly, I felt I could exercise some control over him… I knew by now the dangers to guard against. I had discovered the perils of his impetuous nature. I was now familiar with his method of suddenly arriving at some decision as it were by intuition without any kind of logical examination of the problem… I knew that it would take at least six months for any successor taking over from me to become as familiar as I was with him and his ways. During those six months, anything might happen. I would not suggest that I could exercise any real control over him; I never met anybody that could, but he had grown to have confidence in me and I had found that he was listening more and more to any advice that I gave him.

During the last nine months with Winston I had repeatedly longed to be my own master, to escape from the terrific burden of CIGS' work in war and to return to the open air again to exercise command in the field. And now I had had my chance to fulfil these wishes and I had turned down this chance. I knew my decision was a right one… but it fell far short of soothing the bitter despair that I felt that night… Looking back, I am certain that my decision, hard as it was, was the right one and that by remaining on as CIGS, I was able to render greater service to my country than if I had accepted the more attractive alternative. There is no doubt in my mind that Winston never realized what this decision cost me.

The split of the Middle East Command was one I had been pressing for some time but not for a boundary on the Suez Canal. Such a split was quite unsuitable [since]… strategically Syria, the Lebanon and Palestine formed part of Egypt's eastern flank of defence against any advance through the Caucasus or Turkey. The case of Iraq and Persia was quite different. There lay the oil, and consequently all the motive power for Middle East, Indian Ocean and India. Up to the present, as no threat had existed on this flank, both Iraq and Persia were the poor brethren in the Middle East family. The situation was now changing and the Germans were in the Caucasus… the oil was by far the more important strategic objective… These considerations had convinced me that Iraq and Persia must be detached from the Middle East and given a separate Commander whose sole preoccupation would be the security of the oil.

I had very serious misgivings concerning Gott's appointment in his tired state but was not at that time sufficiently convinced of the degree of this disadvantage to oppose the appointment. I may have been weak".

On 7 August:
"*I received the news that Gott had been killed this afternoon being*

shot down whilst flying back from Burg el Arab! A very hard blow coming on top of all the planning we had been doing. He was one of our linkpins! I do feel sorry for Mrs Gott. After dinner PM, Smuts and I had conference as to how the matter should be settled. Had some difficulty. PM rather in favour of Wilson. However, Smuts assisted me and telegram has now been sent off to Cabinet ordering Montgomery out to take command of 8th Army."

In his Notes, "It seemed almost like the hand of God suddenly appearing to set matters right where we had gone wrong. Looking back on those days with the knowledge of what occurred at Alamein and after it, I cannot but feel that the whole course of the War might have been altered if Gott had been in command of the Eighth Army... I do not think that he would have had the energy and vitality to stage and fight this battle as Monty did."

On 8 August:

"Jacob [Military Assistant Secretary to the War Cabinet] was then sent off with PM's letter to Auchinleck [removing him as Commander-in-Chief, Middle East and offering him the Iraq-Persia command] and instructed to bring back reply.

Result Auchinleck refuses new appointment and prefers retirement. He is I am sure wrong – the Iraq-Persian front is the one place where he might restore his reputation as active operations are more than probable. Back to Embassy again to receive a long lecture from PM with all his pet theories as to how essential it is for Alex to command both ME and 8th Army. I again had to give him a long lecture on the system of the chain of command in the Army! I fear that it did not sink much deeper than it has before!"

In his Notes, "I still think that [Auchinleck] was wrong not to accept the Iraq-Persian Command and although the Germans did not push through on this front it was the vital strategic point at that time. It would also have been a more 'soldierly' act to accept what he was offered in war, instead of behaving like an offended film star."

On the following day:

> "I received a message from the Auk that he had arrived at GHQ and wanted to see me before we went to PM... went round to GHQ where I found him in a highly stormy and rather unpleasant mood. He wanted to know what the decision had been based on and I had to explain mainly lack of confidence in him... After lunch, I had another interview with the Auk and again found him in an unpleasant mood. Later, [Alexander] and I had ¾ hour with Tedder [Commander-in-Chief, RAF Middle East Command] on the air aspect of the proposed new command. Tedder was astonishingly pig-headed and has fallen in my estimation. He is, I am afraid, only a small-brained man."

On 10 August:

> "[Telephone] call from Auk... Had to bite him back as he was apt to snarl, that kept him quiet. Then sent for Dick McCreery to congratulate him on being CGS and to give him a few words of advice. Next, Corbett to tell him that he would be relieved of his job. He asked to finish soldiering as he is tired and yet he is only 54! A poor specimen of a man."

On 11 August, Churchill and Brookie set off for Moscow for their meeting with Stalin. The purpose of the visit was to inform the Russians that no second front would be opened in Europe in 1942. Due to the size of the travelling party, two planes were required. In his Notes, "Our party was unnecessarily large, as Winston on these occasions loved to accumulate a large number of Generals, Admirals and Air Marshalls who were not much connected with the work on hand, but I think he felt it increased his dignity." The first stage of their journey took them to Tehran.

On 12 August, Brookie's plane developed problems after taking off from Tehran: in his Notes, "I had seen Winston's plane disappearing into the distance as it headed for Moscow whilst we turned back to Tehran! I did not like seeing him go off out of my sight without knowing how we were going to follow him." On the following day, he set off again for Moscow. In his Notes, "Our pilot was instructed to fly low... [and] hug the line of the coast to avoid any German fighters that might be about… This suited me admirably as we had a wonderful view of that strip of flat ground some 10 to 20 miles wide between the Caucasus and the Caspian which provides one of the main lines of advance from Russia into Persia. I was very anxious to see what defences were being erected by the Russians. I did not expect very much… I had, however, expected to find more than what I saw… A working party of about a hundred men and two general service horsed wagons were at work. Beyond that nothing to be seen, not a man, gun, lorry, tank or defence of any kind. In fact, the back door seemed wide open for the Germans to walk through for an attack… on the vital Middle East oil supplies of Persia and Iraq."

13 August saw another impeccable judgment, on this occasion Stalin:
"At 11pm we were due to go and meet Stalin in the Kremlin. It was very interesting meeting him and I was much impressed by his astuteness and his crafty cleverness. He is a realist, with little flattery about him and not looking for much flattery either… We remained there till about 1.45am when I was dropping with sleepiness having been up since 3.30am! The discussion ranged mainly round our inability to establish a Second Front and the fact that they cannot understand why we cannot do so.

I do not feel that this evening's meeting was on the whole a success and that it will do much towards drawing us much closer together. The two leaders, Churchill and Stalin, are poles apart as human beings and I cannot see a friendship between them, such as exists between Roosevelt and Winston. Stalin is a realist if ever there was one, facts only count with him, plans, hypotheses, future possibilities mean little to him, but he is ready to face facts even when unpleasant. Winston, on the other hand, never seems anxious to face an unpleasantness until forced to do so. He appealed to sentiments in Stalin which do not, I think, exist there. Altogether I felt we were not gaining much ground and were being accused of breaking our word, lack of courage to open a Second Front, only giving them equipment which we did not want.

Personally, I feel our policy with the Russians has been wrong from the very start, and as begun by Beaverbrook. We have bowed and scraped to them, done all we could for them and never asked them for a single fact or figure concerning their production, strength, dispositions, etc. As a result, they despise us and have no use for us except for what they can get out of us."

In his Notes: "We were shown into a sparsely furnished room of the Kremlin, which reminded me of a station waiting room… We were soon involved in heated discussions concerning Western Second Front and Winston had made it clear that such an offensive was not possible for the present but would be replaced by operations in North Africa. Stalin then began to turn on the heat and through the interpreter he passed a lot of abusive questions such as: 'When are you going to start fighting? Are you going to let us do all the work whilst you look on? Are you never going to start fighting? You will find it is not too bad if you once start!' The effect on Winston was magnetic. He crashed his fist down on the table and poured forth one of his wonderful spontaneous orations… Stalin stood up, sucking at his large bent pipe, and with a broad grin on his face stopped Winston's interpreter and sent back through his own: 'I do not understand what you are saying but, by God, I like your sentiment.'"

On 14 August, Stalin came in for further assessment:

"Anders the Polish general came to see me and we discussed the evacuation of the Polish forces from Russia.

At 9pm we proceeded to the Kremlin for the banquet which was held in one of the state rooms. I kept wandering back into the past and wondering what very different scenes this room must have witnessed in the days of the Tsars… From the beginning, vodka flowed freely and one's glass kept being filled up. The tables groaned under every description of hors d'oeuvres and fish, etc… The evening dragged slowly on, many members getting somewhat the worse for wear! I got so bored and so disgusted looking at food that I almost felt sick! There were 19 courses, and we only got up at 12.15am having been 3¼ hours at the table!

> [Stalin] is an outstanding man, that there is no doubt about, but not an attractive one. He has got an unpleasantly cold, crafty, dead face and whenever I look at him, I can imagine his sending people off to their doom without ever turning a hair. On the other hand, there is no doubt that he has a quick brain and a real grasp of the essentials of war."

In his Notes, "[Anders] had been sent back to Russia to extract the Polish prisoners captured by the Russians in their [1939] invasion of Poland, when cooperating with the Germans. When he came into my hotel sitting room, he beckoned to me to come and sit at a small table with him. He then pulled out his cigarette case and started tapping the table and speaking in a low voice. He said: 'As long as I keep tapping this table and talk like this, we cannot be overheard by all the microphones in this room!' I must confess that till then I had not realized that my sitting room was full of microphones. I learned to realize that all rooms in Moscow had ears! He said he was certain that [the Polish prisoners] were either being liquidated in one of the Siberian Convict Camps or that they had been murdered. It turned out that he was correct [the Soviet regime murdered some 22,000 Polish prisoners].

I was in dread of this banquet and shuddered at the idea of having to spend the evening dodging the effects of vodka... During the first hour we must have got through at least a dozen toasts. Luckily, I had a jug of water in front of me and when I was not being watched I filled up my glass with water instead of vodka."

On the following day:

> "We met Voroshilov and Shaposhnikov [both held the rank of Marshal of the Soviet Union]... for 2½ hours I argued against the possibility of establishing a Western Front in 1942. It was very uphill work as they had no intention of being convinced and hoped to convince us that we were wrong. As they have not got the vaguest conception of the conditions prevailing in France and England nor any real ideas of the implications of amphibious operations, it was a hopeless task from the start.

I had a talk with Shaposhnikov who looks terribly ill and worn out. He has been chief of staff since the start and is a sick man suffering from his heart or something. But he is very charming to talk to and I should think quite a good staff officer. Voroshilov is an attractive personality but the typical political general who owes his life now to his wits in the past.

There is no doubt that they are anxious to get all they can out of us but at the same time have no intention of giving us the smallest help of any kind. They are an astonishingly suspicious type of people and very difficult to arrive at that close cooperation in war which is essential… We have never really got down to discuss the main problems of the war or how we can best circumvent our common difficulties. We agree easily enough that these difficulties exist and must be overcome but since we approach them from diametrically opposed points of view, solutions are hard to find!

I went over… for a second meeting with Voroshilov to discuss the question of the defence of the Caucasus. He had now received permission from Stalin to discuss this point but was still as sticky as could be… He said that there were 25 Russian divisions in the Caucasus with corresponding tanks and air forces. This is the same figure as quoted by Stalin, but I am certain it is not the truth. I am leaving Moscow with no regrets! If Moscow represents Bolshevism, we must certainly look for something better. Even making allowance for war and its effect, the dejection, drabness and lack of any joie de vivre is most marked."

In his Notes: "Voroshilov's military knowledge was painfully limited, as exemplified by his questions, which were entirely childish… I gathered that Voroshilov's position alongside of Stalin was based more on personal friendship… I do not remember a single instance in which Stalin sought his advice in all our meetings. Shaposhnikov was a very different type… He had a well-trained military brain and his questions were far more to the point than those of Voroshilov.

I decided to test [Voroshilov's] veracity over the defences of the

Caucasus. I knew that he would not realize that I had flown up the west coast of the Caspian instead of following the east coast as Winston had done. I therefore began by asking him questions concerning the central passes [and]... then turned to the main approach route between the Caucasus and the Caspian. Here I drew him on and extracted out of him details of their strong lines of defence... A complete pack of lies from what I had been able to see for myself.

Thank heaven, amongst his many mistakes, Hitler lost a golden opportunity by carrying on with the desperate attacks against Stalingrad instead of directing Von Paulus towards Persia and the Middle East oil... he would have found the road leading to one of the greatest strategic prizes practically open and devoid of defences."

On 17 August, the British party returned to Cairo. Brookie enjoyed flying:

"*Another 4.30am rise and off by 6am. We had a wonderful fly back to Cairo averaging well over 200 miles per hour. I went up into the second pilot's seat after we had taken off and remained there till just before landing. We rose steadily to 15,000ft (height of Mont Blanc)... and then remained between 14 and 15 thousand feet up to avoid the bumps owing to heat off desert and hills... We struck the Dead Sea near its northern end... with beautiful visibility. I was able to see the whole Dead Sea from end to end, Jerusalem, Bethlehem and Hebron all at the same time. It was a thrilling sight.*

[Later, in Cairo] I hear from Alexander that [Auchinleck] has been very difficult... Monty I hear is settling down well and going great guns. I pray to God that the new Alexander-Monty combination will be a success, I can think of nothing better. The more I look back at our decision to get rid of Auchinleck, the more convinced I am that we are correct."

On 18 August:

"*Whilst dressing, the PM breezed in in his dressing gown and told me he had been thinking over the urgency of the attack against*

Rommel. He then started producing all the arguments that I have so frequently battled against for speeding up the date. I had to point out that it was exactly 2 days!! ago that [Alexander] had taken over and Monty arrived, and that there was a mess to be put right. I know that from now on I shall have a difficult time curbing his impatience. I then went round to GHQ to meet Archie [Wavell, Commander-in-Chief, India] and explain to him my latest plan. Namely: Iraq and Persia to be handed over at once to India from Middle East so as to free Alex of this responsibility... Archie Wavell agreed with me. Back to the Embassy to see Auchinleck... Did not look forward to this interview, but he was in a much more pleasant mood and the interview went off well. We parted on friendly terms.

I found that PM was evidently again toying with the idea of stopping on here till the 30th!! This is because there is an indication of a possible [German] attack on the 26th and he would like to be here for it!! I had to be as firm as I could with him and told him that he would put himself in an impossible position if he stopped on and would be accused of taking control."

On the next day, Churchill and Brookie visited Montgomery in the desert:

"Monty gave us an excellent appreciation of the situation and what he proposed to do if Rommel attacked... and also his plans in the event of his starting the offensive. He is in tremendous form, delighted at being sent out here and gave me a wonderful feeling of relief at having got him out here."

In his Notes, "Monty's performance that evening was one of the highlights of his military career. He had only been at the head of his Command for a few days and in that short spell he had toured the whole of his front, met all the senior Commanders, appreciated the tactical value of the various features and sized up admirably the value of all his subordinate Commanders. He knew that Rommel was expected to attack... showed us the alternatives open to Rommel... said he considered the first alternative the most likely one [Rommel did choose this alternative]. He explained how he would break up this attack... then drive Rommel back to his present front and no further.

He would then continue with his preparations for his own offensive... [and] would attack on the northern part of his front. It would... take him seven days to break through... I knew my Monty pretty well by then, but I must confess that I was dumbfounded by the rapidity with which he had grasped the situation facing him, the ability with which he had grasped the essentials, the clarity of his plans and, above all, his unbounded self-confidence – a self-confidence with which he inspired all those that he came into contact with."

On 20 August, Brookie and Churchill returned to Cairo:
"At 7pm conference on Iraq-Persia. Committee had sat and produced report on transfer to India. Still impossible to obtain decision from PM!! Usual Air Force difficulties and he will not face up to them. I pointed out that while we are talking, the Germans are walking through the Caucasus."

In his Notes, Brookie provided another insight into Churchill's personality, "The day had been a wonderful example of Winston's vitality. We had been called at 6am. He had started the day with a bathe in the sea; we had then spent a very strenuous day touring the front... Return to camp with another bathe, contrary to his doctor's orders. He was rolled over by the waves and came up upside down doing the 'V' sign with his legs! Then followed a drive to aerodrome and as soon as we had emplaned, he said "I am now going to sleep" and pulled out a bit of black velvet or cloth out of his pocket which he placed over his eyes. The effect was marvellous. He instantaneously went to sleep and never woke up till we had bumped halfway down the Heliopolis runway. Then followed a conference, dinner after which he kept me up till 2am... On our way up to bed he said, "Breakfast on the veranda at 8.30am as usual", which I agreed to and went off to bed dog-tired.

At 7.30am, I woke with my bed shaking and, on opening my eyes, saw [Churchill] standing at the end of my bed shaking it! I thought I had overslept and hurriedly looked at my watch. It was 7.30am. "Come and have breakfast with me," he said, to which I replied, "It is only 7.30; you said breakfast at 8.30." That did not affect him in the least and he continued, "I know but I am awake." I had one more attempt to gain a few more minutes' sleep and said, "Yes but I am not awake, I have not washed or shaved." It was useless, he replied "Never mind, neither have I. Come along, let's eat!" There he was at 7.30am after a long day in the desert, followed by a late night, far fresher than I was."

On 21 August:

"Remained on with PM to settle final details concerning formation of Iraq-Persia Command. Decided to hand it over to Jumbo Wilson to start it. I had sent for Jumbo and went out to probe him to find out whether he was prepared to take it on. He said he was delighted to do so. He is too old really for the job, but I see no alternative to letting him start the show [see 4 August Notes]. It is imperative that something should be done quickly as the Germans are pushing on into the Caucasus rapidly."

On the following day:

"I feel that during the last 3 weeks I have lived through a very full quota!... It has all been intensely interesting, but very hard work when the background of constant contact with Winston is taken into account! And yet nothing could have been kinder and more charming than he has been throughout this trip."

On 23 August, note his 'uncanny feeling':

"I am delighted that we came out as I could never have put matters right here from a distance. It has also been very interesting to meet men such as Smuts and Stalin. Such a contrast! Smuts I look upon as one of the biggest of nature's gentlemen I have ever seen. A wonderful clear grasp of all things coupled with the most exceptional charm. Interested in all matters and gifted with marvellous judgment. Stalin, on the other hand, a crafty, brilliant, realistic mind devoid of

any sense of human pity or kindness. Gives one almost an uncanny feeling to be in his presence. But undoubtedly a big and shrewd brain with clear-cut views as to what he wants and expects to get."

Before flying back to Britain, Brookie demonstrated his man-management skills in a letter which he wrote to the new commander of the Eighth Army,

> My dear Monty,
> Before leaving Egypt, I must just send you a short line to tell you how happy I am to feel that the Eighth Army is in your care. I have had a difficult time out here trying to get things in better shape and am leaving with a great feeling of satisfaction at the thought of Alex and you at the helm.
> You have wonderful prospects out here and I have the fullest confidence that you will make the most of them. You can rest assured that if there is anything I can do from my end to help, it will be done if it is possible.
> Look after yourself, don't work too hard, and may God give you all the help and assistance you may require. God bless you, and the best of luck to you in your great enterprise.
> Yours ever,
> Brookie[1]

24 August illustrated the risks of flying in the 1940s. Note the statistics:
"[As] we approached England... we ran into dirty weather, heavy cloud and electric storms. Wireless failed to function and we were therefore deprived of directions of locations... we struck the coast of Wales north of Pembroke. Most of us thought we were over Cornwall and mistook the Welsh mountains for Dartmoor!

I pray God that the decisions we arrived at may be correct and that they may bear fruit. As regards distance covered in the 3 weeks, I have flown 15,650 miles and have been in the air some 84 hours, the equivalent of 3½ days spent flying."

In his Notes, "This little, short prayer… was not just a figure of speech, it was a very real, deep-felt and agonized prayer written at a moment of considerable mental and physical exhaustion at the end of 3 most memorable weeks!"

In July, Britain and America had agreed that the invasion of north-west Africa, now renamed Operation Torch, should be commanded by an American, Eisenhower, and that the initial landings should be made by American forces in the belief this would minimise resistance from French forces. However, no agreement had been reached on either the invasion date or the landing sites. The British pushed for a date in October and argued in favour of landings at sites inside the Mediterranean on the north coast of Africa: in the words of the British planners, "We must have occupied the key points of Tunisia within 26 days of [the invasion fleets] passing Gibraltar and preferably within 14 days."[2] Those 'key points' were Bizerta and Tunis, both of which the British wanted to seize before the Germans were given an opportunity to occupy them.

In contrast, the Americans adopted a far more cautious approach, preferring a date in November and, initially, restricting the landings to Casablanca on the Atlantic coast. This caution stemmed from their concern that landing at sites on the north coast of Africa may result in their troops not only meeting stiffer resistance from the French but also becoming trapped inside the Mediterranean in the event of a hostile Spanish reaction or Gibraltar being seized by Germany. Two disadvantages of Casablanca were the powerful surf which made amphibious landings there even more hazardous than usual and, secondly, the distance between Casablanca and Tunis was over 1,000 miles and the road and rail links between the two were poor.

26 August saw Brookie back in the saddle:

"A difficult COS meeting trying to find out where we are with Torch operation, things have been going wrong lately and I am not at all happy at the time events have taken! For some reason landings at Casablanca have been abandoned, others of a doubtful nature

at Philippeville and Bone have been inserted. Now the PM steps in and sends a wire to the President settling Oct 14th as a definite date without reference to the COS. We had to have a second COS meeting at 6.30 at which I am afraid I was rather rude to all members of the COS including poor old Dudley Pound – but he is quite maddening and long past retirement."

29 August showed how operations in one theatre could have repercussions on other theatres:

"PM held conference to discuss North African enterprise in the light of latest USA message. Finally agreed that we should examine possibility of doing Casablanca, Oran and Algiers instead of Oran, Algiers and Bone. This is I think a much wiser plan and conforms much more to the USA outlook. The difficulty is that we shall require additional forces for it which can only be found by drawing on Pacific. This will not suit Admiral King. We shall have again to remind the Americans that Germany must remain our primary concern and that the defeat of Japan must take second place."

On 30 August, Rommel launched his expected attack at El Alamein. 31 August was:

"A bad day! Unsatisfactory COS at which I bit First Sea Lord [Dudley Pound] and felt depressed rest of day at having bitten a corpse!

Went [to] 12 Downing Street at 3.30 to discuss President's telegram, which was almost unintelligible… We argued with PM till about 5pm then went off for COS meeting… [and] decided that Americans must do Casablanca, Oran and Algiers. British to follow up… PM decided draft wire in accordance with our proposals… news from the Middle East that Rommel has started his attack!! Not much news of it yet."

In his Notes, "The first [two] lines of this day's diary must never be published. Had I known how ill Dudley Pound was at that time, I should of course never write like that."

1 September saw an interesting observation:

"*Visit from Sir Samuel Hoare [British ambassador in Madrid] on Spain and probable reactions [in Spain] to our re-entry into [northwest] Africa. He painted a gloomy picture. It is very hard to maintain one's determination to carry out an operation when everybody keeps pouring into one's ear all the awful dangers one is likely to meet. It takes far more moral courage than anyone would believe to stick to one's plan and to refuse to be diverted.*

Crerar [commander, 1st Canadian Corps, based in Britain] came to dinner and gave me a very good account of the Dieppe raid and of its difficulties. The casualties were undoubtedly far too heavy – to lose 2,700 men out of 5,000 on such an enterprise is too heavy a cost [the raid, organised by Mountbatten's Combined Operations and largely carried out by Canadian troops, was a disaster]."

On 3 September:

"*Arrived at COS to find that PM had just received President's reply to his wire! He had ordered us to meet him 10 Downing Street at 11am. This was quite useless as the President's wire required examining with experts to arrive at implications. He kept us waiting till 11.15 then talked round the subject till 11.45 when Attlee, Eden and Oliver Lyttelton turned up. We then talked more hot air and at last I obtained leave to withdraw COS to consider the matter and report at 5pm… The new plan contemplated an assault force of some 34,000 at Casablanca, where the surf will probably render a landing impossible, and only 10,000 at Algiers, which is the key to the whole front. We concluded that the Casablanca landing must be cut by some 10 to 12 thousand to make Algiers possible.*"

On 4 September:

"*Received rumours in the morning that the President would probably agree to our proposal except that he would only reduce the Casablanca attack by 5,000 instead of 10 to 12 thousand… Finally, I escaped and went home feeling very weary!*"

The next day was:

> "Spent resting at home. Call from Nye and [special despatch rider] with copies of telegram from President brought me up to date. 'Torch' is now again in full swing and most difficulties have been overcome for the present. Meanwhile news from Alexander continues to be good. Rommel continues to retire."

On 8 September:

> "Not much more news from Middle East. Rommel is now practically back to where he started from. My next trouble will now be to stop Winston from fussing Alex and Monty and egging them on to attack before they are ready. It is a regular disease that he suffers from. This frightful impatience to get an attack launched!"

On the following day:

> "Solitary tête-à-tête with Sikorski [see 3 February Notes]. He was charming as usual… PM sent for me to 10 Downing Street… to discuss the War Office and the Political Under Secretaries, Croft, Sandys [Churchill's son-in-law] and Henderson. He considers Grigg [Secretary of State for War] does not give them enough scope. This is all produced, I think, by Sandys' underhand working and his reporting to father-in-law. It is all a very unhappy situation, and one under which PJ Grigg may well be pushed out in the end. I should be very sorry and, sorrier still, if Sandys were to replace him!!! It would be a desperate situation."

In his Notes, "Poor Grigg at that time was in a very unhappy state… [Sandys] was giving Grigg the impression that he was playing the role of a cuckoo bird, working to push Grigg out of the nest so as to replace him! I cannot say that I had formed any personal affection for Sandys. I would not have trusted him very far!… Of the two there was no comparison. PJ had ten times the ability but what was infinitely more important he was just as straight as they make them. Had Sandys succeeded in replacing PJ, I should have had no alternative but to resign."

On 12 September:

"We discussed the likelihood of being able to carry out the North Africa attack before November 15 and, in that case, the desirability of trying to put in an extra convoy to Russia before it... PM, as usual, trying to get the last ounce out of the Naval forces and consequently wanting to run the convoy if possible.

Adam lunched with me and we discussed difficulties which exist between that objectionable specimen Duncan Sandys and PJ Grigg. It is gradually working to a climax. Sandys reports to PM that S of S is not giving him enough responsibility. PM then tackles Grigg who has no intention of pandering to Sandys and rightly so too. After lunch, long interview with Paget on organization of Army Air Force. Paget has been got at by [Sholto Douglas, RAF] and is prepared to sacrifice all the work we have done of late to secure suitable air forces for the army! Next Bovenschen came to discuss the Sandys-Grigg trouble! Wanted me to discuss with Army Councillors the suggested allocation of duties for Sandys and then put up proposal to S of S. I declined as I consider that this can only be done by S of S himself."

On 15 September:

"At 12.30 we went to meet the PM to discuss the possibility of capturing North Norway in January! He had promised something of this kind to Stalin in his last interview with him! Now he is trying to drive us into it. In my mind, it is quite impossible at the same time as the North African expedition. Shipping alone will make it impossible. He would not agree.

I then went to see Anthony Eden to discuss with him the difficulties S of S is having with [Sandys]. I told him that I feared Sandys was trying to replace S of S and that it would lead to chaos. Also told him that present situation would lead to S of S resigning if we did not watch it, and that we had already had 5!! Ss of S [Secretaries of State for War] since the war started and could not go on changing. He was very nice and promised to help."

In his Notes, "It was about this time that McNaughton [commander, First Canadian Army] arrived one morning to inform me that he had been invited to Chequers for the following weekend to discuss something about Norway. I told him all the back history and the fact that the operation had already been examined twice for Churchill and turned down each time as impracticable. I warned him that he might well now try to have the attack done by Canadian troops. On the following Monday, a limp-looking McNaughton walked into my room and literally poured himself into my armchair… He informed me that he had had a ghastly weekend, he had been kept up all hours of the morning… that [he] had agreed to examine the Trondheim operation… he hurriedly added that he had since sent a telegram to Mackenzie King [Canadian prime minister] asking him on no account to agree to the employment of the Canadian forces in any operations in Norway. This ended Winston's third attempt to have his own way! It did not mean that he relinquished the idea – far from it – he was always hankering after it and the sight of a Norwegian map alone was enough to start him off again.

The Griggs-Sandys situation had become so critical that I felt I must do something about it… I decided to consult Eden. He was most understanding and sympathetic and… said with a twinkle in his eye that he would do what he could with Winston short of accepting Sandys in the Foreign Office! I do not know what he did but… Sandys was moved away from the WO to the infinite relief of all of us."

On 17 September:

"*COS meeting mainly devoted to defeating Winston in his latest venture in North Norway!*"

19 September saw the start of four days' leave which Brookie spent grouse shooting:

"*On returning to the house, found message from PM that I was to go to nearest scrambler [secure telephone] for telephone conversation! This turned out to be at Catterick aerodrome, about 15 miles away. When I got there found bad line and I could only just hear the PM.*

All he wanted was to know what my reactions had been to a wire he had received from Alexander putting off date of attack."

When expanding in his Notes, Brookie provided a further insight into Churchill's personality, "When... he asked me what I thought of Alex's last message I replied, 'I have not seen it.' This met with grave disapproval and he replied, 'You have not seen it? Do you mean to say you are out of touch with the strategic situation?' I replied, 'I told you I was going grouse shooting today and I have not yet solved how I am to remain in touch with the strategic situation whilst in a grouse butt.' 'Well, what are you going to do about it now?' was his next answer, to which I replied, 'If you want to know what I think of Alex's wire, I shall have to have it sent up here tonight and shall let you know tomorrow.' Back came, 'How? Will you send a telegram? Have you got a cipher office with you?' My temper was now beginning to get worn and I replied, 'No I do not take a cipher officer to load for me when I go grouse shooting! I shall come back here tomorrow evening and continue this conversation with you on the scrambler when I have read Alex's wire.'"

On the following day:
 "Drove to Catterick aerodrome for another talk with PM. I had by then received a copy of the telegram and Alexander's reasons, which I thought were excellent. I told him so on telephone and thought he said that he agreed with me. As a matter of fact, he sent a wire to Alex, I discovered afterwards, trying to make him hurry up!"

By 23 September, Brookie was back in London:
 "Started COS work with much reluctance... PM more set than ever on North Norway campaign and now settled to send Andy McNaughton to Moscow! to start staff discussions with Stalin! After lunch, PM sent for me to discuss a reply wire he wanted to send to Alexander. I tried to stop him and told him that he was only letting Alex see that he was losing confidence in him which was a most disconcerting thing before a battle. He then started all his

worst arguments about generals only thinking of themselves and their reputations and never attacking unless matters were a certainty and never prepared to take risks… I had a very unpleasant ¾ hour! At 10pm I was sent for again, this time about tanks for Turkey. We had a hammer and tongs argument which ended on friendly terms."

24 September saw a good example of the 'spellbound and exasperated' Brookie:

"Another COS connected with the mission to Moscow to discuss North Norway attack! McNaughton now not for it! Apparently sent his staff officer by air to Canada to explain details of the attack! We had also further details from Joint Planners as to impossibility of carrying out [the attack] in Feb. We therefore prepared minute for PM on the subject to be sent to him with McNaughton's letter. After lunch… sent for by PM. He had just received telegram from Canadian PM who stated that he did not think it advisable to send McNaughton to Moscow and giving all the reasons for it! I asked him if he had yet seen McNaughton's letter. He said he had not and I told him the contents of it. He then became very worked up about the whole show and in the end was very pathetic. He said this machine of war with Russia at one end and America at the other was too cumbersome to run any war with. It was so much easier to do nothing! He could so easily sit around and wait for work to come to him. Nothing was harder than doing things and everybody did nothing but produce difficulties. He is a wonderful mixture, one never knows what mood he will be in next!"

In his Notes, "We then find him adopting the attitude that he was the only one trying to win the war, that he was the only one who produced any ideas, that he was quite alone in all his attempts, no one supported him. Indeed, instead of supporting him, all we did was provide and plan difficulties. Frequently in this oration he worked himself up into such a state from the woeful picture he had painted that tears streamed down his face! It was very difficult on those occasions not to be filled with sympathy for him when one realized the colossal burden he was bearing and the weight of responsibility he shouldered. On the other hand, if we had not checked some of his wild ideas, heaven knows where we should be now!"

On 25 September:

"I think [Churchill] is giving up the idea of the North Norway attack! At any rate we hope so, but he may well return to the attack."

Over the weekend of 26 and 27 September:

"Early start for home where I unfortunately found you all three the worse for wear for something you had eaten the previous evening. Also followed suit and apparently ate the remainder of that self same something with sad results!"

29 September saw the first of two security threats concerning Operation Torch:

"Alarming information of loss of a Catalina [flying boat] between Lisbon and Gibraltar and bodies washed up at Cadiz with letters in their pockets containing details of North African attack plans! Spent afternoon in the office battling with Portal's latest ideas for the policy of conduct of this war. Needless to say, it is based on bombing Germany at the expense of everything else."

In his Notes, "This instance stimulated the fertile brains of our Cover Plan Branch and led to Operation 'Mincemeat' when a dead gardener was converted into a marine officer and used by means of a submarine to convey false information to German agents in Spain."

On 30 September:

"Hawkes and Lennox from MI5 came to see me with reference to a conversation between Kenneth de Courcy and Raikes which they had intercepted on a concealed microphone in their room. It went very near having discovered all about the North African attack and evidently had been obtained from someone in possession of plans.

At 7pm had to go to 10 Downing St. Arrived there as de Gaulle *was coming out, having just attended a memorable meeting with PM and Foreign Sec where he had adopted a very high-handed attitude and the meeting had almost broken up in disorder!! We then discovered that he was due to broadcast at 8.15pm!! BBC had to be called up by the PM and instructed to cut off broadcast at once if he departed from script!"*

TEN

CIGS: October–December 1942

On 1 October:

> "Whilst I was sitting with the COS, I was sent for by PM. Found him in bed with Duff Cooper [in his Notes, "not both in bed!!"] who had just given him the intercepted conversation between Kenneth de Courcy and Raikes. To my horror, Duff Cooper said that he suspected [John] Kennedy (my DMO) had provided the information on secret operation which de Courcy referred to as having obtained from a 'Director of Plans'… went on to look up Kennedy, who is at present ill, in his flat. To my relief, he said that he had only met de Courcy once… on June 23rd and that so far as he could remember he had said nothing to him at that time. However, as June 23rd was before the operation discussed had even been planned, all was quite safe and Kennedy completely absolved."

On 2 October:

> "Our COS meeting was again mainly taken up with discussing plans for the future feeding of Malta. The present supplies finish about the middle of October. Future supplies will depend on success of Middle East offensive and North African venture. If neither succeeds, God knows how we shall keep Malta alive".

Sunday 4 October was *"a lovely day, spent in collecting apples"* at home. On the following day, future strategy was being addressed:

"Discussed long paper prepared by Joint Planners on operations in 1943 in which they had badly missed the salient points of next year's strategy… meeting at 10pm under the PM for Portal, Sinclair [Secretary of State for Air], PJ Grigg and self to discuss our Army Air support differences. Air Ministry have again gone back on their word. Having at last agreed to provide an Army Support Group they now propose to take it back again!! The meeting was a hopeless one at which Winston never began to understand what we were arguing about."

On 6 October:

"Returned to [War Office] for interview with Harker of MI5 about Kenneth de Courcy. He has now found out that the culprit is one Hannon of the [Special Operations Executive] who has been talking too freely."

On 7 October:

"[Visited] the institution engaged in assisting escapes of our prisoners… [and] interrogation of German prisoners under special means with microphones and 'stool pigeons'. A very well-run and interesting organization, under a live wire."

10 October saw another dry comment, on this occasion a self-deprecating one:

"Went to Staff College to give a talk on the world situation to [senior commanders] of Home Forces. Talked for 1½ hours but for all that most of them were still listening at the end!"

Four days later:

"Porter [gave] me Montgomery's plan for his attack on Rommel [forthcoming battle of El Alamein]."

In his Notes, "I had now received a detailed plan of Monty's attack and also probable date. He asked me to take every possible care that no details of this plan leaked out. As I had no confidence in Winston's ability to keep anything secret, I decided not to tell him".

On 15 October:

"Eisenhower came round to see me… [I wanted] to find out what the arrangements were for the command of American troops in England after [his] departure to Gibraltar [to take command of Operation Torch]. He tells me that Hartle will be in command which does not fill me with joy as I am certain that he is useless [on 6 July, Hartle 'had no grip whatever']!"

On 16 October:

"We again discussed various alternatives open to us in the event of Spain turning sour during [Torch] and decided to prepare special forces to deal with the various eventualities… Then lunched 10 Downing St. PM in the very best of form. After lunch I gave him the details of dates and plans for Middle East attack which had been brought back by Porter."

In his Notes, "I had come to the conclusion that I should not be able to hold Winston and that in his impatience he would wire out to the Middle East and upset Alex and Monty at this critical juncture. He was in a good mood that day so I thought that if I told him I could impress on him the absolute importance of secrecy."

On 19 October:

"At COS, arguments with Portal as regards expansion of Bomber Command at the expense of air forces operating with other services. Heated argument as usual, for once [Dudley Pound] sufficiently awake to support me. Cabinet at 5.30pm when I again approached Smuts and asked him to assist me with reference to Cunningham and Godwin-Austen [see 11 May]. I think that at last we may overcome Winston's objections to employing them again."

On 22 October, discussion returned to the subject of future strategy:

> "I had been expecting that Monty's attack might start last night. Probably will be tonight instead. A heated COS at which I had a hammer and tongs argument with Portal on the policy for the conduct of the war. He wants to devote all efforts to an intensive air bombardment of Germany on the basis that a decisive result can be obtained in this way. I am only prepared to look on the bombing of Germany as one of the many ways by which we shall bring Germany to her knees.
>
> At 12 noon we went round to see PM… I discovered that Winston, after giving me a solemn undertaking that he would not tell anybody what I had told him about details of impending ME attack, had calmly gone and told Eisenhower and Smith [Eisenhower's chief of staff]!! I rubbed his iniquity into him and he was very nice and repentant and said he would send for Eisenhower at once to impress necessity for secrecy on him. I then came back to [War Office] to find that PJ Grigg, the only other person I had told about it, had also gone and told [Deputy Director of Military Intelligence] and the Director of Public Relations!! It is absolutely fatal to tell any politician any secret, they are incapable of keeping it to themselves. Shall be lucky if I get through tonight without being called up by PM to ask how it is the ME attack has not started yet!"

In his Notes, "The newspaper reporter in [Churchill] was coming to the fore. News was not something to sit on, it must be cashed in on at once even if that cash only meant importance. He had no reason whatever to tell Eisenhower, this attack did not concern him in the least at that moment and what is more important, [Eisenhower's] HQ was conspicuously leaky as regards information and secrets at that time."

23 October saw:

> "Another long and difficult COS trying to arrive at agreement concerning future policy for the conduct of the war. We are getting a little nearer but the divergence between Portal's outlook and mine is still very great. He is convinced that Germany can be defeated by

bombing alone… Mountbatten's half-baked thoughts thrown into the discussion certainly don't assist.

This evening after dinner received call from War Office to say that Middle East attack had started! We are bound to have some desperately anxious moments as to what success is to be achieved. There are great possibilities and great dangers! It may be the turning point of the war, leading to further success combined with [Torch] or it may mean nothing. If it fails, I don't quite know how I shall bear it, I have pinned such hopes on these two offensives."

In his Notes, "So much depended on it… and I had such deep hopes of success that I wondered how I should face failure should this be necessary. I knew well that the next few days would mean acute agony of expectation. The anxiety of watching a battle from a distance is far worse than being mixed up in the middle of it and absorbed by running it."

25 October was a "quiet day at home with 3 calls by PM to find out how the Middle East battle was getting on." On 26 October:

"Long COS till 1.15 trying to knock our paper on future strategy into some shape. It is beginning at last to look a little better."

On 27 October:

"Another long COS meeting… [Dudley Pound] more sound asleep than ever! Dined with Churchills… [Winston] showed me answer he had written to PJ Grigg and told me he was prepared to accept his resignation… This was in answer to last letter PJ had sent in. The whole trouble emanated from Duncan Sandys [see 9 and 15 September]. I fear the worst as PJ is not gifted with overmuch tact in these matters. It will be a great mistake to have him out. He is, I think, the best S of S we have had for some time."

On 28 October:

"Interview with Craigie, late Ambassador in Tokyo. He was very interesting in his views about the Japanese, their powers of resistance."

By 29 October, the battle of El Alamein had been raging for almost six days:

> "I was presented with a telegram which PM wanted to send to Alexander! Not a pleasant one and brought about purely by the fact that Anthony Eden had come round late last night to have a drink with him and had shaken his confidence in Montgomery and Alexander and had given him the impression that the Middle East offensive was petering out!!... I was sent for by the PM and had to tell him fairly plainly what I thought of Anthony Eden's ability to judge a tactical situation at this distance!"

In his Notes, "When I went to see Winston… I was met by a flow of abuse of Monty. What was my Monty doing now, allowing the battle to peter out (Monty was always my Monty when he was out of favour!)… Why had he told us he would be through in seven days if all he intended to do was to fight a half-hearted battle? Had we not got a single general who could even win one single battle? When he stopped to regain his breath, I asked him what had suddenly influenced him to arrive at these conclusions. He said that Anthony Eden had been with him last night and that [Eden] was very worried with the course the battle was taking and that neither Monty nor Alex was gripping the situation and showing a true offensive spirit. The strain of the battle had had its effect on me… and my temper was on edge. I felt very angry with Eden and asked Winston why he consulted his Foreign Secretary when he wanted advice on strategic and tactical matters. He flared up and asked whether he was not entitled to consult whoever he wished! To which I replied he certainly could, provided he did not let those who knew little about military matters upset his equilibrium. He continued by stating that he… would hold a COS meeting under his Chairmanship at 12.30 to be attended by some of his colleagues [see 12 October 1941 Notes]."

His 29 October entry continued:

> "At 12.30 we had a COS meeting under PM attended by Smuts, Attlee, Eden and Oliver Lyttelton… Eden made a statement as to

his worst fears. I refuted this statement and the PM then turned to Smuts who (thank God) said, 'You are aware, Prime Minister, that I have had no opportunity of discussing this matter with the CIGS, but I am in entire agreement with all the opinions he has expressed!!' This settled the situation and I was very grateful to him."

Brookie elaborated in his Notes, "[Churchill]… asked [Eden] to express his views. To which Anthony said that he considered that Monty was allowing the battle to peter out, that he had done nothing for the last three days and that now he was withdrawing formations to the rear. I was then asked by Winston what my views were. I replied that the Foreign Secretary's view of the battle must have been very superficial if he had come to the conclusions he had just expressed. He had said that during 3 days Monty had done nothing; he had therefore evidently failed to observe that during that period Monty had withstood a series of determined counter-attacks delivered by Rommel, none of which had made any headway. During that period, Rommel had therefore suffered very heavy casualties, all of which played an important part in securing ultimate success in this battle… Had he not observed that Monty's attack had advanced the front several thousand yards, did he not remember this entailed a forward move of artillery and the establishment of new stocks of ammunition before another attack could be staged? Finally, the Foreign Secretary accused Monty of withdrawing formations. Had he forgotten that the fundamental principle of all strategy and tactics lay in immediately forming new reserves for the next blow? I then went on to say that I was satisfied with the course of the battle up to the present and that everything I saw convinced me that Monty was preparing for his next blow.

The flow of words from the mouth of that wonderful statesman [Smuts] was as if oil had been poured on the troubled waters! The temperamental film stars returned to their tasks – peace reigned in the dovecote! Personally however, I was far from being at peace. I had my own doubts and my own anxieties… but these had to be kept entirely to myself. On returning to my office, I paced up and down, suffering from a desperate feeling of loneliness. I had during that morning's discussion tried to maintain an exterior of complete confidence. It had worked, confidence had been restored... but there was still just the possibility that I was wrong and that Monty was beat. The loneliness of those moments of anxiety, when there is no one one can turn to, have to be lived through to realize their intense bitterness."

His 29 October entry concluded:

"Had to go to PM at 11.30pm... Referring to Middle East he said, 'Would you not like to have accepted the offer of Command I made to you and be out there now?' I said 'Yes' and meant it. And he said, 'Smuts told me your reasons and that you thought you could serve your country best by remaining with me and I am very grateful for this decision.'! This forged one more link between him and me! He is the most difficult man I have ever served with but thank God for having given me the opportunity of trying to serve such a man in a crisis such as the one this country is going through at present."

On 30 October:

"We finally finished off our policy for the conduct of the war in 1943 at this morning's COS. You and the children came to lunch and we went to the Academy to see my portrait by Birley. I am afraid it was a boring afternoon for Miss Pooks and Mr Ti, but I had two very deliciously clammy little hands grasping my hands tightly as we walked through the rooms and I could feel tiny electric impulses registered through those dear hands that they felt they were not in an altogether friendly atmosphere!"

Three days later, attention switched to the forthcoming Torch operation:

"Most of the first flight convoys have now all started and there is no going back. We had a memorable lunch at 10 Downing St... to bid Eisenhower and Clark [Eisenhower's deputy] farewell, for they are off tonight. During afternoon, wire arrived stating Monty had attacked again".

On the next day:

> "Made an early start and motored down to Andover to visit Airborne Division. Started with inspection of Border Regiment, a first class show... After lunch, inspected Parachute [Battalion], grand lot of men... Came away more convinced than ever that there is a great future for airborne forces. Whilst at lunch I was called up by DMI and informed of two recent intercepts of Rommel's messages to [German] GHQ and Hitler in which he practically stated that his army was faced with a desperate defeat from which he could extract only remnants!"

On 4 November:

> "Sent for by PM... to show me an intercept of Hitler saying to Rommel that he was to hold on and that his men should select between 'death and victory'. PM delighted. At 3.30pm he sent for me again to discuss prospect of ringing church bells. I implored him to wait a little longer... More good reports from Alex during the afternoon.
>
> The Middle East news has the making of the vast victory I have been praying and hoping for! A great deal depends on it as one of the main moves in this winter's campaign in North Africa. Success in Libya should put Spaniards and French in better frame of mind to make Torch a success. And if Torch succeeds we are beginning to stop losing this war and working towards winning it! However, after my visit to Cairo and the work I had done to put things straight, if we had failed again, I should have had little else to suggest beyond my relief by someone with fresh and new ideas! It is very encouraging at last to begin to see results from a year's hard labour."

On 5 November:

> "News continues to be good and Monty has now got the whole of Rommel's army on the move: as they are very short of both transport and petrol, he has chances of a tremendous haul. If only luck will be really kind to us! The [Torch] preparations are going well... a great deal of history will be written one way or another during the next week!"

On the next day:

> "We were called to a meeting under the PM to discuss most recent telegram from Sam Hoare [British ambassador to Spain] in which he stated a certain uneasiness prevailed in Madrid as to our probable future action. They knew a hammer was about to fall, but where? Middle East news continues to be excellent and chances of driving Rommel out of Africa are excellent."

On 7 November:

> "All preparations for North Africa proceeding according to plan and with very little interference. It is quite unbelievable that things should have gone so well up to date. It is a great gamble for a great stake and I pray God that it may come off!!"

8 November saw the start of Operation Torch. The Americans, who were leading Torch, had chosen a French general, Henri Giraud, to act as a figurehead in the operation in the belief that his involvement would discourage French forces from opposing the landings. Giraud was only informed late on 7 November that the landings in French north-west Africa were to start early the next day and that Eisenhower was supreme commander of the operation. Giraud regarded Eisenhower's appointment as an affront to his, and France's, prestige and demanded that he be appointed overall commander:

> "This morning the landings at Casablanca, Oran and Algiers, or rather in the vicinity of these places, were carried out almost like clockwork. They met, however, with considerable opposition in places and this opposition has not yet been overcome by any means [the landings at Algiers, the most easterly landing site, met the least resistance: in the event, the Americans' concern about landing troops inside the Mediterranean proved to be misplaced]. Giraud also turned sour and apparently refuses to play unless he is given supreme command of all forces and liberty to use them as he wishes. As one of his intentions appears to be to re-enter France with them, it is pretty clear that such a plan is for the present quite impossible.

However, I am afraid that his personal vanity may well upset some of our schemes!!"

On the following day:

"News of Middle East continues to be very good. That of [north-west] Africa on the whole good, but there are still some dangerous moments in the operation. A lot depends on the extent to which Giraud will succeed in swinging over the military opinion in North Africa. At any rate, Spain is keeping wonderfully quiet. Long Cabinet this evening… at which Winston revelled over our success! But did not give the Army quite the credit it deserved. However, he did finish up by suggesting that the Cabinet might congratulate the CIGS and the S of S for the fine performance put up by the Army."

In his Notes, "I think this is the only occasion on which he expressed publicly any appreciation or thanks for work I had done during the whole of the period I worked for him."

On 10 November:

"The fighting at Oran continued throughout the morning. This evening we received news that Darlan [commander, French forces in north-west Africa] had signed a separate peace with Clark and that he was issuing orders for fighting to stop throughout Africa! Meanwhile, the Germans have started to land forces in Tunisia by air… PM sent for me this evening while he was dressing for dinner to make certain we were taking all necessary steps to take advantage of this situation.

Lunched at Mansion House. PM made very good speech and in referring to good war news he said: 'This must not be considered as the end, it may possibly be the beginning of the end, but it is certainly the end of the beginning'!!"

Two days later:

"Germans are occupying [Vichy] France and Corsica fast and

endeavouring to build up a bridgehead in Tunisia. We are rushing troops over as fast as is possible to evict them out of it."

18 November saw Brookie concerned at the slow rate of progress in Africa:

"*Tunis advance progressing rather slowly and Monty delayed by administrative problems. On the other hand, from secret sources it is plain that Rommel is at present in a very bad state... By the time Monty has overcome his administrative difficulties, the situation will no longer be so rosy.*"

His 19 November entry was in similar vein:

"*COS mainly concerned with support Malta could be expected to give operations directed against Tunis. All dependent on convoy to Malta arriving safely... News from Tunisia rather sticky, only hope Andersen [commander, British First Army in north-west Africa] is pushing on sufficiently fast. Benghazi looks like being captured within next 24 hours.*"

On 20 November:

"*Malta convoy of 4 ships arrived safely, thank God. This puts the island safe again for a bit. Benghazi was also evacuated by Rommel. Attacks against Tunis and Bizerta not going quite as fast as I should like and reinforcements of Germans and Italians arriving fairly freely.*"

On 23 November:

"*Operations in Tunisia not going as fast as they should and on the other hand Monty's pursuit of Rommel badly delayed by weather. As a result, Rommel given more time than I like to re-establish himself.*"

On the next day:

"*Am still very worried with slow rate of progress in Tunisia, in spite of long report from Eisenhower.*"

In his Notes, "Eisenhower seemed to be unable to grasp [the] urgency of pushing on to Tunis before Germans built up their resistance there. It was a moment when bold and resolute action might have gathered great prizes. Eisenhower... was far too much immersed in the political aspects of the situation. He should have left his Deputy, Clark, to handle these and devoted himself to the tactical situation... It must be remembered that Eisenhower had never even commanded a battalion in action when he found himself commanding a group of Armies in North Africa. No wonder he was at a loss as to what to do [in Eisenhower's defence, Allied forces were hampered by serious supply and communication difficulties caused by the terrain, the distances they had to travel, the poor road and rail facilities and the seizure by the Germans of key airfields in Tunisia]... He learnt a lot during the War, but tactics, strategy and command were never his strong points. Where he shone was his ability to handle Allied forces, to treat them all with strict impartiality and to get the very best out of an inter-Allied force... As Supreme Commander, what he may have lacked in military ability, he greatly made up for by the charm of his personality."

29 November was "*a very happy, peaceful Sunday with you.*" 30 November saw the 'spellbound and exasperated' Brookie yet again matching his criticism of Churchill with a compliment, as he reflected on his first year as CIGS:

"*COS at which we examined most recent ideas of PM for a re-entry into the Continent in 1943 and where he is again trying to commit us to a definite plan of action. After lunch, interview with S of S on new proposed manpower cuts of PM. [Churchill] never faces realities, at one moment we are reducing our forces and the next we are invading the Continent with vast armies for which there is no hope of finding the shipping. He is quite incorrigible and I am quite exhausted! Cabinet from 5.30pm to 8pm and now we are off for another meeting with him from 10.30 to God knows when to discuss more ambitious and impossible plans for the reconquest of Burma!*

It is now 1am and I am just back from our meeting. With today, I complete my first year as CIGS, not that I think I shall complete a second one! Age or exhaustion will force me to relinquish the job before another year is finished. It has been quite the hardest year of my life, but a wonderful one in some ways to have lived through! I had only been in the saddle one week when Japan came into the war and by the end of the third week, I thought I was finished and that I could never compete with the job! Then disaster followed disaster and politicians under those circumstances are never easy people to handle. At times life was most unpleasant. The PM was desperately trying at times but with his wonderful qualities it is easy to forgive him all. A hard taskmaster, and the most difficult man to serve that I have ever met but it is worth all these difficulties to have the privilege to work with such a man. And now, at last the tide has begun to turn a little, probably only a temporary lull and many more troubles may be in store. But the recent successes have had a most heartening effect and I start a new year with great hopes for the future."

On 3 December, Churchill wrote a paper in which he advocated launching Operation Round-up, the cross-Channel invasion, in August or September 1943:

"COS meeting at which we were faced with a new paper written by the PM, again swinging back towards a western front during 1943!! After having repeatedly said that North Africa must act as a 'springboard' and not as a 'sofa' to future action [these two words are taken from Churchill's note to the chiefs of staff on 18 November]! After urging attacks on Sardinia and Sicily [Churchill did so in yet another note on 25 November], he is now swinging away from these for a possible invasion of France in 1943! 5.30pm meeting of COS with PM, Attlee, Eden, Leathers. Long harangue by the PM that army must in 1943 fight German army. However, after proving to him small forces that might be made available, [he was] inclined to agree that we might perhaps do more in the Mediterranean unless there are signs of great weakness in Germany."

In his Notes, "I was quite clear in my own mind that the moment for the opening of a Western Front had not yet come and would not present itself during 1943. I felt that we must stick to my original policy for the conduct of the War from which I had never departed. At that afternoon meeting... he said, 'You must not think that you can get off with your 'Sardines' [Sardinia and Sicily] in 1943; no, we must establish a Western Front and what is more, we promised Stalin we should do so when in Moscow.' To which I replied: 'No, we did not promise.' He then stopped and stared at me for a few seconds during which I think he remembered that if any promise was made, it was on that last evening when he went to say goodbye to Stalin and when I was not there!"

Four days later:

"*Situation in North Africa none too good. Eisenhower far too busy with political matters... Not paying enough attention to the Germans who are making far too much progress and will now take a great deal of dislodging out of Tunis and Bizerta!*"

On the next day:

"*Finished off COS fairly early. We were busy deciding line of action to adopt in order to influence the PM to abandon ideas of invasion of France in 1943 for more attractive prospects in the Mediterranean.*"

9 December saw an example of Brookie's analytical skills:

"*Clark Kerr, Ambassador in Moscow, came to see me... He corroborates all my worst fears, namely that we are going to have great difficulties in getting out of Winston's promise to Stalin, namely the establishment of a western front in 1943! Stalin seems to be banking on it and Clark Kerr fears a possible peace between Hitler and Stalin if we disappoint the latter. Personally, I cannot see such a settlement. Stalin is just beginning to get the better of the Boche and would only accept a settlement entailing restoration of old frontiers plus Baltic States... plus many guarantees... which Germany cannot give. On the German side, Germany cannot carry on without grain from Ukraine and oil from Caucasus plus oil from Rumania. I therefore feel that the danger of a peace between Russia and Germany is mainly useful propaganda from either side to secure their own ends!"*

When German forces restarted their offensive in Russia in mid-1942, they concentrated their operations in the south with moves against Stalingrad and the Caucasus. Initially, they made considerable progress but their attack on Stalingrad became bogged down in the devastated ruins of the city. On 19 November, Russian forces launched encircling counter-attacks on either side of Stalingrad and within five days had surrounded and trapped the German forces in what became known as the Stalingrad pocket: the encircled German forces finally surrendered at the end of January 1943. Stalingrad was a disaster for Germany and, taken in conjunction with Rommel's defeat in the desert and Operation Torch, marked the turning point in the War against Germany.

11 December illustrated the contrasting views held by Brookie and Marshall regarding future strategy. This difference in opinion was the root cause of many of the later disagreements:

"This evening received wire from Dill giving insight into Marshall's brain: apparently he considers we should close down operations in the Mediterranean once we have pushed Germans out [of north Africa] and then concentrate for preparing for re-entry into France, combined with a move through Turkey. I think he is wrong and that the Mediterranean gives us far better facilities for wearing out German forces, both land and air, and of withdrawing [German] strength from Russia."

On 15 December:

"We finished off our paper refuting PM's argument for a western front in France and pressing for a Mediterranean policy aiming at pushing Italy out of the war and Turkey into it. By these means, we aim at relieving the maximum possible pressure off Russia. Clark Kerr, the Ambassador in Moscow, gave us an hour on his views of Stalin's reactions if we do not start a western front in France. He argued that

such a course might well lead to Stalin making a separate peace with Hitler. I refuse to believe such a thing is possible and fail to see how any common agreement could ever be arrived at between them which would not irreparably lower the prestige of one or the other in the eyes of their own people. Casey [minister, resident in the Middle East – see 17 April] came and I had a long talk with him about the situation in the Middle East. Probed him as to the rumours of Monty being sticky in his pursuit."

In his Notes, "My enquiries from Casey concerning Monty were due to the fact that at that time there were many rumours afloat that Monty was far too sticky, that he only thought of his own reputation, would never take risks, played for certainties, etc. I discovered that these rumours emanated from the two airmen, Coningham and Tedder, who were responsible for the air support. I felt convinced that they were unjustified and wanted Casey's opinion. I found on several occasions in the war that airmen, entirely disconnected with the administrative problems of supply… and with the very vaguest of conceptions as to requirements of land tactics, were only too free in offering criticisms and accusing the Army of moving too slowly."

On 16 December, future strategy was settled:

"At 6pm we had a COS meeting with PM. Anthony Eden also there. All about policy for 1943. As the paper we put in went straight against Winston, who was pressing for a western front in France, whilst we pressed for amphibious operations in the Mediterranean, I feared the worst!! However, meeting went well from the start and I succeeded in swinging him round. I think he is now fairly safe, but I have still the Americans to convince first and then Stalin next!!"

On 18 December:

"Then interview with old [illegible] to tell him he was getting too old for the job, he took it very well, but the sort of interview that makes me almost sick before starting them!"

Three days later:

"During COS, discussed... report on Anderson [commander, British First Army in north-west Africa] which accused him of lack of cooperation with Commander of the Air. As a result, wrote letter to Anderson. Russian news excellent."

On 22 December:

"I had a very heated discussion in the COS lasting about an hour concerning the role and charter of Mountbatten [Chief of Combined Operations]. The suggestion being that he should command the naval forces for an invasion of France. Portal and Pug Ismay were supporting him and Dudley Pound and I were dead against it on the basis that his job is one of advisor and not of a commander. We finally shook the other two and went a long way towards making the point."

On the following day:

"Had to turn down a very bad plan for the capture of Sardinia worked out by Eisenhower. It never went beyond the landing on the beaches and failed to examine the operations required after the landing is completed. A typical bit of work of the Combined Operations department of Mountbatten's. Instructed Joint Planners to work out complete plan."

After three days' leave over Christmas, Brookie returned to work on 28 December. Note the length of his working day and his opinion of Eisenhower:

"Arrived [War Office] 9.10am, then continual rush till 10.30 studying situation on various fronts, reading all telegrams and looking through briefs for COS meeting. From 10.30 to 1.30pm long and difficult COS all on future strategy and preparing paper to bring the Americans to our way of thinking. From 2.45 to 5.30 continuous interviews then Cabinet till 7pm followed by ¾ hour with PM who now wants to pull Alexander out of Middle East to replace Anderson! at the same time giving Jumbo Wilson the Middle East command!

> *Rushed back to WO to pick up papers, home for dinner followed by 1 hour's hard work before going round to Defence Committee Meeting at 10pm. This lasted till midnight and was mainly filled up with an examination of Eisenhower's situation and his intention to put off attacks for 2 months! I am afraid that Eisenhower as a general is hopeless! He submerges himself in politics and neglects his military duties partly, I am afraid, because he knows little if anything about military matters. I don't like the situation in Tunisia at all!"*

On the next day:

> *"Another long COS at which we considered a telegram to Eisenhower and to Washington concerning Tunisia. Also our future strategy paper which we had had approved by Defence Committee last night and wish to send on to Washington in anticipation of our proposed meetings [forthcoming Casablanca conference]."*

On 30 December:

> *"Interview with Grasett to ask him to take on [a liaison role in the War Office for Allied forces]. I could see he was disappointed and, being one of my best friends, it was naturally a painful interview."*

New Year's Eve proved to be:

> *"A very unpleasant day with continuous annoyances and troubles. First, a ridiculous plan put up by Eisenhower for prosecution of war in Tunisia... [then] interview with Nosworthy who wanted to know why he was not being employed any further. A false idea of his value, consequently some difficulty in making him realize that he had reached his ceiling... From there to S of S and finally with PM for 6.30 to 8.15pm. Back to flat with lots of work after dinner. This is a dog's life!!"*

ELEVEN

CIGS: January–April 1943

The start of a new year prompted Brookie to reflect, yet again:

"*I cannot help glancing back at Jan 1 last year when I could see nothing but calamities ahead; Hong Kong gone, Singapore going, Java, etc. very doubtful, even Burma unsafe, would we be able to save India and Australia? Horrible doubts, horrible nightmares which grew larger and larger as the days went on till it felt as if the whole Empire was collapsing around my head. Wherever I looked, I could see nothing but trouble. Middle East began to crumble, Egypt was threatened. I felt Russia could never hold, Caucasus was bound to be penetrated and Abadan (our Achilles Heel) would be captured with the consequent collapse of Middle East, India, etc. After Russia's defeat, how were we to handle the German land and air forces liberated? England would be again bombarded, threat of invasion revived. Throughout it all, Cabinet Ministers' nerves would be more and more on edge and clear thinking would become more and more difficult.*

And now! We start 1943 under conditions I would never have dared to hope. Russia has held, Egypt for the present is safe. There is a hope of clearing North Africa of Germans in the near future. The Mediterranean may be partially opened. Malta is safe for the future. We can now work freely against Italy and Russia is scoring wonderful successes in Southern Russia. We are certain to have many setbacks to face, many troubles and many shattered hopes but, for all that, the horizon is infinitely brighter.

From a personal point of view life is also now a bit easier. With 13 months of this job behind me, I feel just a little more confident than I did in those awful early days when I felt completely lost and out of place. I pray God that He may go on giving me the help he has given me during the last year."

Three days later:

"Jacob [Military Assistant Secretary to War Cabinet] just back from North Africa came to COS with most recent news. Apparently, Clark [Eisenhower's deputy] has been creating trouble. Very ambitious and unscrupulous, has been egging on Giraud to state that French troops could not fight under British! So as to ensure that he should be given the Tunisian front! Account of Eisenhower's HQ and staff work are pretty shattering. High time I got out there and had a chance of looking around."

In his Notes, "The news about Clark was a bit of an eye-opener… there was no doubt that he was trying to discredit the British in the eyes of the French in order to obtain for himself the command of the Tunisian Front. Eisenhower evidently became aware of this manoeuvre and with his high quality of impartiality rid himself of Clark as his Deputy Commander and sent him back to command the reserve forces in Morocco. Through this action, he greatly rose in my estimation."

On the following day:

"Call from Winston at 7.15pm to vet our telegram to [British Joint Staff Mission in Washington] in which we criticise Eisenhower's strategy. However, we settled the matter by sending the wire and stating that we would await discussions in Casablanca before sending a message to Eisenhower."

On 6 January:

"A very trying COS, arguing about landing craft figures produced by Mountbatten and Dudley Pound. The former was, as usual,

confused in his facts and figures and the latter was as usual asleep! Chairmanship of the meeting was consequently difficult!! You came up for lunch which produced a very beautiful ray of sunshine in an otherwise very cloudy sky. All plans for the departure [to Casablanca] next Monday are progressing well. I foresee that I shall have a difficult time."

On 8 January:

"One of those awful COS meetings where Mountbatten and Dudley Pound drive me completely to desperation. The former is quite irresponsible, suffers from the most desperate illogical brain, always producing red herrings, the latter is asleep 90% of the time and the remaining 10% is none too sure what he is arguing about."

Five days later, Brookie was in Casablanca. One of the principal aims of the Anglo-American conference at Casablanca was to agree military strategy for 1943. Interestingly, when the conference was being planned, Roosevelt had remarked to Churchill, "I am sure that both of us want to avoid the delays which attended the determination on 'Torch' last July."[1] In advance of the conference, the British and the American chiefs of staff had set out their respective proposed strategies in separate papers, both of which are reproduced in the Appendix. The British paper, which clearly bore Brookie's fingerprints, was arguably superb: there was a compelling, overwhelming logic to their proposed strategy combined with a realism in their frank and insightful analysis of the combatant countries.

Many of the views in the British paper were echoed in the American paper. The key point of difference was the American proposal that operations in the Mediterranean should be scaled down once the Allies seized control of north Africa so that their resources could be concentrated on launching a cross-Channel invasion of western Europe in 1943: this was in direct conflict with the British proposal that further operations should be launched in the Mediterranean. Two other American proposals deserve mention, namely their wish to restate the strategy for the Pacific, which doubtless rang alarm bells with the British, and to conduct offensive operations in Burma. In the event, it was the British who were to emerge victorious from Casablanca.

On 13 January:
 "Dined with Marshall and had long talk with him after dinner. Am now tired and very sleepy but must prepare my address to the Combined Chiefs of Staff meeting [tomorrow] on the world situation and proposed policy."

The following day saw Brookie homing in on the American wish to restate the Pacific strategy. Note the British response to King's proposal:
 "I started off with a statement of about 1 hour giving our outlook on the present war situation and our opinion as to the future policy we should adopt. Marshall then followed on with a statement showing where they disagreed with our policy. We... met again at 2.30pm. I then asked them to explain their views as to the running of the Pacific. Admiral King then did so and it became clear at once that his idea was an 'all-out' war against Japan, instead of holding operations. He then proposed that 30 per cent of the war effort should be directed to the Pacific and 70 per cent to the rest. We pointed out that this was hardly a scientific way of approaching war strategy!"

On 15 January, Eisenhower turned up to deliver his situation report to the Combined Chiefs of Staff and was promptly flattened by Brookie:
 "Another hard day. Got up fairly early and by 8.45am started off for a walk with [John] Kennedy to look for birds. Delightful 1½ hours during which we saw goldfinch, stonechat, warblers... Then COS conference till 12 noon.
 After lunch Combined Chiefs of Staff meeting discussing... relative advantages between Western Front in France and Mediterranean amphibious operations. I made a long statement in favour of the latter which went down fairly well and remains to be argued further tomorrow. Eisenhower also came to give statement of operations in Tunisia. I had to criticize his operations against Sfax [Tunisian city]

which is in no way coordinated with either [British] 1st Army or 8th Army operations."

The next day saw Eisenhower's operational plans being changed:

"After breakfast, at 9.30 conference till 10.30 with Eisenhower and Alexander to coordinate the attacks on Tunisia. Eisenhower's previous plan was a real bad one which could only result in the various attacks being defeated in detail. As a result of our talk, a better plan was drawn up. From 10.30 to 1pm Combined Chiefs of Staff meeting at which I had again to put forward all the advantages of our proposed Mediterranean [strategy] and counter arguments in favour of a French front plan. It is a slow and tiring business which requires a lot of patience. They can't be pushed and hurried and must be made gradually to assimilate our proposed policy. From 3.30 to 5.15pm another Combined Chiefs of Staff meeting. I think we are beginning to make some progress.

[Dined] with General Patton, the American general who carried out the landing on the Morocco Front. A real fire-eater and a definite character. Now I am off to bed early for once and feeling dog-tired".

In his Notes, "The whole process was made all the more difficult by the fact… [Marshall] was unable to argue out a strategic situation and preferred to hedge and defer decisions until such time as he had to consult his assistants.

I had already heard of [Patton] but must confess that his swashbuckling personality exceeded my expectation. I did not form any high opinion of him nor had I any reason to alter this view. A dashing, courageous, wild and unbalanced leader, good for operations requiring thrust and push but at a loss in any operation requiring skill and judgment."

17 January was:

"A desperate day! We are further from obtaining agreement than we ever were! Started Combined Chiefs of Staff meeting to be told by Marshall that there was disagreement between the Joint Planners on the question of Burma. Then a long harangue again on the question of the Pacific from Marshall... Had a meeting between [British] Chiefs of Staff and our Joint Planners when we found that the main difficulty rested with the fact that the USA Joint Planners did not agree with Germany being the primary enemy and were wishing to defeat Japan first!!! We have therefore prepared a new paper for discussion tomorrow at which we must get this basic principle settled."

On 18 January, note Marshall's handover of authority to Brookie:
"From 10.30 to 1pm a very heated Combined Chiefs of Staff [CCS] meeting at which we seemed to be making no headway. King still evidently wrapped up in the war of the Pacific at the expense of everything else! However, immediately after lunch I sat down with Dill, I must confess without much hope, trying to define the line of our general agreement. In the middle Portal came in with a better paper. I therefore decided on the spur of the moment, and without a chance of seeing the First Sea Lord, to try to use this proposed policy as a bridge for our difficulties. We met again at 3pm and I produced our paper which was accepted with few alterations!!! I could hardly believe our luck.

[Later, at a meeting with Roosevelt and Churchill] Roosevelt asked me who had been acting as our Chairman and I told him that Marshall had been invited by us to perform that function. He then called on Marshall who at once asked me to expound the results of our meetings. It was a difficult moment... However, the statement went all right, was approved by the Americans and by the President and PM, receiving a full blessing. So, we have reached some results after all. Finished up the day by dining with Giraud [see 8 November 1942]... He is no politician, a very indifferent general but a high-principled gentleman with a whole-hearted desire to defeat the Germans."

In his Notes, "The fact that we had finally secured an agreement with the Americans... was for the greater part due to Dill. I cannot think why I did not give him credit for this in my diary... [After the morning CCS meeting] I was in despair... [and] said to Dill: 'It is no use, we shall never get agreement with them!' To which he replied: 'On the contrary, you have already got agreement to most of the points and it only remains to settle the rest. Let's come to your room after lunch and discuss it.' We sat on my bed... and he went through all the points on which we had agreement and then passed on to those where we were stuck, asking me how far I would go to get agreement. When I replied that I would not move an inch, he said 'Oh yes you will. You know that you must come to some agreement with the Americans and that you cannot bring the unsolved problem up to the Prime Minister and the President. You know as well as I do what a mess they would make of it!' He then put up a few suggestions for agreement and asked me if I would agree to his discussing these with Marshall. I had such implicit trust in his ability and integrity that I agreed. At this juncture, Portal arrived with his proposed plan for seeking agreement which was somewhat similar to some of Dill's suggestions and we decided to adopt it.

Poor Giraud. He was an attractive personality with great charm but the very wildest ideas as to what was possible militarily... We had at that time a strange set-up in North Africa. A C-in-C deficient of experience and of limited ability in the shape of Eisenhower and three possible French leaders, Darlan who had ability but no integrity, Giraud who had charm but no ability and de Gaulle who had the mentality of a dictator combined with a most objectionable personality!"

On 20 January, Brookie's remarks about Marshall are revealing:
"We had a Combined Chiefs of Staff meeting at which we... thrashed out the system of command in Tunisia after arrival of [Montgomery's] Eighth Army, deciding that it must then be transferred to Eisenhower's command. In order to assist in the control and coordination of the [British] First and Eighth Armies and the French and Americans in Tunisia, Alexander to become Eisenhower's deputy. Finally, another walk with Kennedy during which we added three new specimens to our finds in the shape of a wimbrel, sandpiper and yellow wagtail.

The back of the work here is broken and thank God for it!... Now we have got practically all we hoped to get when we came here... Marshall has got practically no strategic vision, his thoughts revolve round the creation of forces and not on their employment. He arrived here without a single real strategic concept, he has initiated nothing in the policy for the future conduct of the war. His part has been that of somewhat clumsy criticism of the plans we put forward. King, on the other hand, is a shrewd and somewhat swollen-headed individual... He does not approach the problems with a worldwide war point of view but, instead, with one biased entirely in favour of the Pacific."

In his Notes, he elaborated on the appointment of Alexander as Eisenhower's deputy. This is the occasion when, as mentioned in Chapter 7, Brookie freely admitted to scheming against the Americans, the reason being the slow progress in north-west Africa under Eisenhower's leadership, "Centralized command was essential to coordinate the actions of the [British] First and Eighth Armies and the American and French forces; but who was to be placed in this responsible position? From many points of view, it was desirable to hand this command over to the Americans but unfortunately up to now Eisenhower certainly did not seem to possess the basic qualities required from such a commander. He had neither the experience nor the tactical and strategical experience required for such a task. By bringing Alexander over from the Middle East and appointing him as Deputy to Eisenhower, we were carrying out a move which could not help flattering and pleasing the Americans in so far as we were placing our senior and experienced commander to function under their commander who had no war experience. Such a plan was consequently quite acceptable to them and they did not at the time fully appreciate the underlying intentions. We were pushing Eisenhower up into the stratosphere and rarified atmosphere of a Supreme Commander where he would be free to devote his time to the political and inter-allied problems whilst we inserted under him one of our own commanders to deal with the military situations and to restore the necessary drive and coordination which had been so seriously lacking of late!"

21 January saw some astute observations, especially the one about 'advice'. This entry had echoes of his 1 September 1942 entry:

"Spent rest of evening preparing for a [British] Chiefs of Staff meeting after dinner… There we had long and protracted arguments as to the relative advantages of Sardinia as opposed to Sicily as an objective. There are a thousand different factors connected with this problem. In my own mind there is not the least doubt that Sicily should be selected but… the majority of opinion is hardening against me. When an operation has finally been completed, it all looks so easy but so few people ever realize the infinite difficulties of maintaining an object or a plan and refusing to be driven off it by other people for a thousand good reasons! A good plan pressed through is better than many ideal ones which are continually changing. Advice without responsibility is easy to give. This is the most exhausting job, trying to keep the ship of war on a straight course despite all the contrary winds that blow is a superhuman job!"

In his Notes, Brookie illustrated his forcefulness, determination and resolve, "We had had many debates on the relative advantages of Sardinia and Sicily… [and] I had obtained general agreement on Sicily. All my arguments with Marshall had been based on the invasion of Sicily and I had obtained his agreement. And now suddenly the [British] Joint Planning Staff reappeared on the scene with a strong preference for Sardinia and expressing most serious doubts about our ability to take on the Sicilian operation! They had carried with them Mounbatten who never had any very decided opinions of his own. Peter Portal and Pug Ismay were beginning to waver… I had a three hours' hammer and tongs battle to keep the team together and to stop it from wavering. I told them that I flatly refused to go back to the American Chiefs of Staff and tell them that we did not know our own minds and that, instead of Sicily, we now wanted to invade Sardinia. I told them that such a step would irrevocably shake their confidence in our judgement. What is more, I told them frankly that I disagreed with them entirely and adhered to our original decision to invade Sicily and would not go back on it."

On the following day:

> "[The Combined Chiefs of Staff meeting] went off far better than I had hoped and the determination to proceed with our plans for Sicily were confirmed... This was really the culmination of all my efforts. I wanted first to ensure that Germany should continue to be regarded as our primary enemy and that the defeat of Japan must come after that of Germany. Secondly that for the present Germany can best be attacked through the medium of Italy in the Mediterranean and thirdly that this can best be achieved with a policy directed against Sicily. All these points have been secured... It has been quite the hardest 10 days I have had".

On 23 January, note his remark about the Torch landings:

> "We motored out to Fedala [village north of Casablanca], the site of one of the American landings. We collected an American Colonel Ratlye to come with us who had actually taken part in this landing. It was most interesting and quite evident that if the French had put up any real resistance, the landing could not have been carried out.
>
> At 5.30pm, we attended meeting with President and PM in the chair. We were congratulated by both of them on the results of our work and informed that we had produced the most complete strategic plan for a world-wide war that had ever been conceived, and far exceeding the accomplishments of the last war... I am convinced that this meeting has achieved a great deal. It has brought us all much closer together and helped us to understand each other's difficulties in a way which we could never have done at a distance."

In his Notes, "The meeting had drawn us far closer together, but we were soon to discover that as soon as we parted we began to drift away from each other... We found that it was essential to have frequent [CCS] meetings".

Roosevelt and Churchill's statement that they 'had produced the most complete plan for a world-wide war' is questionable. There was, arguably, a flaw in the decisions made at Casablanca, namely no agreement had been reached as to what operations should follow the invasion of Sicily.

John Kennedy recorded that the outcome of the Casablanca conference was largely due to Brookie's "personality and drive".[2] According to Ian Jacob, the Americans "were a bit uncertain about CIGS… I think CIGS's extremely definite views, ultra swift speech and, at times, impatience made them keep wondering whether he was not putting something over on them. Nevertheless, I personally thought CIGS handled the conference on the whole remarkably well. He certainly put his back into it and was exhausted by the finish[3]… We had great fun over the CIGS whose birdlike aspect and fast clipped speech lent themselves to caricature. I have never met a man who so tumbles over himself in speaking. He is incapable of reading aloud intelligibly. He cannot make his brain move slowly enough to fit his speech or his reading, especially when his interest is strongly engaged."[4]

On 24 January, Brookie was in Marrakesh:

"I spent a real peaceful afternoon looking for birds in the lovely garden of the hotel and found several very interesting specimens. It is great fun identifying the European specimens in the form of some sub-species with minor variations."

The next fortnight was spent by Churchill and Brookie visiting Cairo, Turkey, Cyprus, Tripoli and Algiers. In the early morning of 26 January, they arrived at the British Embassy in Cairo. In his Notes, "Winston… turned to Jacqueline [British ambassador's wife] and asked her if breakfast was ready. She assured him that it was and led him to the dining room where she offered him a cup of tea. This offer was not at all acceptable and he asked for a glass of white wine! A tumbler was brought which he drained in one go and then licked his lips, turned to Jacqueline and said 'Ah! That is good but you know I have already had two whiskies and soda and 2 cigars this morning.'!! It was then only shortly after 7.30am. We had travelled all night in poor comfort covering some 2,300 miles in a flight of over 11 hours… and there he was, as fresh as paint, drinking white wine on top of two previous whiskies and 2 cigars!!"

On 27 January:

> "Being back here [in Cairo] reminds me the whole time of that nightmare of a first week last August with all the unpleasantness of pushing Auchinleck out and reconstituting the command and staff of the Middle East. Thank heaven that is all over now and this visit is consequently much more pleasant."

Three days later, Churchill and Brookie were in Turkey meeting President Inonu and Field Marshal Cakmak, their aim being to persuade Turkey to enter the War. On 1 February:

> "I never thought that we should make such headway with the Turks. Some of my wild dreams of bringing Turkey along with us no longer look quite so wild!"

In the event, Turkey never did enter the War: as Brookie remarked in his Notes, "My 'wild dreams' about Turkey unfortunately remained wild dreams!"

4 February saw Churchill and Brookie in Tripoli, inspecting Montgomery's troops:

> "The last time we had seen [the 51st Division] was... just after their arrival in the Middle East. Then they were still pink and white, now they were bronzed warriors of many battles and of a victorious advance. I have seldom seen a finer body of men or one that looked prouder of being soldiers... We then took up our position on a prepared stand and the whole Division marched past with a bagpipe band playing. It was quite one of the most impressive sights I have ever seen."

In his Notes, "As I stood alongside of Winston watching the Division march past... I felt a large lump rise in my throat and a tear run down my face. I looked round at Winston and saw several tears on his face from which I knew that he was being stirred by the self-same feelings that were causing such upheaval in me. It was partly due to the fact that the transformation of these men from their raw pink and white appearance… to their bronzed war-hewn countenances provided a tangible and visible sign of the turn of the tide of war."

On 7 February, Brookie returned to Britain. Note his purposefulness:

"We arrived in London where to my great joy you met me. I had finished a journey of some 10,200 miles which had been full of interest and had resulted in agreements with Americans and Turks far above anything I had hoped for. In the last two years, I have flown just under 55,000 miles!! I now foresee some hard work ahead to convert some of the paperwork of the last 3 weeks into facts and actions."

Three days later:

"At this morning's COS we struggled with attempts to put date of attack on Sicily further into June [i.e. bring it forward]. Both President and PM hankering after this, personally I feel we are running grave risks of wrecking the whole show by trying to rush it… Harry Crerar [commander, 1st Canadian Corps] to dinner and a long harangue from him as to the necessity of getting some Canadians fighting soon for Imperial and political reasons. I fully see his point and his difficulties – I wish he could see mine and all their complexities!!!"

In his Notes, "I had to remind him that the main factor that had up to date militated against their use in Africa was the stipulation made by the Canadian Government that the Canadian Army must not be split up and must only be used as a whole… Crerar realized this concept must be broken down".

On 17 February:

"At this morning's COS we had Andrews, the new American General… to discuss the flow of American reinforcements into this country to build up an American force. Something has gone wrong with our Casablanca agreement and the flow has not started at all.

Then General d'Astier de la Vigerie, de Gaulle's second string.

He wanted more planes to drop arms in France, I told him what I thought of the French lack of realization of the true situation and of their failure to get together to fight Germany instead of squabbling amongst themselves… Then Exham just back from Moscow… He corroborated all I knew as to the Russian attitude and their desire to get as much as they could and give as little back as possible."

18 February saw an accurate forecast:

"Bertie Ramsay [commander, Eastern Naval Task Force] just back from North Africa came to our COS meeting and gave us the most recent information about the planning side of the Sicilian operations. Evidently, Eisenhower does not think he can possibly undertake the operation before the July moon in spite of the pressure that is being applied to him to do it in June. In any case, after the recent defeat he has suffered in Tunisia [at Kasserine Pass], I doubt very much whether he can clear Tunisia of Germans before May at the very earliest, if even then!"

On 19 February:

"A long COS meeting at which Dickie Mountbatten gave me a heap of trouble with a proposed attack on the Channel Islands which was not in its proper strategical setting and tactically quite adrift."

21 February saw an example of Brookie's 'abrupt efficiency'. There was a noticeable sharpness in some of his entries during this period:

"Quietly at home but spoilt by bad news from Tunisia. I am afraid the American troops will take a great deal more training before they will be any use and that Andersen [commander, British First Army] is not much good! Sent wire to Alex telling him to get rid of him if he thinks he is no good."

In his Notes, "I had formed a high opinion of [Anderson's] fighting ability in France before Dunkirk but felt that he was not living up to that opinion. From a distance, it was hard to judge".

On 22 February:

> "Cabinet at 6pm, peevish and full of questions about Tunisia… I am not at all happy about Tunisia and very doubtful if Alexander is man enough to pull it straight!"

Two days later:

> "Whilst taking my midday exercise in the Park I ran into Hore-Belisha [former Secretary of State for War]! Looking more greasy and objectionable than ever, he insisted on walking with me which annoyed me as I did not want to talk to him and wanted to look for the scaup duck on the lake".

On the following day:

> "Am very worried by way in which Americans are failing to live up to our Casablanca agreements. They are entirely breaking down over promises of American divisions to arrive in this country."

26 February saw Brookie simultaneously handing out sympathy, support – and a ticking off:

> "I had to attack Portal this morning on the paucity of bomber squadrons with the 1st Army in Tunisia. But unfortunately with the usual results!... After lunch, had interview with Browning [commander, 1st Airborne Division], found he had badly smashed himself up in a bad glider landing! Looked ill, wanted rest. Told him he must take full fortnight's leave at least. Then told him off for causing trouble by writing letters to politicians, he took it very well."

On 1 March:

> "COS mainly concerned with shipping situation… Marshall is quite hopeless… He now proposes to waste shipping equipping French forces which can play no part in the strategy of 1943."

And on 2 March:

> "A long and difficult COS on shipping… we cannot find the

shipping for all our enterprises. Some centralized Shipping Control Board handling the globular shipping is essential."

On 4 March:

"I was expecting an attack by Rommel on Montgomery today. But so far no news about it... Then had to inform Martel that he was for Moscow [as head of the British Military Mission] which he did not appreciate very much!"

On 7 March, he attended a Home Forces exercise:

"Started by motoring to Godalming to see Andy McNaughton commanding Canadian Army and proving my worst fears that he is quite incompetent to command an army! He does not know how to begin the job and was tying up his forces into the most awful muddle. Then went to Newbury to see Crerar and his Corps HQ, a real good show. He has improved that Corps out of all recognition."

Three days later:

"Very heated argument at COS with Mountbatten who was again putting up wild proposals disconnected with his direct duties. He will insist on doing work of Force Commanders and does it infernally badly! Both Portal and I were driven to distraction by him."

Major General Percy 'Hobo' Hobart, a military engineer, was one of the British radicals in the 1920s who foresaw the crucial role that tanks and armoured forces would play in future wars. In 1943, Hobart's 79th Armoured Division was due to be disbanded through lack of resources: however, Brookie intervened and asked him to convert his division into a specialist armoured unit. It was Hobart's division which developed the tanks and vehicles used on D-Day in June 1944. On 11 March:

"Long interview with Hobart to explain to him new job I wish him to take on connected with flotation tanks, searchlight tanks, anti-mine tanks and self-propelled guns."

On 14 March, Brookie fell ill with flu. Eleven days later:

"Had fairly long COS meeting at which we discussed organization for planning [the cross-Channel invasion] and the appointment of a Chief of Staff until such time as we are able to appoint a Supreme Commander [Frederick Morgan, a British lieutenant general, was appointed chief of staff in March and assigned the task of drawing up plans for the cross-Channel invasion]... at 5.15pm, meeting under PM to discuss Eisenhower's new alterations to plans for attack on Sicily and preparation of telegram in which we expressed our disapproval of his proposed plans... had a quiet evening with bird books."

On 29 March:

"Cabinet at 5.30pm after which I had to go and dine with Winston, a tête-à-tête dinner... We discussed the organisation of Europe after the war, his disapproval of Roosevelt's plan to build up China whilst neglecting France. But the main subject was his disappointment about Eisenhower... At 10.30pm we went to a meeting with the Joint Planners to listen to an account of the proposed plan for the capture of Sicily. [Winston] took it fairly well but as usual considered we were using far too much strength and that we ought to be capturing both Southern Italy and Greece at the same time. Now rolling to bed about 1am, dog-tired!!"

On 2 April:

"Visit from... Wilkinson who is sort of liaison officer with [Douglas MacArthur, American general] and quite interesting in his accounts of the prima donna!"

8 April saw future strategy being addressed:

"A difficult COS. We had the Joint Planners in and discussed future Mediterranean policy after capture of Sicily. I had difficulty with Portal and Pound who wandered about in their fluid elements and seldom touched the ground with their feet!"

On the following day:

"5pm to 6pm with Gardiner on plans for Husky [codename for the invasion of Sicily] and the difficulties of arriving at coordinated action owing to Montgomery's egotistical outlook."

On 13 April:

"Tunisian news continues to be excellent. COS meeting at which we discussed future moves after capture of Sicily. This evening, meeting with PM which started being stormy and then improved. Discussed advisability of removing all landing craft from this country to the Mediterranean for 1943 and devoting the whole of our energies to the Mediterranean. Luckily PM finally agreed but we are to put paper up to Defence Committee to prove our case."

Two days later:

"A depressing COS as recent telegrams from America show that we are just about back where we were before Casablanca! Their hearts are really in the Pacific, we are trying to run two wars at once which is quite impossible with limited resources of shipping. All we can hope for is to go all out to defeat Italy and thus produce the greatest dispersal of German forces and make the going easier for the Russians. If we even knew what the Russians hope to do!! But we have no inkling."

On 17 April:

"PM called up concerning ridiculous wire he had received from Marshall concerning advisability of starting attack on Sicily before Tunisia was clear!! Quite mad and quite impossible but PM delighted with this idea which showed, according to him, 'a high strategic conception'. I had half hour row with him on the telephone."

On 19 April, the 'spellbound' Brookie was amused by a Churchillian one-liner:

"Went straight to Hatfield aerodrome where... [we were] shown latest aircraft without propellers driven by air sucked in in front and squirted out behind! Apparently likely to be the fighter of the future. Drove back to London with PM who had forgiven my frankness of Saturday [the 'half hour row' two days earlier]. After dinner hard work till 10pm. Then visit to PM to explain plan of attack in Tunis which starts tonight! After that, meeting with PM to examine plan for recapture of Burma which lasted till close on 1am… Winston did not like the plan… and produced one of his priceless sentences by saying, 'You might as well eat a porcupine one quill at a time'!"*

On the next day:

"No news yet of the start of the Tunis attack. Long discussion at the Chiefs of Staff meeting concerning future moves after capture of Sicily. Very difficult to appreciate what form the collapse of Italy may take and what its implications may mean for us."

On 21 April, Brookie was anticipating future German strategy:

"Remarkably quiet day! Spent most of the afternoon appreciating probable course of action by the Germans during 1943. Not a very easy problem. I think however that their policy will aim at maximum offensive against our shipping at sea and defensive on land and in the air on all other fronts."

23 April saw some interesting observations:

"Archie Wavell [Commander-in-Chief, India], Peirse [Commander-in-Chief, RAF India] and Somerville [Commander-in-Chief, Eastern Fleet] came to discuss the prospects of Burma Campaign… Archie propounded all the difficulties and a very fair estimate of the poor means of solving these problems. Peirse and Somerville apparently have no ideas and take little interest in the solution of the problem! A typical example of the Navy and Air Force dislike for taking any responsibility or producing any ideas and in fact handing over control to Army and yet always up in arms when any idea is put forward for unity of control!

After lunch saw Paget and McNaughton and arranged for

replacing of 3rd Div by a Canadian Division in the plans for attack on Sicily. Although Canadians have continually been asking for this [see 10 February], I received no sign of gratitude from McNaughton!"

Five days later, Burma was again the subject of discussion:

"*A long and very tiring COS… We discussed lengthily the various alternatives open to offensive from India directed against Burma or Sumatra. Came to the conclusion that the offensive for 43/44 must be reduced to a very minor one. To consist mainly in the development of the air route to China from Assam."*

On 29 April, Churchill telegraphed Roosevelt suggesting another Anglo-American conference, this time in Washington. The two pressing issues for discussion were future operations in Europe after the invasion of Sicily and Burma. On the same day:

"*Meeting with PM to try and postpone date of departure. I told him we were not yet ready to discuss the plans on far side yet. He said we should have time on the Queen Mary. Luckily, Transportation said Queen Mary was full of vermin!! Vermin became our allies and our departure is now postponed till next Wednesday."*

TWELVE

CIGS: May–August 1943

On 3 May:

"*Defence Committee till 12.30am to discuss tank production and tank armament. A complete Alice in Wonderland meeting. Clark [Director of Armour] expressing the usual technician opinion entirely detached from tactical and operational requirements. Duncan Sandys [see 9 September 1942] expressing a self-opinionated amateur's view devoid of all sound basis.*"

On 4 May:

"*I am now just off to the station to start on my journey to Washington… I don't feel very hopeful as to results. Casablanca has taught me too much. Agreement after agreement may be secured on paper but if their hearts are not in it, they soon drift away again!*"

On 5 May, the British delegation sailed from Scotland on the *Queen Mary*. Since Burma was one of the main topics for discussion in Washington, the delegation included Archie Wavell. During the six-day journey:

"*Discussed the shipping situation at some length. There is no doubt that unless Americans are prepared to withdraw more shipping from the Pacific, our strategy in Europe will be drastically affected… the bulk of the American navy is in the Pacific and larger land and air forces have gone to this theatre than to Europe in spite of all we have said about the necessity of defeating Germany first!*"

"COS meeting to discuss lines on which we are to approach our American friends to tell them that the reconquest of Burma in 1943/44 is not possible. Just before dinner, good news came in of operations in Tunisia where Alexander's last offensive is making good progress."

"PM had been writing a long paper on our future action against Japan in which he forgot to take into account the basic limitation of our strategy, namely shipping. He also offended Archie Wavell by adversely criticizing the operations in Burma which have just been completed. So much so that Archie was indignant and I had to pacify him. Running a war seems to consist in making plans and then ensuring that all those destined to carry it out don't quarrel with each other instead of the enemy. Capture of Tunis and Bizerta seems to be confirmed [the fall of Tunis on 7 May was significant for two reasons: first, it meant the Allies had finally gained control of the whole of north Africa and, second, it led to the surrender of large numbers of German and Italian troops]."

"More troubles! Archie Wavell's Permanent Assistant arrived while I was shaving with a note from Archie in which he said that he had been unable to sleep and was so upset by Winston's references to the Burma operation that he proposed to send him a letter which he enclosed. In that letter he said that since Winston had lost confidence in him it was better for him to send in his resignation!! I went round and saw him and advised him not to send the letter. Later, he saw Winston, had a talk with him and now all is quiet and I may shave in peace tomorrow!!"

In his Notes, "I told [Archie] that if I were to take offence when abused by Winston and given to understand that he had no confidence, I should have to resign at least once every day! But that I never felt that any such resignations were likely to have the least effect in reforming Winston's wicked ways!"

"I am very very weary with work and at times feel that I just can't face another day of it!"

"We [met] the PM at 11.30 and discussed the Far East strategy… A thoroughly unsatisfactory meeting at which he again showed that he cannot grasp the relation of various theatres of war to each other. He always gets carried away by the one he is examining and in prosecuting it is prepared to sacrifice most of the others. I have never in the 1½ years that I have worked with him succeeded in making him review the war as a whole and to relate the importance of the various fronts to each other.

I do NOT look forward to these meetings, in fact I hate the thought of them. They will entail hours of argument and hard work trying to convince [the Americans] that Germany must be defeated first. After much argument, they will pretend to understand, will sign many agreements and… will continue as at present to devote the bulk of their strength to try and defeat Japan!! In fact, Casablanca will be repeated. It is all so maddening as it is not difficult in this case to see that unless our united effort is directed to defeat Germany and hold Japan, the war may go on indefinitely. However, it is not sufficient to see something clearly. You have got to try and convince countless people as to where the truth lies when they don't want to be acquainted with that fact. It is an exhausting process and I am very very tired and shudder at the useless struggles that lie ahead."

In his Notes, Brookie made an interesting observation, "Where the difficulty rested however was to decide how much effort should be devoted to hold Japan. The holding of Japan provided all the excuse necessary for a continual diversion of effort not truly required for a holding role. I still feel that if at that stage of the war our basic strategy had been more strictly adhered to, we should have finished the war a few months sooner."

On 11 May, the British delegation arrived in Washington. The atmosphere surrounding the conference was one of mutual suspicion: the British believed the Americans were diverting their resources to the Pacific and, therefore, not adhering to the Casablanca agreements whilst the

Americans believed the British were trying to wriggle out of launching cross-Channel operations.

The opening meeting on 12 May saw Roosevelt and Churchill exerting pressure on their military chiefs to maintain the momentum generated by the recent success in Tunisia. Roosevelt is recorded as saying, "the keynote of our plans... should be... to employ every resource of men and munitions against the enemy. Nothing that could be brought to bear should be allowed to stand idle."[1] In perfect harmony, Churchill then emphasised the importance of applying "our vast Armies, Air forces and munitions to the enemy. All plans should be judged by this test. We had a large Army and the Metropolitan Fighter Air Force in Great Britain. We had our finest and most experienced troops in the Mediterranean. The British alone had 13 Divisions in that theater. Supposing that [the invasion of Sicily] were completed by the end of August, what should these troops do between that time and the date 7 or 8 months later, when the cross-Channel operation might first be mounted? They could not possibly stand idle... so long a period of apparent inaction... would have a serious effect on Russia, who was bearing such a disproportionate weight."[2]

Brookie's 12 May entry suggests he was not paying much attention to his political masters:

"Went to the White House to attend meeting with the President at which [Roosevelt and Churchill] laid down their conception of future strategy. I could not help wandering back to eleven months ago when... Marshall came in with news of the surrender of Tobruk!!... And then I wandered through the last 11 months with all their anxieties, hopes, disappointments and worries. And now! At last the first stage of my proposed strategy accomplished in spite of all the various factors that have been trying to prevent it. I felt rather as if in a dream, to be there planning two stages ahead with the first stage finished and accomplished."

The British strategy paper tabled at this conference argued for the continuation of offensive operations in the Mediterranean with the aim of knocking Italy out of the War. The rationale behind this strategy was two-fold. First, it was the most effective way of providing immediate assistance to Russia. Second, if Italy was knocked out of the War, then Germany would be compelled either to transfer some of its forces to defend Italy and the territories occupied by Italy in the Mediterranean or concede these to the Allies. In contrast, the American strategy paper argued that operations in the Mediterranean should be scaled down once Sicily was captured so that Allied resources could be fully concentrated in launching a cross-Channel invasion in the spring of 1944.

On 13 May:

"Leahy [Roosevelt's chief of staff] began by restating the American conception of the global strategy which differs from ours in two respects. First in allowing too much latitude for the diversion of force to the Pacific. Secondly by imagining that the war could be more quickly finished by starting a Western front in France. It is quite clear from our discussion that they do not even begin to realize the requirements of European strategy and the part that Russia must play. I am afraid that we shall have a very difficult time and that we shall leave here having accomplished little towards altering the conception which is deeply rooted in their hearts. I am thoroughly depressed with the prospects of our visit!"

14 May saw chaos rather than progress. Note Brookie's dry comment about Stilwell:

"Started our Combined Chiefs of Staff meeting at 10.30 when we stated that we did not agree with their paper on global strategy. I then had to make a statement on the Anakim operation [large offensive in Burma intended to open up the Burma Road to ensure continuation of supplies to Chiang Kai-shek's Chinese forces].

At 2pm we met President and PM and again discussed the whole of Burma. First President, then PM made statements. Then Wavell was called upon followed by Somervell [American general] who contradicted him! Then Stilwell [American general assigned to Chiang Kai-Shek] who disagreed with both and with himself, as far as I could see! He is a small man with no conception of strategy. The whole problem seemed to hinge on the necessity of keeping Chiang Kai-Shek in the war. Chennault was then called upon followed by more Stilwell and more confusion! President and PM had some more to say about it... and by the time we left, what is not a very simple problem had become a tangled mass of confusion."

In his Notes, "The Americans were trying to make us undertake an advance from Assam [India] into Burma without adequate resources... Except for Wavell, those arguing certainly did nothing to clarify the situation. Somervell had never seen the country and had no conception of the administrative problems. Stilwell was a strange character known as 'Vinegar Joe', a name that suited him admirably... Except for the fact that he was a stout-hearted fighter, suitable to lead a brigade of Chinese scallywags, I could see no qualities in him. He was a Chinese linguist but had little military knowledge and no strategic ability of any kind. His worst failing, however, was his deep-rooted hatred of anybody or anything British! It was practically impossible to establish friendly relations with either him or the troops under his command. He did a vast amount of harm by vitiating the relations between Americans and British, both in India and Burma."

Brookie's criticism of Stilwell was justified. He was a virulent anglophobe, well illustrated by his habit of referring to the British as "pig fucker" and "monocled ass": his contempt was not confined to the British since he referred to Chiang Kai-shek as "peanut".[3] Inevitably, Stilwell fell out with Chiang Kai-shek and Roosevelt was eventually forced to replace him. As for the 'Chinese scallywags', Chiang Kai-shek's regime was riddled with corruption and his forces were poorly trained and equipped, lacked organisation and were led by incompetent commanders.

By 18 May, the American position was hardening:
"It is quite apparent now that we are a long way apart. What

> *is more the Americans are now taking up the attitude that we led them down the garden path taking them to North Africa! That at Casablanca we again misled them by inducing them to attack Sicily!! And now they are not going to be led astray again. Added to that, the swing towards the Pacific is stronger than ever".*

In his Notes, "The Americans still failed to grasp how we were preparing for a re-entry into France through our actions in the Mediterranean. We had now opened the Mediterranean and, in doing so, had regained the equivalent of about a million tons of shipping, thus regaining a great deal of the strategic mobility which we had lost. We had taken a quarter of a million prisoners [in north-west Africa] and inflicted very heavy losses on the enemy both at sea and in the air. We had now opened the way for an attack on Sicily and Italy and we were forcing the enemy to expend forces for the defence of Southern Europe, a region of bad intercommunication… We were in fact taking the best road for the liberation of France and final defeat of Germany.

King had been gaining ground recently and was diverting more and more strength to the Pacific. Any attempts to unduly push our strategy on Marshall had a distinct tendency to drive him into King's Pacific camp. He even stated once or twice that if our strategy was to be one of wasting our time in the Mediterranean, the American forces might well be better employed in the Pacific!"

On 19 May:

> *"At 10.30am we met American COS and started by criticizing each other's papers on the proposed European strategy. Then Marshall suggested the meeting should be cleared for an 'off the record' meeting between Chiefs of Staff alone."*

In his Notes, "The number of [staff officers present in these meetings] had grown far too large… I felt that frequently Marshall did not like shifting from some policy he had been briefed on by his Staff, lest they should think he was lacking in determination."

His 19 May entry continued:

> "We then had heart-to-heart talk and as a result of it at last found a bridge across which we could meet! Not altogether a satisfactory one but far better than a break up of the conference! Our conclusions are that we are to prepare some 29 divisions for entry into France early in 1944 and at the same time a continuance of pressure against Italy in the Med. The latter is a triumph as Americans wanted to close down all operations in Med after capture of Sicily."

On 20 May:

> "11.30 to 1.30 Combined COS at which we reached a complete impasse… They were still pressing for a full-scale advance from Assam into Burma contrary to all administrative possibilities.
>
> 3.30 to 5.00 'Off the record' Combined COS meeting at which we finally reached agreement and obtained practically exactly what we had originally put forward".

On the following day:

> "We had another White House conference with PM and President when we put up the results of our work. It was all accepted and we received congratulations on our work, but I do not think they realized how near we were to a failure to reach agreement!"

On 22 May:

> "Fell down 14 stone stairs with serious bruising all over my body but no real harm."

24 May illustrated the wide divergence of views held by the members of the Combined Chiefs of Staff:

> "Long Combined meeting at which we still had many different opinions which were only resolved with difficulty! I still feel that we may write a lot of paper but that it all has only little influence on our basic outlooks which might be classified as:
> (a) King thinks the war can only be won by action in the Pacific at the expense of all other fronts.

(b) Marshall considers that our solution lies in a cross-Channel operation with some 20 to 30 divisions, irrespective of the situation on the Russian front, with which he proposes to clear Europe and win the war.

(c) Portal considers that success lies in accumulating the largest air force possible in England and that then, and then only, success lies assured through the bombing of Europe.

(d) Dudley Pound on the other hand is obsessed with the anti-U-boat warfare and considers that success can only be secured by the defeat of this menace.

(e) AFB [Brookie] considers that success can only be secured by pressing operations in the Mediterranean to force a dispersal of German forces, help Russia and thus eventually produce a situation where cross-Channel operations are possible.

(f) And Winston??? Thinks one thing at one moment and another at another moment. At times the war may be won by bombing and all must be sacrificed to it. At others it becomes essential for us to bleed ourselves dry on the Continent because Russia is doing the same. At others our main effort must be in the Mediterranean directed against Italy or Balkans alternatively with sporadic desires to invade Norway and 'roll up the map in the opposite direction to Hitler'! But more often than all, he wants to carry out ALL operations simultaneously irrespective of shortages of shipping!

At 4.45pm we went to the White House... to attend conference with President and PM. There the PM entirely repudiated the paper we had passed, agreed to and been congratulated on at our last meeting!! He wished to alter all the Mediterranean decisions! He had no idea of the difficulties we had been through and just crashed in 'where angels fear to tread'. As a result, he created situation of suspicion in the American Chiefs that we had been behind their backs and has made matters far more difficult for us in the future!! There are times when he drives me to desperation!"

In his Notes, "Winston's attitude at the White House was tragic. He had originally agreed entirely to the paper we were discussing and with Roosevelt had congratulated us on it. Now at the eleventh hour he wished to repudiate half of it. Some of the alterations he wished to make were on points we had been forced to concede to the Americans in order to secure more important ones... the American Chiefs might well have believed that we had gone behind their backs in an attempt to obtain these points through Winston."

On 25 May:

"The PM [has] done untold harm by rousing all the suspicions as regards ventures in the Balkans which I had been endeavouring to suppress. He [has] however succeeded in getting the President to agree to Marshall coming with us to North Africa [Churchill and Brookie were due to fly to north Africa after the conference]... This has now become essential as otherwise, after the PM's statements, I feel certain that a visit by the PM and myself to North Africa would be looked upon with grave suspicion as an attempt to swing Eisenhower in our direction at the expense of decisions arrived at in Washington."

By 28 May Churchill, Brookie and Marshall were in Algiers, meeting Eisenhower:

"We had a long discussion as to what our future action in the Mediterranean should be. PM and I were busy trying to impress on Eisenhower what is to be obtained by knocking Italy out of the war. I still do not think that Marshall realizes this, and I am quite certain that Eisenhower does not begin to realize the possibilities that lie ahead of us in this theatre."

On 31 May:

"We... flew to Jejelli and from there on to see 51st [Division]. We found them in a lovely bit of country just east of Bougie. I had no conception that North Africa could be so beautiful. Lovely cork tree forests with carpets of spring flowers, golden field of calendulas, hedges covered with convolvulus and lovely green fields leading to tree-covered

hills on one side and to a lovely blue Mediterranean on the other. A lovely place to rest a war-weary division.

Eden was very nice in congratulating me on the results of Washington, he said he had read the minutes and considered I could not have handled the affairs better. Which is satisfactory."

On 2 June:

"I feel fairly certain that our future plans are on the right lines. We have got the Germans in a definitely difficult position. They must do something in Russia and yet have not got the resources to do anything on a large scale [in early July, Germany launched a major offensive at Kursk, the outcome of which was inconclusive: the battle of Kursk marked the point when Germany lost the initiative on the Russian front]. At the same time, the Italian situation cannot fail to cause them the gravest anxiety. We can at present help Russia by hitting Italy.

I have since the start and in spite of many tribulations aimed at 3 main points:
a) Secure the whole of North Africa (which we have now done)
b) Eliminate Italy (which we may hope to do before too long)
c) Bring Turkey in (which must remain dependent on situation in Russia)

If once we succeed in attaining these three points, a re-entry into France and a conclusion of the war should not be long delayed, all dependent on the situation in Russia."

The next day saw a ticking off for Montgomery:

"[Montgomery]… requires a lot of educating to make him see the whole situation and the war as a whole outside 8th Army orbit. A difficult mixture to handle, brilliant commander in action and trainer of men but liable to commit untold errors of tact, lack of appreciation of other people's outlook. It is most distressing that the Americans do not like him and it will always be a difficult matter to have him fighting in close proximity to them. He wants guiding and watching continually and I do not think that Alex is sufficiently strong and rough with him."

In his Notes, "I discovered that [Eisenhower] was boiling over internally with anger over Monty's insistence on extracting a Fortress aircraft out of him for Monty's personal services. The matter had originated from a remark which Bedell Smith [Eisenhower's chief of staff] had made jokingly whilst visiting Monty. He said to him that if he cleared Sousse of the enemy by a certain date he would earn a Fortress aircraft. This statement had been lightheartedly made and far more as a joke than a real promise. However, Monty reached Sousse by the date mentioned and promptly wired to Bedell Smith for his Fortress aircraft! Bedell Smith still looked upon the matter as a joke and tried to laugh it off in his reply. This apparently did not satisfy Monty who wired back stating that he was still expecting delivery of his aircraft. Bedell Smith was then forced to take the matter to Eisenhower who was infuriated that he should be bounced in this way by Monty! However, being the past master at cementing inter-Allied relations, Eisenhower ordered that Monty should be given the Fortress aircraft together with the American crew to fly it. Monty had thus gained his aircraft but, in doing so, he had annoyed Eisenhower intensely and laid the foundations of distrust and dislike which remained with Eisenhower during the rest of the war.

When I accused Monty of crass stupidity for impairing his relations with Eisenhower… he told me that he had been under the impression that Eisenhower had considered the whole transaction as an excellent joke! I told him that if he had heard Ike express his views to me, he would certainly have had no such illusions. He was as usual most grateful for having his failings pointed out to him. This gratitude was genuine and not assumed, of that I am certain. I am also convinced that with his inability of assessing other people's feelings, through excessive concentration on his own, he was genuinely under the impression that his insistence on obtaining his aircraft was looked on as a joke by Ike."

By 7 June, Churchill and Brookie were back in London:

"A desperate meeting with PM at 10pm about the Azores. We sat for 2 hours and did absolutely nothing!! PM in bad mood, arguing against Foreign Secretary and refusing to make up his mind in any direction."

On 15 June:

> "PM called me in just before the [Cabinet] meeting to tell me that... he wanted me to take the Supreme Command of operations from this country across the Channel [the cross-Channel invasion] when the time was suitable. He said many nice things about having full confidence in me".

In his Notes, "This was the first time that the PM definitely told me that he wanted me to have the Supreme Command of the Liberation Armies when the re-entry into France became possible... This news gave me one of my greatest thrills during the war."

Two days later:

> "Portal informed me that PM had just told him that he had selected Sholto Douglas [RAF] as Supreme Commander for Eastern Asia Command. I am delighted. He should do it well."

On 18 June:

> "Our morning COS was greatly taken up with an interview with the deputy of the Minister of Information in order to try and regulate the press which as usual is discussing the fact that it is inevitable that we should carry out exactly what we propose to do! So far it has worked quite well as a 'double cross' as the Germans cannot imagine that we should be such fools as to give the press such liberty! But we cannot hope to go on fooling them in this way.
>
> Crerar [commander, 1st Canadian Corps] came to dine in the evening and poured his heart out to me as regards his worries connected with the Canadian forces. He is very unhappy about Andy McNaughton who is in a restless mood and undoubtedly quite unsuitable to command an army [see 7 March]. I only wish I could find some job we could remove him to but that is not easy."

On the following day:

> "Adam [Adjutant General]... surprised me by telling me that

Eisenhower had said that although he was very fond of Alexander and admired him, he did not think that he was a big man and that he did not consider him fit to take on a Supreme Commander's job. I did not realize that he had appreciated this fact. He went on to tell Adam that he considered that there were only two men to take on the Supreme Command [of the cross-Channel invasion] in this country and that one was Marshall and the other myself. That also astonished me as I did not believe that he had much of an opinion of me."

By mid-1943, Churchill was running out of patience with Charles de Gaulle. On 21 June:

"*5.30pm Cabinet, mainly preoccupied with de Gaulle's future. Personally, I am convinced that there is only one course to follow and that is to get rid of him at the earliest possible date.*"

Sir Alexander Cadogan in the Foreign Office also attended this cabinet meeting. Eleven months earlier, 26 July 1942, Cadogan had wished that de Gaulle was CIGS: by June 1943, however, "Long discussion about de Gaulle situation. I agree that if you ask me whether we can safely put French army in hands of de G., I answer a thousand times no. If that means that he then resigns from the [French National] Committee, that is altogether deplorable but it can't be helped and we must make the best of it – by blackening de G's face as much as possible. V[ery] unfortunate, but there it is."[4]

The next day saw Brookie buying a well-known collection of bird books:
"*Invested capital in a set of Gould's Birds. It remains to be seen whether my forecast of the set going up in value come[s] true!*"

In his Notes, "My purchase of Gould's Birds was a big venture! There were 45 volumes for which I gave just over £1500 but my forecast was correct and at the end of the war I sold these books for twice their original cost. Meanwhile I had had wonderful value from them as an antidote to the war and to Winston! Whilst looking at Gould's wonderful pictures, I was able to forget everything connected with the war."

On 23 June:

> "PM's conference at 5.30 on the use of special means to counter German air defences in bomber raids [strips of metal ribbon dropped from planes to confuse German radar]. A debatable point as the weapon is two-edged and can be turned onto us. However, in view of heavy losses suffered by Bomber Command, decided to make use of it. I hope that we may have been right."

On 28 June:

> "Cabinet mainly filled with long talk by PM to the effect that he would not let relations with the President be affected by de Gaulle, that he would be quite prepared to dispense with [de Gaulle's] services if he gave trouble. Attlee and Amery were still supporting de Gaulle. Eden, on the other hand, has at last learned wisdom and, I think, sees through de Gaulle now. At any rate, he has different views from this time last year."

Four days later:

> "First a long COS to consider two telegrams from [Roosevelt]. The first suggested sending a whole division plus 400 AA guns and some 14 squadrons of fighters to support Portugal in the event of Salazar [Portuguese prime minister] granting us facilities on the Azores for submarine hunting aircraft. Such action in my mind would inevitably endanger our relations with Spain and bring Germany into Spain to counter what she would consider the first steps towards starting a Peninsular offensive. The whole situation is very dangerous and we may well find ourselves driven into Peninsular war against our wishes! The next telegram for PM was connected with the organization of the new South East Asia Command. There again the proposals cannot meet our requirements [see next entry]."

On 5 July:

> "COS discussion on future Supreme Commander for South East Asia Command. PM wanted Oliver Leese who is quite raw and should

command an Army before going to a Supreme Command. Sholto [Douglas], whom we want, is not being accepted by the President and we feel we must induce PM to approach President again.

After lunch, Stewart, Canadian Chief of Staff, came to see me. Apparently, he realizes that McNaughton is unsuitable to command the Canadian Army! We discussed possible ways of eliminating him, not an easy job!

USA look at present like trying to close Mediterranean theatre if they can after Sicily. We must wait and see how Sicily operations go and what I can do at next Combined Chiefs of Staff [conference]. 10.30pm Staff meeting with PM at which we convinced him of desirability to have one more shot to get Sholto Douglas accepted. Heard today of tragedy of Sikorski's death in an aeroplane accident at Gibraltar. He is a terrible loss and I feel I have lost a great friend."

Two days later, the chiefs of staff dined with King George VI and Churchill:

"[Dudley] Pound in great form and full of stories... when we were saying goodbye, [Churchill]... again told me that he wanted me to take over the Supreme Command of operations out of this country [the cross-Channel invasion], but that I was to stop on as CIGS till January or February and that I should only take over if it looked pretty certain that the operation was possible. He could not have been nicer and said that I was the only man he had sufficient confidence in to take over the job."

On 8 July:

"10.30 [pm] meeting with PM, Eden and Cadogan to discuss latest news from Lisbon as regards use of Azores. However, from 10.30 to 11.20 we listened to a heated argument between PM and Eden as regards recognition of French National Committee in Algiers and a long tirade of abuse of de Gaulle from Winston which I heartily agreed with. Unfortunately, his dislike for de Gaulle has come rather late, he should have been cast overboard a year ago and gave plenty of opportunities for such action! But on every occasion Anthony [Eden] pleaded with him and Winston forgave. We then discussed Lisbon for 10 minutes".

On the following day:

"Irwin who had been sent home from his command on the Burma front [Major General Irwin had been relieved of his command] came to see me. An unpleasant kind of interview which I dislike intensely. However, we did not discuss the future as all reports were not in and confined ourselves to discussing the Burma campaign and all its lessons. I was appalled at listening to what he had to say as regards the morale of the troops and their inferiority complex in relation to the Japs. We shall have to do something very drastic to get matters right. Tonight, the attack on Sicily starts and thank heaven the suspense will be over!"

On 10 July:

"A thrilling day with reports of Sicily coming in. Few people, if any, realize what the weight of responsibility of this attack is like! I feel specially responsible. First, I had to convince the [British] Chiefs of Staff... Then I had battles with the PM to induce him to remain in the Mediterranean and not return to the English Channel! Then finally, whilst busy battling with the American Chiefs of Staff, the Joint Planning Staff went against me and tried to swing back to Sardinia!! It took a lot of will power to keep on with the Sicily objective. And now it remains to prove that I was right or wrong!?! Anyhow the start has been good."

Sunday, 11 July, was "*peacefully spent at home moving bookcases and working hard at repairing the Pook's goat cart to keep my mind occupied and my thoughts away from Sicily. Reports all good, thank heaven.*" On 13 July:

"We were discussing the Commander for South East Asia Supreme Command. The Americans are turning down Sholto Douglas and we do not feel that they have any reason or right to do so. Matter is *rendered more difficult by PM wishing to appoint 'a dashing young Corps Commander from North Africa.'"*

And on the next day:

"Winston will not press President to accept Sholto Douglas against their wishes. I am now turning over Jumbo Wilson, Giffard, Platt and Pownall as possibilities… then to 10 Downing Street for sherry party. PM then asked you how you liked the idea of my becoming Supreme Commander of the invasion of France! And I had not told you anything about it as it was still all so distant and indecisive."

On 15 July, note his dry comment about 'flying nerves':

"At 11.10 we all left for poor Sikorski's funeral at Westminster Cathedral. The service was too theatrical and fussy to stir up my feelings till the very end. But when I saw the empty stand where the coffin had been with 6 [candles] burning round it and, on either flank, representative 'colours' of regiments borne by officer parties it struck me as a sad picture of Poland's plight: both its state and its army left without a leader when a change of the tide seems in sight. I was very fond of Sikorski personally and shall miss him badly.

Went straight from Cathedral to Hendon to fly to Norfolk. Attending funerals in war of victims of air accidents is not a sustaining process to one's flying nerves and should be avoided! Had a bumpy fly. Met by Hobart and taken to see his amphibious tanks [see 11 March]… Delighted to see Hobo so happy and so well employed.

Then at 10.30pm had to go to 10 Downing Street for meeting of COS… discussed [forthcoming conference] with Americans in Quebec in early August and finally again attacked South East Asia Command. Decided to get Sholto Douglas home to answer some of the charges raised against him by the Americans. As I walked out, feeling very weary, PM said 'You look tired, CIGS, are you doing too much?'… Coming from him, a remark like that means a lot and more than compensates for any extra strain."

Brookie's entry on 19 July – nine days after the invasion of Sicily – showed that strategy was now being formulated on a somewhat piecemeal basis:

"A long COS trying to decide what our next best plan should be after Sicily. We were examining a tempting attack direct on Naples. Air cover bad and dependent on carriers [the landing sites in Italy were at the edge of land-based air cover], also plan put forward with only 3 divisions – quite inadequate. Rate of build-up also slower than that of the Germans. Unfortunately, Intelligence Branch are not good at deciding probable enemy moves!

At 8.30pm received new appreciation of attack on Naples which I studied till 9.30pm. A bad paper again! We then met as Chiefs of Staff till 10.30 when PM, Eden, Attlee and Oliver Lyttelton came along to discuss prospects. A real amateur strategists' meeting as far as the last 3 were concerned! Winston, on the whole, very open to reason and on the right lines. We shall have a busy job to knock it into some shape to wire out to Eisenhower and to bring Marshall along with us without frightening him out of the Mediterranean!!"

20 July illustrated how operations in one theatre could impact on other theatres:

"Our COS meeting was mainly concerned with adjusting future planning in accordance with last night's meeting with the PM. We drafted a telegram for Washington supporting Marshall's aspirations for Naples [Marshall was in favour of very limited operations against mainland Italy, namely an amphibious landing near Naples followed by a march on Rome] but pointing out that this must entail certain changes and retentions in the Mediterranean at the expense of operations in Burma and across the Channel. This will not be greeted with great joy!!"

21 July saw an example of Brookie's foresight, on this occasion the need to employ forces experienced in mountain warfare in Italy:

"I went to see Mr Amery [Secretary of State for India and Burma]… and discussed with him ways and means of providing

adequate mountain warfare troops for fighting in mountainous Italy. He was very kind and helpful."

On 22 July:

"*Started with a usual meeting with Joint Planners at the COS at which we discussed the Naples attack and its prospects of success. Came to the conclusion that it was a gamble but probably one worth taking.*"

On 24 July:

"*A very disappointing wire from American COS – Marshall absolutely fails to realize what strategic treasures lie at our feet in the Mediterranean and always hankers after cross-Channel operations. He admits that our object must be to eliminate Italy and yet is always afraid of facing the consequences of doing so. He cannot see beyond the tip of his nose and is maddening.*"

On 25 July, Brookie was with Churchill at Chequers:

"*We then discussed future Mediterranean strategy. We are both in complete agreement but fully realize the trouble we shall have with the Americans. After dinner… came news of Mussolini's abdication!!! Winston dashed off to talk with Eden. A memorable moment and at least a change over from 'the end of the beginning' to 'the beginning of the end'!*"

On 27 July:

"*Stewart, the Canadian CGS, came to see me. He suggested splitting the Canadian force between Home and Mediterranean so as to dispose of McNaughton as an Army Commander! He is right. It is the only way to save the outfit.*"

On 28 July, he finally resolved the issue of Alan Cunningham [see 7 December 1941]:

"*A long COS discussing [armistice] terms which Eisenhower*

proposed to broadcast to Italians before any overtures from Italians. All agreed this was wrong… PM now prepared to take Alan Cunningham in spite of turning him down every time I put him forward!"

On 30 July:

"We were fortunate last night! A wire arrived at 1.30am from Eisenhower about Armistice terms for Italians. PM considered it sufficiently urgent to turn whole War Cabinet out of bed and kept up till 4am!! Thank heaven we escaped and were not sent for."

On 4 August, Brookie set off for yet another Anglo-American conference, this time in Quebec:

"Visit from Wingate [Orde Wingate, commander of the British Chindit forces in Burma], back from Burma to discuss his mobile column tactics… at 8.20 [caught] train for the North to board Queen Mary for Canada."

In his Notes, "[Wingate] had originally been operating in Abyssinia after which he had a nervous breakdown and tried to commit suicide by cutting his throat. He was saved and after some nursing fit for work again. Amery had… asked me whether I would consider sending him out to Burma where he might prove useful… He turned out a great success and originated the long-range penetration forces which worked right in Japanese territory.

[Wingate] explained that he considered that what he had done on a small scale could be run with much larger forces. He required, however, for these forces the cream of everything… I considered that the results of his form of attacks were certainly worth backing within reason."

As Brookie departed for Canada, Henry Stimson, the American Secretary of War, was submitting a report to Roosevelt on his recent trip to Britain and his discussions with Churchill and Eden. In his report, he questioned Britain's commitment to a cross-Channel invasion and made clear his view that the British were looking for ways to avoid launching the operation. Six days later, Stimson followed up on his report by writing a letter to Roosevelt in which he set out the conclusions he had drawn from his trip. The first was that the operation was unlikely to happen if a British commander was placed in charge of it. The second was that opening a front in north-west Europe was the only way of achieving final victory over Germany; Stimson reminded Roosevelt that both America and Britain had given a pledge to Stalin that one would be opened. The third was that Roosevelt should now insist on a cross-Channel invasion in 1944 and, furthermore, that Marshall should be appointed supreme commander of the operation. Stimson handed his letter to Roosevelt in person and recorded in his diary the president's reaction. According to Stimson, Roosevelt stated that he had come to the same conclusions himself, that he also wanted to have an American commander and that this could be achieved if America committed more troops to the operation than the British.

On 5 August, aboard the *Queen Mary*, Brookie was amused by another Churchillian one-liner:

"At dinner this evening the steward was filling tumblers with water before going round with the champagne. Winston stopped him by saying, 'Stop pouring all that water out, it is too depressing a sight'!"

6 August saw Churchill considering a new appointment:

"Started with a COS meeting… we discussed how best to tackle the Mediterranean situation. Decided to relate the action in this theatre to the requirements of Northern France suitable to admit of an invasion. In my mind, it is all so clear and palpable that the policy we must pursue is to complete the elimination of Italy, profit from the situation by occupying as much of Italy as we require to improve bombing facilities of Southern Germany and to force a withdrawal of German forces from Russia, Balkans and France. If we pin Germany in Italy, she cannot find enough forces to meet all her commitments. Spent rest of day reading Morgan's plans for cross-Channel operation. A good plan but too optimistic as to rate of advance to be expected. After tea sent for by PM… He informed me that he now contemplated giving

Dickie Mountbatten the Supreme Command of South East Asia [see 13 July]!! He will require a very efficient Chief of Staff to pull him through!"

On 7 August:

"Spent whole morning with COS discussing the cross-Channel operation and examining the possibility of such an operation and the reduction of German forces in France necessary to render such an operation possible [i.e. reduce the size of the German forces based in France so as to make the cross-Channel invasion practicable]... At 6.30pm a meeting with Winston when I had a hammer and tongs argument with him on the set-up of command in South East Asia. He was upholding the theory that no Army Commander was necessary in Assam, that the commander of land forces of South East Asia working with Supreme Commander, and also responsible for any operations in Malaya, should be capable of doing both jobs from Delhi! After an hour's bitter arguing I partially convinced him".

On 8 August, note Churchill's volte-face and his interest in Sumatra:

"News from Sicily good... A difficult COS at which we discussed the line to take concerning Burma campaign. We got Wingate to come in and discussed what could be done with the Long Range Penetration Group organization and finally arrived at a line of action with which to take on the American Chiefs of Staff and to prove to them that we are in no way neglecting the operations in Burma.

PM sent for me and I had about an hour with him. In the first place he argued with me as regards organization of command in South East Asia and agreed to all he had argued so hard against yesterday. Then he informed me as to his views concerning Sumatra and his wish to localize an offensive... to the north of the island.

Received message from Washington [Dill] that we are to have a very difficult time of it at this conference. Americans determined to carry on with preparations for re-entry into France and for Burma campaign at expense of Italy."

On 10 August, the British party arrived in Quebec. On the following day:

"Meeting with [British] Joint Staff Mission to discuss the background to our coming meeting and to gather from them what lies at the back of all the opposition which we have been meeting lately. As far as I can gather, King is at the back of most of the trouble and with his Pacific outlook is always opposed to most operations in Europe. In addition, Marshall still feels injured that we turned down his plans for cross-Channel operations last year. I am not looking forward to this coming meeting".

12 August saw Brookie admiring nature as the British chiefs of staff "took a day off" and went fishing:

"The country was lovely. Pine tree covered hills leading down to the lake and wild enough for moose to come down to the lake, whilst bears live in the woods and beavers had one of their dwellings on the upper of the two lakes that we fished… I passed a chipmunk within a couple of yards and was fascinated by it, a most delicious creature. Finally on our way home a skunk crossed the road in the beam of the headlights. We got out to look for it but it was gone. By the time we returned to the hotel… we had had a good full 12-hour day away from work. I only wish to heaven I could go on escaping into the country instead of having to face up to a conference with our American friends who have no strategic outlook, cannot see beyond the ends of their noses and imagine that the war can be run by a series of legal contracts based on false concepts as to what may prevail six months ahead! I am tired of arguing with them!"

In his Notes, "This was the first day on which we noticed signs of failing on the part of Dudley Pound. On the way out, he had lost his balance and nearly fallen into a small ravine… He seemed completely exhausted."

On 14 August:

"We had received a telegram from Auchinleck [now Commander-in-Chief, India] giving full details of the floods west of Calcutta. These *floods look like affecting the Burma Campaign drastically and put us in a difficult position in view of the pressure put on us by our American friends to carry out a Burma campaign."*

On 15 August, Brookie received a bombshell:

"The end of a gloomy and unpleasant day… Winston sent for me asking to see me ¼ hour before lunch. He had just returned from being with the President and Harry Hopkins. Apparently, the latter pressed hard for the appointment of Marshall as Supreme Commander for the cross-Channel operations and as far as I can gather Winston gave in, in spite of having previously promised me the job!! He asked me how I felt about it and I told him that I could not feel otherwise than disappointed. He then said that Eisenhower would replace Marshall and that Alexander was to replace Eisenhower, whilst Monty would be required home to take Paget's command. In addition, Dickie Mountbatten had been offered to the President for the Supreme Command of SE Asia and was acceptable to President. He asked me whether I had thought any further about this appointment and I told him that I still considered that he lacked balance for such a job."

When Brookie elaborated in his Notes, written more than a decade later, his bitterness and resentment was still apparent, "This had indeed been a black day. First my interview with Winston before lunch. I remember it as if it was yesterday as we walked up and down on the terrace outside the drawing-room of the Citadel, looking down on to that wonderful view of the St Lawrence River… As Winston spoke all that scenery was swamped by a dark cloud of despair. I had voluntarily given up the opportunity of taking over the North African Command before El Alamein and recommended that Alexander should be appointed instead. I had done so, as I have previously stated, because I felt at that time I could probably serve a more useful purpose by remaining with Winston. But now the strategy of the war had been guided to the final stage, the stage when the real triumph of victory was to be gathered, I felt no longer necessarily tied to Winston and free to assume this Supreme Command which he had already promised me on three separate occasions. It was a crashing blow to hear from him that he was now handing over this appointment to the Americans and had, in exchange, received the agreement of the President to Mountbatten's appointment as Supreme Commander for South East Asia.

Not for one moment did he realize what this meant to me. He offered no sympathy, no regrets at having had to change his mind and dealt with the matter as if it were one of minor importance! The only reference to my feelings in his [memoirs] is that I 'bore the great disappointment with soldierly dignity.' On this same page, he describes the reasons that lay behind this change namely the fact that it was now evident that in the cross-Channel operations the proportion of American forces would be considerably in excess of ours. It was better therefore that the Supreme Commander should be an American. At the time this fact did not soften the blow which took me several months to recover from."

According to Brookie's diary entry, Hopkins had 'pressed hard for the appointment of Marshall' and Churchill 'gave in'. However, in his subsequent memoirs, Churchill offered a markedly different explanation namely that he volunteered the command to Roosevelt. This explanation is almost certainly true because it is corroborated by Stimson's diary; according to Stimson, both Roosevelt and Churchill informed him that the command was voluntarily handed over.

There had been three separate occasions when Churchill had offered command of the cross-Channel invasion to Brookie, the last one being on 14 July. The question, therefore, is why did Churchill change his mind when, on 7 July, he had regarded Brookie as 'the only man he had sufficient confidence in to take over the job'? In a draft of his memoirs, Churchill wrote of his fear that if the cross-Channel invasion proved to be a bloody disaster resulting in huge casualties, then this would have produced an outcry in America and led to a backlash against Britain if the commander had been British: however, if the commander had been American, or America had been invited to choose the commander, Britain would have been spared such a backlash. This explanation is credible since there were occasions during the War when Churchill expressed his fear that the invasion might end in disaster.

Whilst Churchill probably was influenced by the preponderance of American forces in the operation and the fear of a bloody disaster, there was, in truth, another more compelling reason why he changed his mind – South East Asia Command. SEAC was a new inter-Allied command which was to be supervised by the British chiefs of staff and it offered Churchill, who was a passionate believer in the British Empire, the prospect of recovering the colonial territories of Burma, Malaya and Singapore: his interest in recovering these territories is evidenced by his obsession over northern Sumatra, which will shortly become apparent, and his dogmatic insistence in early 1944 that British strategy in the Far East should be based on South East Asia rather than the Pacific. Consequently, the position of supreme commander of SEAC was important to Churchill and in Mountbatten he saw someone who he could influence, direct and cajole. The answer to the 'why' question, therefore, is Churchill decided in late July or August that Mountbatten's appointment at SEAC was more important than Brookie's appointment as commander of the cross-Channel invasion: on 6 August, nine days earlier, "He informed me that he now contemplated giving Dickie Mountbatten the Supreme Command of South East Asia!!" However, Churchill needed Roosevelt's agreement to this appointment. So, he traded Brookie's appointment in order to secure Mountbatten's appointment. Brookie's use of 'in exchange' in his Notes clearly suggests he drew the same conclusion.

Having secured this trade-off, Churchill then had the task of breaking the bad news to Brookie. For Churchill, the solution was simple – lie by putting the blame on the Americans. According to Brookie's entry, 'Apparently, [Hopkins] pressed hard for the appointment of Marshall as Supreme Commander for the cross-Channel operations and as far as I can gather Winston gave in'. His use of 'apparently' and 'as far as I can gather' suggests that Churchill was rather vague when explaining to Brookie what had occurred which is hardly surprising. The next part of Brookie's entry also illustrates Churchill's casual treatment of the truth, 'He then said that Eisenhower would replace Marshall'. Churchill's statement clearly implied the Americans had decided the future roles to be played by Marshall and Eisenhower but, in fact, no decision had been made on that issue and, for some inexplicable reason, the Americans did not decide it for months: they were only galvanised into doing so when Stalin enquired at the Tehran conference in November who would command the cross-Channel invasion and on being informed that this had not yet been decided, he remarked, "Then nothing will come out of these operations."[5] Jolted by this jibe, Roosevelt finally settled the issue on 4 December by keeping Marshall in Washington and appointing Eisenhower commander of the invasion.

After receiving this bombshell at lunchtime, Brookie now had to lead the British team in the afternoon meeting and negotiate with the man who had just replaced him as commander of the cross-Channel invasion:

"It was a most painful meeting and we settled nothing. I entirely failed to get Marshall to realize the relation between cross-Channel and Italian operations and the repercussions which the one exercises on the other [i.e. the Italian operations tied down German forces in Italy which otherwise could be deployed in northern France]... He had not even read the plans worked out by Morgan for the cross-Channel operation and consequently was not even in a position to begin to appreciate its difficulties and requirements. The only real argument he produced was a threat to the effect that if we pressed our point the build up in England would be reduced to that of a small Corps and the whole war reorientated towards Japan. We parted at 5.30, having sat for 3 very unpleasant hours."

Brookie routinely recorded in his diary the names of the people with whom he lunched and dined. There was, therefore, a certain poignancy in the final part of his 15 August entry:

"Dined by myself as I wanted to be with myself! After dinner, discussed with Dill till midnight what our best plan of action was. Dill had been for a private talk with Marshall and had found him most unmanageable and irreconcilable, even threatening to resign if we pressed our point."

The following day saw Brookie employing a brave tactic to break the impasse:

> "At 2.30pm we met [the Americans] in a small session with all secretaries and planners removed. Our talk was pretty frank. I opened by telling them that the root of the matter was that we were not trusting each other. They doubted our real intention to put our full hearts into the cross-Channel operation next spring and we had not full confidence that they would not in future insist on our carrying out previous agreements, irrespective of changed strategic conditions. I then had to go over our whole Mediterranean strategy to prove its objects which they have never fully realized and, finally, I had to produce countless arguments to prove the close relation that exists between cross-Channel and Italian operations. In the end, I think our arguments did have some effect on Marshall."

His tactic appeared to work. On 17 August:

> "We had our meeting with the Americans and started with a closed session with only Chiefs of Staff attending. To my great relief, they accepted the proposals for the European Theatre so that all our arguing has borne fruit and we have obtained quite fair results."

19 August was:

> "Another poisonous day!... went to the citadel to see the PM to discuss South East Asia operations. I had another row with him. He is insisting on capturing the top of Sumatra Island irrespective of what our general plan for the war against Japan may be! He refused to accept that any general plan was necessary, recommended a purely opportunistic policy and behaved like a spoilt child that wants a toy in a shop irrespective of the fact that its parents tell it that it is no good! Got nowhere with him and settled nothing! This makes my arguments with the Americans practically impossible!
>
> From dinner straight to Marshall's room for an hour's talk on the Burma and Japan war. Then to my room where Mallaby was awaiting me... Dill joined us and they remained till midnight. I then

had to… read for an hour to get ready for tomorrow. I feel cooked and unable to face another day of conferences. It is quite impossible to run a conference such as present one with PM chasing hares in the background!"

In his Notes, Brookie provided a good illustration of the confrontational nature of his relationship with Churchill and, also, his ability to manage, and rein in, his wayward political master. Note Brookie's mental agility when replying to Churchill's outburst, "Winston was by now revolving round the northern end of Sumatra as he had done over Trondheim in the past! He had discovered with a pair of dividers that we could bomb Singapore from this point and he had set his heart on going there. It was not a suitable base for further operations against Malaya, but I could not get any definite reply from him as to what he hoped to accomplish from there. When I drew his attention to the fact that when he put his left foot down, he should know where the right foot was going to, he shook his fist in my face saying, 'I do not want any of your long-term projects, they cripple initiative!' I agreed that they did hamper initiative but told him that I could not look upon knowing where our next step was going as constituting a long-term project! I told him he must know where he was going to which he replied that he did not want to know! All this made arguing impossible".

He also recounted in his Notes a humorous incident which occurred at one of the meetings in Quebec, "I suggested to Marshall that we should clear the room… [and] have an 'off the record' meeting… [we] were just breaking up the meeting when Dickie [Mountbatten] rushed up to remind me of 'Habbakuk' [codename for a project making aircraft carriers out of wood pulp and ice]! I therefore asked Marshall if he and the American Chiefs would allow Dickie to give an account of recent developments in 'Habbakuk'. He kindly agreed and we all sat down again.

Dickie now having been let loose gave a signal whereupon a string of attendants brought in large cubes of ice which were established at the end of the room. Dickie then proceeded to explain that the cube on the left was ordinary pure ice whereas that on the right contained many ingredients which made it far more resilient, less liable to splinter and consequently a far more suitable material for the construction of aircraft carriers. He then informed us that in order to prove his statements he had brought a revolver with him and intended to fire shots at the cubes to prove their properties! As he now pulled a revolver out of his pocket, we all rose and discreetly moved behind him. He then warned us that he would fire at the ordinary block of ice to show how it splintered and warned us to watch the splinters. He proceeded to fire and we were subjected to a hail of ice splinters! 'There,' said Dickie, 'that is just what I told you; now I shall fire at the block on the right to show you the difference.' He fired and there certainly was a difference; the bullet rebounded out of the block and buzzed round our legs like an angry bee! It will be remembered that… we had cleared the room of all the attending staff. They were waiting in an adjoining room and when the revolver shots were heard, the wag of the party shouted: 'Good heavens, they've started shooting now!!'"

On 21 August:
"We [met] Winston at 12 noon to discuss [our paper] with him. He was more reasonable and did accept the fact that an overall plan for the defeat of Japan was required but still shouted for the Sumatra operation like a spoilt child! However, he accepted our paper."

23 August saw another outburst from Brookie. These outbursts may well have been a delayed reaction to the 15 August bombshell. The 'Almighty' are Roosevelt and Churchill:

"Last day but one of our conference – and thank God for it!… The strain of arguing difficult problems with the Americans who try to run the war on a series of lawyers' agreements which, when once signed, can never be departed from is trying enough. But when you add to it all the background of a peevish temperamental prima donna of a Prime Minister, suspicious to the very limits of imagination, always fearing a military combination of effort against political dominance, the whole matter becomes quite unbearable! He has been more

unreasonable and trying than ever this time. He has during the sea voyage in a few idle moments become married to the idea that success against Japan can only be secured through the capture of the north tip of Sumatra… We have had no real opportunity of even studying the operation for its merits and possibilities and yet he wants us to press the Americans for its execution! We have struggled all day with a series of COS, Combined COS and Plenipotentiary meetings with PM and President. As a result, we have practically broken the back of all the work and have had our proposals accepted and approved by the Almighty! I am not really satisfied with the results, we have not really arrived at the best strategy but I suppose that, when working with allies, compromises, with all their evils, become inevitable."

On 24 August:

"The conference is finished and I am feeling the inevitable flatness and depression which swamps me after a spell of continuous work and of battling against difficulties, differences of opinion, stubbornness, stupidity, pettiness and pig-headedness. When suddenly the whole struggle stops abruptly and all the participants of the conference disperse in all directions, a feeling of emptiness, depression, loneliness and dissatisfaction over results attacks one and swamps one! After Casablanca, wandering alone in the garden of the Mamounia Hotel in Marrakesh, if it had not been for the birds and the company they provided, I could almost have sobbed with the loneliness. Tonight, the same feelings overwhelm me, and there are no birds!

Winston requested to talk to me on the scrambler. He was in a bad 'prima donna' highly-strung condition… one of Alexander's staff officers had stated that six divisions would not be installed in Naples until about 1st December. The lateness of this forecast sent him quite mad and during a 20 minutes' talk I failed to calm him. I must now go to see him at 10am".

The next day's entry had echoes of his 1 April 1942 entry:

"Reading over what I wrote last night, I feel that I must have been

very liverish! And I should like to remove these pages and should if it did not mean having to write them again in a less despondent strain. The morning started with a conference with Winston… He was still in a very peevish and difficult mood about rate of build up of our divisions in Italy and had already prepared a wire for Alex.

[Later that day, Brookie and Portal went fishing] I was getting on very well in an excellent spot when, to my horror, up turned Winston with Clarke and I had to turn out. I could have shot them both I felt so angry."

On 28 August, Brookie flew back to Britain:

"The morning was spent in packing, visiting old Dudley Pound [who had fallen ill] and running round to a bookshop to collect a book I had ordered on Canadian birds. We are now over the eastern edges of Newfoundland and shall soon be heading off into the Atlantic. It is now my third trip in this direction, but it still has the same thrill as the first crossing".

In his Notes, "Little did I realize on saying goodbye to old Dudley Pound that I should never see him again!… It was very shortly after this that he had his first stroke on arrival in Washington. He travelled back a sick man… and died shortly afterwards. A very gallant man who literally went on working till he dropped… He was a grand colleague to work with and now that I realize how sick a man he was lately, I withdraw any unkind remarks I may have made in my diary concerning his slowness and lack of drive."

30 August saw him back at work in the War Office. That night, he gave vent to his feelings towards Churchill:

"The Quebec conference has left me absolutely cooked. Winston made matters almost impossible, temperamental like a film star and peevish like a spoilt child. He has an unfortunate trick of picking up some isolated operation and, without ever really having looked into it, setting his heart on it. When he once gets in one of those moods, he *feels everybody is trying to thwart him and to produce difficulties. He becomes then more and more set on the operation brushing everything aside and when planners prove the operation to be impossible, he then appoints new planners in the hope that they will prove that the operation is possible. It is an untold relief to be away from him for a bit* [Churchill was in America].

I wonder whether any historian of the future will ever be able to paint Winston in his true colours. It is a wonderful character – the most marvellous qualities and superhuman genius mixed with an astonishing lack of vision at times and an impetuosity which if not guided must inevitably bring him into trouble again and again. Perhaps the most remarkable failing of his is that he can never see a whole strategical problem at once. His gaze always settles on some definite part of the canvas and the rest of the picture is lost. It is difficult to make him realize the influence of one theatre on another. The general handling of the German reserves in Europe can never be fully grasped by him. This failing is accentuated by the fact that often he does not want to see the whole picture, especially if this wider vision should in any way interfere with the operation he may have temporarily set his heart on. He is quite the most difficult man to work with that I have ever struck but I should not have missed the chance of working with him for anything on earth!"

Brookie was still 'spellbound and exasperated'.

THIRTEEN

CIGS: September–December 1943

On 17 August, Sicily fell to the Allies. Four weeks earlier, the American chiefs of staff had agreed to amphibious landings on the Italian mainland at Salerno, near Naples, but had turned down a request that resources earmarked for the cross-Channel invasion be used in these landings: Brookie had feared this would happen on 20 July. The Allies now failed to exploit several opportunities, in part because they were formulating strategy on a somewhat piecemeal basis. First, German and Italian forces in Sicily succeeded in escaping back to the Italian mainland across the narrow Straits of Messina. Second, it was not until 16 August that Montgomery was ordered to cross those Straits and land forces on the southern toe of the Italian mainland: on 3 September, Montgomery's forces landed unopposed and then made slow progress in their advance northwards. Third, Allied landings also took place on 3 September at Taranto and Brindisi on the south-eastern heel of Italy but since these landings were only added at a late stage, they were not fully exploited due to lack of tanks, transport and artillery.

On 8 September, Brookie interrupted his holiday and returned to the War Office:

> "I discovered that all plans were made to announce the armistice with Italy that evening and to invade Naples the next morning [Salerno landings], combined with an airborne landing near Rome. However, in the middle of the day wire arrived from Eisenhower to the effect that Badoglio [Italian prime minister] was ratting... decided

to continue with operations except for the airborne landing outside Rome. The next few days should be momentous ones in the Italian campaign. We are gambling and taking risks, but I feel we are justified in doing so."

On 13 September, four days after the first landings at Salerno:
"This date brought to an end the first real spell of leave that I had had since taking on the job of CIGS. I returned to work with a very flat feeling and a desperate disinclination to work!... Archie Nye took the COS meeting whilst I read hard to bring myself up to date again. A great deal had been going on and a good deal of what I saw I did not like. The Salerno landing in my view seems doomed to failure. The build up of forces has not been fast enough while the Taranto-Brindisi landings are not being made sufficient use of. I am afraid that neither Eisenhower nor Alexander will ever have sufficient vision to be big soldiers. Meanwhile it is hell to have to face being driven out of Salerno at this juncture! Such a setback will do us no good. Cabinet at 5.30pm. A Cabinet under Attlee [Churchill was still in America], how different from those under Winston! In many ways, more efficient and more to the point but, in others, a Cabinet without a head."

On the following day:
"News about Salerno landings is going from bad to worse and I feel we are bound to be pushed back into the sea! It is maddening not to be able to get the Americans to realize that they are going to burn their fingers before they do so. Started again with the morning COS which gave me a feeling of repulsion at the very thought of it."

On 15 September:
"The Salerno news is thank God a little better and the chances of remaining there now seem more hopeful.
I had a visit from Paget [commander, 21st Army Group] who is not improving and is I fear on the decline slope... [Harry Crerar] in a very despondent mood about the Canadians not being sufficiently in

the limelight and the fact that the Americans, although later to enter the war, were playing a greater and more conspicuous part. He made me quite angry with some of his petty criticisms and remarks, however we parted the best of friends."

Three days later,
"Salerno landing now seems safe."

On 21 September:
"Had a talk with PJ Grigg [Secretary of State for War] who is very upset at the thought of having to remove Paget from the Exp Force to make way for Montgomery."

In his Notes, "Paget had been placed in command of the forces in this country destined ultimately for the cross-Channel operations. He had done a marvellous job... and I wish it had been possible to leave him in command for D-Day. I had a great personal admiration and affection for him... He had, however, had no experience in this war of commanding a large formation in action, his abilities in my mind suited him better for the duties of a Chief of Staff than for a Commander. Finally, I felt that it was essential to select some general who had already proved his worth and in whom all had confidence... Grigg was pressing for his retention and although I was in complete sympathy with most of his feelings, I knew I must press for the appointment of Monty... I found it nevertheless a difficult decision to make... Paget of course took it all in a wonderful way and continued giving of his best."

On 27 September:
"Then a visit from Harker [MI5] to give me details of Martel's latest indiscretions through the post in the shape of a letter to that drunkard Mackessie who used to be Military Correspondent to the Daily Telegraph."

In his Notes, "As Mackessie was a close friend of Kenneth de Courcy, whom we had already had trouble with just before the North African landings [see 30 September 1942], all Mackessie's correspondence was being watched."

By 28 September, Churchill had returned to Britain and was making his presence felt. Note his desire to carry out operations in Burma:

"COS at which we discussed PM's wild minute about proposed operations in the Indian Ocean. Now, in addition to the impossible Sumatra operation, he hopes to do Akyab, Ramree and the Rangoon operation all in 1944!! If Germany is defeated by the end of this year, there may be some hope of doing something out there, but Germany is not yet defeated and his wild schemes can have only one result, to detract forces from the main front.

PM's meeting which lasted from 10.30 to 1am. We did practically nothing or, at any rate, nothing that could not have been finished in an hour. He was in a foul mood and convinced that we are finding every excuse we can to avoid doing the Sumatra operation."

On the following day, Churchill appeared to relent:

"I was sent for by the PM after the morning's COS meeting and found him in a much more pleasant and cooperative mood. He started by saying that he was just as anxious as I was about our Mediterranean strategy and for not doing anything that might draw forces away from the Mediterranean. I think he felt that he had been in a very unpleasant mood the previous evening and wanted to make some amends for it."

On 1 October, however, Churchill changed tack again:

"A rushed morning with COS till 12 noon, then meeting with PM, COS, Dickie Mountbatten... This resulted in an hour's pitched battle between me and the PM on the question of withdrawing troops from the Mediterranean for the Indian Ocean offensive. I was refusing to impair our amphibious potential power in the Mediterranean in order to equip Mountbatten for adventures in Sumatra. He on the other hand was prepared to scrap our basic policy and put Japan before Germany. However, I defeated most of his evil intentions in the end!"

On 5 October, Germany's defeat appears to have been viewed as inevitable:

"Cabinet at 5.30... We were by way of discussing Foreign Secretary's paper on line he was to take during his coming visit to Moscow, all concerning post-war handling of Germany... Smuts appeared having arrived in the morning, he raised the interesting point as to whether we really wanted to dismember Germany now or whether a strong Germany in the future might not assist in balancing power in Europe against Russia. He said he had no doubts last year about dismembering Germany but now was doubtful about it."

On the next day:

"Our COS was employed in examining the situation created by the German [capture of] Kos Island [Aegean Sea]... the PM's anxiety to recapture this wonderful trophy and the effect of its loss on the proposed operations to capture Rhodes. It is pretty clear in my mind that with the commitments we have in Italy we should not undertake serious operations in the Aegean... PM by now determined to go for Rhodes without looking at the effects on Italy or at any rate refusing to look the implications square in the face. I had a heated argument with him and no support from Portal, in fact the very reverse!"

His 7 October entry opened in bleak and despairing terms:

"Another day of Rhodes madness. Another 3pm conference, another 1½ hours' battle with PM to hold on to what I think is right. The same arguments brought up again and again! And then finally sent for at 10.30pm to try and swing me and get me to agree in a tête-à-tête interview... He is in a very dangerous condition, most unbalanced, and God knows how we shall finish this war if this goes on."

The following day's entry was in similar vein:

"I am slowly becoming convinced that in his old age Winston

is becoming less and less well balanced! I can control him no more. He has worked himself into a frenzy of excitement about the Rhodes attack, has magnified its importance so that he can no longer see anything else and has set his heart on capturing this one island even at the expense of endangering his relations with the President... and also the whole future of the Italian campaign. He refuses to listen to any arguments or to see any dangers!... The Americans are already desperately suspicious of him and this will make matters far worse... but the worst of the whole matter is that I am afraid matters will go on deteriorating rather than improving. If they do, I shall not be able to stick it much longer!"

In his Notes, "The Americans always suspected Winston of having concealed desires to spread into the Balkans. These fears were not entirely ungrounded! They were determined that whatever happened they would not be led into the Balkans. At times I think that they imagined I supported Winston's Balkan ambitions, which was far from being the case."

On 10 October:

"A quiet day at home!!! with continuous telephone calls connected with Roosevelt's last reply to PM's wire. I spent ½ an hour with [Churchill] on telephone, during which he stated everyone was against him but that the situation was so changed in Italy that we must readjust our thoughts!! Any changes there are only due to everything I have been trying to drill into him during the last week! I can't stick much more of these eel-like tactics!!"

13 October saw another dry comment:

"Bert Harris [Arthur 'Bomber' Harris, Commander-in-Chief, RAF Bomber Command]... came to see us this morning during the COS meeting. According to him the only reason why the Russian army has succeeded in advancing is due to the results of bomber offensive!! According to him I am certain that we are all preventing him from

winning the war. If Bomber Command was left to itself, it would make much shorter work of it all!!"

On 19 October:

"COS at which we received note from PM wishing to swing round the strategy back to the Mediterranean at the expense of the cross-Channel operation. I am in many ways entirely with him, but God knows where that may lead us to as regards clashes with Americans."

On 20 October, Brookie was in low spirits. There was a despondent tone in many of his entries during this period:

"One of those days when even sunshine fails to dispel the gloom that lies on one. All life, and all its enterprises, looked black. In every problem the molehills became mountains and failure seemed to be the inevitable result of all enterprise. A desperate feeling of failure, incompetency and incapacity to carry this burden any longer!"

On the following day:

"Heard news of poor old Dudley Pound's death, it must be a blessing from his point of view as he was deriving little benefit from life in his paralysed state. Cunningham, the new First Sea Lord, now attends the COS. I am still suffering from a dislike for life and even greater dislike for work!"

In his Notes, "[Andrew Cunningham's] arrival in the COS was indeed a happy event for me. I found him first and foremost one of the most attractive of friends, secondly a charming associate to work with and finally the staunchest of campaigners when it came to supporting a policy agreed to amongst ourselves".

On 25 October:

"It is becoming more and more evident that our operations in Italy are coming to a standstill and that owing to lack of resources we shall not only come to a standstill but also find ourselves in a very *dangerous position unless the Russians go on from one success to another. Our build up in Italy is much slower than the German and far slower than I had expected. We shall have an almighty row with the Americans who have put us in this position with their insistence to abandon the Mediterranean operations for the very problematical cross-Channel operations. We are now beginning to see the full beauty of the Marshall strategy!! It is quite heartbreaking when we see what we might have done this year if our strategy had not been distorted by the Americans."*

Brookie elaborated in his Notes, "The winter weather settling in no doubt added to our difficulties, but the main trouble was the American desire to now swing priorities round to the Channel and in doing so render it impossible to gather the full fruits of our present strategic position. We were now firmly established in the lower part of the leg of Italy. We had command of the air and command of the sea. The enemy flanks therefore remained open to [amphibious landings] on both sides throughout the length of Italy. The main artery of rail communication consisted of one double line of railway open to air attack throughout its length. The Italian forces had only one desire and that was to finish with the war. Conditions were therefore ideal for hitting the enemy hard and for enforcing on him the use of [his] reserves in the defence of Italy. We had certainly arrived at the time when the most active planning and preparation was necessary for next year's cross-Channel operation, but these plans and preparations must NOT be allowed to slow down operations in Italy which were themselves one of the most important of the preparations. The American outlook was unfortunately one of, 'We have already wasted far too much time in the Mediterranean doing nothing, let us now lose no more time in this secondary theatre. Let us transfer and allot all available resources to the main theatre and finish the war quickly in Germany.'"

On 26 October:

"I was sent for by Winston at 10am to discuss Alexander's last wire stating that operations in Italy were coming to a standstill. Discussed

with him the best methods of getting the Americans to realize that we must for the present concentrate on the Mediterranean. Then met COS and prepared a wire for Washington.

After lunch attended poor dear old Dudley Pound's funeral and felt, as I sat next to his coffin in the Abbey, that amongst the 3 of the Chiefs of Staff he had certainly chosen the one road that led at last to peace and an end to these worldly struggles, and in some ways I envied him."

Two days later:

"News from Russia continues to be excellent."

In his Notes, "It is rather strange that I did not refer more frequently to the news from Russia. It continued to be the vital point on which the whole of our strategy hinged. If Russia had collapsed all our strategic plans would have gone west. German forces liberated from Russia would have made a cross-Channel operation impossible and would have endangered our position in Italy and Middle East."

On 29 October:

"Met PM to discuss South East Asia operations and thank God succeeded in getting decisions out of him… After our meeting, I asked him whether he would agree to put Dill up for a peerage in the New Year's Honours List. I felt very doubtful how he would react and was surprised to find that he jumped at it… I must now see that he sticks to it."

In his Notes, "This was my first attempt to obtain Dill a peerage. For my next attempt I brought PJ Grigg with me. The results were the same; agreement and promises. Then nothing! I do not believe he had any intention of ever ensuring that Dill received a peerage! And yet there are very few people to whom he owed more than he did to Dill for the exceptional relations he had established with Marshall… I shall never be able to forgive Winston for his attitude towards Dill."

1 November saw Brookie in low spirits, again:

> "Now I am off for another 10.30pm meeting and I am 'sick unto death' of these night meetings! We are to discuss plans for another Combined Chiefs of Staff meeting and the stink of the last one is not yet out of my nostrils! My God! How I hate those meetings and how weary I am of them! When I look at the Mediterranean, I realize only too well how far I have failed in my task during the last 2 years! If only I had had sufficient force of character to swing those American Chiefs of Staff and make them see daylight, how different the war might be. We should have been in a position to force the Dardanelles by the capture of Crete and Rhodes, we should have the whole Balkans ablaze by now [Britain was supplying the partisan resistance movement in Yugoslavia], and the war might have been finished in 1943!! Instead, to satisfy American short-sightedness, we have been led into agreeing to the withdrawal of forces from the Mediterranean for a nebulous 2nd Front and have emasculated our offensive strategy!! It is heartbreaking."

This entry is inconsistent with his entries in early October when he expressed opposition to Churchill's desire to capture Rhodes. The inconsistency is explained in his Notes and also in his 20 November Notes, "I am inclined to think that I cannot have been very far off [a] nervous breakdown at that time. Nevertheless, there is a great deal in what I wrote on the evening of November 1st. If the Americans had cooperated wholeheartedly in the Mediterranean and had been able to appreciate the advantages to be gained, events might well have turned out to our advantage. Unfortunately, just at a moment when there were some fruits to be gained from the efforts we had made, the Americans selected this as a moment to damp down our efforts; troops, landing craft and transport were removed and reallocated. At very little cost, Crete and Rhodes could have been rendered possible operations without affecting operations in Italy whereas, as matters stood, these operations were only possible at the expense of Italian operations and consequently ruled out. Success in Crete and Rhodes might have had the happiest repercussions in Turkey and the Balkans without ever committing a single man in the Balkans; we could have benefited better than before by the actions of the Resistance movements in these countries."

On 2 November:

"A long COS which started with our weekly interview with Joint Intelligence Committee. I had to disagree with a report they had submitted as to number of divisions that could concentrate in Northern Italy. They did not like this and consequently I am very unpopular with them now."

The following day saw Cunningham making his presence felt:

"This morning's COS took a nasty turn in the shape of a long discussion between [Portal] and the new First Sea Lord [Cunningham]!!! Neither would give in and I had a difficult time, I wonder if this is the first of many more of this kind!"

8 November saw a clumsy manoeuvre by the Americans, the aim clearly being to ensure resources were concentrated on the cross-Channel invasion:

"Arrived at WO to find table littered with telegrams from Moscow and from Washington. One from Washington with a ridiculous suggestion by Leahy [Roosevelt's chief of staff] that Marshall should be made Supreme Commander of European Theatre, to combine North Africa with cross-Channel! Luckily, PM was entirely with us and sent back strong telegram to Dill with his views as to the absurdity of the proposal! The trouble is that meanwhile our proposal [to appoint a supreme commander in the Mediterranean] is being sidetracked. Dined out with Bannerman and had a glorious evening of bird talk which I thoroughly enjoyed."

On 9 November:

"Long discussion at our COS meeting on future Mediterranean strategy… Essential that we should clear our minds as to our

recommendations before meeting the American Chiefs [in Cairo, prior to the Tehran conference between Britain, America and Russia]. A few things stand out clearly. First, we must go in Italy till we reach the Pisa-Rimini line. This will entail postponing cross-Channel operations some 2 months. Secondly, we must centralize command of Mediterranean. Thirdly the partisans in Balkans must be rearmed at far greater rate than at present. Fourthly, Turkey must be brought into the war and the Dardanelles opened again. Fifthly, Balkan states must be made to sue for peace. The above seems rough outline to go for."

On 12 November:

"Interview with Ralston [Canadian defence minister] and Stewart [Canadian Army chief of staff]. Apparently former had informed McNaughton that neither I nor Paget had confidence in him as an Army Commander in action. McNaughton had been to see Paget and on the strength of his interview had wired to MacKenzie King [Canadian prime minister] that Ralston and Stewart had fitted up a case against him which was in no way supported by Paget and had given a completely erroneous interpretation of his interview with Paget. It rather looks to me as if McNaughton is going off his head!"

On the same day, Churchill departed for Cairo by sea, his intention being to visit Malta and Italy en route. Three days later, a clearly concerned Brookie was still in London, his departure having been delayed by bad weather:

"Our journey again put off for 24 hours, this is bad as Winston will be off to Italy without me and I want to be there when he sees Alexander and Monty!"

The next day saw military considerations clashing with political objectives:

"Cabinet at 5.30am at which we discussed the question of supporting partisans in Greece. I had considerable difference of opinion with Anthony Eden who is for cutting support to those partisans who

have been doing most of the work as their views are communistic and against the future government of Greece as backed by the Foreign Office. Succeeded in getting Cabinet to agree with me."

By 18 November, both Churchill and Brookie were in Malta. In the event, the planned visit to Italy had to be cancelled:

"PM gave a long tirade on evils of Americans… He was not at his best and I feel nervous as to the line he may adopt at this conference. He is inclined to say to the Americans, all right if you won't play with us in the Mediterranean, we won't play with you in the English Channel. And if they say all right, well then we shall direct our main effort in the Pacific, to reply you are welcome to do so if you wish! I do not think such tactics will pay.

Long military discussions at dinner and after dinner which filled me with gloom! There are times when I feel that it is all a horrid nightmare which I must wake out of soon. All this floundering about, this lack of clear vision… PM examining war by theatres and without perspective, no clear appreciation of the influence of one theatre on another! Then he discusses Command and Commanders and has never yet gained a true grasp of Higher Command organization".

In his Notes, "First of all, the new feelings of spitefulness which had been apparent lately with Winston since the strength of the American forces were now building up fast and exceeding ours. He hated having to give up the position of the dominant partner which we had held at the start. As a result, he became inclined at times to put up strategic proposals which he knew were unsound purely to spite the Americans… There lay, however, in the back of his mind the desire to form a purely British theatre when the laurels would be all ours.

He could not or would not follow how a chain of command was applied. He was always wanting a Commander-in-Chief to suddenly vacate his post and concentrate on commanding one individual element of his command at the expense of all the rest."

20 November saw Brookie in Cairo:

"*[This conference] will be an unpleasant one, the most unpleasant one we have had yet and that is saying a good deal. I despair of ever getting our American friends to have any sort of strategic vision... If they had come wholeheartedly into the Mediterranean with us we should by now have Rome securely, the Balkans would be ablaze, the Dardanelles would be open and we should be... getting Rumania and Bulgaria out of the war. I blame myself for having had the vision to foresee these possibilities and yet to have failed to overcome the American short-sightedness and allowed my better judgement to have been affected by them. It would have been better to have resigned my appointment than to allow any form of compromise. And yet I wonder whether any such action would have borne any fruits. I rather doubt it.*"

He elaborated in his Notes, "Southern Europe was now threatened on all sides; Italy was tottering and seeking for a way out of the war; all partisans in the Balkan states had been... stirred to new activities; Turkey... was showing signs of leaning towards our side. Success breeds success in these cases and the ball was at our feet. A quick elimination of Italy coupled with a show of forces in the approach to the Dardanelles, including the capture of Crete and Rhodes, might well have borne valuable fruits. No liberation of the Balkans should be undertaken. This was unnecessary and would commit too much force. What was wanted was to knock all the props from under the Germans in the defence of the Mediterranean, let them alone to bear this full burden. We had been forced to miss some opportunities through lack of forces in the Mediterranean.

Europe was just one large strategic front with German forces distributed round the perimeter in accordance with the existing threats in each respective theatre. Forces in France watched the Channel approaches, those in Norway and Denmark held down those countries... vast armies contained the Russians, in the south further detachments threatened Turkey and kept peace in the Balkans whilst, finally, considerable force was employed in holding onto Italy and guarding Southern France. All these forces were handled centrally and served by the most perfect East and West railway system in existence. A system which had been built up in the First World War and reinforced by the autobahn system of roads. It was easier for the Germans to convey divisions from the Russian front to the French front than it was for us to convey similar formations from the Italian front by sea to the French front. The North and South communications were, however, nothing like as efficient, comprising only one double line of railway through the leg of Italy and one through the Balkans to Greece.

Our strategy had now become a delicate matter of balancing. Our aim must be to draw as many divisions as possible from the French Channel and to retain them in Southern Europe as long as possible. Any failure to draw full advantage from our present position [in southern Europe] must also fail in drawing [German] reserves away from the Channel. On the other hand, any tendency to weaken our forces in the Mediterranean would at once lead to the move of German forces to the Channel.

I could never get [Marshall] to appreciate the very close connection that existed between the various German fronts. For him, they might have been separate wars, a Russian war on the one side, a Mediterranean war on another and a cross-Channel one to be started as soon as possible."

On the insistence of the Americans, the Chinese leader, Chiang Kai-shek, and his wife, Madame Chiang, attended the Cairo meeting, much to Brookie's disapproval. In his Notes, "We should never have started our conference with Chiang; by doing so we were putting the cart before the horse. He had nothing to contribute towards the defeat of the Germans… We should have started this conference by thrashing out thoroughly with the Americans the policy and strategy for the defeat of Germany. We could then have shown a united front to Stalin and finally, if time admitted, seen Chiang and Madame."

On 23 November, Brookie was, however, clearly intrigued by Madame:
"I was very interested in the Chinese pair. The generalissimo reminded me more of a cross between a pine marten and a ferret than anything else. A shrewd, foxy sort of face. Evidently with no grasp of

war in its larger aspects but determined to get the best of the bargains. Madame was a study in herself, a queer character in which sex and politics seemed to predominate, both being used indiscriminately individually or unitedly to achieve her ends. If not good looking she had certainly made the best of herself and was well turned out".

In his Notes, "She was the only woman amongst a very large gathering of men and was determined to bring into action all the charms nature had blessed her with... she certainly had a good figure which she knew how to display at its best. Also gifted with great charm and gracefulness, every small movement of hers arrested and pleased the eye. For instance, at one critical moment her closely clinging black dress of black satin with yellow chrysanthemums displayed a slit which extended to her hip bone and exposed one of the most shapely of legs.

The trouble... was that we were left wondering whether we were dealing with Chiang or with Madame... whenever Chiang spoke, his General duly interpreted the statement but Madame rose to say in the most perfect English, 'Excuse me gentlemen, but the General has failed to convey to you the full meaning of the thoughts that the Generalissimo wishes to express. If you will allow me, I shall put before you his real thoughts'... I certainly felt that she was the leading spirit of the two and that I would not trust her very far.

[Chiang] was certainly very successful in leading the Americans down the garden path. He and his Chinese forces never did much against the Japs during the war... yet the Americans never saw through all his shortcomings, pinned their hopes to him and induced us to do the same."

His 23 November entry continued:
"After lunch, meeting with CCS [Combined Chiefs of Staff] which became somewhat heated with King on the subject of the Andaman Islands [a string of islands south of Burma] and the possibility of landing craft being diverted from this operation to the Aegean."

The Americans were supporting a proposed attack on the Andamans but were being opposed by the British who wanted to secure agreement over future operations in the European theatre before deciding on the action to take in South East Asia. This 'somewhat heated' meeting was also attended by the anglophobic General 'Vinegar Joe' Stilwell [see 14 May] whose description of it was far more colourful, "Brooke got nasty and King got good and sore. King almost climbed over the table at Brooke. God he was mad. I wish he had socked him."[1]

24 November saw praise for Churchill:

"*We all went over to the President's villa for a meeting with him and the Prime Minister. The President started with a general statement expressing his views as to the conduct of the war. This did not last very long and then the PM gave a masterly statement on his views concerning the European strategy and the best ways of maintaining the pressure on Germany during the winter months*".

On 25 November, note the 'high and mighty' and Brookie's low opinion of politicians and diplomats. Overlord was the codename for the cross-Channel invasion:

"*We went round to President's villa when a series of photos, both still and movie, were taken. First of all, the high and mighty: President, PM and Generalissimo. Then the above with Chiefs of Staff and Chinese Generals. Finally, the above with politicians and diplomats, etc. Not a very attractive lot to look at! I have no doubt that we were not much more beautiful in the military groups, but I pray to heaven that we may have been both individually and collectively less crooked!*

At 2.30pm we had an off the record Combined meeting and made considerable progress. I put forward our counter proposals for continuing active operations in the Mediterranean at the expense of [i.e. which would result in] a postponement of Overlord date. We did not meet with half the reaction we were expecting."

On 26 November:

"*At 2.30 met Americans. It was not long before Marshall and I* had the father and mother of a row! We had to come down to an off the record meeting and we again made more progress. In the end, we secured most of the points we were after. At 5pm attended a tea party given by Chiang Kai-shek and Madame... Had some 15 minutes talk with him through an interpreter. He did not impress me much but hard to tell meeting him like that. Meanwhile Madame holding a court of admirers. The more I see of her the less I like her!"

Since his diary was intended for the eyes of Benita, Brookie could hardly conclude otherwise.

By 28 November, the British and American delegations were in Tehran:
"We [are] very worried with the whole situation. We have not got agreement with the Americans on the main points for discussion and it was evident that we are heading towards chaos. PM has bad throat and has practically lost his voice. At 4pm we went over to the Russian embassy for our first plenary meeting... Stalin turned up in his uniform of Field Marshal but to my mind no more attractive than I thought him last time I saw him.

The President started off with an introductory statement which he followed up by a brief review of the war in the Pacific. To this, Stalin replied that he much appreciated what we were doing in that theatre and that it was only the fact that the Germans fully engaged him that prevented him cooperating with us! This was cheering news and implied Russian help as soon as Germany was defeated. The President then alluded to the Western Front and read a poor and not very helpful speech. From then onwards the conference went from bad to worse! Stalin replied advocating cross-Channel operations at the expense of all else. Winston replied and was not at his best. President chipped in and made matters worse. We finished up with a suggestion, partly sponsored by the President, that we should close operations in Italy before taking Rome. That we should land some 6 divs in southern France at the beginning of April and carry out [the cross-Channel invasion] on May 1st. Turkey, according to Stalin, *was beyond hope and nothing could induce her to come into the war on any account. Dardanelles were apparently not worth opening. In fact, after complaining that we were not holding sufficient [German] divisions away from Russia, Stalin's suggestion was that practically no action should take place during the winter months! We sat for 3 hours and finished up this conference by confusing plans more than they ever have been before!"*

The following section of his Notes illustrated Brookie's analytical skills and good judgment, "This was the first occasion during the war when Stalin, Roosevelt and Winston sat round a table to discuss the war we were waging together. I found it quite enthralling looking at their faces and trying to estimate what lay behind. With Churchill, of course, I knew fairly well and I was beginning to understand the workings of Roosevelt's brain... but Stalin was still very much of an enigma. I had already formed a very high idea of his ability, force of character and shrewdness but did not know yet whether he was also a strategist. I knew that Voroshilov would provide him with nothing in the shape of strategic vision.

During this meeting and all the subsequent ones which we had with Stalin, I rapidly grew to appreciate the fact that he had a military brain of the very highest calibre. Never once in any of his statements did he make any strategic error nor did he ever fail to appreciate all the implications of a situation with a quick and unerring eye. In this respect, he stood out when compared with his two colleagues. Roosevelt never made any great pretence at being a strategist and left Marshall or Leahy to talk for him. Winston, on the other hand, was far more erratic, brilliant at times but far too impulsive and inclined to favour quite unsuitable plans without giving them the preliminary deep thought they required.

Stalin was now evidently far better satisfied with his defensive position. He was beginning to feel that the Germans had shot their bolt; immediate pressure [in] the West was no longer so urgently required. What is more, from his point of view, the entry of Turkey was no longer so desirable. He no longer had (if he had ever had) any great desire for the opening of the Dardanelles. This would bring in the British and the Americans on his left flank in an advance westward through the Balkans. He had by then pretty definite ideas about how he wanted the Balkans run after the war and this would entail, if possible, their total inclusion in the future Union of Soviet Republics. British and American assistance was therefore no longer desirable in the Eastern Mediterranean.

His new outlook on Italy was also interesting. There was now no pressure on our forces to push up the leg of Italy. Such an advance led too directly towards Yugoslavia and Austria, on which no doubt he had by now cast covetous eyes. He approved of Roosevelt's futile proposals to close down operations in Italy and to transfer six divisions to invade Southern France on April 1st, whilst the main Channel operation would take place on 1st May. I am certain he did not approve such operations for their strategic value but because they fitted in with his future political plans. He was too good a strategist not to see the weakness of the American plan. To cease operations in Italy before Rome would at once free [up] the required [German] reinforcements to meet six of our divisions under the precarious conditions of a landing [in southern France] and all the subsequent administrative problems connected with their maintenance on this new front. The potential war effort of our divisions on transfer from Italy to Southern France would in the early stages have been reduced by half. Furthermore, this plan allowed for the whole of the month of April for the annihilation of these six divisions [landing in southern France] whilst fighting in Italy was at a standstill and Overlord had not yet started. I feel certain that Stalin saw through these strategical misconceptions but to him they mattered little; his political and military requirements could now be best met by the greatest squandering of British and American lives in the French theatre.

We were reaching a very dangerous point where Stalin's shrewdness, assisted by American short-sightedness, might lead us anywhere. It is not surprising that I found this series of meetings so difficult. Here we were with the Americans determined to start Operation Overlord on the wrong leg if they possibly could and Stalin inwardly hoping that they would do so."

On 29 November:

> "7 hours spent in conferences and 6 of them through interpreters!! We started the morning with a staff meeting at 10.30 consisting of Leahy, Marshall, Voroshilov, Portal and myself. We spent 3 hours at it, and at the end were no further advanced. Voroshilov's main theme was that the cross-Channel operation must have preference over all others and that the date must remain May 1st. In vain, I argued that by closing operations in the Mediterranean, German forces would be free to proceed to other theatres! Our friend Voroshilov refused to see any of these arguments having been evidently briefed by Stalin... Leahy said nothing and Marshall only stressed the importance that the Americans had always attached to cross-Channel operations.
>
> At 3.30pm we went over to the Russian Embassy to see Winston present the Stalingrad Sword to Stalin. Bands, Guards of Honour, national anthems, etc. Speech by Winston after which he handed sword over in name of King to Stalin. Stalin kissed sword and handed it over to Voroshilov who promptly dropped sword out of its scabbard!... We then sat down at 4pm to another long 3-hour conference! Bad from beginning to end. Winston was not good and Roosevelt even worse. Stalin meticulous with only two arguments. Cross-Channel operation on May 1st and also offensive in Southern France! Americans supported this view quite unaware of the fact that it is already an impossibility. Finally, decided that Americans and ourselves should have another meeting tomorrow with a view to arriving at some form of solution for our final plenary meeting.
>
> I have little hope of any form of agreement... After listening to the arguments put forward during the last 2 days, I feel more like entering a lunatic asylum or a nursing home than continuing with my present job. I am absolutely disgusted with the politicians' methods of waging a war!! Why will they imagine that they are experts at a job they know nothing about! It is lamentable to listen to them! May God help us in the future prosecution of this war, we have every hope of making an unholy mess of it and of being defeated yet!"

In his Notes, "The Americans had forced us to put the cart before the horse in the early stages by meeting Chiang Kai-shek before having our meetings with them. Now the same was occurring with the Russians. We had reached the stage where we had put the horse in the cart and were pulling it around without knowing where we were heading for."

30 November was the last day of the conference. It was also:

"The PM's 69th Birthday. CCS with Americans at 9.30. Here we had a difficult time trying to arrive at some agreement which we could put before our Russian friends in the afternoon. After much argument we decided that the cross-Channel operation could be put off to June 1st. This did not meet all our requirements but was arranged to fit in with proposed Russian spring offensive. We also decided to stage what we could in the way of operations in Southern France. I pressed hard again to obtain the abandonment of the Andaman Island attack so as to render more landing craft available for the Mediterranean. Still same political difficulties [Roosevelt had promised Chiang Kai-shek that an amphibious operation would be staged].

Plenary meeting to report results of our morning meeting... President, PM and Stalin made pretty speeches... One thing is quite clear, the more politicians you put together to settle the prosecution of the war the longer you postpone its conclusion!

We finished the day with a banquet... to celebrate Winston's 69th birthday... We had not been going long when the President made a nice speech alluding to our fathers having known each other when he and I were boys and proposing my health. Stalin then chipped in and said that as a result of this meeting and of having come to such unanimous agreement he hoped that I would no longer look upon Russians with such suspicion and that if I really got to know them I should find that they were quite good chaps!! This was a most unexpected and uncalled for attack and I am certain that Averell Harriman [American ambassador to Russia]... must have been making mischief as he is very busy at the moment trying to improve his USA position at our expense.

> *I could not let this accusation pass… I thanked the President for his very kind words… then turned to Stalin and reminded him that… the PM had said that 'in war the truth must be accompanied by an escort of lies to ensure its secrecy.' I reminded him that he himself had described how in all big offensives he produced masses of dummy tanks and aeroplanes on the fronts he was not going to attack, whilst he moved up forces quietly and under cover of darkness on the front of attack… I felt convinced that he must have been looking at the dummy aeroplanes and guns and had failed to observe the real and true offensive in the shape of real friendship and comradeship which I felt towards him and all the Soviet forces! This went very well and met with some success. After dinner, I returned to the attack and we finished the best of friends with long handshakes and almost with our arms round each other's necks! [Stalin] said that he liked the bold and soldierlike way in which I had spoken and the military strength of my voice! These were true military qualities that he liked and admired".*

In his Notes, "I found it a very trying, nervous test getting up to reply to Stalin's toast… I had, however, by then seen enough of Stalin during our Moscow visits to know that if I remained seated and sat under his insults I was finished in his eyes for good and all and written off as spineless."

By 3 December, Roosevelt, Churchill and their respective chiefs of staff had returned to Cairo for further discussions. Brookie was indignant:

> *We were dumbfounded by being informed that the meeting must finish on Sunday [two days later] at the latest as the President was off! No apologies, nothing. They have completely upset the whole meeting by wasting our time with Chiang Kai-shek and Stalin before we had settled any points with them. And now with nothing settled they propose to disappear into the blue and leave all the main points connected with the Mediterranean unsettled! It all looks like some of the worst sharp practice that I have seen for some time."*

In his Notes, "I withdraw every word connected with 'sharp practice' and am quite certain that the one thing that Marshall would never have tolerated was anything connected with 'sharp practice'. I have seldom met a straighter or more reliable man in my life".

4 December saw Brookie at his most forthright:

> "*Interview with President and Americans. PM gave long discourse and then called on me to express my views. I said that this conference had been most unsatisfactory. Usually at these meetings we discussed matters till we arrived at a policy which we put before the PM and President for approval and amendment... [and] finally putting up a paper for approval which formed our policy for future conduct of the war. This time such a procedure had been impossible. We had straight away been thrown into high-level conference with the Chinese. These had hardly been finished when we were rushed off to Tehran for similar conferences with Stalin and now that we were back we were only given two days to arrive at any concerted policy. We then proceeded with the desirability to give up the Andaman Islands in order to concentrate on the European front. Here at once we came up against political difficulties. The President had made promises to [Chiang Kai-shek] of an amphibious operation and did not like to go back on him. We made no progress!!*
>
> *Finally, asked to dine alone with Winston to discuss questions of command. President had today decided that Eisenhower was to command Overlord whilst Marshall remained as Chief of Staff. I argued with PM that Alexander was not of sufficiently high calibre to take on the new centralized Mediterranean Command. I suggested Jumbo Wilson as Supreme Commander for Mediterranean, Alexander as Commander in Chief Italian Land Forces, Paget for Middle East, Montgomery vice Paget, and Oliver Leese vice Montgomery. He was inclined to agree... I hope he does not change his mind again!"*

In his Notes, "The selection of Eisenhower rather than Marshall was a good one. Eisenhower had now a certain amount of experience as a Commander and was beginning to find his feet. The combination of

Eisenhower [Ike] and Bedell Smith [Eisenhower's chief of staff] had much to be said for it... The removal of Ike from the Mediterranean left a difficult gap to fill. I did not want to touch either Alex or Monty for this job as I required them for the Italian campaign and for the British contingent of Overlord... I therefore introduced Jumbo Wilson for the Supreme Command Mediterranean".

On 6 December:
"To our joy, this morning we discovered that the President had at last agreed to cancel Andaman Islands attack!... this may lead to [Chiang Kai-shek] refusing to carry out his part of the Burma campaign. If he does so, it is no very great loss! At any rate we can now concentrate all our resources in the European theatre... I shall rest very well tonight and feel very satisfied at the final results of this meeting."

On 8 December, Brookie's fear that Churchill might change his mind over the new command appointments proved well-founded:
"All my good work of the [4 December] dinner is gone! [Churchill] is now back again wanting Alexander as Supreme Commander for the Mediterranean and has pushed old Jumbo Wilson aside!... All the trouble has been caused by Macmillan [Harold Macmillan, British minister, resident in the Mediterranean] who has had a long talk with the PM suggesting that Alex is the man for the job and that he, Macmillan, can take the political load off him. [Macmillan] came round to see me for an hour this evening and evidently does not even begin to understand what the functions of a Supreme Commander should be. Why must the PM consult everybody except those who can give him real advice!!"

In his Notes, "This interference on the part of Macmilllan made me very angry. I had been informed by the PM that Macmillan had an excellent solution to the problem of supreme command in the Mediterranean... I at once smelled a rat there and wondered what he was poking his nose into.

I sent for [Macmillan] and... very soon discovered that he had only the haziest of ideas as to what the duties of a Supreme Commander were... I also asked him, when he had these bright ideas on military organization to discuss these matters with me first before seeing the PM. What I did realize very quickly... was that [Macmillan] knew he could handle Alex and that he would be as a piece of putty in his hand; but, on the other hand, Jumbo Wilson was made of much rougher material which would not be so pliable and easy to handle."

On 9 December:

"Last night at the Embassy dinner, [Smuts] pulled me aside to tell me he was not at all happy about the condition of the PM. He considered he worked far too hard, exhausted himself and then had to rely on drink to stimulate him again. He said he was beginning to doubt whether he would stay the course, that he was noticing changes in him. He then said that he fully realized my task was getting more and more difficult with the PM but that I must stick to it and do my best to keep him on the right track. He said that he had been saying things to the PM to try and assist me in my task. He fully realized that I had been correct in sticking to my job when he and the PM had tried to get me to replace Auchinleck, he also fully appreciated what a heavy responsibility it entailed and what a heavy task it was.

I was ordered for a tête-à-tête with PM... he was looking very tired and said he felt very flat, tired and had pains across his loins... he asked me whether I did not think I had better be made a Field Marshal in view of all the responsibility I was carrying! I told him there was nothing I would appreciate more when he considered I had deserved it".

In his Notes, "[Smuts] was realizing far better than anyone, even Moran the PM's doctor, how near Winston was getting to a breakdown! He was at that moment on the verge of his go of pneumonia... I am quite certain... my recommendation for a [field marshal's] baton had probably been started by Smuts".

On 11 December, Churchill and Brookie flew to Tunis:

> "PM very tired and flat, he seems to be in a bad way. I had a very useful conference with Eisenhower and Tedder… mainly on the question of the selection of his successor and of the organization of the Command… Ike's suggested solution was to put Wilson in Supreme Command, replace Alex by Monty and take Alex home to command the land forces for Overlord. This almost fits in with my idea except I would invert Alex and Monty, but I don't mind much."

In his Notes, "I discovered, as I had expected, that [Ike] would sooner have Alex with him for Overlord than Monty. He… could handle Alex but was not fond of Monty and certainly did not know how to handle him. I am surprised… I wrote that between the selection of Alex or Monty for Overlord 'I don't mind much'! I certainly minded a great deal and would have had little confidence in Alex running that show.

I was getting very worried about Winston's health… [and] discussed the matter with Moran who entirely agreed. I therefore… told [Winston] that he was wrong in wanting to go to Italy… [and] was beginning to make a little progress and then I foolishly said, 'And what is more, Moran entirely agrees with me.' He rose up on his elbow in his bed, shook his fist in my face and said: 'Don't you get in league with that bloody old man'!!! [Churchill and Moran were then 69 and 61 years old respectively]"

His 12 December entry suggested Brookie was not a man to wake up in the middle of the night:

> "I was dog-tired last night and sleeping like a log at 4am when I was woken by a raucous voice re-echoing through the room with a series of mournful, 'Hullo, Hullo, Hullo!' When I had woken sufficiently, I said 'Who the hell is that?' and switched on my torch. To my dismay, I found the PM in his dragon dressing gown with a brown bandage wrapped round his head wandering about my room! He said he was looking for Lord Moran, that he had a bad headache. I led him to Moran's room and retired back to bed… This morning… the PM has got a temperature of about 102 and is not in too good a way at all."

On 13 December, Brookie flew to Italy with Alexander. On the next day, he visited Montgomery's HQ:

"Monty strikes me as looking tired and definitely wants a rest or a change... [He] asked me how much importance we attached to an early capture of Rome as he saw little hope of capturing it before March!! To my mind, it is quite clear that Alex is not gripping this show. There is no real plan for the capture of Rome... Frankly, I am rather depressed from what I have seen and heard today."

The problem confronting the Allies was that German forces had dug themselves into well-nigh unassailable defensive positions in the mountain ranges in central Italy.

15 December provided a possible explanation for Alex's failure to 'grip the show':

"My impression of the day is that we are stuck in our offensive here and shall make no real progress till the ground dries unless we make greater use of our amphibious power... Alex has not fully recovered from his jaundice. The offensive is stagnating badly and something must be done about it as soon as I get back."

On 17 December, he visited the front:

"We then motored in our jeeps to within 2500 yards of the Boche and in full view of him without being fired on. Hawkesworth then gave us a description of the attack on Mount Camino from our old front line. We then motored up the slope as far as the jeeps would go and then took to horses to go up a perpendicular mule track to a small plateau below Monastery Hill. Here Brig. Lyne gave us an excellent description of how his brigade of Queen's [battalions] stormed this frightful height. It was all... very vivid as the old Boche trenches and equipment were still lying about and they were even burying Boche still while we were there."

In his Notes, "From the top of Mount Camino, I had been able to see quite clearly Mount Cassino and the country round and had discussed with Alex the very nasty nut we should have to crack there."

By 18 December, Brookie had rejoined the ailing Churchill in Tunisia:
"*Winston started by telling me that the King was very pleased to make me a Field Marshal… He was rather upset when I told him I was off tomorrow morning and I had to be firm as he was suggesting my stopping on for several days! It is now decided that [Jumbo] Wilson becomes Supreme Commander Mediterranean, that Alexander stays in Italy and that Monty comes home to command land forces for Overlord whilst Oliver Leese takes over 8th Army and Paget relieves Jumbo in the Middle East.*"

On 19 December, he was in Gibraltar en route back to Britain:
"*It is very hard to believe that I have not been away quite 5 weeks, it feels more like 5 years!… My brain is feeling tired and confused and a desperate longing for a long rest. I suppose I might as well long for the moon! After dinner, we were told that the weather was good enough for us to fly… Poor Boyle [Brookie's military assistant] had started a go of jaundice so we gave him the only bed available. By 1.30am we were off.*"

Brookie's plane landed in Britain at 9.30am the following day:
"*I went up to the [War Office] where I had an hour's interview with the Secretary of State… The afternoon was spent in getting myself up to date again and in going through recent papers… Am feeling very sleepy and dog-tired*".

In his Notes, "I had some reason for satisfaction… I had got the date of Overlord pushed on to June 1st so that it would not cripple the Italian campaign, then I had turned the South France offensive into something more plastic which could be adjusted without affecting Italy seriously… The present operations in Italy were therefore now on a firmer footing. It must be remembered that to remove a division from the Italian front, to embark it, to transfer it by sea... to unload it in England, locate it in new formations and new training areas and... train it for the most difficult of operations – a combined landing against strong opposition – required a period which could only be measured in terms of months... every division withdrawn from Italy to England for operation Overlord was [therefore] a division washed off the slate for a period of months... the Andaman attack had been put off, thus allowing landing equipment to be assembled in the Mediterranean and not diverted to war against Japan before Germany was defeated. Finally, I had fixed up the intricate problem of command in the Mediterranean... my visit to Italy had brought home to me the importance of making use of our amphibious power in this theatre by opening up a bridgehead near Rome."

On 21 December:
"Attended Chiefs of Staff meeting... made a statement concerning my visit to Italy and necessity for amphibious operations on this front [behind the German defensive line in central Italy]."

After spending Christmas at home, he returned to work on 30 December:
"My recommendations for strong amphibious operations in Rome area are being acted on which is good."

On 31 December:
"Interview with Bedell Smith [Eisenhower's chief of staff] concerning setting up of HQ for cross-Channel operations. He and Eisenhower are anxious to take all the heads of Staff departments out of the Mediterranean!! This will want watching! Considered that Bedell Smith had gone off a lot and was suffering from a swollen head."

In his Notes, "Bedell Smith... was decidedly bumptious and imagined that the Mediterranean HQ could now be robbed of all its best officers to form the new HQ. I had to put Bedell Smith in his place".

FOURTEEN

CIGS: January–May 1944

Brookie's diary entries for 1944 are notable for the sharpness – and frequency – of his criticisms of Churchill. In his Notes, "On reading these diaries, I have repeatedly felt ashamed of the abuse I had poured on [Winston], especially during the latter years. It must, however, be remembered that my diary was the safety valve and only outlet for all my pent-up feelings… During the last years, Winston had been a very sick man… This physical condition together with his mental fatigue accounted for many of the difficulties in dealing with him, a factor which I failed to make adequate allowance for in my diary… Throughout all these troublesome times, I always retained the same unbounded admiration and gratitude for what he had done in the early years of the war… I shall always look back on the years I worked with him as some of the most difficult and trying ones in my life. For all that, I thank God that I was given an opportunity of working alongside of such a man and of having my eyes opened to the fact that occasionally such supermen exist on this earth."

On 1 January 1944:

"Heard on the 8am wireless that I had been promoted to Field Marshal! It gave me a curious peaceful feeling that I had at last, and unexpectedly, succeeded in reaching the top rung of the ladder!! I certainly never set out to reach this position, nor did I ever hope to do so even in my wildest moments. When I look back over my life, no one could be more surprised than I am to find where I have got to!!"

By now, Montgomery had returned to Britain to take command of the land forces for Overlord, the cross-Channel invasion. Two days later:

> "Meeting with Monty to discuss his ideas on plans for invasion... Saw that the scaup [duck] had returned on the St James' Park lake."

On 4 January:

> "A long COS meeting at which we did our weekly review of the threat of the rocket or pilotless plane [German V1 and V2 weapons]. Evidence goes on accumulating... Then Paget came to say goodbye. He is evidently upset and sad at being superseded by Monty but is taking it all very well."

Earlier, 21 July 1943, Brookie had recognised the need to deploy mountain trained troops in Italy. On 7 January, he returned to the same subject. Note his dry comment about Amery and the Alpine Club:

> "A difficult COS as Winston, sitting in Marrakesh, is now full of beans and trying to win the war from there! As a result, a 3-cornered flow of telegrams in all directions is gradually resulting in utter confusion! I wish to God that he would come home and get under control. After lunch, went to see Amery who, having just been appointed President of the Alpine Club, has become more mountain warfare minded than ever! He would almost convert the whole army in Italy into mountaineers! However, there is a great deal in what he says and I don't think that Alexander realizes half enough the necessity of training mountaineers on his front [When the German defensive line in the mountains of central Italy was eventually breached in May, a significant role was played by a French corps which included a Moroccan division experienced in mountain warfare]."

Three days later:

> "The operation for the attack just south of Rome [amphibious landings at Anzio] is now all settled for the 22nd of this month. Pray God that the weather may be fine for it, otherwise it might well end in a bad disaster."

On 11 January:

> "We had our weekly examination at the COS of the prospects of the pilotless plane and of the counter measures. The bombing of the launching emplacements in North France is not going well and the bombing has been very inaccurate."

On 17 January:

> "Eisenhower came round to see me, in very good form. He is apparently quite prepared to face the question of curtailing south of France operation on its merits. Finally Cabinet, the last to be run without Winston who returns tomorrow. I foresee troublesome times the moment he returns. For one thing, he wants again to get Adam out of [Adjutant General] job and wishes to send him to Gibraltar! Luckily, S of S [Grigg] is prepared to fight this alongside of me. He also has some idea of kicking Giffard out [of 11th Army Group] without any reasonable grounds for it."

On 18 January, Churchill returned to Britain from Tunisia:

> "At 12.15 a Cabinet to listen to PM, who rambled on till 1.30pm. He was looking very well but I did not like the functioning of his brain much! Too much unconnected rambling from one subject to another… Then a sad interview with Kenneth Anderson to tell him he would not be commanding the 2nd Army in the forthcoming offensive [Overlord] as Dempsey is to replace him. He took it very well."

19 January saw Brookie close to breaking point. For once, his criticism of Churchill was not matched by a compliment:

> "The PM is starting off in his usual style!! We had a Staff meeting with him at 5.30pm for 2 hours and a Defence Committee from 10.30pm for another two hours. And we accomplished nothing!! I don't think I can stand much more of it. We waffled about with all the usual criticisms, all the usual optimist's plans, no long-term vision and we settled nothing. In all his plans he lives from hand to mouth. He can never grasp a whole plan, either in its width (i.e. all fronts)

or its depth (long-term projects). His method is entirely opportunist, gathering one flower here, another there! My God how tired I am of working for him! I had not fully realized how awful it is until I suddenly found myself thrown into it again after a rest!"*

On 20 January:

"*Operations in Italy going better. Oh! How I hope that the Rome amphibious operation [at Anzio] will be a success! I feel a special responsibility for it [having] resuscitated it after my visit to Italy and found things stagnating there. It may fail but I know it was the right thing to do, to double the amphibious operation and carry on with the outflanking plan.*"

22 January was the day of the Anzio landings:

"*At lunch was called up by WO and told that landing south of Rome had been a complete surprise. This was a wonderful relief!*"

Earlier, 17 January, Eisenhower had been willing to 'face the question of curtailing South of France operation'. This issue, which was to generate considerable controversy, arose again on 24 January after Montgomery recommended that the front for the Overlord landings be broadened. His recommendation meant that assault craft earmarked for use in the landings in southern France would have to be allocated to Overlord:

"*Eisenhower turned up to discuss his paper proposing increase of cross-Channel operation at expense of Southern France operation. I entirely agree with the proposal, but it is certainly not his idea and is one of Monty's. Eisenhower has got absolutely no strategical outlook and is really totally unfit for the post he holds from an operational point of view. He makes up, however, by the way he works for good cooperation between allies. After lunch, Monty came to see me and I had to tell him off for falling foul of both the King and the S of S in a very short time. He took it well, as usual.*

Long Cabinet from 6 to 8.15pm with Winston in great form. He was discussing Stalin's latest iniquities in allowing Pravda to publish the bogus information that England was negotiating with Germany about a peace. He said: 'Trying to maintain good relations with a communist is like wooing a crocodile, you do not know whether to tickle it under the chin or to beat it on the head. When it opens its mouth, you cannot tell whether it is trying to smile or preparing to eat you up.'"

On the next day:

"News of Rome landings continues to be good, but I am not happy about our relative strength in Italy [to that of the German forces]. We have not got a sufficient margin to be able to guarantee making a success of our attacks and the ground unfortunately favours the defence."

On 27 January, Brookie and Eisenhower visited Hobart's specialist unit [see 11 March 1943]:

"We then went on to see various exhibits such as the Sherman tank for destroying tank mines with chains on a drum driven by the engine, various methods of climbing walls with tanks… flame-throwing Churchill tanks… floating tanks, teaching men how to escape from sunken tanks… Hobart has been doing wonders in his present job and I am delighted that we put him into it."

On 28 January:

"At 4.30pm Winston suddenly convened a meeting as he had misread some of the intercepted secret information… He was also full of doubts as to whether Lucas [American commander of Allied forces at Anzio] was handling this landing efficiently. I had some job quieting him down again! Unfortunately, this time I feel there are reasons for uneasiness!"

Three days later:

"News from Italy bad and the landing south of Rome is making little progress, mainly due to the lack of initiative in the early stages. I am at *present rather doubtful as to how we are to disentangle the situation. Hitler has reacted very strongly and is sending reinforcements fast."*

2 February saw Brookie enjoying more Churchillian one-liners:

"Dinner at 10 Downing Street… PM in good form and brought out many gems. I only wish I could remember them. Amongst others:

'Politics are very much like war, we may even have to use poison gas at times.'

'In politics, if you have something good to give, give a little at a time but if you have something bad to get rid of, give it all together and brace the recipients to receive it.'"

On 3 February:

"We had a long COS discussing the wire to send back to American Chiefs of Staff to convince them that with the turn operations have taken in the Mediterranean, the only thing to do is to go on fighting the war in Italy and give up any idea of a weak landing in Southern France."

On the following day:

"Pug [Ismay] wasted a great deal of our time at the COS. He has been having a row with the PM in defending a document we had produced yesterday. Winston had asked us to consider the advisability of pressing de Valera [Taoiseach, head of Irish Government] to sack the German ambassador in Dublin for security's sake. We had discovered that as we had broken the German cipher we could control all cable messages and… it was perhaps better to remain with the devil we knew as opposed to the devil we did not know. Winston apparently wished for another answer and was very angry because he did not get it."

Three days later:

"Usual early start and found my table full of telegrams including some of American Chiefs of Staff disagreeing with us as regards

cancelling the South of France operation. Nothing left but to wire and ask them to come over and discuss. Time now too short for any other course. PM sent for me and kept me for ¾ hour discussing with him the situation in Italy. He was in the depths of gloom and I had a hard time cheering him up."

On 8 February:

"A day spent almost continuously with the PM!... [largely] concerned with a proposed wild venture of his to land 2 Armoured Divisions in Bordeaux 20 days after the cross-Channel operations. I think we have ridden him off this for the present.

Donovan [American brigadier general and intelligence officer]... was interesting: having been on the Rome landing he was able to paint a clear picture of the failure to exercise sufficient drive. I am afraid that Winston is beginning to see some of Alex's shortcomings! It was bound to come some time or other but means difficult times ahead. I wonder how I have succeeded in keeping [Alex] covered up to now!"

On the following day:

"At 5.15pm I was handed a 5-page telegram which PM had drafted for President covering the whole strategy of the war, and most of it wrong! He asked for it to be discussed with him at 10.30pm. Unfortunately, there was a Cabinet at 5.30pm. There I had a royal battle with him concerning the imposition of a ban on visitors to the South Coast [the ban was a security measure to conceal preparations for Overlord]. For some unaccountable reason, he was against the ban and supported Morrison. I had most of the rest of the Cabinet with me... We had a royal scrap and I think I had the best of it. At 7.30pm... a hurried COS meeting to examine PM's wire which required drastic amending."

On 10 February:

"We had a long COS which Eisenhower and Bedell Smith attended at 12 noon. They had prepared a paper showing the requirements for *the cross-Channel operation which coincided with our views. Marshall had also wired that he left it to Eisenhower to take final decision. Therefore, all seems to be going well at present."*

On 11 February:

"Dined with Bannerman… Lodge came to dine… [he] is drawing all the plates for Bannerman's future book of the birds of GB… His plates are quite wonderful and should make a historical book."

14 February saw discussion of British strategy in the Far East. This was another issue which was to generate controversy:

"News of Italy still none too good but I feel the bridgehead south of Rome should hold all right and that ultimately we may score by not having an early easy success. Hitler has been determined to fight for Rome and may give us a better chance of inflicting heavy blows under the new conditions.

Then 10pm meeting with PM to listen to Wedemeyer's plan [Mountbatten's chief of staff] which he had brought back from Dickie Mountbatten. I had long and difficult arguments with the PM. He was again set on carrying out an attack of north tip of Sumatra and refusing to look at any long-term projects or concrete plans for the defeat of Japan… He lives for the impulse and for the present and refuses to look at lateral implications or future commitments. Now that I know him well, episodes such as Antwerp and the Dardanelles no longer puzzle me [two controversial events in the First World War which resulted in extensive criticism of Churchill]! But meanwhile I often doubt whether I am going mad or whether he is really sane. The arguments were difficult as Wedemeyer and his party were of course trying to sell their goods, namely operations through the Malacca Straits and these operations entailed the capture of Sumatra which the PM wanted. But he refused to argue the relative merits of opening the Malacca Straits as opposed to working via Australia. After much hard work, I began to make him see that we must have an overall plan for the defeat of Japan and then fit in the details."

On 15 February, note the attributes which Brookie admired in people:

"Arthur Smith [came] to say goodbye before departure for Iraq-Persia Command. There is no doubt that he is a very fine man, entirely selfless and with only one thought, that of serving his country… Received telegram from Alex that he was not satisfied with Lucas as Commander of Corps in [Anzio] bridgehead south of Rome and asking me to consult Eisenhower. This resulted in a long series of telephone calls to Eisenhower and PM and I only got to bed by 1am."

On 16 February:

"I was sent for by PM who wanted to send Alexander to command the troops in the [Anzio] bridgehead and Wilson to command the main front! I am afraid I rather lost my temper with him over this and asked him if he could not for once trust his commanders to organize the command for themselves without interfering and upsetting all the chain and sequence of command. He gave up his idea for the present but may well return to the attack!!"

On the following day:

"A long COS… mostly concerned with post-hostilities matters and it is not yet easy to concentrate one's thoughts on after-war matters!… I had an interview with Brocas Burrows, who is off to Moscow [as head of the British Military Mission] and found that the Foreign Office had been briefing him on such a completely conciliatory basis that he did not imagine that he was to get anything back out of the Russians! Typical of the Foreign Office – the more I see of them, the more appalled I am at their inefficiency."

On 18 February, the Foreign Office came in for more criticism. British interference in Greek domestic affairs was to cause considerable difficulties for Brookie, as will become apparent:

"Our COS was mainly concerned with the situation in Greece where Mr Leeper [British ambassador to the Greek Government] and the Foreign Office have succeeded in stopping all guerrilla activities *by trying to look for some ultimate settlement which will admit of a political situation suitable for the re-entry of the King [of Greece] at the end of hostilities. In fact, in searching for some ultimate political ideal, we are losing sight of the current military necessities!"*

On 19 February:

"Eisenhower, Bedell Smith, Tedder... came in representing American Chiefs of Staff, to discuss desirability of having an amphibious attack against South of France to coincide with cross-Channel operations. Luckily, I had discovered last night from Monty that he and Bertie Ramsay had foolishly agreed to curtail the cross-Channel operation to allow for a South of France operation. If they had had any sense, they would have realized that the situation in Italy now makes such an operation impossible. They had agreed to please Eisenhower who was pressing for it to please Marshall!!! What a way to run a war! I had a little difficulty with Eisenhower, but not much, to make him see sense as all he required was a little pressure to go back to the plan that he really liked best... I think the matter is now all right."

Two days later, attention returned to the issue of British strategy in the Far East. Brookie's prediction would prove accurate:

"Long COS with Planners discussing Pacific strategy and deciding on plan of action to tackle the PM with, to convince him that we cannot take the tip of Sumatra for him. We shall have very serious trouble with him over this. But we have definitely decided that our strategy should be to operate from Australia with the Americans and not from India through Malacca Straits."

In his Notes, "We were just at the very beginning of the most difficult period I had with Winston during the whole of the war... we had to plan a strategy for the British part in the final operation against Japan as soon as the defeat of Germany made it possible to deploy forces in this theatre. Two major alternative strategies were open to us.

The first consisted of operations based on India, carried out in Indian

Ocean by South East Asia Command with the object of liberating Burma, Singapore and possibly Java, Sumatra or Borneo. The second alternative consisted of operations based on Australia carried out by Naval, Land and Air forces cooperating closely with American and Australian forces in the Pacific. The first of these alternatives was the easiest to stage but limited itself to the recapture of British possessions without any direct participation with American and Australian forces in the defeat of Japan. I felt that at this stage of the war it was vital that British forces should participate in direct action against Japan in the Pacific. First of all, from a Commonwealth point of view, to prove to Australia our willingness and desire to fight with them for the defence of Australia… Secondly, I felt that it was important that we should cooperate with all three services alongside of the Americans in the Pacific against Japan in the final stages of this war. I therefore considered that our strategy should aim at the liberation of Burma by South East Asian Command based on India and the deployment of new sea, land and air forces to operate with bases in Australia alongside of forces in the Pacific.

There was a great deal to be said for all the various alternatives and combinations… The trouble was that Winston… refused to look at any strategy or operation that did not contemplate the capture of the tip of Sumatra as its first stage, or indeed as its only stage, as I never got out of him what his subsequent stage would be… The situation was complicated by the fact that South East Asia Command was ready at all times to foster attacks on Sumatra since this would at least lead to the allotment of forces to that command. The Americans, on the other hand, were not over anxious for our arrival in the Pacific to share their victories in the final stages… they were beginning to feel that they could probably defeat Japan on their own."

22 February saw further discussion of the landings in southern France. Brookie's frank admission regarding Burma is worth highlighting:

"Eisenhower came again to represent the American Chiefs of Staff and to argue their point concerning the Mediterranean. It is quite clear to me from Marshall's wire that he does not begin to understand

the Italian campaign! He cannot realize that to maintain an offensive a proportion of reserve divisions are required. He considers that this reserve can be withdrawn for a new offensive in the South of France and that the momentum in Italy can still be maintained. Eisenhower sees the situation a little more clearly, but he is too frightened of disagreeing with Marshall to be able to express his views clearly.

Wedemeyer came next to argue out and explain the Burma campaigns. I am not a bit happy about the final plans, there is no definite objective and large forces of Long Range Penetration Groups are being launched for no definite purpose. If ever there was a campaign that has been mishandled it is the Burma one and mainly due to the influence exerted by Chiang Kai-shek through the President on the American Chiefs of Staff... I am feeling very weary and old and wish to God the war would finish!"

On 23 February:

"Another long COS... [checked] off telegram to American COS as a result of our meeting with Eisenhower yesterday. We have got all we want but must word the wire to let the Americans 'save face' as much as possible! Finally, Sir Orme Sargent [Foreign Office] to discuss the Greek situation and to try and make some sense out of the present Foreign Office policy in Greece! As this policy is mainly based on the future post-war political regime in Greece, it pays little attention to the requirements of guerrilla warfare!"

25 February was dominated by the issue of British strategy in the Far East. Note Brookie's remark that Churchill 'had packed the house against us':

"I am quite exhausted after spending 7½ hours today with Winston and most of that time engaged in heavy argument... At 12 noon the Chiefs of Staff met the PM... He was still insisting on doing the North Sumatra operation, would not discuss any other operation and was in a thoroughly disgruntled and bad temper. I had a series of heated discussions with him.

At 3pm we met again. This time he had packed the house against us and was accompanied by Anthony Eden, Oliver Lyttelton, and Attlee, in addition the whole of Dickie Mountbatten's party… [they were all] against the Chiefs of Staff! Thank God I have got Andrew Cunningham to support me! It just makes all the difference from the days of poor old Dudley Pound. We argued from 3pm to 5.30pm. I got very heated at times especially when Anthony Eden chipped in knowing nothing about Pacific strategy! Winston pretended that this was all a frame-up against his pet Sumatra operation and almost took it up as a personal matter. Furthermore, his dislike for Curtin [Australian prime minister] and the Australians at once affected any discussion for cooperation with Australian forces… Dewing [British major general and head of Army and Air Liaison Staff, Australia] chipped in and talked unadulterated nonsense and I almost lost my temper with him. It was a desperate meeting with no opportunity of discussing strategy on its merits.

PM called up and asked me to dine. I thought it was to tell me that he couldn't stick my disagreements any longer and proposed to sack me! On the contrary, we had a tête-à-tête dinner at which he was quite charming as if he meant to make up for some of the rough passages of the day. He has astonishing sides to his character. At 10pm another COS meeting which lasted till 12 midnight. PM in much more reasonable mood and I think that a great deal of what we have been doing has soaked in. I hope so at least as I don't want another day like today!"

On 28 February:

"*Cabinet at 6pm when Winston was in an impossible mood with nothing but abuse about everything the Army was doing! Every commander from Jumbo Wilson to last company commander was useless, the organization was useless, the Americans hopeless, etc. It was all I could do to contain my temper. Ramsay then came to dine and gave me some side lights as to how Monty was functioning. He is wandering around visiting troops and failing to get down to basic facts. Shall have to have him up again and kick his backside again!*

Have been awarded the Order of Suvorov (first class) by Soviet Government. As far as I can gather, this was done by specific order of Marshal Stalin!! My speech in Tehran [see 30 November 1943] must have gone deeper than I had thought. Just before going to bed, I received a disturbing wire from Alexander. He evidently is not very happy about [Anzio] bridgehead, proposes to relieve 56th Div by 5th Div and to add extra Div. This at once reacts on number of landing craft available for the cross-Channel operation as if we begin returning those that should go home the bridgehead will be affected! He also proposes to reorganize defence by bringing 8th Army over to Cassino front, in this I think he is right."

29 February saw another Churchillian one-liner:

"*Sent Alex's cable onto the PM knowing it would cause trouble... at 10pm had another meeting with PM... Referring to the Anzio beach head, Winston said: 'We hoped to land a wildcat that would tear out the bowels of the Boche. Instead we have stranded a vast whale with its tail flopping about in the water!'*"

On 1 March:

"*Cabinet... We again discussed the security measures under which we wish to impose a ban on visitors to the [south] coast. Winston waffling badly! I can't make out what is at the back of it all. I feel it must be Beaverbrook again! I cannot think what else would induce him to take such a line.*"

By 3 March, the dispute over British strategy in the Far East was assuming dangerous proportions:

"*I had to discuss [at the COS] the very difficult problem which is brewing up and in which the PM is trying at present to frame-up the War Cabinet against the Chiefs of Staff Committee. It is all about the future Pacific strategy, it looks very serious and may well lead to the resignation of the Chiefs of Staff Committee. I am shattered by the present condition of the PM. He has lost all balance*".

On 6 March, note the 'Yes men':

> "During the COS, we discussed how to handle the PM in the bad mood he has got into concerning the future plans for the war against Japan. We are preparing a reply to the desperate paper he has produced and on Wednesday after dinner we are to have a meeting with him. He is to bring his chorus of 'Yes' men (Eden, Attlee, Oliver Lyttelton and Leathers) with him [Eden, Attlee and Lyttelton also attended the 25 February meeting when Churchill 'packed the house against us']. It will be a gloomy evening and one during which it will be hard to keep one's temper."

In his Notes, "In classifying these four statesmen as 'Yes' men, I was considering them from the point of view of Pacific strategy. None of them had given any deep thought to the matter, had in fact only scratched the surface of the problem as was palpable from their remarks and as for Leathers… no matter what he might have found in scratching the surface he would have continued to trim his sails to whatever wind Winston blew. Somehow the presence of these four 'colleagues' of Winston's at those discussions always infuriated me and put me into a bad temper from the start. It was so palpable that they were brought along by [Churchill] to support him which they proceeded to do, irrespective of the degree of lunacy connected with some of Winston's proposals."

On 7 March:

> "Most of our COS meeting was devoted to preparing notes for tomorrow evening's meeting with the PM concerning the South East Asia strategy. He has produced the worst paper I have seen him write yet. Trying to make a case for an attack on the top of the island of Sumatra! He compared this plan to our outline plan for the defeat of Japan operating with Americans and Australians from Australia… He has now taken Eden, Attlee and Oliver Lyttelton [the 'Yes men'] in tow, none of whom understand anything about it all but who are useful as they are prepared to agree with him! We shall, I feel, have a royal row about this matter.

> *Macmillan came to see me and we concerted as to how we could best save Jumbo Wilson from the PM's wrath! He is angry with [Wilson] as he does not feel he is having sufficient control over him and will not recognize his inter-allied position. I foresee untold trouble over this."*

In his Notes, "Jumbo Wilson was not as pliable in Winston's hands as Alex would have been. Wilson was a tough old specimen and he just let Winston's abuse run over him like water rolls off a duck's back! The only thing that worried me was that I was not quite certain how far Macmillan would cooperate with me in saving Wilson. I felt that he might well be more inclined to cooperate with Winston in getting [Wilson] out."

On 8 March, note Churchill's indecision and Brookie's contempt:

> "At 6pm, Cabinet meeting to discuss security arrangements [on the south coast] for Overlord. Winston in a hopeless mood, incapable of taking any real decision.
>
> The [Far East strategy] meeting consisted of the PM who had brought with him to support him Attlee, Eden, Oliver Lyttelton and Leathers! Our party consisted of Chiefs of Staff. Portal as usual not too anxious to argue against PM and dear old Cunningham so wild with rage that he hardly dared let himself speak!! I therefore had to do most of the arguing and for 2½ hours, from 10pm to 12.30pm I went at it hard arguing with the PM and 4 Cabinet Ministers. The arguments of the latter were so puerile that it made me ashamed to think they were Cabinet Ministers! It was only too evident that they did not know their subject, had not read the various papers connected with it and had purely been brought along to support Winston! And damned badly they did it too! I had little difficulty in dealing with any of the arguments they put forward. Finally, we... succeeded in getting the PM to agree to reconnaissances of Australia being carried out as a possible base for future action and... got him to realize that his plans for the defeat of Japan must go beyond the mere capture of the tip of Sumatra."

On 10 March:

> "I was sent for before COS by PM who wanted to discuss most recent intercept of Kesselring's latest appreciation of the situation [German field marshal]! A most useful document giving his outlook on the whole of the fighting in Italy. PM then told me that he had decided after all to allow the 'visitors ban' [on the south coast] to be imposed!! A triumph after the long battle I had with him... In evening a very useful visit by Monty to tell me how he was getting on with his preparations for the attack. He is making good headway in making plans and equally successful in making enemies as far as I can see! I have to spend a great deal of my time soothing off some of these troubles."

Three days later:

> "Faced again with the PM's restlessness! He now wants to go to Bermuda to meet the President on the 25th of this month! There is nothing special that we want to discuss as Chiefs of Staff. In fact, we do not want to meet American Chiefs until we have arrived at some form of agreement with the PM about the Pacific Strategy. Medically, it is all wrong that he should go, but Moran [Churchill's doctor] has not got the guts to stop him!... PM has now got the Joint Planners with him to discuss the Pacific strategy, heaven knows what he is up to and what trouble he is brewing for us tomorrow!!"

On the following day:

> "Apparently PM... still hopes to go to Bermuda. I had another interview with Moran yesterday to try and stop the PM on medical grounds. He tells me that he is writing to the PM to tell him that there are 3 good reasons why he should not go... However, as he is intent on escaping from the minor worries of parliamentary life, he may well risk all for some peace.
>
> Russian operations continue to go well. Just heard from Alexander that Freyberg's attack [at Monte Cassino in Italy] is to be launched tonight."

On 15 March:

"*The Germans are in a bad way in South Russia. I have said all along that there could be no military reasons to justify their strategy in South Russia and that I could only account for their actions by attributing them to Hitler's orders or to political reasons connected with Romania. Well, it looks now as if the Germans are about to pay the penalty for their faulty strategy!*"

On the next day:

"*We had the Planners in our meeting this morning and discussed with them the instructions the PM gave them on Monday night concerning planning for the capture of Sumatra.*"

On 17 March:

"*We were sent for by the PM… [he] informed us that he had discovered a new island just west of Sumatra, I think it is called something like Simmular. He had worked out that the capture of this island, when once developed, would answer as well as the top of Sumatra and would require far less strength!! However, by the time he had asked Portal his view, he had discovered that from the point of view of the air he had little hope of building up his aerodromes and strength before being bumped off. From Cunningham, he found out that from a naval point of view with the Jap fleet at Singapore he was courting disaster!!! Both Portal and Cunningham were entirely correct and I began to wonder whether I was Alice in Wonderland or whether I was really fit for a lunatic asylum! I am honestly getting very doubtful about his balance of mind… I don't know where we are or where we are going as regards our strategy and I just cannot get him to face the true facts!*"

On the following day:

"*[Churchill] insists on going [to Bermuda] and proposes to fly from there to Gibraltar and then on to Italy, which will probably be the end of him!*"

On 20 March:

> "One of the worst of Cabinet meetings with Winston in one of his worst moods! Nothing that the Army does can be right and he did nothing but belittle its efforts in the eyes of the whole Cabinet. I cannot stick any more meetings like it! He has now produced an impossible document on the Pacific strategy in which he is overriding our opinions and our advice!"

In his 'impossible document', Churchill settled the dispute over Far East strategy by ruling, in his capacity as prime minister and minister of defence, that Britain would pursue a strategy based on the Indian theatre and the Bay of Bengal in the war against Japan.

21 March saw the chiefs of staff considering resignation en masse:

> "We discussed at the COS how best to deal with Winston's last impossible document. It is full of false statements, false deductions and defective strategy. We cannot accept it as it stands and it would be better if we all three resigned rather than accept his solution. We are telling him that it will be essential for us to put in a written reply but that we can, if he likes, discuss with him his paper before we put in our reply. I don't know how tiresome he will insist in being. He may perhaps see some reason otherwise we may well be faced with a most serious situation."

22 March was:

> "A very tiring day. First of all, COS from 10.30 to 1.15 with a long discussion with Planners concerning the latest appreciation by Wilson for the abolition of Anvil [codename for the southern France operation]. Then Eisenhower and Bedell Smith came up to discuss their report which agreed with what we wanted. I now hope... that the American Chiefs of Staff will at last see some wisdom!... Thank heaven Roosevelt cannot meet [Churchill] in Bermuda so our trip next week is off!"

On 23 March, note Churchill's reaction to the American wire:

> "The situation gets more hopeless than ever, Wingate is now

wiring direct to the PM through Mountbatten who expresses no definite opinion on the proposals put forward by Wingate. It looks as if the strain of operations had sent Wingate off his head. Meanwhile, American wire stating that we should push on in Burma and give up all thoughts of Sumatra. PM's reaction was to wire direct to Mountbatten saying if you will conform to American requirements in Burma, I shall back you in Sumatra and see that you are allowed to carry out the operation!!! We stopped that wire but heaven knows where we are going. I feel like a man chained to the chariot of a lunatic!! It is getting beyond my powers to control him.

Martel came to see me about the necessity of appointing a senior general in charge of the Armoured Corps [for Overlord], it was only too clear that in his mind he was the one man for the job!"

On the following day:

"Attended Mansion House lunch to open 'Salute the Soldier Week'... Tomorrow, I have my Trafalgar Square speech to make, and I am not looking forward to it at all!"

In his Notes, "Speaking in public had always frightened me and still frightens me now."

On 27 March:

"Early start. Table crammed with telegrams. News not too good. Wingate reported killed. Marripan threatened by the Japs. Alexander stuck at Cassino. Marshall insisting on doing Anvil operation... Then Monty to dine. He was in very good form and brought all his proposed plans for [Overlord] – I liked his plans."

On 29 March:

"Crerar is just back from Italy and is taking over the [First] Canadian Army. It has been a difficult move to accomplish!! I have had to get rid of Andy McNaughton, give Crerar sufficient war experience in Italy and get Monty to accept him with very limited

active experience. All has now been accomplished with much anguish and many difficulties, but I have full confidence that Crerar will not let me down. I have however, I am afraid, lost a very good friend in the shape of Andy McNaughton. I only hope that he may be able to realize the true situation to rise high enough for me not to lose his friendship."

On 31 March:

"*Telegram from American COS came in, quite impossible to accept. Again, arguing that after uniting Anzio bridgehead and main front [in Italy] we should go on the defensive in Italy and start a new front in Southern France. They fail to realize that the forces available do not admit of two fronts in the Mediterranean! I am afraid that our [British] Joint Staff Mission in Washington are now only acting as a [post office] and not expressing views and opinions of their own. In the afternoon, I received an interesting letter from Wilson and Alexander. Evidently, just as I suspected, Freyberg [New Zealand commander] has been fighting with a casualty-conscious mind. He has been sparing the NZ infantry and hoping to accomplish results by use of heavy bombers and infantry without risking too much infantry. As a result, he has failed.*

In the evening, saw Kenneth Anderson just back from Italy who was very interesting and confirmed all my impressions as to Freyberg's weakness and Clark's [American general] unsuitability for an Army Command."

In his Notes, "[My remarks about Freyberg] in no way reflect on his dash and ability to command. He had already more than proved these qualities in North Africa. The situation was now somewhat changed. The New Zealanders had suffered their full share of casualties for such a small country. It had recently been frequently impressed on Freyberg by the NZ Government that it was most desirable to avoid unnecessary heavy casualties in future. The war was evidently drawing near its close and there was a reluctance to go on risking the lives of gallant men who had already risked them so frequently. All these considerations were weighing heavily on Freyberg and making him loath to risk heavy losses. Unfortunately, it is hard in war to make omelettes without breaking eggs and it is often in trying to do so that we break most eggs!"

On 1 April:

"Had hoped to get off without a COS meeting but found it necessary to meet in order to form our new reply to the last American note about the South of France invasion. Marshall is quite hopeless... The strategy he advocates [go on the defensive in Italy to allow for landings in southern France] can only result in two months without any operations in the Mediterranean, just at the very moment when we require them most owing to the [June] date of the cross-Channel operation."

Two days later:

"Cabinet... at which Winston meandered about, talking continuously to say very little... After dinner another meeting... We again beat round and round the bush... PM aged, tired and failing to really grasp matters. It is a depressing sight to see him gradually deteriorating. I wonder how long he will last, not long enough to see the war through I fear."

In his Notes, "I began to feel at that time that the stupendous burden he had been carrying so valiantly throughout the war was gradually crushing him."

On 5 April, an issue arose over whether the bombing of Germany should be scaled down to allow for the bombing of railways and bridges in northern France, the purpose being to delay and disrupt the movement of German reinforcements to the area of the Overlord landings:

"*Difficulties again with our American friends who still persist in wanting to close down operations in Italy, open new ones in South of France just at the most critical moment. I don't believe they have any tactical or strategical perspective of any kind… At 10.30 had to attend one of those awful evening meetings of the PM. We were kept up till 12.45am discussing use of heavy bombers in support of invasion of France. He is opposed to Tedder's plans to use them on the railways because he does not think that the results to be achieved will be much and, secondly, owing to casualties amongst French civilians which must result from it."*

7 April saw yet another example of Brookie's good judgment:

"At 9am I paraded at St Paul's School to attend a wonderful day Monty ran to run over all the plans for the coming offensive [Overlord]. He started with some very good opening remarks, then we had Ramsay to explain naval plans and Leigh-Mallory to explain air plans. Lunch followed and after that Bradley [American general] and his two Corps Commanders, followed by Dempsey, Bucknall and Crocker [British commanders]. Bucknall was very weak and I am certain quite unfit to command a Corps [Bucknall was removed from his command in August 1944]."

On 8 April:

"Another difficult COS dealing with last reply from American COS on Mediterranean strategy. They have at last agreed to our policy but withdrawn their offer of landing craft from Pacific. This is typical of their methods of running strategy. Although we have agreed that the European theatre must take precedence over the Pacific, yet they use some of their available landing forces as bargaining counters in trying to get their false strategy followed."

On 11 April:

"Alexander turned up to see me, back from Italy. Whenever I meet him again, my first impression is one of marvelling at what a small calibre man he is! He just shatters me, he is floating in the ether with very little realization of what he is doing. And yet the PM has never realized what a small calibre man he is. I discussed Alexander's plan

[for his forthcoming major offensive] with him. It is not ideal. But he is handicapped by all the nationalities he has to deal with. At 10pm we had a meeting with the PM... Our time was spent in going through his telegram to Marshall [attempting to obtain landing craft from the Pacific]. Waste of time as I feel certain the reply will be in the negative."

On 13 April:

"First a long COS at which the Lethbridge Committee attended. They have just been touring the world... studying the requirements for war against Japan. Their report is very good and provides much food for thought and progress.

At 10.30pm went on to Defence Committee to discuss air strategy of bombing railway communications in France prior to [Overlord]. Am far from convinced that we should not be better employed spending that effort on German aircraft industry... I got [Churchill] to agree to my having a week's leave... for the first time since I have held this job I feel thoroughly stale and almost whacked by the work!"

On the following day, British strategy in the Far East was being re-examined:

"We had a long COS meeting attended by the Planners at which we discussed the future Pacific strategy and examined the possibility and advantages of a line of advance on an axis from Darwin towards North Borneo. This might give us a chance of running an entirely British Imperial campaign instead of just furnishing reinforcements for American operations.

Sent for by the PM. He had been drafting a reply to the wire he had received from Marshall about the Mediterranean strategy. It was an awful wire! Giving away all we had been fighting for during the past 6 weeks. I had a hard set to with him... I am finding these battles with him quite exhausting. I came out of this one quite cooked".

On 17 April:

"Lunched with PM at 10 Downing Street. Eisenhower, Bedell

> Smith and Alexander were there. The conversation at once again turned to the Mediterranean strategy and to the American Chiefs of Staff's failure to agree with us as to the necessity to press on with operations in Italy without impairing the prospects by preparations for an offensive against Southern France."

On the following day:

> "A long COS at which we had… the Joint Intelligence Committee to discuss German Forces in Europe and their resources available to meet [Overlord]… Then meeting with Billet, the American Director of Military Intelligence. I found him well on the spot and a good man at his job."

19 April saw blistering criticism of the Americans:

> "At last, all our troubles about Anvil [landings in southern France] are over. We have got the Americans to agree but have lost the additional landing craft they were prepared to provide. History will never forgive them for bargaining equipment against strategy and for trying to blackmail us into agreeing with them by holding the pistol of withdrawing craft at our heads. Am now off for one of those awful night meetings with the PM.
>
> Later: A terrible meeting… as regards bombing of [French] railways, the matter put back for another week's consideration at a time when we are within 5 weeks of [the start of Overlord] and definite decisions are required."

23 April was the start of seven days' leave for Brookie, "I had a heavenly week fishing all day, leaving the house at 9.30 in the morning and not returning till after 11pm… I feel infinitely better." On 1 May:

> "Very reluctantly, I started work again… at 12 noon the opening meeting of the conference of Empire [prime ministers]… by far the most attractive of the lot was dear old Smuts, just the same as ever and with the same dear refreshing outlook on life."

On 2 May:

"Cabinet [meeting]… another long discussion on the bombing strategy of attack on French railways and killing of Frenchmen. More waffling about and vacillating politicians unable to accept the consequences of war."

On the following day:

"Another meeting with PM on bombing of [French] railways which lasted till 1.15am!! Winston gradually coming round to the policy."

Two days later, Brookie was at Chequers with Churchill:

"He sat by the fire and drank his soup. He looked very old and very tired. He said Roosevelt was not well and that he was no longer the man that he had been, this he said also applied to himself. He said he could still always sleep well, eat well and especially drink well! but that he no longer jumped out of bed the way he used to and felt as if he would be quite content to spend the whole day in bed. I have never yet heard him admit that he was beginning to fail. He then said some very nice things about the excellent opinion that the whole Defence Committee and War Cabinet had of me and that they had said that we could not have a better CIGS."

In his Notes, "I appreciated tremendously his kindness in passing on these remarks to me… I did not often get any form of appreciation of my work from him and therefore treasured it all the more on the rare occasions. He was an astounding mixture, could drive you to complete desperation… and then would ask you to spend a couple of hours or so alone with him and would produce the most homely and attractive personality."

On 10 May:

"Dinner at the Ritz to entertain Dominion Military, Naval and Air representatives. I suppose this all serves some purpose in welding Imperial bonds, but I doubt it at times. All these speeches strike me as being so much hot air or, perhaps better, so much alcoholic vapour which goes to everyone's head, producing a beatific and complacent attitude of wonderful imperial understanding. But how much of all this remains there in the bleak reality of the morning after?"

On the next day:

"Tonight at 11pm the Italian attack starts [Alexander's major offensive against the German defensive line in the mountains of central Italy]. I pray to God that it may be successful. A great deal depends on it."

On 12 May:

"Attack started up to time but no news all day! I am now (11.30pm) awaiting a message which is being deciphered. It is very trying having to wait for this information. At morning COS, Blamey [Commander-in-Chief, Australian Military Forces]… came to discuss future operations from Australia. Blamey looked as if he had the most frightful 'hangover' from a debauched night! His eyes were swimming in alcohol! However, we made considerable progress".

15 May saw an interesting assessment of Eisenhower and another dry comment about Bert Harris:

"Went straight from home to St Paul's School to attend Eisenhower's final run over plans for cross-Channel offensive… The main impression I gathered was that Eisenhower was a swinger and no real director of thought, plans, energy or direction! Just a coordinator – a good mixer, a champion of inter-allied cooperation and, in those respects, few can hold a candle to him. But is that enough? Or can we not find all qualities of a commander in one man? Maybe I am getting too hard to please, but I doubt it.

Monty made excellent speech. Bertie Ramsay [Allied Naval Expeditionary Force] indifferent and overwhelmed by all his own difficulties. Spaatz [American Strategic Air Forces in Europe] read every word of a poor statement. Bert Harris [RAF Bomber Command] *told us how well he might have won this war if it had not been for the handicap imposed by the existence of the other two services!! Sholto Douglas [RAF Fighter Command] seemed disappointed at the smallness of his task, and so was I. A useful run through... finished up with Monty dining quietly with me. He was in very good form and bearing his responsibilities well."*

On 16 May:
"Luckily, the Italian news continues to be good".

On 18 May, note Churchill's support for Mountbatten:
"A long COS when we had a meeting of the Planners in order to try and settle a final Pacific strategy to put up to the PM. The problem is full of difficulties although the strategy is quite clear. Unfortunately, the right course to follow is troubled by personalities, questions of command, vested interests, inter-allied jealousies, etc. Curtin [Australian prime minister] and MacArthur are determined to stand together, support each other and allow no outside interference. Winston is determined Mountbatten must be given some operation to carry out, Andrew Cunningham is equally determined that Mountbatten should not control the Eastern Fleet. Americans wish to gather all laurels connected with Pacific fighting, Winston is equally determined that we should not be tied to the apron strings of the Americans!! How on earth are we to steer a straight course between all these snags and difficulties?

From 3 to 4pm, meeting with PM, Eden, Bedell Smith and the Chiefs of Staff to decide how to handle de Gaulle before the invasion whilst still retaining secrecy. Eden, as usual, intended to soften and allow de Gaulle's new Republican Committee to be recognized."

His 19 May entry is slightly garbled but is explained in his Notes:
"Thank heaven the Italian attack is going well and it should play its part in holding [German] formations in Italy and keeping them away from the Channel. At any rate, we have proved that Marshall

and the American Chiefs of Staff were all wrong arguing that the Italians would retire before we could attack them and leave only some 6 divs to cover their rear, leaving us with large forces stranded in Italy which we could not engage! Such a withdrawal may be forced on them later but not, I hope, until we have knocked the stuffing out of them."

In his Notes, "One of [Marshall's] arguments for withdrawing troops from [Italy] was that the enemy would now start withdrawing forces from this front and leave rearguard forces covering this movement. Had this happened we should have been left with some redundant forces in Italy. This was quite a sound argument strategically, but it failed entirely to take Hitler's mentality into account. Nowhere yet had he retired voluntarily on any front and in not doing so [he] had committed grave strategic blunders which led to his ultimate defeat. First Stalingrad, which resulted in the loss of Von Paulus's army of 90,000 men and countless casualties, secondly Tunisia with the loss of 250,000 men and much equipment, shipping and material, thirdly the Dnieper River Bend [southern Russia] where he might have materially increased his reserves by shortening his front. It was not in Hitler's character to retire, he certainly would not give up Italy unless he was driven out of it and he would fight against such a contingency. I therefore felt quite safe in arguing to Marshall that Hitler would not withdraw forces out of Italy unless we went on the defensive and started removing formations, in which case [Hitler] could bring [his] forces on interior lines to counter these moves to meet the new threats [Overlord]."

On 20 May:

"Alexander's news of Italian fighting continues to be excellent. Thank heaven for it! I have staked a great deal on the Italian campaign in all our arguments with the Americans. I felt throughout that we had wonderful opportunities of inflicting a real telling defeat on the Germans which would be worth anything in connection with the cross-Channel operation. The only danger was that the Americans should have their way and plan to withdraw forces from Italy at the critical moment. They nearly succeeded in ruining our strategy and now, I pray God, we may be allowed to reap the full benefits of [it]!"

On the following day, Brookie was anxious:
"Meeting with Joint Intelligence Committee and long discussion with them as to situation in France as regards accumulation of German divisions to meet [Overlord]. Close on 60 divisions accumulated!

Alex's offensive from Anzio bridgehead started this morning together with offensive in Liri Valley. I am rather afraid that he has launched bridgehead offensive too soon and that he may not reap full benefits of favourable situation confronting him. However, he alone can judge being on the spot.

Flew... to Oxford to inspect the Glider Pilot Regiment of which I am Colonel. They are a wonderful lot of men. They gave a demonstration of 20 Hansa Gliders taking off in 14 minutes and subsequently the gliders landing in 8 minutes!"

On 24 May:
"At 10pm we had Chiefs of Staff meeting with [Churchill] to discuss progress made in... Pacific strategy. I think we have at last got him swung to an Australian based strategy as opposed to his old love of the 'Sumatra tip'!"

25 May saw yet another ticking off for Montgomery:
"Dash to Portsmouth... to see the 'Whales', new piers for the invasion... [and] the Phoenixes, the large concrete caissons for the breakwaters for the artificial harbours. A wonderful piece of engineering. From there to Monty's HQ to dine with him. I had to tell him off and ask him to concentrate more on his own job and not meddle himself in everybody else's affairs. Such as wanting to advise Alex on his battle, New Zealand PM on what to do with Freyberg... As usual he took it well.

Just heard Anzio bridgehead and main front are joined up together. Thank heaven for it!!"

On 26 May:

> "*The Italian offensive is going on well, [enemy] reserves are being drawn in and it is performing just the function we wanted with reference to the cross-Channel operation.*
>
> *Meeting with PM, Eden, Attlee, Oliver Lyttelton, Leathers, Curtin [Australian prime minister], Blamey and Chiefs of Staff to consider our future strategy. The meeting started badly as Curtin, who is entirely in MacArthur's pocket, was afraid we were trying to oust MacArthur! He consequently showed very little desire for British forces to operate from Australia. On the other hand, I know this outlook was not shared by the rest of Australia. However, as the meeting went on it took a far better turn and in the end we obtained all we wanted for the present. Namely Darwin and Fremantle to be developed for future operations by us and representatives of our staff to be accepted to work with the Australian General Staff.*
>
> *After lunch, interview with… Admiral Noble from Washington who tells me Dill is showing signs of age and is tired. Then a long talk with Pownall, just back from Mountbatten's HQ in Ceylon with the news that Dickie wants to get rid of George Giffard. I am very sorry for it.*"

In his Notes: "[Dill] had never really recovered from the infection he suffered from after his operation for the hernia… I was more and more distressed every time I saw him… Dickie Mountbatten made a fatal mistake in getting rid of Giffard who would have done him admirably and better than Oliver Leese who replaced him."

On 27 May:

> "*A very full COS which I got through all right by going fast and keeping the ball rolling. By 12 noon I was off for Whit Monday weekend and just longing for a rest of a few hours from continual war responsibility. The hardest part of bearing such responsibility is pretending that you are absolutely confident of success when you are really torn to shreds with doubts and misgivings! But when once*

decisions are taken, the time for doubts is gone and what is required is to breathe the confidence of success into all those around. This is made doubly hard when subjected to the ravings of prima donnas in the shape of politicians who seem to be incapable of having real faith in their own decisions! I never want again to go through a time like the present one. The cross-Channel operation is just eating into my heart. I wish to God we could start and have done with it!!"

Three days later:

"Cabinet. Winston at his worst. Although Alex had brought off a master stroke, not a single word of praise for him, only threats as to what he would think of him if he did not bring off a scoop! I got so angry that I lost my temper."

On the last day of May:

"A long COS attended by Pownall at which we tried to disentangle some of [the] awful South East Asia, Chiang Kai-shek… Commands. The whole show is an awful mess… Mountbatten is quite irresponsible and tries to be loved by all which won't work! He must face facts, ['Vinegar Joe'] Stilwell can't go on functioning in his present treble capacity and the sooner this is made clear to the Americans the better. I am afraid, however, that Mountbatten will be a constant source of trouble to us and will never really fit the bill as Supreme Commander.

News from Italy continues to be very good, I do so hope that Alex succeeds in breaking through on the Vilitri-Valtone front!"

FIFTEEN

CIGS: June–September 1944

On 1 June, Brookie was despondent:

"Long COS meeting at which we discussed the paper we are preparing to put over South East Asia and Pacific strategy to the American COS when they come over next week for [Overlord]. Not an easy paper when we have to steer clear between the rocks of Winston's ramblings in Sumatra, Curtin's subjugation to MacArthur, MacArthur's love of the limelight, King's desire to wrap all the laurels round his head and last but not least real sound strategy! The latter may well get a bad position at the starting gate!! My God, how difficult it is to run a war and to keep military considerations clear of all the vested interests and political foolery attached to it!!

We also discussed the future of Greece and then came across the usual desire of the Foreign Office to support some highbrow ideas as to future governments, entirely unacceptable to the local people, with utterly inadequate forces!! I am tired to death of our whole method of running war, it is just futile and heart-breaking.

Long meeting with Pownall to discuss the heart-breaking situation in Burma. I see disaster staring us in the face with Mountbatten incapable of realizing it, Pownall clever enough but too lazy to appreciate the danger and Giffard, I am afraid, lacking the adequate vision to see where he is going to. Oh! How I wish we had some more men with more vision. Or is it that I am very, very tired and becoming disheartened? If so, it is time I left this job!"

On 2 June:

"COS… was delayed by dear old Andrew Cunningham adopting the Admiralty attitude that a Supreme Commander 'coordinates' but does not 'command'!! It will take several more generations before this outlook can be thoroughly eliminated."

On 4 June:

"Cross-Channel operation was to have started on the night of the 4/5th but the weather was too bad, strong wind and low clouds. The operation has therefore had to be put off which is most regrettable."

On 5 June, the eve of Overlord, Brookie was nervous:

"Left early, news having been received on previous evening that we were in Rome. Winston had returned on Sunday evening in a very highly-strung condition… I found him over optimistic as regards prospects of the cross-Channel operation and tried to damp him down. Similarly, in Italy he now believes that Alex will wipe out the whole of the German forces! A long Cabinet at which we were explained how troublesome de Gaulle was being now that he had been fetched back from Algiers! He is now refusing to broadcast unless Eisenhower alters the wording of his own broadcast!! I knew he would be a pest and recommended strongly that he should be left in Africa, but Anthony Eden would insist on bringing him over!

It is very hard to believe that in a few hours the cross-Channel invasion starts! I am very uneasy about the whole operation. At the best it will fall so very, very far short of the expectation of the bulk of the people, namely all those who know nothing of its difficulties. At the worst it may well be the most ghastly disaster of the whole war. I wish to God it were safely over."

He elaborated in his Notes, "I knew too well all the weak points in the plan of operations. First of all, the weather on which we were entirely dependent; a sudden storm might wreck it all. Then the complexity of an amphibious operation of this kind when confusion may degenerate into chaos in such a short time. The difficulty of controlling the operation once launched, lack of elasticity in the handling of reserves, danger of leakage of information with consequent loss of that essential secrecy. Perhaps one of the most nerve-wracking experiences when watching an operation like this unroll itself is the intimate knowledge of the various commanders engaged. Too good a knowledge of their various weaknesses makes one wonder whether in the moments of crisis facing them they will not shatter one's hopes."

6 June was the start of Overlord:

"*By 7.30, I began to receive first news of the invasion. The airborne landings had been successful, the first waves were reported as going in, opposition not too serious… Throughout the day, information has gone on coming in. On the British front, the landing has gone well and the whole of 3 divisions are ashore. On the American front, the western landing was a success but the Eastern Corps [V Corps on Omaha beach] has failed practically along its whole front! They are now asking to land on [the] western beaches [of the British front]. This will probably have to be done but must inevitably lead to confusion on the beaches. It has been very hard to realize all day that whilst London went on calmly with its job, a fierce conflict was being fought at a close distance on the French coast!*"

7 June saw an interesting observation about the landings and yet another dry comment:

"*The invasion is a day older. I am not very happy about it. The American V Corps seems to be stuck. We are not gaining enough ground and German forces are assembling fast. I do wish to heaven that we were landing on a wider front.*

During afternoon had interviews with… General Bethouart who has come over with de Gaulle. He did not impress me much. A grey, putty-faced, flabby sort of chap with a doleful countenance. However, de Gaulle is enough to depress anybody. News from Alexander continues to be excellent, he is all for dashing off to the Pisa-Rimini Line."

On 8 June:

"We... [met] Winston to discuss future plans. He had put forward a paper with much too early plans for operations on the west coast of France with troops from Italy. But we must first see what happens to our cross-Channel operation and what the final stages of Alex's offensive leads to. In any case we must go on smashing up the German forces in Italy up to the Pisa-Rimini line."

On 9 June:

"The news from France is better. The XXX British and V American Corps have now joined up together. However, I am not yet entirely satisfied with the situation and wish the American front would join up and become a connected whole. At 7.30pm, went to Euston Station to meet Marshall, King and Arnold who had flown over from Washington."

On 11 June:

"Combined Conference [with American chiefs of staff]... Decided Italian campaign to stop at Apennines or Pisa-Rimini line and an amphibious operation to be prepared to land either in Southern France or in Bay of Biscay... It was interesting to listen to Marshall explaining now why the Germans fought in Central Italy! He seemed to forget that I had given him all these arguments several months ago as a prediction of what I was convinced would happen [see 19 May Notes]."

In his Notes: "Now at last we had put the South France operation in its right strategic position. By the time we reached the Pisa-Rimini line, the Italian theatre should have played its part in holding German reserves away from Northern France. We could then contemplate the landing in Southern France to provide a front for French forces from North Africa and to concentrate on southern flank of Overlord operations."

On the next day, Churchill and Brookie sailed to France:

"About 11am we approached the French coast and the scene was beyond description. Everywhere the sea was covered with ships of all sizes and shapes and a scene of continuous activity... It was a wonderful moment to find myself re-entering France almost exactly 4 years after being thrown out for the second time at St Nazaire. Floods of memories came back of my last trip of despair and those long four years of work and anxiety at last crowned by the success of a re-entry into France. We found Monty's HQ and he gave us an explanation on the map of his dispositions and plans. All as usual wonderfully clear and concise.

I was astonished at how little affected the country had been by the German occupation and 5 years of war. All the crops were good... and the French population did not seem in any way pleased to see us arrive as a victorious country to liberate France. They had been quite content as they were and we were bringing war and desolation to the country."

On 13 June:

"Last night Germans used their pilotless planes [V1] for the first time but did little damage... COS meeting where we discussed action to take and decided that we must not let defence interfere with [Overlord]!"

On the following day, there was a familiar whine from Churchill:

"Meeting with the American Chiefs of Staff... We discussed the Pacific strategy and found that they were in agreement with a proposed strategy based on North Western Australia... then on to 10 Downing Street... Winston began one of his long harangues stating that the Army was certain to crowd in 'dental chairs and YMCA institutions instead of bayonets' into the landing in France. What we wanted, he said, were combatants and fighting men instead of a mass of non-combatants. We argued with him that fighting men without food, ammunition and petrol were useless, but he was in one of his foolish moods and not open to conviction. It is appalling the false conception of modern war that he has got."

15 June saw a further meeting with the American chiefs of staff to discuss Burma:

"After the meeting, I approached [Marshall] about the present Stilwell set-up, suggesting that it was quite impossible for him to continue filling 3 jobs at the same time, necessitating him being in 3 different locations, namely: Deputy Supreme Commander, Commander Chinese Corps and Chief of Staff to Chiang Kai-shek [see 31 May]! Marshall flared up and said that Stilwell was a 'fighter' and that is why he wanted him there, as we had a set of commanders who had no fighting instincts! Namely Giffard, Peirse and Somerville all of which, according to him, were soft and useless. I found it quite useless arguing with him.

Monty seems to be meeting with more serious opposition and to have suffered a series of heavy counter-attacks which so far he appears to have resisted."

In his Notes, "Marshall had originally asked us to accept this mad Stilwell set-up… apparently as he had no one else suitable to fill the gaps. I was therefore quite justified in asking him to terminate a set-up which had proved itself as quite unsound. I had certainly not expected him to flare up… and to start accusing our commanders of lack of fighting qualities… especially as he could not have had any opportunities of judging for himself and was basing his opinions on reports he had received from Stilwell. I was so enraged by his attitude that I had to break off the conversation to save myself from rounding on him".

On 16 June:

"Staff meeting with PM [to discuss German V1 pilotless planes]… very few real decisions were arrived at. In my mind it is pretty clear and 3 essentials stand out: a) attacks by what can be spared from Overlord on launching sites, b) barriers of fighters, guns and balloons in succession south of London and c) no sirens and no guns in London. We shall, I hope, eventually get these, but it will take time."

On 19 June:

> "*Arrived up early to find that a pilotless plane had struck the Guards Chapel, Wellington Barracks during Sunday Service and had killed about 60 people!! Amongst them to my great grief Ivan Cobbold! And on my writing table was a letter from him written Saturday… asking me to lunch this week! It all gave me a very nasty turn and I cannot get him and poor Blanche out of my mind. News from France is good, the Cherbourg peninsula has been cut off by the Americans. Long Cabinet at which Winston was in very good form, quite 10 years younger, all due to the fact that the flying bombs have again put us into the front line.*"

In his Notes, "The death of Ivan Cobbold was a ghastly blow to me… made all the worse by the fact that when Brian Boyle was telling me of his death, I was actually picking up Ivan's letter off my blotting pad. His invitation to lunch with him that week made a very large lump rise in my throat."

On 20 June:

> "*Fighting in Cherbourg goes well. In the afternoon, had to inform Laurence Carr that his soldiering days had come to an end, I hated doing it and have a very special feeling for him.*"

On 21 June:

> "*We had a variety of points to consider at the COS, including petty squabbles between Mountbatten and Somerville on questions of command. It is astonishing how petty and small men can be in connection with questions of command.*
>
> *At 2.45 a meeting with the PM and Smuts. PM wanted Smuts to put before us his ideas for the prosecution of the war after clearing the Pisa-Rimini line in Italy. Were we to head for Italy according to Alexander's dreams [drive into north-east Italy and then advance via the mountainous Ljubliana Gap into Austria and on to Vienna] or were we to launch another expedition into France? Although Smuts*

liked the idea of Vienna, he considered it would be better to remove a force from Italy and launch a new cross-Channel expedition across the Calais narrows. He was evidently oblivious of the fact that the port capacity of this country will not support another expedition, that the shipping could not be found… Then Winston, who had evidently been lunching very well, meandered for ¾ hours producing a lot of disconnected thoughts which had no military value. It is hard to keep one's patience on these occasions… back to WO for the unpleasant job of telling Martel that his soldiering days were over."

On the next day:

"We examined Alexander's wild hopes of an advance on Vienna… The proposals he has made are not based on any real study of the problem but rather the result of certain elated spirits after a rapid advance! Am now off for one of the PM's awful 10.30 meetings… We are to discuss Italian strategy and I know that, as usual, it will be a useless waffle round!"

On 23 June:

"We had a long and painful evening of it [last night] listening to Winston's strategic ravings! I have seldom seen him more adrift in his strategic arguments… In the main, he was for supporting Alexander's advance on Vienna. I pointed out that even on Alex's optimistic reckoning the advance beyond the Pisa-Rimini line would not start till after September. Namely we should embark on a campaign through the Alps in winter! It was hard to make him realize that if we took the season of the year and the topography of the country in league against us we should have 3 enemies instead of one.

Cherbourg going rather slower, Alex's advance also slowed up."

Three days later:

"COS at which we had to draft a reply to Americans… We are up against the same trouble again, namely saving Alexander from being robbed of troops in order to land in Southern France!! We shall have great difficulties with Americans, especially as Alex keeps on talking about going to Vienna."

27 June saw another dry comment, on this occasion aimed at Herbert Morrison, the Home Secretary:

"Rather a troublesome night with a series of flying bombs [V1 pilotless planes] coming over between midnight and 3am. One close one made me get out of bed and prepare to get under! After lunch, interview… with Alan Cunningham over from Ireland who considers garrison might be reduced now. He is right and I must find some new home for him.

Cabinet at 6pm… Finished up with a pathetic wail from Herbert Morrison who appears to be a real white-livered specimen! He was in a flat spin about the flying bombs and their effect on the population! After 5 years of war, we could not ask them to stand such a strain, etc.!! In fact, he did not mind if we lost the war much, provided we stopped the flying bombs! However, Winston certainly did not see eye to eye with him!"

In his Notes, "Herbert Morrison's performance was a poor one, he kept on repeating that the population of London could not be asked to stand this strain after 5 years of war. He suggested that our strategy in France should be altered and that our one and only objective should be to clear the north coast of France [the location of the flying bomb launch sites]. It was a pathetic performance, there were no signs of London not being able to stand it and if there had been, it would only have been necessary to tell them that for the first time in history they could share the dangers their sons were running in France and that what fell on London was at any rate not falling on them. Thank heaven Winston very soon dealt with him."

Brookie's uncompromising attitude on this issue was probably shared by Andrew Cunningham, the First Sea Lord: after he attended a war cabinet meeting in April 1944 to discuss civilian casualties likely to be caused by Allied bombing of key communication targets in northern France, Cunningham recorded, "Considerable sob stuff about children with legs blown off and blinded old ladies but nothing about the saving of risk to our young soldiers landing on a hostile shore."[1] Cunningham's comment appears cold-blooded and heartless, but it illustrates the sense of responsibility which commanders feel for their troops.

On 28 June:

"This morning, the American reply to our wire arrived, a rude one at that!! They still adhere to Anvil [landings in southern France] being carried out and want it at once. They produce a series of futile arguments. Amongst others, they argue that we have derived benefit out of the Italian campaign, in spite of the fact that they were always opposed to it, but state that the reason for its success is attributable to Hitler's error in deciding to fight for Southern Italy. They forget that this is exactly what we kept on telling them would happen [see 19 May Notes]!! And now we have the most marvellous intercept message indicating the importance that Hitler attaches to Northern Italy, his determination to fight for it and his orders to hold a line south of the Pisa-Rimini line whilst this line is being developed! Kesselring's army is now a hostage to political interference with military direction of operations; it would be madness to fail to take advantage of it and would delay the conclusion of the war. We spent most of the day drafting a reply refusing to withdraw forces at present for a landing in South France with the opportunities that rest in front of us. Winston is also sending a wire to President backing up our message.

Meanwhile the war goes well. Cherbourg has definitely fallen, the attack for Caen has started well, the Russian attacks are a great success and the Imphal-Kohima Road [in India] is open again!!"

In his Notes, "This is another example of the lack of elasticity in the American method of running the war... There could now be no argument that the Germans were about to retire in front of us in Italy. To my mind, it was all important to keep them occupied there at this juncture and prevent withdrawal of [their] force[s] from Italy to Northern France."

On 29 June:

> "This evening, I collected Rollie... and went to Kew Gardens. It was lovely and peaceful there, I felt it was just what I wanted. Work, troubles, difficulties, differences of opinion, etc., had begun to make life jangle badly. Kew Gardens and contact with God through nature put all at rest again. There are times when I feel that I just can't stand one more day of this job and the burdens of responsibility which it means. On those occasions, contact with nature has a wonderfully strengthening effect."

On 30 June:

> "The President's reply had arrived in the night. It is an interesting document as it is not till you get to the last para that... you find that owing to the coming Presidential election it is impossible to contemplate any action with a Balkan flavour, irrespective of its strategic merits. The situation is full of difficulties, the Americans now begin to own the major strength on land, in the air and on the sea. They therefore consider that they are entitled to decide how their forces are to be employed. We shall be forced into carrying out an invasion of Southern France, but I am not certain that this need cripple Alexander's power to finish crushing Kesselring. I am just off now to a 10pm meeting with Winston to try and arrive at a final decision. He has ordered the Clipper and the York to stand by so we may be flying off to Washington before we are much older, but I doubt it. I think Winston will realize there is nothing more to be gained by argument. It is very unfortunate that Alex and Winston ever started their wild schemes about going to Vienna. This has made our task with the Americans an impossible one.
>
> After lunch went to Ivan Cobbold's memorial service. I do not remember going to a memorial service that upset me more, I miss him most awfully.
>
> Later: just back from meeting with Winston... he looked like he wanted to fight the President. However, in the end we got him to agree to our outlook which is: 'All right, if you insist on being damned fools, sooner than falling out with you which would be fatal, we shall be

damned fools with you and we shall see that we perform the role of damned fools damned well'!"

On 3 July:

"Americans started attack from Cherbourg southwards... at 5.30 record longest Cabinet meeting which lasted till 9.15pm!!! Winston in one of his worst maudlin moods wasted hours... Herbert Morrison as usual painting a gloomy picture of the state of London's morale, quite unjustified."

On the following day:

"A long COS... at which we discussed all the various measures for defeating flying bombs. The fighter aircraft are not proving fast enough, the guns are not hitting them, the balloons may have their cables cut, the launching sites are not worth attacking with bombers, etc. In fact, rather a gloomy and unsatisfactory meeting.

I had two interviews with [Alexander]. I told him that I felt he was missing his chances of smashing up Kesselring before he got back to the Pisa-Rimini line and also that Oliver Leese [commander, British Eighth Army] was not providing the necessary hinge for the 8th Army, which remained continually behind the Americans and the French! I am afraid Alex did not like this very much, but it is very desirable to bring his feet to earth and to make him face the facts confronting him instead of his futurist dreams of an advance on Vienna. PM sent for me at 6.30pm. He was in a bad mood, with all his vindictive spirits aroused, wishing to continue his arguments with the President and longing to have a good row with him!"

On 5 July:

"Considerable excitement today preparing details for Winston's speech on flying bombs. We had to consider advisability of reprisals on small towns in Germany as a deterrent. Personally, I am dead against it... I am afraid however that Winston's vindictive nature may induce him to try reprisals. I hope we shall succeed in stopping him!"

On 6 July:

> "At 10pm we had a frightful meeting with Winston which lasted till 2am!! It was quite the worst we have had with him. He was very tired as a result of his speech in the House concerning the flying bombs, he had tried to recuperate with drink. As a result, he was in a maudlin, bad-tempered, drunken mood, ready to take offence at anything, suspicious of everybody and in a highly vindictive mood against the Americans. In fact, so vindictive that his whole outlook on strategy was warped. I began by having a bad row with him. He began to abuse Monty because operations were not going faster and apparently Eisenhower had said that he was over cautious. I flared up and asked him if he could not trust his generals for 5 minutes instead of continuously abusing them and belittling them. He said that he never did such a thing. I then reminded him that during two whole Monday Cabinets in front of a large gathering of Ministers, he had torn Alexander to shreds for his lack of imagination and leadership in continually attacking at Cassino. He was furious with me, but I hope it may do some good in the future.
>
> It was not till after midnight that we got onto the subject we had come to discuss, the war in the Far East! Here we came up against all the old arguments that we have had put up by him over and over again. Attlee, Eden and Lyttelton [the 'Yes men' – see 6 March] were there, fortunately they were at last siding with us against him. This infuriated him more than ever and he became ruder and ruder. Fortunately, he finished by falling out with Attlee and having a real good row with him concerning the future of India! We withdrew under cover of this smokescreen just on 2am, having accomplished nothing beyond losing our tempers and valuable sleep!!"

In his Notes, "I remember that ghastly evening as if it were yesterday. Winston had driven me to the verge of losing my temper in several Cabinet meetings where he had poured abuse on Alex's head in front of the whole Cabinet. Although I had explained to him the whole of the topography of the front on a raised model, he kept on attacking Alex's plans of attack, his lack of ideas, his continuing to bump his head on the same spot, the incurring of casualties for no results, his lack of vision and many more failings. As most of the Cabinet Ministers had little opportunity of judging for themselves, and took all he said for gospel, there was every danger of their opinion of Alex being seriously affected.

When the whole process was starting again this evening with reference to Monty, although there were only 3 Cabinet Ministers, it was more than I could stand. I think what infuriated me most was that there had not been a single word of approval or gratitude for the excellent work Monty had done in the handling of the land forces in this very difficult amphibious operation. And now he was starting off again with a string of abuse. I lost my temper and started one of the heaviest thunderstorms that we had! He was infuriated and throughout the evening kept shoving his chin out, looking at me and fuming at the accusation that he ran down his generals."

This 'frightful meeting' may well be the incident which was later recalled by Joan Bright Astley, Pug Ismay's assistant, "Brooke in the company of other ministers was far more rude to the PM than he had any right to be – and Churchill was shocked. He broke up the meeting and said to Ismay: 'I have decided to get rid of Brooke. He hates me. You can see the hate in his eyes.' Ismay said: 'I think that he behaved very badly at the meeting but he is under terrific strain. He is bone honest and whatever else his views may be, he doesn't hate you.' Ismay then left to see Brooke and said: 'The PM is frightfully upset and says you hate him.' Whereupon Brooke said: 'I don't hate: I adore him tremendously; I do love him but the day that I say that I agree with him when I don't is the day he must get rid of me because I am no use to him any more.' Asked if these words could be repeated to the PM, he said 'Yes'. Ismay went back and told Churchill what had been said and his eyes filled with tears, 'Dear Brookie.'"

On 7 July,

"Cabinet at 11am where Alexander gave an account of the operations in Italy. He did it very well."

On 8 July, Brookie had a tête-à-tête with Alexander:

> "He is the most delightful person and very attractive, but I am afraid very simple-minded and entirely innocent of any understanding of the politician's underhand methods! I am afraid Macmillan has him entirely fooled, he likes [Macmillan's] company as he believes that he receives from him an insight into political affairs... I fear he has not even begun to understand what politics mean. It is just as well that he does not, a 'soldier must not be politically minded'; but why should not the converse hold good? It seems as reasonable to state that a 'politician must not be militarily minded.'"

10 July saw yet another of Churchill's 'awful 10.30pm meetings':

> "He was in a pleasant mood. We wandered like a swarm of bees from flower to flower but never remained long enough at any flower to admit of any honey being produced... He does not know the situation, has a false picture of the distribution of forces and of their capabilities. A complete amateur of strategy, he swamps himself in details he should never look at and as a result fails ever to see a strategic problem in its true perspective."

On 12 July:

> "Dinner with John Kennedy. Poor Bannerman was there, rather shaken after having been bombed twice in 3 days by [flying bombs]... Apparently he saved himself from being blown to bits by diving under his oak table."

13 July saw an accurate prediction:

> "The capture of Amboina Island in the Pacific and the military backing of Foreign Office policy in Greece were the two topics of discussion at our COS meeting... the latter to try and preserve us against the wild schemes of the Foreign Office and their objectionable ambassador [to the Greek Government] Mr Leeper. This combination, as I see it, is preparing to force on Greece a government of their own [i.e. Foreign Office] selection and to support this government with

military power. I can foresee a very serious military commitment very rapidly increasing."

On 14 July:

"We [met] the PM at 11.30am to discuss Pacific strategy with a view of arriving at a final solution!!! Attlee, Eden, Lyttelton were there as usual, we were there from 11.30 to 2pm and settled absolutely nothing!! We listened to all the PM's futile and empty arguments which we have listened to again and again. Both Attlee and Eden were against him and yet on and on we meandered. In the end, I said to him: 'We have examined the two alternatives in great detail [see 21 February Notes], we have repeatedly examined them for you, we have provided you with all possible information and we are unanimous on our advice to you as to which course to select. They both have certain advantages but, in our minds, we are quite clear as to which course we should select. However, we are even clearer still that one or other course must be selected at once and that we cannot go on with this indecision. If the Government does not wish to accept our advice let them say so but, for heaven's sake, let us have a decision!' He then stated that he must go on thinking about it and would give us a decision within a week! I doubt it!!

In the evening motored out to Chequers for the night to meet Mr Stimson [American Secretary of War]... Stimson quite finished and hardly able to take notice of what is going on round him."

Three days later:

"A long COS... trying to decide policy as regards ELAS organization in Greece [Greek communists actively engaged in subversive activities] and whether time had come to denounce this organization. The whole future Greek policy is full of dangers, the Foreign Office with the Ambassador, Leeper, are likely to brew up a mass of future trouble for us, especially as they insist on retaining the King [of Greece] as their protégé hidden in rear whilst the Greeks are determined not to have him back."

Earlier, 13 June, it had been agreed that the German flying bombs should not influence the course of Allied operations in France. On 18 July:

"Long meeting with Cherwell and Duncan Sandys at the COS… The [V2] rocket is becoming a more likely starter. The tendency is of course to try and affect our strategy in France and to direct it definitely against rocket sites. This will want watching carefully."

18 July saw the start of Operation Goodwood, an attack launched by British and Canadian forces on the eastern side of the Cherbourg peninsular in Normandy. This operation quickly became engulfed in controversy, seemingly because of a misunderstanding as to its true purpose. Montgomery's stated aim was to draw German forces into the Goodwood battle since this would assist the Americans in their planned breakout on the western side of the peninsular: however, other Allied commanders, notably Eisenhower, believed that the British and Canadian attack was itself intended to achieve a breakout. The flames of this controversy were then fanned by stories run by the American media that American troops were bearing a disproportionate share of the fighting and, consequently, a disproportionate share of the casualties.

On 19 July:

"PM sent for me. I found him in bed in a new blue and gold dressing gown but in an unholy rage! What was Monty doing dictating to him? He had every right to visit France when he wanted. Who was Monty to stop him? As Defence Minister, he had full right to visit any front he wanted!

I found it hard to discover what the problem was or to put in a word edgeways. At last, I discovered that Eisenhower had told him that Monty had asked not to have any visitors during the next few days and the PM had argued out that Monty had aimed this restriction mainly at him! Nothing that I could say would make him believe otherwise… He is quite impossible to work with nowadays. I assured him that I could put the whole matter right in 5 minutes with Monty and left him.

[After Brookie's arrival in France] I had a long talk with Monty. First of all, I put matter of PM's visit right by getting Monty to write a note to PM telling him he did not know that he wanted to come and inviting him. Then warned him of tendency in PM to listen to suggestions that Monty played for safety and was not prepared to take risks, mainly fostered by Tedder egged on by Coningham... I found [Monty] in grand form and delighted with his success east of Caen.

[After returning to London] Drove round to leave Monty's letter with PM, could not see him as he was asleep. Got back to flat to find a letter from S of S [Grigg] showing that PM had been unbearable all day on the question of 'Monty trying to dictate to him'!! [Churchill] had finally drafted a foul letter which he wanted [Grigg] to send to Eisenhower notifying him of the intended visit of the PM and of the fact that he would not see Monty, the whole most offensively worded. S of S called me up on telephone, I told him what I had done and while we were talking he received a message from the PM stating that the letter to Eisenhower was not to be sent. Shortly afterwards, PM called me up and said that he was delighted with Monty's letter and felt rather ashamed of himself for all he had said!! And well he might feel ashamed of himself! What a storm in a china cup! All for nothing!"

In his Notes, "I asked [Monty] what he was doing stopping the PM from coming to France. He assured me he was doing nothing of the kind. I then told him that whether he was or not did not matter but the important thing was that the PM was certain he was. Monty then told me that Stimson had visited Bradley's HQ [American general] and had remained with him so long that orders for an attack could not be got out and the attack had to be postponed for 24 hours. Monty had therefore asked Ike to stop visitors for the present.

PJ Grigg also had a sad tale to tell of Winston's abuse of Monty. He read me out part of the letter drafted by Winston which PJ was expected to sign. In it, I remember Ike was to be informed that the PM in his capacity of Defence Minister could visit France when he liked. That he would come on a certain date but that he would not (repeat NOT) visit General Montgomery!"

On 20 July:

"We... considered Winston's minute stating that... he could not give a decision on the Pacific strategy without discussing matters once more with Dickie Mountbatten!! We had sent him a minute stating that Supreme Commanders were not the people to decide world strategy, that these decisions must rest with the Combined Chiefs of Staff and governments concerned. However, he cannot understand strategy and argues the relative advantages of an attack on North Sumatra as opposed to one on Amboina, instead of discussing relative merits of an attack on Japan based on India as opposed to one based on Australia. Now instead of arriving at a decision that is already months overdue he is going off skylarking in France where he can do nothing but disturb commanders who have got important battles to get on with."

On the next day:

"This morning when I turned on the 8am news, I was astounded to hear of the attempt on Hitler's life although this was exactly what I had been expecting for some time. It is hard at present to tell how serious the business may be and how it will ultimately turn out."

On 26 July:

"I was sent for by Winston... Eisenhower had been lunching with him and had again run down Montgomery and described his stickiness and the reaction in the American papers! The old story again: 'He was sparing British forces at the expense of the Americans who were having all the casualties.' However, Winston was in a good mood and receptive to arguments. He even said that on all military matters I was his 'alter ego'!! The first time I had ever heard this or had much reason to suspect it... I was asked to dine tomorrow night to meet Eisenhower and Bedell Smith."

On 27 July, note the 'national spectacles':

> "*I have earned my pay today!... an hour with [Grigg] discussing post-war policy and our policy in Europe. Should Germany be dismembered or gradually converted to an ally to meet Russian threat of 20 years hence? I suggested the latter and feel certain that we must from now onwards regard Germany in a very different light. Germany is no longer the dominating power of Europe, Russia is. Unfortunately, Russia is not entirely European. She has however vast resources and cannot fail to become the main threat in 15 years from now. Therefore, foster Germany, gradually build her up and bring her into a federation of Western Europe. Unfortunately, this must all be done under the cloak of a holy alliance between England, Russia and America. Not an easy policy and one requiring a super Foreign Secretary!*
>
> *Then dinner with PM, Ike [Eisenhower] and Bedell Smith [Eisenhower's chief of staff] intended to bring me closer to Ike and to assist in easy running between Ike and Monty. It did a lot of good. I have offered to go over with Ike if necessary to assist him in handling Monty. My God, what psychological complications war leads to!! The strategy of the Normandy landing is quite straightforward. The British must hold and draw Germans onto themselves off the western flank, whilst Americans swing up to open Brest Peninsula. But now comes the trouble, the press chip in and we hear that the British are doing nothing and suffering no casualties whilst the Americans are bearing all the brunt of the war!! I am tired to death with and by humanity and all its pettiness! Will we ever learn to 'love our allies as ourselves'??!! I doubt it!*
>
> *There is no doubt that Ike is all out to do all he can to maintain the best of relations between British and Americans, but it is equally clear that Ike knows nothing about strategy and is quite unsuited to the post of Supreme Commander, as far as running the strategy of the war is concerned! Bedell Smith, on the other hand, has brains... [and] is certainly one of the best American officers but still falls far short when it comes to strategic outlook. With that Supreme Command set up, it is no wonder that Monty's real high ability is not always realized.*

Especially so when 'national' spectacles pervert the perspective of the strategic landscape."

Brookie followed up on this meeting by writing a letter to Montgomery the next day. His letter is a good example of the direct yet supportive guidance which he gave his commanders: his remark, 'if you see me turn up with him, you will know what it is all about', is wonderful. Note the reference to 'attacking on the whole front' since this was to become yet another contentious issue:

> *Ike lunched with PM again this week and as a result I was sent for by PM and told that Ike was worried at the outlook taken by the American Press that the British were not taking their share of the fighting and of the casualties. There seemed to be more in it than that and Ike himself seemed to consider that the British Army could and should be more offensive. The PM asked me to meet Ike at dinner with him which I did last night; Bedell was there also.*
>
> *It is quite clear that Ike considers that Dempsey [British commander] should be doing more than he does; it is equally clear that Ike has the very vaguest conception of war! I drew his attention to what your basic strategy had been, i.e. to hold with your left and draw Germans on to the flank whilst you pushed with your right [the American breakout on the western side of the Cherbourg peninsular]. I explained how in my mind this conception was being carried out, that the bulk of the [German] armour had continuously been kept against the British. He could not refute these arguments, and then asked whether I did not consider that we were in a position to launch major offensives on each front simultaneously. I told him that in view of the fact that the German density in Normandy was 2½ times that on the Russian front whilst our superiority in strength was only in the nature of some 25% as compared to 300% Russian superiority on Eastern front, I did not consider that we were in a position to launch an all-out offensive along the whole front.*

Evidently, he has some conception of attacking on the whole front, which must be an American doctrine judging by Mark Clark [American general] with Fifth Army in Italy! However, unfortunately this same policy of attacking (or "engaging the enemy") along the whole front is one that appeals to the PM. Ike may, therefore, obtain some support in this direction.

I told Ike that if he had any feelings that you were not running operations as he wished, he should most certainly tell you and express his views. That it was far better for him to put all his cards on the table and that he should tell you exactly what he thought. He is evidently a little shy of doing so. I suggested that if I could help him in any way by telling you for him, I should be delighted. He said that he might perhaps ask me to accompany him on a visit to you! So, if you see me turn up with him, you will know what it is all about.

I feel personally quite certain that Dempsey must attack at the earliest possible moment on a large scale. We must not allow German forces to move from his front to Bradley's front or we shall give more cause than ever for criticism. I shall watch this end and keep you informed but do not neglect this point; it is an important one.[2]

On 28 July:

"*Another of those awful Cabinet meetings which lasted two hours, at which we spent all our time discussing the rocket and flying bomb... what a desperate waste of time! Winston gets more and more prosy relating all his old reminiscences... I remain very fond of him but by heaven he does try one's patience!!*"

Three days later:

"*Cabinet at 5.30 which dragged slowly on till 8.30pm. At least an hour wasted in deciding what a bus driver should do when a buzz bomb was in the offing!... The more I see of Herbert Morrison, the more I despise him [see 27 June]! If England is to be ruled by that type of man, then we are sunk for a certainty!*"

On 1 August:

"August! The month when wars usually start! I wonder whether this one will look like finishing instead [at the end of July, American forces succeeded in breaking out of the western side of the Cherbourg peninsular]!? Flying Bomb Committee... great difficulty as chairman to keep discussion to the point. Portal loves showing his scientific knowledge... Duncan Sandys insists on letting one know that he has a great political future. All that takes up time and bores me to death. Brocas Burrows [head of British Military Mission in Russia] just back from Moscow... confirmed all my views as to how the Russians should be handled."

On 2 August:

"Brocas Burrows attended our COS and we discussed the organization of some staff centre at Moscow although... it is highly unlikely that Stalin will ever agree to any such organization being established.

In the evening, I picked up Rollie at 6pm and we went down to Kew Gardens again, it was lovely down there. We sat on a seat and watched some young water hens being instructed by their mother as to how a bath should be taken! She gave a demonstration first and then those tiny mites followed suit and copied her, a wonderful sight.

News tonight excellent! St Malo, Rennes, Vitre have all been captured, the latter being the last but one HQ that I occupied in France!!!"

On 3 August:

"The war news goes on improving daily... If things go on as they are doing now, we should be able to clear the Brest Peninsula fairly quickly. Beyond that it is rather hard to see what the Boche can do except retire to the line of the Seine and it is also doubtful if he succeeds in doing this, in view of our great preponderance in the air. After lunch, had to have a coloured photograph taken for The Illustrated."

4 August produced an odd incident which has never been satisfactorily explained:

"Today Eisenhower has asked for the famous South of France landing to be cancelled and that same force to be transferred to Brittany instead. That is actually what we had suggested to the Americans and they had turned it down! It is far the best solution. Now Winston starts making work by... calling for a conference tonight... to discuss this change... I cannot see what there is to discuss, it is a matter of taking a decision quickly and the decision in this case is an easy one.

Later: Winston... told us that Eisenhower had lunched with him and read a paper to him with the suggestion that the South of France landing should be transferred to Brittany which Winston thoroughly agreed with. He gave us the impression that Ike had already sent a telegram about it to America. Winston had drafted a telegram to the President supporting this proposition strongly. I told him that although I entirely agreed with the proposal, I was convinced that he was wrong in wiring to the President... He did not agree, decided to send his telegram and asked us to send one to the American Chiefs supporting him!"

Two days later:

"Was called up on the telephone to be told that Eisenhower had never sent any telegram to America and that he was strongly opposed to any change in the South of France attack plan!! Who has been 'double crossing' who? Has Ike fooled the PM or has the PM fooled us!! In any case, we have certainly not improved our relations with the Americans!"

It is difficult to see why Eisenhower would engage in a 'double cross' since he had little, if anything, to gain and a great deal to lose from doing so.

On 7 August:

"Dickie Mountbatten and Wedemeyer came to our COS and explained their Burma strategy. It is clear that now that Stilwell has led us down to Myitkyina [a strategically important town in Burma] we shall have to go on operating in Burma. It is equally clear that the best way of doing so is to take the whole of Burma by an airborne attack on Rangoon. Furthermore, it is clear that such an enterprise must reduce our effort in the Pacific. Finally, as background to it all, when will Germany be finished off and allow us to transfer our strength to the Far East? All these points we discussed repeatedly in a series of conferences all through the day. Now it remains to make up our minds, not the easiest part of the task!"

On the following day:

"At 11am met PM and meeting lasted till 1.30pm. Attended by Eden, Lyttelton, Attlee [the 'Yes men'], Mountbatten and Chiefs of Staff, also Wedemeyer. Meeting resumed again from 6pm to 8.30pm and is due to meet once more from 10.30pm to ? Up to the present we have settled absolutely nothing... We have been discussing the Pacific strategy, recommending the capture of Burma by a landing at Rangoon combined with a Pacific strategy of naval, air and Dominion forces operating from Australia. Winston still hovers back to his tip of Sumatra and refuses to look at anything else.

1am: just back from our evening conference with the PM. It was if anything worse than any of the conferences of the day. I believe he has lost the power of giving a decision. He finds every possible excuse to avoid giving one... Nor has he produced a single argument during the whole of that period that was worth listening to."

9 August saw Brookie scheming in concert with Pug Ismay:

"COS... we discussed previous evening's work and... drafted our conclusions on South East Asia strategy. At 12.30 we met PM [who]... produced a document of his own which he read out. It was not far off ours and I said so and suggested that Pug should draft a document combining our two papers. I told [Pug] privately that he was to draft it mainly on our paper with PM's phraseology.

Meeting with Sosnkowski [Commander-in-Chief, Polish Armed

Forces in the West] who is very upset that we are not providing more assistance to the Underground Army fighting Germans in Warsaw... Meeting with the PM at 10.30pm which lasted till 1.30am, at which we finally arrived at a policy for South East Asia. It is not what we started out for and not ideal, but it saves as much as it can out of the wreck, whilst also meeting... the necessity for liquidating our Burma commitment by undertaking capture of Rangoon. On the other hand, it still gives some scope for... the formation of a British Task Force in the Pacific."

On the next day:

"This morning we drafted carefully our wire to America to put into effect last night's decision. A difficult wire to word as it had to remain acceptable to the Americans whilst remaining within the requirements of the PM. Two opposites very hard to reconcile!! Winston... redrafted our wire to the American COS and put it into a form and words in which it is unmistakable and bound to be recognized as emanating from him and consequently crash any hope of getting it through!!!"

On 11 August:

"We... refuse to accept [PM's amendments] with consequent delay. I then had a busy day... culminating with quite hopeless letters from Dickie Mountbatten to Marshall, which he sent me to look at!! I had to tell him that he could not send any of them and should attend COS on Monday with Wedemeyer and we could tell the latter what he should say to Marshall. Finally, left for home about 7pm... I was feeling absolutely cooked and dog-tired".

The weekend of 12-13 August was *"spent quietly at home with you and resting peacefully. Just heaven after the previous week."* On 14 August:

"News very good and every chance of rounding off the Boche on Monty's front... Tonight, landings in Southern France [Operation Anvil] near Toulon and St Raphael are to take place!!"

On 15 August, his criticism of Churchill was again matched with a compliment:

> "Life has a quiet and peaceful atmosphere about it now that Winston is gone [he was in Italy]. Everything gets done twice as quickly, everybody is not on edge, one is not bombarded by a series of quite futile minutes and the whole machinery settles down to efficient smooth running. I feel that we have now reached the stage that for the good of the nation and for the good of his own reputation it would be a godsend if he could disappear out of public life. He has probably done more for this country than any other human being has ever done, his reputation has reached its climax, it would be a tragedy to blemish such a past by foolish actions during an inevitable decline which has set in during the last year.
>
> Monty's great encircling move in France is making good progress and still holds out great hopes."

On the following day:

> "Most of the COS was taken up with problems as to how to support the Polish underground rising in Warsaw. The Russians appear to be purposely giving no assistance and the Poles here are naturally frantic. The landing at Toulon seems to be going well whilst the operations in Normandy are working up towards a climax. There are great hopes of delivering a smashing blow which might go a long way towards clearing the road for the rest of France."

On 17 August:

> "The Joint Planners came to attend the COS and we discussed all the difficulties facing us if we are to stage a Rangoon attack by next March! The War Office have been raising just one series of difficulties and delays. Their examination proved that it was impossible to do it by that date. I therefore had a 2 hours' meeting this morning to prove to them that it is possible and must be done. It is extraordinary how exhausting it is having to drive a plan through against opposition. First on the part of the PM and now on the part of those responsible

for it in the WO. There are moments when I would give anything just to get in a car and drive home, saying I was fed up with the whole show and they could look for someone else to fill my job! The making of plans is just child's play as compared to putting them into execution. I feel worn out and very glad at the thought of going to Italy for a change and rest."

On 18 August:
"We had a final interview with Dickie Mountbatten to discuss our plans for the capture of Rangoon which is based on our being able to start withdrawing the 6th Division from the European Theatre on Oct 1st. It is a gamble, but I believe one worth taking."

That night Brookie flew to Italy. On the following day, he was in Naples:
"I then had a long talk with Jumbo Wilson… many of my doubts as to the value of Oliver Leese are being confirmed. He is certainly not anything outstanding as a commander."

On 25 August, he returned to London. On the same day, Paris fell to the Allies:
"The news of German decay on all fronts continues to be almost unbelievable!"

28 August saw Brookie alarmed at the prospect of Eisenhower assuming direct command of the Allied land forces in place of Montgomery. Note his prediction of the likely outcome:
"Difficult COS where we considered Eisenhower's new plan to take command himself [of Allied land forces] in Northern France on Sept 1st. This plan is likely to add another 3 to 6 months on to the war! He straight away wants to split his forces, sending an American contingent towards Nancy whilst the British army group moves along the coast. If the Germans were not as beat as they are, this would be a fatal move, as it is it may not do too much harm.

Meanwhile Paris is liberated, Rumania out of the war and

Bulgaria tumbling out next. The Germans cannot last very much longer."

In his Notes, "Up to now [Eisenhower] had been a Supreme Commander with separate commanders for naval, land and air forces. Now he proposed to assume the dual role of Supreme Commander and commander of the land forces. This change was brought about mainly by the American press resenting the fact that Monty was commanding all the land forces. Personally, I consider it wrong for a Supreme Commander to attempt the role of the supreme task on one level and one of the services on the next level."

The Allied land forces in Europe comprised the British and Canadian 21st Army Group, the 12th US Army Group led by General Bradley and the forces landed in the south of France, later to become operational as the 6th US Army Group, led by General Devers. In late August, a disagreement arose between Montgomery and Eisenhower over the deployment of the 21st and 12th Army Groups. Montgomery proposed that they should be kept together and deployed in a single, concentrated, northward thrust. In contrast, Eisenhower wanted to separate them, despatching 21st Army Group on the northward thrust and the 12th Army Group on an eastward thrust.

On 29 August, Brookie flew to France to meet Montgomery. Note the 'political pressure':

"Long talk with [Monty] about recent crisis with Eisenhower. Apparently, he has succeeded in arriving at a suitable compromise by which 1st US Army is to move on the right of 21st Army Group and head for area Charleroi, Namur, Liège, just north of Ardennes. Only unsatisfactory part is that this army is not under Monty's orders and he can only coordinate its actions in relation to 21st Army Group. This may work, it remains to be seen what political pressure is put on Eisenhower to move Americans on separate axis from the British.

Murky fly home through clouds, reaching Hendon at 7.45pm,

having lost my escort of 3 fighters in the clouds. I hope they returned safely."

By 30 August, another Anglo-American conference was looming:

"Apparently, Winston has again got a minor attack of pneumonia. Not much, and they think they can get him right to start by sea in the Queen Mary for Quebec next week... [Churchill] informed me that he wanted to make Monty a Field Marshal, the appointment to coincide with the date of Eisenhower assuming command of the land forces (Sept 1st). He felt that such a move would mark the approval of the British people for the British effort that had led to the defeat of the Germans through the medium of Montgomery's leadership."

Five days later:

"This evening our troops are reported in Brussels and advancing on Antwerp! It is very hard to believe it all!!"

On the next day Brookie travelled up to Scotland with Churchill:

"I am not looking forward to this journey and conference. Winston... has agreed to our airborne campaign on lower Burma but limits his sanction to the capture of Rangoon alone without the clearing of the rest of Burma. This makes the expedition practically useless and what is worse converts it into one which cannot appeal to the Americans since it fails to affect upper Burma where their air route is situated."

On 7 September, the British delegation were en route to Quebec:

"Meeting... to discuss the shipping situation which will arise when Germany is defeated. The call on personnel shipping will be enormous, what with move of forces to the Japanese war, repatriation of our prisoners, return of Americans to USA and on to Japanese war, Canadians to Canada, New Zealanders to their homes and South Africans to South Africa... It is going to be a difficult problem to lay down priorities for all these moves."

On 8 September:

> "[Churchill] looked old, unwell and depressed. Evidently found it hard to concentrate and kept holding his head between his hands. He was quite impossible to work with, began by accusing us of framing up against him and of opposing him in his wishes. According to him… [we] suggested moving troops from Europe for Burma and had never told him that the removal of these forces was dependent on the defeat of Hitler (a completely false accusation). He further said that we had told him only one division was required for Burma, and now we spoke of 5! (Here again a complete misstatement of facts) It was hard to keep one's temper with him, but I could not help feeling frightfully sorry for him. He gave me the feeling of a man who is finished, can no longer keep a grip of things and is beginning to realize it. We made no progress".

On the following day:

> "We received 2 minutes from the PM today which show clearly that he is a sick man… We have come for one purpose only – to secure landing craft for an operation against Istria!! All else of importance fades into the shade of secondary considerations. But what is more serious he now repudiates an agreement which we secured with him weeks ago and which we submitted to the Americans with his approval! Namely the possible formation of a British task force under MacArthur… is now repudiated."

10 September saw blistering criticism of Churchill, yet it was still matched with a compliment. The opening sentence in the second paragraph is highly significant:

> "We had another meeting with Winston… He knows no details, has only got half the picture in his mind, talks absurdities and makes my blood boil to listen to his nonsense. I find it hard to remain civil. And the wonderful thing is that ¾ of the population of the world imagine that Winston Churchill is one of the Strategists of History, a second Marlborough, and the other ¼ have no conception what a public menace he is and has been throughout this war! It is far better

that the world should never know, and never suspect, the feet of clay of that otherwise superhuman being. Without him England was lost for a certainty, with him England has been on the verge of disaster time and again.

And with it all no recognition hardly at all for those who help him except the occasional crumb intended to prevent the dog from straying too far from the table. Never have I admired and despised a man simultaneously to the same extent. Never have such opposite extremes been combined in the same human being."

On 11 September, the British delegation arrived in Quebec:

"Dinner at the Citadel by the Athlones [Governor-General of Canada] for Winston and Roosevelt. All the rank, fashion and clergy of Quebec plus all American Chiefs of Staff. Bad speeches by Athlone and President full of worthless platitudes lacking any sincerity. Am I getting soured against humanity as a whole or am I right that such official banquets are the centres of the most ghastly hypocrisy!?"

On 12 September, note Brookie's description of Marshall:

"We had our first [Combined] COS at 12 noon… It went off most satisfactorily and we found ourselves in complete agreement with American Chiefs of Staff. They were prepared to leave American divisions in Italy till Alex had finished his offensive. They were also prepared to leave LSTs for Istrian venture if required. At 4.30pm we had an ordinary COS to discuss latest minute by PM on Pacific strategy… He now accepts a naval contingent to the Pacific, a Dominion Task Force under MacArthur. At 6.30pm we had to go up to the Citadel for a meeting with him. He was all smiles and friendliness… How quickly he changes. An April day's moods would be put to shame by him! Lunched with Marshall, Leahy and Dill, the former as boring and as charming as usual."

On 14 September, Churchill had driven a member of his inner circle to tender his resignation:

"I started the day by being… told that the PM wanted to see me at 9am and that Pug Ismay would like to see me before that!… Found [Ismay] very upset, having had a ghastly time on previous evening with Winston! PM had, on his own, wired to Dickie Mountbatten to find out how it was he was now wanting 6 divisions to capture Burma having originally said he only wanted 2 from outside. Dickie had wired back giving full details of the series of changes in plans that had occurred. As a result, Winston had accused us all to Ismay of purposely concealing changes of plan from him to keep him in the dark. That we were all against him and heaven knows what not! As a result, Ismay had written out a letter handing in his resignation to him and asked for my advice as to whether he should send it in!!… I agreed it would probably bring Winston to his senses. I then started off to see Winston at 9am, wondering what awful row I should find myself mixed up in. To my surprise, I found him in his bed and in a very good mood… He was in such a good mood that I tackled him about the transfer of Oliver Leese from Alexander to replace Giffard with Dickie and got him to agree!

Combined meeting at 10am… A very successful meeting at which we got the Americans to accept the British fleet in Central Pacific, and also the Burma operation. We had great trouble with [Admiral] King who lost his temper entirely and was opposed by the whole of his own committee! He was determined, if he could, not to admit British naval forces into Nimitz's command in the Central Pacific."

In his Notes, "I believe [Pug Ismay] did hand in his resignation and that Winston refused to take any notice of it."

On 15 September:

"On the whole we have been very successful in getting the agreement which we have achieved and the Americans have shown a wonderful spirit of cooperation… We met the PM at 6pm. A frightful interview!! He did his best to pull the whole of our final report to pieces, found a lot of petty criticisms and wanted to alter many points

> *which we had secured agreement on with difficulty. Anthony Eden was there and he did his best to help us but, unfortunately, Winston was in one of his worst tempers… The tragedy is that the Americans whilst admiring him as a man have little opinion of him as a strategist, they are intensely suspicious of him."*

In his Notes, "I [noticed] at this conference that Dill… seemed to be wasting away and both mentally and physically he was showing signs of slowing up… I was very disturbed to see him in this state but had no idea that this was the last occasion on which we should meet. Thank heaven I did not know – the parting would have been too hard."

By 27 September, Churchill and Brookie were back in London. Note the robust reaction to the German request:

> *"Cabinet at 6pm at which Winston wanted to discuss the desirability or otherwise of responding to German requests to send food for the British population in the Channel Islands. Decided not to send any in and to reply to Germans that it was their duty to keep population reasonably well fed or to surrender if they were unable to do so."*

Two days later:

> *"I am very lucky indeed to have PJ [Grigg] as [Secretary of State for War]. He is wonderfully considerate and very easy to work with… Thank heaven this week is over, I am worn out."*

SIXTEEN

CIGS: October–December 1944

On 2 October, Brookie was forced to review the decision to launch an attack on Rangoon before March 1945. Note his dry comment about the Foreign Office:

"*A longish COS meeting where we discussed the Foreign Office attitude to our paper on dismemberment of Germany. We had considered the possible future and more distant threat to our security in the shape of an aggressive Russia. Apparently, the FO could not admit that Russia might one day become unfriendly.*

10pm meeting with PM to discuss Burma operation. Just before dinner, had received message from Montgomery saying that he could not spare either 52nd, 3rd Divs or 6th Airborne Div [see 18 August]... and drawing our attention to the fact that there is still heavy fighting in front of us before defeating Germany. Operations in Italy are also lagging behind and do not admit of withdrawal of forces. I therefore advised against trying to stage Rangoon operation before next monsoon and PM agreed. It is very disappointing, but I think the correct decision. PM suddenly informed us that he and Anthony Eden were off to Moscow on Saturday next and that he wanted me to come with him!!"

5 October saw Brookie in France, attending a conference organised by Eisenhower:

"*Ike then explained his future strategy which consisted of the capture of Antwerp and advance to the Rhine in the north and south, forcing the Rhine north and south of the Ruhr, capture of Ruhr followed by an advance on Berlin either from Ruhr or from Frankfurt depending on which proved most promising… During the whole discussion, one fact stood out clearly, that Antwerp must be captured with the least possible delay. I feel that Monty's strategy for once is at fault, instead of carrying out the advance on Arnhem [in September] he ought to have made certain of Antwerp in the first place. Ramsay brought this out well in discussion and criticized Monty freely. Ike nobly took all blame on himself as he had approved Monty's suggestion to operate on Arnhem. I thought Ike ran the conference very well indeed, the atmosphere was good and friendly in spite of some candid criticisms of the administrative situation."*

By 7 October, Brookie was in Moscow:

"*I lunched with Brocas [Burrows, head of the British Military Mission]… and discussed with him the Russian dislike for him which has resulted in our having to withdraw him."*

On 10 October, he attended a lunch hosted by the Russians:

"*Stalin himself got up and began a long speech. He referred to Winston's and Harriman's speeches in which they had mentioned the unreadiness for war of Britain and America. Stalin said this was the same in the case of the Russian forces. Why was this? The reason was easy to find, we were all three peace-loving nations with no aggressive thoughts. Germany and Japan both aggressors were ready for war because they wanted war. How was this to be prevented in the future? Only by the cooperation of the three peace-loving nations provided they maintained the power to enforce peace when necessary. It was 5.30pm when we rose from the table, we had sat for 3 solid hours. What had we done? Listening to half-inebriated politicians and diplomats informing each other of their devotion and affection and expressing sentiments very far detached from veracity. Are international friendships based on such frothy products of drunken orgies? If so, God help the future!"*

On 12 October, note Churchill's 'desire to do something for Mountbatten':

> "There is some fable about some hunters going out to shoot a bear who, on the eve of the shoot, became so busy arguing about the sale of the skin and the sharing of the proceeds that they forgot to shoot the bear! I feel this is what we are doing here, ever since we arrived we have been busy discussing post-war settlements and as a result have completely neglected up to date the problem of how we are going to finish the war. During the morning, I went over to see Winston in bed… [and] succeeded in riding him off any idea of trying to withdraw divisions from Italy to still try and carry out the Rangoon attack before the monsoon. He was mainly influenced by his desire to do something for Mountbatten.
>
> In the evening I went to the opera to see Prince Igor. A vast theatre with the stage larger than the auditorium. Very fine music, singing, scenery and dresses; in fact, far better staged than anything that could be done in London. It was a wonderful and most impressive performance. The theatre was packed, all stalls being reserved for commissars and officers. No sergeants allowed in them! [In his Notes, "We had tried to take stalls for some of our sergeant clerks but were informed that they could not be admitted"] And this in a country of supposed equality amongst all?"

In his Notes, "That morning whilst I was with Winston he suddenly looked up at me and asked: 'Why did not the King give Monty his [field marshal's] baton when he visited him in France?' I replied that I did not know… 'No!' replied Winston, 'that is not it. Monty wants to fill the Mall when he gets his baton! And he will not fill the Mall.' I assured him that there was no reason for Monty to fill the Mall on that occasion. But he continued, 'Yes, he will fill the Mall because he is Monty and I will not have him filling the Mall'… It was a strange streak of almost unbelievable petty jealousy on his part. But I had frequently noticed that he liked the limelight to concentrate on him and not to disperse on those that surrounded him. Those that got between him and the sun did not meet his approval. It was all a pretty human failing which somehow made him stand out all the greater".

On the following day, Brookie went to the opera again:

"I could not help wondering what the effect of these wonderfully reproduced episodes of aristocratic life must have on the Communist audience.

It is very distressing to hear from the Mission here how impossible it is to build any sort of social relations with the local inhabitants. They will never come for meals and never ask any of our representatives to come out. A vast gap exists which apparently cannot be bridged."

In his Notes, he recalled a dinner held on 14 October, "Amongst the toasts, Stalin made one which was not translated but which raised peals of laughter from all the Russians there. The toast had been made for Maisky [former Russian ambassador to Britain] and as he sat next to me and had not taken part in any of the laughter, I asked him what all the laughter was about. With a glum look on his face, he replied 'The Marshal has referred to me as the Poet Diplomat because I have written a few verses at times, but our last Poet Diplomat was liquidated – that is the joke!!'"

15 October saw a meeting in the Kremlin to discuss the war against Japan:

"They… consider they may require some 60 divs to deal with the 45 Jap divs they expect. I asked them whether they considered that they could maintain 60 divisions and their strategic air force over the trans-Siberian railway. Antonov [Russian chief of operations] replied in the affirmative but was corrected by Stalin who thought this was doubtful… There was never any doubt that the Russians were [entering the war against Japan] as soon as they could and that they were prepared to discuss plans now. Stalin, however, drew attention to the fact that there was a political aspect to this problem that must also be tackled. What was Russia to get for her help?"

In his Notes, "At our meeting with Stalin that day I was more than ever impressed by his military ability. When I asked Antonov that question as to whether he could maintain 60 divs and the strategic air offensive over the trans-Siberian railway, I felt fairly certain that he knew the answer but was not certain what Stalin might want him to say. He looked round at him for some guidance but got no help, Stalin stood back with a complete poker face. Antonov, at a loss, said that they could and was at once brushed aside by Stalin... He displayed an astounding knowledge of technical railway details, had read past history of fighting in that theatre and from this knowledge drew very sound deductions."

By 16 October, Brookie's work was completed so he was killing time:
"It gets very trying being followed everywhere and completely shadowed by 3 detectives and a major in the Red Army. They are quite nice and supposed to be there to watch over me... Their authority over the crowd is absolute. Whilst shopping the other day, a crowd had collected round me. One of the detectives walked round saying quite quietly, 'It would be better for you not to be here' and they all dispersed and vanished at once!"

On 19 October, the British party left Moscow. After stopping over in Cairo and Naples for conferences, they returned to London on 22 October. Note the statistics:
"I... have covered 10,500 miles since I left [a fortnight earlier]! It has been a remarkably successful trip... I have now got a lot to do to put the results of our conferences and talks into effect... With this flight I have now passed the 100,000 miles in the air! since doing this job."

On the following day, he was in a philosophical mood:
"I am very glad to have been back to Russia again, it is a country with much food for thought. One more of those vast experiments which humanity periodically carries out throughout the annals of history. Experiments which lead to much bloodshed, much upheaval, much suffering and finally, when all is examined, some progress. In my mind Bolshevism, Nazism, Fascism, etc., all have their purpose; they all turn the wheel of destiny one or two more cogs forward. Forward towards the path of general progress. Humanity surges forward like

(l to r) Brookie, Churchill, Jumbo Wilson, Harold Alexander and John Dill in Cairo, January 1943. "I cannot imagine that Alex will ever make a Supreme Commander, he has just not got the brains for it." 17 November 1944

Brookie and John Dill at the Washington conference, May 1943. "I know no other soldier in the whole of my career who inspired me with greater respect and admiration. An exceptionally clear and well-balanced brain, an infinite capacity for work, unbounded charm of personality but, above all, an unflinchable straightness of character"

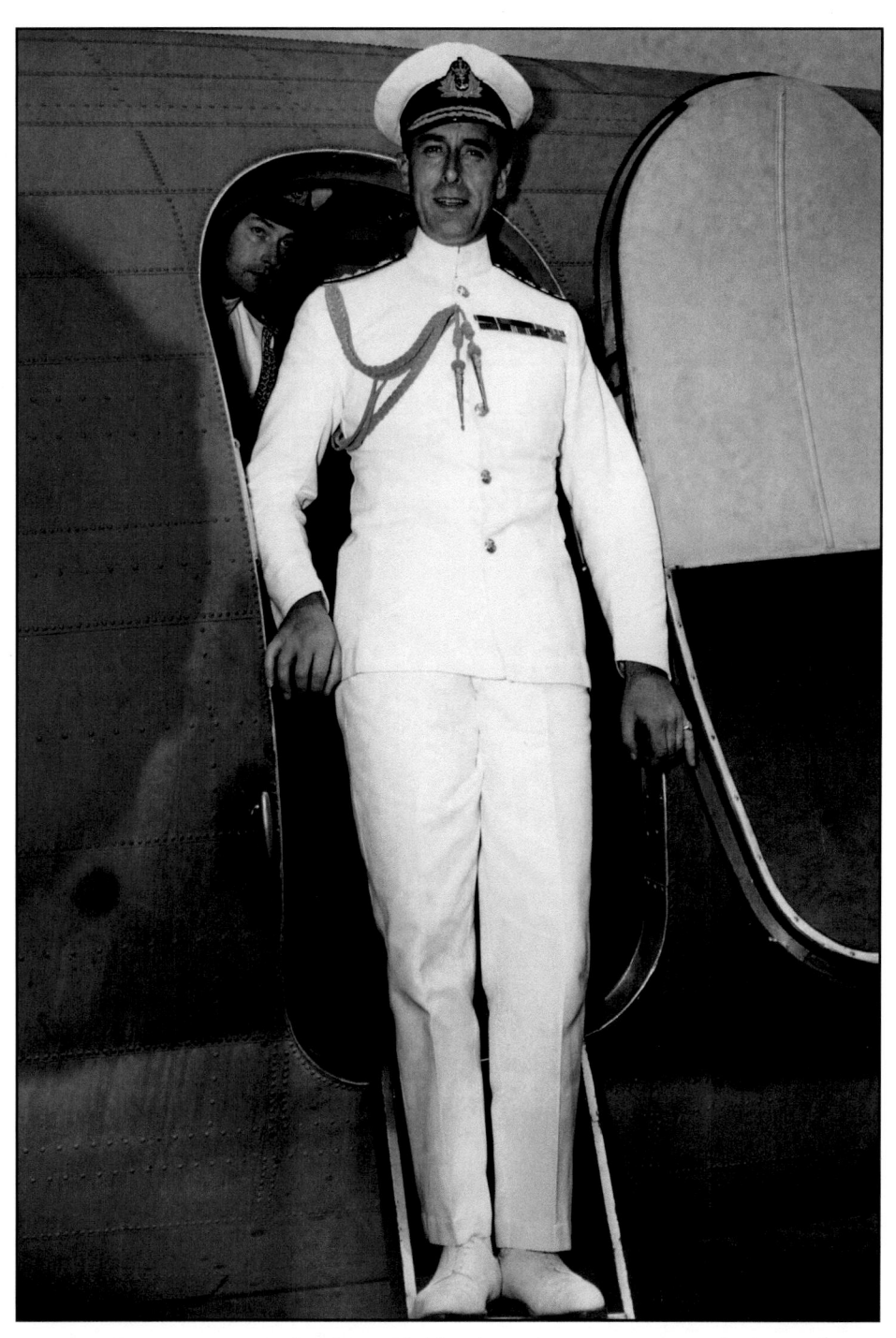

Mountbatten arrives to take charge. "Seldom has a Supreme Commander been more deficient of the main attributes of a Supreme Commander than Dickie Mountbatten." 7 August 1945

Anthony Eden, Foreign Secretary, puffs away whilst reading some papers at Tehran in November 1943. To his right is Sir Alexander Cadogan, the armchair general in the Foreign Office

(l to r) Pug Ismay and Brookie appear to be squaring up to one another as John Dill and Andrew Cunningham, Dudley Pound's successor, look on. Taken in Cairo, December 1943. Brookie's diary is testament to the innumerable disagreements between the members of the British Chiefs of Staff Committee during the War

Montgomery with Brookie in Normandy, 12 June 1944. The body language suggests Montgomery was being ticked-off, yet again. In 1946, Montgomery wrote a letter to Brookie, "I want to say two things. First, I am terribly grateful for all you have done for me. Second, I could never have achieved anything if you had not been there to help me; it has been your wise guidance, and your firm handling of a very difficult subordinate, that really did the business. I could have done nothing alone"

General Dwight D. Eisenhower, United States Army, in November 1944. "I am afraid that Eisenhower as a general is hopeless!" was Brookie's verdict on 28 December 1942 and on 24 November 1944, "Personally, I think he is incapable of running the war even if he tries"

Churchill with the chiefs of staff in the garden at 10 Downing Street, 7 May 1945. Back (l to r), Leslie Hollis, Pug Ismay. Front (l to r), Charles Portal, Brookie, Churchill, Andrew Cunningham

This photograph of Brookie hints at the strength and forcefulness of his character. Yet, look closer and there is sadness in his eyes

This is a rarity, a photograph of Brookie smiling. No prizes for guessing why this lover of nature was so happy. Taken at Sydney Zoo in December 1945 during his world trip

Brookie's statue, bearing the inscription 'Master of Strategy', outside the Ministry of Defence in London. It was unveiled in 1993, thirty years after his death

"I felt throughout the ceremony as if I was in a dream. The white tall pillars of the monument standing out against the ashy grey sky seemed entirely detached from this earth, whilst the two red wreaths of poppies looked like two small drops of blood on that vast monument. They served as a vivid reminder of the floods of blood that had already been spilt on the very ground we were standing, and of the futility of again causing such bloodshed" 11 November 1939
(Reproduced by kind permission of The Airborne Assault Museum – paradata.org.uk)

the tide flowing. Successive waves of one or other 'ism' romp up the beach only to be sucked back almost to where they started from. But in that 'almost' lies the progress forward. It seems essential for humanity to subject itself to untold ordeals in order to achieve even slow progress towards perfection. The path of mankind in learning to 'love its neighbours as itself' is a thorny and rocky one. But for all that, I have not the least doubt that mankind ultimately will reach the top rungs of this long and steep ladder."

2 November saw disapproval of Eisenhower's strategy:

"Unpleasant wire from Mountbatten about his future Chief of Staff to replace Pownall... he wants Swayne or Nye and refuses Slim.

Found out that Ike's plan as usual entails attacking all along the front [this became known as the 'broad front' strategy] instead of selecting main strategic point. I fear that the November attack will consequently get no further than the Rhine at the most!"

On 3 November:

"[Churchill] told me that he had been thinking over the desirability of replacing Dill now that he would be unable to carry on. (It was only yesterday at lunch that he stated that it was unnecessary to replace him and we had all remonstrated with him!). His suggestion now is to send Jumbo Wilson there... [it] will all depend on how Jumbo hits it off with Marshall. Last year in Cairo, Marshall had a good opinion of him. I then tackled the PM on the question of making Jumbo a Field Marshal. He refused at first... however, by working away at him I got him to agree and only hope he does not go back again. I feel Jumbo has certainly earned his baton as much as Ironside or Gort!"

Two days later:

"On the wireless at 9am, the death of Jack Dill was announced, and I had the unpleasant feeling that another of the prominent landmarks of my life was gone, and with it one of my best friends and one to whom I owed more in my military career than to any other. His loss is quite irreparable and he is irreplaceable in Washington. Without him there, I do not know how we should have got through the last 3 years."

In his Notes, "If it had not been for the vital part he played in Washington, we should never have been able to achieve the degree of agreement in our inter-Allied strategy… He was in an ideal position to play the part of intermediary between [Marshall and I] and to bring us together… Any success that I may have had in getting Marshall to finally accept our Mediterranean and Italian strategy were entirely due to Dill's help. Repeatedly, I heard him referred to as the best ambassador we had ever had in Washington."

On 6 November:

"5.30: our usual Cabinet which turned out to be an exciting one. First of all, the PM announced that Lord Moyne [British minister, resident in Middle East] had been shot in the neck in Cairo by terrorists! Then Winston and Amery had a set-to on the India question. Winston had attacked the Viceroy, Amery flared up and told him he was 'talking damned nonsense'!! Winston said that if he had lost his temper to that extent, he better withdraw from the Cabinet! Amery did not move and the situation calmed. Winston then had trouble with John Anderson and became even more sour. Finally, we escaped at 8.15 but I came away with a feeling that Winston is losing his authority in the Cabinet and have not yet seen him with so little authority or control."

On the following day, note 'the error which Eisenhower has just made in France':

"Started our COS with a wire Winston wished to send the President in which he proposed that Wilson should take over Dill's place… and that Alexander should take over from Wilson. So far so good, unfortunately he went on to suggest Alexander should combine the duties of Supreme Commander and his own [as commander of Allied Armies in Italy] at the same time… we had to pull it to pieces badly and *sent it back mutilated with our reasons. He has been unable to send it off but has decided to have a 10.30pm meeting with us which promises to be a fairly heated one! Monty came to lunch with me in very good form but pretty full of criticism of Ike and of his methods of running a war!*

Just back (1am) from our meeting with the PM. Anthony Eden attending… [Eden] had just come back from Italy where he had been seeing Alexander who had, as usual, whined about being crushed by Wilson's HQ, the great duplication of work. As a result, [Eden] had recommended combining the Supreme Commander and Group Commander into one and wanted in fact to commit the error which Eisenhower has just made in France… The problem was complicated by the First Sea Lord… being convinced that [Alexander] is incapable of doing the Supreme Commander's job in the Mediterranean. Personally, I have also serious doubts and feel that he must be given the very best Chief of Staff. After much arguing, I made my point, namely Wilson to replace Dill, Alex to replace Wilson and Clark to replace Alex. It is not ideal, but it is the best that can be made of a very complicated situation with many personal factors (such as PMs admiration for Alex) impinging on it. Anthony Eden behaved well and seeing that he had messed things up did not press his point."

On 8 November, the phrase 'pretending to command' is worth highlighting:

"Joubert de la Ferte [deputy chief of staff, South East Asia Command] gave me some interesting sidelights on Mountbatten's HQ. He said that the Anglo-American relations continued to be bad. The Americans full of criticisms of our management of India and expressing openly the opinion that if they had their way there would be no British Empire after the war!

Cyril Falls, Military Correspondent of The Times, came to see me. He said that he was disturbed at the system of command in France with Eisenhower commanding in two planes namely commanding the Army, Navy and Air Forces in his capacity as Supreme Commander and at the same time pretending to command the land forces, divided into 3 groups of armies, directly. He has hit the nail on the head and found the weakness of this set-up which the Americans have forced onto Eisenhower. Unfortunately, it becomes a political matter and the Americans, with preponderating strength of land and air forces, very naturally claim the privilege of deciding how the forces are to be organized and commanded... It is, however, a very serious defect in our organization and one that may have evil repercussions on the strategy of the war. I do not like the layout of the coming offensive and doubt whether we even reach the Rhine, it is highly improbable that we should cross over before the end of the year."

On 9 November:

"I had a talk with Monty before he returns to France. He still goes on harping over the system of command in France and the fact that the war is being prolonged. He has got this on the brain as it affects his own personal position, and he cannot put up with not being the sole controller of land operations. I agree that the set-up is bad, but it is not one which can be easily altered, as the Americans have now the preponderating force in France and naturally consider they should have a major say in the running of the war. Perhaps after they see the results of dispersing their strength all along the front, it may become easier to convince them that some drastic change is desirable, leading to a concentration of force at the vital point."

10 November saw Churchill and Brookie in Paris:

"In my [hotel] room, I found a set of the most priceless bird books which had been drawn out of the Natural History Library for me to look at!... They are quite lovely and most of them original drawings."

On 12 November:

"[Dined] with Koenig who had two generals dining who had taken a great part in the [French] Resistance movement. They were most interesting about their experiences and lives led under a dozen different names and carried on from a dozen residence[s]. Four months was the most that the majority survived before getting caught by the Gestapo."

In his Notes, "They did not think much of the part [de Gaulle] had played. One of them said to me: 'De Gaulle! What did he do? Evacuated his family to London from the start, where he followed them. There he lived comfortably throughout the war whilst we were risking our lives daily in contact with the Germans... Meanwhile in his safe position he had the impertinence to say *"Je suis la France"*!' They were very bitter".

On 13 November, Brookie visited a section of the Allied front in the Vosges region and was unimpressed by American tactics. Interestingly, his alternative tactics were later employed by French forces:

"On arrival, we were given a description... of the front held by the 1st French Army and the plans for the attack. Considering that the divisions for the attack are on a 30-kilometre front each, have been fighting without rest for 2½ months and also have just been reorganized by absorbing white personnel in lieu of the Senegalese who have to go back to Africa, the whole plan of attack struck me as being fantastic! It is another case of Eisenhower's complete inability to run the land battle as well as acting as Supreme Commander. Furthermore, it is an example of the American doctrine of attacking all along the line. The American Army just north of de Lattre [French general] is attacking in an impossible country in the Vosges, all he will do there is lose men. He ought to establish a defensive front there and concentrate his forces on the Belfort gap. Any successful offensive there would turn the line of the Vosges and render this expensive attack unnecessary. The French realize these errors only too well and are fretting at being subjected to their results. On the way home, we had to visit a training camp where... we saw a battalion of the Legion which marched past. A most impressive sight."

In his Notes, "The one [sight] that remained most rooted in my mind was the march past of the Foreign Legion battalion... The grandest assembly of real fighting men that I have ever seen, marching with their heads up as if they owned the world, lean, hard-looking men, carrying their arms admirably and marching with perfect precision. They disappeared into the darkness leaving me with a thrill and the desire for a division of such men."

On 14 November, Churchill and Brookie met Eisenhower at Rheims:
"We... were met by Ike who drove us out to his camp situated on the golf links built by the big champagne merchants! He went over the dispositions of the front and seemed fairly vague as to what was really going on!

[Following their return to Britain] It was a relief to get the PM safely back from this trip as the security in Paris was far from satisfactory."

On 16 November:
"Started our COS meeting with John Anderson [Chancellor of the Exchequer] on the question of the atomic bomb. He was very interesting and gave us an excellent account of what he knew about the research work going on in Germany, and the likelihood of arriving at some conclusion in the near future, which does not seem to constitute a danger for the present.

We then met the planners to discuss the plans of Mountbatten which are, as usual, half baked."

His 17 November entry is somewhat garbled:
"We found at the morning COS that Winston was still confused about the system of command in Italy and in the Mediterranean. Having tried hard to warp the whole organization while Wilson was Supreme Commander and Alex commanding the Group of Armies so as to try and put Wilson in the saddle for the benefit of Alexander, now that he places Alexander as Supreme Commander he is frightened lest his powers should be restricted in the manner he has endeavoured to reduce those of Wilson!!... I have grave doubts as to the efficiency of

these new appointments! Wilson will, I am afraid, never be able to step into Dill's shoes and I cannot imagine that Alex will ever make a Supreme Commander, he has just not got the brains for it."

20 November saw more criticism of Eisenhower:

"Fairly long COS with... a discussion as to the unsatisfactory state of affairs in France, where Eisenhower completely fails as Supreme Commander and just does nothing. Bedell Smith lives back in Paris quite out of touch, as a result the war is drifting in a rudderless condition. Had a long and despondent letter about it from Montgomery over the weekend. Am preparing case as we shall have to take it up with the Americans before long... Boy Browning came to see me to be informed that he is to go as Chief of Staff to Mountbatten. He took it well, but I doubt whether in his heart of hearts he was thrilled!"

On 21 November:

"Winston... announced that Alex and Wilson would be made Field Marshals. American attacks round the Vosges have been doing better today but I still feel certain that final results will fall far short of our hopes."

The next day saw another dry comment:

"Duncan Sandys [see 9 and 12 September 1942 and 1 August] attended our COS for our fortnightly review of rockets and flying bombs. He does not improve on acquaintance, but no doubt possesses all the necessary qualities for a successful political career! Giffard came to lunch and poured his heart out to me about his treatment by Dickie Mountbatten and, as I thought, he was given a very raw deal. I blame Henry Pownall for a great deal of it, he should have been able to control Dickie better than he did. In any case, I feel certain that most of the credit for the Burma success is due to Giffard."

By 24 November, Brookie had run out of patience with Eisenhower. Note the 'deputation' included Eisenhower's chief of staff, Bedell Smith:

"At the end of this morning's COS meeting I cleared the secretaries out and retained only Pug [Ismay]. I then put before the meeting my views on the very unsatisfactory state of affairs in France with no one running the land battle. Eisenhower, though supposed to be doing so, is detached and by himself with his lady chauffeur on the golf links at Rheims [Kay Summersby had been Eisenhower's chauffeur since 1942: it was rumoured that she and Eisenhower, who was married, were having an affair] – entirely detached from the war and taking practically no part in the running of the war! Matters got so bad lately that a deputation of Whiteley, Bedell Smith and a few others went up to tell him that he must get down to it and RUN the war, which he said he would. Personally, I think he is incapable of running the war even if he tries… Finally decided that I am to see the PM to discuss the situation with him. It is one of the most difficult problems I have had to tackle."

Two days later:

"Monty flew over from Belgium… He came to discuss the situation in France and to try to arrive at the best way of putting it right. We decided that there are three fundamentals to be put right:

a) to counter the pernicious American strategy of attacking all along the line

b) to obviate splitting an army group with the Ardennes in the middle of it, by forming two groups (a northern and a southern) instead of three as at present

c) to appoint a commander for the land forces. The problem is how to get this carried out. What we want is Bradley [commander, 12th US Army Group] as a Commander of Land Forces, Montgomery, Northern Group of Armies… and Devers [American general] commanding Southern Group. Monty is to see Eisenhower on Monday and if he opens the subject Monty is to begin putting forward the above proposals. Meanwhile, I am to have a talk with the PM… Without some such changes we shall just drift on and God knows when the war will end!"

On 27 November:

"Had a long COS, drawn out by a discussion between CAS and First Sea Lord involving inter-service rivalries liable to cause heated blood!... Cabinet at 6.30 to 8.30pm. PM evidently beginning to realize that all is not well in France but incapable of really seeing where the trouble really lies! He is now pressing for clearing Holland during the next few months which he thinks could be done 'in no time with 2 or 3 divisions'!"

On 28 November, note Brookie's concern about the lack of reserves:

"I went to see the PM, having asked for an interview with him. I told him I was very worried with the course operations were taking on the Western Front. I said that when we looked facts in the face this last offensive could only be classified as the first strategic reverse that we had suffered since landing in France. I said that in my mind two main factors were at fault, i.e. a) American strategy and b) American organization. As regards the strategy, the American conception of always attacking all along the front, irrespective of strength available, was sheer madness. In the present offensive, we had attacked on 6 Army Fronts without any reserves anywhere. As regards organization, I said that I did not consider that Eisenhower could command as both Supreme Commander and as Commander of the Land Forces at the same time.

Winston said that he was also worried about the Western Front. He agreed with most of what I had said but was doubtful as to the necessity for a land force commander. I think I succeeded in pointing out that we must take the control out of Eisenhower's hands and the best plan was to repeat what we did in Tunisia when we brought in Alex as a deputy to Eisenhower to command the land forces for him [see 20 January 1943 Notes]. I told Winston that the only way of putting things right was to get Marshall to come over. He agreed, we decided to wait a few more days before doing so."

On the following day:

"Received telegram this morning from Monty. He had had a

talk with Eisenhower [on 28 November]. The latter had agreed that strategy was wrong, that results of offensive were strategic reverse, that front wanted reorganising, would not agree that commander of land forces was necessary. But prepared to put Bradley with a large group north of the Ardennes under Monty's orders, leaving Devers south of the Ardennes. This may be all right, but I still have grave doubts as Ike is incapable of running a land battle and it is all dependent on how well Monty can handle him."

30 November was Churchill's birthday. On 1 December:

"Went to see Winston at 10am to tell him about Monty's wires. Found him in bed having his breakfast, surrounded by birthday presents… He was in a good mood and approved the steps that Monty had taken including the latter's letter to Ike laying down in black and white results of their talk together. If only all Monty thinks he has settled materializes we shall be all right, but I have fears of Ike going back on us when he has discussed with Bedell Smith, Tedder, etc!"

On 2 December:

"I was called up by the PM who had drafted a wire to Eisenhower that he wanted to send. It was a hopeless one referring to the conversations which Monty has been having with Ike and which the latter does not even know that Monty has told me about! It also went on to give Ike advice as to how to run the war, and very bad advice at that! I tried to stop him, explaining to him the harm he would do but he would not agree, stating that [Montgomery and Eisenhower's meeting on 28 November] had been much publicized by the Press, it was a matter for Government decision and not a matter to be settled by military men on their own! It was quite clear that his pride was offended that Monty and Ike had had some limelight turned on them which he had not shared! I got angry and told him that if he treated private wires that way it would make me very reluctant to show them to him again. However, I finally got him to hold his hand until Monday!"

Earlier, 1 December, Brookie had 'fears of Ike going back on us'. On 3 December, his concern proved well-founded:

"A quiet Sunday spoilt by a mass of correspondence sent down by [despatch rider] and several telephone calls. Trouble brewing up in Greece and all my worst forebodings coming true [see 13 July]! Anthony Eden had originally asked for 5000 soldiers, I had told him that he would end by wanting some 4 divisions, which he denied flatly. He has already absorbed over 40,000!! Also, telephone call from Simpson… with Monty's latest news. Monty has now received Ike's reply and it does not look too good, he seems to be changing round since seeing Bradley!"

On 4 December:

"I went off to complete my argument [2 December] with Winston. I found him in a good humour and succeeded in getting him to withdraw an offensive minute he had written to me after our talk on Saturday. He also agreed not to send that wire to Eisenhower and not to do anything till Monty and Ike had had their talk next Thursday. He made some queer statements during our discussion! One was that he did not want anybody between Ike and the Army Groups as Ike was a good fellow who was amenable and whom he could influence! Bradley, on the other hand, was a sour-faced blighter and might not listen to what he said. I replied that I could see little use in having an amenable Supreme Commander if he was totally unfit to win the war for him!"

On 5 December, Leeper's unwarranted remark is worth highlighting:

"The Greek situation is getting more and more confused. Winston spent most of the early hours from 3am onwards sending telegrams to Jumbo Wilson, Scobie [commander, British forces in Greece] and Leeper [British ambassador in Athens]. Meanwhile, Wilson was sending me wires which did not fit in with the instructions Winston was sending him. It is fairly clear that Leeper has got the jitters, having originally asked for 5000 men as being ample to set the Greek Government firmly on its feet, he has now got over 40,000 and considers that 'the military have badly underestimated the strength required' and should send more troops at once. This is exactly what I have been predicting from the very start! Winston had been trying to induce Wilson to leave the Parachute Brigade in Greece whereas it is urgently required for operations in Italy! Added to which these operations are Anglo-American and the approved directive… from the Combined Chiefs of Staff states that the operations in Greece must on no account be allowed to interfere with those in Italy.

I asked for an interview with Winston… He kept me waiting till 12.45 as he was in the House and having a bad time about the Greek situation! When he returned, I put the whole case in front of him. I found him rather rattled about situation, however he agreed that the withdrawal of the Parachute Brigade should be proceeded with as settled. I do not see much daylight yet in that Greek situation. And I feel certain we shall have to send far more troops there!"

On the next day:

"A very long COS which Alexander attended for a bit. I am afraid that it was an eye-opener for him to find some of the problems and difficulties he is to be up against as Supreme Commander in Mediterranean!! He is a mere child at it and does not begin to grasp what his task is! God help him and may God help us! I have been doing my best to get him to shed Harding as his Chief of Staff and take on someone of bigger calibre. I have offered him Monkey Morgan, Budget Loyd, Kirkman, Keightley or Scobie or anybody he likes to choose from… He has practically promised to change him but wants to use Harding to settle him in!

[Later] long interview with Alex in which I asked him to ensure that he did not 'over lie' Clark in the way he had accused Wilson of treating him! I have a great feeling of uneasiness about Alex filling this job adequately!"

On 7 December:

"Another long COS during which we examined the American

plans for the Pacific. They are based on the war in Europe ending before the end of this year and do not bear any very direct relation to facts! They will have to slow up the estimates of their rates of advance. After lunch, I had interview with… Boy Browning prior to his start to act as Chief of Staff to Mountbatten, and a difficult job he is going to have of it!"

On 8 December:

"Called up by Winston to find that he wanted to send a wire to Wilson to reinforce Greece by two brigades. He is doing it without possibly being able to estimate what the situation is. However, one thing is certain, we must now get out of the mess that this Greek venture had led us in. Consequently, I agreed to additional forces being sent since the greater the force the quicker the job will be done. I warned him however that we shall be falling foul of the Americans and that we shall have to have the Supreme Commander Mediterranean's directive adjusted."

On 12 December, note Eisenhower's projected date for crossing the Rhine:

"I have just completed one of those days which should have been one of the key stones of the final days of the war and has turned out as utterly futile! I feel I have utterly failed to do what is required and yet God knows how I could have done anything else. I started by going to the PM at 10am to discuss with him Monty's letter. Found him in bed eating his breakfast… He was quite incapable of concentrating on anything but his breakfast and the Greek situation! I remained till 10.30am, found he had not even read Monty's letter, knew nothing about it. I tried to explain but he kept returning to Greece! 'How wonderful Alex was! What a grasp! What a quick appreciation of the situation! What a master mind!'

Disgusted, I went to the COS which lasted till near 1pm. Was informed during lunch that War Cabinet was to meet at 3pm on Greece. We met and wasted 1½ hours deciding whether the

Archbishop should be appointed as Regent. Finally, Cabinet decided this should be done and drafted minute to that effect to King of Greece who, I understand, refused!

At 6pm met Ike and Tedder [British air chief marshal and Eisenhower's deputy] with PM... [and] whole COS. Ike explained his plan which contemplates a double advance into Germany, north of Rhine and by Frankfurt. I disagreed flatly with it, accused Ike of violating principles of concentration of force which had resulted in his previous failures. I criticized his future plans and pointed out impossibility of double invasion with limited forces he has got. I stressed the importance of concentrating on one thrust... [and] that with his limited forces, any thought of attack on both fronts could only lead to dispersal of effort. Quite impossible to get the PM to even begin to understand the importance of the principles involved. Half the time his attention was concentrated on the possibility of floating mines down the Rhine!!! He cannot understand a large strategical concept and must get down to detail! Ike also quite incapable of understanding real strategy. To make it worse, Tedder talks nothing but nonsense in support of Ike.

Finally dined at 10 Downing St with PM, Ike, Tedder... Conversation again returned to the same topic of the strategy, but I got no further in getting either Winston or Ike to see that their strategy is fundamentally wrong. Amongst other things discovered that Ike now does not hope to cross the Rhine before May!!! [Eisenhower later claimed this date was based on incorrect information]"

On the following day:

"*I was very depressed last night and seriously thought of resigning as Winston did not seem... to attach any importance to my views. I found however today that the situation was far better than I thought. After the COS, I went to see Winston... He told me that he had had to support Ike last night as he was one American against five of us with only Tedder to support him. And also he was his guest. I think he felt that I had been rather tough on Ike but, on the other hand, I found that I had convinced him of the seriousness of the situation. What I had said last night had had far more effect on him than I had thought. He decided that the War Cabinet must assemble... this evening and that I must put before them the whole strategic situation. At 5.30pm we met at 10 Downing St... The date of May for the crossing of the Rhine had a profound effect on the Cabinet. However, it has cleared the air well and the Cabinet now know what to expect, which is a good thing to counter the over-optimistic attitude of the newspapers."*

On 16 December, Germany launched a surprise offensive against American forces in the Ardennes. It took the Allied command in France some time to recognise the scale and seriousness of this offensive which may explain why Brookie first referred to it on 18 December. Note his reference to the lack of reserves [see 28 November], his relatively relaxed reaction to this offensive and his quick appreciation that it might ultimately work to the Allies' advantage which, in the event, is what happened. The phrase – 'a good officer' – was presumably taken from an intercepted German document:

"*Germans are delivering strong counter offensive against Americans who have no immediate reserves to stem the attack with. They ought ultimately to hold it all right and to have an opportunity of delivering serious counter blow which might well finish off Germans. But I am not certain whether they have the skill required, I doubt it. It is a worrying situation, if I felt that the American... Commanders and Staff were more efficient than they are, there is no doubt that this might turn out to be a heaven-sent opportunity. However, if mishandled it may well put the defeat of Germany back for another 6 months. I feel that Rundstedt [German field marshal] in launching this counter offensive feels that as 'a good officer' he is doing the right thing to put off defeat by means of a counter offensive destined to upset the Allied plans. I feel, however, that he must realize the great risks he is taking of achieving exactly the reverse results if the Americans can take advantage of the risks he takes. Perhaps as 'a good German' he considers that there may well be a definite advantage in bringing this* war to an early conclusion and consequently accepts all risks, great as they are, willingly?"

In his Notes, "Rundstedt had proved how faulty Ike's dispositions and organizations were. Spread out over a large front with no adequate reserves and no land force Commander to immediately take charge, we shall see that in his attempts to stop the Germans [Ike] was compelled to withdraw troops from Strasbourg and in doing so to almost create a crisis in the de Gaulle Government. It was a bold stroke on the part of the Germans and had it not been for Monty's prompt action might well have scored a definite success. As it was, Eisenhower was temporarily thrown off his balance. On the other hand, there can be no doubt that after having been keyed up for this offensive by Rundstedt, a definite reaction affected the German morale as a result of its failure."

On 19 December:

"Very little more news of the war in France, Eisenhower seems quite confident and so do his staff that they can deal with this situation. I only hope that this confidence is not based on ignorance! Situation in Greece improving also but it seems pretty certain that we shall have to send additional reinforcements."

On 20 December:

"Received telegram from Monty which showed clearly that the situation in France was serious. American front penetrated, Germans advancing on Namur with little in front of them, north flank of First American Army in state of flux and disorganisation. Also suggesting that he should be given command of all forces north of the penetration. I sent copy to the PM who sent for me at 3.30pm in the Map Room. I found him very much the worse for wear having evidently consumed several glasses of brandy at lunch. It was not very easy to ensure that he was absorbing the seriousness of the situation. We had many references to Marlborough [Churchill's ancestor] and other irrelevant matters. However, I got him to telephone Ike to put the proposal to him that Monty should take over the whole of the Northern Wing whilst Bradley ran the South. Ike agreed and had apparently already issued orders to that effect."

On the next day:

"News of the war in France much better. Provided the two 'gateposts' [north and south of the German offensive] hold on either flank, there may be a chance of annihilating a great many of the sheep that have broken through. If only the Americans are up to it."

On 22 December:

"German offensive appears to be held in the north, but I am a little more doubtful about the south. Patton is reported to have put in a counter-attack. This could only have been a half-baked affair and I doubt it's doing much good. Alexander evidently worried about the Greek war and the instructions he is receiving from the Prime Minister! I predict he will be much more worried before he finishes with his present job!"

Brookie spent the following week on leave. During this period:

"Situation in France gradually improved and Rundstedt's offensive appears to be held, importance now rests in counter strokes to be delivered. Monty has had another interview with Ike. I do not like the account of it. It looks to me as if Monty, with his usual lack of tact, has been rubbing into Ike the results of not having listened to Monty's advice! Too much of 'I told you so' to assist in creating the required friendly relations between them. According to Monty, Ike agrees that the front should now be divided into two and that only one major offensive is possible. But I expect that whoever meets Ike next may swing him to any other point of view! He is a hopeless commander.

Meanwhile, Winston has done a spectacular rush to Greece [Churchill flew to Greece over Christmas] to try and disentangle the mess. He does not appear to have achieved much. The rest of the 46th Div is now off to Greece, this completes the 80,000 men I had *originally predicted! And what are we to get out of it all? As far as I can see, absolutely nothing! We shall eventually have to withdraw out of Greece, and she will then become as communistic as her close neighbours consider desirable. Meanwhile, the campaign in Italy stagnates."*

SEVENTEEN

CIGS: January–April 1945

Brookie returned to work on 1 January:

"*A new year started and let us hope the last one of the war with Germany! I have now done 3 years of this job and am very weary... Not much trouble in getting into my stride as I had had brown bags sent down daily with current news. PM has sent in a regular flow of minutes throughout the afternoon, all of futile nature... As a result, he causes a mass of unnecessary work and clogs the wheels of the machine.*"

2 January saw yet another fatality from a plane crash:

"*[COS] adjourned to meet PM in his Map Room... [He] propounded the wildest of strategy which was purely based on ensuring that British troops were retained in the limelight, if necessary at the expense of the Americans, and quite irrespective of any strategic commitments! Little news from France today but heard that Bertie Ramsay had been killed in a plane crash in Paris; his is a desperate loss.*"

On 3 January, Churchill and Brookie flew to Paris to meet Eisenhower and de Gaulle:

"*We found a very worried Ike as de Gaulle had taken exception to his proposed dispositions in Alsace and Lorraine [see 18 December Notes]: to withdraw front to the Vosges leaving only an outpost line. De Gaulle stated that such an abandonment of Strasbourg and of the Alsatians and Lorrainians would lead to an outcry throughout*

France which [would] bring his government crashing to the ground!... [he] painted a gloomy picture of the massacres that would ensue if the Germans returned to portions of Alsace or Lorraine. However, Ike had already decided to alter his dispositions so as to leave the divisions practically where they are... I remained on for a discussion with Eisenhower about his front. He seemed worried about the turn of affairs, but I avoided returning to any questions of command organization or strategy, as it is quite useless.

[PM] said that he was beginning to see that any operation from Italy towards Vienna had little prospects!... He then went on about Alex saying that he could not leave him in Italy once this front had become a subsidiary one with only small forces there. He suggested that as Tedder was wanted back by the Air Ministry, we might replace him with Alex. This... might assist in keeping Ike on the rails [see 28 November 1944]."

On 4 January:

"On the whole, the counter-attacks [against the German offensive] appear to be making some progress towards narrowing the corridor at Bastogne. Unfortunately the air unable to function owing to this foul weather... Winston put the move of Alex to replace Tedder forward to Ike who said he would welcome him."

On the next day:

"Monty... seemed quite pleased with his attack which had started yesterday... [and] fairly confident that between him and Bradley they could deal with the Western end of the German salient but said that the base of the salient would present a more difficult problem. I told him about... the possible scheme of Alex replacing Tedder. He said that he was all for such a plan which might go some way towards putting matters straight."

Three days later, Brookie was back in London:

"Monty's offensive seems to be progressing very favourably, but I

am not so certain that matters are all right in Alsace and Lorraine. Alexander is also worrying me by committing more and more troops in Greece without much hope of getting them out!

Had to go round to PM at 10.30pm. He wanted first of all to gloat over the reply from Stalin promising an offensive middle of Jan. which he had received to the wire he had sent asking for information and promising he would only divulge reply to Eisenhower and myself. By the way he had already told Anthony Eden and was contemplating telling the President!!! He was already in bed when I arrived, sipping coffee, drinking brandy and smoking his cigar… We then discussed all the evils of Monty's press interview [Montgomery created the impression in this interview that he and the British Army had come to the rescue of the American forces in the Ardennes]… at 1.30am, we all withdrew, what had we accomplished beyond getting sleepy?! I know not."

On 9 January:

"COS at which I pointed out the necessity to draft a new directive to Alex telling him to finish off Greek enterprise at earliest possible moment, rest troops in Italy, prepare offensive, drive Kesselring back to Adige [river] and provide troops for France."

12 January was:

"A very nice quiet day for a change which gave me an opportunity to write a long letter to Alexander. He has now become completely lost in this damned Greek business and has forgotten the whole war on the strength of it. He relies on Macmillan as his confidential advisor on all matters including military ones and, as a result, loses all military perspective. The more I see of him the more I marvel at the smallness of the man. I do not believe that he has a single idea in his head of his own!"

In his Notes, "[Alex] held some of the highest qualities of a Commander: unbounded courage, never ruffled or upset, great charm and a composure that inspired confidence in those around him... One could not help being fond of Alex and of enjoying being with him. I think however, that it was just on account of all these outward qualities that on knowing him one realized the deficiency of brains and character. I have often described him as a beautiful Chippendale mirror, with the most attractive and pleasant frames but when you look into the mirror you always find the reflection of some other person who temporarily dominates him, be it a Monty, an Oliver Leese or a Macmillan. I think that many of my criticisms of him are probably too hard, but on the one side I had so much affection and admiration for him that I was always angry that the other side of him did not live up to this charming exterior. There is no doubt that he may well be proud of what he achieved in the war."

On 15 January, Brookie was scathing:

"Cabinet at 5.30. Great deal of the time spent in listening to Herbert Morrison lamenting about the rockets. 'London had already suffered too much and could not be expected to suffer much more! Something must be done to lighten this burden! More energy must be displayed! It was all very well stating that the Army and the Battle required the support of our Air Force, London required such support and should not be denied it!' In fact, never mind if we have to put off defeating Germany but let us at any rate defeat the few rockets that land in London! If there are many like him in England, we deserve to lose the war!"

Sir Alexander Cadogan, the armchair general in the Foreign Office, also attended this cabinet meeting. He was equally scathing but for a different reason, "PM not there at first so Morrison and others make a stink about V2's... PM came in about 6 and when we reverted to the subject, the protagonists had lost their fire!"[1]

On the next day:

"Good news coming in from Russia, it looks as if they had started their winter offensive in earnest. I hope so as it should make all the difference towards speeding up the end of the war."

On 17 January:

> "We had a specially long COS as we had Boy Browning back from Kandy, having been sent by Dickie to plead his case for more transport aircraft for the Burma operations. There is no doubt that the operations there have taken quite a different turn and there is now just a possibility of actually taking Rangoon from the north! This is due to the Japanese forces beginning to crumple up and to be demoralized. One of our difficulties arises through the fact that the transport aircraft belong to the Americans and that the reconquest of lower Burma does not interest them at all. All they want is north Burma and the air route and pipeline and Ledo road into China. They have now practically got all of these".

18 January saw Brookie in a philosophical mood:

> "A long meeting with COS preparing our directive for Alex in the Mediterranean and trying to clamp down his misplaced ardour in Greece! It is hard to tell at present who is Supreme Commander in the Mediterranean! Is it Macmillan or is it Alex? Surely it is Macmillan?... His new charger [Macmillan] may carry him over the political fences (perhaps) but will certainly crash him over the military ones!
>
> My God, how difficult war is to run owing to the personalities one has to handle, and how terribly dull it would be if they were all soulless cog wheels without any personal idiosyncrasies! But to handle them you must be young and full of vigour and enthusiasm, whereas every day I feel older, more tired, less inclined to face difficulties, less capable to face problems! What did Kipling say? 'If you can make your nerves and sinews serve you long after they are gone' or something of that kind... Youth seems difficult enough to cope with when one is young, middle age is just one series of problems, but are not those of old age and decline the hardest to face bravely and, most important of all, with a balanced mind? Is not the inferiority complex of old age more difficult to size up and appreciate than that of youth?"

On the following day:

> "As I returned home, found call from PM wanting to see me!! So off I started again. I found it was in connection with Greece and the fears he had that we should 'frame up' with the American Chiefs of Staff against him in an effort to pull out of Greece prematurely. I assured him that although strongly opposed to our original venture into Greece, now that we were committed, I fully realized the difficulty and impossibility of extracting forces out of Greece until such time as the Greek forces had been organized and trained to take on the job. It was a commitment which we had incurred against my military advice, no doubt based on excellent political reasons. But now that we were committed, I fully realized all implications."

Earlier, 10 September 1944, Brookie had noted Churchill's failure to give 'recognition' to 'those who help him' and on 2 December 1944 Churchill had been 'offended that Monty and Ike had had some limelight turned on them which he had not shared'. On 20 January, he returned to the same subjects:

> "It is a strange thing what a vast part the COS takes in the running of the war and how little it is known or its functions appreciated. The average man on the street has never heard of it. Any limelight for it could not fail to slightly diminish the PM's halo! This may perhaps account for the fact that he has never yet given it the slightest word of credit in public.
>
> Arrived home for late lunch and spent afternoon gumming in book plates in my bird books. Wonderful news from Russia continues to come in... However, I feel that this offensive may still fall short of final victory and necessitate another double offensive, East and West, in the Spring."

On 22 January:

> "Eisenhower's appreciation... leaves us again with a most confused picture, still hankering after the Frankfurt line of advance [as well as an advance in the north], and in the end backing both and being

insufficiently strong for either. At 5.30pm War Cabinet, drawn out by the usual endless statements by Winston. My God! How I loathe these Cabinet meetings! The waste of time is appalling."

Sir Alexander Cadogan's description of this cabinet meeting was in similar vein, "Cabinet as discursive and useless as usual".[2]

Exasperated by Eisenhower, the British chiefs of staff now decided that the Combined Chiefs of Staff [CCS] should issue a new directive to him. To this end, they prepared their own draft specifying that Allied resources should be concentrated on one single thrust in the north and that a land forces commander, responsible to Eisenhower, should be appointed.

On 23 January:

"I don't feel that I can stand another day working with Winston, it is quite hopeless… We met him this morning to try and get from him some decisions prior to our meeting with the American Chiefs of Staff [in Malta, in advance of the Yalta conference]. We wanted… approval to our proposed Directives to the Supreme Commanders. The first was one to Alexander, laying down that forces should be withdrawn from Greece as soon as political situation admitted and that some 6 divisions should be transferred from Italy to France. I had obtained full agreement from him before to these moves, now he began to hover… He did not know what he wanted but would not agree to anything. Then Eisenhower's directive urging that only one offensive should be carried out, and that in the north, a much more debatable point, he took little interest in it and it was the only point he expressed any sort of agreement with… Finally the conversion of the Long Range Penetration Groups to an Airborne Division for operations in Burma, a flat refusal to give decision… and a statement that he would send a decision in writing!! A matter of complete detail which he ought to have nothing to do with at all."

On 25 January:

"We have been unable to get agreement with PM over moves of

divisions from Italy to France… the whole matter is mixed up with the reduction of Alexander's command and the difficulty of finding another appointment for Alexander. In fact, strategy is now being warped by personalities… [Churchill] has no alternative strategy for Italy and agrees that it must now become a secondary front and yet he cannot drive himself to taking a decision. Monty… is again very depressed with the American strategy and Eisenhower's inability to retain a definite policy without waffling about."

On the following day:

"Monty came to lunch and I had a good talk with him. The old trouble keeps turning round and round in his head. Lack of organization of command on the part of the Americans and their failure to concentrate their efforts on the vital point."

30 January saw the start of the Anglo-American conference in Malta:

"Met the Americans at 2.30. We discussed the Western Front and Ike's Appreciation. Started with Bedell Smith [Eisenhower's chief of staff]… giving a description of Ike's plans. This description was very much in line with what we have always asked for but not in line with what Ike had put down as his plan. This resulted in considerable discussion. Bedell Smith had to agree that Ike's paper did not entirely agree with what he had been propounding. As a result, I said that we would probably be prepared to approve Bedell's statement as taken down in the minutes of the meeting but that we could not approve the appreciation by Eisenhower.

[Churchill] said that he was now entirely with us [on the issue of withdrawing divisions from Italy]".

On 31 January:

"We started the day with our COS meeting where we had some difficult points to consider. There was the question of the Western Front strategy, of Eisenhower's awful appreciation which points to no decisive action. Then there was Bedell Smith's interpretation which

was very close to our own views... We decided to adopt Bedell's statement and ignore Ike's appreciation.

However, when we met [the Americans] at 2.30pm the situation was more confused than ever as Bedell Smith had sent another wire to Ike which was also impossible and Ike had wired back!! So we were again stuck. However, we made good progress with the directive for Alexander withdrawing divisions from Italy for France and also in getting the South East Asia directive approved, contemplating clearing of Burma and then proceeding with Malaya.

After the meeting, I had a long and useful interview with Alex... told him that some of us had doubts as to whether Macmillan or Alexander was Supreme Commander of Mediterranean! This had, I think, the required effect. But, my God, how I loathe being unpleasant in this way.

[I] was just off to bed when Bedell Smith came in and we had at least an hour's talk trying to find some settlement to the difference that lies between us."

On 1 February:

"*CCS meeting at 2.30. There we had more difficulties about the Western Front. Marshall wished to go into 'closed session', he was opposed to cramping Eisenhower's style by issuing any directive to him! He wanted us to approve his quite unacceptable appreciation and plan. I refused to do this but said I would be prepared to 'take note' of it. Which we finally settled to do. However, this allowed Marshall to express his full dislike and antipathy to Montgomery!"*

In his Notes, "I did not approve of Ike's appreciation and plans yet, through force of circumstances, I had to accept them. The 'force of circumstances' was that we were dealing with a force that was predominantly American and it was therefore natural that they should wish to have the major share in its handling. In addition, there was the fact that Marshall clearly understood nothing of strategy... Being unable to judge for himself, he trusted and backed Ike and felt it his duty to guard him from interference.

My talk with Bedell Smith on the previous evening had at any rate shown to me that Bedell was quite able to appreciate the dangers of Ike's strategy and I felt… he would use his influence to guide him [in the event, Eisenhower did allocate priority to an attack in the north by Montgomery's 21st Army Group]… one further consideration weighed with me, namely… after the failure of Rundstedt's offensive, German morale had deteriorated and that we could from now on take greater liberties with him. Under these new circumstances, an advance on a wider front might present some advantages."

2 February saw another fatality from a plane crash. This one was to affect Brookie deeply:

"This morning when I went to my office, Brian Boyle met me with the ghastly news that the plane Barney [Barney Charlesworth, Brookie's long-standing aide-de-camp, friend and flatmate] was travelling in had crashed last night in the sea near Pantelleria! Of the 20 passengers, only 7 had been saved… it was not till just on 8pm that I obtained the news that Barney was amongst those killed. It is a frightful blow as Barney had grown to be a most intimate companion, I always knew I could discuss anybody or anything with him without any fear of his ever repeating anything. He was always cheerful and in good humour no matter how unpleasant situations were. He had grown to know me well and was of the greatest help, I shall miss him most awfully and feel so very, very sorry for Diana. On top of that, the day has been a very busy one and I have found it extremely difficult to concentrate my thoughts and not let them wander off to Barney.

At 5.30pm… an interim Plenary Meeting. Winston, as usual, had not read the paper although he had had it since this morning! He made most foolish remarks about it which proved he had not read it… However, the paper was passed".

In his Notes, "The loss of Barney Charlesworth was one of the worst blows I had during the war. He had come to me in France, we had been through Dunkirk together and since then had lived in the same flat".

On 3 February, the British and American delegations arrived in Yalta:

"*I forgot to write down yesterday that after the Plenary Meeting Winston asked me to stop on to discuss with him and the President and Marshall the proposal for Alexander and Tedder to change round. The President and Marshall considered that politically such a move might have repercussions in America if carried out just now. It might be considered that Alex was being put to support Ike after his Ardennes failure! However, they were quite prepared to accept the change in about 6 weeks' time after future offensive operations have been started by Ike and the Ardennes operation more forgotten.*"

On 4 February:

"*At 5pm we met at the American Headquarters. They are living in the old Yalta Tsar's Palace. Marshall is in the Tsarina's bedroom and King in her boudoir, with the special staircase for Rasputin to visit her! We had a round table conference... Meeting started with the usual compliments followed by an opening statement by Stalin calling in Antonov [Russian chief of operations] to give a statement of the war. He gave an excellent and very clear talk*".

On 5 February:

"*Last night Stalin showed great reluctance to propose the King's health stating that he was a republican, Americans failed to take our part in this connection! Meanwhile, Macmillan is donning the coat of Supreme Commander of the Mediterranean and submitting wild schemes for employing further forces in Greece, quite forgetting that we are fighting Germany!!! My God! how tired I am of it all!*"

On 7 February, Brookie visited the Crimean War battlefields:

"*There was... on our immediate left the site of the Charge of the Heavy Cav Brigade and, on our right, the site of the memorable Charge of the Light Cav Brigade!!... I had luckily brought with me diagrammatic sketches of the battles [and]... with the help of these, it was easy to reconstruct both the two memorable cavalry charges...*

I was thrilled! It has been an intensely interesting day but one when the thought of dear old Barney still remained as a black cloud in the background. He would so much have loved to have been with us. I only hope that he may have been there in spirit. This conference has been a nightmare with his loss hanging over me the whole time. I do so funk the thought of returning to the flat [in London] and realizing more than ever that he is gone!"

On 8 February, Stalin hosted a banquet:

"*The standard of the speeches was remarkably low and most consisted of insincere, slimy sort of slush! I became more and more bored and more and more sleepy, and on and on it dragged.*"

In his Notes, "Amongst the various toasts that Stalin proposed was one which he dedicated to 'those to whom we all look to in war for our security, those on whom our very security depends, the heroes of all the women and the centre of all things as long as hostilities continue only to be forgotten and lapse into oblivion as soon as hostilities cease – our soldiers.'"

9 February saw another unflattering reference to Marshall [see 12 September 1944]:

"*[Dinner] at 9pm with Winston who had invited Marshall and Alexander also to dine. It was a dull dinner party, Marshall's never-ending accounts about details connected with his life and work... I was left alone with Alex [and] took advantage of this occasion to give him more advice on how to carry on as a Supreme Commander... He took it very well, but it is not easy to give him advice as he is very 'naif' and unsuspecting of the ways of politicians!*"

On 10 February, Brookie flew to Malta, en route back to Britain:

"*I went straight to the cemetery where Barney had been buried and laid a wreath on his grave and also on the other three War Office officers who had been killed. My last words to Barney were haunting* me, as I left Northolt ahead of him I had said 'Well, we shall meet in Malta.'"

On 13 February:

"Rollie Charrington came to dinner and like the brick he is offered to take Barney's place as [aide-de-camp]. I should love to have him but wonder whether he would be happy at it. I shall have to think this over very, very carefully."

Over the next few days:

"We had a record COS for shortness and finished it in 30 minutes!... Finally home to a lonely dinner. This is a very trying week and the absence of dear old Barney just haunts me the whole time!"

"I never realized... what an awful void [Barney's absence] would leave in my life."

"I had poor Diana Charlesworth to lunch. It was a very heartbreaking lunch for both of us. She is wonderfully plucky outwardly, but it was only too clear that inwardly she was torn in two with grief. I wish I could have done more to help her."

On 18 February:

"Rollie Charrington came over and I fixed up with him to come and replace poor old Barney on the understanding that either of us can finish the agreement at any time."

Two days later:

"There are certainly a few small cracks that are beginning to appear in the German fighting machine, but no indications of a general cracking up. It is quite impossible to estimate how long it may last.

Visit from Kopanski [chief of staff to the Commander-in-Chief, Polish Armed Forces in the West]... He said the Poles wished to go on fighting with us but were not prepared to return to Poland until they knew that it was entirely free and not a vassal of Russia in any shape or form."

On 22 February:

"The Dutch Ambassador came to see me about 2 additional ships for relief of Dutch in occupied Holland [German-occupied Holland was suffering acute food shortages]. Heaven knows they deserve it, but the difficulty is to find spare ships.

Finally, a very trying hour with General Anders [commander, 2nd Polish Corps], who is back from Italy. He had been to see the PM yesterday but was still terribly distressed. According to him the root of the trouble lay in the fact that he could never trust the Russians after his experiences with them whilst Winston and Roosevelt were prepared to trust the Russians. After having been a prisoner and seeing how Russians could treat Poles, he considered that he was in a better position to judge what Russians were like than the President or PM. He said that he had never been more distressed since the war started. When in a Russian prison he was in the depth of gloom, but he did then always have hope. Now he could see no hope anywhere. Personally, his wife and children were in Poland and he could never see them again, that was bad enough. But what was infinitely worse was the fact that all the men under his orders relied on him to find a solution to this insoluble problem! They all said 'Oh! Anders will go to London and will put matters right for us' and he, Anders, saw no solution and this kept him awake at night. I felt most awfully sorry for him, he is a grand fellow and takes the whole matter terribly hard. He is to see Winston again next Wednesday and then he is to see me afterwards. I shudder at the thought of this next interview."

On the next day:

"We had one of our usual monthly examinations of the rocket threat… It is pretty clear that no air action has much effect on this form of enemy attack… There is only one way of dealing with them and that is by clearing the area from which they come by ground action and that, for the present, is not possible."

On 27 February:

"Morgan came to see me in the afternoon prior to departure for Italy to take over Chief of Staff to Alexander. I had to again ground him as to how he was to take charge of Alex and protect him against his lamentable lack of vision."

2 March saw Churchill and Brookie at Montgomery's HQ on the continent:

"After dinner, we attended the interview which [Montgomery] holds every evening with his liaison officers. It was most interesting and most impressive. After completing this interview, he dictates his daily wire to me based on his conception of the situation arrived at from the liaison officers' reports. The battle is going wonderfully well and there are signs from all sides of decay setting in on the German Army."

On 6 March, Brookie met with Eisenhower:

"There is no doubt that he is a most attractive personality and at the same time a very, very limited brain from a strategic point of view. This comes out the whole time in all conversations with him. His relations with Monty are quite insoluble, he only sees the worst side of Monty and cannot appreciate the better side. Things are running smoothly at present, but this cannot last and I foresee trouble ahead before long. For all that, to insert Alex is only likely to lead to immediate trouble for all I gather [see 3 February]! The war may not last long now and matters may run smoothly until the end. Therefore, I feel now that it is best to leave Alex where he is. I think that Winston is now of the same opinion.

[After returning to London] Cabinet at 5.30pm which lasted till 8.15pm and, as far as I could see, accomplished nothing! How ministers can afford to waste time in this way in times of war passes my understanding. What is more, Winston is by far the worst offender."

The following day saw a familiar whine from Herbert Morrison, the Home Secretary:

"Morrison attended the COS to discuss what could be done to save London from rockets and buzz bombs. He painted a lurid picture of the awful 5 years London had suffered and how wrong it was to expect her to go on suffering! He seemed to forget that theatres, cinemas, restaurants, night clubs, pubs, concerts, etc. have been in full swing for the last few years and very little affected by enemy action. We listened as sympathetically as we could and then explained to him our difficulties in trying to deal with this threat either by air or land action."

On 9 March:

"Our main problem at the COS was the Dutch PM's lament to Winston concerning the starvation of the Dutch population and urging a reconsideration of our strategy so as to admit of an early liberation of Holland! One more of the continual repercussions of political considerations on strategical requirements. And many of them we have already had to compete with!! However, it is pretty clear that our present plans for Monty's crossing of the Rhine cannot be changed. After the crossing of the Rhine, again from a military point of view, there is no doubt that we should work for the destruction of Germany and not let any clearing up of Holland delay our dispositions.

I had poor Diana Charlesworth to lunch and did what I could for her to assist her in disentangling her life. I am so sorry for her. She would like to go to Brussels and I have asked Adam to find out if there is any opening for her there."

On 10 March:

"Just as I was rushing to make an early start home, a telegram turned up from Alex with certain underground peace proposals. These suggested the surrendering of the whole of Kesselring's army in Italy. However, as Wolff [SS commander in Italy] was the main instigator and he is a rabid SS follower of Himmler, it does not seem very plausible. We are following it up for the present and sending representatives to Switzerland to the selected spot."

12.3.45!

"*It is sad that this date will not return for another 100 years. It looks so nice.*

A rushed morning with COS and Cabinet, the latter luckily run by Attlee which shortened matters considerably. Long letter from Monty with all his plans for the attack across the Rhine on the 24th of this month. Also an invitation to the PM to come for it and stop with him. This is as a result of the letter I had written to him telling him the PM would get into another of his rages if he felt that Monty was again trying to... stop him from coming out!"

On 13 March, Brookie's 'fears' about Leese would prove well-founded:

"*Jack Swayne [chief of staff to Auchinleck, Commander-in-Chief, India] came to see me and we had a long talk together about India. It is very satisfactory to hear that relations between the Auk and Dickie [Mountbatten] are good. But he confirms my fears that we may possibly have trouble later on between Oliver Leese and Dickie! If we do, it will be Oliver's fault.*"

On 14 March:

"*We again discussed the underground movements towards capitulation of German forces in Italy. Somehow the whole business looks pretty fishy and not very promising.*"

The following day saw another dry comment:

"*Our COS was again concerned with trying to extricate divisions out of Greece. I am afraid that Alexander, being now entirely in Macmillan's clutches, has forgotten the main object of this war and no longer remembers that there are such people as the Germans!*"

Six days later:

"*Adam came to lunch and told me about the arrangements that he had made for Diana Charlesworth to go to Rheims to start a hotel for inter-Allied soldiers.*"

On 22 March:

> "Tomorrow, I start off with PM on this visit to France for him to see operation connected with the Rhine crossing. I am not happy about this trip, he will be difficult to manage and has no business to be going on this trip. All he will do is to endanger his life unnecessarily... get in everybody's way and be a damned nuisance to everybody. However, nothing on earth will stop him!"

The next day saw Churchill and Brookie at Montgomery's HQ:

> "We found Monty there, very proud to be able to pitch his camp in Germany at last... Monty described plan of attack for the crossing of the Rhine which starts tonight... Crossings take place throughout the night and the guns have already started and can be heard indistinctly in the distance. After dinner Monty went off to bed early and Winston took me off... We went back over some of our early struggles, back to Cairo when we had started Monty and Alex off. How he had had to trust my selection at that time. The part that the hand of God had taken in removing Gott at that critical moment. He was in one of his very nicest moods and showed appreciation for what I had done for him in a way in which he had never before.
>
> I am now off to bed. It is hard to realize that within some 15 miles hundreds of men are engaged in death struggles along the banks of the Rhine, whilst hundreds more are keying themselves up to stand up to one of the greatest trials of their life! With that thought in one's mind, it is not easy to lie down to try and sleep peacefully!"

On 24 March:

> "Started off in Monty's plane for a fly round to look at the front. We flew very low over the Meuse from Venlo to Gennep, looking at the wonderful defences the Germans had built.
>
> Later: attended Monty's conference with his liaison officers. From their reports, there is no doubt that the operations have been an outstanding success... One of the outstanding successes of the day has been the employment of the airborne divisions in close proximity, and

closely connected, to the attack... I am quite certain that the end of the Germans is very near indeed and I would not be surprised to see them pack up at any moment. In a few days, I feel that coordinated defence north of the Rhine will cease and that we shall be in a position to let Monty's 8th Armoured Division operate boldly through North Germany maintained by air supply."

On the following day, Churchill and Brookie were at the Rhine:
"We were met by Eisenhower, Bradley and Simpson [commander, US 9th Army]. [Eisenhower] wanted to know whether I agreed with his present plans of pushing in the south for Frankfurt and Kassel. I told him that with the Germans crumbling as they are the whole situation is now altered from the time of our previous discussions. Evidently, the Boche is cracking and what we want now is to push him relentlessly wherever we can until he crumples. In his present condition, we certainly have the necessary strength for a double envelopment strategy which I did not consider as applicable when he was still in a position to resist seriously.

We... motored to the main road bridge over the Rhine into Wesel. The bridge had been broken in several places but partly boarded over so that one could scramble about on it. Winston at once started scrambling along for some 40 yards. We found however that Wesel was still occupied and that considerable sniping was going on inside the town... We decided that it was time to remove the PM who was thrilled with the situation and very reluctant to leave! However, he came away more obediently than I had expected.

The news of Patton's advance in the south is a clear indication that the Germans are cracking fast."

He elaborated in his Notes, "[In] Eisenhower's *Crusade in Europe* [Eisenhower's war memoirs, published in 1948], he refers to a conversation which took place between us on the day this diary entry was written. I feel certain that he did not write down at once the statement which he attributes to me and I can only assume... he did not remember clearly what I had said. According to him when we stood together on the bank of the Rhine on March 25th, I said to him: 'Thank God, Ike, you stuck by your plan. You were completely right and I am sorry if my fear of dispersed efforts added to your burdens. The German is now licked. It is merely a question of when he chooses to quit. Thank God you stuck by your guns.' I think that when this statement is considered in connection with what I wrote in my diary that evening, it will be clear that I was misquoted. To the best of my memory, I congratulated him heartily on his success and said that as matters had turned out his policy was now the correct one, that with the German in his defeated condition no dangers now existed in a dispersal of effort. I am quite certain that I never said to him 'You were completely right', as I am still convinced that he was 'completely wrong', as proved by the temporary defeat inflicted on him by Rundstedt's counter stroke which considerably [delayed] the defeat of Germany.

I failed to record a picture which is as vivid in my mind as it was on that day. It is the picture of the USA General Simpson, on whose front we were, coming up to Winston and saying 'Prime Minister, there are snipers in front of you, they are shelling both sides of the bridge, and now they have started shelling the road behind you. I cannot accept the responsibility of your being here and must ask you to come away.' The look on Winston's face was just like that of a small boy being called away from his sandcastles on the beach by his nurse! He put both his arms round one of the twisted girders of the bridge and looked over his shoulder at Simpson with pouting mouth and angry eyes! Thank heaven he came away quietly, it was a sad wrench for him, he was enjoying himself immensely!"

On 26 March:

> *"It was a strange feeling motoring along the east bank of the Rhine with [Neil Ritchie] and looking back to our retreat to Dunkirk together! I reminded him of it and how little we then dreamed that 5 years later we should be on the Rhine together with Germany beat! I find it almost impossible to believe that after these 6 years of endless, heartbreaking struggles that we are now at last on the threshold of the end!*

It has been a wonderful trip and one which gave me a feeling of realization that all the last few years' toil and agony were at least producing results beyond my wildest hopes."

On the same day, Churchill and Brookie returned to Britain. In his Notes, "It was a relief to get Winston home safely. I knew that he longed to get into the most exposed position possible. I honestly believe that he would really have liked to be killed on the front at this moment of success. He had often told me that the way to die is to pass out fighting when your blood is up and you feel nothing."

On 29 March:

"A very long COS meeting with a series of annoying telegrams. The worst of all was one from Eisenhower direct to Stalin trying to coordinate his offensive with the Russians. To start with, he has no business to address Stalin direct, his communications should be through the Combined Chiefs of Staff, secondly he produced a telegram which was unintelligible and, finally, what was implied in it appeared to be entirely adrift and a change in all that had been previously agreed on. At 5.15pm we were sent for by the PM to discuss Ike's telegram to Stalin… He was in a hopeless mood and kept us 2 hours to settle what we could have got through in 20 minutes! He drives me quite frantic and I can only just keep my temper nowadays. He meanders about, always grasping onto details and failing to see the leading points. Quite incapable to really grasp strategy and its implications… I feel that I just can't stick another moment with him and would give almost anything never to see him again! The last three years are beginning to tell and the strain of dealing with him is taking effect!"

On 1 April, note the 'nationalistic outlook of allies':

"We sat in conference with PM… discussed his wire to Ike, Ike's reply to him and Ike's official reply to the CCS. Now that Ike has explained his plans it is quite clear that there is no very great change except for the fact that he directs his main axis of advance on

Leipzig instead of on Berlin… Most of the changes are due to national aspirations and to ensure that the USA effort will not be lost under British command. It is all a pity and the straightforward strategy is being affected by the nationalistic outlook of allies. This is one of the handicaps of operating with allies. But, as Winston says, 'There is only one thing worse than fighting with allies and that is fighting without them!' After lunch we had to go on drafting a reply to the American Chiefs' rather rude message."

3 April saw Brookie employing his analytical powers and mental agility to devastating effect. Tedder never stood a chance:

"Tedder attended COS and tried to explain that Ike was forced to take immediate action [i.e. communicate direct] with Stalin as Monty had issued a directive Ike did not agree with! I said that I was astonished that Ike found it necessary to call in Stalin in order to control Monty! Furthermore, I could not accept this excuse as the boundaries of [Montgomery's] 21st Army Group and [US] 9th Army still remained the same in Ike's order as in Monty's, the only difference being the transfer of the 9th Army from Monty to Bradley! Surely Stalin's help need not be called in for such a transfer!!"

On 6 April:

"During our COS we had a visit by General Hurley, the USA Ambassador in China. He is an outstanding personality, good-looking, tall, clear-cut features, well dressed and a very merry twinkle in his eye… Hurley was in tremendous form towards the end of lunch and most amusing. A born 'raconteur' with a great sense of humour and a good memory. After lunch, to my great joy, I collected a copy of Phillips's A Natural History of the Ducks. A book I had been looking for for a long time."

On the following day:

"I had made all plans to escape early and was just starting off when a message came through from the PM that we were to report

on Dickie Mountbatten's last wire! There was absolutely no hurry and absolutely no necessity for a Saturday meeting of the COS. He was told so but insisted that we should meet, thereby again showing his complete lack of consideration for others... On these occasions my feelings for him are hard to describe!"

Three days later:

"Another long and very boring agenda for the COS. Amongst other items we appointed Monty as the 'Gauleiter' for the British occupied zone [the Allies had agreed to break Germany up into four zones of occupation]. May heaven help him with that job!!... The war has started another of its rather more sticky periods... [and] looks like dragging on unless Stalin kicks off again which I have every reason to believe he will do before long!"

On 12 April:

"We had to consider this morning at the COS one of Winston's worst minutes I have ever seen. I can only believe that he must have been quite tight when he dictated it. It brought out all his worst qualities and was based on a complete misappreciation of existing organization. It went back to Ike's direct approach to Stalin, he abused Tedder for having allowed him to do so without referring to us [and] stated that Tedder failed entirely to realize that he was intended to act as the main link between Ike and us. Again forgetting that he himself had entirely undermined Tedder's position by continually communicating direct with Ike and cutting Tedder out!... But then matters such as 'chain of command' and 'loyalty to one's superiors' are unknown factors to him!! My God! how little the world at large knows what his failings and defects are! And thank heaven they don't or we should not be where we are now!

PJ [Grigg, Secretary of State for War]... asked me to stop on as CIGS with him if the Conservative Gov was returned, as Winston had asked him to come back as S of S. I told him I was quite ready to do if he wanted me but that I did not feel that I should remain after the end of the year... He was very kind in things he said as regards my influence with Winston and as to my being one of the few he had seen whom Winston would listen to. However, you were there to hear what he said so I need not write about it!"

On 20 April, Brookie's forecast regarding the effect of Hitler's suicide would prove correct:

"The Russians are now moving properly and it should not be long before we meet up with them on the Berlin-Dresden front. I feel that we shall still have several more weeks in front of us before we finish off the war. Several centres of resistance in Austria, Czechoslovakia, Denmark, Holland and Norway... may give us considerable trouble. On the other hand, Hitler's suicide might well bring the end on rapidly. Anyhow I am off on leave tomorrow morning early for a week on the Dee and I pray and hope that I may not be recalled!"

On 30 April:

"The usual early start and back to work again refreshed by a week away but with a great disinclination to start work again! A long COS and an unpleasant Cabinet with Winston in a bad mood. In spite of the fact that Alex had made the greatest advance he had yet brought off, he was abused for not having taken Trieste!!"

On the following day:

"The crumbling of Germany is fast. Forces in Italy may surrender to Alex tomorrow. At same time Bernadotte [Folke Bernadotte, vice-president of the Swedish Red Cross] is carrying on negotiations with Himmler. The end must come soon."

EIGHTEEN

CIGS: May 1945–June 1946

On 2 May:

"Last night, on the midnight news, Hitler was reported as dead. After longing for this news for the last 6 years and wondering whether I should ever be privileged to hear it, when I finally listened to it, I remained completely unmoved. Why? I do not know. I fully realized that it was the real full stop to the many and long chapters of this war but I think that I have become so war weary with the continual strain of the war that my brain is numbed and incapable of feeling intensely.

The surrender of the German Army in Italy to Alex… did not take place owing to Kesselring stepping in and sacking local commanders. However, Kesselring is prepared to carry on but asks for 48 hours more. Meanwhile, Monty reaches the Baltic and it is possible that Boche will surrender Northern forces to him. I doubt whether Germany will last over the weekend! Meanwhile in Burma the landings south of Rangoon are going well."

On the next day:

"Germany crumbles. The Italian front has surrendered, Monty takes 100,000 prisoners, Hamburg gives in and negotiations with Monty look like the rest of Northern Germany and Denmark giving in!"

4 May was:

> "A memorable day in so far as it will probably be one of the last ones of the second war with Germany! Monty met Keitel [German field marshal] this morning who surrendered unconditionally Holland, all North Germany, Schleswig Holstein, Denmark, Friesian Islands and Heligoland! Keitel then went on to Ike's HQ to discuss surrender of Norway.
>
> We were sent for for a COS meeting with PM in Cabinet room… he was evidently seriously affected by the fact that the war was to all intents and purposes over as far as Germany was concerned. He thanked us all very nicely and with tears in his eyes for all we had done in the war and all the endless work we had put in 'from El Alamein to where we are now'. He then shook hands with all of us."

On the following day:

> "Another flood of telegrams necessitated our having a Saturday COS meeting. The telegrams were mainly concerned with Alexander's difficulties with Tito about Trieste. Also masses about the negotiations for surrender… Difficulty of carrying the Russians along with us, combined with great reluctance on the part of the Germans to surrender to the Russians of whom they are terrified. Monty faced with difficult problem of surrender of Denmark occupational troops, over 1 million German soldiers, 400,000 Russian prisoners, 2 million excess German population in Schleswig Holstein."

On 7 May:

> "Although all documents had been signed and hostilities were to cease from today, the Russians made difficulties saying that the negotiations should be signed in Berlin and repudiating those documents which their representatives had accepted.
>
> PM had invited Chiefs of Staff with Pug Ismay and Hollis to lunch at 10 Downing St to celebrate the culmination of our efforts… Winston discussed the pros and cons of elections in June [general elections had been suspended during the War]. We stressed the 'cons'

from the military point of view, stating that it could lead only to dispersal of effort which would be better concentrated onto the war.

So this is at last the end of the war!! It is hard to realize. I can't feel thrilled, my main sensation is one of infinite weariness! A sort of brain lethargy which refuses to register highlights and remains on an even, dull, flat tone. And yet at the back of it all there is a feeling of only partially digested wonderful restlessness, a realization of something I have been striving endlessly for with hardly any hope of realization for month after month. The most acute feeling is one of deep depression such as I have experienced at the end of the strain of each Combined Chiefs of Staff Conference."

8 May was Victory in Europe Day, VE Day:

"Left [War Office] for Buckingham Palace… [for] a meeting of War Cabinet and Chiefs of Staff with the King. I… battled my way down the Mall and came into an impenetrable crowd outside the Palace… PM was very late as he insisted on coming in an open car! The King made very nice little speech of congratulation, finishing up with a reference to the Chiefs of Staff as that organization which probably only those present in the room had any idea what their real part had been in securing the success of this war.

Then back to the WO to finish off work. I had to go and see PJ [Grigg, Secretary of State for War] and on coming out Lady Grigg collared me and brought me into the passage. She said, 'I watched you getting into your car this morning from the window with a crowd looking at you, and none of them realizing that beside them was the man who had probably done most to win the war against Germany!' She said it was all wrong that they should not realize it, 'I do, and lots of people do, tell Lady Brookie from me.' It was very nice of her, she said it so nicely and I wish you had been able to hear her.

There is no doubt that the public has never understood what the Chiefs of Staff have been doing in the running of this war. On the whole, the PM has never enlightened them much and has never once in all his speeches referred to the Chiefs of Staff or what they have been doing in the direction of the war on the highest plane. It may be inevitable, but I do feel that it is time that this country was educated as to how wars are run and how strategy is controlled. The whole world has now become one large theatre of war and the Chiefs of Staff represent the Supreme Commanders, running the war in all its many theatres, regulating the allocation of forces, shipping, munitions, relating plans to resources available, approving or rejecting plans, issuing directives to the various theatres. And, most difficult of all, handling the political aspect of this military action and coordinating with our American allies.

It is all far less spectacular than the winning of battles by commanders in the field and yet if the COS make any errors the commanders in the field will never be in a position to win battles. Their actions are not in the limelight, indeed most of the time they are covered by secrecy. We therefore find the COS... working incessantly, shouldering vast responsibilities, incurring great risks without the country ever realizing we were at work. It has been a wonderful experience, of never-ending interest. At times the work and the difficulties to be faced have been almost beyond powers of endurance. The difficulties with Winston have been of almost unbearable proportions, at times I have felt that I could not possibly face a single other day. And yet I would not have missed the last 3 years of struggle and endeavour for anything on earth.

I remember the night Winston offered me the job of CIGS... I was so overcome that my natural instinct was to... pray to God for his assistance in my new task. I have often looked back during the last 3½ years to that prayer and thanked God for the way he had listened to me and provided me with the help I had asked for and without which I should have floundered in the first year. I am not a highly religious individual according to many people's outlook. I am however convinced that there is a God all powerful looking after the destiny of this world. I had little doubt about this before the war started but this war has convinced me more than ever of this truth... The suffering and agony of war in my mind must exist to gradually educate us to the fundamental law of 'loving our neighbour as ourselves'. When that lesson has been learned, then war will cease to exist. We are however many centuries from such a state of affairs. Many more wars and much suffering is required before we finally learn our lesson."

9 May was:

"VE2 Day, namely the second day of victory in Europe, a national holiday. The majority of Englishmen apparently enjoy spending such a holiday by crowding together into the smallest possible place. Personally, the less I see of the human species, the more content I am! I went home, found you busy putting up wonderful flagstaffs and decorations and, incidentally, cutting your hand badly! We had a happy and peaceful afternoon together looking after goats and chickens."

On the following day:

"Returned to work early and on the whole had a fairly easy day… Only trouble connected with Syria and Lebanon which are brewing up for trouble. De Gaulle evidently determined to do all he can to lay his clutches again on this part of the world. The time has now come when we must decide whether friendship of France in Western Europe is of more importance than friendship of the Pan Arabic League in the Middle East. A difficult problem to decide but one which requires a definite solution either one way or the other. I fear that we shall hover between the two."

On Saturday, 12 May, *"Spent the morning in complete peace mending an old rabbit hutch! After lunch went to Turgis Green where I met Mussens [who] had nests of hawfinch, not ready to photograph, and nightingale, bullfinch… I spent 1½ hours photographing the bullfinches".* On 13 May:

"Winston had a War Cabinet to discuss the Yugoslav situation. He had received a telegram from Truman [Harry Truman, the new American president: Roosevelt died in April], full of bellicose views and ready to be rough with Tito. Winston delighted, he gives me the feeling of already longing for another war! Even if it entailed fighting Russia!"

Two days later:

> "*Tito still refuses to withdraw out of Istria. Truman, after adopting a strong attitude... last week, now states that he could not dream of asking America to start hostilities unless the Yugoslavs attacked us first. Meanwhile, de Gaulle insists on stirring up trouble in Syria by sending French reinforcements there. He also infuriates the Italians by refusing to withdraw his troops from North West Italy. In fact, the vultures of Europe are now crowding round and quarrelling over bits of the Austro-German-Italian carcass which they are endeavouring to tear off. Meanwhile, they gather round a table at San Francisco to discuss how to establish universal peace [the United Nations Conference on International Organization attended by 50 Allied nations]!*"

On 16 May, Brookie was enjoying more Churchillian one-liners:

> "*Went for a meeting with the PM and Eisenhower... Winston in one of his meandering moods... A series of good catch words such as, 'When the eagles are silent, the parrots begin to jabber' – Tito and de Gaulle being the latter! Or again, 'Let the Germans find all the mines they have buried and dig them up. Why should they not? Pigs are used to find olives (!!!)'. We had to remind him that truffles were what pigs hunted for. We were then told that the children in Russia were taught a creed:*
>
> *I love Lenin.*
> *Lenin was poor and therefore I love poverty.*
> *Lenin went hungry therefore I can go hungry.*
> *Lenin was often cold therefore I shall not ask for warmth.*
> *'Christianity with a tomahawk' said Winston.*"

Earlier, 19 August 1944 and 13 March, Brookie had expressed reservations about Oliver Leese. In May 1945, a furore broke out within the ranks of the British Fourteenth Army in Burma, commanded by Lieutenant General Slim: it arose after Leese, commander of Allied land forces in South East Asia, decided that Slim, who had been in Burma since 1942 and was very popular with his troops, would not command the Fourteenth

Army in the forthcoming invasion of Malaya. On 17 May:

"Interview with Auchinleck about appointment of Slim to Burma Command. Leese is going quite wild and doing mad things, prepared a fair rap on the knuckles for him!"

On 23 May:

"Winston insists on retaining that portion of the Russian zone [of occupation] which we have been able to occupy in our advance as a bargaining counter with the Russians. Considering that the only reason why we secured this ground was due to the fact that the Germans used their available forces to resist the Russians thus facilitating our advance, and also considering that we have already agreed with the Russians as to the Zones of Occupation in Germany, I consider that Winston is fundamentally wrong in using this as a bargaining counter! But this is a political matter and politics are as crooked as rams' horns!"

24 May saw Brookie examining the prospect of waging war against Britain's ally, Russia:

"A long COS meeting with the Joint Planners in. We were discussing future operations in the Pacific after the capture of Singapore. We want, if possible, to participate with all 3 services in the attacks against Japan. It is however not easy to make plans as the Americans seem unable to decide between a policy of invasion as opposed to one of encirclement. It also remains to be seen what attitude Winston may take. I have no idea what his reaction will be. For the present, he is absorbed in this mad election [a general election had been called for 5 July] and for the next few months he will be unable to devote much attention to war plans!

This evening I went carefully through the Planners' report on the possibility of taking on Russia should trouble arise in our future discussions with her. We were instructed to carry out this investigation. The idea is of course fantastic and the chances of success quite impossible. There is no doubt that from now onwards Russia is all powerful in Europe."

In his Notes, "A few weeks earlier, when examining the desirability of dismembering Germany after her defeat, the COS had then looked upon Russia as our future potential enemy. This paper had created a considerable stir in the Foreign Office who considered it very remiss of us to look upon our present ally as our probable future enemy. We might even have been asked to withdraw this paper had we not asked for an interview with Anthony Eden who approved our outlook. Now… Winston had come to us expressing his anxiety at seeing 'that Russian bear sprawled over Europe' and instructing us to examine from the military point of view the possibility of driving him back to Russia before the Americans and ourselves demobilized our forces… Here I was… a few days after VE Day, examining the results of the Planners' work on this problem. The result of this study made it clear that the best we could hope for was to drive the Russians back to about the same line the Germans had reached. And then what? Were we to remain mobilized indefinitely to hold them there?"

On 28 May, the Foreign Office came in for more criticism:

"*COS mainly concerned with the situation in the Levant which is getting daily worse. This in my mind is all due to the Foreign Office not taking a firm attitude with de Gaulle. Meanwhile, Paget [Commander-in-Chief, Middle East] is being left in a very difficult position. I was sent for by PM… Eden wishes the military to step in once the French and Syrians have started a proper row! Winston holds different view and considers we should stand aside, watch our own interests and let the French and Syrians cut each other's throats. Personally, I feel Winston is in this case right. If we step in now, we shall have to shoot up both sides to stop the fight and shall increase our unpopularity with both. There is only one spot to stop the trouble and that is in Paris, by putting it across de Gaulle in no measured terms.*"

30 May saw another dry comment:

"*Situation in Syria is deteriorating rapidly… Winston convened a Cabinet at 6.30pm. I missed this treat by being out fishing! Decided* to step in and stop the trouble but first of all to ensure American participation or, at any rate, approval of our actions."

On the following day:

"We again discussed the 'unthinkable war' against Russia at this morning's COS and became more convinced than ever that it is 'unthinkable'!... Meanwhile, Paget has been ordered to take action to stop any further bloodshed in Syria and Lebanon. Goodness knows where this may end if the Foreign Office does not unite with US State Department and set about de Gaulle in the way he deserves."

On 7 June:

"A long and difficult survey of personnel shipping... with [the] redeployment of USA, Canadian, South African and New Zealand forces together with the repatriation of prisoners and our movement of troops to the Far East, the claims of long overseas service men, leave and civil travel are very hard to fit in!! The whole matter becomes a bad headache!"

On 11 June:

"PJ Grigg's statement in the House last week in which he shortened the tour abroad [for servicemen]... has raised an outcry from Dickie [Mountbatten] saying he cannot now stage his offensive on the fixed date owing to the loss of personnel this will produce. I am afraid there is something in what he says.

At 5.30pm a Cabinet in which Winston gave a long and very gloomy review of the situation in Europe. The Russians were further West in Europe than they had ever been except once. They were all powerful in Europe. At any time that it took their fancy, they could march across the rest of Europe and drive us back into our island. They had a 2 to 1 land superiority over our forces and the Americans were returning home. The quicker they went home, the sooner they would be required back here again. He finished up by saying that never in his life had he been more worried by the European situation than he was at present."

12 June saw Brookie reassessing his opinion of Eisenhower:

"After COS rushed off to the Guildhall for Eisenhower's presentation of the freedom of the City. Ike made a wonderful speech and impressed all hearers… He then made an equally good speech of a different kind outside the Mansion House and a first-class speech at the Mansion House lunch. I had never realized that Ike was as big a man until I heard his performance today!"

Six days later:

"Drafted letter to Mountbatten advising him to get rid of Oliver Leese who has proved to be a failure in South East Asia Command. It is very disappointing."

On 19 June:

"The elections continue to have a fatal effect on operations. The S of S's statement in the House reducing service abroad in India from 3 years and 8 months to 3 and 4 has had a most pernicious result on the prospect of our operations for the recapture of the Malay peninsula! We are now releasing more men than we have shipping to bring home! We therefore lose them from the fighting forces and disgruntle them by failing to bring them home! And all this just for some electioneering vote catching!"

On 21 June:

"We had a long struggle this morning with the Planners trying to tidy up our policy for the prosecution of the war after the capture of Singapore. It is essential in my mind that we should provide some form of land force for operations against Japan proper and yet the difficulties produced by the Principal Administrative Officers almost make it impossible. It is exhausting driving people on to make them overcome difficulties!"

On 27 June:

"A long COS... on questions of organization of command in Burma. Dickie [Mountbatten] had put up a foolish scheme which we had to down."

Two days later:

"I had to go to PM at 3pm to tell him that we should have to withdraw Oliver Leese from South East Asia... We are now ordering Oliver home, appointing Slim in his place and sending out Dempsey as the additional Army Commander... I told [Winston] that I considered I should go at the end of the year. He said that if as a result of the election he got in again he would not hear of my going and that I was quite young (!!) and required to carry out the reorganization of the army!"

2 July saw yet more criticism of the Foreign Office:

"We are now faced with difficulties ahead concerning future of Polish Forces! In a few days we shall be recognizing the Warsaw Government officially and liquidating the London one. The Polish forces then present a serious conundrum which the Foreign Office has done little to solve in spite of repeated applications for ruling ever since May!"

On 4 July, note Brookie's remark about Churchill's 'fertile brain':

"Meeting with the PM at 12 noon to get him to approve our proposed policy for war after capture of Singapore. We are suggesting that we should send a force of some 5 divisions to take part in the direct attack against Japan. The exact composition of the force to depend on our conversations with the Americans when we meet them in Berlin [forthcoming Potsdam conference]... Winston very tired after all his electioneering tours... At last, we got onto our problem and he confessed he had not even read the paper which we had prepared for him with such care! (And yet if the proposed strategy in the long run turns out successful, it will have originated in his fertile brain!! This has happened so frequently now!)

> *Finally, home for a dinner with John Kennedy and wife... The former informed me of a rumour... that I was to be made the next Governor General of Canada!!! I had been told that Harry Crerar was to take that job on and very well he would do it too."*

On 6 July:

> *"Cabinet at 3pm to give details about Canadian riots in Aldershot during last two nights. Winston had already called me up at 9am and been abusive on the telephone. At the Cabinet, he again started being abusive: 'Why could we not keep better order?... Were we going to let these wild Canadians break up the homes of these poor inoffensive shopkeepers?'... It is only as a very last resort that I should order British troops to rough handle Canadians who are giving trouble... In such cases, Canadians must deal with their own nationals... I was very annoyed and I hope he realized it from my answers."*

On 10 July:

> *"A long COS with the Joint Intelligence Committee reporting on the ability of Japan to carry on with the war. Somewhat depressing report but one which held out some hope of shortening the war if it were possible to find some more suitable definition for 'Unconditional Surrender'. One making it clear that we had no evil intentions on the [Emperor of Japan], the Japanese religion or Japanese society as a whole.*
>
> *At 6pm poor Oliver Leese came to see me, having just arrived back. Very sad and repentant. He took it all wonderfully well. Ready to go back to private life or any lower rank or anything that might suit best. Shall have a difficult job to find employment for him."*

On 15 July, Brookie flew to Berlin for the Potsdam conference. The following day brought disappointing news:

> *"[Churchill] sent for me... [and said] he had heard from Lascelles [King George VI's private secretary] that the King wanted Alex to*

replace Athlone as Governor General of Canada. This is the job that John Kennedy had told me that Lascelles had said that they wanted me for. A job I would have given a great deal for. However, I agree that Alex is ideally suited for it and told the PM so. Consequently, it is pretty well settled that he goes there, and I remain with a few heartburns which I think Kipling's If has taught me by now to overcome.

At 2.30 we had our first meeting with the Americans... An easy meeting with no controversial points... we then went on to Berlin for a tour round. It was most interesting. I was very impressed by the degree of destruction. We went to... the Chancellery which was even more interesting. It was possible to imagine the tragedies which had occurred there only some 2 months ago. Hitler's study in ruins with his marble top writing table upside down!... In one part of the apartments, masses of Iron Crosses on the floor and medal ribbons. On the way up, I was handed a German decoration in its box by a Russian private soldier!!... the whole afternoon seemed like a dream and I found it hard to believe that after all these years' struggles I was driving through Berlin! The population did not look too thin but on the whole pathetic and surly. I saw many sights of refugees returning to Berlin which brought back to me vividly the picture of the French refugees rushing back to Lille as we arrived from Brussels. In every way throughout this war the Germans have been made to suffer the same misery as they inflicted on others, but with 100% interest."

On the next day:

"COS at which we discussed new [American] papers... The first was the American reply to our desire to participate in the direct attack on Japan. The reply was far better than we had hoped for and the offer is accepted in principle. The second was a question of command in the Pacific. There I foresee more trouble ahead.

Alexander came to lunch and I had a chance of asking him afterwards how he liked the idea of the Canadian Governorship. He was delighted with the thought of it, and well he might be."

On 18 July:

> "At 2.30 we had a Combined Chiefs of Staff meeting... We then turned to questions of command in the Pacific and we were on much thinner ice! We had asked for a quarter share in the control of operations in the Pacific and the Americans showed every sign of reluctance to afford us such facilities. However, Marshall made a very nice speech pointing out the difficulties of control in the Pacific and the desirability to simplify the control and avoid delays. They would be prepared to discuss strategy, but final decisions must rest with them. If the plan for the invasion of the Tokyo Plain did not suit us, we could withhold our forces but they would still carry on."

On the following day:

> "We went back to Berlin to visit... Hitler's [underground bunker] where he is supposed to have died. A sordid and unromantic spot. Absolute chaos outside... Down below even worse chaos. It is however possible to make out one large sitting room probably used for meals, a study for Hitler, a bedroom of Hitler's opening into two separate bath and WC rooms, connecting through to Eva Braun's room... Outside, we were shown where Goebbels and his family were found, also where a body was found which was taken for Hitler. However, the Russian in charge said that he considered that Hitler was now in Argentina and that Eva Braun had never died, but a mistress of Goebbels. I wonder if the truth will ever be known. We also... had a drive round Berlin. The more one sees of it, the more one realizes how completely destroyed it is."

On 21 July, Churchill and Brookie inspected British troops in Berlin:

> "We returned to the stand and then the [7th Armoured] Division marched past. I suppose I ought to have been gripped by what this all meant. Here were British troops who had come from Egypt through North Africa and Italy to France (a real example of the strategy I had been working for) parading where masses of German forces had goosestepped in the past! Somehow it left me cold."

23 July saw an interesting assessment of Anthony Eden:

"I was completely shattered by the PM's outlook! He had seen the reports of the American results of the new TA secret explosive experiments [Tube Alloys, codename for the atomic bomb] which had just been carried out in the States. He had absorbed all the minor American exaggerations and, as a result, was completely carried away! It was now no longer necessary for the Russians to come into the Japanese war, the new explosive alone was sufficient to settle the matter. Furthermore, we now had something in our hands which would redress the balance with the Russians! The secret of this explosive and the power to use it would completely alter the diplomatic equilibrium which was adrift since the defeat of Germany! Now we had a new value which redressed our position (pushing his chin out and scowling), now we could say if you insist on doing this or that, well we can just blot out Moscow... And now where are the Russians!!!

I tried to crush his over-optimism based on the results of one experiment and was asked with contempt what reason I had for minimizing the results of these discoveries. I was trying to dispel his dreams and as usual he did not like it... During lunch, Anthony Eden came in hot from his discussion with Molotov and Byrnes, I am afraid that he added to my gloom. Delightful as he is, in my opinion he always seems to just miss the point.

Spent the afternoon reading over the minutes of the meetings of the big three and they are very interesting reading, the one fact that stands out more clearly than any other is that nothing is ever settled!! Finally, the day finished up with a big dinner... Truman proposed my health coupled with Antonov [Russian chief of operations]. I had to reply and in doing so reminded Stalin of his Yalta toast 'to those men who are always wanted in war and always forgotten in peace – the soldiers'... I reminded the politicians and diplomats that even in peace there might be a use for soldiers. And finally proposed the toast to the hope, perhaps a pious hope, that soldiers might not be forgotten in peace!! This went down well with Stalin who replied at once that soldiers would never be forgotten. After dinner, we had the menus signed up and I went round to ask Stalin for his signature, he turned round, looked at me, smiled very kindly and shook me warmly by the hand before signing."

In his Notes, "Winston's appreciation of [the value of the atomic bomb] in the future international balance of power was certainly far more accurate than mine. But what was worrying me was that with his usual enthusiasm for anything new, he was letting himself be carried away by the very first and rather scanty reports of the first atomic explosion… This attitude brought out all my reactionary sentiments which led me into a failure to fully realize the importance of the new discovery."

24 July saw another assessment:

"On the whole I liked [President Harry Truman], not the same personality as his predecessor but a quick brain, a feeling of honesty, a good businessman and a pleasant personality. Last night in one of his quick remarks, Stalin had said about him 'honesty adorns the man' and he was not far wrong.

At 2.30pm we had a meeting with the Russian Chiefs of Staff… Antonov informed us that the Russians were coming into the war [against Japan] in August.

Thus finished our Combined Chiefs of Staff Meeting in Berlin!! where we had never hoped to meet in our wildest dreams in the early stages of this war. And now that we are here, I feel too weary and cooked to even get a kick out of it. It all feels flat and empty. I am feeling very, very tired and worn out."

In his Notes, "It had been much the easiest of any of our meetings… There now only remained the Pacific problems to coordinate and as in this theatre [the Americans] had always been much more of a predominant partner, it was more a matter of conforming to their strategy. Looking back at the conference, I remember only too well those feelings of unaccountable flatness that hung over me. I had a feeling that my mind was not registering properly the magnitude of the occasion… There is no doubt that I was suffering from extreme exhaustion by that time".

By 25 July, Brookie was back in London:

"I find my brain quite exhausted nowadays and have to read each paper two or 3 times to make any sense of it."

On 26 July, the result of the general election was declared – Churchill and the Conservatives had lost and a new Labour Government, led by Clement Attlee, voted into office:

"The Conservative Government has had a complete landslide and is out for good and all!! If only Winston had followed my advice he would have been in at any rate till the end of the year! But what was my advice to him a mere soldier!!! Now he is gone, and PJ [Grigg]. Who shall I be dealing with in future, Attlee? as PM and who as S of S? I feel too old and weary to start off on any new experiments. It is probably all for the good of England in the long run, any government in power during the next year is not going to last long. But what a ghastly mistake to start elections at this period in the World's History! May God forgive England for it."

27 July was:

"A day of partings! First a COS to which Dickie [Mountbatten] came and did not contribute greatly to. After lunch, I had a long interview with [Grigg]. It was a sad one and I hate to see him go. We have worked wonderfully together and I have grown to know him well and to appreciate his high qualities. I am genuinely fond of him and very sad at our parting. Then at 5.30pm had to go and see Winston at 10 Downing St with other Chiefs of Staff. It was a very sad and very moving little meeting at which I found myself unable to say much for fear of breaking down. He was standing the blow wonderfully well."

In his Notes, "The thought that my days of work with Winston had come to an end was a shattering one. There had been very difficult times and times when I felt I could not stand a single more day with him... No doubt Winston must frequently have felt that he could stand me no longer, and I marvel even now that... he did not replace me. There are few things that can bind two individuals more closely than to be intimately connected in a vast struggle against overwhelming odds and to emerge on top of all... Providence was indeed kind to me during the war to have placed PJ [Grigg] at the helm in the WO. It would have been hard to find a man with whom I would sooner have worked."

After this 'sad and very moving little meeting', Brookie wrote a letter to Churchill which elicited the following reply,

> My dear Brookie,
> I am deeply grateful for all you have done for me and for the country. Your charming letter has touched me deeply and cheered me. I shall always value your friendship, as I do my memories of Ronnie and Victor [two of Brookie's brothers] in those young and far off days. Our story in this war is a good one, and this will be recognized as time goes on.

On 28 July, bird photography was the order of the day:

> "Met Hosking at 8.30... and went on to the hide at once. A huge erection 26 feet high! but within 12 feet of the nest. There are 3 young birds. By 9am I was established. At 10.45 the hen came for the first time and was at nest feeding for 10 minutes. At 12.15 she returned and was again there for close on 10 minutes. I took a lot of photographs and only hope that they may be good. It was... I believe, the first time that a coloured cine picture of a hobby has been taken!"

Two days later:

> "Usual early Monday start, left my priceless films with Kodak, I do pray that they may be good!"

31 July saw a lambasting for the Foreign Office:

"*Combined Intelligence Committee… warned of the gathering clouds on the northern Greek frontier. Seven Yugoslav Divisions close to frontier, many more behind, 19 Bulgarian divisions, 350-400,000 Russians all in Bulgaria. It looks too much like power politics to be pleasant. Meanwhile, Foreign Office as usual going adrift! We were originally told to send 10,000 troops to Greece to back the Government. I said it would require at least 80,000 to do what they wanted. I was informed politely that I knew nothing about it as it was a political matter and that 10,000 would be ample to give the necessary backing to the Government. We eventually sent about 90,000 into Greece!!! Now having originally sent forces into Greece to restore law and order internally, we are informed that these self-same forces are required to also defend the frontiers of Greece!! We are on a slippery slope, with one task leading into another all requiring more and more forces which we have not got. And at the same time we receive instructions to accelerate our own demobilization!*"

1 August saw another example of Brookie's ability to read people well:

"*By 7.30am, Rollie and I were off, heading for the hobby's nest! By 9.15, I was again up in the hide 22 feet above the ground and glad to have the climb up behind me! By 9.45, the hobby was back feeding and I exposed about 100ft of Kodachrome.*

Freyberg [New Zealand commander] came to see me this evening to assure me that he was the one man to command the [Imperial] Corps for the invasion of Japan!"

On the following day:

"*I collected my precious film of the hobby taken last Saturday. I am glad to say that it has turned out very good and I am delighted with it. During the afternoon… long discussion with Simpson on plans for our Imperial Expedition for the invasion of Japan with a corps of 1 British, 1 Canadian and 1 Australian Division.*"

7 August was:

> "A long and somewhat weary day. First of all, a Chiefs of Staff meeting with Mountbatten and Lloyd of the Australian Army. The latter was quite excellent and clear-headed. The former was as usual quite impossible and wasted a lot of our time. Always fastening onto the irrelevant points, repeating himself, failing to recognize the vital points. Seldom has a Supreme Commander been more deficient of the main attributes of a Supreme Commander than Dickie Mountbatten. Then our first Cabinet meeting [of the new Labour Government]!... I was asked many questions... all of them mainly influenced by political as opposed to military motives."

In his Notes, "I remember being very impressed by the efficiency with which Attlee ran his cabinet. There was not the same touch of genius as with Winston but there were more businesslike methods. We kept to the agenda and he maintained complete order with a somewhat difficult crowd."

On 8 August:

> "I found Dickie Mountbatten waiting for me [at the War Office]. As usual, he wanted me to pull the chestnuts out of the fire for him and expected me to tackle First Sea Lord to draw aircraft carrier from the Pacific Fleet for his purposes! I called his bluff and told him to do his own dirty work."

On the following day:

> "Then a meeting with Slim prior to his departure for India. I rubbed into him my dislike for 'prima donna generals' and 'film star generals', I hope he will take it to heart."

On 10 August:

> "Started with a long COS attended by Mountbatten, I find it very hard to remain pleasant when he turns up! He is the most crashing bore I have met on a committee, is always fiddling about with unimportant

matters and wasting other people's time. Just before lunch, BBC intercepts of Japanese peace offers were received in the shape of an acceptance of the Potsdam offer. There was, however, one rather obscure clause concerning the prerogatives of the Emperor being retained.

PM convened a Cabinet for 3pm when the message was examined... Cabinet were unanimous that... if [the Americans] were of the opinion that the clause affecting the Emperor was acceptable we should agree... The Chiefs of Staff were liberated from the Cabinet at 4 and we convened a COS meeting for 5pm to be attended by Joint Planners. I told them the general outline of what was required and instructed them to prepare a paper to be ready Sunday evening and considered Monday morning covering the various actions required... One of the main points of urgency is that of providing a force for the rapid occupation of Hong Kong."

Two days later:

"All going well, reply has been sent to Japan, we now await their final acceptance. Meanwhile, our plans for the Japanese surrender are progressing. MacArthur as Supreme Commander to work through the Emperor and Fraser [Commander-in-Chief, British Pacific Fleet] to be our representative with him. Force for Hong Kong progressing... It is hard to realize that by the end of the coming week the war with Japan may be over!"

14 August saw another dry comment:

"Announcement appeared this morning of the 3 Chiefs of Staff having been created Barons [they were nominated by Churchill in his resignation honours list: Brookie took the title Alanbrooke of Brookeborough, the name of the village in Northern Ireland where his family home was located]! When you look at some of the other Barons and Viscounts, one wonders whether it is such an honour and a distinction!

Have just heard that midnight wireless announces Japan's final acceptance of the terms!! Can this really be the end of the war?"

Japan's surrender on the following day prompted Brookie to reflect:

> "The end of this war for certain. Six very, very long years of continuous struggle, nerve-wracking anxiety, dashed hopes, hopeless bleak horizons, endless difficulties with Winston finished with! When I look back at the blackest moments, it becomes almost impossible to believe that we stand where we do. One thing above all others predominates all other thoughts, namely boundless gratitude to God and to His guiding hand which has brought us where we are.
>
> [Jack Lawson, the new Secretary of State for War] again asked me to stop on for another year, I again pressed for situation to be reviewed at the end of this year."

Four days later, he attended a Thanksgiving Service for Victory in St Paul's Cathedral:

> "Cunningham, Portal and I took our seats in a landau pulled by 4 bays in the King's procession to St Paul's. It was an interesting experience to go through and to look at the crowd instead of being one of them!"

On 21 August:

> "Hong Kong and its relief by British forces before the arrival of either Chinese or American forces filled most of our COS discussion."

23 August saw Brookie fretting about money:

> "We finished our COS with a private meeting discussing future of COS, our own successors and probable dates of our departures. We all favoured the period between January and March for the end of our tours. The following were possible successors:
> CNS – Tovey too obstinate, John Cunningham the best, Fraser a little later after more experience.
> CAS – Tedder best, Slessor possible but better to wait for couple of years.
> CIGS – Monty very efficient from Army point of view but very unpopular with large proportion of the Army. Archie Nye very

capable but after 7 years in War Office must have some outside experience. Of these two, Portal and Cunningham strongly in favour of Monty.

Pug – only two real alternatives. Jo Hollis or Ian Jacob. Pug favoured first, personally I feel certain Jacob is best.

We then discussed the cost of becoming a Baron. Apparently, I can't get out of it under £200 which appals me."

On 28 August:

"I struggled with the COS trying to get the other two to realize the dangers of the Foreign Office policy in Greece, where they now suggest that we should take on frontier defence as well as our internal task of supporting the Gov, maintaining law and order and distributing food. It is shattering how little sailors and airmen are able to understand the problems connected with land warfare!"

Two days later:

"We had representatives from the Dominion Office in whilst we discussed Australia's latest claim to run an occupational force quite separate from ours in Japan. We were recommending another attempt to... get Australia to join with our Commonwealth united force. They are trying to run out on their own. Dominion Office are not showing much guts in returning to the attack. I recommended to [Wavell] that he should put up [Auchinleck] for Field Marshal and he agreed with me."

In October 1945, Brookie departed on a 40,000-mile world trip, the purpose being to conduct a review of Britain's overseas military commitments: his trip included visits to Greece, the Middle East, Iran, India, Burma, Hong Kong, Japan, Australia, New Zealand, Singapore, Kenya and Italy. Two days before his departure:

"Dashed off to see Winston in his new flat as I felt he might be hurt if I started for Far East without visiting him. I found him very bitter against the Labour Party."

Given his love of flying and visiting foreign countries, this trip would have appealed to Brookie. However, it meant separation from Benita. On 26 October:

> "Started for home to spend my last evening with you before my departure. How I hate those last hours! Overwhelmed by thoughts that one may not return, wondering whether any of these are rising to the surface, trying to be cheerful and retain usual manners. Inwardly racked by the thought that similar thoughts are going through your brain… It is agony when two souls closely linked together live through such hours! I hope that our partings of this kind will now come to an end."

In Japan, he met the American, General Douglas MacArthur:

> "I came away with the impression that he is a very big man and the biggest general I have yet seen during this war. He is head and shoulders bigger than Marshall and if he had been in the latter's place during the last four years, I feel certain that my task in the Combined Chiefs of Staff would have been far easier."

In his Notes, "MacArthur was the greatest general and best strategist that the war produced. He certainly outshone Marshall, Eisenhower and all other American and British generals including Montgomery. As a fighter of battles and a leader of men, Monty was hard to beat but I doubt whether he would have shown the same strategic genius had he been in MacArthur's position… I had kept a very careful watch on MacArthur's strategy in the Pacific and the more I saw of it the more impressed had I become. The masterly way in which he had jumped from point to point leaving masses of Japs to decay behind him had filled me with admiration, whereas any ordinary general might have eaten up penny packets of Japs till he had such indigestion that he could proceed no further. The points he selected for his jumps were always those best suited for the efficient use of the three services… From everything I saw of him that day, he confirmed the admiration I already had. A very striking personality, with perhaps a tinge of the actor, but any failing in this direction was certainly not offensive". There was, perhaps, more than a 'tinge of the actor' in MacArthur since:

"He finished by presenting me with a signed photograph of himself."

In Kenya, the nature-loving Brookie visited a game reserve:

"We found a solitary [rhinoceros] and stalked him with the car... I had just asked Ritchie to stop so as to snap him when he turned and came for the car like an express train! I just had time to take one snapshot... before [Ritchie] swung the car away from the rhino. I looked out of the opposite window and found the native tracker sitting on the back seat with the rifle getting ready to shoot but could see no rhino. I then looked through the back window and in the middle of a cloud of dust of the car saw the old rhino's head closing fast on to the back of the car. It was a thrilling moment... Thus finished two of the happiest days I had had for a long time."

In January 1946, Brookie, Portal and Cunningham were created viscounts. With Brookie's retirement now fixed for the summer of that year, a commanders-in-chief conference at the end of March gave him the opportunity to say farewell to many of his colleagues. In his Notes, "It had been a very long association and through momentous days, and it was all I could do to prevent myself breaking down and my goodbye had consequently to be shortened."

On 10 April;

"Received a letter from Lascelles [King George VI's private secretary] stating that the King wished to confer the Order of Merit on me in his Birthday Honours List."

In his Notes, "Of all the orders and decorations that I received, none of them have ever seemed in the same category. I felt intense gratitude that my services should have been recognised in such a manner."

In May, he vacated the London flat which had been his home since January 1942:

"The walls are stripped of their pictures, most of the chairs are *gone, the writing table removed and memories of the last four and a half years surge round me... those horrible wakeful moments in the early hours when all life looks at its worst and doubts swamp one's confidence... and many solitary hours when I communed with myself and wondered how correct I was in the policies I was pursuing."*

On 8 June Brookie, Portal and Cunningham participated in the Victory Parade in London.

"Cunningham, Portal and I... had insisted on travelling in the same car. They had... offered one car for First Sea Lord and CIGS and a separate one for the Chief of the Air Staff. But we refused and said we had been united as a trinity throughout the War and could not be separated on such an occasion!"

25 June 1946 was the day of Brookie's retirement:

"My last day as CIGS... There have been moments when I wondered whether I should last the course – times of intense fatigue when work had become an unbearable burden, when responsibility weighed heavier than ever and when it became more and more difficult to make decisions. My feelings were so mixed that I found it hard to disentangle them. But above everything the longing for rest predominated over all other feelings. The last day was necessarily a trying one. Thus ended my active military career."

Part Three

NINETEEN

Alanbrooke

Diaries tend to reveal a great deal about their authors, especially those maintained over a period of years: this is particularly true of Alanbrooke's diary since he wrote openly and freely in the belief it would only be read by Benita. It is, therefore, possible to draw a portrait of Alanbrooke's character from his entries.

Identifying the reasons why he started his diary is a helpful first step. There were two, the first of which was his enforced separation from Benita. In his opening dedication to her, "I should feel quite lost without an occasional opportunity of a talk with you". Benita was the central and pivotal figure in his life: she was the magnetic star around which he orbited, as he admitted in his letter which appears in the Introduction, "As usual, my darling, you are being my mainstay and anchor in life. Without you I should be able to do nothing. Your example and life is the most wonderful inspiration to me and my whole life just hinges around you." The diary was his umbilical cord to Benita, hence why his 'talks' with her were "quite sacred" to him and why he was prepared to breach wartime regulations and create a security risk by keeping one.

On 1 October 1939, four days after leaving Benita, "Still no letters today and I am longing to hear from you, it is a horrid feeling to suddenly find yourself cut clean off from those you love and all that means everything to you in the world." In marked contrast, on 5 October 1939, "I received two letters from you today, the first two, they transformed the whole day and seemed to make the sun shine brighter." On 1 February 1940, "No mail this evening and consequently no letter from you and, as a result, a colourless day! The receipt of your letter is the hub round which the day revolves. Without its hub, the day turns with an aimless wobble!" and on 11 February 1940, "Sunday again, our day when we should be together... Life without your comradeship is just one long blank."

3 September 1940 was the first anniversary of the start of the War, "Looking back, it has been a year of heartbreaking partings from you which stand out for me above all else". 27 September 1940 was the first anniversary of his departure for France, "I can see your car driving off now when I shut my eyes and can again feel that ghastly desolation that froze into my heart at our having to part." Little wonder, therefore, that when he returned to London from Washington on 27 June 1942, it was "such a joy to be back with you" and, likewise, when he returned on 7 February 1943, "to my great joy you met me."

The second reason was that a diary provided Alanbrooke with the only means by which he, a corps commander based in France, could express his intense dislike of war: Alanbrooke practised an art which he firmly believed was futile. In his first entry on 28 September 1939, "I found it quite impossible... to realize that I was starting off for the war... It is all too ghastly even to be a nightmare. The awful futility of it all, as proved by the last war!... I suppose that... we have still got to be taught more fully the futility of war." On 11 November 1939, he attended an armistice ceremony, "the two red wreaths of poppies... served as a vivid reminder of the floods of blood that had already been spilt on the very ground we were standing, and of the futility of again causing such bloodshed." His belief that war was futile stemmed from his experiences in the First World War which had left him appalled by its brutality and horrors. On 15 December 1939, he read about a battle in 1214 which had been fought "just to the left of my Corps front... it is possible to carry oneself back some 720 years... and follow the whole combat right to the end of the dreadful carnage that resulted from it". Those experiences also left him appalled by the destruction caused by war. On 6 March 1940, he visited an old fort near Verdun which "brings home to one better than anything I have yet seen what the last war meant as regards devastation and destruction". He made the same point later in the War, 2 August 1942, when he visited Malta, "The destruction is inconceivable and reminds one of Ypres, Arras, Lens at their worst during last war."

There was a possible third reason, namely a diary allowed him to express his emotions and feelings in writing. This was important to Alanbrooke because he was prone to lose self-control when talking about his feelings. On 28 September 1939, he recalled "that day we spent together, our dinner at the County Hotel which kept coming back to my mind again and again during the last few days without my daring to refer to it lest I might break down". When, in November 1941, he said farewell to his colleague, General Paget, at Home Forces HQ, he "had tears in his eyes" and "rushed from the room unable to finish his farewell." After Churchill lost the 1945 General Election, 27 July 1945 was "a day of partings… had to go and see Winston at 10 Downing St… It was a very sad and very moving little meeting at which I found myself unable to say much for fear of breaking down." In March 1946, Alanbrooke bid farewell to his colleagues prior to his retirement, "it was all I could do to prevent myself breaking down and my goodbye had consequently to be shortened."

An incident in Alanbrooke's childhood hinted at his inability to talk about his emotions and feelings. His sister, Hylda Wrench, recalled the occasion when he was bitten by a wild dog which prompted concern that he may have contracted rabies, "The point of the story is that Alan never said anything on the subject… so I was very much taken aback when, three weeks later, he one day said to me: 'Now there is no longer any danger is there of my going mad?' It just showed what he had been going through inside without ever saying a word." This weakness may explain, at least in part, why Alanbrooke became a distant and uncommunicative father to his children following Janey's death in 1925.

However, he was perfectly capable of expressing his emotions and feelings in writing and when he did, they gushed out. On 31 December 1940, "I thank God for one thing above all others in life and that is for having allowed me to meet you and thus realize what perfection could be realized on this earth." Further examples occurred on 6 November 1939, 9 December 1939, 19 and 20 October 1940.

Some of Alanbrooke's attributes – intelligence, strong analytical powers, good judgment, energy and drive, steely determination and resolve – have already been highlighted. In addition, he was adept at managing senior commanders. Alexander observed, "I could not have had a wiser, firmer or more understanding military chief"[1]: his choice of adjectives was instructive. To this list can be added ten further attributes.

The first was a strong sense of service and duty. On 29 October 1942, "[Churchill] is the most difficult man I have ever served with but thank God for having given me the opportunity of trying to serve such a man in a crisis such as the one this country is going through". Likewise, on 30 November 1942, Churchill was a "hard taskmaster, and the most difficult man to serve that I have ever met". It was this strong sense of service and duty which lay behind his decision to turn down Churchill's offer of command in Egypt on 6 August 1942, "I feel therefore that, tempting as the offer is, by accepting it I should definitely be taking a course which would on the whole help the war the least. I… am quite convinced… I can do more by remaining as CIGS." It also explained his reaction to Auchinleck's refusal of the Iraq-Persia command: in his Notes, 8 August 1942, "It would have been a more 'soldierly' act to accept what he was offered in war, instead of behaving like an offended film star." In similar vein, when France was on the point of collapse on 14 June 1940, Alanbrooke was flabbergasted that General Weygand, the man "destined to minister to France in her death agonies", was far more concerned about damage to his "successful career". Such attitudes were anathema to Alanbrooke.

This strong sense of service and duty could be seen in the way he viewed his relationship with the prime minister and senior politicians: they were "the highest", 2 February 1940, and on 25 November 1943 Churchill was one of "the high and mighty". He accepted that he was at Churchill's beck and call, hence his frequent use of "sent for", and dutifully complied with Churchill's summonses. Alanbrooke saw his role as that of an adviser to "the highest". On 6 August 1942, "after working with the PM for close on 9 months I do feel at last that… he is beginning to take my advice" and on 26 July 1945 after Churchill lost the general election, "If only Winston had followed my advice he would have been in at any rate till the end of the year! But what was my advice to him a mere soldier!!!" The best illustration of how he defined his role was the statement attributed to him by Joan Bright Astley in early July 1944, "the day that I say that I agree with [Churchill] when I don't is the day he must get rid of me because I am no use to him any more."

Alanbrooke's sense of service and duty manifested itself in several ways. First, he remained loyal to Churchill, notwithstanding their confrontational relationship and endless arguments. Second, he was protective of Churchill. On 14 November 1944, "It was a relief to get the PM safely back from this trip as the security in Paris was far from satisfactory": he expressed a similar sentiment on 22 March 1945. Alanbrooke saw himself as Churchill's military chaperone and he became concerned when he was separated from his charge. In his Notes, 10 August 1942, "I had seen Winston's plane disappearing into the distance as it headed for Moscow whilst we turned back to Tehran! I did not like seeing him go off out of my sight without knowing how we were going to follow him": a further instance occurred on 15 November 1943. Third, there was a notable lack of self pity in his diary. He frequently recorded how "exhausted", "cooked" and "tired" he was yet, rarely, did he feel sorry for himself. Few and far between were comments such as those on 31 December 1942, "This is a dog's life!!", and on 17 August 1944, "There are moments when I would give anything just to get in a car and drive home, saying I was fed up with the whole show and they could look for someone else to fill my job!"

As an aside, Alanbrooke was possessive and territorial of his military domain and he reacted sharply when politicians encroached on it. 8 December 1943 saw Harold Macmillan meddling in the appointment of a supreme commander for the Mediterranean, "[He]... evidently does not even begin to understand what the functions of a Supreme Commander should be" and in his Notes, "This interference on the part of Macmillan made me very angry". He was likewise angry when Anthony Eden encroached upon his military domain on 29 October 1942 and 7

November 1944. Whilst he accepted that his political masters had the final word on major decisions, he clearly believed that a demarcation line existed between military and political matters and that this line should not be crossed. On 8 July 1944, "a 'soldier must not be politically minded'; but why should not the converse hold good? It seems as reasonable to state that a 'politician must not be militarily minded.'"

It was this strong sense of service and duty, combined perhaps with his steely determination and resolve, which helped Alanbrooke revive his spirits when he became downcast. On 31 March 1942, he was very despondent but on the following day, "Looking back at what I wrote last night, I wonder whether I was liverish! Life looks yellow at times but as long as one can prevent one's thoughts and actions being tinged with yellow all is well! We have got to choose between pulling through and sinking and it does not take long to make that choice!" A further example occurred on 24/25 August 1943.

The second attribute was realism. When, on 13 August 1942, Alanbrooke recorded his first impressions of Stalin, he could have been describing himself, "He is a realist, with little flattery about him and not looking for much flattery either… Stalin is a realist if ever there was one, facts only count with him, plans, hypotheses, future possibilities mean little to him but he is ready to face facts even when unpleasant." 'Facts only counted' for Alanbrooke as well. On 7 February 1943, he returned to London after the Casablanca conference, "I now foresee some hard work ahead to convert some of the paperwork of the last 3 weeks into facts and actions." On 31 May 1944, "[Mountbatten] must face facts". 4 July 1944 saw him criticising Alexander, "it is very desirable to bring his feet to earth and to make him face the facts confronting him". On 28 November 1944, he told Churchill that "when we looked facts in the face, this last offensive could only be classified as the first strategic reverse that we had suffered since landing in France." On 10 May 1944, he attended a formal dinner, "All these speeches strike me as being so much hot air… which goes to everyone's head, producing a beatific and complacent attitude of wonderful imperial understanding. But how much of all this remains there in the bleak reality of the morning after?"

Alanbrooke dealt with facts and situations as they were, not as he might hope them to be. On 28 November 1939, "On arrival in [France] and for the first two months, [II] Corps was quite unfit for war, practically in every respect": he made similar observations on 4 October and 26 November 1939. On 30 January 1940, "[Martel] was wondering why we were not more concerned with preparing offensive measures to attack the Siegfried Line; and seemed quite oblivious of the fact that instead of attacking this spring, we are far more likely to be hanging on by our eyelids in trying to check German attacks!" His prediction proved to be correct.

He was brutally realistic in his assessments of commanders. On 31 March 1942, "Half our Corps and Divisional Commanders are totally unfit for their appointments and yet if I were to sack them, I could find no better. They lack character, imagination, drive and power of leadership." On 2 October 1941, "I am... disappointed at the way Higher Commanders are handling [the armoured divisions]. They have all got a great deal to learn and the sooner they learn the better." His draft letter to British commanders-in-chief in mid-February 1942 was likewise brutally realistic, "Too many officers have been, and are being, promoted even to high command because they are proficient in staff work, because they are good trainers, because they have agreeable personalities or because they are clever talkers... We must be more ruthless in the elimination of those who seem unlikely to prove themselves".[2] Alanbrooke was rooted in reality.

It was this realism which explained Alanbrooke's methodical and workmanlike approach: as Lord Moran observed, "a craftsman by instinct, he knew exactly what could be done with the resources at his command and he had the craftsman's respect for method."[3] On 3 September 1942, Churchill demanded an immediate meeting to discuss Roosevelt's wire about Operation Torch, "This was quite useless as the President's wire required examining with experts to arrive at implications... at last I obtained leave to withdraw COS to consider the matter and report at 5pm." On 23 August 1943, Churchill was fixated on capturing northern Sumatra, "We have had no real opportunity of even studying the operation for its merits and possibilities and yet he wants us to press the Americans for its execution!" On 22 June 1944, he examined Alexander's plan to advance from northern Italy into Austria, "The proposals he has made are not based on any real study of the problem but rather the result of certain elated spirits after a rapid advance!"

A comparison with Rommel helps illustrate Alanbrooke's methodical and workmanlike approach. One observer described a tactical manoeuvre carried out by Rommel in the north African desert as "a gamble that had the elements of genius and the wildest possible folly".[4] This was not Alanbrooke's approach: he did not strive for genius and he certainly avoided folly. Instead, he measured risk. On 10 February 1943, pressure was being exerted to bring forward the date of the attack on Sicily, "I feel we are running grave risks of wrecking the whole show by trying to rush it." On 22 July 1943, amphibious landings on the Italian mainland were being examined, "Came to the conclusion that it was a gamble but probably one worth taking." On the eve of those landings, 8 September 1943, "We are gambling and taking risks, but I feel we are justified in doing so." And on 18 August 1944, "It is a gamble, but I believe one worth taking."

In the 1930s, Alanbrooke was described as "essentially deliberate in his methods as a tactician".[5] If this is a weakness in a military commander, which is debatable, then in Alanbrooke's case it was more than counterbalanced by his intelligence, analytical skills and good judgment: he demonstrated these on 13 November 1944 when he assessed American tactics, "Considering that the divisions for the attack are on a 30-kilometre front each, have been fighting without rest for 2½ months and also have just been reorganized by absorbing white personnel in lieu of the Senegalese… the whole plan of attack struck me as being fantastic!… The American Army just north of de Lattre [French general] is attacking in an impossible country in the Vosges, all he will do there is lose men. He ought to establish a defensive front there and concentrate his forces on the Belfort gap. Any successful offensive there would turn the line of the Vosges and render this expensive attack unnecessary."

The downside to Alanbrooke's realism was a lack of vision and, perhaps, imagination. In his Notes, 22 February 1942, he freely admitted that his initial scepticism of the new Combined Chiefs of Staff organisation was misplaced. On 19 April 1943, he attended a demonstration of a new type of aircraft which was "driven by air sucked in front and squirted out behind! Apparently, likely to be the fighter of the future." Most telling of all, on 23 July 1945 he failed to appreciate the full significance of the new atomic bomb.

The third attribute was single-mindedness. Archie Nye attested to his "singleness of purpose" and Eisenhower recorded that he was "earnestly devoted to the single purpose of winning the War."[6] For Alanbrooke, factors such as nationalistic attitudes, personal reputations, private agendas and vanity were irrelevant, and he despaired whenever these factors influenced the strategic decision-making process. 1 June 1944 saw discussion of British strategy in the Far East, "We have to steer clear between the rocks of Winston's ramblings in Sumatra, Curtin's subjugation to MacArthur, MacArthur's love of the limelight, King's desire to wrap all the laurels round his head and last but not least real sound strategy! The latter may well get a bad position at the starting gate!! My God, how difficult it is to run a war and to keep military considerations clear of all the vested interests and political foolery attached to it!!" On 1 April 1945, "Most of [Eisenhower's] changes are due to national aspirations… It is all a pity and the straightforward strategy is being affected by the nationalistic outlook of allies." On 19 February 1944, when he discovered that Montgomery and Ramsay had "foolishly agreed to curtail the cross-Channel operation to allow for a South of France operation" in order "to please Eisenhower who was pressing for it to please Marshall", Alanbrooke's reaction was, "What a way to run a war!"

The fourth – objectivity – was one of his greatest strengths. In his biography of Alanbrooke, David Fraser made an interesting observation, "he developed an objectivity which is not the universal characteristic of his profession or those who rise therein":[7] since Fraser was a professional soldier for forty years, his remark carries weight.

A very good example was his assessment of countries' armed forces: they were judged by the objective criteria of training, efficiency, leadership and effectiveness and Alanbrooke was strictly impartial when making his judgments. On 31 August 1940 he was "very much impressed" by a New Zealand division, on 10 April 1941 Canadian forces were "excellent material", on 20 August 1941 Polish forces were "very good and promise well for the future" and on 7 July 1942 American troops were "excellent material", even if they did "require a great deal more training." In marked contrast were his many criticisms of units in the British Army. On 27 July 1940, he visited the 46th Division, "Found it in a lamentably backward state of training, barely fit to do platoon training" and on 10 September 1941, he witnessed "one of the worst divisional advances that I have seen in the last year!" There was little, if any, nationalism or xenophobia in Alanbrooke.

On 29 January 1940, he watched a French Army film "mainly intended as propaganda" but this had no effect on him whatsoever: he had seen and assessed for himself the state of the French Army and his fears regarding it proved correct. As for Germany's armed forces, Alanbrooke was never in any doubt as to their efficiency and fighting qualities. On 23 May 1940, "the success they have achieved is nothing short of phenomenal. There is no doubt that they are most wonderful soldiers." His respect for the German Army was also apparent in his entries on 9 and 19 October 1939, 28 and 29 January 1940 and it remained undiminished throughout the War: on 24 March 1945, he was admiring their "wonderful defences". This respect was justified since, according to a post-War analysis, German combat effectiveness was notably superior to that of both British and American forces.

He applied the same objectivity and impartiality when assessing individuals. 17 April 1942 saw an assessment of the Australian, Richard Casey, "I was very much impressed by him and by his grasp of things – he should be excellent in the ME." On 18 April 1944, he met the American, Billet, "I found him well on the spot and a good man at his job." In contrast, on 25 January 1940, the commander of a British battalion recently arrived in France "struck me as being no use at all" and on 7 April 1944 one of the British corps commanders was "very weak and I am certain quite unfit to command a Corps." On 7 August 1945, "Chiefs of Staff meeting with Mountbatten and Lloyd of the Australian Army.

The latter was quite excellent and clear-headed. The former was as usual quite impossible and wasted a lot of our time. Always fastening onto the irrelevant points, repeating himself, failing to recognize the vital points".

To Alanbrooke, the nationality of an individual was irrelevant. Fellow countrymen such as Churchill, Pound and Mountbatten attracted constant criticism whereas a South African, a Pole and a Russian drew respect. The South African was Smuts who, on 4 August 1942, was "the most delightful old man with a wonderfully clear brain" and on 23 August 1942 "one of the biggest of nature's gentlemen I have ever seen. A wonderful clear grasp of all things coupled with the most exceptional charm. Interested in all matters and gifted with marvellous judgment." The Pole was Sikorski. On 3 February 1942, "The more I see him, the more I like him" and in his Notes, "I had the greatest admiration for his ability". When he learnt of Sikorski's death on 5 July 1943, "He is a terrible loss and I feel I have lost a great friend" and at his funeral ten days later, "I… shall miss him badly."

The Russian was Stalin. Alanbrooke disliked Stalin but he respected his ability, particularly his military ability. At their first meeting on 13 August 1942, "I was much impressed by his astuteness, and his crafty cleverness" and on the following day, "He is an outstanding man, that there is no doubt about, but not an attractive one… there is no doubt that he has a quick brain and a real grasp of the essentials of war". On 23 August 1942, "a crafty, brilliant, realistic mind devoid of any sense of human pity or kindness… But undoubtedly a big and shrewd brain with clear-cut views as to what he wants and expects to get." On 29 November 1943 at Tehran, "Winston was not good and Roosevelt even worse. Stalin meticulous with only two arguments." Alanbrooke's respect for Stalin was evident in his 23 July 1945 entry, "After dinner, we had the menus signed up and I went round to ask Stalin for his signature, he turned round, looked at me, smiled very kindly and shook me warmly by the hand before signing." Further examples can be seen in his Notes, 28 November 1943 and 15 October 1944.

Alanbrooke tended to judge people according to the clarity of their thought, analysis and speech. On 28 January 1942, "Wonderful what a clear and active mind old Milne has maintained in his old age." On 4 February 1945 Antonov, the Russian chief of operations, delivered "an excellent and very clear talk." On 18 January 1944, "I did not like the functioning of [Churchill's] brain much! Too much unconnected rambling from one subject to another."

He also attached importance to a person's age: he equated old age with inefficiency and infirmity. On 29 June 1940, "Why do we in this country turn to all the old men when we require a new volunteer force? Old men spell delay and chaos!" On 17 June 1941, he attended a commanders' conference which turned out to be a meeting of "moth-eaten old Admirals!" On 17 February 1942, Dudley Pound was "an old dodderer". On 4 August 1942, Jumbo Wilson was "too old and to be replaced" and on 15 September 1943, Paget was "not improving and is I fear on the decline slope."

It was this objectivity which probably explains the element of detachment in Alanbrooke's character. One manifestation of this detachment was his habit of referring to people as 'specimens': on 3 October 1940 Finch was a "poisonous specimen", on 16 December 1941 de Gaulle was "a most unattractive specimen", on 10 August 1942 Corbett was "a poor specimen of a man", on 12 September 1942 Duncan Sandys was an "objectionable specimen" and on 27 June 1944 Herbert Morrison was a "real white-livered specimen". Occasionally, this element of detachment was striking, almost 'Spock-like' in nature. On 1 April 1941, he visited Portsmouth, "Was very much impressed by the results of bombing on Portsmouth, the place has been badly smashed up." When he returned home on 26 September 1942, "I unfortunately found you all three the worse for wear for something you had eaten the previous evening. Also followed suit and apparently ate the remainder of that self-same something with sad results!" On 12 July 1944, after learning that Bannerman had been "bombed twice in 3 days", Alanbrooke airily noted, "Apparently he saved himself from being blown to bits by diving under his oak table." Two days later, Henry Stimson, the American Secretary of War, was "quite finished and hardly able to take notice of what is going on round him."

His remark on 9 May 1945, "Personally, the less I see of the human species the more content I am", suggests he was none too keen on his fellow human beings. However, that was far from the case since he enjoyed the company of 'personalities'. On 6 April 1945, General Hurley was "an outstanding personality, good looking, tall... and a very merry twinkle in his eye... A born 'raconteur' with a great sense of humour". On 22 November 1939, Gort was a "very definite personality, full of vitality, energy and joie de vivre". On 7 October 1942, the institution that he visited was run by a "live wire" and on 16 January 1943 General Patton was "a real fire eater and a definite character." Alanbrooke was an unusual mix – at times distant and detached, at other times interested and engaged.

The fifth attribute was a strong sense of propriety. His sister, Hylda Wrench, recalled the eight-year-old Alanbrooke insisting that his nephew, Basil, call him "Uncle Alan". In his Notes, he was "terrified of doing the wrong thing" at the Royal Military Academy at Woolwich. Alanbrooke disliked improper conduct. On 29 April 1942, he had a heated discussion with the Secretary of State for Air, "I should have liked to have told him even more plainly that he was deliberately speaking untruths!" 6 August 1942 saw a hint of prudishness, "Whilst I was dressing and practically naked, the PM suddenly burst into my room." When, on 3 December 1943, he discovered the Anglo-American meeting in Cairo must end within two days, he was "dumbfounded... It all looks like some of the worst sharp practice that I have seen for some time." On 30 November 1943, at Tehran, the "quite good chaps" taunt levelled at him by Stalin was a "most unexpected and uncalled for attack". On 19 April 1944, he was outraged by the Americans "trying to blackmail us into agreeing with them by holding the pistol of withdrawing [landing] craft at our heads!" On 29 March 1945, he was appalled when he learnt of Eisenhower's telegram to Stalin, "he has no business to address Stalin direct, his communications should be through the Combined Chiefs of Staff".

Alanbrooke deplored "sharp practice", yet he was perfectly willing, if he felt it necessary, to scheme in a way which almost amounted to sharp practice: this was well illustrated by his actions as BEF commander-in-chief in France in June 1940 and, much later, the surreptitious installation of Alexander into Eisenhower's command on 20 January 1943. This was a contradiction in Alanbrooke's character and, as will become clear, it was the first of a number of contradictions.

His dislike of improper conduct probably explains his dislike of rudeness. On 23 November 1939, Montgomery had used "such obscene language" in his VD circular to his troops. On 5 November 1941, Beaverbrook was "all smiles having written a most abusive memo in reply to [Dill's] memorandum". On 26 August 1942, he apologised for his own rudeness, "I am afraid I was rather rude to all members of the COS". On 28 June 1944, "the American reply to our wire arrived, a rude one at that!!" On 6 July 1944, Churchill was infuriated "more than ever and he became ruder and ruder." On 19 July 1944, Churchill had drafted a "foul letter" which was "most offensively worded". On 4 December 1944, he persuaded Churchill to "withdraw an offensive minute he had written to me" and 1 April 1945 saw another "rather rude message" from the Americans.

Yet the same man who disliked rudeness expressed trenchant opinions that were tantamount to rudeness. Haining, Pound, Elliot and Hartle were dismissed as "useless" on 13 February 1941, 3 March 1941, 28 August 1941 and 15 October 1942. Page had "the mentality of a greengrocer" on 19 December 1941, Pile was "a repulsive creature" on 14 July 1942 and Hore-Belisha was "greasy and objectionable" on 24 February 1943. Herein lay the second contradiction in Alanbrooke.

The sixth attribute was self-assurance. On 20 January 1944, two days before the Anzio landings in Italy, "It may fail but I know it was the right thing to do". On 14 June 1940, he told Dill "there was only one course open to us, namely re-embark the BEF as quickly as possible" and over the next six days he never entertained the slightest doubt over that decision. This self-assurance was apparent in his Notes in mid-January 1941, "I was criticized by many for [appointing Budget Loyd as my chief of staff] owing to the fact that Budget had had a nervous breakdown... [I] felt sure that Budget would not break down with me and that he would fill the job admirably." On 16 December 1942, the chiefs of staff met Churchill to decide strategy for 1943, "I feared the worst!! However, meeting went well from the start and I succeeded in swinging [Churchill] round": for Alanbrooke, it was now just a case of persuading others to agree with his views, "I think he is now fairly safe, but I have still the Americans to convince first and then Stalin next!!"

This self-assurance has fuelled the claim that Alanbrooke was self-opinionated – convinced that his own views were correct, he dismissed the views held by other people out of hand. The evidence in support of this claim appears compelling. On 20 November 1943, "I despair of ever getting our American friends to have any sort of strategic vision... I blame myself for having had the vision to foresee these possibilities and yet to have failed to overcome the American shortsightedness and allowed my better judgement to have been affected by them." On 10 May 1943, he was en route to the Washington conference, "it is not sufficient to see something clearly. You have got to try and convince countless people as to where the truth lies when they don't want to be acquainted with that fact" and on 1 November 1943, "When I look at the Mediterranean, I realize only too well how far I have failed in my task during the last 2 years! If only I had had sufficient force of character to swing those American Chiefs of Staff and make them see daylight, how different the war might be".

Three factors tend to support this claim. First, Alanbrooke was forthright and forceful. Second, he was reluctant to compromise: in his Notes, 18 January 1943, "[Dill asked] me how far I would go to get agreement... I replied that I would not move an inch". Compromise was unpalatable to Alanbrooke but on 23 August 1943 he reluctantly acknowledged it was unavoidable, "I am not really satisfied with the results, we have not really arrived at the best strategy but I suppose that, when working with allies, compromises, with all their evils, become inevitable." However, by 20 November 1943, he regretted having done so, "It would have been better to have resigned my appointment than to allow any form of compromise." Third, he was completely unmoved if discussions with the Americans descended into violent disagreement. His matter-of-fact descriptions of these disagreements suggest they were just water off a duck's back to him. The highly acrimonious meeting on 23 November 1943 was, in Alanbrooke's words, "somewhat heated" and three days later he blithely recorded, "It was not long before Marshall and I had the father and mother of a row".

Yet, there is clear evidence which rebuts this claim. His remark on 10 July 1943, the day of the invasion of Sicily, was hardly that of a man convinced of the correctness of his own views, "It took a lot of will power to keep on with the Sicily objective. And now it remains to prove that I was right or wrong!?!" In similar vein were his remarks on 14 January 1940 "We may or may not have been right", on 11 February 1942 "I wonder if I was right?", on 24 August 1942 "I pray God that the decisions we arrived at may be correct" and on 23 June 1943 "I hope that we may have been right." When he vacated his London flat in May 1946, he recalled the "many solitary hours when I communed with myself and wondered how correct I was in the policies I was pursuing."

The claim is also undermined by the fact that Alanbrooke was plagued by doubts, worries and misgivings. On 29 July 1941, he was fretting about "all the worries and doubts which endeavour to swamp one's mind and are not always easy to keep down. Those horrible question marks which seem to be everywhere at times! Have I really taken the proper dispositions for the defence of this country?" 20 October 1940 was the end of "a week of worries, responsibilities, doubts as to whether I am doing all I can". On 16 November 1941, when he was asked to replace Dill as CIGS, he had "doubts whether I shall be able to compete with [the job]… the consequences of failures or mistakes are a nightmare to think about." 1 January 1943 saw him reflecting on the previous twelve months, "Horrible doubts, horrible nightmares which grew larger and larger as the days went on". On 15 August 1945, he recalled the "nerve-wracking anxiety" of the previous six years and in May 1946 he remembered "those horrible wakeful moments in the early hours when… doubts swamp one's confidence".

As an aside, Alanbrooke went to great lengths to conceal his doubts, worries and misgivings. On 27 May 1944, he explained why, "The hardest part of bearing such responsibility is pretending that you are absolutely confident of success when you are really torn to shreds with doubts and misgivings! But when once decisions are taken, the time for doubts is gone and what is required is to breathe the confidence of success into all those around." He made the same point much earlier on 15 September 1940. These two entries explain General Blacker's remark that "he was one of those whose brief presence was sufficient to make one perfectly sure that all would come right in the end."[8]

The claim is further undermined by his willingness to adopt the ideas and advice offered by others: self-opinionated people tend to have closed minds, but Alanbrooke had an open and enquiring mind. On 27 July 1943, he was dealing with the tricky issue of General McNaughton, "Stewart, the Canadian CGS, came to see me. He suggested splitting the Canadian force between Home and Mediterranean so as to dispose of McNaughton as an Army Commander! He is right. It is the only way to save the outfit." On 26 November 1940, someone else was "right", "Lord Trenchard came… to discuss with me steps he was taking to rehabilitate the army in the eyes of the country. He is quite right: it has become far too much a habit to run down generals and the army in the press". On 27 June 1944, yet another person was "right", "interview [with] Alan Cunningham over from Ireland who considers garrison might be reduced now. He is right and I must find some new home for him." On 19 March 1942, he met Lord Milne, the former CIGS, whose "advice on all matters is most valuable." On 7 January 1944, Amery was "more mountain warfare minded than ever! He would almost convert the whole army in Italy into mountaineers! However, there is a great deal in what he says".

Alanbrooke's open and enquiring mind was apparent in his reaction to the rumours that Montgomery was being overcautious in his pursuit of Rommel's forces in late 1942. Given his high opinion of Montgomery, he might have been inclined to ignore these rumours but, instead, he investigated them. On 15 December 1942, "I had a long talk with [Casey]… Probed him as to the rumours of Monty being sticky in his pursuit." It was also apparent when, on 12 June 1945, he revised his opinion of Eisenhower, "I had never realized that Ike was as big a man until I heard his performance today!"

It was his open and enquiring mind which prompted him to philosophise. On 23 October 1944, following his return from Moscow, "I am very glad to have been back to Russia again, it is a country with much food for thought. One more of those vast experiments which humanity periodically carries out throughout the annals of history. Experiments which lead to much bloodshed... and finally... some progress. In my mind Bolshevism, Nazism, Fascism, etc., all have their purpose; they all turn the wheel of destiny one or two more cogs forward. Forward towards the path of general progress." Alanbrooke was interested in "progress". On 13 April 1944, the Lethbridge committee reported their findings on the war against Japan, "Their report is very good and provides much food for thought and progress". 19 October 1940 saw him philosophising about the futility of war, "And yet through all its destruction, uselessness and havoc, I can see some progress. Progress that could never be achieved without the upheaval of war. Long-standing institutions and social distinctions are shattered by war and make room for more modern methods of life. Those that would never release what they hold in peace are forced to do so in war, to the benefit of the multitude."

Richard Casey provided one of the more perceptive assessments of Alanbrooke when he described him as "a man of unusual quality and intensity".[9] Casey was right: there was an "unusual... intensity" about Alanbrooke which ran like a thread through his character, shaping his actions, feelings, thoughts, beliefs and behaviour. It could be seen in his relationship with the perfect mother, in his feelings for Benita, in his relationship with Churchill and in his reaction to the deaths of Janey in 1925 and Barney Charlesworth in 1945. It was this intensity which explained his "restless energy", his inability to control his emotions in public, his loss of temper and his fast speech. Ian Jacob observed, "I have never met a man who so tumbles over himself in speaking... He cannot make his brain move slowly enough to fit his speech or his reading, especially when his interest is strongly engaged."[10] And it was this same intensity which explained his seemingly dogmatic views and the forceful way he expressed them. Alanbrooke undoubtedly appeared to be self-opinionated but that was a misleading impression: in truth, he was just "a man of unusual… intensity."

The seventh attribute was an acute awareness of the weight of his responsibilities. 31 December 1940 saw him reflecting, "Personally, I feel that it is the year of my life in which I have had to shoulder the heaviest burdens and face the greatest responsibilities." On 19 July 1940, he was appointed Commander-in-Chief, Home Forces, "I find it hard to realize fully the responsibility that I am assuming… The idea of failure at this stage of the war is too ghastly to contemplate." On 8 September 1940, he was fearing a German invasion, "The responsibility of feeling what any mistakes or misappreciations may mean in the future of these Isles and of the Empire is a colossal one! And one which rather staggers me at times." On 19 November 1941, following his appointment as CIGS, he felt a "ghastly responsibility hanging as a black thunder cloud over me" and on 27 May 1944, he was "longing for a rest of a few hours from continual war responsibility."

He felt the weight of his responsibilities even more acutely at the start of operations which he had advocated. 10 July 1943 saw the invasion of Sicily, "Few people, if any, realize what the weight of responsibility of this attack is like! I feel specially responsible". On 20 January 1944, two days before the Anzio landings in Italy, "Oh! How I hope that the Rome amphibious operation will be a success! I feel a special responsibility for it [since I] have resuscitated it after my visit to Italy and found things stagnating there." Herein lay the third contradiction in Alanbrooke: behind his self-assurance was a man acutely conscious of the weight of his responsibilities and, furthermore, plagued by doubts, worries and misgivings.

It is noticeable how often Alanbrooke invoked God's assistance in his diary. On 1 January 1942, "I pray God that He may give me sufficient strength to devote the energy and drive that [the next year] will require" and on 1 January 1943, "I pray God that He may go on giving me the help he has given me during the last year."

Was Alanbrooke religious? These two entries would suggest he was, yet in his Notes, 16 November 1941, he admitted "I am not an exceptionally religious person" and on 8 May 1945, "I am not a highly religious individual according to many people's outlook. I am however convinced that there is a God all powerful looking after the destiny of this world." In an early section of his Notes, when recalling his time in India in the early 1900s, "I have certainly obtained more religious and spiritual help throughout my life by close contacts with nature and all its beauties and wonderful conceptions than through books or my contacts with churches and clergy." This suggests that whilst not religious in the conventional sense, he did believe there was a God or Maker since this explained how nature came to be created. His 29 June 1944 entry tends to support this, "This evening I… went to Kew Gardens. It was lovely and peaceful there, I felt it was just what I wanted… Kew Gardens and contact with God through nature put all at rest again. There are times when I feel that I just can't stand one more day of this job and the burdens of responsibility which it means. On those occasions, contact with nature has a wonderfully strengthening effect."

An alternative explanation is that he chose to refer to God because the person for whom he wrote his diary, Benita, was religious in the conventional sense. On 3 September 1940, "I do thank Him for having allowed me to meet you and through you to be able to get closer to Him", on 22 September 1940 "Then went home, where I found you all singing hymns" and on 31 December 1940 he referred to "your sublime… confidence in God".

The eighth attribute was sensitivity. For a man famed for his "abrupt efficiency",[11] Alanbrooke was, paradoxically, a remarkably sensitive man: this attribute may explain why he was acutely aware of the weight of his responsibilities. On 16 November 1941, he was invited to replace Dill as CIGS, "I hated the thought of what this would mean for [Dill]." Likewise, when Churchill demanded Neil Ritchie's removal from command of Eighth Army on 22 June 1942, "I… hate to think of the disappointment this will mean to him". On 6 August 1942, he turned down Churchill's offer of command in the Middle East, "I could not bear the thought that Auchinleck might think that I had come out here on purpose to work myself into his shoes!" On 31 August 1942, "Unsatisfactory COS at which I bit First Sea Lord and felt depressed rest of day at having bitten a corpse": for "depressed", read guilty. On 30 October 1942, "You and the children came to lunch and we went to the Academy to see my portrait by Birley. I am afraid it was a boring afternoon for Miss Pooks and Mr Ti, but I had two very deliciously clammy little hands grasping my hands tightly as we walked through the rooms, and I could feel tiny electric impulses registered through those dear hands that they felt they were not in an altogether friendly atmosphere!"

On 19 June 1944, he learnt that 60 people had been killed by a German pilotless plane, "Amongst them to my great grief Ivan Cobbold! And on my writing table was a letter from him written Saturday… asking me to lunch this week! It all gave me a very nasty turn and I cannot get him and poor Blanche out of my mind": eleven days later, "I do not remember going to a memorial service that upset me more, I miss him most awfully." The death of Barney Charlesworth produced a similar reaction. On 7 February 1945, "This conference has been a nightmare with his loss hanging over me the whole time. I do so funk the thought of returning to the flat [in London] and realizing more than ever that he is gone!": three days later, he flew to Malta, "I went straight to the cemetery where Barney had been buried and laid a wreath on his grave… My last words to Barney were haunting me, as I left Northolt ahead of him I had said 'Well, we shall meet in Malta.'"

This sensitivity was evident in his descriptions of difficult interviews with colleagues: he clearly disliked having to convey disappointing news to them. A very good example occurred on 18 December 1942, "interview with old [illegible] to tell him he was getting too old for the job, he took it very well, but the sort of interview that makes me almost sick before starting them!" There were numerous other instances. 9 July 1943 saw "an unpleasant kind of interview which I dislike intensely." On 20 June 1944 he told Laurence Carr that "his soldiering days had come to an end, I hated doing it and have a very special feeling for him" and on the following day he had "the unpleasant job of telling Martel that his soldiering days were over." Further examples occurred on 18 November 1939, 19 August 1940, 15 April 1941, 12 December 1941, 10 March 1942 and 30 December 1942.

It was also evident in the concern he showed as to how his colleagues reacted in these difficult interviews. After ticking off Montgomery for his VD circular on 23 November 1939, "he took it wonderfully well." On 18 August 1942, he met Auchinleck following the latter's removal from command in the Middle East, "Did not look forward to this interview, but… the interview went off well. We parted on friendly terms." On 26 February 1943, he "told [Browning] off for causing troubles by writing letters to politicians, he took it very well." On 2 November 1943, he disagreed with a report prepared by the Joint Intelligence Committee, "They did not like this and consequently I am very unpopular with them now." On 20 November 1944, he informed Browning that he was to become Mountbatten's chief of staff, "he took it well but I doubt whether in his heart of hearts he was thrilled." Further examples occurred on 4 and 18 January 1944.

Yet, Alanbrooke could be abrasive. In his Notes, he recounted his conversation with Marshall at the May 1943 Washington conference, "Marshall said to me, 'I find it very hard even now not to look on your North African strategy with a jaundiced eye!!' I replied, 'What strategy would you have preferred?' To which he answered, 'Cross channel operations for the liberation of France and advance on Germany, we should finish the war quicker.' I remember replying, 'Yes, probably, but not the way we hope to finish it!'" On 9 February 1945, "I told [Alexander] that at times I had grave doubts as to who was Supreme Commander, he or Macmillan! He took it very well". Herein lay the fourth contradiction in Alanbrooke: behind his abrasiveness was a remarkably sensitive man.

The ninth attribute was a sense of fairness and consideration for other people. In 1939, Alanbrooke thought it unfair that his volunteer troops in the Anti-Aircraft Corps were "being required to honour a liability for which they did not contract." On 26 November 1939, he inspected a British battalion recently arrived in France, "It is totally unfit for war in every respect… I told [Hore-Belisha] that I considered [sending it out in such a state] was neither fair to the units, the BEF or our allies, the French." On 16 January 1940, he "inspected the Indian Mule Company to find they were badly housed, huts unfinished, no glass in windows, stove pipes missing and no palliasses to sleep on. Administered a few 'bites' [reprimands] and hope situation will improve shortly."

On 9 July 1942, after Churchill ordered the Canadian, General McNaughton, to examine the capture of north Norway, an operation previously rejected by the British chiefs of staff, "I... informed [McNaughton] privately how matters stood as I did not want him afterwards to imagine that we were suggesting that the Canadians should undertake an operation which we considered impracticable." On 15 July 1942, he interviewed Ritchie following the latter's removal from command: in his Notes, "I told him that I considered that he had been pushed on much too fast by Auchinleck, to be put in command of 8th Army in the field when he had never even commanded a division in action. I told him he must regain confidence in himself... [and when he had done so], I would give him a Corps. This is just what happened." On 17 January 1944, "[Churchill] also has some idea of kicking Giffard out without any reasonable grounds" and on 22 November 1944 Giffard "poured his heart out to me about his treatment by Dickie Mountbatten and, as I thought, he was given a very raw deal". On 13 February 1945, Rollie Charrington offered to replace Barney Charlesworth, "I should love to have him but wonder whether he would be happy with it": five days later, he accepted his offer "on the understanding that either of us can finish the agreement at any time." In October 1945, he visited Churchill prior to departing on his world trip, "I felt he might be hurt if I started for Far East without visiting him." Further examples occurred on 11 February 1940, 17 November 1941, 7 December 1941, 24 April 1942, 2 February 1945, 16 February 1945 and 19 June 1945.

Herein lay the fifth contradiction in Alanbrooke: behind the daunting, formidable figure with the forthright and abrupt manner was a man with a sense of fairness who was considerate of others.

The final attribute was impatience. Alanbrooke could be easily irritated, especially by those who were slow, wasted time or lacked clarity of thought and speech. On 1 December 1941, "Dudley Pound the slowest Chairman I have ever seen" and on 2 April 1942 "[Pound] is always lagging about 5 laps behind even when he is not sound asleep". 23 October 1942 saw future strategy being debated, "Mountbatten's half-baked thoughts thrown into the discussion certainly don't assist" and on 6 January 1943, Mountbatten was "as usual, confused in his facts and figures". Two days later, "One of those awful COS meetings where Mountbatten and Dudley Pound drive me completely to desperation. The former is quite irresponsible, suffers from the most desperate illogical brain, always producing red herrings, the latter is asleep 90% of the time and the remaining 10% is none too sure what he is arguing about": as an aside, his 8 August 1945 entry hinted that he may have carried Mountbatten during the War, "As usual, [Mountbatten] wanted me to pull the chestnuts out of the fire for him and expected me to tackle First Sea Lord to draw aircraft carrier from the Pacific Fleet for his purposes! I called his bluff and told him to do his own dirty work."

Yet, Alanbrooke displayed remarkable patience in his relationship and dealings with Churchill. After their clash over Norway in October 1941, he tolerated Churchill's flaws, abuse, sarcasm, indecision and ramblings for almost four years: as he noted, somewhat belatedly, on 21 June 1944, "It is hard to keep one's patience on these occasions" and on 28 July 1944, "I remain very fond of him but by heaven he does try one's patience." On 8 October 1943, "I am afraid matters will go on deteriorating rather than improving. If they do, I shall not be able to stick it much longer". Yet, Alanbrooke 'stuck it' for almost two more years. On 19 January 1944, "I don't think I can stand much more of it. We waffled about with all the usual criticisms, all the usual optimist's plans, no long-term vision and we settled nothing... My God how tired I am of working for him! I had not fully realized how awful it is until I suddenly found myself thrown into it again after a rest". On 10 September 1944, "He knows no details, has only got half the picture in his mind, talks absurdities and makes my blood boil to listen to his nonsense. I find it hard to remain civil" and on 29 March 1945, "I feel that I just can't stick another moment with him and would give almost anything never to see him again!"

He displayed a similar level of patience with Montgomery. On 10 March 1944, "He is making good headway in making plans, and equally successful in making enemies as far as I can see! I have to spend a great deal of my time soothing off some of these troubles." Montgomery was a constant source of trouble for Alanbrooke throughout the War, well illustrated by the number of tickings-off he received. The first, on 23 November 1939, was followed by others on 3 June 1943 and 24 January 1944. On 28 February 1944, the long-suffering and exasperated Alanbrooke remarked, "Shall have to have him up again and kick his backside again" and on 25 May 1944, "I had to tell him off and ask him to concentrate more on his own job and not meddle himself in everybody else's affairs." After the War, Montgomery acknowledged Alanbrooke's patience, "there have been moments when I have gone 'off the rails'… You always pulled me back on to the rails, and I started off down the course again. I know very well that when I used to go 'off the rails', it increased your own work and anxieties 100 per cent. But you never complained." Herein lay the sixth contradiction in Alanbrooke: behind his impatience was a remarkably patient man.

These were not the only contradictions. Behind all his criticisms of Churchill was a man "spellbound"[12] by his political master. Behind his "abrupt efficiency"[13] and steely determination and resolve was a man who needed, and relied upon, the support of Benita. Finally, and perhaps most contradictory of all, behind the professional head of the British Army who injected energy and drive into the national war effort and single-mindedly dedicated himself to the task of winning the War was a man who held an intense dislike of war, convinced it was utterly futile.

There are three descriptions of Alanbrooke which suggest the most likely explanation for these contradictions. According to Lieutenant General Horrocks, "We regarded him as a highly efficient military machine. It is only since I have read his diaries that I appreciate what a consummate actor he must have been. Behind the confident mask was the sensitive nature of a man who hated war, the family man-cum-birdwatcher in fact."[14] According to Joan Bright Astley, Pug Ismay's assistant, "As he ate toast with caviar and drank Russian tea laced with vodka, he teased and talked and laughed. After a morning or two of silent surprise we realised that instead of a formidable and distant figure, we had with us a delightful, amusing and easy companion who treated us with equal and courteous attention".[15] According to Montgomery, the incident when Alanbrooke broke down and wept in the sandhills at Dunkirk was "one which will remain with me all my life. I was allowed to see the real Brookie."[16]

All three observers were making the same point. Behind the professional soldier, or in their words the "military machine" and "formidable and distant figure", there lay another Alanbrooke: "the real Brookie", according to Montgomery. It was the ever-observant Lord Moran who accurately identified this alter ego in Alanbrooke when he described him as "a simple, gentle, selfless soul – a warning to us all not to give up hope about mankind."[17]

There were two Alanbrookes – the professional soldier and the simple, gentle, selfless soul – and the contradictions in his character were explained by the markedly different nature of those two personas. The professional soldier was perfectly willing, if necessary, to scheme in a way which bordered on sharp practice: in contrast, the simple, gentle, selfless soul deplored sharp practice. The professional soldier voiced trenchant opinions of others which were tantamount to rudeness: in contrast, the simple, gentle, selfless soul disliked rudeness. The professional soldier was self-assured, breathing confidence into those around him: in contrast, the simple, gentle, selfless soul was acutely conscious of the weight of his responsibilities and plagued by doubts, worries and misgivings. The professional soldier could be abrasive: in contrast, the simple, gentle, selfless soul was sensitive. The professional soldier was the daunting, formidable figure with the forthright and abrupt manner: in contrast, the simple, gentle, selfless soul possessed a sense of fairness and was considerate of others. The professional soldier was impatient: in contrast, the simple, gentle, selfless soul was remarkably patient.

It was the professional soldier who criticised Churchill and was "exasperated"[18] by him: in contrast, it was the simple, gentle, selfless soul who was "spellbound"[19] by his political master. It was the professional soldier who displayed "abrupt efficiency"[20] and steely determination and resolve: in contrast, it was the simple, gentle, selfless soul who needed, and relied upon, the support of Benita. And it was the professional soldier who injected energy and drive into the British war effort and single-mindedly dedicated himself to the task of winning the War: in contrast, it was the simple, gentle, selfless soul who held an intense dislike of war, convinced it was utterly futile.

Of his two thousand or so diary entries, there is one – 11 November 1939 – which perfectly captured these two personas in Alanbrooke. The first paragraph, written by the professional soldier, provided a crisp, factual record of the events at the armistice ceremony which he attended. The second, written by the simple, gentle, selfless soul, described his innermost feelings. The contrast in tone, style and language is such they could have been written by two different people,

> *The suspense continues, more threats to Belgium and Holland, but no further moves on the part of the Germans. This morning I took part in an Armistice ceremony at the Canadian Memorial at Vimy Ridge. We had two guards of honour, a French one formed by the 51st Division and a British one from the Black Watch. General Pagezy came from Lille for the ceremony. He and I laid wreaths of poppies on the Memorial, the French guard then presented arms whilst their bugles sounded a 'Sonnerie', this was followed by the Black Watch guard presenting arms whilst their pipers played the 'Flowers of the Forest'. The ceremony ended with inspection of each other's guards and by a march past of the guards.*
>
> *I felt throughout the ceremony as if I were in a dream. The white tall pillars of the monument standing out against the ashy grey sky seemed entirely detached from this earth, whilst the two red wreaths of poppies looked like two small drops of blood on that vast monument. They served as a vivid reminder of the floods of blood that had already been spilt on the very ground we were standing, and of the futility of again causing such bloodshed. I suppose that it is through such punishments that we shall eventually learn to 'love our neighbours as ourselves'.*

Alanbrooke's two personas could also be seen in his markedly different reactions to Auchinleck's removal from the Middle East command. 17 August 1942 saw the professional soldier's reaction,

> "The more I look back at our decision to get rid of Auchinleck, the more convinced I am that we are correct."

27 January 1943 saw the simple, gentle, selfless soul's reaction,

> "Being back here [in Cairo] reminds me the whole time of that nightmare of a first week last August with all the unpleasantness of pushing Auchinleck out and reconstituting the command and staff of the Middle East. Thank heaven that is all over now and this visit is consequently much more pleasant."

In similar vein was his contrasting treatment of another British commander, Kenneth Anderson. 21 February 1943 saw the professional soldier,

> "I am afraid… that Anderson is not much good! Sent wire to Alex telling him to get rid of him if he thinks he is no good."

18 January 1944 saw the simple, gentle, selfless soul,

> "Then a sad interview with Kenneth Anderson to tell him he would not be commanding the 2nd Army in the forthcoming offensive… he took it very well."

18 June 1945 saw the professional soldier dealing with Oliver Leese, commander of Allied land forces in South East Asia,

> "Drafted letter to Mountbatten advising him to get rid of Oliver Leese who has proved to be a failure".

10 July 1945 saw the simple, gentle, selfless soul dealing with Leese, after he had been removed from command,

> "Poor Oliver Leese came to see me… very sad and repentant. He took it all wonderfully well. Ready to go back to private life or any lower rank… shall have a difficult job to find employment for him."

Both personas appeared in his 31 January 1945 entry. The professional soldier was roughing up Alexander, the newly appointed supreme commander of the Mediterranean, much to the dislike of the simple, gentle, selfless soul,

> "I had a long and useful interview with Alex... told him that some of us had doubts as to whether Macmillan or Alexander was Supreme Commander of Mediterranean! This had, I think, the required effect. But, my God, how I loathe being unpleasant in this way."

They also appeared in his 16 November 1939 entry. As the professional soldier interviewed the officers under his command, the simple, gentle, selfless soul harboured the "terrible feeling" and "haunting thought",

> "In every case interviewed all the officers and had a few words with them. While talking to them, I always have the terrible feeling that I may at one time or another be instrumental towards the issue of orders that may mean death to them. It is I think one of the most trying sides of commanding in war, the haunting thought that you may at any time be forced to issue orders that mean probable death to your friends."

23 February 1942 saw two markedly different reactions to Margesson's removal as Secretary of State for War. The professional soldier thought it would "make for efficiency" whereas the simple, gentle, selfless soul was "sorry to see [him] go",

> "Then went to say goodbye to Margesson who has been replaced by James Grigg. A good change which will make for efficiency, but I was sorry to see Margesson go as he seemed so very upset and took it so well."

On 25 February 1944, Alanbrooke spent "7½ hours with Winston and most of that time engaged in heavy argument." That night, the professional soldier wrote a long, highly critical entry, but it was the simple, gentle, selfless soul who penned the final sentence,

> "I think that a great deal of what we have been doing has soaked

in [to Churchill]. I hope so at least as I don't want another day like today!"

On 10 July 1944, the simple, gentle, selfless soul was concerned as to how his alter ego may react in a meeting with Churchill later that night,

"I only hope I shall not lose my temper with him this time."

On 8 September 1944, the professional soldier was struggling to contain his temper with Churchill whilst the simple, gentle, selfless soul just felt "frightfully sorry" for him,

"[Churchill] was quite impossible to work with... According to him... we also suggested moving troops from Europe for Burma and had never told him that the removal of these forces was dependent on the defeat of Hitler (a completely false accusation). He further said that we had told him only one division was required for Burma, and now we spoke of 5! (Here again a complete misstatement of facts). It was hard to keep one's temper with him, but I could not help feeling frightfully sorry for him. He gave me the feeling of a man who is finished, can no longer keep a grip of things and is beginning to realize it."

On 20 January 1945, the professional soldier kept an eye on the progress of the War, as the simple, gentle, selfless soul worked on his bird books,

"Arrived home for late lunch and spent afternoon gumming in book plates in my bird books. Wonderful news from Russia continues to come in."

These were not the only instances in the diary when the simple, gentle, selfless soul peeked out from behind the professional soldier. On 3 March 1940, "At dinner this evening, I had the fun of hearing my own voice on the wireless on the evening news delivering a bit of my French speech and I wondered whether you were also listening, and hoped you were." 29 August 1944 saw "a murky fly home through clouds reaching Hendon at 7.45pm, having lost my escort of 3 fighters in the clouds. I hope they returned safely." On 22 February 1945, he spent a "very trying hour" listening to the "terribly distressed" Polish commander, General Anders, "I felt most awfully sorry for him... He is to see Winston again next Wednesday and then he is to see me afterwards. I shudder at the thought of this next interview". On 12.3.45, "It is sad that this date will not return for another 100 years! It looks so nice." On 23 March 1945, he was at Montgomery's HQ to watch Allied forces cross the Rhine, "I am now off to bed. It is hard to realize that within some 15 miles hundreds of men are engaged in death struggles along the banks of the Rhine, whilst hundreds more are keying themselves up to stand up to one of the greatest trials of their life! With that thought in one's mind, it is not easy to lie down to try and sleep peacefully!"

Alanbrooke's love of nature and his hobbies of fishing, birdwatching and photography were manifestations of his simple, gentle, selfless soul. On 16 April 1940, "I went for a walk in the woods nearby and imagined you were at my side. We discussed the lovely carpet of anemones and all the nice green young shoots. In the garden, M. Rosette has found a blackbird's nest that I am watching. I wish I could take photographs of it." On 24 January 1943, at Casablanca, he spent the afternoon "looking for birds in the lovely garden of the hotel and found several very interesting specimens. It is great fun identifying the European specimens in the form of some sub-species with minor variations." On 31 May 1943, in north Africa, "We found [the 51st Division] in a lovely bit of country just east of Bougie. I had no conception that North Africa could be so beautiful. Lovely cork tree forests with carpets of spring flowers, golden field of calendulas, hedges covered with convolvulus and lovely green fields leading to tree-covered hills on one side and to a lovely blue Mediterranean on the other. A lovely place to rest a war-weary division." On 2 August 1944, "I picked up Rollie at 6pm and we went down to Kew Gardens again, it was lovely down there. We sat on a seat and watched some young water hens being instructed by their mother as to how a bath should be taken! She gave a demonstration first and then those tiny mites followed suit and copied her, a wonderful sight."

The simple, gentle, selfless soul in Alanbrooke manifested itself in other ways. First, he enjoyed carrying out mundane tasks at home.

On 29 September 1940, he was "sawing wood and just basking in the sunshine of happiness spread by the presence of you and the wee ones". Christmas Eve 1940 was "a lovely evening preparing stockings for children". 4 October 1942 was "a lovely day, spent in collecting apples". On 11 July 1943, he was "moving bookcases and working hard at repairing the Pook's goat cart." On 9 May 1945, he and Benita spent a "happy… afternoon together looking after goats and chickens". Three days later, he spent the morning "mending an old rabbit hutch!"

Second, he derived great satisfaction from calculating the distances that he travelled. On 22 July 1941, "Have now been C-in-C Home Forces for 1 year and 2 days. Have flown just under 14,000 miles during that period and motored some 35,000 miles in my own car. As I have certainly done at least as much in other people's cars… my total road mileage must be somewhere near 70,000 miles in the year." Further examples occurred on 24 August 1942, 7 February 1943 and 22 October 1944.

Third, he could be easily 'thrilled'. On 17 August 1942, "I went up into the second pilot's seat after we had taken off… I was able to see the whole Dead Sea from end to end, Jerusalem, Bethlehem and Hebron all at the same time. It was a thrilling sight." On 28 August 1943, he flew back to Britain from America, "It is now my third trip in this direction, but it still has the same thrill as the first crossing". On 7 February 1945, he was "thrilled" when he visited the Crimean battlefields. After the War, when his car was chased by a rhinoceros during his visit to a Kenyan game reserve, "It was a thrilling moment".

The fourth was his lack of ambition. His sister, Hylda Wrench, remarked that "he did not seem to have any ambition" and Lord Moran observed he was "without ambition".[21] This lack of ambition was evident in his reaction on 16 July 1945 to the news that he had lost out to Alexander for the governor generalship of Canada, "A job I would have given a great deal for. However I agree that Alex is ideally suited for it and told the PM so… I remain with a few heartburns which I think Kipling's *If* has taught me by now to overcome."

The fifth was his dislike of anything "unpleasant": it is noticeable how often this adjective appears in his diary. On 2 February 1942, there were "most unpleasant remarks by various ministers", 24 July 1942 saw "an unpleasant reply" from Stalin, on 9 August 1942 Auchinleck was "in a highly stormy and rather unpleasant mood", 30 November 1942 saw him reflecting on his first year as CIGS, "At times life was most unpleasant" and 2 November 1944 saw an "unpleasant wire from Mountbatten". Further examples occurred on 19 August 1940, 1 April 1942, 18 August 1942, 27 January 1943, 9 July 1943, 21 June 1944 and 31 January 1945.

Sixth, he was publicity-shy and did not enjoy being the object of public scrutiny. On 24 March 1944, "Tomorrow, I have my Trafalgar Square speech to make, and I am not looking forward to it at all!": in his Notes, "Speaking in public had always frightened me and still frightens me now."

The seventh was his disdain for politicians and diplomats: politicians and their methods did not appeal to the simple, gentle, selfless soul at all. 25 November 1943 saw the delegations at the Cairo conference being photographed, "First of all the high and mighty: President, PM and Generalissimo. Then the above with Chiefs of Staff and Chinese Generals. Finally, the above with politicians and diplomats, etc. Not a very attractive lot to look at! I have no doubt that we were not much more beautiful in the military groups, but I pray to heaven that we may have been both individually and collectively less crooked!" On 22 November 1944, Duncan Sandys attended the COS meeting, "he does not improve on acquaintance, but no doubt possesses all the necessary qualities for a successful political career!" On 23 May 1945, "this is a political matter and politics are as crooked as rams' horns!"

The eighth was his dislike of insincerity and hypocrisy. On 11 September 1944, he attended a formal dinner in Quebec, "Bad speeches by Athlone and President full of worthless platitudes lacking any sincerity. Am I getting soured against humanity as a whole or am I right that such official banquets are the centres of the most ghastly hypocrisy!?" On 10 October 1944, he was in Moscow "listening to half-inebriated politicians and diplomats informing each other of their devotion and affection and expressing sentiments very far detached from veracity." And on 8 February 1945, at the Yalta conference, most of the speeches at the banquet "consisted of insincere, slimy sort of slush!"

Alanbrooke occasionally philosophised about war and how it could be avoided in the future: his antidote was always the same. On 8 May 1945,

> "The suffering and agony of war in my mind must exist to gradually educate us to the fundamental law of 'loving our neighbour as ourselves'. When that lesson has been learned, then war will cease to exist."

It was a delightfully simple, arguably naive, theory conceived by a simple, gentle, selfless soul.

TWENTY

Strategy

Five aspects of Anglo-American strategy are examined in this chapter but before doing so, there are two issues relating to Alanbrooke's first year as CIGS which warrant mention.

The first is that he struggled in the months following his appointment in December 1941 and the evidence for this claim is, ironically, provided by Alanbrooke himself: diaries can be very revealing. 30 November 1942 saw him reflecting on his first year, "I had only been in the saddle one week when Japan came into the war and by the end of the third week, I thought I was finished and that I could never compete with the job!" A few weeks later, 1 January 1943, "With 13 months of this job behind me I feel just a little more confident than I did in those awful early days when I felt completely lost and out of place." And on 8 May 1945, Victory in Europe Day, "I have often looked back… and thanked God for the way he… provided me with the help I had asked for and without which I should have floundered in the first year." Interestingly, Arthur Bryant did not include this 1 January 1943 entry in his books based on Alanbrooke's diary and whilst he did reproduce the long 8 May 1945 entry, he edited out the above section: his editing of the diary was selective.

Alanbrooke's first year can, broadly, be broken down into four phases, the first of which ran from December 1941 to March 1942. Japan's entry into the War, seven days after his appointment as CIGS, was hugely significant since it was bound to result in Britain suffering losses in the Far East, due to lack of resources. The next three months saw Alanbrooke overwhelmed by a tsunami of defeats as Hong Kong fell on 25 December

1941, closely followed by the fall of Malaya, Singapore and then Rangoon in Burma. With Britain also suffering setbacks in the Middle East, he came under acute pressure. On 2 February, "5pm Cabinet meeting. As usual most unpleasant remarks by various ministers in connection with defeats of our forces! As we had retired into Singapore Island… besides being pushed back in Libya, I had a good deal to account for!" According to Sir Alexander Cadogan, the British Army was "the mockery of the world"[1] and Alanbrooke, as its professional head, bore ultimate responsibility.

His 11 February entry captured the central theme of this first phase, "I certainly never expected that we should fall to pieces as fast as we are". By 31 March, "we have already lost a large proportion of the British Empire, and are on the high road to lose a great deal more of it… There are times when I wish to God I had not been placed at the helm of a ship that seems to be heading inevitably for the rocks."

The second phase ran from April to July 1942. During this period, Alanbrooke remained on the back foot as Britain 'hung on by its eyelids', to borrow one of his phrases. He had to contend with Burma, the Japanese threat in the Indian Ocean, Malta, mounting shipping losses, the growing clamour to open a second front in Europe, the surrender of Tobruk and Rommel's success in driving British forces back into Egypt. With Alanbrooke on the back foot, the initiative was seized by others: April saw the Americans table their proposals for cross-Channel operations and June saw Roosevelt and Churchill championing Operation Gymnast [Torch] at the Washington conference.

The third phase, August 1942, saw Alanbrooke 'gripping the show', to borrow another of his phrases. On 6 August, his use of "at last" is significant, "after working with the PM for close on 9 months, I do feel at last that I can exercise a limited amount of control on some of his activities and that at last he is beginning to take my advice." Admittedly, he did on the same day accede to Churchill's appointment of Gott as commander of the Eighth Army despite his own reservations, "Considering everything, this is perhaps the best solution. I accepted it", and in his Notes, "I may have been weak." However, when Gott was killed the following day, Alanbrooke refused to accede to Churchill's wishes again and seized the opportunity to instal Montgomery. Twelve days later, "[Montgomery]… gave me a wonderful feeling of relief at having got him out here."

The final phase, which ran from September to December 1942, saw Alanbrooke firmly in the saddle and taking charge: this is evident from the tone and content of his entries during this period which became far more assertive and definite. On 1 September, "It takes far more moral courage than anyone would believe to stick to one's plan and to refuse to be diverted." On 23 September, he "had a hammer and tongs argument" with Churchill. On 22 October, "I am only prepared to look on the bombing of Germany as one of the many ways by which we shall bring Germany to her knees." According to his Notes, 3 December, when Churchill claimed that "we" had promised Stalin a second front, he pulled Churchill up in front of two members of the war cabinet by replying "No, we did not promise".

It is a near certainty that whoever had been appointed CIGS in December 1941 would have fared no better in contending with the events that occurred in the first half of 1942. Moreover, the difficulties faced by Alanbrooke during this period were not of his own making. His observation on 12 February 1942 was more than justified, "We are paying very heavily now for failing to face the insurance premiums essential for security of an Empire! This has usually been the main cause for the loss of Empires in the past."

The second issue is that Alanbrooke is open to criticism on two matters. The first is irrefutable: he should have visited Egypt much earlier than August 1942. In January 1942, he was already concerned with the situation in Cairo and the handling of operations in the desert, well illustrated by his 21 January letter to Auchinleck and his 30 January entry, "The Benghazi business is bad and nothing less than bad generalship on the part of Auchinleck." He expressed further concern in his 5 February letter to Auchinleck and in his entries on 29 January, 4 February, 5 February and 24 March. Yet seven months elapsed between January and his eventual visit in August.

In his defence, it was probably impractical for Alanbrooke to be absent from London between December 1941 and February 1942 given the calamitous events in the Far East. Equally, he needed to be in London in April for the visit of Marshall and Hopkins and in Washington for the June conference. However, he could – and should – have visited Cairo much earlier than August since north Africa was a key theatre throughout this period. On 13 March 1942, "[Churchill]… would not agree to Auchinleck's suggestion that I should go out with [Portal]." That was a mistake: Alanbrooke should have insisted that he and Portal visit Cairo. As he later admitted on 23 August 1942, "I could never have put matters right [in Egypt] from a distance."

It is possible he knew by the summer of 1942 that he was at fault for not having visited Egypt. This would explain his violent reaction to the visit of Julian Amery on 3 July 1942, "a most objectionable young pup turned up who was Amery's son, just back from Cairo. He calmly said… that two things were necessary to secure the Middle East, first more equipment and secondly better morale… and that [raising morale] could only be done by the PM flying out to Egypt!! The cheek of the young brute was almost more than I could bear." In drawing attention to the problems in Egypt, Amery may have touched a raw nerve in Alanbrooke. Furthermore, when he addressed this issue in his Notes, 30 June 1942, he appeared distinctly defensive, "It is strange that I did not write more about my probable visit… This impending visit was so constantly in my thoughts that I may not ever have thought it necessary to refer to it in my diary": this explanation sounds weak and unconvincing. In a later section of his Notes, 15 July 1942, he claimed he was held back from visiting Cairo because of the difficulty in securing Churchill's permission: this also sounds unconvincing.

The second matter on which Alanbrooke is open to criticism is far more arguable: following Japan's entry into the War, should Burma have been reinforced at the expense of Singapore? On 17 December 1941, "Personally I do not feel that there is much hope of saving Singapore but feel that we ought to try and make certain of Burma" and in his Notes, 23 January 1942, he admitted, "I think we were wrong to send [18th Division] to Singapore and that it would have served a more useful purpose had it been sent to Rangoon."

Militarily, a strong case can be made out that Britain should have relinquished Singapore and concentrated its limited resources on defending Burma since the latter provided a first line of defence for India and a supply route to the Chinese nationalist forces. Given all the problems which the Burmese theatre caused in the War, hindsight suggests Alanbrooke should have been more vociferous in advocating this strategy. Politically, however, it was well-nigh impossible since such a course of action had potentially catastrophic ramifications in Britain and abroad, notably in Australia and New Zealand. It is, therefore, harsh to criticise him on what was, in truth, a real conundrum. Yet, the fact remains that Britain allowed itself to fall between the two stools of Singapore and Burma and ended up losing both.

This matter had echoes of an earlier incident in the War. When, in 1939, it was proposed the BEF should advance into Belgium in the event of a German invasion, Alanbrooke's instinct on 19 October 1939 was against the proposal. However, he relented when the alternative plan of advance was proposed on 19 November 1939 and 15 January 1940. Alanbrooke had a good instinct, probably derived from his good judgment, and he should, perhaps, have been more steadfast in following it.

The first of the five aspects of Anglo-American strategy is posed as a question – did a Mediterranean strategy exist in December 1941? The eminent British military historian, the late Professor Sir Michael Howard, has argued that the Mediterranean strategy was only conceived in late 1942 and emerged for the first time at the Casablanca conference in January 1943. The chiefs of staff did indeed draft their paper on future strategy during late 1942: on 30 October, "we finally finished off our policy for the conduct of the war in 1943". Furthermore, since this Mediterranean strategy formed one of the central planks of the British paper tabled at Casablanca, Professor Howard's argument appears compelling.

However, Alanbrooke's entry on 3 December 1941, his third day as CIGS, clearly suggests a Mediterranean strategy was already in existence by that date: it may not have been committed to paper, but it certainly existed in Alanbrooke's mind. It should be remembered that Japan and America had not entered the War by 3 December 1941:

> "COS meeting at 10.30 where Pug Ismay produced memo from PM to the effect that 18th and 50th Divs were to be offered to the Russians for their Southern front!... This would probably mean having to close down the Libyan offensive whereas I am positive that our policy for the conduct of the war should be to direct both our military and political efforts towards the early conquest of North Africa. From there we shall be able to reopen the Mediterranean and to stage offensive operations against Italy.
>
> Cabinet Defence Committee meeting at 5.30... Tried to begin to make them realize that we must have one definite policy for the conduct of the war. I must get the PM to see the advantages of a real North African offensive policy."

His use of "positive" regarding the policy which should be pursued is worth highlighting as is his use of "definite" and "real". In his Notes, "it was already clear to me that we must clear North Africa to open the Mediterranean and until we had done that we should never have enough shipping to stage major operations." For Alanbrooke, the key issue was the shortage of shipping, a subject to which he made frequent reference in his diary namely on 25 December 1941, 3, 4 and 10 February 1942, 15 September 1942, 30 November 1942, 2 March 1943, 15 April 1943, in early May 1943 during his journey to Washington and on 24 May 1943. His reasoning was that if the Mediterranean could be re-opened as a sea route, then one million tons of shipping would be freed up which would enable offensive operations to be launched "against Italy." However, re-opening the Mediterranean was dependent on the "early conquest of North Africa", hence the need for a "real North African offensive policy".

Moreover, there are later entries which are entirely consistent with what Alanbrooke wrote on 3 December 1941. On 20 December 1941,

> "My hopes of carrying on with the conquest and reclamation of North Africa are beginning to look more and more impossible every

day. From now on the Far East will make ever increasing inroads into our resources."

On 12 May 1943, five days after Tunis fell to the Allies, the "conquest of North Africa" was finally achieved,

> "At last the first stage of my proposed strategy accomplished in spite of all the various factors that have been trying to prevent it. I felt rather as if in a dream, to be there planning two stages ahead, with the first stage finished and accomplished."

On 2 June 1943, "since the start" is highly significant,

> "I have since the start and in spite of many tribulations aimed at 3 main points:
> a) Secure the whole of North Africa (which we have now done),
> b) Eliminate Italy (which we may hope to do before too long),
> c) Bring Turkey in (which must remain dependent on situation in Russia).
>
> If once we succeed in attaining these three points, a re-entry into France and a conclusion of the war should not be long delayed, all dependent on the situation in Russia".

And on 21 July 1945, after he inspected British troops in Berlin,

> "Here were British troops who had come from Egypt through North Africa and Italy to France (a real example of the strategy I had been working for) parading where masses of German forces had goosestepped in the past!"

If the Mediterranean strategy did exist in December 1941, then this does beg the question of why it spent almost a year in cold storage. The answer is that the outbreak of war in the Far East forced the strategy to be shelved: Alanbrooke's 20 December 1941 entry, quoted above, and his 24 December 1941 entry testify to this, "Auchinleck struggling along with the forces at his disposal… little knowing that his activities must shortly be curtailed".

The second aspect falls out of Roosevelt's remark to Churchill in December 1942, shortly before the Casablanca conference, "I am sure that both of us want to avoid the delays which attended the determination on Torch [Gymnast] last July".[2] Roosevelt's remark was more than justified: there had been "delays" and they were caused by a conspicuous lack of sound planning and open, honest debate between March and July 1942. The second aspect is that the formulation of Anglo-American strategy during this period was somewhat shambolic.

First, the process which led to the drafting and tabling of the Marshall Memorandum was rushed and ill-conceived. Eisenhower's paper recommending that American resources be concentrated on cross-Channel operations was approved on the same day it was submitted, 25 March 1942. Within two days, outline plans for those operations, later described as "a very simple sketch of the operations",[3] had been hastily prepared. The Americans then chose to bypass the Combined Chiefs of Staff organisation by presenting their proposals direct to the British Government. On 8 April, a mere fourteen days after Eisenhower submitted his paper, Marshall and Hopkins arrived in London to advocate these operations, despite no detailed planning or examination having been undertaken. It is possible their proposals were a reaction to the modest strategy agreed at the December 1941 Washington conference, "it does not seem likely that in 1942 any large-scale land offensive against Germany except on the Russian front will be possible",[4] since treading water was always likely to jar on the American psyche.

In effect, the Americans were signalling a statement of intent, 'this is what we want to do, let's now decide to do it and then examine whether it's feasible'. This approach was not devoid of merit but it did place the British in a quandary: should they express their reservations over the feasibility of the proposals frankly in which case America might withdraw from the Germany First principle and divert its forces to the Pacific, or suppress their reservations and endorse the proposals. Disingenuously, they chose the latter and, by doing so, sowed the seeds of distrust in the Anglo-American relationship.

Second, it was clear from the Marshall Memorandum that the key operation in the American proposals was Round-up, the 1943 cross-Channel invasion, and that Sledgehammer, the emergency 1942 cross-Channel operation, was only to be considered if Russia was collapsing or there was a severe deterioration in Germany's situation. Yet – somehow – Sledgehammer lost its emergency status and was allowed to acquire an importance that was unwarranted for such a questionable, arguably suicidal, operation. As a result, it not only became a time-consuming distraction but also tended to undermine the merits, such as they were, of Round-up: the demarcation line between the two operations became blurred.

Third, in late March, Roosevelt had approved the proposed cross-Channel operations which, in effect, ruled out launching any major operation in 1942 except, possibly, Sledgehammer. Yet, by the time of the Washington conference some ten weeks later, he was insistent that American troops must engage German forces in 1942. The most likely explanations for this volte-face are that either he changed his mind – there is some evidence that his approval was not whole-hearted – or had pinned his hopes on Sledgehammer being carried out in 1942 but, by June, realised this was not going to happen or his priorities had altered. Of these, the latter appears the most likely: mid-term elections were due in November, and he needed to justify the Germany First policy to the voters.

Fourth, after the British concluded that Sledgehammer was impractical, Mountbatten was despatched to America to inform Roosevelt of this decision. Within days of his return to Britain, Churchill and Alanbrooke then flew to Washington in June 1942 for a conference convened on short notice: according to Alanbrooke's 16 June Notes, "we were both somewhat doubtful why we were going [and]… what we should achieve while we were there". With Sledgehammer sidelined, Churchill and Roosevelt now resurrected Gymnast notwithstanding the agreement reached two months earlier regarding cross-Channel operations. Unsurprisingly, the outcome of the conference was a fudge – planning for cross-Channel operations was to continue whilst Gymnast was re-examined.

Fifth, believing the British to be lukewarm about their cross-Channel plans, Marshall and Stimson then proposed that America withdraw from the Germany First policy and concentrate its resources in the Pacific. After Roosevelt rejected this, he despatched Hopkins, Marshall and King to London in July, a mere twenty-three days after the Washington conference, with a presidential directive that agreement must be reached with the British which ensured that American troops engage German forces in 1942: on 15 July, Alanbrooke noted, "Hopkins is for operating in Africa, Marshall wants to operate in Europe and King is determined to strike in the Pacific!". Boxed in by Roosevelt's directive, Marshall advocated Sledgehammer and when the British rightly turned it down, Gymnast was selected.

It had taken almost five months and three conferences to make this decision. It could be argued that this is a good illustration of the difficulties which confront wartime allies when trying to agree a strategy or, alternatively, of Churchill's ability to win people round to his own view. Perhaps, but far more persuasive is the argument that the planning and formulation of strategy during this period was somewhat shambolic.

The third aspect is the role played by Roosevelt in determining the course of Anglo-American strategy in the War. On 18 May 1943, Alanbrooke observed, "the Americans are now taking up the attitude that we led them down the garden path taking them to North Africa!" In one sense, the Americans were right since they were steered towards north Africa in mid-1942 by Churchill and the British. In another sense, however, the Americans were wrong: they were taken to north Africa by their own president. It was Roosevelt who made the policy decision that American troops must engage German forces in 1942. It was Roosevelt who resurrected Gymnast just before the start of the Washington conference. It was Roosevelt who included his confidante Harry Hopkins in the American delegation sent to London in July 1942: Alanbrooke's 21 July entry was revealing, "I had to go back to 10 Downing Street. Both Eden and Hopkins there, I was not allowed to join them for fear that Marshall and King should hear of it and feel that I had been briefed by Hopkins against them according to President's wishes [Hopkins was in favour of "operating in Africa"]!!" It was Roosevelt who then steered his military advisors towards Gymnast: on 23 July, "Roosevelt had wired back accepting fact that western front in 1942 was off. Also that he was in favour of attack in North Africa and was influencing his Chiefs in that direction." And it was Roosevelt who, ultimately, made the decision to invade north-west Africa.

His decision was hugely significant because it triggered a chain reaction of events. If the Allies were victorious in north-west Africa, then it was inevitable that Roosevelt and Churchill would pressurise their military chiefs to launch new offensives as soon as possible: victory signalled that the Allies had seized the initiative in the War and lack of momentum meant loss of that initiative. Unsurprisingly, therefore, when it became clear on 12 May 1943 that victory was assured, Roosevelt and Churchill were exhorting their military chiefs to take the fight to the enemy: in Churchill's words, Allied forces "could not possibly stand idle".[5] With American and British armies now encamped in north-west Africa, where were they to be deployed next? Sicily beckoned since this reopened the Mediterranean as a sea route, thereby increasing Allied shipping stocks. And once Sicily was captured, then the case for some form of operations against mainland Italy became overwhelming, almost unarguable.

Roosevelt's decision was also significant because, as he had been warned by Marshall and Stimson, invading north-west Africa might result in the deferral of the 1943 cross-Channel invasion of Europe. Consequently, the Americans needed the campaign in north-west Africa to be short and swift to allow time to prepare for that invasion in the summer of 1943. Yet, they were uncharacteristically cautious in their choice of landing sites when planning Torch. In contrast, the British were far bolder, pressing for landing sites as far east inside the Mediterranean as was practicable with the intention of occupying "the key points of [Bizerta and Tunis] within 26 days of [the invasion fleets] passing Gibraltar and preferably within 14 days."[6] This American caution contributed to the campaign becoming protracted since Allied forces had to cover long distances over difficult terrain to reach those "key points". As a result, Eisenhower quickly became engulfed in supply and communication difficulties.

There were, admittedly, other reasons why the campaign became protracted, namely the speedy despatch of reinforcements to Tunisia by Germany and, to a lesser extent, bad weather. To these should be added, if Alanbrooke is to be believed, Eisenhower's poor handling of the Allied forces. On 24 November 1942, "Am still very worried by slow rate of progress in Tunisia" and in his Notes, "Eisenhower seemed to be unable to grasp [the] urgency of pushing on to Tunis before Germans built up their resistance there." By 28 December 1942, "Eisenhower as a general is hopeless!"

Roosevelt's decision to invade north-west Africa cast the die on the future course of Anglo-American strategy and furthermore, in terms of cause and effect, it was the combination of that decision and American caution in the planning stages of Torch which rendered a cross-Channel invasion in 1943 impossible.

The fourth aspect is the British attitude towards the cross-Channel invasion. It is not easy to form a definitive view of Churchill's attitude to it since pinning him down on this issue is akin to nailing jelly to a wall. In his 3 December 1942 paper to the chiefs of staff, he was clearly in favour of a 1943 invasion and thirteen days later he "was pressing for a western front in France [in 1943]". Yet, there is clear evidence that at other times he viewed the operation with foreboding.

As for Alanbrooke, it appears to have been a case of when, not if, to launch the invasion. On 24 May 1943, "success can only be secured by pressing operations in the Mediterranean to force a dispersal of German forces, help Russia and thus eventually produce a situation where cross-Channel operations are possible" and nine days later, "a re-entry into France and a conclusion of the war should not be long delayed, all dependent on the situation in Russia."

However, there are entries which suggest he had considerable misgivings about it. On 25 October 1943, he described it as "very problematical" and on 1 November 1943 he was complaining about having to withdraw forces from the Mediterranean for "a nebulous 2nd front". Furthermore, he displayed far more anxiety about Overlord than other major operations such as El Alamein, 23 October 1942, Torch,

7 November 1942, Sicily, 9 July 1943 and Italy, 8 September 1943 and 20 January 1944. On 27 May 1944, "I never want again to go through a time like the present one. The cross-Channel operation is just eating into my heart. I wish to God we could start and have done with it!!" and on the eve of Overlord, 5 June, "I am very uneasy about the whole operation… it may well be the most ghastly disaster of the whole war. I wish to God it were safely over." Given the magnitude and the significance of Overlord, his anxiety was perfectly understandable, but these entries hint that Alanbrooke had significant reservations about the operation. John Kennedy confirmed this to be the case in his memoirs: he, in effect, let the cat out of the bag when he wrote, "Had we had our way, I think there can be little doubt that the invasion of France would not have been done in 1944."[7] As Director of Military Operations in the War Office, Kennedy was in a better position than most to know the British attitude towards the invasion.

The final aspect concerns Eisenhower and his handling of the Allied campaign in north-west Europe. In his criticisms of Eisenhower, Alanbrooke identified three weaknesses. The first was hesitancy, perhaps explained by his lack of experience of field command. On 28 December 1942, seven weeks after the Torch landings, Alanbrooke noted "his intention to put off attacks for 2 months!" and on 12 December 1944 he "discovered that Ike now does not hope to cross the Rhine before May [1945]!!!"

The second was lack of drive and grip. On 15 May 1944, Alanbrooke thought "Eisenhower was a swinger and no real director of thought, plans, energy or direction!" On 14 November 1944, Eisenhower "seemed fairly vague as to what was really going on!" Ten days later, Alanbrooke complained that he was "entirely detached from the war and taking practically no part in the running of the war!" and on 25 January 1945, he referred to "Eisenhower's inability to retain a definite policy without waffling about."

The third was that he tended to change his mind. His style of leadership was consultative and he was prone to being influenced by the views of his senior commanders. On 30 November 1944, "I have fears of Ike going back on us when he has discussed with Bedell Smith, Tedder": three days later, Alanbrooke's fears proved correct, "he seems to be changing round since seeing Bradley!" At the end of December 1944, "Ike agrees that… only one major offensive is possible. But I expect that whoever meets Ike next may swing him to any other point of view! He is a hopeless commander."

When Overlord was being planned, it had been agreed that Eisenhower would have separate commanders-in-chief for his naval and air forces, but the issue of who was to command his land forces had been fudged: the Americans were insistent that their land forces, which would quickly outnumber all other Allied troops, should not be under British command. However, they did not have an American commander with the necessary experience or gravitas to perform this role. Consequently, it was agreed that Montgomery would command the land forces for the initial landings and operations in Normandy and thereafter the British and American army groups would fall under national command. It was also loosely agreed that Eisenhower would assume direct command of all Allied land forces when they reached the River Seine.

After the Allies swept across France in August 1944, they were presented with an opportunity of driving into Germany and seizing the Ruhr industrial region which would have hastened Germany's defeat. However, the opportunity was lost, in part because of two events which occurred in mid-August 1944. First, Washington exerted pressure on Eisenhower to assume direct command of Allied land forces which he agreed to do from 1 September: the timing could not have been worse. Second, Montgomery and Bradley, the respective commanders of the British and American army groups, disagreed over the strategy to pursue after the Allies crossed the Seine and this resulted in Eisenhower choosing a course of action which amounted to a compromise of their different strategies. If the issue of command of Allied land forces had not been fudged, and a single land forces commander-in-chief had been in place, this opportunity would have been exploited to the full although it is questionable whether it would have led to seizure of the Ruhr, given the severe supply difficulties being experienced by the Allies at the time.

At this point, it is worth recalling General Paget's remark that if Alanbrooke had been supreme commander in Europe, "he would have won the war in Europe a year earlier. He would have been decisive and have closely directed the campaign". A similar sentiment was expressed by Andrew Cunningham, the First Sea Lord, "I… feel that had it come his way in the later stages of the war he would have been one of our most brilliant commanders in the field"[8] and by General Franklyn, "he would have made a great Commander-in-Chief in the field."[9]

These remarks raise the question of whether Alanbrooke should have been appointed commander-in-chief of Allied land forces in Europe? It would certainly have been preferable to the fudged arrangement that was set up. He undoubtedly had the skills and experience to perform the role and by mid-1944 there was no compelling need for him to remain as CIGS in London. He would have injected more purpose and drive into the campaign than Eisenhower and he also had the force of personality to keep the Allied generals, notably Montgomery, under better control. It could be argued he was too senior to act as a commander under Eisenhower but that is a tenuous ground of objection: in any event, his diary creates the impression that Eisenhower was slightly in awe of him and that Alanbrooke knew how to handle Eisenhower.

However, it is highly unlikely that the Americans would have agreed to his appointment, and not merely because of their insistence that an American command their land forces or because the commanders-in-chief of the naval and air forces were both British. America was emerging from the War as a global superpower and Americans were sensitive to anything which diminished their country's stature and prestige. This was apparent in their response on 3 February 1945 to the British proposal that Alexander be appointed Eisenhower's deputy, "The President and Marshall considered that politically such a move might have repercussions in America if carried out just now. It might be considered that Alex was being put to support Ike after his Ardennes failure! However, they were quite prepared to accept the change in about 6 weeks time after future offensive operations have been started by Ike and the Ardennes operation more forgotten." It was also apparent in their response on 1 February

1945 to Britain's draft directive to Eisenhower stipulating the action he should take as land commander, "[Marshall] was opposed to cramping Eisenhower's style by issuing any directive to him!" The Americans were outraged that Eisenhower, who was the physical embodiment of America's stature and power, needed instruction from the British on matters of strategy: consequently, they circled their wagons around him. The likelihood is that the Americans would not have agreed to his appointment.

Decades after the event, speculating on this issue might appear an academic exercise which belongs in the 'what if' compartment of history. Perhaps, but the period between September 1944 and the German surrender in May 1945 saw a high rate of casualties in Europe, both military and civilian. There was considerable force in Paget's observation and, arguably, the Allies missed a trick in failing to make use of Alanbrooke's talents.

Alanbrooke was also highly critical of Eisenhower's broad front strategy of launching simultaneous attacks across the entire front. On 12 December 1944, "Ike explained his plan which contemplates a double advance into Germany, north of Rhine and by Frankfurt. I disagreed flatly with it, accused Ike of violating principles of concentration of force which had resulted in his previous failures. I criticized his future plans and pointed out impossibility of double invasion with limited forces he has got. I stressed the importance of concentrating on one thrust. I drew attention to the fact that with his limited forces any thought of attack on both fronts could only lead to dispersal of effort." Further examples occurred on 28 August 1944, 2 November 1944, 9 November 1944 and 28 November 1944.

Two further factors militated against Eisenhower's broad front strategy. First, Allied supply lines were extremely stretched with the result that simultaneous attacks across the entire front could not be adequately supported. On 5 October 1944, Alanbrooke noted the "candid criticisms of the administrative situation" and the importance of seizing a large port, "one fact stood out clearly, that Antwerp must be captured with the least possible delay." Second, the strategy left Eisenhower operating with insufficient reserve formations. On 28 November 1944, "In the present offensive, we had attacked on 6 Army Fronts without any reserves anywhere" and on 18 December 1944, "Germans are delivering strong counter offensive against Americans who have no immediate reserves to stem the attack with."

In Eisenhower's defence, it is easy to overlook the enormous responsibilities that were thrust on him during the War. Furthermore, it is indisputable that he worked tirelessly for the Allied cause and was entirely non-partisan in his efforts to secure cooperation and unity between the Allies: in that regard, as Alanbrooke observed on 15 May 1944, "few [could] hold a candle to him". However, the impression created by the diary is that Eisenhower was as much a diplomat and politician as he was a field commander. Alanbrooke was certainly never in any doubt as to his military abilities. On 4 December 1944,

"[Churchill] made some queer statements during our discussion! One was that he did not want anybody between Ike and the Army Groups as Ike was a good fellow who was amenable and whom he could influence... I replied that I could see little use in having an amenable Supreme Commander if he was totally unfit to win the war for him!"

TWENTY-ONE

1945–1963

After the War, Alanbrooke experienced several difficulties and disappointments. Some of his diary entries hinted that money was a cause of anxiety for him: on 22 June 1943, he was concerned whether his "big venture" of purchasing the full collection of Gould's bird books would prove a successful investment and on 23 August 1945 he was "appalled" that it cost £200 to become a baron. In 1945, he was asking an army colleague who was about to resume his business career, "Can you give me some sort of job when I [retire from the army] for I can't afford not to work and goodness knows who will have me when all this is over."[1] On retirement, he was due to receive a gratuity of £311, which is approximately £13,500 in today's money, and his pay would be cut by one half.

In January 1946, he informed his nephew's wife, "I am looking for some means of making money as I am broke (and forced to sell off bird books). I hope to find something in the line of a directorship which will help me along." With Kathleen and Victor still in their teens, and his retirement pay and gratuity insufficient to meet all his outgoings, Alanbrooke and Benita were compelled to sell the family home in Hampshire and move into the nearby gardener's cottage which they intended to purchase. However, the sale of their home took longer than expected, in part because of a fire which destroyed the stables, so he was forced to sell his Gould bird books. In his Notes, "I had the whole complete collection of Gould's works, 45 volumes. It nearly broke my heart having to part with them. But, as I had to buy my house to live in, I could not afford to keep this capital locked up in books."

In his 15 July 1945 entry, Alanbrooke had revealed his disappointment at losing out to Alexander for the governor generalship of Canada. Alexander was duly appointed in 1946 and in the same year John Kennedy became governor of southern Rhodesia. Shortly thereafter, Mountbatten, now Lord Mountbatten of Burma, was appointed Viceroy of India and Pug Ismay was installed as his chief of staff. As the great and the good departed to take up their new appointments in the dwindling British Empire, he was dealt another blow. In 1947, a new governor general of Australia was due to be appointed and Alanbrooke was, according to King George VI's private secretary, the King's "first choice" for this appointment. However, the Australian prime minister was insistent that the appointee should be a native Australian.

Alanbrooke did acquire several company directorships, most notably with the Midland Bank, the Anglo-Iranian Oil Company, Belfast Banking Company and the Hudson Bay Company. He was appointed a director of Hudson Bay in 1948 and in the following year conducted an inspection of Hudson's operations in Canada: Hudson Bay's chairman later commented he and his fellow directors had been "astonished by the way he had sized up the men in charge. Time had proved the accuracy of his appraisements."[2] Alanbrooke always was a good judge of his "fellow men".

One particularly memorable event was an official trip that he and Benita made in February 1947 to Bagnères-de-Bigorre, the place of his birth in south-west France. Seven years earlier, the Bagnères Municipal Council had learnt that one of the British generals in the BEF, then stationed in France, had been born in their town and at the end of the War the councils of both Bagnères and Pau decided to award Alanbrooke the freedom of their towns. In Bagnères, Alanbrooke and Benita were greeted by a French guard of honour and then shown a plaque set in the wall of the chalet where Alanbrooke had been born,

Dans ce chalet est né le 23 Juillet 1883
Le Field Marshal Viscount Alanbrooke
Chef de L'Etat Major Imperial Britannique
De 1942 à 1945

The perfect mother would have been proud: her youngest son had achieved the goal she had set him when he was a boy.

Following his retirement, Alanbrooke was appointed Master Gunner, St James's Park, a largely ceremonial position in the Royal Regiment of Artillery, and Colonel Commandant of the Honourable Artillery Company. 1947 saw his appointment as chancellor of Queen's University Belfast, a position he held until his death, and in 1950 he was appointed Lord Lieutenant of the County of London and Constable of the Tower: three years later, he was made Lord High Constable of England for the coronation of Queen Elizabeth II. In addition, he was president of the Royal United Kingdom Benevolent Association, the Forces Help Society, the Star and Garter Home for Disabled Servicemen and the London Union of Youth Clubs. Inevitably, he continued to pursue his hobbies of fishing, bird watching and bird photography – he developed a notable expertise in the latter – which led to his appointment as president of both the London Zoological Society and the Severn Wildfowl Trust and vice president of the Royal Society for the Protection of Birds.

Outside of military circles, Alanbrooke remained a largely unknown and little recognised figure in the post-War years and there is little doubt that he was perfectly content with this anonymity: when, in 1951, the Royal Regiment of Artillery commissioned Arthur Bryant to write his biography, Alanbrooke consented on condition that it was only written and published after his death. Alanbrooke was heading for the exit marked obscurity and it is well-nigh certain he would have passed through it, had it not been for the actions of two men, Winston Churchill and Arthur Bryant.

After Churchill lost the 1945 General Election, he began writing his six volumes of war memoirs which were published between 1948 and 1954 under the title, *The Second World War*. His memoirs were a highly personalised record of the War and left any reader of them under no illusion that Churchill had played a central – and perhaps the vital – role in the Allied victory. It is safe to assume that, in common with most political leaders, he was keen to secure his place in history and, consequently, had an eye on posterity when writing them.

Towards the end of the War, Alanbrooke had noted Churchill's failure to recognise and give credit to others for the role which they played in the conflict. On 10 September 1944, "And with it all no recognition hardly at all for those who help him except the occasional crumb intended to prevent the dog from straying too far from the table." On 20 January 1945, "It is a strange thing what a vast part the [Chiefs of Staff Committee] takes in the running of the war and how little it is known or its functions appreciated. The average man on the street has never heard of it. Any limelight for it could not fail to slightly diminish the PM's halo! This may perhaps account for the fact that he has never yet given it the slightest word of credit in public." On 8 May 1945, Victory in Europe Day, "the PM has never enlightened [the public] much and has never once in all his speeches referred to the Chiefs of Staff or what they have been doing in the direction of the war on the highest plane." More ominous was Alanbrooke's observation on 4 July 1945, "[Churchill] confessed he had not even read the paper which we had prepared for him with such care! (And yet if the proposed strategy in the long run turns out successful, it will have originated in his fertile brain!! This has happened so frequently now!)"

This failure to recognise and give credit to others for their role in the War was to be repeated by Churchill in his memoirs. By analogy to the theatre, they amounted to a one-man show or monologue with Churchill centre stage throughout whilst the rest of the cast was consigned to the shadowy background, barely discernible to the awestruck audience. The memoirs were, in truth, a very good illustration of the notable streak of self-centredness which existed in Churchill. Alanbrooke provided an example of this Churchillian flaw in his Notes, 20 August 1942, "At 7.30am I woke with my bed shaking and, on opening my eyes, saw [Churchill] standing at the end of my bed shaking it… "Come and have breakfast with me," he said, to which I replied, "It is only 7.30; you said breakfast at 8.30." That did not affect him in the least and he continued, "I know but I am awake." I had one more attempt to gain a few more minutes' sleep and said, "Yes but I am not awake, I have not washed or shaved." It was useless, he replied "Never mind, neither have I. Come along, let's eat!" For Churchill, prior agreements could be unilaterally revoked at his whim – he wanted breakfast and he wanted company whilst he ate: consequently, everyone around him was expected to fall into line with his changed requirements, regardless of their own situation. In similar vein was Churchill's habit of keeping his entourage up until the early hours of the morning – he enjoyed staying up late, therefore everyone else was expected to fit in with his wishes.

Churchill's self-centredness manifested itself in several ways. First, he was prone to overreact if he perceived any challenge to his prestige and authority. On 19 July 1944, Montgomery's request for a ban on visits to France produced a remarkably petulant reaction from Churchill which included a "foul... most offensively worded" letter. Furthermore, the importance which Churchill attached to his own prestige and authority led him to be unduly suspicious that others were conspiring against him. On 8 September 1944, "he was quite impossible to work with, began by accusing us of framing up against him and of opposing him in his wishes." Further examples occurred on 23 August 1943, 14 September 1944 and 19 January 1945.

Second, Churchill wanted, perhaps needed, to be the centre of attention and he was reluctant to share the limelight with others. On 2 December 1944, "It was quite clear that his pride was offended that Monty and Ike had had some limelight turned on them which he had not shared!" In his Notes, 12 October 1944, Alanbrooke recalled Churchill's "almost unbelievable petty jealousy" of Montgomery, "'he will fill the Mall because he is Monty and I will not have him filling the Mall'!"

Third, Churchill could be insensitive and offhand when dealing with people. Lord Moran hinted at this when describing him in these terms, "Winston happened to be a genius, trampling down like a bull elephant everything that got in his way."[3] Churchill did indeed rampage in the style of a bull elephant and he trampled over anything, and anyone, that "got in his way". In May 1943, during the sea journey to Washington, Wavell drafted his letter of resignation since he "was so upset by Winston's references to the Burma operations". 14 September 1944 saw a "very upset" Pug Ismay driven to tender his resignation, which was then blithely ignored.

A good example of this insensitive and offhand streak in Churchill appeared in the second volume of his memoirs when he explained the circumstances which led to Alanbrooke's appointment as Commander-in-Chief, Home Forces. After praising Alanbrooke for his actions in France in 1940, Churchill then wrote at some length in footnotes about Alanbrooke's older brothers, Ronnie and Victor, who had been his friends decades earlier. Significantly, he did so in far warmer and more endearing terms than he used in relation to Alanbrooke, thereby creating the impression that whilst he valued and enjoyed his friendships with Ronnie and Victor, he tolerated their younger brother. This tactless and somewhat wounding slight, which doubtless was unintentional, was typical of the self-centred Churchill: his own feelings always prevailed over the feelings of others.

Churchill's reference to Ronnie and Victor in his memoirs was not an isolated one since he also referred to them in his letter to Alanbrooke in mid-November 1941, following the latter's appointment as CIGS. In late July 1945, Churchill wrote another letter to Alanbrooke, after the general election result severed their wartime association which had spanned nearly four years. With final victory in the War imminent, here was the moment for Churchill to cast his own personal feelings aside when writing to his loyal lieutenant yet,

> My dear Brookie,
> I am deeply grateful for all you have done for me and for the country. Your charming letter has touched me deeply and cheered me. I shall always value your friendship, as I do my memories of Ronnie and Victor in those young and far off days. Our story in this war is a good one, and this will be recognized as time goes on.

In the circumstances, Ronnie and Victor were completely irrelevant but that did not matter to Churchill: he referred to them because he enjoyed recalling his old friends. Incidentally, his claim, "I shall always value your friendship", appears disingenuous since Lord Moran later remarked, "I cannot recall a single occasion [after the War] when he brought up Alanbrooke's name. It was as if he had cut this opinionated soldier out of his life and only wanted to forget him."[4]

When Arthur Bryant was commissioned in 1951 to write Alanbrooke's biography, it was agreed that his researcher, Marian Long, should start her work immediately. She began by approaching Alanbrooke's colleagues and friends for their opinions of him. General Pug Ismay informed her, "You have taken on a tricky job... Brookie is one of those reserved chaps who keeps his thoughts and emotions to himself." In similar vein was Lieutenant General Freddie Morgan's reply, "To the best of my recollection, I don't believe there is or was anybody whatever who really knew Brookie. I well remember that his own personal staff used to complain at times that they could never get near him in the human sense at all, even after years of association." More revealing was the reply she received from Major Aitken since it confirmed Alanbrooke's two personas, "the most delightful companion... completely unselfish, intensely human with a wonderful sense of humour and gift of description, most entertaining and amusing. And when this far away from his busy life, it is difficult to believe that he can present to the official world the stern efficiency which lied behind these most lovable characteristics."

Perplexed by the feedback she was receiving, Marian Long sought help. In January 1953, she wrote to Colonel Bevan, "As you will probably realise, 'Brookie' is not an easy personality to capture and put on paper. There are so many different facets to him and sometimes when interviewing people, I wonder if they are talking of the same man" and in May 1954, she wrote to Lieutenant General Ian Jacob, "The Brookie problem, as you say, is a fascinating one... The Brookie that I have got to know these last two years is amusing, witty, an entertaining raconteur, a brilliant mimic and cartoonist. Very different from the glimpses I had of him during the war... Why is [it] that the Army as a whole appear to respect and I think fear Brookie, but he appears to have few real friends except for one or two who he knew as subalterns in India 1908–14. Yet his personal friends can't understand this, they know the amusing and lighter side of him and say he was the best company in the world. I suspect, but tell me if I'm wrong, that Brookie in a strange illogical way felt that his lighter and more sentimental side was a weakness in a soldier. That as he climbed the ladder of promotion, he hid behind a mask of isolation, felt he mustn't let his judgment be influenced by personal feelings and, therefore, shunned close personal friendships with other soldiers. Of course, it is up to Arthur Bryant to draw the final conclusions – not me, but I feel he's going to need a lot of material to get a true insight to Brookie as a character before he can draw a true picture of him which will be recognised by all who knew him." Marian Long's suspicion that Alanbrooke "hid behind a mask of isolation" was probably correct since he informed her in a letter written in June 1955, "Both as a C-in-C and as a CIGS, I considered [it] essential never to disclose outwardly what one felt inwardly."

Even more revealing was the reply Marian Long received from Cynthia Brookeborough, the wife of Alanbrooke's nephew, "[Alan] said too that his increasing hostility (I think this is perhaps too strong a word) was very largely due to [Churchill's] absolute unfairness to several people and failure to award them any credit – or even to give them a fair deal – both in his [memoirs] or at the time. He instanced Dill [and] Alan Cunningham as two examples of this [and] said there were others. Also [Churchill's] completely egotistical outlook, WC first all of the time – I think you're right – that though Alan admired him, he never felt warm towards Winston [and] I don't think that the daily visitation accounted for it – I do remember though his mentioning with much amusement and appreciation WC coming in on trips at 2am in his dragon-embroidered dressing gown or paddling like a child in [north] Africa. But we agree with you, [Winston's memoirs] hardened Alan's heart considerably – I think for their egoism – [and] lack of praise for underlings – or more, his equals – perhaps. Does that help? He thought [Churchill] very jealous towards equals."

In late 1954, by which time all six volumes of Churchill's memoirs had been published, Bryant suggested he should use Alanbrooke's diary to write a short book narrating the story of the War between Dunkirk and El Alamein and that, once written, this book should be published immediately. This suggestion was not made on a whim since Bryant crafted a lengthy, detailed proposal which he sent to Alanbrooke. Cynthia Brookeborough's remark that Churchill's memoirs "hardened Alan's heart considerably" may explain Alanbrooke's reaction: he replied stating he was "delighted with your suggestion and thrilled with the idea".

In the event, Bryant used the diary and autobiographical Notes to write the story of the entire War, publishing it in two volumes, *The Turn of the Tide* [1957] and *Triumph in the West* [1959]. The foreword to *The Turn of the Tide*, written by Alanbrooke himself, made clear that the aim of the books was to raise public awareness of the role played by the British chiefs of staff in the War. Whilst this was a perfectly reasonable rationale, it did carry two risks. First, the books might prove controversial since that rationale inevitably brought Churchill's approach to strategy into play which, in turn, brought his judgment and his stewardship of the British war effort into play. The second risk was that the books might overstate the British chiefs of staff's contribution in the War. To minimise these risks, Bryant needed to be balanced, measured and nuanced in his writing of them. Unfortunately, he failed: according to Lord Moran, Bryant gave "too much credit to Alanbrooke for his share in the conduct of the war".[5] These were not the only difficulties confronting Bryant. His books inevitably fell into the slipstream of Churchill's memoirs which had already been published. Churchill had gained first mover advantage and his memoirs had reinforced in peoples' minds the common perception that he was the successful leader who had delivered victory.

Consequently, when *The Turn of the Tide* was presented to a slightly startled world in 1957, it was greeted with the reaction – who was this Alanbrooke to challenge the record and, moreover, question Churchill's godlike status by asserting that his judgment was suspect and his stewardship of the British war effort far from faultless. Controversy loomed and became inevitable when *The Turn of the Tide* was serialised in a national newspaper. In America, *Time* magazine's review of the book was savage.

Arguably, Bryant was guilty of a more fundamental error: put simply, he wrote the wrong book. Instead of using the diary to write the story of the War, he should have used it to write a book setting out all the lessons which could have been learnt from Alanbrooke's experiences in the War. There was a powerful rationale for this alternative book which, perhaps ironically, appeared in Alanbrooke's diary: on 2 February 1940, he wrote, "History is repeating itself in an astonishing way... We shall apparently never apply the lessons of one war to the next." That rationale also appeared in his foreword to *The Turn of the Tide* since he claimed that the lessons to be learnt from the experiences of the Chiefs of Staff Committee in the War were "of enduring value in the life of our nation."[6]

As a wartime CIGS and chairman of the Chiefs of Staff Committee, Alanbrooke was well-qualified to identify those lessons and, moreover, pass comment on them: he had a compelling story to tell about his experiences and it was one which, had it been written, offered four advantages over Bryant's published titles. First, it would have offered invaluable guidance to future generations of military leaders. Second, given its rationale, it would have been very difficult to criticise the book. Third, it avoided falling into the slipstream of Churchill's memoirs since it addressed the War from an entirely different standpoint. Fourth, it would not have contained the element of self-aggrandisement which permeated from Bryant's titles.

The first lesson was that the relationship between political leaders and military chiefs was, at best, uneasy and, at worst, almost irreconcilable. On 18 June 1940, Alanbrooke sailed back to England after commanding the second British Expeditionary Force in France, "To try and relate political considerations, with which you are not fully informed, with military necessities, which stare one in the face, is a very difficult matter when these two considerations pull in diametrically opposed directions. Politically, it may have been desirable to support [France] to the very last moment even to the extent of being involved in the final catastrophe and annihilation. Militarily, it was self-evident from the start that the very small forces at our disposal could do nothing towards restoring the military situation." And on 10 July 1941, "I remember always considering that Sir Henry Wilson's description of what he called the 'Frocks' [politicians] must be exaggerated. Now I am surprised how true to life his descriptions are! It is impossible for soldiers and politicians ever to work satisfactorily together – they are, and always will be, poles apart."

The second was to understand the role and function of senior military advisors. On this issue, Alanbrooke had few difficulties since he accepted that matters of policy were settled by politicians and that his role was to advise on the military aspects and consequences of those policies. A good example was the British Government's decision to interfere in Greek domestic affairs. Whilst Alanbrooke clearly doubted the wisdom of this policy, he nevertheless accepted it. On 19 January 1945, "I assured [Churchill] that although strongly opposed to our original venture into Greece, now that we were committed, I fully realized the difficulty and impossibility of extracting forces out of Greece".

This British interference in Greek domestic affairs was also a good example of the third lesson, namely politicians were prone to ignore the advice and predictions of their military advisors. From the outset, Alanbrooke was concerned this policy would not only necessitate a commitment of troops far greater than the politicians anticipated but also have a detrimental effect on other theatres. The history of this policy is well illustrated by stitching three of his entries together: as an aside, these demonstrate Alanbrooke's foresight and consistency on this issue. On 13 July 1944,

"The capture of Amboina Island in the Pacific, and the military backing of Foreign Office policy in Greece were the two topics of discussion at our COS meeting... the latter to try and preserve us against the wild schemes of the Foreign Office and their objectionable ambassador Mr Leeper. This combination, as I see it, is preparing to force on Greece a government of their own [i.e. Foreign Office] selection and to support this government with military power. I can foresee a very serious military commitment very rapidly increasing."

Two days later,

> "*It is fairly clear that Leeper has got the jitters, having originally asked for 5000 men as being ample to set the Greek Government firmly on its feet, he has now got over 40,000 and considers that 'the military have badly underestimated the strength required' and should send more troops at once. This is exactly what I have been predicting from the very start!*"

31 July 1945 saw,

> "*gathering clouds on the northern Greek frontier. Seven Yugoslav Divisions close to frontier... 19 Bulgarian divisions, 350-400,000 Russians all in Bulgaria. It looks too much like power politics to be pleasant. Meanwhile, Foreign Office as usual going adrift! We were originally told to send 10,000 troops to Greece to back the Government, I said it would require at least 80,000 to do what they wanted. I was informed politely that I knew nothing about it as it was a political matter and that 10,000 would be ample to give the necessary backing to the Government. We eventually sent about 90,000 into Greece!!! Now having originally sent forces into Greece to restore law and order internally, we are informed that these self-same forces are required to also defend the frontiers of Greece!! We are on a slippery slope, with one task leading into another all requiring more and more forces which we have not got. And at the same time we receive instructions to accelerate our own demobilization!*"

The fourth lesson was the importance of military leaders being resolute in their dealings with the prime minister and senior politicians. Political leaders tend to be persuasive individuals – Churchill being a prime example – and, consequently, military leaders are at considerable risk of agreeing to a course of action against their better judgment. In his Notes, 14 June 1940, Alanbrooke described his first conversation with Churchill, "The strength of his power of persuasion had to be experienced to realize the strength that was required to counter it."

The fifth was the importance of identifying the weaknesses of political leaders, and then managing those weaknesses. There is so much criticism of Churchill in Alanbrooke's diary that the reader could be forgiven for not attempting to disentangle it. However, the exercise is well worth undertaking.

First, he was opportunistic, impulsive and intuitive. On 19 January 1944, "In all his plans he lives from hand to mouth. He can never grasp a whole plan, either in its width (i.e. all fronts) or its depth (long-term projects). His method is entirely opportunist" and on 14 February 1944, "He lives for the impulse and for the present and refuses to look at lateral implications or future commitments." His 10 July 1944 entry was in similar vein.

Second, Churchill was an aggressive, combative personality who craved offensive action against the enemy: as a result, he harassed field commanders. On 8 September 1942, "My next trouble will now be to stop Winston from fussing Alex and Monty and egging them on to attack before they are ready. It is a regular disease that he suffers from, this frightful impatience to get an attack launched!" Furthermore, any perceived inaction or delay by field commanders resulted in a fusillade of Churchillian criticism. On 2 March 1942, "PM had drafted a bad wire for Auchinleck in which he poured abuse on him for not attacking sooner". Further examples occurred on 11 July 1942, 18 August 1942, 20 and 23 September 1942 and 29 October 1942.

Third, Churchill's criticism and abuse of field commanders undermined cabinet ministers' confidence in those commanders. On 6 July 1944, "He began to abuse Monty because operations were not going faster... I flared up and asked him if he could not trust his generals for 5 minutes instead of continuously abusing them and belittling them. He said that he never did such a thing. I then reminded him that... in front of a large gathering of Ministers, he had torn Alexander to shreds for his lack of imagination and leadership". In his Notes, "As most of the Cabinet Ministers had little opportunity of judging for themselves, and took all [Churchill] said for gospel, there was every danger of their opinion of Alex being seriously affected." Further examples occurred on 28 February 1944, 30 May 1944, 30 April 1945 and in his Notes, 2 February 1942.

His criticism and abuse was not confined to field commanders. 9 February 1942 saw "nothing but abuse for the army". At the cabinet meeting on 8 July 1942, "PM ran down ME army in shocking way" and on 20 March 1944, "Nothing that the Army does can be right and he did nothing but belittle its efforts in the eyes of the whole Cabinet."

Fourth, the imaginative and enthusiastic Churchill could easily be carried away by optimism: a good example was his 15 June 1942 paper on Operation Round-up. On 23 May 1942, "he was... establishing lodgements all round the coast from Calais to Bordeaux with little regard to strengths and landing facilities."

The fifth Churchillian weakness was his tendency to focus on one theatre of war to the exclusion of all others: he failed to appreciate the interrelationship that existed between different theatres. On 10 May 1943, "He again showed that he cannot grasp the relation of various theatres of war to each other. He always gets carried away by the one he is examining... I have never in the 1½ years that I have worked with him succeeded in making him review the war as a whole and to relate the importance of the various fronts to each other." Further examples occurred on 30 August 1943, 18 November 1943 and 14 February 1944.

Sixth, Churchill did not understand the chain of command. On 8 August 1942, "Receive[d] a long lecture from PM with all his pet theories as to how essential it is for Alex to command both ME and 8th Army. I again had to give him a long lecture on the system of the chain of command in the Army! I fear that it did not sink much deeper than it has before!" In his Notes, 18 November 1943, Alanbrooke hinted this may have been deliberate, "He could not or would not follow how a chain of command was applied": since a chain of command is not the most difficult concept to understand, he may well have been right. If so, the most likely explanation is that Churchill chose to ignore it when it suited his purposes to do so. Further examples occurred on 7 August 1943, 18 November 1943, 16 February 1944, 17 November 1944 and 12 April 1945.

The seventh Churchillian weakness was indecision. On 20 August 1942, a decision was urgently required on the new Iraq-Persia command, "Still impossible to obtain decision from PM!!... I pointed out that while we are talking, the Germans are walking through the Caucasus." On 7 June 1943, "We sat for 2 hours and did absolutely nothing!! PM in bad mood… and refusing to make up his mind in any direction." Churchill's indecision became more pronounced as he declined in the latter stages of the War. On 14 July 1944, Alanbrooke squared up to him on the issue of Far East strategy, "'If the Government does not wish to accept our advice let them say so but, for heaven's sake, let us have a decision!'" Further examples occurred on 8 March 1944, 19 April 1944, 20 July 1944, 8 August 1944 and 6 March 1945.

Eighth, Churchill immersed himself in matters of detail. On 10 July 1944, "A complete amateur of strategy, he swamps himself in details he should never look at and as a result fails ever to see a strategic problem in its true perspective." Further examples occurred on 12 December 1944, 23 January 1945 and 29 March 1945.

Ninth, he had a casual attitude to security. On 22 October 1942, Alanbrooke was horrified that Churchill "had calmly gone and told Eisenhower and Smith" details of Montgomery's forthcoming offensive. A further example occurred on 8 January 1945.

Churchill's final, and perhaps his greatest, weakness was his determination to micromanage the British war effort. In contrast, Roosevelt, despite being commander-in-chief of American forces by virtue of his presidency, tended to decide overall policy objectives and then let his military chiefs determine how they could best be achieved. Alanbrooke alluded to these different styles of leadership in his Notes, 10 April 1942, when he ruefully remarked, "[Marshall] informed me that he frequently did not see [Roosevelt] for a month or six weeks. I was fortunate if I did not see Winston for 6 hours."

When Churchill was appointed prime minister, one of his first acts was to appoint himself minister of defence which, in effect, gave him control over the management and direction of the British war effort. In his memoirs, Churchill claimed it had been "understood and accepted" that he should be given this control "subject to the support of the War Cabinet and of the House of Commons".[7] He also claimed that he had taken care to ensure that his rights and duties as minister of defence were not defined. It is fair to assume he took this step because lack of definition meant lack of boundaries: that suited Churchill since he enjoyed having the freedom to act as he pleased. In his Notes, 9 July 1941, Alanbrooke commented on Churchill's decision to appoint himself minister of defence, "One of his first acts, however, was virtually to convert the democracy into a dictatorship! Granted that he still was responsible to a Parliament and granted that he still formed part of a Cabinet; yet his personality was such, and the power he acquired adequate, to place him in a position where both Parliament and the Cabinet were only minor inconveniences which had to be humoured occasionally, but which he held in the palm of his hand, able to swing both of them at his pleasure."

Alanbrooke's claim of a "dictatorship" had some validity. Not only was Churchill autocratic by nature and in style but he was also a domineering individual who fought tenaciously to have his own way in the management of the British war effort, the most notable instance being in March 1944 when, in his capacity as prime minister and minister of defence, he overruled the chiefs of staff on the issue of British strategy in the Far East: interestingly, he did so after consulting the defence committee but not the war cabinet whose support was, on his own admission, a pre-condition to the exercise of his powers. Furthermore, a comparison of Churchill with Hitler reveals considerable similarities. Both men understood the power of oratory and used it to great effect, both increased their own powers by appointing themselves to positions of authority, both were domineering personalities who exercised a persuasive hold on those around them, both were intuitive, both thought they were strategic geniuses, both berated their generals and then sacked their generals, both sought to micromanage the conduct of the War, both personally interfered in the running of military campaigns, both immersed themselves in matters of detail, both were prone to be indecisive, especially in the latter stages of the War, and both were nocturnal animals who displayed little consideration for their entourage by keeping them up until the early hours of the morning.

Yet, instances such as the one in March 1944 were the exception. Churchill was undoubtedly aggressive, combative and bullying, but he did submit to discussion and debate and was willing to be persuaded by argument: he rarely overruled. It is, therefore, probably more accurate to say he hovered on the cusp of dictatorship during the War but, crucially, shrank back from it and allowed himself to be reined in. Perhaps he did so because the British checks and balances designed to constrain prime ministers were effective and too well entrenched? Perhaps he did so because he believed in democratic government? As is so often the case with Churchill, it is difficult to pin him down, largely because he was so inconsistent and volatile. The most likely explanation is that he did believe in democracy provided it came in a form which gave him wide freedom of action.

In marked contrast, Hitler deliberately dismantled all the checks and balances designed to curb his powers as chancellor, assumed supreme and unbridled power as Führer and then embarked on a course of action which culminated in his, and Germany's, oblivion. Had Churchill been given free rein and allowed to follow his instincts, he would probably have tacked in a similar direction and ended up making as many mistakes as Hitler since he was an impulsive opportunist with a back history of serious misjudgments: on 14 February 1944, "Now that I know him well, episodes such as Antwerp and the Dardanelles no longer puzzle me!" But the fact remains he did not. Churchill has rightly been feted for his resolute leadership, his inspirational speeches, his spirited defiance and his resilience. However, he also deserves to be feted for allowing himself to be reined in when he was on the cusp of dictatorship: therein, arguably, lay Churchill's greatest achievement.

Moreover, it is difficult not to feel a twinge of sympathy for Churchill. Here was a mercurial, self-confident, passionate individual brimming with imaginative ideas yet when he advanced them, he was repeatedly opposed. At the cabinet meeting on 4 December 1941, "we were told that we did nothing but obstruct his intentions, we had no ideas of our own and whenever he produced ideas, we produced nothing but objections" and on 10 October 1943, he complained that "everyone was against him". For Churchill, the process of being reined in was highly frustrating: he must have felt as if he had been put on a leash from which he was unable to break free. On 24 September 1942, "He then became very worked up about the whole show and in the end was very pathetic. He said this machine of war with Russia at one end and America at the other was too cumbersome to run any war with. It was so much easier to do nothing! He could so easily sit around and wait for work to come to him. Nothing was harder than doing things and everybody did nothing but produce difficulties." Alanbrooke elaborated in his Notes, "We then find him adopting the attitude that he was the only one trying to win the war, that he was the only one who produced any ideas, that he was quite alone in all his attempts, no one supported him. Indeed, instead of supporting him, all we did was provide and plan difficulties, etc. Frequently in this oration he worked himself up into such a state from the woeful picture he had painted that tears streamed down his face!"

The sixth lesson concerned the weaknesses of the cabinet. Its members were quick to voice their opinions on subjects of which they had limited knowledge, often with unfortunate results. 7 July 1942 saw a "dreadful exhibition of amateur strategy by Cabinet ministers! Bevin quite at his worst… Eden and Cripps offering criticism as if they were leading authorities on strategy!" On 31 March 1942, "Politicians still suffer from that little knowledge of military matters which gives them unwarranted confidence that they are born strategists! As a result, they confuse issues, affect decisions, and convert simple problems and plans into confused tangles and hopeless muddles". In similar vein, on 24 July 1942, "Eden and Cripps thought they saw a flaw in [the Combined Chiefs of Staff document], they began to argue about things they did not understand, others joined in and very soon we had one of those situations I have now seen frequently in the Cabinet where the real issue is completely lost in arguing out some detail which is misquoted and distorted in the discussion." Further examples occurred on 19 July 1943, 29 November 1943, 8 March 1944 and 10 July 1944.

They also attached too much importance to politics. On 9 July 1941, "The more I see of politicians the less I think of them! They are seldom influenced directly by the true aspects of a problem and are usually guided by some ulterior political reason!" and on 31 March 1942, "Party politics, party interests still overrule larger war issues."

Furthermore, members of the cabinet interfered in matters which clearly fell within the military domain. On 29 October 1942, an impromptu chiefs of staff meeting was convened because Anthony Eden "had shaken [Churchill's] confidence in Montgomery and Alexander and had given him the impression that the [El Alamein] offensive was petering out": Eden interfered again on 7 November 1944. Occasionally, politicians did so for their own devious purposes. 8 December 1943 saw Harold Macmillan lobbying for the appointment of Alexander as supreme commander in the Mediterranean. In his Notes, "[Macmillan] knew he could handle Alex and that he would be a piece of putty in his hand".

In addition, they were unable to appreciate the risks of dispersing their armed forces. On 2 February 1940, five months after sending a poorly equipped BEF to France, the British Government was contemplating the despatch of troops to Scandinavia, "Apparently, various expeditions to other theatres of war are being considered by the highest [politicians], most of which would it strikes me lead to a dispersal of effort and provide better chances than ever for our losing the war. History is repeating itself in an astonishing way… the same tendency to start subsidiary theatres of war and to contemplate wild projects!!"

Cabinet members also dithered and were indecisive. On 2 May 1944, four weeks after the issue of bombing French railways and communications had first been raised, "Cabinet… another long discussion on the bombing strategy of attack on French railways and killing of Frenchmen. More waffling about [with] vacillating politicians unable to accept the consequences of war." At Tehran, on 30 November 1943, "One thing is quite clear, the more politicians you put together to settle the prosecution of the war, the longer you postpone its conclusion": he made the same point at Potsdam on 23 July 1945.

Alanbrooke identified another weakness on 15 September 1942 when he pointed out to Anthony Eden how many politicians had held the position of Secretary of State for War since 1939, "we had already had 5!! Ss of S since the war started and could not go on changing."

If ever there was a prime minister who needed to be challenged and, if necessary, faced down by his cabinet, it was Churchill: yet his cabinet was submissive and allowed itself to be dominated and browbeaten by him. Sir Alexander Cadogan clearly had a low opinion of them. On 2 February 1942, "After last week's debate, PM hectors more brutally a more subservient Cabinet. He flew at Amery. Latter said 'Is that the view of the Cabinet?' PM said 'Yes'. No one else said anything".[8] At the 15 January 1945 cabinet meeting, "PM not there at first so Morrison and others make a stink about V2's… PM came in about 6 and when we reverted to the subject the protagonists had lost their fire"[9] and on 22 January 1945, "Cabinet as discursive and useless as usual."[10]

Alanbrooke appeared to have an equally low opinion of the cabinet. On 31 March 1942, he referred to "a government with only one big man in it". On 27 June 1944, the cabinet meeting "finished up with a pathetic wail from Herbert Morrison who appears to be a real white-livered specimen" and on 31 July 1944, "the more I see of Herbert Morrison, the more I despise him!" On 6 March 1944, "on Wednesday after dinner we are to have a meeting with [Churchill]. He is to bring his chorus of 'Yes' men (Eden, Attlee, Oliver Lyttelton and Leathers) with him": in his Notes, "Somehow the presence of these four 'colleagues' of Winston's at these discussions always infuriated me… It was so palpable that they were brought along by [Churchill] to support him which they proceeded to do". His use of "always" is understandable because Churchill had involved these "Yes men" in earlier meetings on 12 October 1941, 3 September 1942, 29 October 1942, 3 December 1942, 19 July 1943 and 25 February 1944 and he did so again in subsequent meetings on 6 July, 14 July ["Attlee, Eden, Lyttelton were there as usual"] and 8 August 1944.

7 March 1944 saw forthright criticism of the "Yes men", "[Churchill] has now taken Eden, Attlee and Oliver Lyttelton in tow, none of whom understand anything about it all but who are useful as they are prepared to agree with him". On the following day, Alanbrooke was contemptuous, "The meeting consisted of the PM who had brought with him to support him Attlee, Eden, Oliver Lyttelton and Leathers!… from 10pm to 12.30pm I went at it hard arguing with the PM and 4 Cabinet Ministers. The arguments of the latter were so puerile that it made me ashamed to

think they were Cabinet Ministers! It was only too evident that they did not know their subject, had not read the various papers connected with it and had purely been brought along to support Winston! And damned badly they did it too! I had little difficulty in dealing with any of the arguments they put forward."

It was not until mid-1944 that the "Yes men" began to assert themselves. On 6 July 1944, Alanbrooke's use of "at last" is significant, "Attlee, Eden and Lyttelton were there, fortunately they were at last siding with us [the chiefs of staff] against him [Churchill]" and eight days later, "Both Attlee and Eden were against [Churchill]". Eventually, on 6 November 1944, the cabinet flexed some muscle, "usual Cabinet, which turned out to be an exciting one… Winston and Amery had a set-to on the India question. Winston had attacked the Viceroy, Amery flared up and told him he was 'talking damned nonsense'!! Winston said that if he had lost his temper to that extent he better withdraw from the Cabinet! Amery did not move and the situation calmed. Winston then had trouble with John Anderson and became even more sour… I came away with a feeling that Winston is losing his authority in the Cabinet". If Alanbrooke's diary is to be believed, the chiefs of staff were far more effective than the cabinet in challenging and, when necessary, facing down Churchill.

The seventh lesson was the extent to which political considerations influenced strategic and operational decisions during the War: it was noticeable how often this occurred. On 15 June 1940, when Alanbrooke was commanding the second BEF in France, "I… was again told that for political reasons it is desirable that the two Brigades… should not be re-embarked for the present… pointed out to them that from a military point of view we were committing a grave error". On 25 February 1942, he attended a cabinet meeting to discuss sending 72 Hurricanes to Russia, "As usual, failed to have any deduction made and informed that political aspect of keeping our promise to Russia overtook all strategical considerations! Personally, I consider it absolute madness." Further examples occurred on 15 September 1942 and 9 March 1945.

Political considerations included elections. 30 June 1944 saw

Alanbrooke examining a telegram from Roosevelt, "it is not till you get to the last para that... you find that owing to the coming Presidential election it is impossible to contemplate any action with a Balkan flavour irrespective of its strategic merits." On 19 June 1945, "The elections continue to have a fatal effect on operations. The S of S's statement in the House reducing service abroad in India from 3 years and 8 months to 3 and 4 has had a most pernicious result on the prospect of our operations for the recapture of the Malay peninsula!"

Alanbrooke was adept at predicting when political considerations may influence future operational decisions. 27 October 1939 saw him second-guessing what might happen if the Allies advanced into Belgium, "Therefore, for political reasons, we may well be forced to abandon what strategy dictates and thus court disaster." A further example occurred on 18 July 1944.

There were a few occasions when he managed to subordinate political considerations to military requirements. One was on 25 June 1942, "I was able to convince PM that military aspect of this problem and its advantages outweighed the political considerations." Another was on 6 December 1943 when the Andaman Islands operation was cancelled.

The eighth lesson concerned the Chiefs of Staff Committee. It was vital that this committee spoke with a single, unified voice and presented a unanimous front to the prime minister and cabinet and to allies: as Alanbrooke remarked in his Notes, 17 February 1942, "It is essential that these three men should work together as a perfect trinity." Consequently, any differences between its members had to be reconciled in private session, even if that necessitated "hammer and tongs" arguments. In the main, the committee proved highly effective, notwithstanding the presence of the ailing Dudley Pound. However, it was not flawless. Even as late as 28 August 1945, Alanbrooke was noting, "It is shattering how little sailors and airmen are able to understand the problems connected with land warfare!"

The ninth related to field commanders. They needed to be protected and defended from political interference and criticism. On 24 March 1942, "It is very exhausting, this continual protecting of Auchinleck, especially as I have not got the highest opinion of him" and on 8 February 1944, "I wonder how I have succeeded in keeping [Alexander] covered up to now!" On 6 July 1944, "I flared up and asked [Churchill] if he could not trust his generals for 5 minutes instead of continuously abusing them and belittling them." Field commanders also needed to be guided and supported. Alanbrooke had a talent for providing clear and incisive guidance, well illustrated by his 28 July 1944 letter to Montgomery. Finally, there was considerable truth in his observation on 21 February 1942, "I know well from personal experience that whatever we may say, the man on the spot is in the end the only one who can judge": he made the same point on 23 May 1944.

The tenth was relationships with allies. Successful inter-allied relationships were built on openness, healthy debate and, crucially, trust: incidents such as the disingenuous British approval of American cross-Channel plans in April 1942 were counterproductive since they bred suspicion and distrust which soured future relations. On 16 August 1943, Alanbrooke provided a good example of the degree of candour required, "Our talk was pretty frank. I opened by telling [the Americans] that the root of the matter was that we were not trusting each other."

On 18 May 1944, he cited various factors which undermined inter-allied relationships, "personalities, questions of command, vested interests, inter-allied jealousies". However, the one which drew most criticism was nationalistic attitudes. On 27 July 1944, "now comes the trouble, the [American] press chip in and we hear that the British are doing nothing and suffering no casualties whilst the Americans are bearing all the brunt of the war!!… 'national' spectacles [are] pervert[ing] the perspective of the strategic landscape" and on 1 April 1945, "the straightforward strategy is being affected by the nationalistic outlook of allies. This is one of the handicaps of operating with allies."

The eleventh was identified by Alanbrooke on 23 August 1943, "the Americans… try to run the war on a series of lawyers' agreements which, when once signed, can never be departed from": he made the same point on 17 July 1942. The Americans, who valued clear objectives, firmness of purpose and commitment, tended to adopt a rigid approach to strategy. In contrast, the British were far more flexible and willing to adapt to changed circumstances: 28 June 1944 provided a good example of their different approaches. Whilst each approach had its advantages, Alanbrooke was probably justified when he complained to the Americans on 16 August 1943 that they would "in future insist on our carrying out previous agreements irrespective of changed strategic conditions."

The final, and most important, lesson to be learnt from Alanbrooke's experiences in the War was that he created an invaluable template as to how military leaders should handle their political masters. He willingly adopted the position of an advisor whose role was to serve his political masters, yet he was never in servitude to them. He reserved the right to speak his mind openly and freely on all military matters and he never wavered from that position: this was well illustrated by the incident in early July 1944 when, in the opinion of Joan Bright Astley, "Brooke was far more rude to the PM than he had any right to be". Portal clearly approved of Alanbrooke's approach, "I have an unbounded admiration for… the forcefulness and complete sincerity and the clearsightedness and soundness with which you always dealt with Ministers on our behalf", as did Cunningham, "Straight, absolutely honest and outspoken… he always spoke out fearlessly and fluently against what he knew to be wrong."[11]

An important element of this template was to view one's dismissal or resignation with indifference. On 25 February 1944, "PM called up… I thought it was to tell me that he couldn't stick my disagreements any longer and proposed to sack me!" On 21 March 1944, after Churchill overruled the chiefs of staff on British strategy in the Far East, "it would be better if we all three resigned rather than accept his solution". Alanbrooke was willing to play the ultimate card in his hand.

The importance of these lessons has been illustrated by the recent wars in Afghanistan and Iraq since these twenty-first century conflicts show that many of the lessons have either still not been learnt or, perhaps, forgotten. Alanbrooke's observation, "History is repeating itself in an astonishing way", has as much application today as it did on 2 February 1940.

First, following the 9/11 attacks on America in 2001, American and British forces, supported by other countries, invaded Afghanistan in October 2001 with the aim of destroying al-Qaeda's base of operations and overthrowing the Taliban. Initially successful, America and Britain then switched the focus of their military operations away from Afghanistan and in March 2003 launched a full-scale invasion of Iraq. As a result, the pressure on the Taliban eased and by mid-2003 the first signs of their resurgence started to appear. This contains more than an echo of Alanbrooke's 11 November 1940 entry, "Why will politicians never learn the simple principle of concentration of force at the vital point and the avoidance of dispersal of effort?"

Second, by 2004, America and Britain had recognised the need to increase their military presence in Afghanistan. However, with forces now simultaneously engaged in the two theatres of Iraq and Afghanistan, British resources were stretched: as one British general later remarked, "We called it the perfect storm… we were heading for two considerable-size operations and we really only had the organisation and manpower for one."[12] This contains more than an echo of another of Alanbrooke's entries. On 17 June 1941, he learnt that large-scale operations were to be undertaken simultaneously in both north Africa and Syria, "How can we undertake offensive operations on two fronts in the Middle East when we have not got sufficient for one? From the moment we decided to go into Syria we should have to put all our strength on that front to complete the operation with the least possible delay. If the operation is not pressed through quickly, it may well lead to further complications."

Third, in 2006, Britain despatched over 3,000 troops to secure and stabilise Helmand province in Afghanistan, but the size and terrain of the province was such this number proved hopelessly insufficient for the task. Consequently, additional forces were despatched and by 2009 some 9,000 British troops were deployed there, yet this still proved insufficient. According to one senior British Army commander, the number of troops sent to Helmand was capped on the insistence of the British Government. In the event, Helmand was only brought under control after a significantly larger force of American marines was despatched to the province. The history of this deployment contains more than an echo of Alanbrooke's 31 July 1945 entry, "We were originally told to send 10,000 troops to Greece to back the [Greek] Government, I said it would require at least 80,000 to do what they wanted. I was informed politely that I knew nothing about it as it was a political matter and that 10,000 would be ample to give the necessary backing to the Government. We eventually sent about 90,000 into Greece!!!"

Fourth, between late 2001 and April 2010, a period during which British forces were on active service in both Afghanistan and Iraq, Britain had five different Secretaries of State for Defence: of these, four held office between May 2005 and April 2010. This contains more than an echo of Alanbrooke's entry on 15 September 1942 when he informed Anthony Eden that "we had already had 5!! Ss of S since the war started and could not go on changing."

Fifth, in relation to both the Afghanistan and Iraq campaigns, it has been claimed that British military chiefs were too willing to comply with the demands and instructions of their political masters and insufficiently robust when questioning and challenging their decisions and policy objectives. Alanbrooke demonstrated the level of robustness required of military leaders when dealing with politicians in what is, possibly, the most notable section of his autobiographical Notes, 19 August 1943, "Winston was by now revolving round the northern end of Sumatra as he had done over Trondheim in the past! He had discovered with a pair of dividers that we could bomb Singapore from this point and he had set his heart on going there. It was not a suitable base for further operations against Malaya, but I could not get any definite reply from him as to what he hoped to accomplish from there. When I drew his attention to the fact that when he put his left foot down, he should know where the right foot was going to, he shook his fist in my face, saying, 'I do not want any of your long-term projects, they cripple initiative!' I agreed that they did hamper initiative but told him that I could not look upon knowing where our next step was going as constituting a long-term project! I told him he must know where he was going to which he replied that he did not want to know!"

Sixth, the post-war planning carried out prior to the 2003 invasion of Iraq, such as it was, is widely regarded as woeful. Alanbrooke attached great importance to forward planning, as was apparent by his use of the 'left foot, right foot' metaphor in his Notes, quoted above. On 15 April 1942, "[Marshall's] plan does not go beyond just landing on the far coast [of France]... I asked him this afternoon – do we go east, south or west after landing? He had not begun to think of it!!" and on 23 December 1942, "[Eisenhower's] very bad plan for the capture of Sardinia... never went beyond the landing on the beaches and failed to examine the operations required after the landing is completed".

Seventh, history also repeated itself in the political sphere. Like Churchill, Tony Blair also dominated his cabinet, albeit in a different way. Whereas Churchill browbeat his cabinet, well illustrated by Cadogan's observation on 2 February 1942 "PM hectors more brutally a more subservient Cabinet",[13] Blair largely kept his cabinet in the dark during the period leading up to the invasion of Iraq in March 2003. The result, however, was the same – in the face of a dominant prime minister, both cabinets proved weak and ineffectual. On 25 January 2011, the Iraq Inquiry heard evidence from Lord Wilson, Cabinet Secretary from 1998 until September 2002, and Lord Turnbull, his successor. According to Lord Wilson, "what the Blair years illustrate is that Prime Ministers, if their Cabinets let them be extremely strong, can be extremely strong. And this Cabinet allowed Mr Blair [to] be extremely strong."[14] He testified there was only one substantive discussion about Iraq in the cabinet in the twelve months prior to September 2002. This occurred on 7 March 2002 when the cabinet, apparently concerned as to what may be taking place behind the scenes, "raised all sorts of issues, not political issues particularly, issues about the legal position... what would be involved in military action... about the United Nations": significantly, Lord Wilson then added, "I felt quite proud of the Cabinet at that time for doing their job".[15] Yet that appears to have been the only occasion when it did. The combined testimony of Lords Wilson and Turnbull tell a story of how Blair's cabinet was neither provided with briefing papers nor given any further opportunity to discuss Iraq until the cabinet meeting on 17

March 2003, two days before the start of the invasion, by which time it was, in Lord Turnbull's words, "pretty much imprisoned".[16]

Furthermore, the 'sofa' style of government practised during Blair's tenure as prime minister – informal discussions with selected individuals rather than formal, minuted meetings – contains more than an echo of Churchill's style of government. Marian Long, Arthur Bryant's researcher, interviewed Lieutenant General Ian Jacob, Military Assistant Secretary to the War Cabinet, who informed her, "Churchill didn't like formal committees. He preferred to invite Ministers ad hoc [the "Yes men"?] and to keep all matters of strategy between himself and the Chiefs of Staff. Also, [the] Defence Committee was not set up constitutionally but emerged and made use of as Winston found necessary: they, unlike the War Cabinet and the COS Committee, had no executive powers."

Finally, in his testimony to the Iraq Inquiry, Lord Wilson stated, "If you had said to me 'Is the Prime Minister as the man who devises and drives through strategy serious about military action?' I would have said 'There is a gleam in his eye which worries me.' I think I used that phrase at the time".[17] The "gleam in his eye" contains more than an echo of a phrase which Alanbrooke used in relation to Churchill: on 30 August 1943, "He has an unfortunate trick of picking up some isolated operation and, without ever really having looked into it, setting his heart on it… He becomes then more and more set on the operation brushing everything aside" and, likewise, on 8 October 1943, "[he] has set his heart on capturing [Rhodes]". Perhaps this is one reason why history repeats itself? Political leaders develop a "gleam in the eye" or "set [their] heart" on a military course of action and then, having convinced themselves of the necessity for such action, brush aside all the lessons they can learn from history as to the dangers and risks of taking such action. If so, then history will continue to repeat itself.

In his letter to Alanbrooke written after the War, Budget Loyd predicted, "Few people will ever realize what you have achieved in this war": time has proved the accuracy of his prediction. Of his many achievements, five stand out. The first is the decisive role which he played in saving the

BEF in France in May 1940. According to Sir James Grigg, "By almost universal testimony, it was due largely to his skill and resolution that not only his own Corps but the whole... BEF escaped destruction in the retreat to Dunkirk."[18] Lieutenant General Horrocks made the same point, "The more I have studied this campaign, the clearer it becomes that the man who really saved the BEF was our own corps commander".[19] When this achievement is viewed in conjunction with his actions as commander-in-chief of the second BEF in June 1940, Alanbrooke played a crucial role in averting two disasters. His detractors would doubtless point out he was at the centre of two defeats and humiliating withdrawals but that misses the key point: Britain needed to avoid losing the War in its early stages.

Second, as CIGS, Alanbrooke instilled more purpose, focus and drive into the War Office, the Chiefs of Staff Committee and the British war effort. On 30 September 1940, prior to his appointment as CIGS, he attended a chiefs of staff meeting, "This organization works surprisingly slowly considering there is a war on! We seem to meander along and there is no snap about it." Following his appointment, he was, according to John Kennedy, "quick and decided; his freshness made a new impact; he infected the War Office and the Chiefs of Staff with his own vitality; the change of tempo was immediate and immense."[20] Furthermore, Alanbrooke maintained the same level of purpose, focus and drive throughout the entire War. On 21 January 1943, "This is the most exhausting job, trying to keep the ship of war on a straight course despite all the contrary winds that blow is a superhuman job!" and on 17 August 1944, "The War Office have been raising just one series of difficulties and delays [regarding the proposed attack on Rangoon]. Their examination proved that it was impossible to do it by that date. I therefore had a 2 hours' meeting this morning to prove to them that it is possible and must be done. It is extraordinary how exhausting it is having to drive a plan through against opposition". He made the same point again on 21 June 1945.

Third, he replaced Churchill's opportunistic and intuitive management of the British war effort with a far more coherent and structured strategy

– and it was a strategy which proved successful. If there is one person who can be described as the principal architect and proponent of the British Mediterranean strategy in the War, which is a highly arguable proposition, then that person is Alanbrooke. Moreover, if it is accepted that a cross-Channel invasion before 1944 was impracticable, then he was almost certainly right to advocate it. His detractors will point to the slow and gruelling campaign which ensued on the Italian mainland between 1943–45 but that campaign served an invaluable purpose: as he noted on 26 May 1944, eleven days before Overlord, "The Italian offensive is going on well, [enemy] reserves are being drawn in and it is performing just the function we wanted with reference to the cross-Channel invasion."

Fourth, the heated nature of the debates at the Anglo-American conferences tends to overshadow the fact that Alanbrooke and the British chiefs of staff largely won those debates. In tandem with others, he beat off the proposed 1942 cross-Channel operation. In January 1943, the British prevailed at Casablanca. On 19 May 1943, at Washington, "Our conclusions are that we are to prepare some 29 divisions for entry into France… [and] a continuance of pressure against Italy in the Med. The latter is a triumph as Americans wanted to close down all operations in Med after capture of Sicily" and on the following day, "we… obtained practically exactly what we had originally put forward." On 17 August 1943, at Quebec, "all our arguing has borne fruit and we have obtained quite fair results." On 26 November 1943, at Cairo, "In the end we secured most of the points we were after" and on 6 December 1943, again at Cairo, "I… feel very satisfied at the final results of this meeting."

Alanbrooke's final achievement – and it is one which has been widely recognised – was his management of Churchill. According to Lord Moran, "If anything had happened to him, I do not know any other soldier who would have stood up to the Prime Minister so effectively."[21] In managing his political master, Alanbrooke employed the very same weapons which Churchill himself used, namely assertiveness, confrontation and argument: as Churchill remarked, "When I thump the table and push my face towards him, what does he do? Thumps the table harder and glares back at me".[22]

The scale of this final achievement is best illustrated by comparing Alanbrooke with Field Marshal Keitel who was, loosely, his German counterpart. Whilst they were similar in that both men were motivated by a strong sense of duty, they were polar opposites in two crucial respects: Alanbrooke was strong-willed and spoke his own mind whereas Keitel was weak and obsequious. Keitel was born in 1882 into a middle-class, land-owning family. His interests were riding, hunting and farming and his sole ambition in life appears to have been managing the family's 600-acre farm estate. However, he was steered towards a career in the German Army. After he was wounded in the early stages of the First World War, he was posted to the general staff in 1914. At the end of the war, Keitel was keen to leave the army but was persuaded from doing so. Shortly afterwards, he was posted to the Reich Ministry of Defence.

In 1934, Keitel's father died. Since he was due to inherit the family estate, Keitel applied to resign his commission but, yet again, was persuaded from doing so. In the following year, he was appointed to the administrative post of head of the Armed Forces Office in the Ministry of Defence. In 1936, this ministry was renamed the Ministry of War. In 1938, after Hitler assumed the position of commander-in-chief of Germany's armed forces, the Ministry of War was replaced by a new high command organisation known as OKW and Keitel was installed as its head. In that position, which he held until the end of the War, Keitel took his orders direct from Hitler.

Keitel's nickname was 'Lakeitel', a play on his name and the German word 'lakai' meaning lackey. According to well-placed observers, he was "pathetic"[23] and a "yes man and sycophant"[24] who was guilty of "zombie-like acquiescence"[25] and "senseless chatter"[26]. Another description was, "Keitel allowed himself to be totally dominated by Hitler. Deep down, he was undoubtedly an honest, pleasant man but his intellectual gifts were at best limited… I always had the feeling that Hitler put him into a blue funk and that he was forever trying, like an apprentice, to placate his dreaded employer. His submissive behaviour was almost shameful… At briefings where he should have been the principal advisor, he lent a ready ear to everything Hitler said. I never heard him express the slightest personal opinion. He was, however, an extremely conscientious administrator… Methodical and meticulous, he had a boundless admiration for Hitler, clearly stupefied at his master's agility of mind and imagination. His nickname of Lakeitel unfortunately suited him only too well."[27]

Albert Speer offered this opinion of Keitel, "Constantly in Hitler's presence, he had completely succumbed to his influence. From an honourable, solidly respectable general, he had developed in the course of years into a servile flatterer with all the wrong instincts. Basically, Keitel hated his own weakness; but the hopelessness of any dispute with Hitler had ultimately brought him to the point of not even trying to form his own opinion… In 1943–44 when Schmundt, Hitler's Chief Adjutant, tried… to replace Keitel by the much more vigorous Kesselring, Hitler said he could not do without Keitel because the man was 'loyal as a dog' to him."[28]

According to General Guderian, "Keitel was basically a decent individual who did his best to perform the task allotted him. He soon fell under the sway of Hitler's personality and, as time went on, became less and less able to shake off the hypnosis of which he was a victim… It was Keitel's misfortune that he lacked the strength necessary to resist Hitler's orders when such orders ran contrary to international law and to accepted morality. It was only this weakness on his part that permitted the issuing to the troops of the so-called 'Commissar Order' [directing them to execute captured Russian political commissars] and other notorious decrees. He paid for this with his life at Nuremberg".[29]

After the War, Keitel faced four charges at the International Military Tribunal in Nuremberg. Whilst accepting full responsibility, he pleaded the defence that he was merely following orders issued to him by Hitler. On 1 October 1946, he was found guilty on all four charges and sentenced to death. Prior to his execution, he wrote about the sense of betrayal which he felt: it was belated recognition by a weak and misguided man that he had been manipulated, exploited and then left to face the music,

Suicide: how often I have found myself seriously confronted with this as a possible way out, only to reject it because – as suicides have always demonstrated – nothing is changed and nothing bettered by such action. Quite the contrary, the armed forces, whose counsellor and mediator I had so often been, would have labelled me a deserter and branded me a coward.

Hitler himself chose death rather than accept responsibility for the actions of the OKW, of Colonel-General Jodl and myself. I do not doubt that he would have done us justice and identified himself wholly with my utterances [at Nuremberg]; but for him – as I learned only later – to have committed suicide when he knew he was defeated, shunning thereby his own ultimate personal responsibility upon which he had always laid such great stress and which he had unreservedly taken upon himself alone, instead of giving himself up to the enemy; and for him to have left it to a subordinate to account for his autocratic and arbitrary actions, these two shortcomings will remain for ever incomprehensible to me. They are my final disillusion.[30]

TWENTY-TWO

The Reluctant Warrior

Taken at face value, Alanbrooke is not a character for whom one instinctively feels sympathy: certainly, historians have shown little inclination to do so. Yet, on closer analysis, there are many reasons for sympathising with him.

First, if left to his own devices, the young Alanbrooke would have pursued a career in medicine rather than the army. His sister, Hylda, stated in her account of his childhood, "He surprised us one day by announcing he was going to be a Doctor" and then added, significantly, "and this idea he stuck to for some years." Hylda's statement was corroborated by Lord Moran, "Alanbrooke told me that before he took up soldiering he wanted to be a surgeon."[1] Hylda used strange, almost coded, language when describing how Alanbrooke came to enter the army, "He had by now decided to become a soldier but he took it all very calmly so that one had no idea of the possibilities lying under that quiet exterior": the clear implication was that someone either steered him towards the army or made the decision for him. The answer was provided by Benita in an interview with Marian Long, Bryant's researcher, after the War. Long recorded in her notes, "Lady Alanbrooke mentioned that as a boy Alanbrooke had always wanted to be a doctor or a surgeon, in which he had been encouraged by his mother. It was his brother Victor [Alanbrooke's "hero"] who turned his thoughts to the Army and finally tipped the scale in its direction." Long's notes also quote Benita making this revealing observation, "Alan is obviously much more like [his mother] and the Bellinghams, than the Brookes."

There is an entry in Alanbrooke's diary which suggests the army was not his first choice of career. He was at his most revealing on new years and anniversaries since these prompted him to reflect on the past. On 1 January 1944, he listened to a radio broadcast announcing his promotion to field marshal, "It gave me a curious peaceful feeling that I had at last, and unexpectedly, succeeded in reaching the top rung of the ladder!! I certainly never set out to reach this position, nor did I ever hope to do so even in my wildest moments. When I look back over my life, no one could be more surprised than I am to find where I have got to!!"

Second, Hylda's account of Alanbrooke's childhood contained little sign of the daunting and formidable personality which emerged in adulthood. He was "dreamy and elusive" and during lessons "he sat there dreamily playing with his eyelashes, a far-away look in his big eyes". According to Hylda, "One never quite knew what was going on in Alan's little mind, one of the tantalising things about him was his un-get-at-able quality… at this time he certainly showed no indication of the very masculine being he was going to become". Yet, when she met him towards the end of the two-year course at the Royal Military Academy in Woolwich, she noted that "he had developed very much… He had quite outgrown his delicacy." Hylda's observations raise the possibility that Alanbrooke's forthright and abrupt manner – the characteristic by which he has come to be defined – was not a feature of his natural character but was embedded into him by the culture and disciplines of the army.

Alanbrooke had a sheltered upbringing, largely due to his overprotective mother choosing to keep him close to her side for her own selfish reasons. Hylda noted "It does not seem to me on looking back that he had any little boy friends those early years, I mean not of his own age." As a result, he had limited exposure to the outside world. In his Notes, "At the age of 16, I went to a crammer at Roehampton… Whilst at the crammers and at the [Academy], I felt that I was not quite one of the herd, I had missed something that they had all had. As a result, I was inclined to suffer from an inferiority complex which I found very hard to battle against and which stuck to me through my early life. This failing was accentuated by being intensely shy": according to one of his contemporaries at Woolwich, Alanbrooke "lived on his nerves and found it difficult to relax". The "something" that he "had missed" may have been a public school education, as he claimed in his Notes, but it is just as likely to have been experience of life. The element of immaturity in his letters to Victor, his brother, and the perfect mother during his early adult years, and his use of a catapult on railway journeys when he was in India, point to the likelihood that Alanbrooke was a late developer. Consequently, when he entered the Academy at the age of seventeen, and then the army two years later, he was bound to be shaped and influenced by their culture and disciplines: it was, quite literally, a character-forming experience.

The third is his engagement to Janey in 1908. Four facts raise the suspicion that this may have been 'arranged' or that he was pressurised into this engagement: Alanbrooke and Janey were markedly different personalities, their respective families were neighbours, he had been in India since late 1906 and they became engaged whilst he was on leave. Alanbrooke's lukewarm remark in his Notes, "we had known each other for many years", tends to heighten rather than assuage those suspicions, especially when it is compared to what he wrote about Benita, "It would be quite impossible for me to find words that would do justice to the immeasurable part she has played in shaping my life ever since the day we were married… she has stood as a rock inspiring me with strength and resolution and quite especially as a lighthouse always burning brightly to guide me through life towards those things that really matter and count during our stay on this earth." One is left with a strong sense that his marriage to Janey may not have been the most blissful union.

The fourth relates to Alanbrooke's wish to leave the army in 1927. In his Notes, "I had reached a restless stage in my career… promotion was slowing up… I could see no great prospects of making much of my military career. I seriously contemplated migrating to New Zealand." Whilst this explanation is almost certainly genuine since he cited it in his 30 April 1927 letter to his former colleague, Captain Short, there was another reason why he wanted to leave the army. His experiences in the First World War had left him nursing an intense dislike of war: the horrors, brutality and destruction that he witnessed between 1914 and 1918 had turned him into a reluctant warrior. This was well illustrated by the following letter which he wrote in 1918,

> Yesterday we attacked Cambrai… I followed into the town at 10am… the scene was beyond description. The contrast between war and peace was the thing that struck me most, one dilapidated house with its end blown off and the inside wrecked but sitting on the mantelpiece of one of the rooms, as if no war was on, a stuffed jay with its head on one side.
>
> One trip up to Lens where I wandered among the ruins… such ruin and desolation. I climbed onto a heap of stones which represents the place where the Church once stood and I looked down on the wreckage. One could spend days there just looking down picturing to oneself the tragedies that have occurred in every corner of this place. If the stones could talk and repeat what they have witnessed, and the thoughts they had read on dying men's faces, I wonder if there would ever be any wars.

In his Notes, "Twenty-one years later, I was to stand in the same spot alongside of the rebuilt Church. Stones had remained silent and we were starting the Second World War." The sentiment which lay behind his observation, "I wonder if there would ever be any wars", reappeared in his diary on 2 April 1940, "It is a very strange war, but I sometimes wonder whether if it lasts much longer in its present state we may not on both sides realize that there are better ways of settling our differences than by resorting to war… I am a firm believer that we can ultimately cease from war on this earth". His "firm belief" was more likely his fervent hope.

Alanbrooke clearly wished to leave the army in 1927 but, and herein lies the reason for sympathising with him, he was unable to do so because Janey's death two years earlier had left him a single parent with sole responsibility for two young children: he was boxed in. It is possible that he also considered leaving the army at the end of the First World War, but he was again boxed in, on this occasion by the birth of his first child, Rosemary, in October 1918. If Alanbrooke did feel trapped within the army, which admittedly may be an overstatement of the case, then this would explain why Benita was such an important figure in his life, why he relied so heavily on her and why spending Sundays with her was so important to him: she was his refuge from the army.

The fifth reason for sympathising with Alanbrooke follows on from the previous one. Scarred by his experiences in the First World War, he was horrified when he learnt of Germany's invasion of Poland on 1 September 1939: in his Notes, "I was overwhelmed by a flood of memories of the last war and stood in the passage motionless and aghast at the thought that it was all to be started again." On 28 September 1939, he sailed to France to join the BEF, "It is all too ghastly even to be a nightmare. The awful futility of it all, as proved by the last war!" For this reluctant warrior, the outbreak of war in September 1939 marked the beginning of what was to become a six-year endurance test.

Alanbrooke's "nightmare" was compounded by the fact he was returning to the very locations in France where he had fought in the First World War with the result that all his memories of that conflict were reawakened. On 5 November 1939, he attended an armistice service "at the spot where Germans came out with a white flag in 1918… there was something in it that gripped one, mainly I think the past against the present." On the following day, he visited "our old Canadian Corps HQ occupied during Battle of Vimy. I saw my old office, the window I used to look out of to see HQ staff playing baseball… and my bedroom hut. It brought back floods of memories and made me feel that the war had never stopped." On 24 November, he visited Raudicourt chateau, "The last time I had been there was when we moved out in 1918 to begin the final advance of the war! I felt a desperate longing to have reached the same stage of this war!" On 14 December, he was in the vicinity of Neuve Chapelle "with all its memories of fighting in 1915. I… went past the first billet I ever occupied near the front in 1914… I saw the old ditch into which the trench ambulance had fallen on that first night… It was just a mass of memories which were given a bitter twinge through the fact that I was back again starting again what I thought at the time I was finishing for good and all."

The eight months spent by Alanbrooke in France in 1939–40 was a highly unpleasant experience for him: he may even have hated it. The depth of his discontent was illustrated by the tone and language of his entries describing his two spells of leave during this period. Leave meant escape from war and reunion with Benita. On 2 April 1940, "I still don't dare let myself be carried away in a wild flood of joy at the thought of being on my way home… It is the ghastly fear that something might yet crop up at the eleventh hour to stop me… I would feel as if the bottom of the world had dropped out if I was now stopped from coming back to you." Ten days later, "The end of a week in the most perfect heaven with you came to an end this morning at 9.45am just outside Waterloo platform… I felt a great tidal wave surging up in my throat which I had to gulp down hard… After the last 6 months of it, I know so well what it means being away from you, the awful longings to be back with you… If it was not for your wonderful courage and wonderful calm way of facing trials and difficulties, I do not know what I should do. You are just a tower of strength to me." His entries on 21 December 1939 and 2 January 1940 were in similar vein.

Interestingly, whenever he took periods of leave during the War, he always returned to work downcast. On 29 July 1941, "Motored back to London with a distinct 'going back to school' feeling" and on 13 September 1943, "I returned to work with a very flat feeling and a desperate disinclination to work!" Further examples occurred on 23 September 1942, 1 May 1944 and 30 April 1945.

Alanbrooke escaped from war again when he was evacuated from Dunkirk. In his Notes, he described his car journey to London after arriving in Dover on 31 May 1940, "It was a most lovely English spring morning, with all the country looking as it only can in spring. Everywhere around us were those spring sights and smells of nature awaking after her winter slumbers. The contrast of this lovely sunlit country and its perfect peacefulness when compared with those Belgian roads crammed with distressed and demoralized humanity, horizons shrouded in smoke-clouds from burning villages, continuous rumbling of guns, bombs and aircraft, smashed houses, dead cattle, broken trees and all those war scars that distort the face of nature. To have moved straight from that inferno into such a paradise… made the contrast all the more wonderful": unsurprisingly, the reluctant warrior then added, "That drive will always remain one of my most cherished memories".

His remark, "all those war scars that distort the face of nature", suggests he also disliked war because it led to the desecration of nature. This would explain why he occasionally juxtaposed his love of nature with his dislike of war in his diary. On 3 February 1940, "The first feelings of spring. A lovely mild day which makes it harder than ever to realize that humanity can be so mad as to be at war again". On 22 March 1940, "Weather getting more springlike, daffodils coming up and bushes sprouting which makes war even more objectionable". 10 May 1940 was the day of the German invasion of Holland and Belgium, "It was hard to believe on a most glorious spring day with all nature looking quite at its best that we were taking the first step towards what must become one of the greatest battles of history" and on 23 March 1942, "spring sun shining which made the war all the more unpleasant."

The distress felt by Alanbrooke when nature was desecrated can be traced back to the early 1900s when he participated in hunting trips in India. In this section of his Notes, the key phrase is "and yet from the very start", "I derived the most intense thrill from the pursuit of wild game, and the pitting of my own intelligence against that of wild animals on their own ground. And yet from the very start, I had experienced pangs of regret and repentance when a hunt was brought to a successful end by the destruction of some wild creature that I had been the cause of. Strange feeling of deep dissatisfaction with oneself… I had been finding recently that by replacing the rifle more and more by the camera, I still obtained all the thrills of the chase without any of the personal reproaches at its outcome." He then recalled the incident when he chose to take three photographs of a buffalo rather than shoot it: his final sentence was revealing, "I have lost most of my shooting trophies and do not miss them much, but I still have those 3 snapshots and they always stir up the happiest memories when I look at them."

His escape from war on 31 May 1940 was, however, short-lived. Two days later, "I walked into Dill's room with a light heart… and asked him what he now wished me to do. His reply was, 'Return to France to form a new BEF'. As I look back at the war, this was certainly one of my blackest moments": the reluctant warrior was returning to war. When he arrived in France on 13 June, "heartbreaking to find oneself back amongst [the refugees]." Six days later, he returned to Britain, "we set foot on British soil and thanked God for again allowing us to come home." Alanbrooke had, yet again, escaped from war.

His reaction to Germany's defeat was notable. On 2 May 1945, "Last night, on the midnight news, Hitler was reported as dead. After longing for this news for the last 6 years and wondering whether I should ever be privileged to hear it, when I finally listened to it, I remained completely unmoved. Why? I do not know." On 21 July 1945, he inspected British troops in Berlin, "We returned to the stand and then the Division marched past. I suppose I ought to have been gripped by what this all meant… Somehow it left me cold." Three days later, "Thus finished our Combined Chiefs of Staff Meeting in Berlin!! where we had never hoped to meet in our wildest dreams in the early stages of this war. And now that we are here, I feel too weary and cooked to even get a kick out of it. It all feels flat and empty." Exhaustion was not the only explanation for his deflated reaction. If, as Alanbrooke believed, war was futile then by logical extension being victorious in war must also be futile: consequently, no satisfaction could be gained from it. Little wonder, therefore, that when Germany surrendered on 7 May 1945, "So this is at last the end of the war!!… I can't feel thrilled".

The sixth, and the most compelling, reason for sympathising with Alanbrooke is that he endured an internal conflict throughout the entire War. This conflict arose because his two markedly different personas pulled him in opposite directions – whilst the professional soldier practised the art of war, the simple, gentle, selfless soul just yearned for peace. 2 January 1940 saw a "New Year beginning and pray God that it may bring us

Peace". On 3 February 1940, he wanted to "wake up out of this nightmare of war and find myself at your side again with the world at peace". On 31 May 1940, following his evacuation from Dunkirk, "Wonderful feeling of peace after the last 3 weeks [of war]". On 19 October 1940, "I am very tired of this war and long for peace". On 24 January 1943, after the Casablanca conference, "I spent a real peaceful afternoon looking for birds in the lovely garden of the hotel". On 26 October 1943, he attended Dudley Pound's funeral, "he had certainly chosen the one road that led at last to peace and an end to these worldly struggles, and in some ways I envied him." On 29 June 1944, he visited Kew Gardens, "It was lovely and peaceful there. I felt it was just what I wanted."

And the one place where the simple, gentle, selfless soul found peace was at home in the company of Benita: they were his sanctuary from the War, a place to which he could escape. On 27 December 1941 and 13 June 1942 he "escaped home", on 4 September 1942 he "escaped and went home" and on 7 April 1945 he "had made all plans to escape early". On Sunday, 8 September 1940, "It is so wonderful being able to get into such surroundings for a bit and to forget the war and all its horrors. Motored back [to London]… It seemed so strange leaving you and all the wonderful peace and happiness connected with our combined lives". 29 September 1940 was "a lovely and peaceful day… These Sunday afternoons with you are the most wonderful tonic… When with you [at home], I am able to forget everything connected with the war". 19 October 1940 saw him longing for "A peace that will allow us to spend the remaining years of our life quietly together in a small cottage with a garden to work in, some trees to look after and perhaps a stream close by where I can watch the fish even if I don't catch them! And above all somewhere where I can bask in the sublime happiness of the sunshine of your company!"

28 December 1941 was "a lovely peaceful day with you… [which] fitted me up to stand another week of this strain!" On 8 March 1942, "Lovely peaceful quiet day at home, forgetting there is any war". 29 November 1942 was a "happy peaceful Sunday with you." The weekend of 12 and 13 August 1944 was "spent quietly at home with you and resting

peacefully. Just heaven after the previous week." On 9 May 1945, as the population of Britain celebrated victory, Alanbrooke and Benita spent "a happy and peaceful afternoon together looking after goats and chickens". Three days later, he "spent the morning in complete peace mending an old rabbit hutch!" Derivatives of 'peace' appear more than thirty times in Alanbrooke's diary for those days spent at home during the War. This may not seem many but, given he was in France for the first nine months of the War and thereafter was often overseas for lengthy spells, it is significant.

It was this yearning for peace which prompted Alanbrooke to lash out against humanity for waging war. On 19 October 1940, "Another day gone and thank God for it! Every day that passes must at least be one day less of this war. But there are times when the madness and folly of war choke one! Why human beings must behave like children at this stage of the evolution of the human race is hard to understand." On 26 May 1942, he attended the ceremonial signing of a new Anglo-Russian treaty, "Many toasts and many speeches. Somehow the whole affair gave me the creeps and made me feel that humanity has still many centuries to live through before universal peace can be found" and on 23 October 1944, "It seems essential for humanity to subject itself to untold ordeals in order to achieve even slow progress towards perfection."

This internal conflict is evidenced by Alanbrooke's frequent use of two phrases in his diary. The first was 'had to'. Admittedly, he used this phrase when describing something which he disliked. For example, since he was a private man who was uncomfortable with publicity, he did not enjoy being photographed so on 21 July 1940 "had to suffer photographer and cine man", on 13 March 1941 "I had to pose" and on 3 August 1944 "had to have a coloured photograph taken".

More significant, however, was his use of this phrase when the professional soldier performed a task which the simple, gentle, selfless soul found unpleasant. On 23 November 1939, "Started the day by having to tell off Monty". Why did he 'have to' tell off Monty – it would have been easier and quicker to record 'Started the day by telling off Monty'? The answer was that the professional soldier had done something which the simple, gentle, selfless soul found unpleasant: consequently, it 'had to' be performed.

On 11 January 1940, "Had to break the news to [Franklyn] that his division would be leaving the II Corps. I am sorry he is going". On 19 February 1940, "Had to reprimand [illegible] for contravening censorship in letter home." August 1942 saw considerable unpleasantness in Cairo. On 8 August, "I again had to give [Churchill] a long lecture on the system of the chain of command in the Army", on 9 August, he met Auchinleck who had just been informed of his removal from command, "He wanted to know what the decision had been based on and I had to explain mainly lack of confidence in him" and on the following day, "had to bite [Auchinleck] back as he was apt to snarl". On 29 October 1942, Eden sowed disquiet over the progress of the El Alamein battle, "I... had to tell [Churchill] fairly plainly what I thought of Anthony Eden's ability to judge a tactical situation at this distance!" On 23 December 1942, "Had to turn down a very bad plan for the capture of Sardinia worked out by Eisenhower."

On 15 January 1943, at Casablanca, "I had to criticise [Eisenhower's] operation against Sfax". On 26 February 1943, "I had to attack Portal this morning on the paucity of bomber squadrons". On 4 March 1943, "had to inform Martel that he was for Moscow which he did not appreciate very much!" On 2 November 1943, "I had to disagree with a [Joint Intelligence Committee] report... They did not like this". On 24 January 1944 and 25 May 1944, he "had to" give further tickings off to Montgomery. On 29 March 1944, "I have had to get rid of Andy McNaughton [Canadian commander]". On 20 June 1944, "had to inform Laurence Carr that his soldiering days had come to an end, I hated doing it". On 11 August 1944, "I had to tell [Mountbatten] that he could not send any of [his "quite hopeless letters"] and should attend COS on Monday." On 7 November 1944, "we had to pull [Churchill's draft wire] to pieces badly and sent it back mutilated".

The second phrase was 'I am afraid'. Alanbrooke occasionally used this when he sympathised with the plight of others. On 13 November 1939, "I am afraid Dill feels the situation acutely... he is torn between loyalty to his commander and loyalty to his Corps" and on 18 May 1940, "The Germans unfortunately got into the 15/19 Regt today and I am afraid did in the HQ and at least 1 squadron."

He also used it in a way which was tantamount to an apology. On 26 August 1942, "I am afraid I was rather rude to all members of the COS" and on 16 February 1944, "I am afraid I rather lost my temper with [Churchill]". On both occasions, the simple, gentle, selfless soul was lamenting the professional soldier's lack of propriety.

Most noticeable of all, however, was Alanbrooke's repeated use of this phrase when he found fault in others: this was the simple, gentle, selfless soul regretting the criticisms made by his alter ego, the professional soldier. In July 1940, he inspected Plymouth's defences, "Green must I am afraid go. He has not got the required qualities." On 9 August 1942, "[Tedder] is, I am afraid, only a small-brained man." On 28 December 1942, "I am afraid that Eisenhower as a general is hopeless… partly, I am afraid, because he knows little if anything about military matters." On 21 February 1943, "I am afraid the American troops will take a great deal more training before they will be any use, and that Anderson is not much good!" On 13 September 1943, "I am afraid that neither Eisenhower nor Alexander will ever have sufficient vision to be big soldiers." On 29 March 1944, "I have had to get rid of Andy McNaughton… All has now been accomplished with much anguish and many difficulties… I have however, I am afraid, lost a very good friend".

On 31 March 1944, "I am afraid that our Joint Staff Mission in Washington are now only acting as a [Post Office] and not expressing views and opinions of their own." On 31 May 1944, "I am afraid however that Mountbatten will be a constant source of trouble to us and will never really fit the bill as Supreme Commander." On 1 June 1944, "Giffard, I am afraid, lacking the adequate vision to see where he is going to". On 4 July 1944, he met Alexander and criticised his handling of operations in Italy, "I am afraid Alex did not like this much": four days later, "[Alexander] is… I am afraid very simple-minded and entirely innocent of any understanding of the politician's methods!" On 17 November 1944, "Wilson will, I am afraid, never be able to step into Dill's shoes."

On 15 March 1945, "I am afraid that Alexander… has forgotten the main object of the war and no longer remembers that there are people such as the Germans!" And on 23 July 1945, "I am afraid that [Anthony Eden] added to my gloom. Delightful as he is, in my opinion he always seems to just miss the point."

Quite understandably, Alanbrooke felt it necessary to conceal this internal conflict from public view: the outside world was only allowed to see the professional soldier dispensing "abrupt efficiency".[2] This may, in part, explain his remark to Marian Long in 1955 that he "considered [it] essential never to disclose outwardly what one felt inwardly." However, his guard was bound to slip during the six years of the War and when the simple, gentle, selfless soul did peek out from behind the professional soldier, Joan Bright Astley saw "a delightful, amusing and easy companion"[3] and Montgomery saw "the real Brookie".[4]

His concealment of this internal conflict may also explain the occasional feelings of loneliness which he suffered. On 19 November 1941, his appointment as CIGS was announced, "now that I am stepping up onto the plateau land of my military career, the landscape looks cold, black and lonely". On 24 August 1943, at the end of the Quebec conference, "a feeling of emptiness, depression, loneliness and dissatisfaction over results attacks one and swamps one! After Casablanca, wandering alone in the garden of the Mamounia Hotel in Marrakesh, if it had not been for the birds and the company they provided, I could almost have sobbed with the loneliness. Tonight, the same feelings overwhelm me, and there are no birds!"

It was, of course, the professional soldier who emerged victorious from the internal conflict which he endured: even for this reluctant warrior, duty and service had to – and did – prevail. In his biography of Alanbrooke, David Fraser captured this point well when describing him as "the imprisoned bird which had so often had to beat its wings against the iron cage of duty he had so firmly constructed."[5]

The seventh reason for sympathising with Alanbrooke is that fate handed him the task of managing the charismatic and mercurial Churchill. By analogy to the business world, he was ordained to play the role of finance director whose job was to question and challenge the ideas of his chief executive and, when necessary, kill off the wild ones. It is a fact of life that people are attracted to colourful, larger than life personalities such as Churchill and find it easy to overlook or excuse their flaws: paradoxically, the more genius there is in a person, the more flaws there are. It is also a fact of life that the vital role played by those who guide and, in truth, sustain such personalities is always underappreciated. Given his close proximity to Churchill, it was predestined that Alanbrooke would pale into insignificance which is exactly what has happened.

The eighth is the incident in August 1943 regarding command of the cross-Channel invasion. Churchill offered this command to Alanbrooke on three separate occasions in mid-1943 but then, unilaterally and without warning, handed it over to the Americans in return for securing Mountbatten's appointment as supreme commander in South East Asia. This was a devastating blow to Alanbrooke from which it took him "several months to recover", according to his 15 August 1943 Notes. Moreover, it was the way Churchill handled this incident which Alanbrooke found so wounding. In the same section of his Notes, "Not for one moment did he realize what this meant to me. He offered no sympathy, no regrets… and dealt with the matter as if it were one of minor importance!" Churchill's indifference and insensitivity were made more reprehensible by the fact he knew at the time that Alanbrooke had come to regret his earlier decision to turn down the offer of command in the desert [29 October 1942]. However, such was Churchill's style: as Lord Moran observed of this incident, "In that moment there was revealed to Brooke the crushing indifference of these monolithic figures [Churchill] to the lower forms of life."[6]

Ninth, one attribute for which Alanbrooke has received barely any credit is that he was a team player: he dedicated himself to the task of achieving victory for the Allies to the exclusion of his own self-interests. Ismay attested to his "selflessness"[7], Montgomery and Moran described him as "selfless"[8] and Cunningham observed, "Alan Brooke was always actuated by the highest motives… Jealousy in any shape or form did not enter into his composition."[9] In marked contrast to many other leading individuals, he refused to be influenced by factors such as self-promotion or personal fame. On 18 May 1944, British strategy in the Far East was being planned, "Unfortunately, the right course to follow is troubled by personalities, questions of command, vested interests, inter-allied jealousies... How on earth are we to steer a straight course between all these snags and difficulties?" Twelve months earlier, 8 May 1943, he dryly remarked, "Running a war seems to consist in making plans and then ensuring that all those destined to carry it out don't quarrel with each other instead of the enemy". It would be quite impossible to make a film about the role played by Alanbrooke in the War and title it *Alanbrooke – Lust for Glory*.

Allied to this selfless dedication was his refusal to act in a way that would endear him to others. Alanbrooke understood that an essential part of his role as CIGS was to inject energy, drive and purposefulness into the British war effort which, inevitably, meant confrontation. He also understood that efficiency and popularity were mutually exclusive for a man in his position, hence his observation on 31 May 1944, "Mountbatten is quite irresponsible and tries to be loved by all which won't work!" Alanbrooke deliberately chose the former and, in doing so, he paid a price: popularity and self-interest were sacrificed at the altar of efficiency.

Tenth, it is difficult to avoid the feeling that Alanbrooke received poor reward for his invaluable services to Britain. It could be argued that titles and medals – and he received his fair share of these – are all that members of the armed forces can and should expect. Perhaps, but a gratuity of £310 appears paltry, almost miserly. Furthermore, there was a strong whiff of unfairness, almost injustice, in his losing out on the governor generalships of Canada and Australia and then being forced to sell his house and his beloved collection of Gould bird books so soon after the War. The fact that Alanbrooke's statue outside the Ministry of Defence in London was only erected in 1993, thirty years after his death and thirteen years after Montgomery's statue was unveiled, says it all.

It is also difficult to avoid the feeling that he was poorly served by Arthur Bryant, the author of *The Turn of the Tide* and *Triumph in the*

West. His books lacked the essential ingredient of balance with the result that they cast Alanbrooke in a negative light: Pug Ismay thought there was "a danger that posterity… will get the idea that Brooke was self-satisfied, self-pitying, ungenerous and disloyal"[10] and Lord Moran believed the books left "the reader with a misleading picture of Alanbrooke… his friends protested… it was hardly credible that this self-effacing man, who never spoke of himself or took credit for anything in the war, should in cold print claim the landing in North Africa as 'my strategy.'"[11] Moran was probably correct when he observed that Alanbrooke should have written the books himself because only he, as author of the diary, "could get the feel of things and be able to measure his words."[12] As a consequence, Alanbrooke found himself in the minefield of a public controversy which is unlikely to have been a pleasant experience for the publicity-shy field marshal. In fairness, Alanbrooke must bear some of the blame since by handing his diary over to Bryant and then allowing him too much free rein in the writing of the books, he was, in effect, giving Bryant stewardship of his name and reputation: for once, his impeccable judgment deserted him. However, this is not the first time that a military man has stumbled when making the transition from the military to the civilian world. Neither, in all probability, will it be the last.

Unsurprisingly, Bryant's books were viewed by some as an exercise in self-aggrandisement by Alanbrooke. This may partly explain the coolness which historians have tended to show towards Alanbrooke and their readiness to find fault in him. Writing in the twenty-first century, Sir Max Hastings offered this description, "A man of notable vanity, which suffused his diaries, he overrated his own talents and was ungenerous in his estimate of Churchill's. But a significant part of his achievement – and it was a remarkable achievement – lay in his willingness to fight Churchill day or night when he believed him wrong. If Brooke was a cautious soldier, who might not have prospered as a field commander, he had provided a superb foil for the prime minister, preserving him from many misfortunes. His contribution to Britain's war effort had been substantial… He was unable, however, to accept that the price of serving a towering historical figure was to be obscured by his shadow."[13]

This description is quite typical of historians' treatment of Alanbrooke in the decades since the War. The positives are there, but they are drowned out by the negatives and, of course, it is the negatives which are remembered. Was Alanbrooke "a man of notable vanity"? Did he "overrate his own talents"? Was he "ungenerous in his estimate of Churchill's [talents]"? Why speculate that he "might not have prospered as a field commander"? These claims are questionable, not least the one that he was "unable to accept that the price of serving a towering historical figure was to be obscured by his shadow." The "spellbound and exasperated"[14] Alanbrooke was never in any doubt about Churchill's stature or, for that matter, his flaws. The only thing he was "unable to accept" was Churchill's egotism and his failure to recognise and give credit to others for the role which they played in the War. That grated on Alanbrooke's sense of fairness.

There is an alternative explanation for the coolness which historians have tended to show Alanbrooke: they have just taken him at face value and failed to appreciate that there was far more depth and complexity to the man than the daunting, formidable figure who projected "abrupt efficiency"[15] in forthright manner. If this is correct, they can hardly be criticised for doing so, given the lengths Alanbrooke went to conceal his inner soul from public view.

The eleventh reason for sympathising with Alanbrooke is that death was such a prominent feature of his life: it seemed to stalk him. He experienced a series of deaths as a child, most notably the premature death of his father. He suffered the loss of his "hero" brother, Victor, in the First World War and, in common with many others, witnessed death on a massive scale on the Western Front between 1914 and 1918. This was followed by the death of Janey in 1925, which left him guilt-ridden, and by the deaths of close friends such as Barney Charlesworth, John Dill and Ivan Cobbold during the War. Sadly, death continued to stalk Alanbrooke after the War since his daughter, Kathleen, was killed in 1961 in a riding accident.

In 1963, a group of Alanbrooke's friends pooled their resources to buy some of the treasured Gould bird books as an eightieth birthday present for him. However, it was not to be. On 17 June, Alanbrooke suffered a heart attack whilst drinking a cup of tea in bed at home and died, instantly and peacefully.

Benita was inundated with letters of condolence. One female sympathiser hit the bullseye,

> It was with much sorrow that I heard of your great loss. I know well what it must mean to you. Seldom surely has any man done so much for our country and the world and also carried the admiration, respect and affection of all who worked with him. I am quite certain he could never have achieved so much and withstood the strain of the war years without you as his companion to sustain, encourage and help him. I do hope that this knowledge will be of some comfort to you and help you to bear the parting.

A few days later, and with Alanbrooke's funeral set for 26 June 1963 in St George's Chapel at Windsor Castle, Benita received a letter from Montgomery, "I fear it will not be possible for me to be with you on Wednesday next, 26 June. I will have to speak in the Foreign Affairs debate in the House of Lords. My present intention is to pay a quiet visit to the grave on Monday morning, 8 July. I am so distressed about it that I want to go there quite alone. There will I hope be somebody on duty in the church or cemetery who will help me to find the grave."

In early July, Benita received a further letter from Montgomery: true to form, he had "gone off the rails" again, "I visited the grave this morning. It could not be in a better spot, looking out over England's green and pleasant land. I was early. But a very nice young lad then arrived, sent, I imagine, by you to be my guide. But one of the gardeners had taken me to the grave. I fear I was not very talkative as I was feeling sorrowful, and he may have been offended. I would like to write to him, and apologise, and thank him. Will you tell me who he was and give me his address?"

Benita survived Alanbrooke for five years. The circumstances of her death in May 1968 would have appalled him: bearing an eery similarity to Janey's death in 1925, Benita was killed in a car accident whilst being driven by a female companion.

The final reason for sympathising with Alanbrooke is that he never had the chance to read the following letter which Benita received in early 1967. If he had, then he would have known that his "6 years of endless, heartbreaking struggles" [26 March 1945] had not been in vain,

To Lord Alan Brooke,
Viscount, Ex Field-Marshal,
Commodore in Chief General Staff Imperial,
of Great Britain.

Dear Sir:

The writer is an Italian (one of your ex-enemy). I fairly fought against your country from 10th July to 8th September 1943 – like non-commissioned officer of Admiralty on board of submarines. Like most Italian people I did not felt the war that Mussolini and [illegible] ordered us to do against the Allies; but my country was in arms, as I loved it, I did my duty: (to obey and fight).

Really I never detested you, neither when during the fight I risked to die from Allies.

After the armistice of 8th September I remember that I prayed God so that you will be the winners and I was happy to know that you defeated the Germany; now I can say that if the Allies would not have won Hitler and Mussolini would have kept on with the wars and now we should not have the peace. With the peace the Allies gave back to the European people their liberty and I, as a free man, wish to say thank you to the American and English people; but especially I wish to say thank you to the late Sir Winston Churchill and also to you Marshal Alan Brooke.

Of late I read with emmotion all books that Prof. Arthur Bryant got from your war-diary. I admired your strategy, your courage, the character and the noble feelings that you have had during those long

and terrible years. Rightly as you say in some of your memories God gave you his help and you Mr Marshal Alan Brooke, have used this help very well and therefore you have deserved it.

By your deeds you honoured your country and you handed down an example of high virtue to posterity but particularly you contributed to save people from horrors of Nazism. From your deeds Prof. Bryant had drawn wonderful pages of history that now all the world knows.

As to perform my duty I am writing to you this letter to make known to you my gratitude. God grant you have a quiet and long old-age.

Excuse me if my letter is too long but it was impossible for me to be short and at the same time tell to you that I would like and that my heart feel and think of you.

I will finish with some phrases your diary:

"I went to see PJ and while I was going out Lady Grigg took me on arm and drew aside and she said to me: 'This morning behind the window, I saw you to get on the car, all people were observing you but nobody knew you and that you did to win the war against the Germany. It is not right that people does not know all this. I think so and like me a lot of other people, tell this to Lady Brooke from my part.'"

The thought of Lady Grigg is also mine.

Yours faithfully

Romeo Meregalli

The "phrases" quoted by Romeo Meregalli came from Alanbrooke's entry on 8 May 1945, Victory in Europe Day,

I had to go and see PJ [Grigg, Secretary of State for War] and on coming out Lady Grigg collared me and brought me into the passage. She said, 'I watched you getting into your car this morning from the window with a crowd looking at you, and none of them realizing that *beside them was the man who had probably done most to win the war against Germany!' She said it was all wrong that they should not realize it, 'I do, and lots of people do, tell Lady Brookie from me.' It was very nice of her, she said it so nicely and I wish you had been able to hear her.*

The final sentence was written by Alanbrooke because he wanted to share the praise with Benita, in recognition of the role she had played as his "lighthouse" and "mainstay and anchor" throughout the War.

The final sentence was written by a simple, gentle, selfless soul.

APPENDIX

The British strategy paper tabled at Casablanca in January 1943[1]

American-British Strategy in 1943

1. Our combined resources have increased to the point where we have been able to wrest the initiative from Germany and Italy, and to pin down the Japanese in the Southwest Pacific. The days of plugging holes are over. We must now agree on a plan that will lead to victory, quickly and decisively.

2. The main factors bearing on the conduct on the war are:
   (a) The fighting power of Germany is on the wane and her oil situation is at the moment critical. What she needs above all is a period for recuperation.

   (b) All that stands between Germany and the opportunity for recuperation with an abundant oil supply is Russia. The Russian war effort is also the greatest single drain on the power and hope of Germany and must be sustained and assisted at all costs.

   (c) The Japanese war effort is incapable of much expansion provided communications with Germany are kept severed.

   (d) The offensive power of the United States is growing. The main problem is to decide how her armed forces can best be deployed against the enemy.

(e) The war potential of the British Empire is not capable of much more overall expansion. The bulk of the British armed forces are already directed against Germany. As long as Germany is in the field, a considerable proportion of these forces must continue to be located in the United Kingdom and Home Waters.

(f) Shipping is vital – not only to maintain the British war effort but to deploy the forces of the United Nations against the enemy.

(g) Submarine warfare is now the only means whereby Germany could cripple our offensive action.

3. The resources of the United Nations are insufficient to defeat Germany and Japan simultaneously. We must therefore either concentrate on defeating Germany while holding Japan, or vice versa. The arguments may be summarized as follows:

(a) If Germany were allowed breathing space to recuperate, she might well become unbeatable. Provided we maintain limited pressure on Japan, she can never become unbeatable.

(b) By concentrating on Germany, we uphold Russia. By concentrating on Japan we should cause little, if any, relief to the Russians. Moreover, for a given amount of shipping, more United States forces can be deployed against Germany than against Japan.

(c) In order to defeat Japan, we should need to concentrate against her so large a naval force that the security of the United Kingdom and of Atlantic Sea communications would be seriously jeopardized.

(d) If we do not bring sufficient pressure to bear on Japan, there is a risk of China dropping out of the fight. We must therefore continue to give China such support as will ensure that she will not give up the struggle.

(e) Important though China is as an ally against Japan, Russia is far more important as an ally against Germany. Moreover, after the defeat of Germany, Russia might be a decisive factor in the war against Japan, whereas China could never help us in the war against Germany.

4. It is clear from the above that we should persist in the strategic policy adopted at the first Washington Conference, namely that we should bend all our efforts to the early and decisive defeat of Germany, diverting only the minimum force necessary to hold Japan.

Holding Japan

5. The operations in the Southwest Pacific during the last few months have forced the Japanese to make this area their principal theater of operations. These have directly relieved the threat to Australasia, India and the Indian Ocean, and have indirectly assisted Russia by staving off a Japanese attack on the Maritime provinces. The best way of holding Japan is to continue limited offensive operations on a scale sufficient to contain the bulk of the Japanese forces in the Pacific. It is necessary to define the broad action required to implement this strategy.

6. The only way of bringing material help to China is to open the Burma Road. The reconquest of Burma should therefore be undertaken as soon as resources permit.

Defeat of Germany

7. The occupation of Germany will ultimately be necessary. For the

present, however, Northwest Europe may be likened to a powerful fortress which can be assaulted only after adequate preparation. To make a fruitless assault before the time is ripe would be disastrous for ourselves, of no assistance to Russia and devastating to the morale of occupied Europe. We cannot yet bring to bear sufficient forces to overcome the German garrison of France and the Low Countries, which can rapidly concentrate against us in superior strength and behind powerful coast defenses.

8. The alternatives which lie before us are:
   (a) To devote our main effort towards building up in the United Kingdom a force of sufficient size to invade the Continent, or

   (b) To devote our main effort towards undermining the foundations of German military power, simultaneously building up in the United Kingdom the maximum United States and British forces which our remaining resources allow in order to return to the Continent as soon as German powers of resistance have been sufficiently weakened. The effect of each of these courses of action is discussed in the following paragraphs.

Invasion of the Continent

9. If we go for the maximum "Bolero" with the intention of assaulting the Continent in 1943 we must be ready to strike by September. Thereafter weather conditions will progressively deteriorate. The strongest Anglo-American force which we could assemble in the United Kingdom by that date for an attack upon Northern France would be some 13 British and 9 United States divisions with perhaps a further 3 United States divisions collecting in the United Kingdom. 6 divisions are probably the maximum which could be organized as assault forces.

10. The assembly of the above forces would have the following effects:

APPENDIX

On the Axis

(a) We should have to accept only a small increase in the scale of bomber offensive against Germany and Italy from now onwards. This would be due to giving a higher priority to the passage of United States soldiers across the Atlantic and to the need for bringing over larger proportion of army support types of United States aircraft.

(b) We should have to abandon all amphibious operations in the Mediterranean, thereby giving Germany the opportunity she so desperately needs for rest and recuperation, and Italy a chance to steady her morale.

On Russia

(c) We could run a limited number of convoys to North Russia.

(d) The Axis might well make advantage of the relaxation of pressure to transfer forces from the Mediterranean to Russia.

On Turkey

(e) There would be sufficient Allied Forces left over in the Mediterranean to support Turkey but these could not be used for offensive operations owing to lack of shipping and assault craft. The reduction of our offensive in the Mediterranean would make Turkey all the more reluctant to join in the war on our side.

On Spain

(f) Relaxation of Allied pressure in the Mediterranean would make Spain more inclined to yield to German pressure.

11. Even if we accepted the above curtailment of our activities in other

theaters, we should probably find that the expedition which we had prepared was inadequate to overcome the scale of German resistance existing when the time came for the assault. The scale of "Roundup" as originally planned was a total of 48 British and United States divisions; since then the defenses of the French Coast and the German garrison in France have been increased to some 40 divisions. In short the adoption of this strategy would mean a relaxation of pressure on the Axis for 8 or 9 months with incalculable consequences to the Russian Front and at the end of the period no certainty that the assault on France could, in fact, be carried out. Or even if it were carried out, that it would draw out land forces from the Russian Front.

Attrition of Germany

12. Apart from operations to clear the enemy out of North Africa, our attrition of Germany has hitherto comprised bombing, blockade, raids and subversive action. All these methods strike at the enemy's industrial and economic system, submarine construction, sources of air power and, last but not least, at the morale of the German people – and all can be intensified.

13. The bomber offensive is susceptible of great development and holds out most promising prospects. For this purpose we should aim at an Anglo-American bomber force of 3,000 heavy and medium bombers in the United Kingdom by the end of 1943.

14. Our success in North Africa opens up wide possibilities of offensive operations against the Southern flank of the Axis. In particular we may be able to detach Italy from the Axis and induce Turkey to join the Allies. If we force Italy out of the war and the Germans try to maintain their line in Russia at its present length, we estimate that they will be some 54 divisions and 2,200 aircraft short of what they need on all fronts. If the defection of Italy were followed by that of

other satellite powers, these deficiencies would be still larger.

15. While we follow this policy of bombing and amphibious operations in the Mediterranean, our surplus resources can be devoted to the build-up of Anglo-American forces in the United Kingdom to take advantage of any deterioration in German military power. Any decision to re-enter the Continent would have to allow 3 months for the collection of landing craft and other preparations. We estimate that under favorable conditions a force of 12 British and 6 United States divisions could be made available in the United Kingdom by September with a further 3 United States divisions collecting in the United Kingdom.

16. The effects of devoting our main effort initially to this undermining of German military power will be:

On the Axis
    (a)   We can substantially increase the weight of the bomber offensive.

    (b)   By amphibious operations in the Mediterranean aimed at bringing about the collapse of Italy, we can give the maximum relief to Russia, wear out the German Air Force and ultimately threaten Axis economic resources in the Balkans.

    (c)   The build-up of forces in the United Kingdom, though below the maximum rate, would still be sufficient to pin down substantial German Forces in Northwest Europe, and would permit us to take advantage in the autumn of a pronounced decline in German fighting power.

On Russia
    (d)   During the period of amphibious operations in the Mediterranean convoys to North Russia will be limited to the extent that the United States can provide escort vessels.

On Turkey

(e) We should have forces available in the Mediterranean which we could use to support Turkey. Turkey is more likely to come into the war on our side if we succeed in eliminating Italy – as we hope to do during 1943. With Turkey on our side, we should be well placed for offensive action against the Balkans.

On Spain

(f) Germany will have no forces to spare to invade Spain. Spain is less likely to yield to German pressure if we keep the German Forces fully extended by a vigorous offensive in the Mediterranean.

Conclusion

17. Our proposals for the conduct of the war throughout 1943 are these:

(a) The defeat of the U-boat menace to remain a first charge on our resources.

(b) The expansion of the Anglo-American bomber offensive against Germany and Italy.

(c) The exploitation of our position in the Mediterranean with a view to –
(1) knocking Italy out of the war,
(2) bringing Turkey into the war, and
(3) giving the Axis no respite for recuperation.

(d) The maintenance of supplies to Russia.

(e) Limited offensive operations in the Pacific on a scale sufficient only to contain the bulk of Japanese Forces in that area.

(f) Operations to reopen the Burma Road to be undertaken as soon as resources permit.

APPENDIX

(g) Subject to the claims of the above, the greatest possible concentration of forces in the United Kingdom with a view to re-entry on to the Continent in August or September 1943 should conditions hold out a good prospect of success, or anyhow a "Sledgehammer" to wear down the enemy Air Forces.

The American strategy paper tabled at Casablanca in January 1943[2]

Basic Strategic Concept For 1943

1. The Joint Chiefs of Staff have reviewed, in the light of current developments, [earlier CCS papers and memoranda] covering the evolution of United Nations strategy, for the purposes of determining what adjustments, if any, are necessary or desirable at this time in the basic strategic concept.

Conclusions and Recommendations

2. The present basic strategic concept of the United Nations, reduced to its simplest form, has been stated,

"To conduct the strategic offensive with maximum forces in the Atlantic-Western European theater at the earliest practicable date, and to maintain the strategic defensive in other theaters with appropriate forces."

In the opinion of the Joint Chiefs of Staff, this concept, while basically sound, should be restated with a view to setting forth more exactly the strategic concept as regards the Pacific theater. The following statement is proposed:

"Conduct a strategic offensive in the Atlantic-Western European theater directly against Germany, employing the maximum forces consistent with maintaining the accepted strategic concept in other theaters. Continue offensive and defensive operations in the Pacific

and in Burma to break the Japanese hold on positions which threaten the security of our communications and positions. Maintain the strategic defensive in other theaters.

It is well understood that the strategic concept contained herein is based on the strategic situation as it exists and can be foreseen at this time, and that it is subject to alteration in keeping with the changing situation."

3. It is recommended that the following (see paragraph 4) be approved as the strategic objectives of the United Nations in support of the basic strategic concept as stated above. In arriving at its recommendations the Joint Chiefs of Staff have taken note:

   (a) That Germany is our primary enemy;

   (b) That Russia is exerting great pressure on Germany and is absorbing the major part of her war effort;

   (c) That Russia's continuance as a major factor in the war is of cardinal importance;

   (d) That timely and substantial support of Russia, directly by supplies and indirectly by offensive operations against Germany, must be a basic factor in our strategic policy;

   (e) That until such time as major offensive operations can be undertaken against Japan, we must prevent her from consolidating and exploiting her conquests by rendering all practicable support to China and by inflicting irreplaceable losses on Japanese naval, shipping and air resources;

   (f) That a prerequisite to the successful accomplishment of the strategic concept for 1943 is an improvement in the present critical shipping situation by intensified and more effective anti-submarine warfare.

4. Strategic objectives:
   (a) Western Hemisphere and United Kingdom.
   Maintain the security, the productive capacity, and the essential communications of the Western Hemisphere and of the British Isles.

   (b) Western Europe.
   Insure that the primary effort of the United Nations is directed against Germany rather than against her satellite states by:
   (1) Conducting from bases in United Kingdom, Northern Africa, and as practicable from the Middle East, an integrated air offensive on the largest practicable scale against German production and resources, designed to achieve a progressive deterioration of her war effort.
   (2) Building up as rapidly as possible adequate balanced forces in the United Kingdom in preparation for a land offensive against Germany in 1943.

   (c) North Africa.
   Expel the Axis forces from North Africa, and thereafter:
   (1) Consolidate and hold that area with the forces adequate for its security, including the forces necessary to maintain our lines of communication through the Straits of Gibraltar against an Axis or Spanish effort;
   (2) Exploit the success of the North African operations by establishing large-scale air installations in North Africa and by conducting intensive air operations against Germany and against Italy with a view to destroying Italian resources and morale, and eliminating her from the war;
   (3) Transfer any excess forces from North Africa to the UK for employment there as part of the build-up for the invasion of Western Europe in 1943.

   (d) Russia.
   Support Russia to the utmost, by supplying munitions, by

rendering all practicable air assistance from the Middle East and by making the principal offensive effort of 1943 directly against Germany in Western Europe.

(e) Middle East.
   (1) Maintain Turkey in a state of neutrality favorable to the United Nations until such time as she can, aided by supplies and minimum specialized forces, insure the integrity of her territory and make it available for our use.
   (2) If Turkey can then be brought into the war, conduct offensive air operations from bases on her northern coast in aid of Russia and against German controlled resources and transportation facilities in the Balkans.

(f) Pacific.
Conduct such offensive and defensive operations as are necessary to secure Alaska, Hawaii, New Zealand, Australia, and our lines of communications thereto, and to maintain the initiative in the Solomon-Bismarck-East New Guinea Area with a view to controlling that area as a base for further offensive operations and involving Japan in costly counter operations.

(g) Far East.
Conduct offensive operations in Burma with a view to reopening the supply routes to China, thereby encouraging China and supplying her with munitions to continue her war effort, and maintain, available to us, bases essential for eventual offensive operations against Japan proper.

Bibliography

This is not an exhaustive bibliography: it is, principally, a list of sources. Those in bold were the most helpful.

The primary source is Alanbrooke's diary together with his autobiographical notes and papers held in the archive catalogue, **Alanbrooke, FM Alan Francis, 1st Viscount Alanbrooke of Brookeborough**, at the Liddell Hart Centre for Military Archives, King's College London.

Secondary sources are as follows:

Alexander, Harold, *The Alexander Memoirs 1940–1945* McGraw-Hill (New York) 1962 (published in UK as *The Memoirs of Field Marshal Earl Alexander of Tunis 1940–1945* Cassell 1962)

Astley, Joan Bright, *The Inner Circle: a view of war at the top* The Quality Book Club 1972

Bryant, Arthur, *The Turn of the Tide* The Reprint Society Ltd 1958

Bryant, Arthur, *Triumph in the West* The Reprint Society Ltd 1960

Casey, Richard Gardiner, *Personal Experience 1939–1946* Constable 1962

Churchill, Winston S., *The Second World War* Book Club Associates 1985

Colville, John, *The Fringes of Power: Downing Street Diaries Vol 2 1941–April 1955* Sceptre 1987

Cunningham, Andrew Browne, *A Sailor's Odyssey* Hutchison & Co 1951

Danchev, Alex, *Establishing the Anglo-American Alliance*, Brassey's (UK) 1990

ed. Danchev, Alex, and Todman, Daniel, *War Diaries 1939–1945* Field Marshal Lord Alanbrooke Phoenix Press 2002

ed. Dilks, David, *The Diaries of Sir Alexander Cadogan 1938–1945* Cassell & Company 1971

Eisenhower, Dwight D., *Crusade in Europe* William Heinemann 1948

Engel, Gerhard, *At the Heart of the Reich* Greenhill Books 2005

Foreign Relations of the United States 1933–1945, *The Conferences at Washington, 1941–1942, and Casablanca, 1943* (FRUS 1) eds Fredrick Aandahl, William M. Franklin, William Slaney, Washington: Government Printing Office 1958. Office of the Historian – https://history.state.gov

Foreign Relations of the United States 1933–1945, *Conferences at Washington and Quebec, 1943* (FRUS 2) eds William Slaney and Richardson Dougall, Washington: Government Printing Office 1970. Office of the Historian – https://history.state.gov

Fraser, David, *Alanbrooke* HarperCollins Publishers 1997

Guderian, Heinz, *Panzer Leader* Penguin 2009

Hastings, Max, *Finest Years: Churchill as Warlord 1940–45* HarperPress 2010

Horrocks, Sir Brian, *Escape to Action* St Martin's Press 1961 (published in UK as *A Full Life* Collins 1960)

Howard, Michael, *The Mediterranean Strategy in the Second World War*, Greenhill Books 1993

Ismay, *The Memoirs of Lord Ismay* William Heinemann 1960

Keitel, *The Memoirs of Field Marshal Wilhelm Keitel* ed. Walter Gorlitz, Cooper Square Press 2000

Kennedy, Sir John, *The Business of War* Hutchison & Co 1957

Leasor James, *War at the Top* Michael Joseph 1959

Liddell Hart, B.H., *History of the Second World War* Papermac 1992

Liddell Hart, B.H., *The Liddell Hart Memoirs Vol. 11 The Later Years* G.P. Putnam's Sons (New York) 1965 (published in UK as *The Memoirs of Captain Liddell Hart* Cassell 1965)

Loringhoven, Bernd Freytag von, *In the Bunker with Hitler* Weidenfield & Nicholson 2006

Matloff, Maurice, and Snell, Edwin, *United States Army in World War 11: Strategic Planning for Coalition Warfare 1941–42*, The War Department 1953

McMeekin, Sean, *Stalin's War* Penguin Books 2022

Montgomery, Viscount, *The Art of Leadership* Pen & Sword Military 2009

Moorehead, Alan, *The Desert War* Aurum Press 2009

Moran, Lord, *Winston Churchill: The Struggle for Survival 1940–1965* Sphere Books 1968

Richardson, Charles, *From Churchill's Secret Circle to the BBC* Brassey's (UK) 1991

Roberts, Andrew, *Masters and Commanders* Allen Lane 2008

Sebag-Montefiore, Hugh, *Dunkirk* Penguin Books 2007

Speer, Albert, *Inside the Third Reich* Sphere Books 1975

BIBLIOGRAPHY

Spitzy, Reinhard, *How We Squandered The Reich* Michael Russell (Publishing)

Stimson, Henry L., and Bundy, McGeorge, *On Active Service in Peace and War* Harper 1948

Stoler, Mark A., *George C. Marshall* Twayne Publishers 1989

The Economist, Statesman and Soldier, 23 February 1957

Warlimont, Walter, *Inside Hitler's Headquarters 1939–45* Weidenfield & Nicholson 1964

Weinberg, Gerhard L., *A World at Arms* Press Syndicate of the University of Cambridge 1995

Wilmot, Chester, *The Struggle for Europe* The Reprint Society Ltd 1954

Notes

The vast majority of the quotes that appear in this book have been sourced from Alanbrooke's diary, his autobiographical notes and other papers in the archive catalogue, *Alanbrooke, FM Alan Francis, 1st Viscount Alanbrooke of Brookeborough*, held at the Liddell Hart Centre for Military Archives, King's College London. This archive catalogue, which is extensive, comprises fifteen sections. Quotes have been taken from

Section 1 Childhood and early military service
Section 2 Letters
Section 5 Diaries
Section 7 Post-war life and career
Section 8 Personal correspondence
Section 11 Notes made by Marian Long, Arthur Bryant's researcher
Section 12 Correspondence and papers relating to *The Turn of the Tide* and *Triumph in the West*

Many of the photographs reproduced inside this book were taken from Section 13 of the archive catalogue.

Sources for the other quotes are as follows:

Introduction
1. Moran p.746
2. ed. Danchev and Todman
3. *The Economist*
4. Horrocks p.80
5. Weinberg p.928 (Bibliographic Essay)
6. Horrocks p.80

7   Montgomery p.127
8   Fraser p.113
9   *The Economist*
10 Fraser p.268
11 Horrocks p.80
12 Fraser p.94
13 Cunningham p.661
14 Fraser p.114
15 Alexander p.79–80
16 Astley p.103–104
17 Astley p.164–165
18 Fraser p.112
19 Fraser p.187
20 Casey
21 Cunningham p.661
22 Eisenhower p.185
23 Bryant, *The Turn of the Tide* p.116–117
24 Bryant, *The Turn of the Tide* p.117 footnote
25 Roberts p.37
26 Bryant, *The Turn of the Tide* p.278
27 Leasor p.11
28 Horrocks p.80–81
29 Ismay p.317–318
30 Kennedy p.181
31 Montgomery p.127–128
32 Montgomery p.131–132
33 Moran p.747
34 Moran p.753
35 Moran p.752
36 Moran p.754
37 Moran p.132
38 Kennedy p.317
39 Fraser p.501

Chapter 1
1   Moran p.754
2   Fraser p.16

Chapter 2
1. Fraser p.32
2. Fraser p.94
3. Fraser p.530 notes and p.64–65
4. Fraser p.67
5. Fraser p.82
6. Fraser p.71
7. Fraser p.69
8. Liddell Hart, *Memoirs* p.41
9. Ismay p.317

Chapter 3
1. Sebag-Montefiore p.14

Chapter 4
1. Fraser p.133

Chapter 5
1. Colville p.401 (Biographical Notes)
2. Bryant, *The Turn of the Tide* p.214
3. Kennedy p.169–170
4. Kennedy p.63
5. Fraser p.174
6. Kennedy p.179
7. Kennedy p.162
8. Fraser p.174
9. Fraser p.175
10. Leasor p.83

Chapter 6
1. Kennedy p.181
2. Kennedy p.114–115
3. Kennedy p.115
4. Kennedy p.186
5. Kennedy p.189
6. FRUS 1, Document 115
7. Churchill, *Volume IV, The Hinge of Fate* p.51

8   Dilks p.430
9   Dilks p.430
10 Dilks p.432–433
11 Churchill, *Volume IV, The Hinge of Fate* p.87–88
12 Dilks p.433
13 Kennedy p.198
14 Kennedy p.199–200

Chapter 7
1   Kennedy p.208
2   Kennedy p.205
3   Kennedy p.207
4   Moran p.754
5   Matloff and Snell p.183
6   Churchill, *Volume IV, The Hinge of Fate* p.283
7   Churchill, *Volume IV, The Hinge of Fate* p.289–290
8   Dilks p.449
9   Roberts p.175
10 Dilks p.456

Chapter 8
1   Dilks p.458
2   FRUS 1, Document 291
3   Roberts p.175
4   Stimson and Bundy p.419
5   Danchev p.158
6   FRUS 1, Document 296
7   Danchev p.159
8   FRUS 1 Document 273
9   Dilks p.458
10 FRUS 1, Document 270 (first version) page 478–479 (revised version)
11 Dilks p.461
12 Dilks p.461
13 Dilks p.464

Chapter 9
1   Bryant, *The Turn of the Tide* p.398
2   Liddell Hart, *History of the Second World War* p.327

NOTES

Chapter 11
1 Churchill, *Volume IV, The Hinge of Fate* p.599
2 Kennedy p.286
3 Richardson p.167
4 Richardson p.164

Chapter 12
1 FRUS 2, Document 29
2 FRUS 2, Document 29
3 Stoler p.134
4 Dilks p.538
5 McMeekin p.503

Chapter 13
1 Roberts p.437

Chapter 15
1 Roberts p.476
2 Bryant, *Triumph in the West* p.194

Chapter 17
1 Dilks p.695
2 Dilks p.697–698

Chapter 19
1 Alexander p.79
2 Kennedy p.199
3 Moran p.752
4 Moorehead p.242
5 Liddell Hart, *Memoirs* p.41
6 Eisenhower p.185
7 Fraser p.20
8 Fraser p.112
9 Casey
10 Richardson p.164
11 *The Economist*
12 Colville p.401 (Biographical Notes)
13 *The Economist*

14 Horrocks p.80–81
15 Astley p.164
16 Montgomery p.128
17 Moran p.132
18 Colville p.401 (Biographical Notes)
19 Colville p.401 (Biographical Notes)
20 *The Economist*
21 Moran p.754

Chapter 20
1 Dilks p.433
2 Churchill, *Volume IV, The Hinge of Fate* p.599
3 Matloff and Snell p.183
4 FRUS 1, Document 115
5 FRUS 2, Document 29
6 Liddell Hart, *History of the Second World War* p.327
7 Kennedy p.305
8 Cunningham p.661
9 Bryant, *The Turn of the Tide* p.117

Chapter 21
1 Bryant, *Triumph in the West* p.417
2 Moran p.753
3 Moran p.756
4 Moran p.747–748
5 Moran p.752
6 Bryant, *The Turn of the Tide* p.vii
7 Churchill, *Volume II, Their Finest Hour* p.15
8 Dilks p.430
9 Dilks p.695
10 Dilks p.697–698
11 Cunningham p.661
12 Lord Dannatt, www.bbc.co.uk/news/uk-29714738 (dated 23 October 2014)
13 Cadogan p.430
14 Iraq Inquiry, Witness Transcripts, Lord Wilson of Denton, 25 January 2011, p.70 https://webarchive.nationalarchives.gov.uk/ukgwa/20171123123302/http://www.iraqinquiry.org.uk/the-evidence/witness-transcripts/

15 Iraq Inquiry, Witness Transcripts, Lord Wilson of Denton, 25 January 2011, p.72–73 https://webarchive.nationalarchives.gov.uk/ukgwa/20171123123302/http://www.iraqinquiry.org.uk/the-evidence/witness-transcripts/

16 Iraq Inquiry, Witness Transcripts, Lord Turnbull, 25 January 2011, p.39 https://webarchive.nationalarchives.gov.uk/ukgwa/20150122085226/http://www.iraqinquiry.org.uk/media/51794/20110125-turnbull-final.pdf

17 Iraq Inquiry, Witness Transcripts, Lord Wilson of Denton, 25 January 2011, p.42 https://webarchive.nationalarchives.gov.uk/ukgwa/20171123123302/http://www.iraqinquiry.org.uk/the-evidence/witness-transcripts/

18 Roberts p.37
19 Horrocks p.80
20 Kennedy p.181
21 Moran p.752
22 Fraser p.174
23 Engel p.93 and 136
24 Spitzy p.164–165
25 Spitzy p.305–306
26 Warlimont p.246
27 Von Loringhoven p.109–110
28 Speer p.338–339
29 Guderian p.464
30 Gorlitz p.235

Chapter 22

1 Moran p.752
2 *The Economist*
3 Astley p.164
4 Montgomery p.128
5 Fraser p.496
6 Moran p.755
7 Ismay p.318
8 Montgomery p.131: Moran p.132
9 Cunningham p.661
10 Ismay p.318
11 Moran p.749
12 Moran p.749

13 Hastings p.569
14 Colville p.401 (Biographical Notes)
15 *The Economist*

Appendix 1
1   FRUS 1, Document 401
2   FRUS 2, Document 399

Acknowledgements

This book could not have been written without Alanbrooke's diary. So, the first acknowledgement is to Alanbrooke for his self-discipline and dedication in maintaining a diary throughout the entire War and then supplementing it with his autobiographical notes in the 1950s: he created an historical record of considerable value and importance in so many different ways. The second is to the Liddell Hart Centre for Military Archives, based at King's College London, for taking custody of, storing, preserving and protecting Alanbrooke's diary and papers for more than fifty years. The third is to everyone who works, or previously worked, in the Liddell Hart Centre since they could not have been more helpful and cooperative when dealing with my enquiries and requests; their assistance is much appreciated. Finally, I am extremely grateful to the Trustees of Lord Alanbrooke's Settlement and the Trustees of the Liddell Hart Centre for Military Archives for their kind permission to publish the many extracts from Alanbrooke's diary and papers.

Responsibility for any mistakes that appear in the text of this book is mine and – unfortunately – mine alone.